Economy in Society

Economy in Society: Economic Sociology Revisited

by

Jacek Tittenbrun

Translated by Jacek Tittenbrun and Barbara Jazienicka

CAMBRIDGE SCHOLARS
PUBLISHING

Economy in Society:
Economic Sociology Revisited,
by Jacek Tittenbrun

This book first published 2011

Cambridge Scholars Publishing

12 Back Chapman Street, Newcastle upon Tyne, NE6 2XX, UK

British Library Cataloguing in Publication Data
A catalogue record for this book is available from the British Library

ISBN (10): 1-4438-3145-X, ISBN (13): 978-1-4438-3145-1

Translation funded by the Polish Foundation of Science

TABLE OF CONTENTS*

* The abbreviation "I" refers to what is termed in the present book sociology of the economy, whereas "II" denotes economic sociology. Both concepts are explained in the first section of Chapter Two

FOREWORD

This book is, in a sense, a rather odd animal. The reason for this is that its author attempts what is commonly considered an impossible mission—he would like the book to be all things to all people.

Well, perhaps a more modest formulation would be appropriate. The book may be read in at least two different ways. Firstly, its author does not hide the fact that it is meant to be not only an overview of the discipline's historical background and both old and contemporary achievements, but also as a novel perspective within the field, and hopefully a ground-breaking one. Its socio-economic approach, based on a new and in many respects theoretical and conceptual apparatus, is not only valuable in its own right, but casts light on many phenomena and conceptions providing a range of fresh insights. From this perspective the book may be treated as a (not altogether typical) textbook on what has come to be known as economic sociology.

However, it should have at least some appeal for the so-called common or average reader, as another strength of the book lies in the fact that it is both scientifically rigorous and written in an accessible style. It manages, hopefully, to avoid mathematical and other jargon so common in economics and sociology which should broaden its potential readership. Both from the viewpoint of the academic and the general reader, however, the book will be, at least such are the author's hopes and expectations, considered as thought-provoking. It follows that the author is well prepared for the fact that his product may stir some, or even a storm of controversy. After all, it is only owing to sometimes harsh debate and discussion that any progress in science, social science included, can emerge.

CHAPTER I.1.

ECONOMIC SOCIOLOGY: TRADITIONS AND ORIGINS

I.1.1. Pre-classical Economics

Economic sociology, as a specific sub-discipline of sociology, crystallised not so long ago. Published in 1937, the Encyclopaedia of Social Sciences contained no article on the sociological approach to economic phenomena and processes. Published thirty years later (1968), the International Encyclopaedia of Social Sciences, despite containing the term "economy and society," still lacked the term "Economic Sociology." In the following three decades, the position of economic sociology was very different, demonstrated by the establishment in 2001 of the economic sociology section of the American Sociological Association, a fact testifying to the established position and authority of a given field of research. Economic sociology's growing institutionalization is also manifested in its presence at leading American universities such as Harvard, Stanford, Cornell and others. An important event, or even turning point in the development of economic sociology, took place in 2005, prompting the following commentary: "If a relatively new (sub-) discipline is able to produce an encyclopedia covering a vast range of topics, one can indeed say that it has come of age" (Dolfsma 2006).

The young age of economic sociology as a distinct field of sociology does not mean that one cannot talk about its shorter or longer history, proto-history, or even traditions or sources. The greatest, although not exclusive, role in the formation of the sub-discipline was played by, unsurprisingly, sociology and economics. For proof of the latter just look at the standard definition of economics, which in one of its wordings states that this science "seeks to answer three basic questions: what to produce and in what quantities? How to produce—using what techniques and technologies? Who and to what extent will use the social product produced?"

In principle, all, especially the last two questions, overlap the field of interest of sociology. Even the first question, the allocation of scarce resources, considered a classic economic problem, does not, or at least should not be the exclusive domain of economists, because both at a micro and macro level it assumes presuppositions in the form of rationality, criteria and motives of choice of both means and objectives of action, each of which has obvious social content. Similarly, production and work processes in general are not only technological in nature, but, as we shall see in further chapters, are native objects of study of economic sociologists. The answer to the third question, at least from the perspective of a sociologist assuming the same theoretical and methodological principles as the author of this study, is difficult to put in terms other than of ownership-class relations.

The origins of economic thinking, including socio-economic thinking, can be seen in ancient Greece. The poet Hesiod (seventh century BC) should be mentioned in this context not only owing to his maxim "no work dishonours, idleness brings shame." Incidentally, as we shall see, it cannot be regarded as an expression of the typical Greek attitude towards work. In his poem *Works and Days*, Hesiod explains the problem of scarcity of goods as a result of an error by Pandora, who according to Greek mythology opened a box received from the gods. She persuaded her husband to this deed, thus releasing all the evils of the world and from then on men have faced the scarcity of resources against unlimited needs.

In Christian culture a similar idea can be found in the myth of original sin, as the first parents were expelled from paradise because of their disobedience to the will of God. The first woman persuaded her husband Adam to disobey God's will and pick fruit from the forbidden tree. As a consequence, from then on they had to work, and men have been in need of many goods, a need that appeared only with the departure from paradise. The abundance of goods as an attribute of paradise means, in socio-economic terms, the dominance of property (which will be discussed later) over labour.

Hesiod also dealt with the effectiveness of management, formulating in this context the principle of maximum effect with minimum effort. Greater production efficiency, according to Greek thought, can be achieved through the division of labour. Perhaps the most famous figure in the pantheon of Greek philosophers, Socrates, formulated a concept of exactly this social division of labour: "Let shoemakers make shoes, let blacksmiths forge iron, but let the state government be appointed from among the best … the wisest."

The historian Xenophon, who lived four hundred years after Hesiod in Athens, and was a disciple of Socrates and remained under the strong influence of his work, divided labour according to professional qualifications, expressing contempt for manual labour. Physical labour dishonours the "free" man, distorts the body and leaves no time for political, social and cultural concerns. Xenophon was also the first author to explicitly refer to "a science of economy." Xenophon created a work entitled *Oikonomikos* (*oikos*—house, farm; *nomos*—law), or "Host" (hence the word "economist"). Xenophon's work is primarily a manual of household, or city-state management (in this case, Athens). It contains, in addition to a range of management guidelines, a handful of economic thoughts. At the very beginning, Xenophon quotes from his master, Socrates, that: "'economy,' like the words 'medicine,' 'carpentry,' 'building,' 'smithying,' 'metal-working,' and so forth, is the name of a particular kind of knowledge or science." By "economists" we now generally understand political economists, macro-economists or micro-economists, but in this case the word refers to domestic economy. Property or estate management requires knowledge, like "medicine, blacksmithing and carpentry" (Xenophon 2008, 1). Thus management is a knowledge-based craft.

The above-mentioned name was propagated by Aristotle. Through it he understood teachings about the phenomena of household management, contrasting it with "chremastics" as a science and art of wealth acquisition or money making through market exchange. The latter was contrary to Aristotelian ethics because its purpose was the pursuit of money. The Greek philosopher thus raised the question of a fundamental distinction between two economies: the natural and the commodity-money economy. The distinction is taken up at a later stage of thought by, among others, Max Weber in his dichotomy of *Haushalten* and *Erwerben*, or Karl Marx who distinguished use values and exchange values. At the same time, formulating the above opposition, Aristotle was in a perverse way opposed to the latter, including the most recent, theoretical tendency to associate the economy with the principle of maximizing profit, and by the same token treating the relation to it of the household as highly problematic.

The above-mentioned affinity of the great Greek thinker to another great scholar who lived many centuries later in fact extends still further, becoming apparent when one takes into consideration early insights in the labour theory of value in Aristotle´s *Politics*. He developed a "theory of the value of labour," holding that the value of labour skills is given by the goods they command in the market. He maintained that value is not created solely by the expenditure of labour in the production process, but also that utility and labour skills are pertinent to the determination of exchange values and exchange ratios (Jaffe & Lusht 2003). Other issues of a socio-economic character that were of interest to the ancient Greek thinkers were property and social classes.

Solon (638–558 BC) was a statesman credited with having laid the foundations for Athenian democracy. Solon broadened the financial and social qualifications required for election to public office. The Solonian constitution divided citizens into four political classes defined according to assessable property. That classification might previously have served the state for military or taxation purposes only. The standard unit for this assessment was one *medimnos* (approximately twelve gallons) of cereals, and yet the kind of classification set out below might be considered too simplistic to be historically accurate:

- **Pentacosiomedimni**
    - valued at 500 medimnoi of cereals annually
    - eligible to serve as Strategoi (Generals)
- **Hippeis**
    - valued at 300 medimnoi production annually
    - approximating to the mediaeval class of knights, they had enough wealth to equip themselves for the Cavalry
- **Zeugitai**
    - valued at a 200 medimnoi production annually
    - approximating to the mediaeval class of Yeoman, they had enough wealth to equip themselves for the infantry (Hoplite)
- **Thetes**
    - valued 199 medimnoi annually or less
    - manual workers or sharecroppers, they served voluntarily in the role of batman, or as auxiliaries armed for instance with the sling or as rowers in the Navy.

According to Aristotle, only the *Pentacosiomedimnoi* were eligible for election to high office as archons and therefore only they gained admission into the Areopagus. A modern view affords the same privilege to the hippeis. The top three classes were eligible for a variety of lesser posts and only the Thetes were excluded from all public office.

Depending on how the historical facts known to us are interpreted, Solon's constitutional reforms were either a radical anticipation of democratic government, or they merely provided a plutocratic flavour to a stubbornly aristocratic regime, or else the truth lies somewhere between these two extremes. Be that as it may, Solon’s taxonomy should be regarded as a mix of what is probably the earliest theory of stratification with a class perspective rather than one of classes pure and simple. Plato, however, divided the ideal state into three classes: rulers, soldiers and breadwinners. In this elitist-egalitarian utopia, rulers and soldiers must not hold private property, should only be subject to the common property so as to avoid conflicts over ownership, and focus only on the state. Slaves and craftsmen must work to maintain the ruling classes.

By contrast, Aristotle presented what may be seen as an ideological justification of private property. In *Politics*, Book II, Part V, he argued that:

> Property should be in a certain sense common, but, as a general rule, private; for, when everyone has a distinct interest, men will not complain of one another, and they will make more progress, because every one will be attending to his own business... And further, there is the greatest pleasure in doing a kindness or service to friends or guests or companions, which can only be rendered when a man has private property. These advantages are lost by excessive unification of the state. (Aristotle 350 BC)

The obligatory mode of Plato's statement is not accidental; ancient Greeks treated economic considerations as a part of philosophy (understood as an all-embracing science) and were ethical and normative in nature, assessing what was good in economic life and what was wrong, and showing how it should be. As we have seen, while one can find many more or less sound observations on economic topics in their writings, the Greeks did not form any coherent theory of economics. Certain views on the economy, however, must have been assumed by their flourishing activity within a variety of areas of the economy. Among other things, they knew certain forms of insurance and credit operations, and were excellent merchants.

Even more practical were the Romans. From the very beginning, they were a farming people, therefore most of the works on the widely understood economic sector written by Roman authors were concerned with estate management. Ancient Rome also gave Europe the Roman law, and particularly the theory of contract and property (*jus utendi et abutendi*).

The Middle Ages did not lead to fundamental changes in views on economic phenomena. Agriculture, crafts, trade, and money as a source of wealth were still the subject of interest, now considered in the context of ethical and moral principles of the Christian religion. Thomas Aquinas (1225–1274) dealt with the ethical side of economic activities. He condemned usury—*Iustum pretium* is a just price, i.e. reflecting the value of the goods. Opposed to the community doctrine of original Christians, he defended feudal ownership. However, at the same time he stressed that property carries the burden of care for the poor.

Scholastic economics was a stage of development highly regarded by Joseph Schumpeter, who published the influential *History of Economic Analysis*. Its history begins with the Franciscan St. Bernardine of Siena (1380–1444), who dealt with, among other things (of course through the prism of morality) the role of the entrepreneur. A figure linking Bernardine with late Scholastics is Thomas De Vio, Cardinal Cajetan (1468–1534), who described the contemporary theory of money.

From this the thought moved to Salamanca and the Dominican founder of the school of Salamanca, Francisco de Vitoria (1485–1546). It is this sixteenth-century Spanish School of Salamanca, the main centre of learning and commerce, that is considered to be the peak moment of the development of scholastic economic thought. For example, the Dominican Domingo de Soto (1494–1560) stated that, "the price of goods is not determined by their nature, but how they serve humanity." He believed also that the natural law of man is "to hand over objects that are lawfully his in a chosen manner."

In the preface to the significant work of Alejandro Chaufen on the subject of late Scholastic economic thought, the philosopher Michael Novak suggests that a relationship exists between the Austrian economic school and a nascent interest of the late Scholastics in economic enterprise and entrepreneurial economics. This convergence is combined with another involving, common for both schools of thought, methodological individualism and subjectivism. Late scholastics are therefore linked to the late period of the nineteenth century Austrian school by, among others, the theory of economic value according to which the value of any product or service lies not so much in objectively existing properties of the product as in how people personally relate to that product. This means that the economic value is the result of individual intentions and states of mind, and therefore, ultimately, is subjective.

Sociologists of economy should criticize this approach not so much for its subjectivism *per se* as for its idealistic interpretation, i.e. not just in reference to the individual but restriction of this relation to a relationship with their psyche, while at the same time disregarding their objective needs and interests. Meanwhile relativism, in contrast to absolutism or immanentism that regards values as inherently belonging to given material or ideal objects is, in our opinion, a correct approach to the nature of social values. Transferring such an understanding of value into the field of economy, however, can be regarded as an expression of a specific sociological imperialism, which can be as harmful as its economic counterpart critically assessed later in the book; value in the sociological sense need not be a value in the economic sense. To be specific, values understood in such a way have much in common with the use value of economists, as opposed to exchange value. Hence, another accusation against the said approach is the confusion of different levels of understanding of economic value.

A significant breakthrough in the development of economic thought was brought about by the Renaissance, fostered by the change of intellectual climate, and encouraged thorough inquiry and profound changes in socio-economic conditions. The latter consisted of significant acceleration of the development of agricultural production, craft and trade as a result of increasing processes of the replacement of natural economy with commodity-money economy (initiated by the replacement of tribute by rent) and as a result of geographical discoveries. This created a demand for economic knowledge corresponding to the new situation and social needs. Among economic issues, problems of trade, especially foreign trade as well as money, were brought into the forefront.

At the beginning of the seventeenth century the first coherent set of economic views emerged, called Mercantilism, which saw sources of wealth in bullion, accumulated through trade considered the main area of economic activity, and changes within economic policy opting for a strong protectionism, limiting the freedom of economic activity of individuals.

Marx, in his *Theories of Surplus Value* (chapter IV), elucidates both the core of the current under consideration and its historical socio-economic context:

> The basis of their theory was the idea that labour is only productive in those branches of production whose products, when sent abroad, bring back more money than they have cost (or than had to be exported in exchange for them); which therefore enabled a country to participate to a greater degree in the products of newly-opened gold and silver mines. They saw that in these countries there was a rapid growth of wealth and of the middle class. What in fact was the source of this influence exerted by gold? Wages did not rise in proportion to the prices of commodities; that is, wages fell, and because of this relative surplus-labour increased and the rate of profit rose—not because the labourer had become more productive, but because the absolute wage (that is to say, the quantity of means of existence which the labourer received) was forced down—in a word, because the position of the workers grew worse. In these countries, therefore, labour was in fact more productive for those who employed it. This fact was linked with the influx of the precious metals; and it was this, though they were only dimly aware of it, which led the Mercantilists to

> declare that labour employed in such branches of production was alone productive.
>
> The remarkable increase (of population) which has taken place … in almost every European State, during the last fifty or sixty years, has perhaps proceeded chiefly from the increased productiveness of the American mines. An increased abundance of the precious metals" (of course as a result of the fall in their real value) "raises the price of commodities in a greater proportion than the price of labour; it depresses the condition of the labourer, and at the same time increases the gains of his employer, who is thus induced to enlarge his circulating capital to the utmost of his ability, to hire as many hands as he has the means to pay;—and it has been seen that this is precisely the state of things most favourable to the increase of people… Mr. Malthus observes, that 'the discovery of the mines of America, during the time that it raised the rice of corn between three and four times, did not nearly so much as double the price of labour.' The price of commodities intended for home consumption (of corn for instance) does not immediately rise in consequence of an influx of money; but as the rate of profit in agricultural employments is thus depressed below the rate of profit in manufactures, capital will gradually be withdrawn from the former to the latter: thus all capital comes to yield higher profits than formerly, and a rise of profits is always equivalent to a fall of wages.
>
> (John Barton, Observations on the Circumstances which Influence the Condition of the Labouring Classes of Society, London 1817, 29)

So, firstly, according to Barton, in the second half of the eighteenth century there was a repetition of the same phenomenon as that which, from the last third of the sixteenth century and in the seventeenth, has given the impulse to the Mercantile system. Secondly as only exported goods were measured in gold and silver on the basis of its reduced value, while those for home consumption continued to be measured in gold and silver according to its former value (until competition among the capitalists put an end to this measuring by two different standards), labour in the former branches of production appeared to be directly productive, that is, creating surplus-value, through the depression of wages below their former level.

Economic and social developments conditioned changes not only in content, but even in the very name of discipline. Antoine Monchrentien de Vateville (1615) wrote the "Treatise on Political Economy" in which he considered economics to be a political science. This was during the development of absolute monarchy in France, which was still building its power. Therefore, the state interfered in the economy. This purposeful intervention in the social life was to increase state revenue.

From our point of view, it will not be without significance to mention that in Polish literature, political economy was sometimes also referred to as the science of a "social economy." This term can be found, among others, in the title of the book by J. Supiński, *School of Polish Social Economy (1862–1865)* and S. Grabski's *Social Economy* (Marciniak 2001).

In 1730 there appeared a work considered to be the first general economic treatise, the "Essay on the Nature of Commerce" by Richard Cantillon, an Irish-born emigrant to France, educated in the scholastic tradition. His work confirms relationships of this tradition with the later Austrian school, as evidenced by, among others, the recognition of the market as an entrepreneurial process. Cantillon's thought, however, is notable not only for that reason. He implicitly accepted what was a *de facto* concept of the value of labour power by acknowledging the role of class struggle.

However, it is the school of the Physiocrats, a word from Greek meaning "government of nature," who held that agriculture was the source of wealth, considered to be the first school of political economy as they studied economic phenomena in the sphere of production and perceived the existence of objective economic laws. The physiocrats placed particular stress upon patterns that emerge from *laissez-faire*, stating that: "the movements of society are spontaneous and not artificial, and the desire for joy which manifests itself in all its activities unwittingly drives it towards the realization of the ideal type of State" (de la Riviere 1767; cited in Gide & Rist 1948, 30).

Among the outstanding achievements of this theoretical stream one should consider the "Tableau Économique" by Francois Quesnay, the first account in the history of economics of social wealth flow between branches of production. This is the first scheme of simple reproduction (repeated from period to period at the same size). Quesnay was first to adopt the assumption of constancy of prices, production and net product as well as the capitalist system of land lease.

The economic tables are based on a quantitative analysis, and feature the flow of wealth between classes in an accounting way, which shows their socio-economic nature. In this combination of economic with sociological analysis the scheme under consideration, regardless of its outdated characteristics such as an over-emphasis on agriculture, appears more modern than many arch-modern economic accounts. Quesnay distinguishes between large circulation (circulation of manufactured product between classes) and small circulation (circulation within each class).

Social classes according to Quesnay are:

The king, landowners (lay and clergy). This class owns the land, which they then lease and for which they receive rent equal to the value of net product, i.e. surplus (over the cost of production).

Productive class. The class of farmer's tenants—only they produce net product. They lease the land and make necessary capital expenditure. Only this class augments social wealth.

Sterile class, which includes industrialists, artisans, merchants. This class does not increase social wealth but only processes the generated wealth. As a result of its activity it generates only the equivalent of used resources of consumption.

Passive class, which includes the urban proletariat and the poor. The existence of this class depends on the economic situation of the three main classes. It is, to use Marx's phrase, the reserve army of free wage labour.

Quesnay's diagram of interbranch flows as in the following:

The class of farmers (tenants) allocates two billion lire. They hand over the sum to the proprietary class as rent for the cultivated land; for one billion lire the class buys from the sterile class (industrial) tools needed for production.

The proprietary class allocates the two billion lire from farmers: one billion goes to the purchase of consumer goods, for consumption in the class of farmers; one billion for the purchase of industrial products from the sterile class (industrial).

The sterile class allocates the two billion lire from farmers and proprietors: one billion goes to the purchase of consumer goods from the class of farmers; one billion for the purchase of raw materials necessary for industrial production also from the class of farmers.

Thus, farmers get back three billion lire, which after reinvestment can be used for production.

Quesnay treated the "economic tables" as a kind of method that allows for the creation of economic theories and to establish conditions for the process of simple reproduction.

Quesnay's "Tableau Économique" represent an ideal state of the economy—economic equilibrium. Quesnay believed that the implementation of the principles of "Tableau Économique" would remove all economic difficulties. However, he was aware that the reality deviates from the ideal presented in the tables, because the class of landowners spends more than half their income on buying industrial articles and the sterile class buys not from domestic farmers but abroad. The class of farmers get less resources than the amount that would guarantee the process of simple reproduction.

Karl Marx, while finding a number of logical and arithmetic errors in Quesnay's scheme, appreciated the accomplishments of the scheme which is apparent from, *inter alia*, his statement in his "Theories of Surplus Value":

> And this is the great merit of Physiocracy. The Physiocrats put themselves the question: how is surplus-value (for him [the anonymous writer] it is revenue) produced and reproduced? The question how it is reproduced on an enlarged scale, that is, increased, comes up only in the second place. Its category, the secret of its production must first be revealed.

Quesnay:

> definitely denies that economies made by the wage-earning classes have the faculty to increase capital, and the reason he gives for this is that these classes should not have any means on which to make economics, and that if they had a surplus, an excess, this could only be due to an error or to some disorder in the society's economy

Quesnay's Physiocratic system:

> regards the consumption of artisans, and even of those who merely consume, as meritorious, because this consumption, even though in an indirect and mediated way, contributes to the growth of the nation's revenue; since but for this consumption the consumed products would not have been produced from the land and could not have been added to the revenue of the landowner.

And in the *Theories of Surplus Value* (chapter IV) further praise can be found to the effect that:

> … the Physiocrats put forward the correct view that from the capitalist standpoint only that labour is productive which creates a surplus—value; and in fact a surplus—value not for itself, but for the owner of the conditions of production; labour which produces a net product not for itself, but for the landowner, for the surplus-value or surplus labour-time is materialised in a surplus-produce or net product. But here again they have a wrong conception of this; [...] Surplus-value itself is wrongly conceived, because they have a wrong idea of value and reduce it to the use-value of labour, not to labour-time, social, homogeneous labour. Nevertheless, there

> remains the correct definition that only the wage-labour which creates more value than it costs is productive. (Marx 1863)

Physiocracy recognised the principle of full freedom of business activity. However, a crystallized doctrine that put forward an individual as an economic agent, while at the same time criticized the intervention of state appeared only at the turn of the eighteenth and nineteenth century, at the end of French absolutism. This was Economic Liberalism. While intervening, the state infringes on the basic mechanism of the economy—the market mechanism (the activity of an individual, violating its freedom to act). English Liberalism, whose standard exponent is Adam Smith, proclaimed that society is the sum of free individuals.

I.1.2. Classical Political Economy

Although owing much to the physiocrats, as well as to the teaching of Frances Hutchinson (1694–1746) and David Hume (1711–1776), Adam Smith (1723–1790) is credited for having secured the foundations of classical economics, not least for his rejection of Quesnay's representation of agriculture as the source of wealth. For Smith, human activity in general, rather than agricultural activity in particular, is the original source of economic value. The influence of Bernard de Mandeville (1670–1733) is manifested in *The Theory of Moral Sentiments* (1759), where Smith explains how general welfare is served by the pursuit of private interests. However, it is with *The Wealth of Nations* (1776) that Smith ultimately "eclipsed the tentative efforts of his predecessors" (Gide & Rist 1948, 69). Its general thesis is that economic prosperity is a manifestation of spontaneous social interaction. Prosperity is enhanced by the free exchange of a vast array of differentiated commodities secured through the division and specialization of labour. However, that achievement is possible only where there is a supportive institutional framework: the "Smithian" mode of argument for free market policies, starting from a realistic view of man and his psychology, and recognising the all-persuasiveness of ignorance in human affairs, gives as important a place in its objectives to freedom and the Rule of Law as it does to some kind of ideal, optimal economic efficiency (Hutchinson 1984, 162).

It is thanks to Smith that economics began its career as an independent science. Smith accomplished a synthesis of accumulated economic thought, and developed and amended certain elements of it, thus forming a coherent theoretical framework whose foundation was the issue of wealth. This theory became the basis of a system of economic views known as the classical school of political economy, amongst whose exponents one should mention especially David Ricardo. The major achievements of classical political economy are the development of market theory, the development of the theory of value based on labour,[1] and a thorough

[1] For the sake of historical accuracy and fairness it is worth noting that the ideal of work as the basis for the value of goods had already been formulated by, among others, Benjamin Franklin and Martin Luther. In its more mature form the theory has been traced back to *Treatise of Taxes*, written in 1662 by Sir William Petty and to John Locke's notion, set out in the *Second Treatise on Government* (1689), that property derives from labour through the act of "mixing" one's labour with items in the common store of goods, though this has alternatively been seen as a labour theory of property. Other writers (including Joseph Schumpeter) have traced the concept back even further to Ibn Khaldun, who in his *Muqaddimah* (1377), described labour as the source of value, necessary for all earnings and capital accumulation, obvious in the case of craft. He argued that even if earning "results from something other than a craft, the value of the resulting profit and acquired (capital) must (also) include the value of the labour by which it was obtained. Without labour, it would not have been acquired."

Adam Smith accepted the LTV (labour theory of value) for pre-capitalist societies but saw a flaw in its application to capitalism. He pointed out that if the "labour embodied" in a product equalled the "labour commanded" (i.e. the amount of labour that could be purchased by selling it), then profit was impossible. David Ricardo (seconded by Marx) responded to this paradox by arguing that Smith had confused labour with wages. "Labour commanded," he argued, would always be more than the labour needed to sustain itself (wages). The value of labour, in this view, covered not just the value of wages (what Marx called the value of labour power), but the value of the entire product created by labour.

Ricardo's theory was a predecessor of the modern theory that equilibrium prices are determined solely by production costs associated with "neo-Ricardianism." Based on the discrepancy between the wages of labour and the value of the product, the "Ricardian socialists"—Charles Hall, Thomas Hodgskin, John Gray, and John Francis Bray—applied Ricardo's theory to develop theories of exploitation. Marx expanded on these ideas, arguing that workers work for a part of each day adding the value required to cover their wages, while the remainder of their labour is performed for the enrichment of the capitalist. The LTV and the accompanying theory of exploitation became central to his economic thought.

Nineteenth century American individualist anarchists based their economics on the LTV, with their particular interpretation of it being called "Cost the limit of price." They, as well as contemporary individualist anarchists in that tradition, held that it is unethical to charge a higher price for a commodity than the amount of labour required to produce it. Hence, they proposed that trade should be facilitated by using notes backed by labour.

Adam Smith held that, in a primitive society, the amount of labour put into producing goods determined its exchange value, with exchange value meaning in this case the amount of labour a good can purchase. However, according to Smith, in a more advanced society the market price is no longer proportional to labour cost since the value of the goods now includes compensation for the owner of the means of production: "The whole produce of labour does not always belong to the labourer. He must in most cases share it with the owner of the stock which employs him. Nevertheless, the "real value" of such a commodity produced in advanced society is measured by the labour which that commodity will command in exchange. But Smith disowns what is thought of as the genuine classical labour theory of value; that labour-cost regulates market-value. This theory was Ricardo's, and his alone. Classical economist David Ricardo's labour theory of value holds that the value of goods (how much of another good or service it exchanges for in the market) is proportional to how much labour was required to produce it, including the labour required to produce the raw materials and machinery used in the process. Ricardo stated it as, "The value of a commodity, or the quantity of any other commodity for which it will exchange, depends on the relative quantity of labour which is necessary for its production, and not as the greater or less compensation which is paid for that labour" (Ricardo 1817).

In this, Ricardo seeks to differentiate the quantity of labour necessary to produce a commodity from the wages paid to the labourers for its production. However, Ricardo was troubled with some deviations in prices from proportionality with the labour required to produce them. For example, he said "I cannot get over the difficulty of the wine which is kept in the cellar for three or four years (i.e., while constantly increasing in exchange value), or that of the oak tree, which perhaps originally had not 2 s. expended on it in the way of labour, and yet comes to be worth £100" (Quoted in Whitaker). Of course, a capitalist economy will stabilize this discrepancy until the value added to aged wine is equal to the cost of storage—if anyone can hold onto a bottle for four years and become rich, it will be done so much that it is hard to find freshly corked wine. There is also the theory that adding to the price of a luxury product increases its exchange-value by mere prestige.

The labour theory as an explanation for value contrasts with the subjective theory of value, which has been hinted at earlier and will be discussed at more length later in the book. This theory holds that value of goods is not determined by how much labour was put into it but by its usefulness in satisfying a want and its scarcity. Ricardo's labour theory of value is not a normative theory, as are some later forms of the labour theory, such as claims that it is "immoral" for an individual to be paid less for his labour than the total revenue that comes from the sales of all the goods he produces.

In fact it is not clear to what extent these classical theorists embraced the labour theory of value as it is commonly defined. For instance, Ricardo theorised that prices are determined by the amount of labour but found exceptions for which the labour theory could not account. In a letter, he wrote: "I am not satisfied with the explanation I have given of the principles which regulate value." Adam Smith, as noted above, theorised that the labour theory of value holds true only in the "early and rude state of society" but not in a modern economy where owners of

analysis of ground rent. High appraisal of the achievements of classical economics does not mean uncritical relationship to it. Ricardo distinguished between use value (the objective ability of goods to meet individual needs) and exchange value. He claimed that the basis of value is either the scarcity of goods, which concerns a small group of economic goods (unique goods such as works of art) or the amount of labour expended to produce particular goods, which applies to the majority of commodities.

Ricardo noticed that the amount of value is not constant, that it varies with technical progress, and on this basis he formulated a statement known as Ricardo's Law: value of a product is directly proportional to the effort and inversely proportional to labour productivity (the claim is correct, since in the latter case, production costs are lower). Ricardo was so consequent in his standpoint on the labour theory that he believed that both in "petty-commodity" society and capitalist society value is determined by the amount of labour. The basis of this standpoint however is his false assumption that capital existed in the primitive society, the natural economy. Ricardo construes capital ahistorically, identifying it with every work tool (means of production), even with the stone of the Primitive man.[2] Ricardo failed to see the social content of capital, consisting in the fact that the means of production become capital when used for the employment of wage-labour.

It is also Ricardo himself who was criticised by Marx (in the chapter on "Relative Surplus-Value" in *Capital*), who drew attention to the fact that:

> Ricardo never concerns himself about the origin of surplus-value. He treats it as a thing inherent in the capitalist mode of production which, in his eyes, is the natural form of social production. Whenever he discusses the productiveness of labour, he seeks in it not the cause of surplus-value, but the cause that determines the magnitude of that value. On the other hand, his school has openly proclaimed the productiveness of labour to be the originating cause of profit (read: Surplus-value). This at all events is progress as against the mercantilists who, on their side, derived the excess

---

capital are compensated by profit. As a result, "Smith ends up making little use of a labour theory of value."

[2] See an ironic remark by Marx in *Capital*: "By a wonderful feat of logical acumen, Colonel Torrens has discovered, in this stone of the savage the origin of capital. 'In the first stone which he (the savage) flings at the wild animal he pursues, in the first stick that he seizes to strike down the fruit which hangs above his reach, we see the appropriation of one article for the purpose of aiding in the acquisition of another, and thus discover the origin of capital'.

> of the price over the cost of production of the product, from the act of exchange, from the product being sold above its value. Nevertheless, Ricardo's school simply shirked the problem, rather than solving it. In fact, these bourgeois economists instinctively saw, and rightly so, that it is very dangerous to stir too deeply the burning question of the origin of surplus-value.

This criticism does not detract from the scientific merits of the school being discussed. It could be argued, for instance, that the particularly interesting part, from the perspective of sociology of the economy, of the achievements of classics—translating directly into the theory of social classes—was the articulation of the laws governing the division of social product. Adam Smith, for example, wrote not just about classes, highlighting the class of creators of inventions and improvements or, as we would say, anticipating terminology introduced later in this work, producers of the ideal means of production or performers of conceptual work. In addition, this is in a language that the uninitiated reader, unaware of the identity of the author of the statements in question, would probably have taken for Marxian, regarding the class struggle.

Of course, however, the concept of class struggle is usually connected with the names of Karl Marx and Friedrich Engels, which can be treated as a separate school of thought, and is often counted among the mainstream of classical political economy as apart from criticism of certain aspects of the latter (after all, the main work of Marx has the subtitle "critique of political economy"), and it took over a significant part of its output. Among the achievements of Marx and Marxism important for sociology of the economy one must mention the theory of surplus value derived from the theory of value based on labour, the concept of the mode of production and economic formation of society as well as the theory of social classes. We are not dwelling at this point over the content of these categories, as they will, although not always in the meaning entirely consistent with the original, be deployed in this work.

I.1.3. Historical School of Economics

Criticism of classical economics was also taken up by the historical school, the nature of which criticism should not be surprising in a country of creators of empirical and inductive methods such as Bacon and Macaulay. This kind of approach was bound to conflict with abstract theoretical constructions present in the work of Adam Smith, David Ricardo and John Stuart Mill.

Advocates of the historical school (which in its English version has a lot in common but is not identical to its mainland counterparts, especially in Germany and France) accused the school of classical political economists of an ahistorical understanding of economic laws, in particular. Their idiographism and empiricism led them to concentrate on historical and economic research, resulting especially in the birth of economic history, a very useful discipline for the sociology of the economy as providing the ample material for research.

Among the exponents of the English historical school are:

Richard Jones, 1790–1855. Jones attacked Ricardo's supporters, among others, for their theory of rent, lack of empirical content and the pretensions of scientific universalism; his views were characterized by inductionism, relativism, and evolutionism.

William Whewell, 1794–1866;

Walter Bagehot, 1826–1877;

Thomas E. Leslie, 1825–1882;

John Kells Ingram, 1823–1907. Ingram accused classical political economy of abstractionism, and at the same time scientism and ideologism. He himself was an advocate of the sociology of Auguste Comte from which he drew the principle of the need to recognise the historical and context of the economy.

Edwin Thorold Rogers, 1823–90. Author of the monumental, eight volume quantitative study of English prices in agriculture and works whose titles are cited to illustrate the usefulness of the achievements and direction of economic history in general for the sociology of the economy, such as: *Work and Wages in England*, *Six Centuries of Work and Wages in England*, and *Economic Interpretation of History*.

Arnold Toynbee, 1852–1883. Toynbee was the first researcher to name and study the industrial revolution. His works which deserve mention include the research on monopolies and oligopolies. He observed closely the induction method.

William Richard H. Tawney, 1880–1962. Economic historian, social critic and Fabian socialist, Tawney is famous for the work on the role of religion in the emergence of capitalism, explored also by Max Weber and the German historical school.

German and English historical streams had much in common, both in terms of their positive content and the type of debate with a powerful adversary in the form of classical political economy, although in both these respects they were far from being identical.

Classical political economy was based on the doctrinal and methodological assumptions of individualism, treating society as the sum of individuals and social welfare as the sum of the well-being of individuals. Meanwhile, the German social philosophy (from the late eighteenth and early nineteenth century) was grounded in opposite assumptions, namely holism. The focus was not an individual, but an independent public entity.

This idea was already evident in the notions of economists whose thought underpinned the development of German historicism. A.H. Müller stressed that the economy is aimed at obtaining the means to achieve ideal purposes of the existence of a society in the form of the state. Müller's idea, that sets him closer to the category of contemporary proponents of human capital, deserves citation, although not necessarily literal acceptance (see a critique of that notion later in this work). The idea highlights that having only three factors of production (land, capital and labour) is incomplete; he proposed to add a fourth factor, namely, the spiritual capital in the form of knowledge, talents, culture, civilization, and others, as he captured it, the perfect goods of human nature (Marciniak 2001). According to Müller, this type of capital is the most important factor of production. He believed, therefore, the distinction made by Smith, of productive labour creating the material means to meet needs and non-production labour producing intangible objects to meet needs, to be false. This latter type of work is, according to Müller, as productive as the former, and even more important. Apparent in this criticism is a fairly widespread confusion in identifying the distinction: productive–non-productive, with the opposition: useful–useless, or important–unimportant. Nevertheless, this remark points to the controversial character of the concept of productive labour, and since an attempt to solve this problem will be presented further in this work, we will not remain here any longer on this issue. Müller held also that the value of goods is determined not by the amount of work invested in it, but its importance for society, namely usefulness.

Müller's views had a great influence on Friedrich List (1789–1846) and the so-called older historical school. Like Müller, List condemned Smith for the individualistic approach to society and for cosmopolitanism. According to List, there is an interface (not taken into account by Smith) between the individual and humanity. However, in his opinion, each nation goes through five stages of development:

The period of savagery
The shepherd period

The agricultural period
The agricultural and handicraft period
The agricultural, craft and trade period.

It is only when a society reaches the fifth stage of development that it becomes a normal nation.

The second basic premise of the argument of List was his idea of productive powers. In his opinion, the classic concept of wealth is as static, not accounting for the future. Equally important, in fact, are sustainability and sustainable development of national wealth. This, on the other hand, is determined by manufacturing abilities and productive forces. In this latter concept, List included qualitative economic factors, including the parliamentary system, the state of morality and culture, freedom of conscience and work. He opposed his concept to the materialism of Smith. This idea of List can be criticized especially for confounding factors affecting the development of productive forces with their internal components, for example that a certain political factor affects the condition and functioning of productive forces does not make it a part of the latter, and thus the economy.

Another comment is also relevant in this context. The term "culture," of course used not only by the above-mentioned thinker, is essentially superfluous within our theoretical framework; our socio-economic structuralism uses instead the notion of "social consciousness" which comprises most of what is usually regarded as cultural objects, the caveat being that these, in our terms, products largely of the ideational structure (this as well as other terms pertinent to our theoretical and methodological approach will be explicated later in the text) may change their societal location according to what specific actions use them as their necessary means. For instance, particular religious norms or texts may wander essentially throughout the entire society, including, if we are to believe Weber for example, the economy. This, however, must be established separately on a case-by-case basis, for which reason, contrary to Pierre Bourdieu's intentions, his statement refers to a special rather than general case:

> the true object of a real economics of practices is nothing other, in the last analysis, than the economy of the conditions of production and reproduction of the agents and institutions of economic, cultural and social production and reproduction or, in other words, the very object of sociology in its most complete and general definition. (Bourdieu 2005)

This criticism does not mean, though, any underestimation of valuable contributions of the thinker in question—in particular those related to its apparent historicity combined with the category of a nation—that he introduced to economics and sociology of the economy, with the view of the need to take account of the past in the study of the latter.

In 1843, Wilhelm Roscher made a step forward, explicitly raising the issue of the need to use the historical method in economics, the essential element of which should be a comparative approach. Roscher argued that economic behaviours are dependent on their historical and social context, causes that in their studies should be used not only in an economic but also a historical and sociological approach. The first task of a researcher is therefore to immerse oneself in history to get as wide a knowledge of economic facts as possible, and on that basis determine the relationship between the economy and society. This explains why so much effort of the representatives of the so-called older historical school, notably Bruno Hildebrand and Karl Knies, focused on describing the stages of the historical development of society. There is often talk of the methodological assumption common to most representatives of this school of thought, shared by their English counterparts, which was a denial of the existence of universally valid economic laws in conjunction with the emphasis on the importance of individual facts.

Roscher in 1843 proclaimed that the economy is not an abstract and deductive explanatory science, but a descriptive science which must develop in close connection with other social sciences, including geographical and historical aspects of the economy. The first proponents of the historical school strongly denied the nomothetic nature of economics. Its later representatives, such nomo-German historians as Schmoller and Schoenberg, were in their convictions less methodologically dogmatic. Schmoller permitted the possibility of the existence in economics of the so-called periodic laws, i.e. acting in a certain period of time related to certain developmental periods such as the Middle Ages or capitalism (Marciniak 2001). Representatives of the younger historical school, especially Schmoller, made a major contribution to the sociology of the economy. According to Joseph Schumpeter, as cited by Swedberg (1991), no economist before Schmoller had approached the task of specific description and analysis of the economic process with such attention. Others could formulate such programme objectives, but only Schmoller, according to Schumpeter, made a serious attempt to bring this program into effect. Schmoller painstakingly collected statistical data and historical documents, wrote specialized monographs and tried to synthesize all of his extensive knowledge in a treatise titled "*Grundriss der Allgemegemein WirtschaftsLehre*."

To recapitulate the main differences between schools of classical and Historical economics, they may be reduced to the following:

The Classical School recognised the theoretical nature of the science of economics and applied the method of deduction based on the *a priori* assumptions of economic man and free competition and the principle of universality—that economic laws are universal, absolute and therefore are valid always and everywhere. Proponents of the school stood on the position of economic liberalism (free competition, free trade). They were characterised by methodological individualism—treatment of socio-economic developments through the prism of the behaviour of economising individuals.

The Historical School is an idiographic approach, emphasizing the description of specific facts. Its proponents used the research method of induction, i.e. a detailed description of economic phenomena in the historical context. This was related to the merit of this school which was the development of a series of monographs focusing on a selected problem in the field of economic history. They emphasized relative and historical character of economic laws and their historical variability. They were supporters of state intervention in economic life and the idea of tariff barriers (customs protectionism). The school was characterized by methodological holism, conceiving the socio-economic phenomena through the prism of social collectivities.

These features of the historical school caused it to find itself under fire from the Austrian School, also in opposition to classicism but from a different angle. Its founder, Karl Menger, started a dispute known as *Methodenstreit* with Schmoller and his work. Menger considered the deductive method and creating general theories applicable within a broad context to be an appropriate approach in economics. In economics, the subjective and atomic approaches were to be applicable as well. No collective notion had a right to exist, unless it was brought down to its individual components. Among the key conditions of economics were to be found the principle of maximization of self-interest and the perfect knowledge of an economising subject.

I.1.4. Neoclassical economics

The Principles of Economic Science by Karl Menger (1871) was one of the economic works that appeared at approximately the same time representing a similar approach signalling a new period in development of this discipline. Apart from this work were *Theory of Political Economy*, by William Jevons (1871) and *Elements of Pure Economics* by Leon Walras (1877). They all created a radical break with classical political economy. They dropped studies of wealth of the nation, the division between main social classes for the benefit of research on a micro scale (individuals or firms), and the study of objective laws governing the economy was replaced by an investigation of individual choices and valuations, thus opting for subjectivity. Within the framework of this approach the main attention is drawn not to production but consumption. The primary tool is not a great aggregate concept, but changes at the margins, hence the name of the direction: "marginalism."

This simultaneous appearance of several important works heralding a breakthrough in economics can be accounted for by both its internal contradictions as well as those which arose between it and reality. In the second half of the nineteenth century classical economics was in a state of stagnation, and economies described by the theory more and more experienced economic crises the sources of which it was unable to explain. Some inconsistencies of the classical theory became apparent, demonstrating gaps in explanations or even its inability to acknowledge the specific phenomena within the economic sphere. In addition, its revision was urged by the need to oppose the socialist doctrine, which was gaining in popularity especially in its key thesis that only labour is a productive factor of production, while land and capital are not. These factors *inter alia* influenced the rise of the modern microeconomic theory in the last thirty years of the nineteenth century, whose origin is commonly referred to as being subjective marginal revolution (also known as marginal revolution). This revolution created a new analytical tool kit used by economists to the present day. This change transformed classical economics into neoclassical economics, and thus into a renewed and restructured version of classical economics.

Leaders of neoclassical school are Marshall (1842–1929), Jevons[3] (1835–1881), Clark (1847–1938) and Pigou (1887–1959). Marshall in 1890 published the work *Assumptions of Economics*, the term "economics" being used to show it as an exact science, similar to life sciences.

Smith and Ricardo's economics is called classical economics. Marshall and post-Marshallian economics is called neoclassical economics because it draws to a degree on classical economics, among others in terms of the

[3] Ironically, it was Jevons who in 1879 first used the term "economic sociology"; only later it appeared in the writings of such classics of economic sociology, or sociology of the economy, as Emile Durkheim, Max Weber and Georg Simmel.

price-setting role of production costs. Specifically, Marshall believed that he drew on the school of Ricardo, but the fact of the matter is he reduced Ricardo's theory of value incorrectly to the theory of production costs. Marshall, in his deliberations, combined a subjective and objective point of view.

Price of a product is determined on the one hand by its marginal utility, and on the other by the marginal cost of production, by which onc understands the cost of the last unit of production. Marshall studied separately forces shaping supply and demand. Literature defines the marginal theory of economics also as subjective or subjectivist. This reorientation of the economics of the 1870s is referred to as the establishment of a subjective marginal thought, with the concept of subjective characterized by a new perception of economic phenomena. Subjective marginal economics in the formulation of general economic laws, appealed to the laws of the human psyche, to human psychology, individual subjective experiences, different assessments, estimates, feelings and emotions in each individual.

It should come as no surprise that the key concept of marginal utility has been criticised as unobservable, unmeasurable and untestable. This is illustrated by the theory of value, which in classical economics, as we know, was reduced to the value or quantity of labour, thus to a certain objective factor. However, in subjective marginal economics, value was shaped by subjective factors, by how the individual assesses and perceives goods. Value was reduced to the subjective level and was determined on the basis of subjective feelings and the reactions of economizing individuals.

The difference between classical and subjective marginal economics is evident when one compares the list of issues and theories dominant in each. In classical political economy the object of studies was primarily economic development, and more precisely the factors and types of policies that either facilitate or hinder this economic development. It was, speaking in modern terms, developmental macroeconomics with an emphasis on institutions, the mechanisms that ensure economic growth or slow it down. The object of interest was primarily groups and social classes, whose behaviour was used to explain economic processes. In particular, the theory of value had an important place in the analysis as well as the conception concerning the distribution of social product.

Meanwhile, subjective marginal economics completely changed the research view. The individual became the centre of analysis. It tried to understand what motives the individual is driven by, what the motives of human action are, what determines its economic behaviour, why a person acts, takes such decisions and not others, why they work in a particular way. Marginal economists came to the conclusion that the dominant motive is the desire to maximize utility, that each individual acts in such a way so as to maximize his or her utility, to avoid trouble. A human being does for this purpose some kind of calculation, an economic calculus to compare trouble with pleasures, costs with benefits and tries to select a course of action that will provide maximum benefits with minimum effort. Economists of the "new wave" concluded that the classical theory of value, a value based on the amount or the time of labour is wrong, because value is not objective in character but is something subjective, something that has been assigned (or, as they would have it, imputed) to a certain good by the economising individual, economising individuals.

Emphasis was placed on the freedom of consumer choices—definitions of economics that arose at that time defined its subject matter as an analysis of human choice in conditions of scarcity of goods. In other words, economics was identified with and dominated by the problem of allocation, i.e. an efficient allocation of production factors and consumer goods between the competing consumer needs and production needs processes. Strictly speaking, the problem of allocation can be defined as a problem of management of rare resources of many competing uses, and as a problem of management of limited resources against unlimited wants.

It was Eugen von Böhm-Bawerk who gave perhaps the most widely known description of the marginal theory of value:

> A pioneer farmer had five sacks of grain, with no way of selling them or buying more. He had five possible uses: as basic feed for himself, food to build strength, food for his chickens for dietary variation, an ingredient for making whisky and feed for his parrots to amuse him. Then the farmer lost one sack of grain. Instead of reducing every activity by a fifth, the farmer simply starved the parrots as they were of less utility than the other four uses; in other words they were on the margin. And it is on the margin, and not with a view to the big picture, that we make economic decisions. (Böhm-Bawerk 1899, 143)

Böhm-Bawerk describes a mechanism for price formation—in a situation where prices are not formed, the farmer can neither buy nor sell their output. If the farmer produced within a capitalist economy it would be the price of his output, not its use, i.e. its exchange value not its use value which determined whether he sold it or consumed it. If he could sell grain for a higher price than the cost of food, chickens, whiskey or parrots, he would sell the grain and buy the food, chickens, whiskey and parrots. The price that the farmer receives for his output would be something entirely separate from its utility for him, consequently the latter cannot determine its price.

Furthermore, the vast bulk of production in a modern market economy is by capitalists employing workers, not by simple commodity producers like small self-employed farmers.
Capitalists produce not to consume their output but to sell it, the utility of the commodities they produce is immaterial to them, all that matters is the amount of profit it yields on their investment. Workers do not own the production they produce for the capitalist as they have already alienated their labour power in the act of employment. In neither case does the choice Bohm Bawerk describes apply.

The novelty or, if you will, the revolution of the marginal analysis is particularly evident in the case of the aforementioned subjective marginal value theory. According to marginal economists, the classical theory of value was insufficient to indicate how the price is created in the case of goods of fixed supply (i.e. such that there cannot be more of them—their supply is rigid). The classical theory could indeed say very little about it (as we remember, Ricardo excluded these kinds of goods from his analysis—indivisible goods, non-reproducible by work—and simply did not consider them; in his analysis he focused on only those goods that are proliferable by work), while supporters of the new subjective marginal approach tried to find the general rule that governs the value of goods, meaning that some goods are extremely valuable, explaining why they have a high value while others have little value even though we sometimes are in great need of them. According to the subjectivist theory of value, the theory of value based on marginal factors, the value does not depend on production costs of the goods, nor on the time in which it is produced, but on the utility. It is the usefulness of good that is decisive of its value.

The core notion of the theory under consideration can be clarified by the famous diamond-water paradox, i.e. the observation that even though water is essential to human life, the price of water is relatively low. Diamonds (apart from industrial diamonds) are frivolous and unimportant for human existence, yet the price of diamonds is substantially higher. The marginalist theory of value explains the "paradox" by arguing that it is not the usefulness of water as a whole that affects price (not necessarily monetary), but the usefulness of one unit of water, not total utility but marginal utility. If a person has ten gallons of water, then the usefulness of any particular gallon is lower to them than it would be if only one gallon was available. Another way of saying this is that because water is in large supply, the marginal utility is low and therefore the price is proportionally low. On the other hand, because diamonds, which are not as useful, are scarce, each diamond is more useful in satisfying human wants than each gallon of water. The benefit someone forfeits by losing one gallon of water when they have ten gallons is less than the benefit lost if he or she loses one diamond out of ten diamonds. The marginal utility of water is lower than that of diamonds. This corresponds with water having a lower price than diamonds, because people are willing to pay less for things they value the least (whether it be payment with money, goods, or their own labour).

David Ricardo, as a supporter of the labour theory of value, maintained that value of goods is dependent on the amount of labour required to attain them. It follows that diamonds are expensive because they require a lot of labour to find and mine. In other words, it can be argued that the reason that diamonds are more expensive than water is not because of their relative natural abundance but because of their cost of production. The reason water is available abundantly and diamonds in relatively smaller quantities is because one is inexpensive to produce and one very expensive. Critics therefore claim that the reason water is cheaper than diamonds is simply because it costs less to produce. If diamonds could be produced cheaply from carbon, as modern technology may make possible in the short term, then the price of diamonds will fall, even though the demand for their use has not altered. Therefore, as these critics would claim, it is the cost of production which determines price, not the marginal utility.

It does not follow, as we already know, that the classics ignored the problems of usefulness of goods, they simply considered it from another angle. The labour theory of value distinguishes between exchange value and use value. By the third volume of *Capital*, Marx had developed a critique of the confusion between the use value or "utility" of an object and its "exchange value" which forms the basis for marginal utility theory, demonstrated very clearly, for example, in Marx's discussion around the effect of supply and demand on prices:

> If supply equals demand, they cease to act [...] . Whenever two forces operate equally in opposite directions, they balance one another, exert no outside influence, and any phenomena taking place in these circumstances must be explained by causes other than the effect of these two forces. If supply and demand balance one another, they cease to explain anything, do not affect market-values, and therefore leave us so much more in the dark about the reasons why the market-value is expressed in just this sum of money and no other. (Marx 1967)

Therefore to really explain the price of a commodity, it is necessary to consider some other factor—for Marx the labour time necessary for a commodities production—other than supply and demand.

One of Marx's followers, Maurice Dobb, writing in his 1973 *Theories of Value and Distribution*, provided a further critique of marginal utility theory. Dobb pointed out that prices derived through marginal utility theory assume a pre-existing distribution of value. Consumers with different amounts of money have vastly divergent abilities to express their different preferences. A different distribution of income would produce different prices. As marginal utility theory asserts that prices arise in the act of exchange it is unable to explain how the distribution of income affects prices and consequently it cannot explain prices.

Dobb also exposed the ideological function of marginal utility theory. Jevons, one of its key originators alongside Marshall and Walras, wrote: "so far as is consistent with the inequality of wealth in every community, all commodities are distributed by exchange so as to produce the maximum social benefit." Dobb and other Marxist and radical critics contend that this statement (and other similar claims) indicate that marginalism is intended to logically insulate market economics from criticism by making prices the natural and optimal result of a given income distribution.

These criticisms, of course, do not alter the fact that it is precisely utility that constitutes a key category, if one does not count the much earlier utilitarian doctrine, in the subjective marginal revolution. It can be defined as a kind of satisfaction resulting from the consumption of goods, the feeling of satisfaction of a want that someone gets when consuming goods, and the subjectively felt or assessed ability of goods to meet our needs.

Evident here is, already mentioned above, the limitation or, if you will, the opposition of subjectivist concept to objectivist concept of use value, which in particular may be the basis for a general sociological theory of value (which, as has already been stressed, should not be confused with the economic theory of value). From the point of view of the subjectivist theory, alcohol or drugs may have the same or an even greater ability to give pleasure to an individual than, say, a healthy soy steak.

In formal terms, the utility is in fact a subjective measure of satisfaction, with individual psychological feeling being unique for each individual, of completely different value. Carl Menger stated:

> The measure of value is entirely subjective in nature, and for this reason a good can have great value to one economising individual, little value to another, and no value at all to a third, depending upon the differences in

> their requirements and available amounts … Hence not only the nature but also the measure of value is subjective. Goods always have value to certain economising individuals and this value is also determined only by these individuals. (Menger 1994)

Hence the general law was introduced that goods are more useful the more intensely they meet a particular want of a human being.

From the standpoint of a marginal analysis the value of goods are, however, not determined by total utility, i.e. utility derived from the consumption of all units of those goods by an individual, but the marginal utility associated with the last consumed unit of a good by an economic actor. The law of diminishing marginal utility was formulated which states that the utility associated with the consumption of the last unit decreases with the increase in consumption (the more one consumes given goods, the more the utility of successive units is decreasing for a given consumer).[4]

For a long time, marginal analysis was used in economics primarily for the analysis of the demand side, the analysis of the consumer. However, it was also found applicable when it comes to the theory of production, the supply side of the economic process. It was also found that in the theory of production there is a similar law to that of diminishing marginal utility. Because it relates to production, it is termed the law of diminishing marginal productivity. On its basis one can develop an argument leading to the conclusion that all factors of production, i.e. not only labour but also capital and land, are productive and must be paid according to their contribution made in the production process.

Subjectivism is closely related to the methodological individualism of the neoclassicists.

They believe that all statements about collective social phenomena should be reduced to statements about the behaviour of individuals, of dispositions, beliefs, and attitudes of individual human beings. Psychology of individuals is the basis for explanation of social phenomena, an ultimate frame of reference of collective phenomena. This means the dependencies formulated on the microeconomic level are moved to a global, macroeconomic level.

This approach to the analysis of economic phenomena is also characteristic of the other contemporary theoretical streams, such as the Austrian school and the Lausanne school. Among the leading representatives

---

[4] With all the real or imaginary scientific aspects of equipment used to justify this law, it is hard to resist the impression of its commonsensical nature, resulting from subjectivization of the methodological approach, as a result of which there are as many examples of its truth as there is evidence—according to the Polish proverb "once you start you can't stop"—of its falsity.

of the Austrian school it is worth mentioning Böhm-Bawerk (1851–1914) and Wieser (1851–1926). The creators of the Lausanne school, often referred to as the mathematical school, are Walras (1834–1910) and Pareto (1848–1923). It was the first to attempt to feature a static picture of the economic system in the form of a system of equations. The concept of general economic equilibrium boils down to the proposition that the system of economic data has the ability to return to equilibrium. Leon Walras, as the originator of the theory of general equilibrium,[5] has left a lasting though certainly controversial mark on economic thought. This theory showed all participants of the economic game and all goods in a system of enormous number of equations. His successor, Vilfredo Pareto, created the normative basis of welfare economics. Pareto optimum is such a case of allocation of resources in which you cannot improve the situation of a unit without worsening the situation of another one.

Let us look at this, at first sight very convincing, concept, as an economic sociologist. It involves the concept of perfect competition representing a description of the ideal market structure in neoclassical economics. The model assumes a large number of sellers and buyers in the market, none of whom have the possibility to influence the price with (1) excellent and equal for all access to information on product features and prices, and (2) the absence of barriers limiting market access. Businesses

---

[5] However, an opinion of Michio Morishima, fluent both in Walrasian and Marxian economics, is worthy of mention: "Marx … should in my opinion be ranked as high as Walras in the history of mathematical economics. It has rarely been pointed out that the general equilibrium theory was formulated independently and simultaneously by Walras and Marx. It was in 1874 that Walras' *Elements d'Économie Politique Pure* was first published; whilst it was early in the 1860s that Marx began to investigate the problem of 'reproduction and circulation of the aggregate social capital.' The fact that Marx's work was only published after his death—by Engels, in volumes II and III of *Capital* in 1885 and 1894 respectively—does not affect the greatness of his achievement at all. Indeed, Marx's theory of reproduction and Walras' theory of capital accumulation should be honoured together as the parents of the modern, dynamic theory of general economic equilibrium. [...] It has often been pointed out that Walrasian microscopic equilibrium theory is rather sterile, since it is too general and complicated to be able to derive definite conclusions. It is no exaggeration to say that before Kalecki, Frisch and Tinbergen no economist except Marx, had obtained a macro-dynamic model rigorously constructed in a scientific way. His micro-model, the foundation of his macro-model, might on the other hand, as I have mentioned, be compared with Walras' general equilibrium model of capital formation and credit. These are the most elaborate models we have ever had" (Morishima 1974).

and consumers are perfectly mobile, i.e. everyone can at any time enter or exit the market, and contributions to production can be substituted at no extra cost. All companies in a given sector produce identical products, therefore a consumer is guided only by the price. Excellent competitive equilibrium allows the achievement of Pareto optimality condition (i.e. an ideal state in a market where one entity cannot increase production of one good or its own utility without reducing the production of another good, or reducing the utility of another market participant. In other words, Pareto formulated a definition of economic efficiency, expressed as a mathematical formula, which allows the determination of the optimum in the allocation of resources.

The starting point for the model was a few assumptions of conditions that must be met for optimal allocation of resources to be achieved. One of them (i.e. the aforementioned so-called Pareto optimum) was the theoretical assumption that economic efficiency is achieved if the allocation of benefits for one firm or individual does not reduce the benefit of another market participant (Pareto assumed an ideal state. Such an assumption is far from the reality of the market). Pareto's definition assumes that economising individuals or businesses and competition in the market self-limit and optimise maximalization of individual benefits. Thus, competitive markets maximize well-being of society as a whole. This scientific criterion of economic efficiency is expressed in a mathematical formula based on the assumptions adopted *a priori*, and not on the basis of empirical research.

The definition of Pareto efficiency was modified by two other economists, Nicholas Kaldor and John Richard Hicks, where the parameters of efficiency were relaxed and compensation for victims was taken into consideration. For example, compensation for the death of a child is reimbursement of the funeral costs. The principle of economic efficiency became a scientific criterion of economic prosperity and laid the foundations for a new welfare economics, in contrast to its "old" variant of material prosperity based on a comparison of well-being of individuals where the security of needs, health, etc. were measured and compared and where the key issue was growth with redistribution (Pigou 1920; 1937; 1947).

In neoclassical economics the engine of prosperity is egoistic self-interest and unlimited, continuously new desires of competitors in the market, as well as the assumption that the market is moving in the direction of perfect balance, so in the long run everyone will benefit. Such a definition of prosperity is measured with the stream of money. The optimality criterion discussed above assumes, however, a pre-set distribution of resources. If it is uneven, inequalities, according to Matthew, effecting where the rich get richer and the poor get poorer, can be exacerbated. The situation in which Pareto optimality is accompanied by social non-optimality, i.e. huge income disparities and lack of material conditions of existence of numerous groups of people, is not taken into account, for which the new welfare economics was criticized by Amartya Sen. It should be added that while inside the market as a system of mediated money exchange there is a rule of resource scarcity, outside the market, for example, the contribution of women or resources of nature are treated as infinitely flexible, having no price, and therefore no limits to their use. This reveals the same methodological property that created an occasion for a critique of Ricardo and other classical economists—the division of goods into two disjoint categories treated completely differently.

In neoclassical economics the market is, therefore, conceived of as a mechanism of exchange (trade) organized on the principle of supply and demand, which under certain conditions reaches a state of perfect equilibrium and ensures optimal allocation of resources and their efficient use. Relative scarcity of resources is assumed, and the assumption is also made that each trading entity has resources, which does not allow for an analysis of inequalities in the initial endowment of resources. Business agents make decisions based on a rational choice, led by their own preferences and utility maximization. Infinite desires of consumers are assumed. Comparison of the quality, usefulness of various goods and their mutual interdependence is not included in the parameters of the constructed model of market mechanism. Utility is transitive (substitutability), which means that each good or input to production can be replaced by another. Prices serve as information signals that determine the market value of goods and inputs. Markets should be characterized by perfect competition.

Perfectly competitive markets, however, do not exist in reality. Prices are unable to reflect the real value of all types of goods for the people. Markets cannot operate without the (free) contribution of mainly women in human reproduction, and without the use of natural resources free of charge, because the ad hoc market value does not reflect the cost of irreparably damaged environment, or transferring costs to current or next generations (Slownik Pojec 2007).

Decisions are not made on the basis of rational choice and perfect access to information, because they are made also with some level of uncertainty and inability to determine all the consequences. People, to whom we will return later, are guided by the scale of values and altruism, or the common good, not just self-interest and utility maximization (indicated by none other than Adam Smith). Persuasive advertising mobilizes emotions and harnesses people to maximization of profits. The functioning of markets depends on social institutions (cultural norms, laws, knowledge, forms of organization). Market mechanism is not the work of God's giving, does not come from the so-called natural law and is not analogous to the laws of physics. Markets and economic knowledge are historically and socially constructed (by humans).

I.1.4.1. The general equilibrium theory

Walras' theory still equally arouses interest and opposition. It is based on numerous wildly unrealistic assumptions. It has to be noted that while for many the general equilibrium analysis of Léon Walras (1880–1910) represents the apogee of neoclassical economics, formal proofs came only in the 1950s, when Kenneth Arrow (1921–) and Gerard Debreu (1921–) structured a mathematical model of a market economy, wherein the hire of factors of production and the production of goods and services are planned so as to maximize welfare. The model specifies agents with perfect foresight; agents whose choices are independent (no one's welfare is affected by what happens to someone else (Steel 2004).

It is worth pausing over Walrasian theory because of its unquestionable role not only in the history of economics. In *Elements of Pure Economics* (1874), Walras distinguishes three sections of economic behaviour: industry (production), the exchange and institutions. In his opinion, industry is not the subject of economics as a science, because it represents the art, e.g. in the form of management practices. Similar disqualification awaits institutions because ethical considerations, for example while creating laws, are inseparable from them. What remains as the subject of economics is only the exchange, which, as proposed by Walras, can best be understood by using a highly competitive model, such as the Paris stock exchange. Economics based on this model is to be, according to Walras, a scientific approach that resembles in all respects physics or mathematics; the task of the researcher should be to discover the laws which acts of purchase and sales on the market are automatically subjected to. For this purpose, according to Walras, we should accept the existence of perfect competition in the market, just as in mechanics the existence of a friction-free machine is assumed. Walras summarizes the action of these laws in the form of a mathematical model of general equilibrium.

These considerations allow us to supplement the previously formulated assessments of neoclassical economics, important, let us stress it again, due to its hegemonic position occupied for a long time in economics, which could not remain, and has not remained, without impact on the development and shape of another discipline claiming to deal with a given sector of social life, i.e. sociology of the economy. Indeed, one may look at the split between the two disciplines from the standpoint of the sociology of knowledge:

> The project of divorcing the economy from society and polity was spearheaded by capitalists and politicians but also by philosophers and social observers. As Karl Polanyi argued in *The Great Transformation* (1944), British industrialization depended on the idea that the economy could be wrenched free of society so that a free labour market could be constructed by breaking traditional links between lords and serfs as well as on the concrete public policies and capitalist practices. One manifestation of the intellectual side of the project of splitting economy from society was the division of economics and sociology into distinct disciplines. In the nineteenth century, the dividing line between economics and sociology was difficult to draw. Most of the people who are now part of sociology's heritage studied economic behaviour, and called themselves economists. Karl Marx was interested in how capitalism emerged from feudalism, Max Weber in how religious institutions hastened the development of capitalism, and Émile Durkheim in the consequences of the division of labour. Empirical studies typically showed that the economy was not a distinct realm, but that it was enmeshed in social life. In their struggle against this idea, economists increasingly turned to abstract theorizing in which they modelled behaviour "as if" the economy could be treated as a world apart. Sociologists continued to see economy and society as intertwined, but even sociologists came to accept the emerging division between the disciplines. Sociologists were inductive, deriving theories of social behaviour by observing behaviour. Economists were deductive, deriving theories of economic behaviour from the axiom that self-interest drives individual behaviour. Economics thus came increasingly to resemble physics. (Dobbin 2004)

Considering the nature of neoclassical economics, it in fact cannot claim any right to be the study of the economy, as it sterilizes the latter from the fundamental economic and social content. Such a key element of the economic structure as property relations does not exist in the neoclassical view of the economy. As a result, for the neoclassical theory it does not matter whether its claims refer to the private sector or public, its large mesh of categories are penetrated equally by employee-owned firms, companies with single or majority owners, and those with deconcentrated or dispersed ownership, etc. Firms are only technologically determined resultants of production function; money is not granted any theoretical role; similarly, the distribution of wealth and income is not only treated as externally given and therefore is not analyzed, but as indifferent to the performance of the economy, i.e. regardless of the initial state of possession of various participants, the economy will bring results consistent with the Pareto optimum; people were reduced to individualistic arch rational monads resembling giant calculators or computers whose behaviour is not subject to influence of social norms and who passively respond to market incentives; labour is treated as a factor of production fundamentally not different to others, which not only blurs the differences between them, a side effect of which is the blurring of the nature of the basic relationship between capital and wage labour on which the capitalist mode of production relies, but also between the capacity and willingness to work, i.e. labour power, and the labour itself, i.e. in the jargon of labour economists between resource categories and stream. Finally, the entire system is "mechanistic: once the initial assumptions and conditions are met, the end result is logically preordained and determined by an "'invisible hand' that efficiently coordinates the actions of individuals in the same way that the G-force coordinates the movements of the sun and planets" (Mirowski 1989).

The neoclassical school, which eventually became the basis for the so-called neoclassical synthesis,[6] more or less identified with the so-called mainstream economics and is characterised by an eclectic approach, i.e. the use of heterogeneous methodology. This is reflected in attempts to reconcile objective and subjective aspects. In this way the school partially absorbed the achievements of classical economics based on the results of the analysis of objective factors, and the accomplishments of psychological school, characterised by extreme subjectivity in the analysis of economic phenomena. It also adapted the achievements of the developing mathematical school, its attempts to use mathematics in economics.

I.1.5. Institutionalism

With all their rapidly growing influences, marginalism and neoclassicism, most likely due to the naturalness of the reaction caused by each hegemony, soon found their critics. Among them was the American institutional school, especially interesting for us because of the very close

---

[6] At the beginning of the second half of the twentieth century, under the influence of Keynes's theory, neoclassical economics expanded into macroeconomics. This synthesis was made by Paul Samuelson in his work *The Foundation of Economic Analysis* 1947.

relationship, if not downright adherence of many works of this current, to the sociology of economy.

The institutional school developed in the United States in the late nineteenth century under the influence of the English and German historical school, whose traditions were bought onto American soil by and Richard Ely and Edwin Seligman. These relationships are at first sight apparent in the initial assumption of the said critique, which was the accusation of negligence by the neoclassicists of the impact of social conditions on human activities. The American institutionalists argued that human needs are not the result of a rational choice, but are determined by social arrangements and institutions. One of the founders of this school, John Commons, insisted that it represents a return to the true spirit of the theory of Adam Smith, lost by his alleged successors under the sign of neoclassical economic tradition and political economy. Smith, Commons pointed out, saw the wood, while the later economists only trees, i.e. they focused on the logic of the market, ignoring the existing social relations within the economy and the institutional framework in which it operated (1924, 363).

In terms of institutional economics, each economic system operates within institutions such as property, a system of production and distribution of social income, and the division of labour. These institutions and their methods influence the situation of social groups, the objectives of economic activities, and individual and social preferences. The variety and variability of the institution in time means that there are no universal economic laws. Members of the school of thought stressed the importance of socio-historical and institutional factors determining the action of the so called economics "laws." Economic reality, they argued, is not immutable, but is subject to the influence of ever-changing history exerted on individuals through the institutions and society within which it operates.

This position not only presupposed the need for an interdisciplinary approach, taking into account alongside economics other social sciences such as sociology, psychology and history, but also what goes with it, the emphasis on change, a category impossible to handle on the basis of the marginal theory. Neoclassical theory, being too narrow and individualistic, was not, according to the institutionalists, able to cope with empirical reality. An example was business cycles, a favoured research object of one of the main proponents of the American institutional school, Wesley C. Mitchell, whose point of view was that general economic theory could, in his mind, only be an obstacle. The basis was to be empirical approach, represented by the National Bureau of Economic Research founded in 1920, whose staff painstakingly gathered data on economic history to measure business cycles. Studies over the business cycle are at the same time for obvious reasons a certificate of interest of Mitchell's in the category of change. He is famous for saying that in business cycles the past and present are organically linked with each other, and crisis is born of prosperity. The interest in social change is also shown by the fact that Mitchell chaired a social committee which published in 1934 an interdisciplinary volume called *Recent Social Trends*.

Another prominent American institutionalist, Thorstein Veblen, was also concerned with the business cycle. In his paper "The Theory of Business," analysing long-term trends he noticed that during the period of prosperity there is excessive credit expansion, because too great an importance is placed on "the elusive ability of corporations to make profits." A gap is revealed between the profitability of capital and its value expressed by share price, and the decline in production and employment and reduction of credit lead to determining the value of the firm on a more realistic level.

According to Veblen, a person is guided in their activities by four main instincts: care, workmanship, idle curiosity, and greed. This notion provided Veblen with one of the cornerstones of his periodization of history. In an era of peaceful savagery, communities were primarily guided by the instinct of care over the family and tribe, and through the instinct of workmanship, primitive production techniques allowed them to operate without the need for the institution of private property. Technological changes slowly gaining momentum meant that the dominant instincts became idle curiosity and workmanship and thus the predatory phase begins, with its institutions of private property and state-owned property. Looting became a habit, because there is a surplus of wealth, which is worth fighting for in order to gain advantage over others. Hunting and war are transformed into social institutions, sanctioning deceit and violence as a practice. It is then that two classes appear: the working class and the leisure class. The change is brought about by the feudal system, looting activities are displaced by industrial activity, and society becomes more peaceful and with an increased importance on the ownership of the means of production.

Veblen was a supporter of the concept of economics as an evolutionary science, however, as the preceding argument may suggest, and the following only reinforce the belief that evolutionism should not in any way be equated with historicism. This is demonstrated, amongst other things, by probably the most popular product of Veblen: his theory of the leisure class. As Veblen's commentator writes:

> The leisure class is people who, despite the substantial financial resources and ostentatious consumption do not live off work of their own hands. They live off work of other people. In every society where there is but a shadow of stratification (sociology and social anthropology cannot even imagine a perfectly egalitarian society), where there are only two steps of hierarchical ladder, there always appears the leisure class … a class that enjoys the privilege of [...] living in luxury without having to undergo a regime of physical toil. Once they were the owners of slaves, another time lords, then the bourgeoisie. (Szlendak 1996)

All these categories killed free time, which they had plenty of, with ostentatious consumption, which Veblen minutely examines starting from ostentatious idleness to a system of higher education as a derivative of ostentatious idleness. Life for the showoff which, incidentally, always resulted in development of art and science, is possible only after the fulfilment of two basic conditions: a substantial financial security that does not come from work of one's own hands and free time, which has an identical source as property—namely, someone else grapples for us with a factory machine, a field of rape, with oil pump or a stinking garbage dump.

Therefore, as in the Preface to Polish edition of the book writes Kłoskowska, Veblen derived the psychology of the leisure class from the barbarians, whose predatory culture was based on contempt for productive labour, and on expropriating the results of someone else's work. In the industrial society there is:

> … tremendous growth of opportunities for aggression, however, the exploitation of the masses takes place of marauding expeditions as a means of acquiring property. Wealth is sought as a source of prestige and plays its role fully only if it is manifested ostentatiously. The most obvious evidence of physical power and importance is leisure—having free time. (Kłoskowska)

Without denying the brilliance with which the satirical pen of Veblen paints the portrait of the leisure class, one should pay attention to the ahistorical nature of the concept, covering not only classes but social estates (e.g. clergy) of different periods of history very differently.

For sociology of the economy, more valuable than the best-known work of Veblen are other studies in which he makes interesting observations about the changes in contemporary capitalism, or engages in the constructive debate with popular views on productive labour. He writes that from the perspective of this notion, inherited from the classics of political economy, there are three factors of production: work, capital and the land, the productivity of which is assessed on the basis of the existence of three respective forms of income: wages, profits and rent. Later, economics added to this scheme a fourth factor of production—an entrepreneur. Meanwhile, Veblen shows that such a view ignores the essential role played in production by, according to his words, the collective resources of knowledge which are a product of the past and are passed on in an undivided form. Only fragments of the common resources may be subject to private appropriation in the form of patents or trademarks; the resource is not an individual property of any person (Veblen 2001, 20).

It is noteworthy that Veblen implicitly applies here a socio-economic approach to property which, like the proprietary nature of science, is more fully analyzed later in the book. It is with the relevance of knowledge and technology to production that Veblen's notion of the role of engineers, translating this knowledge into practical applications in the production process, is closely linked. He writes about the gaining of class consciousness by the technicians, the basis of which is constituted by the sense of their indispensability in the industrial system, while the direct manifestation is a sense of waste and chaos in the management of industry by the financial agents of the absentee owners (Veblen 2001:46).

I.1.5.1. Institutionalism and Tayloryzm

In Veblen's thinking, in fact, engineers had not always stood in the forefront. Frederick Winslow Taylor came up with his theory of scientific management in 1911, suggesting in it a detailed empirical analysis of each work process to determine the time required for the execution of individual operations and developed a system of incentives to achieve production standards.

Contrary to widespread opinion, Taylor himself was a man of progressive views, believing that his system would contribute to higher wages and better working conditions, including the reduced working time of workers (Belinger 2006). Taylorism did not, therefore, have an anti-worker or anti-unionist edge. Again, contrary to popular belief, Taylorism did not intend to, nor in effect did not lead to an overall loss of skills, which in our language would translate into the expropriation of workers from property in their labour power. In the eyes of many thinkers contemporary to Taylor, his scientific management system was a modern, technocratic, empirically grounded scientific solution to economic problems.

Veblen, like many radicals contemporary to him, welcomed Taylorism with open arms because he believed that it would help to plan and rationalize production, increase productivity and improve the material conditions of the labouring classes (1904, 313). He did not believe that the process of engineering led to deskilling or stupefaction. Other institutionalists, however, did not share the enthusiasm and approached Taylorism with greater caution. With the benefit of hindsight, we know that too much and too mechanical fragmentation of work process pertaining to Taylorism could harm the motivation and creativity of the workforce (Vroom & Deci 1970). The European institutionalist John Hobson noted the possible outcome of Taylorism as early as 1914. He stated that if scientific management was implemented rigorously throughout the entire field of traditional industries, not only would the cost of labour increase, but industrial progress would probably be hampered, if not halted, because the great assistance granted to technology through observations and experiments of an intelligent worker would cease under a constant stream of suggestions for detailed improvement and creative elements pertaining to work routine would disappear.

Hobson drew attention to the mechanisms of motivation and innovation that had been omitted in Veblen's approach to work and machine production. He emphasized the sphere of autonomy and decision-making present in every act of exploitation of practical skills. He criticized total separation of the mental aspect of management from labour proposed by Taylorism, claiming that infringement of this autonomous sphere would make productivity and creativity suffer. Hobson argued that the monopolisation by managers of all the knowledge associated with the process of work, as suggested by Taylorism, would be neither desirable nor feasible.

Other leading institutionalists also took part in this discussion on Taylorism. At the request of Commons, a student of Veblen and, incidentally, one of two co-authors of the name "institutional economics," Robert Hoxie, endeavoured in 1914 to write a report on Taylorism for the U.S. Federal Industrial Relations Commission. Taylor believed that workers and trade unions should be involved in the detailed study of working time. While Commons was decidedly against any direct participation of workers and trade unions in management, on the other hand he made the case for a system of consultations between the employer and trade union activists at a level by definition higher than the shopfloor to which the previous proposal applied. With a debt of gratitude to Commons, Hoxie wrote a report in a tone corresponding to his views. After the publication of the report, it met with a critical reception due to this bias, i.e. the inadequate representation of the Taylor position. The author of the report felt so devastated by the criticism that he committed suicide by cutting his throat (Belinger 2006).

In the posthumously published work entitled *Trade Unionism in the United States*, Hoxie, among others, considered Veblen's thesis according to which involvement in modern machine production would contribute quietly to the implementation of reasonable and non-traditional habits of thinking. Hoxie noticed that Veblen's argument would imply that the unionists, because of their proximity to the manufacturing process, were less likely than their employers to accept arguments justifying property on the grounds of natural rights (Belinger 2006).

Meanwhile, in his study of American trade unions, Hoxie concluded that this claim does not entirely correspond to reality. He came to the conclusion that the leading motive of action of union members was to obtain the maximum reward for their toil. Employees were at least equally interested in wages as material causality. In view of this criticism, Veblen modified his views, shifting the focus from machine workers to the well-educated engineers as agents of social change (Hodgson 2006, 225–6).

I.1.5.1.1. Commons' Theory of Transactions

The interest in change characteristic of Mitchell and Veblen was shared by another leading adherent of American institutionalism. John R. Commons in this respect shared the same methodological position, demonstrated by his multi-volume work on the history of industrial society and the labour movement in the United States. He also emphasized the desirability of an analysis of not only individual but also collective economic behaviour. Commons even made the concept of collective action the basis of his definition of the central category for the whole school discussed, i.e. institution.

He defined, with a good deal of dialectical thinking, an institution as "collective action in control, liberation and expansion of individual action" (Commons 1931, 648). Examples of institutions are for Commons both informal habit and formal organization, such as a corporation or the stock exchange. Institutions are ordinances, prohibitions, or acquiescence of behaviour of an individual and the common feature for all types of institutions is the disposal of collective sanctions.

This concept of an institution as containing in itself collective rules or, as we might say otherwise, social norms objectified towards an individual, is combined by Commons with the criticism of classical and neoclassical economics; it presupposes a radical change of the unit of analysis the transition from the goods and individual to transactions. In both criticized schools of thought the starting point, according to Commons, was man's relation towards nature, only institutional economics was based on the relationship between human beings. In classical economics the foundation was goods generated by labour, in hedonistic neoclassical economics the same goods were considered through the prism of not the producer but the consumer. In the former case it was the objective, in the latter the subjective side of the same relationship between man and the forces of nature.

According to institutionalism, the link between labour of the classics and the pleasure of their hedonistic successors is the transaction owing to which people implement their control over their access to natural forces. Transactions do not rely simply on the exchange of goods but on the sale and acquisition of rights to property and liberty created by society. Transactions must therefore be negotiated and concluded between relevant parties before a direct manufacturer can start producing goods, before a physical exchange can take place and before the consumer can consume it.

It follows, then, that the theory under consideration represents *par excellence* the sociological approach, as Commons' transactions are in each case mediated by society, i.e. by social relations.

In Commons' approach transactions can be reduced to three types[7]:

(1) Bargaining transactions
(2) Managerial transactions
(3) Rationing transactions.

The bargain is a typical market transaction, where the ruling principle is scarcity of goods. Commons does not idealise the market; he writes about conflicts of interests inseparable from transactions, of inequality of bargaining power of the parties, of the possibility of unfair pricing, etc.

Disputes arising in connection with this may be settled in court. Commons was very much interested in law, and among his comments on this subject there is at least one view that deserves to be mentioned according to which the Supreme Court's rules of procedure vary depending on, among others, the change of the nature of class domination.

The role of scarcity in bargaining transactions is taken over by another universal principle within managerial transaction—efficiency. A superior, either the owner or manager, master or another executive gives orders to a

[7] A clear echo of the typology of Commons is found in the well-known work of the representative of the neoinstitutional thought Williamson, in *Markets and Hierarchies*.

subordinate; the orders may be reasonable or not, and can be followed willingly or not.

However, rationing differs from management in that the supervisor is collective here, while individuals are subordinate, although according to Commons examples of such transactions are not only dictatorial decrees, but also the preparation of the budget of a corporation, the decisions of the court or a mediator, the distribution of pork barrel or log-rolling taking place in democratic legislatures, all of which rely on rationing of wealth or purchasing power without a bargain, which does not preclude negotiations between the parties. Commons notes that the latter are often conflated with bargaining, which should not occur since they presuppose the existence of argument, persuasion, claims contained within an approach based on order and obedience, and not, as in the case of market bargaining transaction, equality and freedom.

To return to more general considerations, the features mentioned above such as the departure from the theory of society as a whole which, at least implicitly, had been adopted by classical political economy, and the focus on a psychologically perceived individual, sometimes meant through extreme formalization that the domination of economics through the neoclassical paradigm was disastrous from the perspective of sociology of the economy, causing a persistent gap between the two disciplines. Sociological studies on economic relations developed largely owing to the potential partner's indifference to sociology, in isolation from the economic theory. That gap, however, was quite varied in a cross-national and even continental perspective; certainly to a relatively lesser extent the lack of contact with and knowledge of economics could be attributed to representatives of German sociology.

I.1.6. German *Wirtschaftssoziologie*

The founder of the younger historical school, Schmoller, was repeatedly but rather unfairly charged with sheer epistemological nihilism. As a matter of fact he did not oppose theory to facts; in his work are present not only historical facts, but also analytical generality (Swedberg 1991). In addition, the entire German sociology of economy can be seen as an attempt to reconcile the methodological dispute between theory and history.

Wirtschaftssoziologie, which is perhaps most distinctly embodied in the works of its flagship exponent, Max Weber, was to serve as a bridge between the two perspectives which clashed with each other in *Methodenstreit*, based on both historical research and analytical theory.

Between 1890 and 1930, the research program attracted many of the most creative German scholars of social science such as Karl Buecher, Joseph A. Schumpeter, Otto Hintze, Werner Sombart and Georg Simmel. But even among such an outstanding panel, the figure of Max Weber stood out. It is Weber with whom the term *Wirtschaftssoziologie* will be always associated. He wrote not only perhaps the most widely known and discussed work in the field about the role of the Protestant ethic in the formation of capitalism, the fundamental treatise *Wirtschaft und Gesellschaft*, containing a systematic exposition of his economic sociology, but also a lot of works on specific topics within sociology of the economy or economic sociology, such as medieval trading, the stock market, a case study on farming labourers, the economic history of antiquity, and the economic ethics of major world religions.

The above-mentioned exposition of the basic theoretical categories of Weber's sociology of the economy is presented in an official-like, not to say, bureaucratic style, in the form of successive definitions. Therefore, the reaction of German students should not come as a surprise, who, while listening to lectures of Weber himself at the end of the first decade of the previous century, considered them to be far too abstract.

Wanting to put socio-economic flesh on the theoretical bones, Weber prepared a series of lectures on economic history, delivered in the years 1919 and 1920. These lectures were translated by Frank Knight into English and were published under the title *General Economic History*. Many topics that Weber dealt with were also of interest to other German scholars of that period; with the problem of the causes of the emergence of capitalism taken up by, for example, W. Sombart.

A recurring theme of German social sciences was the relationship between the state and the economy, which was dealt with by Otto Hintze in his study of eighteenth-century policy of Prussia. While Hintze described the role of the state in the construction of the national market (Swedberg 1991), Schumpeter analyzed the budget and the imperialistic undertakings conducted under the aegis of the state. In his work entitled *Capitalism, Socialism and Democracy* he endeavoured, inspired by Marx and Weber, to draw out contradictions of modern capitalism.

Schumpeter was particularly attracted by the function of an entrepreneur in the economy. Entrepreneurship in his view is the core of the capitalist economy. The fate of capitalism depends on how it will be able to provide new opportunities for profit. Otherwise, it would be doomed to extinction and be replaced by some form of bureaucracy and socialism. The essence of capitalism is the process of creative destruction, the constant replacement of old firms with new ones.

One result of the above-mentioned conflict was an unsuccessful revolution in Germany in connection with which Karl Buecher published in 1919 a brochure on the nationalisation of factories. Buecher was also, through his analysis of non-market exchange and gift, one of the founders of non-market economics.

I.1.6.1. Simmel's Sociology of Money

The single most important contribution to the sociology of the measure of market exchange, i.e. money, was Georg Simmel's treatise on *The Philosophy of Money* in which he also presented his pioneer analysis of the role of trust in the economy. But while *Wirttschaft und Gesellschaft* by Weber is primarily a description of the basic categories used for the analysis of the economy, the work of Simmel,[8] presenting as it does money's ties with almost every conceivable social phenomenon, shows the relevance of economy for society as a whole. Among other observations, Simmel, one of the masters of dialectical thinking, stresses how money, which is essentially a means of exchange may, due to its unlimited potential as a medium of exchange, become an end in itself. Thus quantity transforms into quality, hunger for money and greed spread not only in the market, but also outside it, leading to the phenomenon of what Simmel calls the commodification of social life, or bringing quality down to quantity.

On the other hand, Simmel demonstrates the positive side of money as leading to an increase in individual liberty. Money does not involve the whole personality of an individual, but only its specific aspects, as we would say, related to the performance of a specific role: the buyer or seller. In relations on the basis of money there occurs the transfer of property. Thus freedom is based ultimately on ownership, the possession of goods and/or money which enables the development of constantly new social relations, to expand circles of social interaction of an individual participating in them and developing thanks to them.

Money, with its unlimited convertibility properties, can overcome physical and social barriers and distances between individuals. Money frees the individual from participating in any particular community, enabling her or him to engage in a whole network of various groups and social categories.

That freedom understood as no restrictions dialectically implies, however, sterilization, glut, burn-out, boredom, lack of a sense of meaning, loss of

[8] This section draws in part on Deflem (2003).

ability to enjoy the new relationships. The motto to this part of Simmel's argument could be an excerpt from the famous Rolling Stones' hit, "I Can't Get No Satisfaction."

In the network of relationships in which money circulates, it creates new relationships between its participants, but also leads to mutual estrangement and the creation of new divisions. Money gives birth to new social relations, but also reifies them and reduces them to the balance of costs and benefits. Monetisation of social life leads to the spread of the phenomenon of the evaluation of individuals in monetary terms. People are measured objectively and absolutely on the basis of the monetary value that they represent.

Money, Simmel shows, imprints its mark on most spheres of social life. Legal powers are transformed into monetary claims, work is useful only as long as it earns money in the form pay. All of life, Simmel argues, is under an overwhelming influence of money, subject to the process of rationalisation, the displacement of the emotional content for the benefit of computability and countability. Culture of people is replaced by a culture of things, and the creativity of the spirit, the creativity of mind is subject to the inevitable reification, reduction to the countable matter. The process of rationalisation and intellectualisation is accompanied by the transformation of all objects into commodities.

Both of these principles are the most extremely visible in the modern metropolis, the habitat of the money economy in which, Simmel writes, a person, the participant of countless relationships is treated as a number. The anonymity of contacts in a city, derived from their plurality reaches its climax. Urban life is fraught with mutual strangeness; repulsion of its participants may at a time of a closer physical contact, result in hostility and aggression.

Rationalisation that accompanies expansion of the money economy leads to disintegration of the substance of interpersonal relationships, and their transformation into impersonal relationships.[9] This also applies to the basic socio-economic relation underlying the economic system described by Simmel. The author of *The Philosophy of Money* states that: "Money creates both unprecedented economic impersonality of all economic property and also increased independence and autonomy of the personality" (Simmel 1991, 18). Simmel also drew attention to the disparity between the general progress of culture on the collective level, whether in science, technology or life comforts, etc. and its much poorer reflection amongst individuals, even those belonging to higher social estates, explaining it

[9] This view parallels Weber's famous "iron cage" argument.

through the growing division of labour, requiring from individuals more one-sided and narrow skills, the development of which too often has disastrous consequences for their personality.

I.1.7. French sociology of the economy

In this aspect, Simmel's views intersect with the thought of another classic of sociology, Emile Durkheim, who took up the issue of division of labour in his doctoral dissertation, placing it in the context of historiosophical thesis, drafting the model of the evolution of societies from mechanical to organic solidarity, i.e. replacing the bond between identical, interchangeable elements with the relationship between different, functionally specialized parts. Of course, from the viewpoint of the sociologist, other aspects of Durkheim's approach must not be underestimated, as Wilson & Dixon, for example, remind us.

A re-evaluation of the self and its acts lies at the heart of the formation of sociology. For Durkheim, in particular, a sociology of action was to be the necessary antidote to what he saw as the ultimate sterility of the Hobbesian assumptions of political economy, assumptions that "detach the individual from the rest of the world ... (that) clos(e) off every horizon," and thus lead to a palpable motivational and affective deficit in the theorisation of individual behaviour (Durkheim 1972, 94). Durkheim is quite clear: an adequate social theory must begin with a "moral individualism," with the presumption of an individuality that is social through and through.

Arguably, though, Durkheim's promise of an irreducibly social conception of human behaviour is never satisfactorily mapped out. Instead of supplying a richer conception of the self, a self that would want to behave in a more complex fashion than *homo economicus*, Durkheim's actor is somehow forced to behave in that way. The behaviour of Durkheim's actor is more complex because he or she is subject to "social facts." Indeed, a "social fact," according to Durkheim, "is to be recognised by the power of the external coercion which it exercises" (1982, 56). In a strategy reminiscent of modern socio-economics, then, Durkheim has the "social" characteristics of the individual somehow added on to a "natural" (i.e. Hobbesian) character; for what is distinctive about human, as against animal, society for Durkheim is that not all human motives are instinctive and/or internal, but rather that some are "imposed ... from the outside," are "added on to his own nature" (1982, 248). Thus, Durkheim wants to insist on an irreducibly social self (2008).

Less well known than the general view but still forming a valuable contribution to the sociology of the economy is Durkheim's discussion regarding co-operation. Co-operation in terms of the French sociologist is sharing a common task. If the division is of relatively qualitatively homogeneous tasks, it is a simple division (the division of the first degree), and if tasks are qualitatively different, heterogeneous division of labour is complex and involves specialization (Durkheim 1999, 158). Implicitly, Durkheim speaks about the categories of socio-economically understood property, noting that the division of labour connects the work of an individual with the work of all members of society, thanks to the benefits that an individual's work brings to society and the benefits that an individual derives from the social work of others. This issue is a point of contact between the German and French tradition of the sociology of the economy.

Such convergence can be traced, as for example by Swedberg (1991), in the role played in both these traditions by, on the one hand, a method of understanding (*Verstehen*) and, on the other the concept of collective representations, which Swedberg interprets as a common recourse to the cultural and symbolic dimension of reality. The matter does not appear to be that simple, however. While Durkheim's collective representations clearly belong to, in terms of socio-economic structuralism, social consciousness, i.e. supraindividual symbolic realm, with Weber's subjective motives of agents, even understood as ideal types, the issue, as discussed at more length in the next chapter, is more complex and not as straightforward as the former case. In addition, drawing attention to similarities should not obscure the differences that exist between the two traditions of thought.

Thus, if German-speaking theorists such as Weber, Sombart and Schumpeter talked about capitalism and its contradictions, the authors gathered around Durkheim preferred the term industrial society and wrote about its lack of coherence. This difference was caused, as Swedberg aptly notes, by different intellectual sources from which both traditions of thought took inspiration. In the first case, it was Marxism, and the German historical school, while in Durkheim's case, the school was, among others, Saint-Simon's conception of industrial society, whose inspiration can also be traced in the Durkheim's analysis of the division of labour.

For the treatment of the problem of industrial society, it was argued by Comte, another thinker whose accomplishments provide ideal means of production used later by the French sociology of the economy, that one needs a general theory of society which can only be delivered by sociology, in contrast to economics which deals with only one sector of society. (Such an approach, incidentally, present also in Parsonian theory, deserves to be named sociological imperialism and was alien to German sociology of the economy, which did not seek to absorb economics by sociology).

Meanwhile, the approach of the French sociologists to the sister discipline, much harsh truth as it contained, can only be described as antagonistic and hostile. In his influential *Course of Positive Philosophy*, Comte launched a stinging attack on economic theory as ideological, scholastic and sterile. Later, this criticism was repeated by Durkheim and also his colleague Francois Simiand who, as Swedberg notes, wrote in the strongest terms that:

> mathematical economists do not hesitate to call what they do science even before checking whether their hypothetical constructs are justified by facts, even if they are not justified by the facts, and even if they are contrary to the facts.
>
> It is no exaggeration to identify this as a methodological scandal, since we are dealing with a science, which aspires to explain the reality, after all. (Swedberg 1991)

Among other economic sociologists belonging to the Durkheim school are Mauss, Halbwachs, and the Bourgin brothers.

The master himself, in addition to studies already mentioned (and the notion that sources of respect for property derived, in his somewhat idiosyncratic opinion, from the religious taboo) was not, unlike some of his students and colleagues, particularly interested in economic sociology. Within the Durkheim school a study of gift by Marcel Mauss was made, being an analysis of not only the gift but also other exchanges, and the role of the economy in primitive society in general. Also noteworthy is Mauss's view, paralleled by the views of the role of history by the previously discussed German thinkers, on the need to supplement the economic sociology with anthropological research.

Simiand, less quoted today, had at one time a significant impact on the Annales historic school with the view according to which social sciences should, rather than focus on particular individual events, take the long-term perspective. This view was strongly pushed by Simiand in the pages of his gigantic statistical study of salaries in France from 1790 to 1930. The author described, from a different point of view, the methodology used in his work as a positive method; it was supposed to rely on the exclusion from the analysis of all elements of subjectivity.

This approach, however, strongly differed from that represented by the Annales school, and therefore met criticism, such as that formulated by

Marc Bloch, who said that treating numbers as objective would impose harmful limitations on the sociology of the economy. The school, in the works of its representatives, such as Braudel, Duby and others, seems to benefit more from the concept of collective representations than the aforementioned positive method.

An echo of another view deriving from the Durkheim school can be found, as mentioned above, in the notion formulated by Fernand Braudel as three forms of history, in which he distinguished:

(1) Short time, relating primarily to political events
(2) Cyclical time, relating primarily to business cycles
(3) Long duration, characteristic of changes in social structures and history of civilization.

Another theory of Braudel is related directly to the concept of long and short duration, concerning space (the concept of the centre and peripherals). In the course of his exploration of capitalism, Braudel introduced and described the forms of analysis of the economic system as a factor organizing the world: the world economic system in the sense of the global system, system economy, in which the economy is a part of the world, organizing a designated space, influencing the whole of the world. Braudel had a major impact on sociological thought, mainly through his disciple Immanuel Wallerstein.

II.1.7.1. Emmanuel Wallerstein's Theory of the World System

Wallerstein developed the theory of the world system, basing it in particular on the classic theory of dependence, which he enriched, distinguishing in addition to the centre and peripheral countries also semi-peripherals, competing with the centre countries. This novel notion has, however, remained relatively undeveloped.

The following extensive excerpt from his work should allow us to consider both pros and cons of his approach:

> A world-system is a social system, one that has boundaries, structures, member groups, rules of legitimation, and coherence. Its life is made up of the conflicting forces which hold it together by tension and tear it apart as each group seeks eternally to remold it to its advantage. It has the characteristics of an organism, in that it has a life-span over which its characteristics change in some respects and remain stable in others. [...]
>
> What characterizes a social system in my view is the fact that life within it is largely self-contained, and that the dynamics of its development

> are largely internal. The reader may feel that the use of the term "largely" is a case of academic weaseling. I admit I cannot quantify it. Probably no one ever will be able to do so, as the definition is based on a counterfactual hypothesis: If the system, for any reason, were to be cut off from all external forces (which virtually never happens), the definition implies that the system would continue to function substantially in the same manner. Again, of course, substantially is difficult to convert into hard operational criteria. Nonetheless the point is an important one and key to many parts of the empirical analyses of this book. Perhaps we should think of self-containment as a theoretical absolute, a sort of social vacuum, rarely visible and even more implausible to create artificially, but still and all a socially-real asymptote, the distance from which is somehow measurable. (Wallerstein 1976)

From this strange position, which might perhaps be best described as a mix of organicism and platonism its author draws equally remarkable conclusions:

> Using such a criterion, it is contended here that most entities usually described as social systems—"tribes," communities, nation-states—are not in fact total systems. Indeed, on the contrary, we are arguing that the only real social systems are, on the one hand, those relatively small, highly autonomous subsistence economies not part of some regular tribute-demanding system and, on the other hand, world-systems. These latter are to be sure distinguished from the former because they are relatively large; that is, they are in common parlance "worlds." More precisely, however, they are defined by the fact that their self-containment as an economic-material entity is based on extensive division of labor and that they contain within them a multiplicity of cultures. (Wallerstein 1976)

No less subversive are the following conclusions to the effect that:

> It is further argued that thus far there have only existed two varieties of such world-systems: world-empires, in which there is a single political system over most of the area, however attenuated the degree of its effective control; and those systems in which such a single political system does not exist over all, or virtually all, of the space. For convenience and for want of a better term, we are using the term "world-economy" to describe the latter. (Wallerstein 1976)

Whilst Wallerstein's terminology is certainly idiosyncratic, he hastens to translate it into more common terms:

> Finally, we have argued that prior to the modern era, world-economies were highly unstable structures which tended either to be converted into

empires or to disintegrate. It is the peculiarity of the modern world-system that a world-economy has survived for 500 years and yet has not come to be transformed into a world-empire—a peculiarity that is the secret of its strength.

This peculiarity is the political side of the form of economic organization called capitalism. Capitalism has been able to flourish precisely because the world-economy has had within its bounds not one but a multiplicity of political systems.[...] The only alternative world-system that could maintain a high level of productivity and change the system of distribution would involve the reintegration of the levels of political and economic decision-making. This would constitute a third possible form of world-system, a socialist world government. This is not a form that presently exists, and it was not even remotely conceivable in the sixteenth century. [...] We have defined a world-system as one in which there is extensive division of labor. This division is not merely functional—that is, occupational—but geographical. That is to say, the range of economic tasks is not evenly distributed throughout the world-system. In part this is the consequence of ecological considerations, to be sure. But for the most part, it is a function of the social organization of work, one which magnifies and legitimizes the ability of some groups within the system to exploit the labor of others, that is, to receive a larger share of the surplus. [...]

World-economies then are divided into core-states and peripheral areas. [...]

The division of a world-economy involves a hierarchy of occupational tasks, in which tasks requiring higher levels of skill and greater capitalization are reserved for higher-ranking areas. Since a capitalist world-economy essentially rewards accumulated capital, including human capital, at a higher rate than "raw" labor power, the geographical maldistribution of these occupational skills involves a strong trend toward self-maintenance. (Wallerstein 1976)

The preceding, in Wallerstein's judgment, supports the following startling conclusion:

the modern world-economy is, and only can be, a capitalist world-economy. It is for this reason that we have rejected the appellation of "feudalism" for the various forms of capitalist agriculture based on coerced labor which grow up in a world-economy. Furthermore, [...] we will [...] regard with great circumspection and prudence the claim that there exist in the twentieth century socialist national economies within the framework of the world-economy [...] If world-systems are the only real social systems (other than truly isolated subsistence economies), then it must follow that the emergence, consolidation, and political roles of classes and status groups must be appreciated as elements of this world system. And in turn it follows that one of the key elements in analyzing a class or a status-group

> is not only the state of its self-consciousness but the geographical scope of its self-definition.
>
> Classes always exist potentially (an sich). The issue is under what conditions they become class-conscious (fur sich), that is, operate as a group in the politico-economic arenas and even to some extent as a cultural entity. (Wallerstein 1976)

The main criticism of Wallerstein's approach is that its central notion of the world system is a Hypostase (greek: *hypóstasis*). It is by no means holism as such but a special, distorted variety that makes this charge credible. Wallerstein conceives of his key concept as a self-contained, autonomus whole, he equates it to "organism." Even as a metaphor it is not particularly fortunate, but Wallerstein is dead serious about his notion. This personalisation of sorts leads to other grave errors. Having labelled his world system as capitalism, there is no room in Wallerstein's framework for such historically existing economic formations of society as feudalism and socialism. It is one thing to wonder to what degree the so-called "real socialism" of Central and Eastern Europe was real rather than formal,[10] it is quite another to write it out of existence. As we already know, the theory divides the world into the core, the semi-periphery, and the periphery. This division started to emerge in the sixteenth century, together with the rise of capitalism. The latter emerged owing to the actions of a select group of European elites to suppress egalitarian trends in socio-economic development. While these actions were not "consciously verbalized," they proved highly successful (Wallerstein 1984, 42). Since then, the upper strata of Europe (and, since the late nineteenth century, the United States) has been busy creating a capitalist world system designed to extract surplus value from the periphery and transfer it for accumulation by the capitalists of core countries. National, cultural, and intellectual

[10] This alludes to the Marxian distinction between real and formal capitalist mode of production. As the latter was based on historically inherited means of production and types of labour power, its existence was not yet sustainable. It was only with the formation of industrial capitalism based on machinery that the capitalist mode of production generated adequately for its character and development productive forces. Similarly, it may be argued that the socialist mode of production in its existing shape has never achieved the real stage, i.e. disposing of qualitatively new means of production that would adequately express its class character. To put it in a nutshell, it would be adapted to the needs and interests of its nominal class hegemon, i.e. the working class. On the contrary, it did not go beyond the stage of mimicking the capitalist means of production and industrial organisation. This, accidentally, was in the long run the fundamental cause of its failure and eventual collapse.

developments in the last five hundred years or so have been completely subordinated to the process of extraction, distribution, and accumulation of surplus value. By the late nineteenth century, the world had become one enormous capitalist enterprise where different states, nations, and ethnic and racial groups existed only insofar as they facilitated the capitalist division of labour (Wallerstein 1984, 128; 1995, 142).

World system theory, using accumulation of capital as the main criterion, can classify any country in the world system as capitalist, thus enabling us to see beyond ideological labels and into the very nature of relations of production. Every economy in the modern world has to accumulate. Which group is in charge of accumulation determines what kind of capitalism exists. Thus, Soviet-type economies are classified as state capitalist, as accumulation is performed by the state. Wallerstein, while subscribing to Marx's theoretical frame of reference, is rather selective in relation to it, as the above example shows. In his account, economic property relations, Marx's key criterion for distinguishing different modes of production and economic formations is, strangely enough, missing. On the other hand, a common criticism (for example Mann [2010]) of economic determinism levelled against Wallerstein's theory deserves scrutiny. There are, sadly, quite a large group of authors in whose eyes any mention of the economy's role in society and history smacks of economism or economic determinism. Meanwhile, each proposition or approach suspected of such a thing must be assessed on an individual basis rather than in terms of a sweeping generalisation. In the particular case of Wallerstein, one should object not to his talk in economic terms, since it is by no means a fault, but rather to the absence of dialectics in his general approach. To be more precise, one has to do not with a total lack but rather insufficient utilisation of dialectics.

Wallerstein speaks of particular nation states, classes, even class struggle. The point is, however, that the role of the economy or technology (as it is strongly accentuated by him) for that matter should be always conceived as mediated by the internal state and contradictions of specific societal structures subject to its influence. By the way, Wallerstein, unfortunately, commits an error—which though common remains unjustified—when he uses the term of status groups rather than social estates, as will be explained in due course. It is also such seemingly minor mistakes that may be responsible for some of the weak spots in his theory. When one disposes of no adequate conceptualisation of the military, for instance, it is rather difficult to capture the historical and societal role of that group. There are some other questions raised by Wallersteinn's theory, for example the notion of unequal exchange, derived from one of its theoretical roots, with which, frankly speaking, due to its key role in his theoretical scheme, Wallerstein's whole conception stands and/or falls. This assumes the Marxian theory of value based on labour which one would like to see in action, i.e. in its empirical application to the relations of international commerce, terms of trade, etc. Having expressed all the above criticisms, one must finally admit that Wallerstein's scholarly undertaking is truly impressive, especially as regards is historical horizons. At the same time, its methodological foundation is identified by his term "unidisciplinarity," highlighting an important property of his approach—a lack of deference to the traditional boundaries of the social sciences, which he has long considered to be arbitrary, artificial and historically contingent (2004, 19). This terminological innovation is nothing more than a confirmation of the research practice of such giants of the social sciences as Marx, Weber, Simmel or Toennies. However, he appears to commit a mistake opposed to that of Granovetter discussed later in the book. While the latter lacks any valuable macrostructural theory, in Wallerstein it is the microsociological and microeconomic perspective that is largely missing, or when present is inadequate.

Still, we cannot leave without comment on one of Wallerstein's critics who opposes his alleged economic determinism as a: "macro-sociology in which four sources of social power, ideological, economic, military and political, were given equivalent status in overall social causation" (Mann 2010). As a matter of fact, one can hardly imagine a worse solution to the issue of social and historical causation. In order to grasp it, let us suppose, for the sake of argument, that the critic is right and economic determinism, as he would have it, should be rejected out of hand. Mann fails to comprehend that his own approach repeats, or more precisely, even multiplies the supposed flaws of his target. For all practical purposes, there is no significant, if any, difference between a mono-causal approach and a series of such mono-causations, which in effect Mann has proposed. If the former is flawed, the more is the latter.

I.1.7.2. Theories and categories of Pierre Bourdieu

Habitus, one of the most fundamental categories of the French theorist, is a complex concept. In the simplest terms, it could be understood as a structure of the mind characterized by a set of acquired schemata, dispositions and taste. The habitus is, by definition, isomorphic with the structural conditions in which it emerged. It has been described as a "second sense," a "practical sense" or "second nature" (Johnson 1993) that equips social actors with a practical "know-how." Habitus is manifest in styles of standing and moving, taking up space, in ways of speaking (idioms, as well as accents), in styles of dress, and so on (Bourdieu 1986, 1990). It is not, however, confined to the body, since it also involves a series of dispositions, attitudes and tastes. As such, habitus is a concept which cuts across conventional mind/body splits. It also cuts across conventional distinctions between conscious and unconscious, since much of its force derives from non-conscious elements:

> The process of acquisition (of habitus)—a practical mimesis (or mimeticism) which implies an overall relation of identification and has nothing in common with an imitation that would presuppose a conscious effort to reproduce a gesture, an utterance or an object explicitly constituted as a model—and the process of reproduction—a practical reactivation that is opposed to both memory and knowledge—tend to take place below the level of consciousness, expression and the reflexive distance which these presuppose … (The body) does not represent what it performs, it does not memorize the past, it enacts the past, bringing it back to life. What is "learned by the body" is not something one has, like knowledge that can be brandished, but something that one is. (Bourdieu 1990, 73)

As this quotation indicates, habitus carries the concept of history; both personal history and social, or collective, history. Elsewhere, Bourdieu defines habitus as "embodied history, internalized as a second nature and so forgotten as history" (Bourdieu 1990, 56). For Bourdieu, "the subject is not the instantaneous ego of a sort of singular cogito, but the individual trace of an entire collective history" (1990, 91).

The emphasis on history makes the concept of habitus appear as the carrier of the weight of dead generations, a means of more or less, straightforward reproduction. For Bourdieu, however, to be forced to act does not nullify action (Fuller 1988).

The theory of habitus challenges the foundations of the concept of free will, on the grounds that it assumes limited (by disposition or willingness to act) choice. The concept of habitus draws attention to the fact that there are unlimited possibilities for action, which a person would never have thought about.

For Bourdieu, habitus mediates between objective structures of social relations and subjective, individual action of agents thus becoming an attempt to solve one of the perennial oppositions of social sciences: between subjectivity and objectivity, between structure and agency, etc. Through this, in its creator's intention, the breakthrough character of the concept under investigation is shown, *inter alia*, by the following quotation:

> It is the primary function of the concept of habitus to break with the Cartesian philosophy of consciousness and thereby overcome the disastrous mechanism, [...] or, in other words, the alternative of determination by causes and determination by reasons; or, to put it another way, between so-called methodological individualism and what is sometimes called (among the 'individualists') holism - a semi-scientific opposition that is merely the euphemistic form of the alternative (undoubtedly the most powerful in the political order) between, on the one hand, individualism or liberalism, which regards the individual as the ultimate autonomous elementary unit, and, on the other, collectivism or socialism, which are presumed to regard the collective as primary. In so far as he or she is endowed with a habitus, the social agent is a collective individual or a collective individuated by the fact of embodying objective structures. The individual, the subjective, is social and collective. The habitus is socialized subjectivity, a historic transcendental, whose schemes of perception and appreciation (systems of preferences, tastes, etc.) are the product of collective and individual history. (Bourdieu 2005, 211)

> Reason (or rational) is limited not only, as believed by Herbert Simon, because the human mind is species limited (there is nothing new in this idea), but because it is socially structured and determined, and consequently limited.
>
> In short, if there is any universal property, it consists in the fact that agents are not universal, because their properties and in particular, their preferences and taste are the product of their position and movements within the social space and hence the collective and individual history. (Bourdieu 2005, 210)

Whatever reservations one may have over Bourdieu's approach to class, and he is not flawless in that regard, as is argued in two places in the present book, it is certainly noteworthy how Bourdieu understands this socio-cultural grounding of habitus:

> So deeply rooted are these dispositions in individuals that they are experienced as natural and their social origins (the fact that they are a product of the objective structure of society) remain unrecognised. In this instance misrecognition derives from the tendency to see only differences in lifestyle between different individuals since their position in the class structure of society is obscured. These different cultural tastes are themselves a product of the specific class habitus which everyone develops according to their relationship to economic necessity. The dominant class asserts its lifestyle (based on refined, distinguished pleasures) as the benchmark of 'good taste' to which others must aspire, and in so doing legitimises class differences under the guise of individual virtue or ability.

> The imposition of such arbitrary norms and values through symbolic violence is neither recognised as, nor reducible to, economic factors alone. Indeed, argues Looc Wacquant, "culture is no longer a passive and mystifying reflection of class relations operating through the dominance of the 'commodity form' (Marx) but an arena [...] in which [...] "the individual or collective classification struggles aimed at transforming the categories of perception and appreciation of the social world and, through this, the social world itself are indeed a forgotten dimension of the class struggle." (Wolfreys 2000)

Whatever its failings, there is no denying that building on the concept being discussed, Bourdieu's approach finds itself at the heart of economic sociology as a field oscillating between a rock and a hard place. According to the saying attributed to Bertrand Russell (but also to James Duesenberry): "While economics is about how people make choice, sociology is about how they don't have any choice to make." According to Bourdieu:

> Economic behavior socially recognised as reasonable is the product of some economic and social conditions. Only by linking it to its individual and collective genesis can you understand the economic and social conditions of existence of its possibilities and as a result both the need and sociological borders of the economic reason and seemingly unconditional concepts such as needs, preferences, or calculation. (Bourdieu 2005, 202)

However, the concept of habitus suffers from some limitations, which has profound implications for other parts of Bourdieu's theoretical framework. Bourdieu himself replied to "Those who will be first to point out that this is nothing new," by pointing out that they should ask themselves why economic theory has remained so solidly deaf to all reminders of these anthropological findings.

> For example, even in his day, Veblen defended the idea that the economic agent is not a "bundle of desires" but "a coherent structure of propensities and habits," and it was James S. Duesenberry who observed that the explanation for consumer choices was to be found not in rational planning, but rather in "learning and habit formation". And it was Veblen again, [...] who, like Jevons and Marshall, long ago enunciated the effects of structure, or of position within a structure, on the definition of needs and hence on demand. (2005, 209).

His numerous protestations to the contrary notwithstanding, Burdieu's much-trumpeted overcoming of the dilemma: subjectivism vs. objectivism that precisely the just mentioned concept purportedly permits, is illusory.

Bourdieu, who as most French Marxists, neo-Marxists and post-Marxists, whatever it would mean, is largely incapable of dialectical thinking, which demonstrates his dependence on the Althusserian formalism, style of thought that has exerted a huge influence on now already generations of especially French thinkers.Be that as it may, the Bourdelian statement reproduced below is a blatant example of determinism, thinking along the lines of "iron laws".

> "The passions of the dominated habitus, a somatized social relationship, the law of the social body converted into the law of the body, are not of a kind that can be suspended by a simple effort of will, founded on a liberatory awakening of consciousness" (2000, 179-80).

A critic points out that "in Bourdieu's accounts of bodily hexis, the body appears as a sort of physiological template that is "written by" culture and that reciprocally reproduces culture. [...] Bourdieu presents us with a sophisticated, yet deterministic, cycle of causation that runs from culture to the body, and back to culture" (Fries 2005). Thus,Bourdieu' position is a curious and unsustainable mix: on the one hand, his emphasis on the body, and "habitus deterministically connected with the body(Fries 2005)" represents a crude form of materialism, or physicalism; on the other hand, considering the fact that the body is conceived of as a mere extension of culture, as it were, it is a form of culturalism, i.e. idealism.

Such criticisms should cause to think twice all those who see the concept in question as a universal magical wand, applicable to all imaginable problems. Bourdieu, for example, contends that:

> The concept of habitus also enables us to escape the dichotomy between finalism—which defines action as determined by the conscious reference to a deliberately set purpose and which, consequently, conceives all behaviour as the product of a purely instrumental, if not indeed cynical, calculation—and mechanism, which reduces action to a pure reaction to undifferentiated causes. [...] But the task of reconciling the irreconcilable is made easier here by the fact that the two branches of the alternative are really only one [...]
>
> Habitus is a highly economical principle of action, which makes for an enormous saving in calculation (particularly in the calculation of costs of research and measurement) and also in time, which is a particularly rare resource when it comes to action. It is, therefore, particularly well suited to the ordinary conditions of existence which, either because of time pressure or an insufficiency of requisite knowledge, allow little scope for the conscious, calculated evaluation of the chances of profit. [...;] this practical sense cannot be assessed outside of the practical conditions of its implementation. [...] the habitus [...] lies below the level of the dualism of

> subject and object, activity and passivity, means and ends, determinism and freedom—in which the habitus determines itself in determining what determines it, is a calculation without calculator and an intentional action without intention, for which there is much empirical evidence. In the particular (and particularly frequent) case in which the habitus is the product of objective conditions similar to those under which it operates, it generates behaviours that are particularly well suited to those conditions without being the product of a conscious, intentional search for adaptation. [...] In this case, the effect of the habitus remains, so to speak, invisible, and the explanation in terms of habitus may seem redundant in relation to explanation in terms of the situation (one may even have the impression that we are dealing with an ad hoc explanation along the lines of the explanation of sleep by some "dormitive property"). (Bourdieu 2005, 114; author's emphasis)

Half-jokingly, the above passage may serve as crown proof of how far French sociology has been Americanised—Bourdieu's self-confidence and optimism speak for themselves. Fortunately, in the same mood, his baroque style is uniquely French.

Even putting aside Bourdieu's apparent tendency to "solve" theoretical problems by means of linguistic games, it appears that for the purposes of economic sociology much more useful is an older typology by Weber that does not, unlike Bourdieu, prejudge predominance of any particular type of action, such as habitual or instrumentally rational, for that matter. According to the author of *Economy and Society*:

> Social action, like other forms of action, may be classified in the following four types according to its mode of orientation: (i) in terms of rational orientation to a system of discrete individual ends (zwecfyational), that is, [...] the successful attainment of the actor's own rationally chosen ends; (2) in terms of rational orientation to an absolute value (wertrational); involving a conscious belief in the absolute value of some ethical, aesthetic, religious, or other form of behaviour, entirely for its own sake and independently of any prospects of external success;) in terms of affectual orientation, especially emotional, determined by the specific affects and states of feeling of the actor; traditionally oriented, through the habituation of long practice. (Weber 1947, 88)

Although Weber wrote far earlier than Bourdieu, the position of the former thinker on the role of consciousness in the context of the type of action under consideration is much subtle and dialectical:

> Strictly traditional behaviour, like the reactive type of imitation [...] is very often a matter of almost automatic reaction to habitual stimuli which guide

> behaviour in a course which has been repeatedly followed. The great bulk of all everyday action to which people have become habitually accustomed approaches this type. [...] attachment to habitual forms can be upheld with varying degrees of self-consciousness and in a variety of senses. (Weber 1947, 88)

Thus, we find Weberian taxonomy more empirically sensitive and allowing for a much wider spectrum of behaviour than Bourdiu's rigid conception, one-sidedly favouring what for Weber would be only one, albeit empirically widespread, type of action.

Related to the above commentsIn, the following specific criticism (with wide ramifications) may be levied against Bourdieu's beloved concept:

> Bourdieu's stress on the unconscious incorporation of objective structures leaves little room for conscious action to break out of the circle imposed by the pattern of Habitus-Practice-Structures-Habitus (HPSH). [...] the apparently relentless manner in which they are able to reassert themselves means that no sooner has the prospect of transformation been opened up than the revolving door of HPSH closes it off and domination is reasserted:
>
> > "struggle to impose the legitimate way of perceiving the power relations [...] can help to perpetuate or subvert these power relations."
>
> What is unclear, however, is what constitutes these power relations and in particular, what role economic factors play in their configuration. Despite his emphasis on the role played by "the symbolic aspect of the acts and relations of production … to prevent the economy from being grasped as an economy, that is, as a system governed by the laws of interested calculation, competition or exploitation," Bourdieu's conception of the economic field, as Andreani has noted, remains vague. Since he rejects the notion that economic factors determine the social structure as a whole … it becomes very hard to see either what gives rise to domination (human nature? psychological 'interests'?) or how forms of domination may change in different societies. (Wolfreys 2000)

In the face of such a powerful critique, one wonders how Bourdieu's commentator can consider the concept in question an useful one:

> It is the absence of any real sense either of what drives the system to reproduce itself, besides the mechanical process of reproduction itself, or of what may subvert or revolutionise this process, which makes the otherwise fruitful concept of habitus appear trapped in a circular process, as Bourdieu's own explanations frequently seem to underline:
>
> > "Habitus is thus at the basis of strategies of reproduction that tend to maintain separations, distances, and relations of order(ing), hence concurring in practice (although not consciously or deliberately) in

> reproducing the entire system of differences constitutive of the social order."
>
> [...] It is perhaps not surprising then that Bourdieu himself should appear so cautious about the prospects for self emancipation:
>
> "Dominated individuals … assent to much more than we believe and much more than they know. It is a formidable mechanism, like the imperial system--a wonderful instrument of ideology, much bigger and more powerful than TV or propaganda."
>
> (Wolfreys 2000)

Indeed, Bourdieu seems to focus on only one type of change, i.e. reproduction, whereas any qualitative transformation is difficult to articulate within his conceptual framework.

This may suggests not only that the notion of habitus cannot be regarded as a successful attempt to solve the dilemma of agency vs. Structure,[11] but that this relative failure has something to do with the quality of the notion of the latter or, in Bourdieu's terminology mentioned above, the field. It means a section of a social structure which is characterized by the fact that it brings together individuals and groups focused on similar efforts, and competing for a position within it, and indirectly in society as a whole, according to existing criteria in the section, around the central assumptions and objectives considered to be particularly important.

Bourdieu sometimes calls these objectives a stake in the game that goes on in the field and the assumption of the priority nature of this stake as illusions applicable in this field. In each field, the game is played according to a stake that is considered a priority in the field. For example, in the field of power one such central objective and criterion is power. In the field of political power it is political power. In the field of economic power it is the economic power. In the field of cultural production it is the specific criteria for this field, e.g. intellectual value or artistic value of creations, recognition of equal status of other artists and intellectuals, who stand alone in possession of sufficient fluency in the issues of the field (this is one of the forms of cultural capital especially inherent in that field).

A key feature of the field of power is the principle of distinction. Distinction rests in deepening and highlighting the differences between the

[11] This is not the same, as Bourdieu appears to surmise, as the opposition between methodological individualism and holism, for to effectively overcome the latter, much more detailed analysis, based on a richer conceptual apparatus, is indispensable. Notably, one should address the thorny question of levels of social reality (micro, meso and macro) and, above all, their inter-relationships.

dominant and subordinated classes, primarily by rejecting desirability, understood in a straightforward manner, as well as rejecting practical usability and moving the focal point to the aesthetic and pleasure dimensions—the refusal of practicality. It may consist of demonstrable waste (noticeable is the debt incurred by the French sociologist with Veblen), accumulation of "useless" (from a practical point of view) works of art, and the collection of cultural capital, including in the body the difference in social position by avoiding an open demonstration of naked physical force (and thus avoiding building excessive muscle tissue for such sports as golf or tennis).

In relations with intellectuals (i.e. within the field of cultural production) the field of power emphasizes its more rational, "life" or "masculine" stance, stressing the "feminine" and "irrational" nature of the attitudes presented by the intellectuals. On the other hand it needs them as providers of the aesthetic lifestyle, which gives the field of power the symbolic legitimacy (in its own eyes) of its own dominant position in relation to the subordinated classes.

In opposition to the intellectuals, the field of power is placed in the position of nature (against culture represented by intellectuals). In opposition to the dominated classes, in order to justify its dominance it adopts, using the products of the field of cultural production, the position of culture, leaving the position of nature to subordinate classes, and therefore a state somewhat deprived of culture. The field of power effects subordinate classes thanks to symbolic capital accumulated by the groups functioning in it through a mechanism of the so-called symbolic violence, the demonstration of its aesthetic approach to life thus hiding biological necessity and practicality. Therefore, subordinate classes react to it with the refusal to mimic the aesthetic impractical attitude of the dominant classes.

Symbolic violence is the most effective form of governance over the subordinate classes, since as a rule they do not even see that it is a form of violence. They are convinced that this is a natural order, that individuals and social groups with a large symbolic capital are simply better, and their better social position is normal, and they therefore do not give it consideration. An illustrative example is the relationship between sexes in which there is also the phenomenon of symbolic violence. In Bourdieu's rather sexist opinion, most women wish for a man who is taller, richer, stronger and mindlessly recognises that such a finding is in their personal interest, while such an arrangement places them in a subordinate position to a male (and men in general), a situation which is more in the interest of man.

This is the classic case of symbolic violence, because women have such ideas as a result of the impact of culture based on male domination. This in Bourdieu's view explains why even scandalous exploitation in the worst periods of feudalism so rarely aroused public opposition, although in some countries in the Middle Ages aristocracy and nobility together accounted for only a few percent of the population (2% in France, therefore measures of physical coercion, which they had at their disposal, were insufficient to dominate the rest of the society). The most important part of the task was performed by symbolic violence. Peasant masses did not revolt because they were imposed with categories of perception and evaluation justifying such injustice. It is difficult to see why this much-trumpeted concept enjoys such wide admiration. After all, it does not seem to go in any material way beyond the Marxian notion of ruling ideology. The field of cultural production can be described as consisting of a number of subfields: the literary field, the artistic field, the scientific field (academic), etc. It all depends on what exactly we want to describe; Bourdieu analyzed them in different ways, both as a whole and the individual parts. This methodological relativism seems to imply a serious flaw in the concept under consideration. Such suspect methodological fluidity always betrays a lack of precise criteria for identifying particular (in this case) fields.

The field of cultural production in France became an autonomous part of social structure in the nineteenth century, which Bourdieu calls symbolic revolution. A surplus of people with higher education in relation to the needs for official and similar positions led to the establishment of a separate field, comprised of intellectuals. Since then, they can be regarded as a *de facto* separate social class.

Bourdieu's theoretical views constitute a peculiar mix of his efforts to produce some conceptual innovations that would render his position unique and supposedly original whilst yielding to the pressure of (not always properly understood) tradition. This appears to apply also to the just mentioned case of intellectuals. Bourdieu wants to underline their position in society at large, and the only way he can think of to do this is to define them as a social class, class being a well-established concept in social science. Why his remarkable innovative capacities did not extend to this case, we don't know. What is sure enough, though, is his rather cavalier use of the concept of class. The fact of the matter is that Bourdieu lacks a separate well-defined concept with which to determine the societal position of groups acting in the extra-economic realm such as the notion of social estate proposed in this book.

Gaining of autonomy by the field was associated with the rejection of binding in the illusion of money and economic success as an indicator of quality and position. The field of cultural production replaced them with their own specific criteria which can be described as recognition from their peers, i.e. those involved in the issues of the field, such as artistic and intellectual work; imposition of these specific criteria on the whole of society and depriving the field of power or market mechanisms of the right to any meaningful assessment of works of art and works of an intellectual character; rejection of bourgeois morality, the category of *raison d'etat*, profitability and other concepts from the register of the field of power and replacing them with specific values of the field of cultural production, and the creation of alternative social norms inherent to that specific field, such as greater freedom of culture, rejection of bourgeois conventions, and condemnation of all forms of discrimination. Figures who played a huge role in this stage are Charles Baudelaire and Gustave Flaubert. As for obtaining a specific authority giving the right to speak on matters of social life and even social expectations to take such standpoint by representatives of the field, the turning point was the Dreyfus case of Émile Zola, entitled "*J'accuse!*" ["I Accuse!"].

Whilst Bourdieu's account The value of this account would be higher were it not for Boudieu's persistent tendency to over-generalise and decontextualise his argument, to reify it in terms of some elusive "fields" instead of viewing it as a case of estate-class struggle against not the "field of power" but the capitalist forces.

The field of cultural production finds itself in the left part of the field of power, or to the left of the field of power. As a result of its genesis, the structure of the field causes that leftist views are appropriate to it, because intellectuals occupy an ambivalent position of the dominated within the dominating group, which allows them to understand the position of dominated groups. Yet it is well-known that not all people involved in intellectual creativity have left-wing views. In Bourdieu's theory they are recognised as "right-wing intellectuals," with the mandatory quotation marks, or (more systemic) representatives of the field of power in the field of cultural production.

The fact that Bourdieu distances himself from the division of left-wing–right-wing suggests one of the following: either a holder of such a view does not dispose of any criteria to identify these two opposite political and ideological camps, or they constitutes a target of an observation by another famous French intellectual, Jean Paul Sartre, who said: "If I hear that the division between the left and the right has no sense,

I know that this is said by someone from the right." As the latter alternative obviously does not apply in Bourdieu's case, there remains the former possibility, more damaging to him in cognitive terms. Be that as it may, Bourdieu's "right-wingers" are people that use measures appropriate to the field of cultural production in order to express the goals and viewpoint of the field of power. Such people therefore do not represent the interests of the field of cultural production. For Bourdieu a key example was Raymond Aron.

The first thing to note is the rather loose or fuzzy use of the concept of power; there is power as such, political power and economic power in connection with which one wonders if it really constitutes the primary objective of economic agents. What about profit, capital accumulation and pay as the ends of various classes? An even more serious weakness of Bourdieu's otherwise interesting notion of the field is its lack of clear explanation of the relationship between it and the concept of structure. Bourdieu once used the two concepts in a parallel way; at other times he spoke of the structure of the field, and anything like convincing proof that his conceptual innovation permits one to say something about reality that cannot be said by the category of structure is missing. The problematic character of this term, however, pales in the shadow of another questionable characteristic of a different quality of the theoretical system of Bourdieu: an almost magical ability with which he multiplied the concept of all kinds of capital.

In the[12] panorama apart from the acceptable, as related to the economy, in financial, commercial, technological and technical (the difference between the two remaining unexplained) capital, there was no lack of (attributed to the state) "the capital of physical force," social capital to which Bourdieu claims copyright, cultural capital, supplemented with informational and scientific as well as symbolic capital (to which he claims an analogous copyright) and even such bizarre creations as legal capital. Ironically, the author of a book under the same title seems to fail to recognise the distinction between the particular and the general for, on the one hand, he associates the state with its specific capital in the form of force, but on the other simultaneously identifies: "the different types of capital (or power, which amounts to the same thing)" (Bourdieu 1986).

It is paradoxical that Bourdieu is able to criticise Becker for his concept of human capital, without noticing that the weapon he uses is

[12] An extensive, in-depth critique of human capital, social capital, etc. can be found in my forthcoming books: "Karl Marx's Posthumous Revenge? The Proliferation of Capitals in the Social Sciences" (Brill) and "Anti-Capital [Human, Social and Cultural]" (Ashgate).

double-edged. This proliferation of terms is subject to the criticism by Baron & Hannan (1994, 1124) who describe the puzzling efforts by rational choice sociologists, including exchange theorists, to expand the types of capital, stating that they are "baffled that sociologists have begun referring to virtually every social feature as a form of capital."

From our theoretical point of view, the concept of all kinds of capitals of Bourdieu represents a confusion of non-economic phenomena (e.g. belonging to the ideational structure), including objects of estate and non-economic ownership relations, apparent in the following definition: "cultural capital, i.e. [...] a means of acquiring exclusive advantages" (Bourdieu 1986), with elements associated to the economic structure, including aspects of ownership of labour power. Indeed, this example clearly shows the harmful consequences of a lack of the notion of economic property which is repeatedly conflated with that of capital as such:

> the structure of the distribution of the capital among the various directors (*dirigeants*) of the firm, that is, between owners and "functionaries"—managers—and, among these latter, between the holders of different species of cultural capital: predominantly financial, technical or commercial, that is to say, in the French case, between the various elite corps and the schools where they received their training: the Ecole Nationale d' Administration, the Ecole Poly technique or the Ecole des Hautes Etudes Commerciales. (Bourdieu 2005)

Bourdieu's inability to recognise that in the above case various degrees of labour power are at stake is, as a matter of fact, hardly surprising given his flawed understanding of ownership in general which stems, on the one hand, from his dependence on the jurisprudential notion of property and, on the other, from the stance which may be dubbed "pandominationalism," i.e. transforming almost each relationship under investigation into one or another form of power or force, for that matter, which is clearly demonstrated, *inter alia*, by the following statement:

> The evolution of the relations of force between the major agents in the field of power within firms: most notably one sees, first, a pre-eminence of entrepreneurs with a mastery of new technologies, capable of assembling the funds required to exploit them, then the increasingly inevitable intervention of bankers and financial institutions, and finally the rise of managers. However, apart from the fact that one must analyze the particular form the configuration of the distribution of powers among firms assumes at each state of each field, it is by analysing, for each firm at every moment, the form of the configuration of powers within the field of power

> over the firm that one can fully understand the logic of the struggles in which the firm's goals are determined. It is, in fact, clear that these goals are stakes in struggles and that, for the rational calculations of an enlightened "decision-maker," we have to substitute the political struggle among agents who tend to identify their specific interests (linked to their position in the firm and their dispositions) with the interests of the firm and whose power can no doubt be measured by their capacity to identify, for better or for worse (as the Henry Ford example shows), the interests of the firm with their interests within the firm. (Bourdieu 2005, 207)

And these conceptual drawbacks seem to express more general weaknesses pertinent to the general theory of society of Bourdieu. Of course, one could try to counter this objection, stating that the author of *Social Structures of the Economy* has no obligation to accept a theory such as that proposed in this book, because they have their own. The point, however, is that this notion lacks complexity, consequence and structure.

Somewhat similar objections may also be addressed towards the theory of class that Bourdieu employed. Declaratively, the French thinker distanced himself against Marxism, but in practice he took a considerable part of Marx's legacy in the field of class theory, using, for example, categories such as the petty bourgeoisie or working class. Interestingly enough, capitalists are replaced by entrepreneurs, and, worse, the concepts of classes mingle with professional groups and strata such as the middle classes, higher classes etc. Meanwhile, the basic model, instead of making them more prominent, rather obliterates the boundaries between classes and estates, which derives from its dependence on the concept of multiple capitals criticised above. Bourdieu distinguishes the dominant class due to the size of the economic capital and cultural heritage. These include industrialists, managers of the private sector and university professors. At the opposite extreme is the working class including labourers and farm workers. Between these classes emerges the middle class, i.e. small business owners, technicians, secretaries or primary school teachers. The French sociologist also divides the dominant class due to the predominance of the capital. Industrialists and trade staff have a larger stock of economic capital compared to professors and artistic producers, but in turn those have a larger stock of cultural capital (Weininger 2002, 123–124).

The under-specified, to say the least, relationship between such concepts as class, ownership and capital (due, amongst other things, to the latter's exuberance) cannot but affect his particular theories and arguments.

> In 1970 the highly influential Reproduction (Bourdieu and Passeron 1977) [...] offered a theory of how cultural reproduction fosters the social reproduction of the relations between groups and classes. The central but curiously ill-defined explanatory gambit of this text is the use of the concept of 'capital'. Different forms of capital appear through the book, each without proper definition: economic capital (implicitly), cultural capital, linguistic capital, scholastic capital, social capital. Cultural capital is the most developed of these, being used to explain how the cultural 'judgement' of the dominant group is presented as universal and selectively endowed, allowing it to legitimize its domination.(Field, Schuller, Baron, Field 200)

The failings identified above are neither accidental nor exceptional, as the following criticism clearly shows:

> The contrast between sophisticated theoretical claims and weak empirical data is stark. Mechanisms of cultural reproduction and social reproduction are operationalized through the simple crosstabulation of percentages of, for example, working/middle/upper class students by male/female by above/below twelve out of 20 in a particular test (Bourdieu and Passeron 1977: 81, Table 5). While statistical analysis later became more complex, the problem of operationalizing non-tangible 'capitals' has remained significant. (Field, Schuller, Baron 2000)

Complex, too, became his theory of capital(s):

> In Distinction, forms of capital are presented as real entities: 'the overall volume of capital, understood as the set of actually useable resources and powers— economic capital, cultural capital and also social capital' (Bourdieu 1984: 114). In this formulation 'also' is the key word as social capital effectively drops from Bourdieu's vision, being subsumed under economic and cultural capital. In Language and Symbolic Power, a series of essays written between 1977 and 1982 (Bourdieu 1991 b), social capital appears along with economic capital, cultural capital, and symbolic capital as the principal fields which combine to constitute the social position of any particular person, but the inter-relation of these concepts is not explored. The elaboration of forms of capital continues in Homo Academicus (Bourdieu 1988), with social capital now appearing alongside yet new forms of capital such as academic capital or the capital of services rendered. Social capital, however, is also highlighted in the text in that it constitutes half of the domain from which the highly orthodox, explanatory quantitative variables are drawn (Bourdieu 1988: Table 1, Appendix 1).
>
> The evocative use of the concept 'capital', with its promiscuous proliferation of varieties, was reined in by Bourdieu in 1983 in an essay on 'The Forms of Capital' (Bourdieu 1997). While acknowledging the primacy of

> economic capital in his previous work, Bourdieu had tended to stress cultural capital, with social capital a very distant third. In a subtle shift of position Bourdieu posits a unitary capital which 'can present itself in three fundamental guises' (1997: 47), economic, cultural, and social. (Field, Schuller, Baron 2000)

Yet the above move is much more than just a minor shift in emphasis,, rather, it is a logical conclusion of Bourdiu's scholastic approach far from being inconsequential in that "the use of the concept of capital is often metaphorical rather than analytically disciplined. When applied by Bourdieu to empirical research the substantial problems of operationalizing the concept make this important theoretical corpus appear ill-founded" (Field, Schuller, Baron 2000).

And indeed, Such flaws in Bourdieu's analytical framework have inevitable empirical implications:

> Bourdieu and Passeron (1977), in developing the concept of cultural capital and habitus sought to explain how schools, despite their relative autonomy from social structures, reproduced economic and social relations. [...] However, empirical evidence for this explanation is weak. Similarly, the treatment of the cultural capital of elites as unproblematically dominant without any attention to resistant other cultures means that we are still far from understanding how cultural capital works. (Munn 2000)

But this is not the end of the story:

> One influential social reproduction argument concerns the special importance of cultural capital (Bourdieu and Passeron 1970; Bourdieu 1997 [1983]): that the odds in school are stacked particularly heavily in favour of children and youth whose parents are the well-placed insiders in a society's educational and cultural institutions, the cultural elite. [...] It would seem that the further one's origin is from a country's cultural elite, the fewer are one's chances of doing well in school. By this line of reasoning, immigrant children should be destined to fail in school.
>
> Very often, immigrant parents do not speak with ease the language of the country to which they have moved, let alone master its more socially exclusive nuances. Not being familiar with the education system from their own experience, immigrants should be at a disadvantage in helping their children navigate through it. Excepting those few who belong to a jet-setting international elite, the parents' grasp of the life-style subtleties of the form of cultural capital into whose ambit they have moved would be poor.[...]
>
> [...] Does the weight of research evidence support such pessimistic hypotheses?

> Findings of poor achievement are not dominant in international research literature on the educational achievement of immigrant youth. Sometimes immigrant youth from certain backgrounds lag behind others in school, but they typically do better than might be expected when account is taken of their parents' social class circumstances and level of schooling.
>
> […] Quantitative survey research in the United States has corroborated the theme of immigrants trying harder and having high educational ambitions. […] Most of the immigrant groupings examined outperform their peers. […] in Norway. In Sweden, in a study of whole cohorts of people born in Sweden during 1953-70, Simila (1994) found that those of immigrant background obtained higher rates of upper academic-secondary schooling than those of non-immigrant parentage, after controlling for parental socioeconomic status (SES). Intriguingly the sole exceptions were those of Finnish, Norwegian and Danish parentage, groups which had come from just across the border. (LAUGIQ 2000)

Indeed, "social history is replete with examples concerning certain religious minorities as well as certain immigrant groups who in the space of two to three generations have risen from humble beginnings to a preponderance in middle-class professions: for example, Japanese Americans, Chinese Americans, immigrant Jews who started in the sweatshops of New York's garment district or in London's Spitalsfield. Social reproduction is a reality, but so also are the forces that defy it" (LAUGIQ 2000).

Overall then, to return to more general conclusions, even though relations between the European sociology and economics can hardly be described as idyllic (the latter often became the target of criticism of the representatives of the former), then at least sociologists did not respond in kind to the growing "undersocialisation," so to speak, of economics, i.e. turning its back to the economy, with the result that the European sociology of the economy could boast significant achievements.

I.1.8. The origins of sociology of the economy in the U.S.

In the United States at the turn of the century, sociology of the economy was still in its infancy. None of the founding fathers of American sociology published any material work in this field. Reasons for the delay of the development of American economic sociology economy were many, among them traditions of thought about society apart from the old continent; they lacked trends, like Marxism or the historical school, which would deal with the issue. Another reason was an openly xenophobic and sectarian attitude of economists,[13] later replaced by indifference in relation to the attempts of sociologists to enter what they regarded as their own proprietary territory. Economists blandly advised sociologists to stay away from economic issues and to focus exclusively on social topics such as family, poverty or deviance (Swedberg 1991, 266).

Fortunately, not everyone complied with this advice. Charles Horton Cooley wrote his doctoral thesis in economics on the theory of transport, which contributes not only to human ecology but also the sociology of the economy. For Cooley's work in this field it was typical, according to his theoretical position, to emphasize the role of communication in economic relations (Swedberg 1991). Also worthy of mention are works on transport and communications from the first half of the twentieth century by the proponents of social ecology, including those related to the Chicago school such as Robert Park and W.F. Ogburn. The researchers of the Chicago School generally respected social division of labour between sociology and economics leaving economic issues as a monopoly of economists. However, they made an important contribution to two new substantive areas which were the subjects of two respective branches of sociology of the economy: sociology of the professions and the industrial sociology.

Everett C. Hughes is considered the founder of the former sub-discipline, while industrial sociology had its source in studies of Elton Mayo and his Harvard colleagues in the Hawthorne plant owned by the Western Electric Company, conducted in the late 1920s and 30s. While it is fair to say that subsequent studies of industrial sociologists on performance and staff morale were based largely on the foundations created by this research, it was the Chicago sociologists that made a groundbreaking contribution to the field of industrial sociology, both theoretically and methodologically. The latter consisted of participant

[13] The strength of that derogatory attitude is shown by the following anecdote: “An Indian-born economist once explained his personal theory of reincarnation to his graduate economics class. 'If you are a good economist, a virtuous economist,' he said, 'you are reborn as a physicist. But if you are an evil, wicked economist, you are reborn as a sociologist.'" For the economist, the pinnacle of the academic pyramid had become the most pristine science with the most immutable laws. Economists spelled out how people would behave if they followed pure principles of self-interest. Like physicists, they thought they were identifying universal laws. Like philosophers, they imagined an ideal world and worked out the details of how people would behave in it. They came to play the role that prophets played in another age, conjuring up a perfect world and its rules of behavior” (Dobbin 2004).

observation technique, the former on the recognition that the relationship between employees and the management can often take a conflicting form.

I.1.9. American Economics and Sociology

An attempt at a realistic treatment of at least certain aspects of the capitalist economy can also be found in the works of the follower of the institutional way of thinking, John Kenneth Galbraith, who coined the concept of countervailing power, which, in his opinion, is created by trade unions for the growing power of corporations and its ruling technostructure. Another example of this phenomenon, occurring this time in the product market, is the ability of major buyers such as car manufacturers in relationships with steel manufacturers and retailers nationwide in dealing with food manufacturers to obtain price discounts and rebates. This introduces significant modifications to the textbook model of free competition, since it enables us to conceive of the existing capitalist economy in terms of bilateral monopoly / oligopoly.

This is an example of the general theoretical and methodological approach of Galbraith, who conceived of capitalism historically, speaking of the various phases of its development, from early to contemporary. In a modern capitalist economy in his opinion there are two distinct sectors—planning and market. The first (which could be described as oligopolistic or monopolistic) is created by large corporations. The market sector on the other hand consist of medium-sized and small companies. Mega-corporations have the ability to administer a large part of the supply and demand, becoming an independent regulator. Following in the footsteps of technocracy of Veblen, Galbraith also put forward the thesis of the inevitability of those big, technically complex corporations to find themselves under the control of technostructure, i.e. an elite group consisting of engineers, technicians, middle and senior management, accountants and lawyers as the only ones competent enough to make rational economic decisions.

This thesis, whose weakness is the lack of precision of the term technostructure which does not represent a single force but involves various class groups, also fits into the framework of a notion already formulated by other institutionalists Berle & Means, in the famous work *The Modern Corporation and Private Property*, of separation of ownership and management or control, which was also taken up by Burnham in his theory of managerial revolution. In a somewhat different shape it can also be found in the so called agency (principal-agent) theory or, more generally, in the views of the theory of property rights.

From the standpoint of economic and sociological content, however, the work of Galbraith, let us note, was an exception against the background of the development of economic thought as of the 1930s. The victory of the school of neoclassical economics over the historical school in Europe and the institutional school in the U.S. meant the suspension of relations with sociology, which could not fail to affect the quantity and quality of the work of economists addressing sociological issues. Economists dealing with questions important from the socio-economic point of view followed two paths: a minority consisting of, among others, JK Galbraith, Gummar Myrdal, Raoul Prebisch and Robert L. Heibroner continued the tradition of old institutionalism.

I.1.9.1. Neoinstitutionalism

Meanwhile, increasing popularity was gained by so-called neoinstitutionalism, the direction of thinking with a somewhat confusing name in that it refers to its predecessor in a perverse way, literally reversing its standpoint.

The new institutionalism uses theorems of neoclassical economics to explain the history, social relations and the formation of institutions, while the former does the opposite, explaining the economic actions and relations on the basis of these socio-historical conditions. The said current unfolded for good only in the 1970s, but its origins should be linked to an article, as we shall see also in a later chapter, relevant to sociology of the economy. Ronald Coase published his essay "The Nature of the Firm" in 1937, long before the work of Galbraith, in which he described the planning sector.

Coase, who studied the organizational structures of such companies as Ford or General Motors, saw that their organization is barely different from the Soviet type of economic organization as a result of centralization of decision-making, planning and control. Coase sought to understand why these almost self-sufficient giants are created—at the time, even rubber plantations were owned by Ford! He wondered why otherwise sensible people conducted their business on the model of the Stalinist state. Trying to find reasons, Coase reached the conclusion that they are stuck in market "resistances," later called transaction costs (transaction cost economics was developed especially by Oliver Williamson). Coase identified three types of transaction costs:

Search costs, which the company has to pay to reach potential partners. How to find reliable suppliers? Who knows them, and may issue a certificate? Even if you managed to find these potential cooperators, their check would require time and money.

Contracting costs alone explain why the execution of certain operations is easier within a company than outside it. The costs of contracting are lawyers' fees, time spent on negotiations and other costs that have to be borne to buy a larger consignment of goods. If one needs to repeat this each time, it's not surprising that firms prefer to do it on their own.

Coordination costs are time and effort the company must take to combine supply of materials and other means of production, employees and any other factors. We should also realize, as pointed out by the author whose commentary I am drawing on here, that in those days, even in the United States, trying to coordinate all this would lead to considerable phone bills, and even then no one could guarantee that what you ordered would be sent to the customer, and you would not be outbid by a competitor: “It was easier to give an order to a daughter plant” (Kuszweyko 2001).

Each of these costs was an argument to do everything on your own and not use the intermediary market. Hence, the statement that later gained the name the Coase Law: a company should grow as long as the cost of transaction within the company is lower than the cost of transaction outside it. This could be regarded as a theoretical justification for the establishment of the mega corporations later described by Galbraith. However, in order to give this statement a scientific value, you need to justify theoretically its second component, which in this form is a purely descriptive, empiricist, claim. Its author would not avoid this challenge. Taking the bull by the horns, he referred, first of all, in the spirit of the marginal theory, to the principle of declining revenues from management, i.e. the increase in the cost of organizing additional transaction within the company. Secondly, the increase in the number of transactions organized within a company can cause those managing it to fail to make the best use of factors of production available to them. And so, like the previous case, the cost of organizing the next transaction within the company becomes in the end equal to the cost of carrying out the transaction on the open market (or of implementing it by another entrepreneur), in this case at some point the cost of wastage is aligned with the cost of the exchange transaction on market, or loss resulting from its takeover by a competitor. Thirdly and finally, the price of the supply of one or more factors of production may rise, because the advantage a large company seems to dispose of in this section may be inadequate compared with the advantages available to a smaller company (Coase 1937, 26).

This interesting notion of Coase requires comment. It explores, as we shall see in the appropriate chapter, some economic and ownership benefits stemming from the existence of a company, but not all. For example it omits the advantages of a unit division of labour. One could point to a drawback of the above-mentioned notion consisting in the fact that its author does not consider non-contractual relationships, as between friends or family. More importantly, new light on the Coase law is also cast by the appearance of new ideal work resources, especially indirectly material work. What consequences for the optimal size of a company does computerisation of the economy have? On the one hand, management based on computerized work should reduce the cost of running a large company. On the other, however, the lowered cost of searching for partners due to broadening and improving the market through the internet launches the opposite tendency, to reduce the size of the company. Transaction costs are still there, only they are often larger within a company than on the market. Product search is now entering the name of the product you are searching into a "window" on the relevant website of a stock exchange; you do not need to go from city to city. We need information about the company's credibility, and reports of analysts, consulting firms, companies specializing in assessments and in the certification are all available on the internet. The costs of contracting, what steel is needed and how much and when, whether glass panes or varnish are needed, how much, what type, when, what price—all of these can be input in appropriate boxes. With regard to coordination costs, each supply can be traced without the need to move away from the desk, and the "networked" supplier can give us access to the information in their production management system. It is worth noting that the internet also reduces transaction costs within the company. The CEO may at any time look into what is happening on the production line anywhere in the world, even through the use of installed cameras connected to the computer network, not to mention access to information about the inventory, sales volume and receivables from customers (Kuszweyko 2001).

The proof that the analysis of economic phenomena cannot be confined to a purely economic point of view, and that the sociological viewpoint must also be taken into account, is the fact that the vested interests, born in the industrial age, are quite resilient, thus considerably slowing down the speed in which new mechanisms for quality control and resource allocation are introduced. But the phenomena connected to the internet have implications for the concept of transaction costs for yet another reason.

The notion of transaction costs explains why the economy is composed of a number of companies, and not many more individuals, who offer their services. Open source software development and transfer of that model to internet projects (e.g. Wikipedia), or cultural goods (the creative commons license) have been described in at least a few critically acclaimed works from the point of view of the new model of production and the economic mechanisms behind it.

Works by Eric S. Raymond (*The Cathedral and the Bazaar*, *The Magic Cauldron*), Professor Yochai Benkler ("Coase's Penguin, or Linux and The Nature of the Firm," *The Wealth of Networks: How Social Production Transforms Markets and Freedom*) and Don Tapscott & Anthony Williams (*Wikinomics*) state that on the market a new model of goods production appeared of a quality comparable to that of products from the traditional commercial model (Linux vs. Windows, or Wikipedia vs. Britannica).

In 2002, Yochai Benkler (professor of law at Yale University) published an essay regarding a possible IP law change caused by the emergence of a new model of production called peer production. Peer production is a term that describes a new mode of production, different from the market where cooperation of often large groups of people through the internet, whose participants are mostly financially unrewarded, leads to substantial undertakings.

To come back to our topic of interrelations of two adjacent social sciences, the relationship and the state of both disciplines may be demonstrated by a speech from 1936 by the President of the American Sociological Association Henry Pratt Fairchild, who lamented the mutual estrangement of the two fields of research, noting that it is time to change the existing state of affairs and thereby implement the convergence of economics and sociology. In his opinion, economic institutions should be included in sociology on a par with the family, the state and school (1937, 7). According to Fairchild, economists would continue to explore economic relations, while sociologists should focus on the investigation of social organizations within which these relations take place. Let us note immediately a certain limitation of such delineation of demarcated fields of interest of economics and sociology of the economy. Luckily, not all representatives of the latter shared this point of view, as we could partly and will continue to see.

First and foremost, the eminent American sociologist Talcott Parsons should be mentioned in this context. His doctoral dissertation of 1927 was a declaration of his socio-economic interests, titled "*Der Kapitalismus bet Sombart und Weber*." In a later work entitled *The Structure of Social Action*, Parsons took up among other things the issue of the relationship of economics and sociology. Even before *The Structure of Social Action* (1937; 1949a) was published, Parsons had produced a series of theoretical essays in leading economics journals in which he dealt critically with economic action theory and with the impact of "noneconomic factors" on the economy. In the 1940s more essays followed regarding economic action theory (1949b, 1954a) and professions (1951; 1954b) (Beckert 2006).

After a few years, sociology of the economy started to take shape in the USA as an independent academic discipline. In 1951, Parsons' student Francis X. Sutton and economist James Duesenberry began classes at Harvard University, called "A Sociological Analysis of Economic Behaviour." Sutton managed to persuade other significant economists such as Carl Kaysen, James Tobin and Seymour E. Harris to join the project, the result of which was the 1956 publication *American Business Creed*, which includes the thesis that the ideology of American businesses is the result of tensions in their social role. Parsons himself made a personal contribution to the new (in the American academic field) discipline in 1953 in a series of the so-called Marshall lectures, which became the basis for a book published shortly after, titled *Economy and Society*, co-authored by Neil Smelser. Because a separate part of this book is devoted to the theory expounded in the pages of that work, we confine ourselves at this point to a remark about the change in point of view on the interrelation of economics and sociology, which compares the said work with *The Structure of Social Action* mentioned above. In the latter work, Parsons presented himself as a supporter of an analytical factor view. This approach would rely on different points of view of economics and sociology, the first of which would consider the alternative use of scarce resources to meet needs, while the second would focus on values, i.e. fundamental common ends. By contrast, in *Economy and Society* economics is no longer regarded as a science equivalent or alternative to sociology but as a special case of a general theory of social system.

Details and implications of this approach will be considered in the above-mentioned chapter, so that at the present moment we confine ourselves to a brief discussion of subsequent research interests of the two sociologists mentioned above, in terms of their relationship to the sociology of the economy (and economic sociology for that matter). Parsons in that regard restricted himself essentially to the interest in money, mainly through the prism of his theory of interchanges.

Smelser's interest in sociology of the economy proved more enduring. In *Social Change in the Industrial Revolution*, he highlighted the importance of sociological analysis of changes in the study of the economy. In 1963, he published the first textbook of economic sociology, and two years later the first reader in that discipline. Among Smelser's subsequent contributions in this field one should mention his co-authorship of the 1994 *Handbook of Economic Sociology*.

Before we go on to discuss later fortunes and misfortunes of our discipline, we ought to mention some others, apart from those in the most basic economics and sociology disciplines, whose contribution should not be neglected.

I.1.10. Economic anthropology

Anthropologist and economic historian Karl Polanyi is known primarily as the author of *The Great Transformation*, featuring a sharp critique of capitalism, especially in its unbridled variety. He wrote, among other things, that "the license to the market mechanism to be the sole manager of the fate of human beings and their natural environment … can have devastating effect in the form of society's devastation" (Polanyi 1944, 73). However, although this aspect of his work probably brought him the widest acclaim, from a scientific point of view, for sociology of the economy the most important thing seems to be, most likely drawing on a parallel Weberian distinction, the distinction made between two meanings of the term "economics." In the formal meaning, economics is a logic of rational action and decision-making based on rational choice between alternative uses of scarce (rare) resources. Meanwhile substantive, the second meaning highlighted by Polanyi, does not necessarily assume either rational decision making or the condition of scarcity, but refers simply to the various processes of securing the necessities of life by people in the context of their natural and social environment. Processes of acquisition of the means of subsistence by the society that assume adaptation to their physical conditions may, but do not have to, include the maximization of utility or preferences as understood by conventional economics identified with the formalist position. In its broader sense, which Polanyi as an anthropologist and a historian opted for, the subject of economics is the process of satisfaction by the society of their material needs.

Polanyi's term "great transformation" refers to the gap between modern societies dominated by the market and non-capitalist, non-Western pre-industrial societies. Economics in the material sense applies only to the latter, similar to those based on the centrally planned economy, for example. The activities of economic agents in these societies are determined not so much by the principle of profit maximization, but social ties, cultural values, moral considerations, politics or religion.

Production in most of the peasant and tribal societies is production for own use, and operates on the principles of natural economy and not for-profit. According to Polanyi, in modern capitalist economies the substantive approach can be identified with a formalist approach, since the way in which people acquire the means of subsistence is based here on the rule of rational choice.

By contrast, in non-capitalist, pre-industrial societies such convergence cannot be found; in contrast to capitalist Western societies, transfer of goods and services between people is based here not on a market commodity exchange, but a redistribution or the rule of reciprocity. Reciprocating with goods and services is a type of non market exchange that occurs within a long-term relationship or association. Redistribution implies the existence of a strong political centre, such as kinship-based leadership, and receiving and distributing the means of subsistence in accordance with culturally specific rules.

In societies based on the non-market economy one can usually encounter two types of exchange. By contrast, in modern industrial societies the dominant form of economic ties and coordination of economic life is commodity exchange. While the principle of reciprocity can still persist here in family relations as well as in the relations between households, and redistribution to some extent is implenented by the state and charitable institutions, from the viewpoint of methodological substantivism, as opposed to formalism, each of these three types of circulation of goods and service requires a separate group of analytical category. However questionable a too rigid division between the two types of societies, assuming that in capitalism social factors do not affect the price governed by pure logic of supply and demand, the value of this particular contribution to the sociology of the economy is undisputable.

The substantive approach as conceived of by Polanyi and his followers frames economic activities as embedded in the social and cultural reality and the socio-historical conditions of economic life. The economy is not an isolated domain, but is included in a broader social system—for example, exchange takes place not in a social vacuum, but within the framework and is regulated by the society. The functioning of the economy is affected not only by economic institutions but also by politics and religion, in the process of acquiring the means of subsistence by people an important role is played by standards and socio-cultural values. Consequently, any examination of the economy as being an analytically isolated entity separated from its socio-cultural and political context is doomed to failure.

Methodological substantivism, supported by Polanyi, focuses on a variety of social institutions on which the process of gaining means of subsistence by the people is based; market is just one of many institutions defining the nature of economic relations. The notion of embeddedness made a real impact, not only in anthropology, but also sociology, illustrated by Michael Chibnik with an example of a study of the ethnic Chinese network of economic relations in Indonesia by Mark Granovetter. The author discovered that individual economic activities are rooted in a network of strong personal relationships. Cultivating personal relationships between merchants and customers becomes of equal if not greater importance than economic transactions as such. Acts of economic exchange occur not between strangers, anonymous individuals, but between those involved in a long-term bond. Granovetter criticized the conventional neoclassical definition of economic activity as separating the economy from society and culture, and thus leading to the atomisation of human behaviour, an "undersocialized" concept of the individual: human individuals do not take decisions or actions as atoms outside and independently of social context.

I.1.11. Economic psychology

It is also properly understood that psychology can contribute to our field of interest. After all, when this science deals with mechanisms of conduct of humans acting in the economy, it deals with their behaviour within one of the substructures of society and thus becomes social psychology. The findings of psychology will be repeatedly recalled in later chapters; however, let us at this point approach the issues that are the subject of the discipline called by its students economic psychology. For that purpose, let's use a sketchy and incomplete overview of the issues raised in a textbook of the same title.

In a collective work edited by Zbigniew Tyszka the authors discuss, among others, the issue of decision-making, both in terms of certainty and risk, as well as from the perspective of the time horizon. At the same time, it is worth pointing out that the authors seek to portray actual behaviour of people from the perspective of the theory of discounted utility by Irving Fisher, the general result of which appears to be at odds with the simple model of *homo economicus*. This will be the subject of our later separate discussion, so here we make only a remark regarding the volume under consideration that similar conclusions also result from the subsequent chapters, making for a total image of a man as a being full of restrictions and contradictions, led by emotions, not just intellect and reason.

This treatment, let us add, parallels criticisms put forward by some other commentators, such as Steel who contends that the dominance that has been achieved by neoclassical economics might be attributed to a desire to match the analytical achievements of physical science (2004). In the event, it delivers little more than mathematics. In the pursuit of pseudo-scientific tractability, neoclassical economics neglects the dynamic aspects of the social realm and delivers a static utilitarian calculus. In the context of its earlier classical usage, utility, "usefulness," implies that potential benefits are conditional upon social circumstances. In its neoclassical connotation, "satisfaction," the pseudo-social objective becomes the greatest satisfaction (by intensity and duration) of the greatest number. The driving concept is that of a "Pareto optimum" (Vilfredo Pareto, 1843–1923), which is such that no individual can be further advantaged without some other individual suffering disadvantage. In reaching that optimum, the utilitarian drive is directed by a "hedonistic calculus of pleasure and pain" (that is, by the logic of pure choice) that underpins every aspect of the neoclassical theory of human behaviour. So, for example, the undesirability of work *per se* is offset by earnings that enable desired purchases to be made, but time must also be allocated to recuperation. Hence, the precise calculation of hours of work, rest, and play: a hedonistic calculus with a rational economic man intent upon maximum satisfaction. Yet the limitations of this "psychology" are suggested by its own redundancy of expression: pleasure (pain) is negative pain (pleasure). The human condition is poorly represented by such monochromic shades.

Without omniscience optimization fails. Even with omniscience, the hedonistic calculus is inoperable in the presence of incommensurability; and, in pursuit of the greatest satisfaction of the greatest number, interpersonal transfers must be addressed. Here, the possibility has been mooted of replacing subjective preferences with some objective standard, "a kind of majority rule," that is determined by "a majority of interests suitably weighted for intensity" (Nagel 1979, 112). Of course, this risks the subordination of personal freedom to some nebulous concept of public good. Who is to decide? Furthermore, the utilitarian concentration upon individual choice ignores the important issue of which preferences are worth having. In conflating preferences and values, neoclassical economics denies the relevance of ethics. Automata may optimize but, uniquely among sentient/sapient beings, man is able to decide what needs to be optimized. This issue, the question of which preferences are worth having, raises an important distinction: unreflective tastes ("wanton preferences" or "appetites") and meta-preferences ("values") that are supported by reflective consideration. In regard to values, a re-examination of rational behaviour can be explored. It is one that demands a reversion to the wider remit of political economy and to the values that constrain an individual's actions.

Indeed, for example in decisions about investing funds, people, as it turns out, take into account not only profits they can count on, but also the social implications of such decisions, which may manifest in, amongst other things, refraining from the purchase of shares of a corporation accused of inhumane treatment of animals. A wider issue of financial markets is also discussed in the volume under consideration, pointing to anomalies occurring in them, and the resulting cognitive tendencies of market participants and the influence on their decisions are considered. This thesis is connected with the so-called behavioural approach to finance, as seeking psychological mechanisms of behaviour of participants of the financial markets.

In the section on the field considered to be the flagship for economic psychology, consumer behaviour, various categories of consumer choices are discussed. One can immediately indicate the fact, which will be emphasized thanks to the structural theory of society outlined later, of the necessity to distinguish, drawing upon the categorisation by Max Weber, between: firstly, economic phenomena, which are part of the economic structure; secondly, economically conditioned phenomena; and thirdly, economic relevance, i.e. affecting the economy leading to the conclusion that consumer behaviour is undoubtedly on the one hand conditioned by the economic processes, and on the other that this consumer behaviour influences the level and direction of production. It is, however, not in itself a part of the economy, in contrast to the activities of the character irrefutably adherent to this sphere, the focus of one of the chapters of the work being discussed.

The chapter in question considers personality traits of entrepreneurs. The author describes among other things the importance of psychological characteristics such as achievement motivation and location of control. In addition, he presents external factors as often having a big part in deciding on the establishment of own business. The focal point of the chapter is the issue of information gathering and decision making by entrepreneurs. At this point, the author shows the differences in the perception of potential gains and losses by entrepreneurs and managers who decide the fate of the company.

Much as one should welcome, in accordance with the reference to social aspect of psychology, the recognition of the multiplicity of social roles performed by actors of the social structure created by the capitalist firm, ironically at the same time one needs to pay attention to the characteristic discrepancy in relation to the notion that probably inspired the Polish manual. A leading American practitioner of the discussed discipline uses language explicitly referring to the identification of a class, writing about "Business owners" and "executives" in the context of decisions on production, prices and capital investment.

Worth citing is the self-characterisation of the methodological approach of economic psychology given by George Katona. He contrasts it with pure economics and its normative approach which, in his opinion, answers the question of how to make a profit. However, the point of view of economic psychology in the American scholar's understanding is both broader and narrower than those of orthodox economics. Broader because the first, as opposed to the second, does not accept any presuppositions about the orientation of the economic decisions on maximizing and even achieving profit. At the same time it is also more restricted, since it is not aimed at the formulation of universal laws valid always and everywhere, but examines instead all the factors influencing specific decisions in specific circumstances (Katona 1951, 241).

Though the state of mutual relations between sociology and economics over a large part of their history would surely be more accurately rendered by a metaphor for England's neighbours, who jealously guard the borders of their domestic fortresses and are misanthropically disinterested in their neighbour's garden, this brief and necessarily incomplete presentation of the situation within certain social sciences close to economics does not alter the primary significance for economic sociology of the disciplines that are most associated with it, but that live with one another, historically speaking, not on the best terms, namely sociology and economics.

The work published in 1956, which was intended as a synthesis of these disciplines, has met with a rather muted reaction and, quite independent of its intrinsic value, which we will assess individually, did not become, objectively speaking, a milestone in the development of our discipline. Beckert points out that: "This is a remarkable legacy for economic sociology! However, at the time of their publication, neither the works from the 1930s nor *Economy and Society* were great successes for Parsons" (Parsons 1977; Smelser 1981). Later, when the importance of *The Structure of Social Action* was recognised in sociology, it was not the economic sociology entailed in it that was considered interesting. Rather, his rendering of sociological classics and the rejection of utilitarianism as a theory of social order became influential in sociological discourse.

A probable reason for Parsons' work being overlooked is the fact that economic sociology, although it had an excellent debut with classic sociologists such as Durkheim, Marx, Simmel and Weber, received little attention for many decades from the late 1930s onward. How could someone then become seriously interested in Parsons' significance as an economic sociologist? Only during the last thirty years or so did the situation in economic sociology change dramatically. It developed from a marginalised area of sociological research to an innovative and prominent field. This is especially true for the United States, where today "the new economic sociology" is an important field of sociological scholarship (Guillén et al. 2003; Smelser and Swedberg 1994; Zukin and DiMaggio 1990). In this scenario, it would have been expected that as a part of the increasing interest in economic sociology the works of Talcott Parsons in this area of scholarship would have received late credit. His works on the economy were indeed debated in the 1980s and 1990s (Deutschmann 1999; DiMaggio and Powell 1991; Ganssmann 1989, 1996; Granovetter 1985, 1990; Holton 1986, 1992; Saurwein 1988; Swedberg 1987; Zelizer 1994). However, all in all, these receptions were mostly critical. Important proponents of the new economic sociology distanced themselves from Parsons, even defining today's economic sociology against his theoretical framework. Perhaps it was published too early, did not hit at the right time, as in the 1960s the mutual isolation of sociology and economics reached, in the judgment of Swedberg, its peak (1991, 260). The cold war between the two sciences never acted in favour of the development of the discipline inherently situated at their interface, from this point of view, and open conflict and exchange of blows was preferable, which at least constituted some form of dialogue.

I.1.12. New economic sociology

This dialogue, moreover, not limited to disputes, commenced, or to be more specific, was revived, in the 1970s, and intensified over the following decade. Its flagship example was the sketch by Mark Granovetter on embeddedness (1985), whose author interpreted the ensuing recovery in the field of sociology of the economy, not without a great dose of cheek, in the same year as nothing less than "new sociology of economic life." Granovetter's essay contained a critique of Neoclassical Economics and derived from it a New Institutional Economics. The latter collective name involves a few currents of thought developed mainly by economists, revolving around such concepts as transaction costs discussed above or, a large part of which will be considered in greater detail in subsequent parts of this work, agent principal (representative), asymmetry of information, etc.

These various notions, however, share certain characteristics, one of which can be regarded as an assumption of the efficiency factor as accounting for the existence of certain organizational forms. Granovetter rightly points out that this kind of reasoning, embodied for example in the argument according to which "every evolutionary economic problem requires for its solution a social institution" (Scho 1981, 2) is loaded with functionalist error. Function, functionality, rationality, reasonableness or effectiveness is used to explain origins, to explain why X was created. That reasoning which has its source, we should add, in vulgar Hegelianism (all that exists is rational, or in this case efficient) implies, as correctly pointed out by Granovetter, thinking straight from common Darwinism: "effective solutions ... have the ability to survive similar to the ability forced in biological world by natural selection" (1985, 502). And so, although it is acknowledged that "not all managers of companies accurately perceive their economic opportunities and accurately respond to them" it turns out to be of little significance, because "after some time, greater ability to survive is within moves [of those managers, in this case of vertical integration] that are more reasonable in terms of transaction costs and economies of scale" (Williamson & Ouchi 1981, 38). It is the polemics of one of the most popular representatives of the new institutional economics, Oliver Williamson, that Granovetter focuses on in the text under consideration. It allows us to see all the strengths, but also essential weaknesses of his conceptual framework. The question Williamson asked, in the tradition of Coase, was in what circumstances economic functions are implemented within hierarchically organized companies, and in what market processes.

His response, entirely in the spirit of the new institutional economics, is a statement that in any case this will be the form of organization that most effectively addresses the issue of economic costs of a transaction. These, whose results are uncertain, are repeated frequently and require substantial transaction-specific investments in the form of money, time, energy, etc. which cannot easily be transferred to interactions with other partners, and will most likely occur within hierarchical organizations, while simple transactions not involving specific investments and not repeated, such as one-time purchases of standard equipment, will be carried out between firms. According to this notion, the first type of transactions are positioned within hierarchically organized firms for two reasons. The first is the limited rationality of economic agents—the inability to accurately predict the complex sequences of potential circumstances that may be relevant for long-term contracts. If they are moved to the inside of the company, anticipation of these eventualities becomes unnecessary. Instead of complex negotiations, one can deal with them under the masterful structure of the company. The second reason is opportunism, which Williamson understands as the rational pursuit on the part of economic operators of their own benefits by using all means at their disposal, including deceit and fraud. This opportunism becomes mitigated and limited in a situation when the transaction partners belong to a single corporate body, both because of their greater (compared with the transaction on the open market) mutual identification and the power relations pertinent to the company.

Authority, or legitimate power particular to a company as a hierarchical structure, also makes it a much more efficient instrument for settling disputes between the parties, compared to market. In disputes between companies, non-judicial agreements are not always possible, and the law-suits can be very expensive. In the meantime, to resolve a disagreement within an organization a decision may suffice (Williamson 1975, 30). Williamson reckons that complex repeated transactions require long-term relations between non-anonymous individuals, while noting that these relations are threatened by opportunism in his sense of the word. Adaptations to changing market conditions crucial over the duration of the relationship are too complex and unpredictable to be pre-determined, and promises of good will, in the absence of an overriding authority, are unenforceable.

Granovetter criticizes Williamson's conception, using the language deployed, amongst others, by Dennis Wrong in his critique of Parsons, as being at the same time both over- and under-socialised (1985, 493–4). On the one hand the American economist overplays in his view the effectiveness of hierarchical authority in the company (as does Hobbes in relation to the sovereign in his *Leviathan*), whereas on the other, he depicts the market in the colours that recall Hobbes' state of nature—it is an atomized and anonymous market of classical political economy minus a discipline, the result of competition, which in effect gives the de-socialised picture of the economy, "omitting the role of social relations between individuals" (Granovetter 1985, 494).

Although Williamson, according to his critic, is aware that the picture of the market presented by him is not entirely adequate, he notes that:

> norms of trustworthy behaviour sometimes expand to the market and are to some extent enforced by group pressure. Multiple personal contacts outside the organizational boundaries assume a certain level of courtesy and respect between the parties … Moreover, the expectations of multiple business contacts discourage the seeking of a narrow advantage in any single transaction.

> Individual aggressiveness is bridled by the perspective of ostracism among partners on both professional and social ground. Protected resource of a company is also its reputation for honesty. (Williamson 1975, 106–8)

Such observations open the way, according to Granovetter, to an analysis of the impact of social structure on market behaviour. Williamson, however, does not follow this path, and treats his examples as exceptions, and moreover does not see to what extent the relationships described by him are themselves rooted in a broader system of social relations (Granovetter 1985, 496).

Based on this analysis, Granovetter argues that "the anonymous market of neoclassical models of economic life basically does not exist, and transactions of all kinds abound as described [above] with social interactions" (1985. 497). The American sociologist highlights (easy to find because life around him is full of it) evidence of mixing economic and social relations: trade associations, interlocking directorates, mixtures of professional and social relations, as manifested in, for example, rumours about competitors, market shortages and raises mentioned during meetings of suppliers and wholesalers (Granovetter 1985, 495). Granovetter also illustrates his general point with the results of studies of housing construction industry in Massachusetts, showing not only the presence of long-term relationships with subcontractors, but also limitation to hiring two or three suppliers, which according to him must be related to the pleasure derived from co-operation with a permanent partner as opposed to the daily exchange of subcontractors arising from the selection of companies on a competitive basis: "Similarly to other sectors of the economy … the layer of social relations imposed on the transaction plays a decisive role, initiated as purely economic" (1985, 497).

These considerations, including concrete examples specified by the author of his key categories of the proposed approach allow for their critical examination. Granovetter's own criticism of economics is largely correct, especially when he points out its asociologism, although its drawback is putting classical and neoclassical economics in one bag, whereas they are distinct in (and not only) this respect.

Granovetter's positive programme designed to overcome this shortcoming, however, is not free of weaknesses, the basis of which is the identification of social relations in which economic relations are to be embedded with interpersonal relations. Granovetter, moreover, has repeatedly used the formula of "personal relations," and in the programme declaration states that "most behaviour is closely embedded in networks of interpersonal relations," an approach that in his opinion avoids the extreme of both liberal and "over-socialised rendering of human action" (1985,

500). From this point of view, the bitterness over Granovetter's attack is difficult to comprehend, as he and his adversary have very much in common as far as their basic analytical framework is concerned; Williamson (1993, 56) states: "Transaction cost economics mainly works out a dyadic set-up. Albeit adequate and instructive for studying many complex transactions, provision for larger numbers of actors and interaction is sometimes needed."

To add insult to injury, the above claim is in fact an understatement; regrettably, in the battle over the meaning of "embededness" it is not Granovetter but Williamson that emerges the victor. Williamson (1998), proposed a four-tier analytical schema. At the lowest level, "third order economising," is resource allocation theory appropriately addressed by neoclassical economics: "get the marginal conditions right." It is set within the context of second-order economising, which is devoted to contracting, and analytically subject to transactions cost economics: "get the governance structure right." This in turn is determined by first-order economising, concerned with the formal rules of the game, to be examined by the economics of property rights: "get the institutional environment right." Finally, social theory is the broadest first tier, encompassing "embeddedness: informal institutions, customs, traditions, norms, religion." It appears to eschew economising and is the subject of social theory. Williamson also provides for feedback mechanisms between adjacent tiers. Williamson's notion of embeddedness is far more sociological (in the sense of adopting a much broader societally view) than Granovetter's, irrespective of Fine's correct objections to the effect that:

> this is clearly arbitrary, and there is no reason why one tier should be privileged over another and why all should not be determined simultaneously. Indeed, the whole analytical schema is a consequence of taking third-order economising as the starting-point and, partly by design and partly of necessity, moving to 'higher' levels of analysis which might, on a more circumspect approach, be considered to be more appropriate to begin with. (Fine 1999)

We will return immediately to the other part of the opposition outlined by Granovetter, but first let us finish the commentary regarding the understanding of social relations adopted by him in the wake of this: the network of social relations in which economic relations are to be embedded and the title concept of social structure.

Interpersonal relationships, personal, direct contacts and acquaintances comprise undoubtedly a category, but still only one major, but not the only, category of social relations.[14] One can say that the American sociologist sent for the war against economic man of the economic theory, in spite of the appearances of his profession; not a social man but merely a sociable man. The author of this work devoted an entire book to the criticism of such an approach and its implications (Tittenbrun 1983). Note that this "sociable" or "interactive" focus often derived from the past (and perhaps this also applies to Granovetter) in the search by sociologists of a pure social stuff that would be an exclusive, particular subject matter of their science. This kind of approach, however, as the case of Granovetter shows, leads to odd outcomes according to which, as is clear from his work, economic relations are not social relations; in order to become partly social, they must get that social, or, more precisely sociable overlay.

And yet, are economic relations the relations between people within the economic structure, and the relationships between people not social relations, as such? In reality, a variety of relationships make up the economic structure and its individual substructures, all of which are social relations, as part of the society as a whole, just as the structures within which these relationships take place. It follows that the economic structure is certainly not opposed to the notion of social structure, and is itself a social structure. Moreover, such a social structure is not only a company operating within the economic structure but also, more broadly, agents involved in economic activity in the form of individuals,[15] not to mention their collectives and groups.

Questioning the meaning of each and every primary concept of Granovetter's, we have finally reached the popular "embeddedness" theory that in the form proposed also proves to have too narrow an empirical reference compared to the actual place of economy in social life.

---

[14] For that reason Zelizer's criticism is clearly insufficient: "treating only two-person relations one set at a time missed the large impact of third parties on the forms and qualities of intimacy as well as the character and significance of the economic activity involved" (2006, 31). To overcome the initial dyadic frame of reference it is not sufficient to extend it to include "third parties"; what must be taken account of, as indicated earlier, is the overwhelming presence in social life of suprapersonal relations that play out at an entirely different that a face-to-face level.

[15] In contrast to the small social structures, the smallest, and in this sense the atomic social structure, could, by analogy with the terminology of natural sciences and engineering, be called nanostructure. That an individual is a social structure is known not only to the author of the "Theses on Feuerbach," who wrote about the individual as: "a totality of social relations, not only to Freud as the creator of the concept of the superego, Parsons with his concept of socialization, but probably every sociologist, not only as a reader of the mentioned authors."

Granovetter's conceptual apparatus is also too poor to render the difference in the nature of the relationship between the economy and the society as a whole. These categorial deficiencies regard, among others,[16] the notion of property, which is one reason why in Granovetter's account the aforementioned diversity of these relationships is missing. Specifically, Granovetter realizes the existence of such differences, but does not dispose of any conceptual apparatus that would allow him to describe them theoretically. For example, he indicates that the impact of personal relations on economic relations is particularly evident in countries such as Japan, which in his view must be explained by cultural peculiarities (1985, 496). In fact, we are dealing here with a specific model of capitalism based on specific economic and property relations (Tittenbrun 2011). Granovetter recognises, moreover, the shortcomings of his analysis, omitting historical and macro-structural issues; however, he does not notice that these gaps are not irrelevant to the content of this analysis; whilst there is a possibility of a different focus of concentration either on the macro, or on the microstructural issues, the two types of analysis are closely related to each other (Tittenbrun 1983). Conditioning of the analysis on the micro social level through a macro structural analysis applies not only to small social groups, but also to the structure of the individual.

Granovetter, as already suggested by the quotation cited above, sets himself apart from not only from the asocial neoclassical theory, but also from the, in his opinion, overly socialized concepts and considers that:

> a fruitful analysis of human action requires avoidance of atomization assumed by the theoretical extremes of under and over-socialised concepts. Individuals do not take actions or decisions independently of social context, nor slavishly pursue a scenario prescribed to them by actual social positions occupied by them. Attempts of deliberate action, meanwhile, are embedded in specific systems of social relations. (Granovetter 1985, 486)

Here again there is a problem of misunderstanding by the author of the relationship of the terms "individual" and "structure," although his text does not reveal his knowledge of the work of French structuralists, this

[16] This charge also holds as regards his later texts, although Granovetter's contention to the effect that "action driven by interests as well as that driven by trust or power, occur and have outcomes in ways determined by larger contexts than those in which they are located. individuals who find themselves in situations determined by forces beyond their control, and often far beyond their lifespan" (2001) obviously goes in the right direction.

approach of the American sociologist seems to assume the way of thinking manifested in some extreme formulations of the latter[17] as well as their critics.

Granovetter seems thus to understand structures, systems or social wholes in the image and likeness of some superhuman entities functioning regardless of and above human individuals. This image is naturally completely untrue; social structures are nothing else than collections of human relations. This ontological argument has methodological implications—not only is knowledge of a social structure, composed fully or partially of human beings, impossible without an examination of individuals functioning as parties to the relationships that comprise the whole, but also the knowledge of an individual will be the fuller, the more complete, the more structures in which the individual participates or has to do with are taken into account in its description.

In this sense, there is no opposition, not only between individuals and other social structures which may be called, following Kozyr-Kowalski, anthropic, but also non-human structures: both material and ideal. The more of all types of structures we consider the more our description of the individual will be faithful and accurate, more fully reflecting its function in a society. Thus we do not kill the individual, as implied by Lacan's well-known proclamation, and do not dispel its individuality, but on the contrary we extract it fully. With each step of the description we learn more about the individual: we find that he or she is a member of a particular nation, then put him or her in a particular class or social position. We find that he or she belongs to a certain family, works in such and such plant or office, resides in a particular city, is a member of a political party, such and such organizations and voluntary associations.

This same relationship applies to object (material and ideal) structures: we enrich our knowledge of the individual of interest to us, finding out in which apartment or house he or she lives, what collection of books he or she has, what household utensils, clothes, etc. Meanwhile, Granovetter suggests that if one in his or her examination of social influences on the individual takes account of what he calls "social categories" to which the individual belongs, one has no other option than approaching these social determinants in an oversocialised fashion.

Granovetter cites two examples of exactly such approaches: the theory of labour market segmentation according to which participants in different segments of this market are characterized by different styles of decision-making, and those governed by custom, order or rational choice,

[17] The most famous is perhaps Lacan's saying: "Man is dead."

depending on the class subcultures from which they come. The attribution of individual modes of thinking and action to different social classes and identification of the latter may be in the above notion more or less justified, as well as completely wrong, but this does not undermine the fruitfulness of searching for this kind of social conditioning. Therefore, however well founded Granovetter's remarks formulated in relation to the segmentation theory would be, the idea itself remains in force. He considers the view attributing the ability of "rational choice" only to managers, professionals and technicians to be wrong, and rightly draws attention to the fact that behaviour apparently appearing irrational may be quite reasonable after taking into account situational constraints. In addition, instrumental, rational action does not necessarily have to be oriented to economic objectives, since there may be targets such as approval, social status or power, etc., which are rarely considered rational by economists, as suggested by Granovetter.

The second test cited in the polemical context by Granovetter is also concerned with class determinants. Samuel Bowles and Herbert Gintis, in a study on the American education system, recognised as one of the consequences the diversity of cognitive processes of individual classes.
Granovetter this time makes no specific charges against the above study, restricting himself to an overall assessment, intended to target the previous study and potentially, it seems, any attempt to refer the action or awareness of social agents to their macrostructural, mainly (this is the conclusion of the selection of examples to illustrate the alleged "oversocialisation") class conditions. The following complaint of Granovetter prejudges the issue, which is certainly not a foregone conclusion, and studies that make class their foundation may well avoid mistakes and simplifications indicated by Granovetter, who accuses "oversocialised" concepts of impact of society on individual behaviour of mechanicism:

> The moment we know the social class or sector of the labour market of an individual, the whole of behaviour is explained automatically, because people are so well socialized.
>
> The social impact is seen here as an outside force, which similarly to a god of deists sets things in motion, [...] a power that haunts the minds and bodies of individuals (as in the film 'Body Snatchers'), transforming their way of decision-making.
>
> As soon as we know the exact nature of their impact on the individual, relationships and social structures [in which it participates] become irrelevant.

> Any social influences are included in the head of an individual, so that in real decision-making situations it may be as atomized as any *homo economicus*, although probably on other rules of decision-making. (Granovetter 1985, 485)

This general conclusion is an unwarranted over-generalisation, based on some personal biases rather than a comprehensive analysis of the matter.

Granovetter's paper has been selected as an example of "new economic sociology" both for its representativeness and because it has made it possible for us to correct more than one ill-conceived notion. In fact, similar criticism might be addressed against many other notions employed by the so-called new economic sociology; for instance, the following advice: "even the strictest neoclassical economist should accept today the idea of a market as a network of people, knowing each other personally" (Richter 2004). It does not follow that an equally harsh verdict should apply to the entire "new sociology of economic life." After all, even the essay by Granovetter contains, as we have underscored, many sound points. It is also, this time tacitly, the term "embeddedness" that is referred to by another proponent of "new economic sociology," but differently, structrurally, understood: "The construction of courses of action depends greatly on the position of actors within the structure of the organization, which forms the interests and identities of actors" (Fligstein 1990, 11).

One of the favourite subjects of the research stream under consideration is what is called the social construction of markets and certain other economic institutions. For example, in his fine paper Milan Zafirovsky has aimed to "show that market-based and (superficially) gain-seeking production, just as distribution, exchange and consumption, is a dependent variable of certain social conditions rather than being a natural universal" (Zafirovsky 2002).

Within the field of inquiry under consideration a few distinct theoretical perspectives have established themselves. One of those approaches is Joe Podolny's (1993) status perspective. He defines status as "deference relations," which means that one actor accepts a social relation with another. Podolny states that status firms can make more money because their status enables them to charge more for their products or services than firms with less status. With reference to markets where this concept is applied by its advocate, Podolny's approach boils down to the well-known economic notions of product differentiation and brand. Similarly, no new insight seems to be offered by Podolny's related point that status, in his terminology, "leaks," which means that when a high-status firm interacts with a low-status firm, the status of the latter increases, while the high-

status firm diminishes (Aspers 2007). This point, only without Podolny's terminology, has been long made, for instance, by observers of many failed mergers.
This criticism, however, pales into insignificance compared with the much-hailed but trivial "discovery" by Granovetter that "our acquaintances (weak ties) are less likely to be socially involved with one another than are our close friends (strong ties)" (1973).

More original, but arousing rather mixed feelings, is Michel Callon's (1986; 1988) performativity approach, that: "the economy is not a passive object that social scientists develop theories about." In fact, Callon claims that we have got it wrong; it is the other way around: the theories we have developed are implemented in the world so that it mirrors these theories. This is what Callon refers to when he says that the economy is performed. His idea, moreover, implies that we should conduct anthropological studies of economists and the corresponding body of knowledge represented by economics, rather than of "the world" (Aspers 2007). In its extreme implication the theory represents an untenable semantic idealism which should be discarded. In its moderate form, however, it clearly has a point. Take the stock exchange, which is a by no means purely economic institution, but must be analyzed in socio-economic terms insofar as stock prices depend to a large or even overwhelming extent on the collective assessment of public opinion represented by a plethora of bodies: the media, analysts, central bankers, and leading investors whose moves are followed by others. This social dependency is shown, for instance, in the fact that a given company's stock price depends not on its absolute amount of earnings or volume of sales but on how those financial data are mediated by the collective market evaluation. Thus, when a corporation has high quarterly earnings but lower than those expected by the market, its stock price will most likely drop. This perspective is also applicable to the recent crisis:

> Keynes seventy years ago [stated]: "Practical men, who believe themselves to be quite exempt from any intellectual influence, are usually the slaves of some defunct economist. Madmen in authority, who hear voices in the air, are distilling their frenzy from some academic scribbler of a few years back."
>
> What the "madmen in authority" heard this time was the distant echo of a debate among academic economists begun in the 1970s about "rational" investors and "efficient" markets. [...] it was a debate won by the side that happened to be wrong. (Kalecki 2009

And the ominous significance of that victory was that:

And on those two reassuring adjectives, rational and efficient, the victorious academic economists erected an enormous scaffolding of theoretical models, regulatory prescriptions and computer simulations which allowed the practical bankers and politicians to build the towers of bad debt and bad policy …

Which brings us to the causes of the present crisis. The reckless property lending that triggered this crisis only occurred because rational investors assumed that the probability of a fall in house prices was near zero. Efficient markets then turned these assumptions into price-signals, which told the bankers that lending 100 per cent mortgages or operating with 50-to-1 leverage was safe. Similarly, regulators, who allowed banks to determine their own capital requirements and private rating agencies to establish the value at risk in mortgages and bonds, took it as axiomatic that markets would automatically generate the best possible information and create the right incentives for managing risks …

The scandal of modern economics is that these two false theories—rational expectations and the efficient market hypothesis—which are not only misleading but highly ideological, have become so dominant in academia (especially business schools), government and markets themselves. (Kalecki 2009)

CHAPTER I.2.

"WIRTSCHAFT UND GESELLSCHAFT" BY MAX WEBER

I.2.1 Sociology of the economy and economic sociology

In the previous chapter we used almost exclusively the term "sociology of the economy," and therefore one of the two terms mentioned in the subtitle of the work that can be used as the name of a specific sub-discipline of sociology, which we deal with here. Meanwhile, much more popular among students of the discipline in Poland, as evidenced by titles of books and textbooks, the names of departments and faculties, and educational courses, seems to be the latter term, but which so far in our considerations has been on the back burner. This situation, however, seems to be based on a misunderstanding or a mistake in translation.

The names "industrial sociology," "urban sociology" and "rural sociology" we translate as "*socjologia przemysłu*" (literally "sociology of industry"), "*miasta*" ("of city"), "*wsi*" ("countryside"), and not "*socjologia miejska*" ("urban sociology") or "*wiejska*." By analogy, "economic sociology" in Polish is "*socjologia gospodarki*" ("sociology of the economy"), rather than "*socjologia ekonomiczna*" ("economic sociology"). However, if the whole problem was limited to this linguistic correction the whole matter could end on that note. Meanwhile, we want to propose here an attempt to get out of the existing situation, to in a sense reconcile supporters of the two competing terms, to demonstrate that they need not compete with each other. An even more important goal of what follows is to persuade the general sociological community that alongside the essentially universally accepted term "economic sociology," another term is also useful to define the field of study of the sub-discipline under consideration. This rapprochement can be achieved by appropriate definition of their respective fields of inquiry. Thus, sociology of the economy in our view could be defined as the sociological approach to the economic structure.

One could also include in it the issues treated by the socio-economics of Etzioni—the impact of factors of non-economic nature on business phenomena and processes. The weakness of the approach of Etzioni, valuable as it is, is the lack of an explicit theory of society at large, which causes an impression that these independent social variables that influence the dependent variables from the sphere of the economy are selected fairly randomly and irregularly. An outline of such a theory is presented later in this book. In addition, this scheme informed by the ideas of Parsons and Marx is discussed among others in Tittenbrun (2005). The theoretical and methodological standpoint of the author can be best described as a socio-economic structuralism, the meaning of which will be defined more precisely in one of the following chapters of the text.

One of its key aspects is revealed by the above mentioned definition of the sociology of economy that conceives of the economy as a structure situated in its social context. Moreover, the economy itself is treated here as consisting of many substructures such as the means of work and production, ownership relations, etc. Such an approach reveals the rather dubious revolutionary character of the already considered concept of the social embeddedness, supported especially Granovetter, whose innovation, according to some commentators (Swedberg 1991) would go so far as to form the basis of a new perspective worthy of a distinct label dubbed: "the new sociology of economic life." Meanwhile, treatment of economic actors as exactly embedded in respective systems of economic and social relations comprising particular structures not only pertained to many "old masters" of sociology, including those who have been mentioned in the present book,[1] but is an inherent property of the theoretical and methodological position taught for years, though not under that name and in the version put forward here, in the circle of Poznań-based sociologists?

Ownership relations, for example, are not some superhuman entities determining human individuals, but a set of relations between the means of production or other type of economic activity, which in themselves constitute a structure and their human beneficiaries, and indirectly between them and other categories of persons, for example individuals putting in motion these resources of material work, and so always between specific individuals conceived in the aspect of their social roles.

The flagship motto of every sociologist, that man is a social being, means nothing more than a multilateral dependence of every human being

---

[1] Suffice it to mention but one Marx's statement in Appendix I of "A Contribution to the Critique of Political Economy": "production is always appropriation of nature by an individual within and with the help of a definite social organisation."

upon others—his or her nation, city, family, workplace, etc. In the latter example, we can distinguish two lines of sociation: horizontal or technological, also known as functional sociation, based on the co-operation in the production process or other work processes; and vertical sociation, consisting of subordination within the hierarchy of decision-making. In other words, an individual employee is within horizontal sociation dependent on his or her co-workers in a team, at the assembly line for example, and within vertical sociation one is dependent on his or her superiors issuing commands to them on the basis of subordination. Sociation or, more precisely, collectivization, as we mostly are dealing with the context of job performance of the wider or narrower factory or office collective (the brigade, the whole workforce, or, more broadly, employees in the other branches of the economy, those involved in the supply chain, etc.) also takes place at the level of compensation in various forms of collective fringe benefits, profit sharing, etc.

In connection with the above remarks, one should consider the fact that throughout the book, chapters qualifying as sociology of the economy have been marked with the numeral I, while the chapters pertaining to economic sociology are preceded by the numeral II. Perception of the economy in its social context, however, may also be understood differently, in the sense that is shown by the proposed definition of economic sociology. Unlike sociology of the economy, it would focus on the influence of the economic structure on the non-economic structures of social life. Socio-economic structuralism assumed here takes as its central thesis the contention concerning the conditioning of all social life by the economy.

This claim, however, by no means signifies the adoption of some form of economic determinism or economism; it merely means that no phenomenon of the non-economic sphere can be scientifically understood and explained without reference to the economic structure and, therefore, knowledge of the economic structure in a given society. According to the plan of this work we will now go on to discuss a number of examples of theories representing these two strands of research operating at the interface between sociology and economics. First the classic theory of Max Weber which falls within the scope of sociology of the economy, but also contains references to economic sociology and has been objectivized first of all in his monumental treatise.

One of the fundamental merits of Weber's work is his broad context in the form of a general theory of society. Conceptualization of the economy in this broader framework locates Weber's deliberations on an intellectual shelf inaccessible to most contemporary influential and fashionable social science celebrities each of whom has, according to Andy Warhol's famous saying, their fifteen minutes of fame which are minuscule in comparison with Weber's giant intellectual legacy. The German sociologist and economist is characterised by his "intellectually sophisticated allowance for the immense complexity of the problems, for [his] ability to draw clear and definite conclusions from such complex materials and yet not fall into dogmatic over-simplification" (Weber 1947).

At the same time the combination of terms in the title of Weber's work prompts questions about their relationship, more specifically on how to delineate the boundaries of the economy as part of society. The fact that Weber introduces his concept of the economy as a part of the logical sequence of systematic definitions on the one hand is not surprising, given that the whole book has such a textbook-like character, but on the other hand does not exempt, as it will turn out, the author from objections and reservations that one may have in relation to his work. In science there are no holy cows immune from criticism, even if this concerns figures of such monumental posture as Max Weber.

I.2.2. The economy, the state and law

Weber starts with the following definition: "Action will be said to be 'economically oriented' so far as, according to its subjective meaning, it is concerned with the desire: for 'utilities' (*Niitsleistungcn*)" (Weber 1947). This definition contains at least two concepts requiring some further clarification. Firstly, economic utilities are, he says, of three classes: goods, services, and a residual category of objects of rights not fitting into either of the other classes. This includes such intangibles as "good will" and the advantages of participating in all manner of social relationships so far as these can be the object of economic orientation. Goods are physical objects of economic significance, and services the actions of human beings in the same context. More complex, or indeed, as we shall see, ambiguous, is Weber's notion of "subjective meaning" which is crucial for his so-called interpretive approach. It figures prominently in his definition of sociological science. According to Weber, "sociology (in the sense in which this highly ambiguous word is used here) is a science which attempts the interpretive understanding of social action in order thereby to arrive at a causal explanation of its course and effects" (Weber 1947, 88).

Thus, Weber's essential starting point is an acceptance of the subjective point of view, of *verstehende Soziologie*, i.e. a system of sociological categories couched in terms of the subjective point of view, that is of the meaning of persons, things, ideas, normative patterns, and motives from the point of view of the persons whose action is being studied (Weber 1947, 89).The fact that *prima facie* the above-cited statements may appear to be clear should not obscure the circumstance that the key idea is not devoid of ambiguity. The term in question seems, to be sure, suggestive of specific interpretation. The matter, as we shall see, is not that simple. Note, namely, Weber's statement to the effect that: "in all the sciences of human action, account must be taken of processes and phenomena which are devoid of subjective meaning, in the role of stimuli, results, favouring or hindering circumstances" (Weber 1947). So far, so good. Weber adds, however, that:

> To be devoid of meaning is not identical with being lifeless or non-human; every artefact, such as for example a machine, can be understood only in terms of the meaning which its production and use have had or will have for human action; a meaning which may derive from a relation to exceedingly various purposes. Without reference to this meaning such an object remains wholly unintelligible. That which is intelligible or understandable about it is thus its relation to human action. (Weber 1947)

The above pronouncement contains an idea according to which subjective meaning could be understood as reference to human action, or comprehending various material and ideal objects from the viewpoint of an actor or agent. This "activist" or "actionist" as opposed to psychologistic interpretation is highlighted by the following contention referring to such objects as functioning:

> … in such roles as ends, means, obstacles, and by-products. It is not, however, permissible to express this by saying, as is sometimes done, that economic action is a "psychic" phenomenon. The production of goods, prices, or even the "subjective valuation" of goods, if they are empirical processes, are far from being merely psychic phenomena. But underlying this misleading phrase is a correct insight. It is a fact that these phenomena have a peculiar type of subjective meaning. This alone defines the unity of the corresponding processes, and this alone makes them accessible to subjective interpretation. (Weber 1947)

From the perspective of socio-economic structuralism adopted here there can be no quarrel, therefore, with the following rendering of Weber: "Weber rejects psychological reductionism in the course of emphasising that motives should be viewed as discrete psycho-historical, or psycho-cultural, entities" (Campbell 2006).

Our anti-subjectivistic interpretation of Weber is confirmed, too, by Peukert who draws attention to the fact that:

> The concept of understanding is not developed in a subjectivist or hermeneutical tradition. [...] Weber did not adhere to his official interpretative principles and analytical framework. His studies on agrarian social relations, on antiquity, and the development of the concept of Agrarverfassung demonstrate that his substantive studies and his methodological claims (methodological individualism, value neutrality, etc.) diverge. He was also a structuralist; for example, his studies implicitly hold that an internal logic rules at different times in history, existing independently of individual consciousness. (Peukert 2004)

The latter conclusion was confirmed by Mary Fulbrook in her *British Journal of Sociology* article, "Comparing One Aspect of Max Weber's Explicit Conception of 'interpretive sociology' with His Actual Practices in his Substantive Investigations". The author was able to:

> show that Weber's overt emphasis on the importance of meanings and motives in causal explanation of social action does not correspond adequately with the true mode of explanation involved in his comparative-historical studies of the world religions. Rather, the ultimate level of causal explanation in Weber's substantive writings is that of the social-structural conditions under which certain forms of meaning and motivation can achieve historical efficacy. (Fulbrook 1978)

But let us come back to our main task in this subchapter, that is to say, the determination of demarcation lines of the economic structure. From this point of view, the following definition is of cardinal importance: "'Economic Action,' (*Wirtschaften*) is a peaceful use of the actor's control over resources, which is primarily economically oriented" (Weber 1947).

What is worth stressing here as both sound and crucial from the viewpoint of the above-mentioned purpose is Weber's reference to the term "peaceful." Its usefulness for the purpose under consideration is shown, among others, by the following outline of interelations between the heading substructures of the present subchapter, distinguished by Weber:

> from "economic action" as such, the term "economically oriented action," which will be applied to two types: (a) every action which, though primarily oriented to other ends, takes account, in the pursuit of them, of economic considerations; that is, of the consciously recognised necessity for economic prudence. Or (b) that which, though primarily oriented to economic ends, makes use of physical force as a means. It thus includes all

> primarily non-economic action and all non- peaceful action which is influenced by economic considerations. (Weber 1978)

Weber goes on to say that "type of action, including the use of violence, may be economically oriented. This is true of war-like action in such cases as marauding." He praises "Franz Oppenheimer, in particular, for the fact that he has rightly distinguished economic means from political means." It is essential to distinguish the latter from economic action. The use of force is unquestionably very strongly opposed to the spirit of economic acquisition in the usual sense. Hence the term:

> "economic action" will not be applied to the direct appropriation of goods by force and the direct coercion of the other party by threats of force. [...] Furthermore, the formally peaceful provision for the means and the success of a projected exercise of force, as in the case of armaments and economic organization for war, is just as much economic action, as any other. (Weber 1978)

Weber makes use of the concept when he points out that "Every course of rational political action is economically oriented with respect to provision for the necessary means, and it is always possible for political action to serve the interest of economic ends" (Weber 1947). Similarly, while Weber points out that "though it is not necessarily true of every economic system, certainly the modern economic order under modern conditions could not continue if its control of resources were not upheld by the legal compulsion of the state; that is, if its formally 'legal' rights were not upheld by the threat of force." However, one cannot agree more with Weber when he states that the above-mentioned circumstance does not blur or eliminate irreducible distinction between the economy and the non-economic structures in question:

> But the fact that an economic system is thus dependent on protection by force, does not mean that it is itself an example of the use of force. It is entirely untenable to maintain that economic action, however defined, is only a means by contrast, for instance, with the state, as an end in itself. This becomes evident from the fact that it has been possible to define the state itself only in terms of the means which it attempts to monopolize, the use of force. (Weber 1947)

On these grounds Weber clarifies some other important conceptual distinctions. In particular, the term "economy" will be distinguished from that of "technology." The term "technology" applied to an action refers to the totality of means employed as opposed to the meaning or end to which the action is, in the last analysis, oriented. [...]

> "Rational" technique is a choice of means which is consciously and systematically oriented to the experience and reflection of the actor, which consists, at the highest level of rationality, in scientific knowledge. (Weber 1978)

The following statement corrorobates our earlierinsight concerning Weber's structural or holistic approach, which in the following case combines with his dialectical style of thinking.

> What is concretely to be treated as a "technology" is thus variable. The ultimate significance of a concrete act may, seen in the context of the total system of action, be of a "technical" order; that is, it may be significant only as a means in this broader context. Then concretely the meaning of the particular act lies in its technical result; and, conversely, the means which are applied in order to accomplish this are its "techniques." In this sense there are techniques of every conceivable type of action. [...] All these are capable of the widest variation in degree of rationality. The presence of a "technical question" always means that there is some doubt over the choice of the most efficient means to an end. Among others, the standard of efficiency for a technique may be the famous principle of "least action," the achievement of the optimum result with the least expenditure of resources. (Weber 1978)

Weber's account contains several rather simple truths, but also some ambiguity—as the following passage shows—concerned with the similarity of the terms "economising", "economical" and "economic", which permits, nay, encourages slips from one of these meanings to either of the remaining two:

As long as only questions of technology in the present sense are involved, the only considerations relevant are those bearing on the achievement of this particular end, the pursuit of which is accepted as desirable without question. Given this end, it is a matter of the choice of the most "economical" means, account being taken of the quality, the certainty, and the permanence of the result. Means, that is, are compared only in terms of the immediate differences of expenditure involved in alternative ways of achieving the end. As long as it is purely a technical question, other wants are ignored.

Thus, in a question of whether to make a technically necessary part of a machine out of iron or platinum, a decision on technical grounds alone would, so long as the requisite quantities of both metals for this particular purpose were available, consider only which of the two would in this case bring about the best result and would minimize the other comparable expenditures of resources, such as labour. But once consideration is extended to take account of the relative scarcity of iron and platinum in relation to their potential uses, as every technologist is accustomed to do even in the chemical laboratory, the action is no longer in the present sense purely technical, but also economic. (Weber 1947)

Despite Weber's best intentions, the manner he frames his distinction contributes to the obliteration of the economy's boundaries rather than their clear delineation. The latter task would be helped by an adoption of, for example, Polanyi's substantive approach discussed earlier. From this viewpoint some actions of laboratory scientists may indeed be included in the economy inasmuch as they nanufacture concrete material goods, say, medicines, or engage inthe type of work later defined as pre-material. This, however, is not a criterion Weber would use.

From the economic point of view, "technical" questions always involve the consideration of "costs." This is a question of crucial importance for economic purposes and in this context always takes the form of asking what would be the effect on the satisfaction of other wants if this particular means were not used for satisfaction of one given want. [...] The question of what, in comparative terms, is the cost of the use of the various possible technical means for a single technical end depends in the last analysis on their potential usefulness as means to other ends. This is particularly true of labour.[2] A technical problem in the present sense is, for instance, that of what equipment is necessary in order to move loads of a particular kind, or in order to raise mineral products from a given depth in a mine; further, among the alternatives it is a question of knowing which is the most efficient, that is, among other things, which achieves a given degree of success with the least expenditure of effort. It is, on the other hand, an economic problem how, on the assumption of an exchange economy, this equipment can be paid for in money through the sale of goods; or, on the assumption of a planned economy, how the necessary labour and other means of production can be provided without damage to the satisfaction of other wants held to be more urgent. In both cases, it is a problem of the comparison of ends. Economic action is primarily oriented to the problem of choosing the end to which a thing shall be applied, of choosing the appropriate means.

---

[2] Recognising this special importance of labour, Weber moves closer to his arch-rival's position.

> For purposes of the theoretical definition of technical rationality it is wholly indifferent whether the product of a technical process is in any sense useful. In practice this is not the case, however, since economic elements are also involved in concrete cases. (Weber 1947)

Thus, Weber himself acknowledges that the distinction concerned is not as clear-cut as he would have us to believe.

In the present terminology there could well be a rational technique even of achieving ends which no one desires. It would, for instance, be possible, as a kind of technical amusement, to apply all the most modern methods to the production of atmospheric air, and no one could take the slightest exception to the purely technical rationality of the action. Economically, on the other hand, the procedure would under normal circumstances be clearly irrational because there was no demand for the product. (Weber 1947)

It may seem paradoxical that Weber, considering his impressive historical erudition, uses here categories peculiar to only one type of historically existing modes of economic activity, the commodity-money economy, which is best exemplified by its most developed variant in the form of the capitalist mode of production.[3] To generalise Weberian considerations, one would have to use the notion of use value instead of his category of demand which implies that a given good has exchange value. But again, by no means all economies, as Weber is perfectly aware, were organised on exchange principles. Thus, it follows that we must return to the topic of defining the economy if such a definition is to be satisfactory from the standpoint of socio-economic structuralism.

I.2.3. The problem of rationality

The above deliberations involve one of Weber's central notions, which must be discussed at some length, not only for its own sake, but also for more general implications in terms of Weberian approach. A German scholar has carried on a thorough analysis of this question. His conclusions, relevant to the above arguments, are as follows:

[3] However close is the relationship of the two, it is not one of identity, which is overlooked by the following comment to Blaug's observation that: "'The history of economic thought … is nothing but the history of our efforts to understand the workings of an economy based on market transactions' (1985, 6).
Accordingly conventional economics can be seen as the theoretical construction of capitalism" Li Xing & Jacques Hersh 2003).

That abstract theory starts with the modern occidental type of man and his economy. It tries to understand the elementary phenomena of the "economically fully educated" man (1990, 29). Weber does not say here that abstract theory is only a heuristic advice. He underlines the idea of a single logic of economic action. This logic is most fully expressed in occidental societies. What Weber describes seems to be a real and not an ideal type of description. Weber is not historical, insofar as he does not assume different types of systematic economic action in different economic systems … In the most-often-quoted passage of his deliberations on economics, he enumerates the well-known idealizations: all noneconomic motives are excluded; full knowledge of the situation, maximization (the use of the best means available), and full use of all energies …

This is an unrealistic image, analogous to a mathematical ideal figure (1990, 30). For Weber, the neoclassical model of man is in the center of theoretical analysis. His remark on the unrealistic character makes no difference, because no serious neoclassical economist doubts that we are dealing with an idealization. Weber himself states just previously that the action of this idealized economic man formulates the transhistorical logic of systematic or rational economic behavior and that, at least for the time being, the occident converges to this model …

The notion of rationality [...] presupposes a world without surprise, corresponding to Schumpeter's closed circuit and not to discontinuous change, novelty, surprise, and uncertainty.[4] [...] he often talks of complete calculability.

He identifies capitalists, managers, and organizers, but he does not reflect on the role and function of the entrepreneur. [...]

he tries to apply the rationality concept in every aspect of analysis. Sometimes the reader begins to doubt if we know more as a result of the introduction of the notion of rationality compared with more traditional descriptions. For example, he talks about the limitations of the free recruitment of the labour force as limitations on the formal rationalization of economic activity and continues with limitations on technical rationality in this sphere (1968d: 128). (Peukert 2004)

1.2.4. The formal and substantive rationality of economic action

While considerations of rationality in general are certainly of crucial importance, at least equally relevant for the purposes of sociology of economy is the distinction alluded to in the claim cited above. As we shall

[4] These notions are characteristic concepts of the Austrian school that is the subject of one of the subsequent chapters.

see, the author of the present book has in this matter a rather different view than the above-mentioned German scholar:

> Weber's distinction has been much acclaimed, but in our view it is not so spectacular and also ambiguous. It is not spectacular because no market theorist questions the indifference of the market with regard to distribution or that market allocations may lead to unacceptable results[5] (working poor, etc.).
>
> On the other hand, if Weber accepts the Austrian story of the market economy, formal rationality is to a great extent identical to substantive rationality.
>
> This is because the economy serves the final consumer and competition wipes out profits, so that the ethical substantive standard of the market economy since Adam Smith (i.e., the procurement of cheap goods) is realized. (Peukert 2004)

This conception of Weber can, however, be looked at from a different angle. Although the right-wing convictions of Weber are well-known, in practice he would not shy away from recognising a number of fundamental contradictions of a market economy or capitalism, for that matter. Thus, he pointed out that:

> It is necessary to formulate the concept of economic action in such a way as to include the modern market economy; so it is not possible to take consumers' wants, and their 'satisfaction,' as a point of departure. The concept must take account, on the one hand, of the fact that utilities are actually sought after—including among them orientation to pecuniary acquisition for its own sake. But, on the other hand, it must also include the fact, which is true even of the most primitive self- sufficient economy, that attempts, however primitive and traditionally limited, are made to assure the satisfaction of such desires by some kind of activity. (Weber 1947)

The purpose of what is in fact a criticism of the capitalist system is served, among others, by the aforementioned dichotomy. Weber points to one of the fundamental contradictions in the modern economy, what he calls the tension between the "formal" and "substantive" (materiel) rationality of the economy. At the same time, Weber's distinction, not accidentally parallel to that of Polanyi, mitigates somewhat not only our, as we have

---

[5] This claim is unfounded as, *inter alia*, an example of Hayek whose views on the matter were explored in an earlier chapter, definitely shows. All this seems rather odd given that Peukert, as his paper amply demonstrates, has an extensive knowledge of Austrian economics.

seen, charge of insufficient historical sensivity of his approach. By the term formal rationality he means the extent to which it is possible to carry through accurate rational calculation of the quantities involved in economic orientation, and hence to act upon the results of such calculation. By substantive rationality, on the other hand, he means the extent to which it is possible to secure what, according to a given system of values, is an adequate provision of a population with goods and services, and in the process remain in accord with the ethical requirements of the system of norms. The tension arises from the fact that a high level of formal rationality can be attained only under certain specific substantive conditions, which are always in some important ways in conflict with the interests and moral sentiments implied in a high level of substantive rationality.

The prices which are an essential basis of rational accounting are, as he says, not so much "claims to unspecified utilities" without relation to the conflict relations of human beings, as they are "estimates of the chances of success" in a situation of the conflict of interest with other competitors.[6] The outcome of such a competitive conflict can never be guaranteed to be strictly in accord with the standards of substantive rationality. (Weber 1947)

From a comparative point of view, note note how many common points there are between Weber and Marx- structural and dialectical approach, a key aspect of the latter being the category of contradiction or conflict, for that matter. On the other hand, ideological and class positions of the two thinkers are far apart; Weber reckons that because of its enormous simplification of the goals and standards of success of economic activity, the highest degree of formal rationality takes the form of capital accounting. The thing Weber emphasizes immediately is the dependence of this in turn on the highest possible degree of market freedom, that is of the absence of impingement on the market of economically irrational interests or influences, or of economically rational ones which, like monopolies, by restricting market freedom interfere with the access of

[6] And yet, for all his merits, Weber, it has been observed, "reduces that relationship to a conscious, considered interaction between competitors investing in the same object ('all parties potentially interested in the exchange'). [...] The point is [...] to subordinate this 'interactionist' description of strategies to a structural analysis of the conditions that delimit the space of possible strategies—while, at the same time, not forgetting that competition among a small number of agents in strategic interaction for access (for some of them) to exchange with a particular category of clients is also, and above all, an encounter between producers occupying different positions within the structure of the specific capital" (Bourdieu 2005).

others to the conditions of high calculability. In addition, capital accounting implies, Weber notes, a high level and stability of discipline in the functioning of the enterprise, and stable relations of appropriation of all the important elements in the situation, materials, premises, equipment, labour, legal rights, and privileges, etc.

On the other side, though, the differences concerned are not as wide as is often thought. Finally, third, it is not, according to Weber, "need" or "desire" as such which influences the production and marketing of goods, but "effective demand." There is in the first place no guarantee that any given distribution of purchasing power is in accord with the standards of substantive rationality. This is true not only between individuals but also between impersonally organised interests. For instance, so far as higher education and research are dependent on private support through gifts and endowment there would seem to be no reason to suppose that the relative funds available to institutions for this purpose at all accurately reflect the valuation of the goals in the society at large.[7] Too many fortuitous circumstances influence their income. Furthermore, there is reason to believe that the processes of a competitive market economy themselves influence the distribution of income in ways contrary to any given set of substantive standards, notably through the cumulative tendency to increasing inequality[8] which operates unless control of it is more stringent than there seems to be any realistic possibility of attainment.

The tension operates reciprocally. The process of extension of formal rationality, and of the conditions underlying it, creates situations and stimulates types of action which in various ways come into conflict with whatever substantive norms there are in the society and the sentiments and symbols associated with them. As a result of this conflict there are at various points tendencies to "interference with the operation of the free market economy. Under relatively stable conditions these forces may be held in a state of relative balance, even though it is precarious, but under other conditions it is quite possible for the interfering tendencies to enter upon a cumulative development such as to lead to a far-reaching process of change, undermining many of the essential conditions of the market economy" (Weber 1947).

The above statement shows how far Weber would go in his realistic socio-economic assessment of capitalism. The intellectual honesty of the

---

[7] This criticism of capitalism, in turn, may be compared to that of Galbraith, implied in his distinction between private opulence and public squalor.

[8] This assertion alone suffices to show that Weber, contrary to Peukert and other critics, does go beyond conventional economics.

author is remarkable, all the more so as this statement contradicts his other, rather sceptical assessments of the capacity of collective action of the working class as an agent of change:

> "Profit-making" (*Erwerben*)[9] is activity which is oriented to opportunities for seeking new powers of control over goods on a single occasion, repeatedly, or continuously.[...] There is a form of monetary accounting which is peculiar to rational economic profit-making; namely, "capital accounting." Capital accounting is the valuation and verification of opportunities for profit and of the success of profit-making activity.
>
> "Capital" is the sum of money in terms of which the means of profit-making which are available to the enterprise are valued. (Weber 1947)

This technical definition of capital is disappointing, as, after all, we are dealing here with one of the most eminent social scientists of all time. From the sociological, or, more precisely, socio-economic viewpoint, capital is not simply a sum of things or money, for that matter. It is, rather, a social relation between the labour power and his/her employer, as an owner of the means of production, services etc.

This does not mean that Weber, as a general rule, does gloss over important socio-economic distinctions.

As distinguished from the calculation appropriate to a budgetary unit, the capital accounting and calculation of the market entrepreneur are oriented not to marginal utility, but to profitability. To be sure, the probabilities of profit are in the last analysis dependent on the income of consumption units and, through this, on the marginal utility of the available income of the final consumers of consumer goods.

> As it is usually put, it depends on their "purchasing power" for the relevant commodities. But from a technical point of view, the accounting calculations of a profit-making enterprise and of a consumption unit differ as fundamentally as do the ends of want satisfaction and of profit-making which they serve. For purposes of economic theory, it is the marginal consumer who determines the direction of production. In actual fact, given the actual distribution of power this is only true in a limited sense for the modern situation. To a large degree, even if the consumer is in a position to buy, his wants are "awakened" and "directed" by the entrepreneur.[10]

---

[9] The editors note that "In common usage the term *Erwerben* would perhaps best be translated as 'acquisition.' This has not, however, been used as Weber is here using the term in a technical sense as the antithesis of Haushalten" (Weber 1947).

[10] It can be seen that Weber rather mercilessly treats one of the favourite capitalistic myths of "consumer sovereignty."

> In a market economy [...] the double entry form of bookkeeping which is the most highly developed from a technical point of view. [...] in the system of accounting, there is introduced the fiction of exchange transactions between the different parts of a single enterprise[11]; [...] in order to develop a technique of estimating the bearing of each particular measure on the profitability of the enterprise. [...] In an economy which makes use of capital accounting and which is thus characterized by the appropriation of the means of production by individual units, that is by property,[12] profitability depends on the prices which the "consumers," according to the marginal utility of money in relation to their income, can and will pay. It is only possible to produce profitably for those consumers who, in these terms, have sufficient income. A need may fail to be satisfied, not only when an individual's own demand for other goods takes precedence, but also when the greater purchasing power of others, in relation to any kind of demand, withdraws the relevant good from the market. Thus the fact that competition on the market is an essential condition of the existence of rational money accounting further implies that the outcome of the economic process is decisively influenced by the ability of persons who are plentifully supplied with money to outbid the others, and of those more favourably situated for production to underbid their rivals on the selling side. The latter are particularly those well supplied with goods essential to production or with money. (Weber 1947)

This implicit reference to class deserves to be stressed, again in contrast to orthodox economics in which this notion is conspicuous by its absence. Meanwhile, as we have seen, Weber takes account of differentiation in property and class terms not only among consumers but also producers, i.e. capitalists.

I.2.5. Capitalism and its genesis

The most essential features of capitalism as an economic order were for Weber the deferral of consumption and rational accounting. Weber argues that ascetic Protestantism (or some other form of innerworldly asceticism) was a necessary but not sufficient condition for the emergence of Capitalism as a socio-economic formation. According to this view, capitalism was the unintended consequence of religious ethics.

---

[11] In modern parlance, this would be referred to as transfer prices.

[12] It should read: private property, as property of the means of production, or, more generally, means of economic activity is present, albeit in a variety of forms, under all economic formations of society.

Let's take into account the contrast between attitudes toward wealth in the medieval & modern worlds. In the former case, wealth was looked down on morally. What wealth generated was for consumption. However, capitalism is based on the supremacy of wealth over the individual, the valuing of production without consumption. This change did not occur, Weber reckons, because of change in the economic structure. [...] Weber came out from the general principle that ethics influence action.

Christian ethics revolve around the issue of salvation. Catholisism accorded the highest salvation to those who withdrew from the world (one worked in the monastery for discipline, not profit). Penance was a way to salvation, not work in the world. Ordinary folks could reach salvation through good works, charity, and financial support of the church. It was precisely the corruption of this last act that produced the Reformation. In Lutheranism, by contrast, the highest value is not withdrawal from the world; instead: work is one's "calling." One has a duty to serve God whatever one's station. It laid stress on innerworldly life, not otherworldly, but still no ascetic drive which would rationally order one's life. Calvinism assumed the premises that work is one's calling, and while one cannot influence salvation, one can know if one is saved by carrying out God's commands. Thus, one rationalises one's life and conduct by way of success, showing one's salvation takes hard work; wealth is acceptable, but, mind you, only if you don't enjoy it! It provides a useful temptation, which will be resisted only by the saved.

Weber recognized that capitalism requires capital accumulation, specifically, reinvestment of profit for the sake of the enterprise, not for the capitalist. Thus, it is Weber's contention that inner-worldly asceticism has an "elective affinity" for capitalism. In other words, Weber argued that there obtains a close parallel between the ethics of Calvinism and the ethics of the capitalist. When one notices the historical priority of the former, and the former's absence in other civilizations, which supposedly had all the other prerequisites, the causal importance of Protestantism for the development of capitalism follows.

Weber's thesis may also be couched in the following terms:

> Weber emphasized that money making as a calling had been "contrary to the ethical feelings of whole epochs ..." (Weber 1930, 73; further Weber references by page number alone). Lacking moral support in pre-Protestant societies, business had been strictly limited to "the traditional manner of life, the traditional rate of profit, the traditional amount of work ..." (67). Yet, this pattern "was suddenly destroyed, and often entirely without any essential change in the form of organization ..." Calvinism, Weber argued,

changed the spirit of capitalism, transforming it into a rational and unashamed pursuit of profit for its own sake. (Frey 2001)

According to Weber, a key feature of Calvinism, uncertainty about salvation:

had the psychological effect of producing a single-minded search for certainty. Although one could never influence God's decision to extend or withhold election, one might still attempt to ascertain his or her status. [...] If one[...] conformed to what was known of God's requirements for this life, then that might provide some evidence of election. Thus upright living, which could not earn salvation, returned as evidence of salvation.

The upshot was that the Calvinist's living was "thoroughly rationalized in this world and dominated by the aim to add to the glory of God in earth ..." (118). [...] This singleness of purpose left no room for diversion and created what Weber called an ascetic character. "Only activity serves to increase the glory of God, according to the definite manifestations of His will" (157). Only in a calling does this focus find full expression. "A man without a calling thus lacks the systematic, methodical character which is ... demanded by worldly asceticism" (161). A calling represented God's will for that person in the economy and society.

Such emphasis on a calling was but a small step from a full-fledged capitalistic spirit. In practice, according to Weber that small step was taken, for "the most important criterion (of a calling) is ... profitableness. For if God ... shows one of His elect a chance of profit, he must do it with a purpose..." (162). This "providential interpretation of profit-making justified the activities of the business man," and led to "the highest ethical appreciation of the sober, middle-class, self-made man" (163).

A sense of calling and an ascetic ethic applied to labourers as well as to entrepreneurs and businessmen. Nascent capitalism required reliable, honest, and punctual labor (23–24), which in traditional societies had not existed (59-62). That free labor would voluntarily submit to the systematic discipline of work under capitalism required an internalized value system unlike any seen before (63). Calvinism provided this value system (178–79).

Thus, the Protestant ethic ordered life according to its own logic, but also according to the needs of modern capitalism as understood by Weber. (Frey 2001)

The famous Weberian thesis has been hotly debated.

British scholar R. H. Tawney in *Religion and the Rise of Capitalism* (1926) noted that Weber treated multi-faceted reformed Christianity as though it were equivalent to late-era English Puritanism, the period from which Weber's most telling quotes were drawn. Tawney observed that the "iron collectivism" of Calvin's Geneva [indeed, some go even further,

> calling Calvin's sect a totalitalian one: note- J.T.] had evolved before Calvinism became harmonious with capitalism: "(Calvinism) had begun by being the very soul of authoritarian regimentation. It ended by being the vehicle of an almost Utilitarian individualism" (Tawney 1962, 226–7). [...] Roland Bainton [...] disputed Weber's psychological claims. Despite the psychological uncertainty Weber imputed to Puritans, their activism could be "not psychological and self-centered but theological and God-centered" (Bainton 1952, 252–53). That is, God ordered all of life and society, and Puritans felt obliged to act on His will. And if some Puritans scrutinized themselves for evidence of election, "the test was emphatically not economic activity as such but upright character ..." He concludes that Calvinists had no particular affinity for capitalism but that they brought "vitality and drive into every area ... whether they were subduing a continent, overthrowing a monarchy, or managing a business, or reforming the evils of the very order which they helped to create" (255). (Frey 2001)
>
> Somewhat similarly, Samuelsson (1993: 27–48), argued that Puritan leaders did not truly endorse capitalistic behavior. Rather, they were ambivalent. Given that Puritan congregations were composed of businessmen and their families (who allied with Puritan churches because both wished for less royal control of society), the preachers could hardly condemn capitalism. Instead, they clarified "the moral conditions under which a prosperous, even wealthy, businessman may, despite success and wealth, become a good Christian" (38). But this, Samuelsson makes clear, was hardly a ringing endorsement of capitalism. (Frey 2001)

However, apart from Weber's possible misinterpretation of Puritanism, there is also another question- that of his misinterpretation of capitalism as a result of exaggerating the importance of asceticism. Weber's favourite exemplar of capitalism, Benjamin Franklin, did advocate unremitting personal thrift and discipline. There is no denying that some quarters within capitalism did advance by personal thrift. However, Samuelsson (83–87) argues that thrift could not have contributed even in a minor way to the creation of the large fortunes of capitalists.

Frey argues that: "Perhaps more important than personal fortunes is the finance of business. The retained earnings of successful enterprises, rather than personal savings, probably have provided a major source of funding for business ventures from the earliest days of capitalism." All his counterarguments notwithstanding, Frey ends up *de facto* undermining Weber's interpretation of the capitalist spirit: "And successful capitalists, even in Puritan New England, have been willing to enjoy at least some of the fruits of their labours. Perhaps the spirit of capitalism was not the spirit of asceticism" (Frey 2001). And, unfortunately, Weber's thesis cannot be saved by, according to the researcher being cited, its last pillar. It is true that:

> Weber was influenced by the writings of Benjamin Franklin, [...] Weber quoted Franklin early in his work and based many of his ideas on Franklin's writings: For six pounds a year you may have the use of one hundred pounds, provided you are a man of known prudence and honesty. He [...] Weber then said, "Truly what is here preached is not simply a means of making one's way in the world, but a particular ethic ... It is not mere business astuteness, that sort of thing is common enough, it is an ethos. The earning of money within the modern economic order is, so long as it is done legally, the result and the expression of virtue and proficiency in a calling; and this virtue and proficiency are, as it is now not difficult to see, the real Alpha and Omega of Franklin's ethic". (Pierotti 2003)

However, Weber's interpretation of Franklin has met with criticism to the effect that "far from demonstrating a commitment to the 'spirit of capitalism,' and the accumulation of wealth as an end in itself and moral duty, Franklin's writings are in fact evidence against the existence of such a spirit" (Dickson and McLachlan 1989). The two aforementioned writers point out that the title of the work from which Weber quoted is "Necessary Hints to Those That Would Be Rich." They assert, "This suggests that what Franklin is offering is prudential advice, rather than insisting on a moral imperative. The gist of Dickson's and McLachlan's argument is that Weber misinterpreted Franklin's writings as moral ends. They deny that Franklin was preaching a Protestant work ethic and assert that all Franklin was saying was that if a person is interested in being successful in life and commerce, here are some virtues to follow.

Dickson and McLachlan conclude with a clear statement of their criticism of Weber's hypothesis: "It seems clear to us that Weber misinterprets Franklin and that the latter was not imbued with the ethos which Weber attributes to him. It is not in dispute that a methodological lifestyle is conducive to the accumulation of wealth. What is at issue concerning Weber's Protestant Ethic thesis is the impetus for such a lifestyle". Weber's misinterpretation of Franklin does not in itself, to be sure, invalidate his methodology or his thesis. Nonetheless, it does suggest a rather cavalier attitude towards evidence, particularly as the writings of Franklin are the only "'evidence' that he presents in his original essays to demonstrate the existence of the 'spirit of capitalism'" (Pierotti 2003).

Indeed, Weber was not able to show (empirically) that Calvinists became capitalists: not in the 1600s, nor in 1905.

While this doesn't undermine the logic itself, it raises questions about the data. An even more troublesome problem for Weber's theory arises from a question: To what extent can religious doctrine be seen as a reflection of changing medieval economic conditions?[13] Putting it differently, one should ask to what extent was the response to Luther and Calvin economically determined. Did the followers use these religious ideologies to justify working in the world and not donating to churches?

This more far-reaching argument is at odds with the logic of Weber's reasoning. Weber's thesis is weakened still further in confrontation with a more elaborate and magnified version of the above-mentioned counter-argument:

> R. H. Tawney, perhaps Weber's most famous critic, agreed with Weber that capitalism and Protestantism were connected. However, Tawney overturned Weber's view as to their relationship. In his 1926 work, *Religion and the Rise of Capitalism*, he states that Protestantism adopted the risk-taking, profit-making ethic of capitalism, not the other way around. Tawney claims, with some good measure:
>
> "There was plenty of capitalist spirit in fifteenth century Venice and Florence, or in south Germany and Flanders, for the simple reason that these areas were the greatest commercial and financial centers of the age. The development of capitalism in Holland and England in the sixteenth and seventeenth centuries were due, not to the fact that they were Protestant powers but to large economic movements, in particular the Discoveries and the results which flowed from them."
>
> ... in Europe prior to the Reformation, [t]he Italian merchants and the Dutch clothiers operated under a rational economic system. Double-entry bookkeeping was invented in Italy and adopted by other merchants throughout Europe ... it is obvious that several factors were at work in Europe during the long sixteenth century, which led to the growth and dominance of capitalism. (Pierotti 2003)

Thus, one fairly widespread line of attacking Weber's thesis boils down to a contention that modern capitalism might have arisen before reformed Protestantism or in places where the reformed influence was much smaller than Weber (which is rather strange given Weber's enormous historical knowledge; but, sadly, many scholars indulge in taking consideration of merely such datathat are consistent with their preconceptions) believed:

> During the early twentieth century, historians studied the timing of the emergence of capitalism and Calvinism in Europe. E. Fischoff (1944, 113) reviewed the literature and concluded that the "timing will show that Calvinism emerged later than capitalism where the latter became [...] powerful," suggesting no cause-and-effect relationship. [...] Bainton also

[13] Indeed, as Antonio Labriola aptly noted, "ideas do not fall from heaven."

> suggests that the Reformed contributed to the development of capitalism only as a "matter of circumstance" (Bainton 1952, 254). The Netherlands "had long been the mart of Christendom, before ever the Calvinists entered the land." Finally, Kurt Samuelsson (1957) concedes that "the Protestant countries, and especially those adhering to the Reformed church, were particularly vigorous economically" (Samuelsson, 102). However, he finds much reason to discredit a cause-and-effect relationship. Sometimes capitalism preceded Calvinism (Netherlands), and sometimes lagged by too long a period to suggest causality (Switzerland). Sometimes Catholic countries (Belgium) developed about the same time as the Protestant countries. Even in America, capitalist New England was cancelled out by the South, which Samuelsson claims also shared a Puritan outlook.
>
> Weber himself, perhaps seeking to circumvent such evidence, created a distinction between traditional capitalism and modern capitalism. The view that traditional capitalism could have existed first, but that Calvinism in some meaningful sense created modern capitalism, depends on too fine a distinction according to critics such as Samuelsson. (Frey 2001)

As a matter of fact, it is not that the above distinction is too fine but rather that both critics and defenders of Weber's thesis lack sufficiently fine conceptual apparatus to effectively address such questions. In particular, what would be incredibly useful in the context under consideration is a distinction between, on the one hand, capitalist modes of production and more generally economic activity and, on the other, the capitalist economic formation of society as comprising all those modes. We have used a plural mode, because historically there were (and there still are) a variety of different bourgeois modes of production, e.g. a slave-capitalist mode (and of economic activity), usually regarded as a universal base on free labour power, i.e. semi-slave labour power and so forth. Suffering from such glaring gaps in one's theoretical framework, one has no other option but to conclude that in light of rigorous canons of science, and: "because of the impossibility of controlled experiments to firmly resolve the question, the issue will never be completely closed" (Frey 2001).

The strongest link that Tawney saw between capitalism and Protestantism was rationality. Protestantism was a revolt against traditionalism and as such advocated rationality as an approach to life and business. Tawney proposed that the rationality inherent in capitalism became a tenet of Protestantism because rationality was diametrically opposed to the traditionalism of Catholicism. Others regarded rationality as a value label, which functioned to place value on Western civilisation, and devalue others. Academics used this political aspect of "modernization" to create a critique of all theories that had a "modernization" component. Weber was interpreted as embodying this perspective of "modernization" by such intellectuals. And because the modernisation theory went out of fashion (together with functionalism which promoted it), some sociologists have levelled criticism against him for this perspective. At the same time, other commentators drew attention to the existence of the different types of rationality in *The Protestant Ethic and the Spirit of Capitalism.* For example, in Roger Brubaker's *The Limits of Rationality* (1984), he discussed several different types (deliberate, systematic, calculatable, impersonal, exact, purely qualitative, rule-grounded, predictable, methodological, sober, scrupulous, logical, intelligible, consistent, anti-emotional, and conscious self-scrutiny).

To return to Tawney's important work, he reckoned that early Protestant leaders recognized that hard work and rational organization of time were capitalist virtues which fit very nicely into the concept of living one's life in the service of God. Tawney saw the capitalist concepts of division of labour and planned accumulation as being reflected in the dogma of Protestantism which urged its followers to use one's calling on earth for the greater glory of God. According to Tawney, capitalist precepts and Protestant dogma fit hand in glove.

As a historian, Tawney did not see a linear relationship between capitalism and Protestantism, however. He considered Weber's thesis, though, to be a little too simplistic to explain historical events. History tends to be non-linear, and attempts to draw straight casual lines between events are shaky at best.

That Weberian methodological approach was contestable is also evidenced by other scholars' arguments, two of whom wrote commentaries on the original 1904–5 thesis: Karl Fisher in 1907 and Felix Rachfahl in 1909 (Chalcroft 2001). They interpreted Weber as arguing that the development of religious thought in Protestantism caused (in a mono-causal and linear fashion) capitalism. Both of these writers admonished Weber on his use of concepts such as the "capitalist spirit," the "protestant ethic" and Luther's "calling."

The historian Carlo Antoni even argued that Weber's methodology held him back from discovering the true nature of the phenomena that he wanted to investigate. His methodology created a theory that reduced logical struggles and grand dialectics to mere psychological origins, and discarded the modern (in terms of the search for natural laws) for the classical (the use of "ideal types," which Antoni, and not without reason, identified with the archetype-models of Plato) (Antoni 1959).

To comment briefly on the latter point, not dwelling on what Weber himself had to say on the status of his ideal types, one should note that genuine sociological research, as opposed to metaphysical deliberations, precludes any use of anything like Platonic ideas since concepts deployed in an empirical investigation, by definition, have to have some empirical referent.

> To return to Tawney's rejoinder to Weberian methodology, he was of an opinion that "The Protestant ethic, with its insistence on hard work, thrift, etc., had contributed to the rise of capitalism, but at the same time Protestantism itself was being influenced by an increasingly capitalistic society." As Tawney's proposition stands, it sticks firmly within the bounds of interactionism which is as equally a simplistic form of thinking as the unilinear approach allegedly pursued by his opponent. For the said proposition to move beyond those narrow bounds, it should be subordinated to a dialectical approach whose outline we have attempted to lay out below. By the same token this remark applies to others who have contended that Weber "in his work employed a multi-causal explanation model (in the words of Daniel W. Rossides [1978], a model of "pluralistic sociocultural positivism" [353]) that was superior to the mono-causal model that was often associated with positivism" (Gannon 2002–3)

An even more radical, if at all possible, U-turn was performed by economic historian Jacob Viner (1976), who used pre-eighteenth century Scotland as a case study to demonstrate that where Calvinism was a state religion, it tended to have a restraining rather than freeing effect on economic development. He quotes a letter from John Keats in support of his thesis: "... the ecclesiastical supervision of the life of the individual, which, as it was practised in the Calvinistic State Churches almost amounted to an inquisition, might even retard that liberation of individual powers which was conditioned by the rational ascetic pursuit of salvation, and in some cases actually did so." Viner points out that until well into the eighteenth century, Scotland was a desperately poor country. Contemporary commentators often remarked on the lack of economic initiative and ambition and on the general lack of enterprise and economic discipline of the population. Several of these reporters attributed Scotland's economic backwardness in large part to the deadening effect of Calvinist doctrine as forcibly applied by both Church and State. Viner quotes Henry T. Buckle who, in his 1857 treatise *Introduction to the History of Civilization in England*, wrote concerning the economic teachings of Scottish Calvinists in the seventeenth century as follows:

> To wish for more than was necessary to keep oneself alive was a sin as well as a [...] violation of the subjection we owe to God. [...] He was no lover of riches[...] To be poor, dirty, and hungry, to pass through life in misery, [...] to suffer constant affliction, and to be tormented in all

> possible ways; to undergo these things was deemed proof of goodness, just as the contrary was a proof of evil. (Pierotti 2003)

The opposition of Scottish Calvinism to capitalism was so well known in Europe that some English commentators such as Roger L'Estrange urged English businessmen to look at the record of the Scottish Presbyterians in interfering with commerce and industry for religious reasons before supporting Cromwell's cause.

To be fair to Weber and his thesis, one should point out that there are also other case studies leading to opposite conclusions,(specificallly, Norway) which, though, will not be discussed here.

> review of economic historians shows that they have given little explicit attention to Weber in recent years. However, they show an interest in the impact of cultural values broadly understood on economic growth. In this connection it is indicated that a modified version of the Weber thesis has also found some support in empirical economic research. Granato, Inglehart and Leblang (1996, 610) incorporated cultural values in cross-country growth models on the grounds that Weber's thesis fits the historical evidence in Europe and America. They did not, to be sure, focus on Protestant values, but accepted "Weber's more general concept, that certain cultural factors influence economic growth..." Specifically they incorporated a measure of "achievement motivation" in their regressions and concluded that such motivation "is highly relevant to economic growth rates" (625). Conversely, they found that "post-materialist" (i.e., environmentalist) values are correlated with slower economic growth. (Frey 2003)

This research, one cannot fail to notice, suffers from serious methodological limitations which render it implausible. What is most problematic about these and other similar studies is their way of collecting data. The empirical status of the latter is, as a matter of fact, very suspect, as they come from statistical surveys, and this sociological technique suffers from unalienable problems. Survey designers and executors fail to realise that each such a survey constitutes in fact a kind of experiment (Szczurkiewicz 1969) which underlies an artefactual and epiphenomenal nature of its results—surveys take place in an artificial environment forcefully detached from their respondents' social environment. Subjects are not investigated as embedded in complex social networks but, conversely, artificially isolated from those settings. Survey respondents may not have any particular view on the matters touched by the questions put to them and so they frequently *ad hoc* generate respective answers in the form of verbal utterances. Those are unavoidably incredible as indexes of actual behaviour. For one thing, respondents may not understand questions they face, they can also simply tell lies or, in a more complex but equally frequent case they are not able to articulate their own attitudes whether owing to their lack of semantic competence or, as both Freud and Bourdieu, amongst others, would have it, because such attitudes function at a subconscious level. For all those reasons, it is most unlikely that a collector of such verbal utterances would reveal real practical efficacy, i.e.functioning at a level of actual behaviour, demonstrating motives of human action. However, the above objections do not apply to Barro's (1997, 27) study as it referred not to purportedly individual, but instead to social consciousness. The researcher modified Solow growth models and found that a "rule of law index" is associated with more rapid economic growth. This index is a proxy for such things as "effectiveness of law enforcement, sanctity of contracts and … the security of property rights." As a corollary, "recalling Puritan theologian William Ames' definition of a contract, one might conclude that a religion such as Puritanism could create precisely the cultural values that Barro finds associated with economic growth" (Frey 2001).

Be that as it may, the enduring appeal of Weber's thesis can be measured by how many fine minds have participated in the debate over its meaning and validity. Thus, still another limitation to Weber's approach, corresponding to our above critical comments on conventional sociological methodology, lies in the fact that he focuses on the motives imbedded in the leaders' doctrines, not on the followers' actual ideas and motives of conduct. In addition, Weber's examples of ethical change do not come from the bourgeoisie, but from the petty bourgeoisie. The saying that a "Penny saved is a penny earned" has little in common with capital accumulation of the real bourgeoisie. Furthermore, Weber's examples are from the 1700s, two hundred years after the Reformation, and by then doctrines had been watered down.

If we are to believe his critics (and their arguments are not easy to dismiss), Weber committed more such historical errors.

H. M. Robertson, a historian at the University of Cape Town, asserted in "A Criticism of Max Weber and His School" that the Roman Catholic and Protestant Churches stressed the same precepts in the sixteenth and seventeenth centuries. He states that Weber's assertion that the concept of the "calling" was novel to Luther and Protestantism was not established in Weber's writings. Robertson supports his thesis by quoting Aquinas: "There seems to be no essential difference between the doctrine of the Catholics and the Puritans on this point (the calling). St. Thomas Aquinas' teaching on distributive justice was that:

This division of men in different occupations occurs in the first place through divine providence, which distributes the condition of men in such a way ... and also in the second place from natural causes, as a result of which it happens that there are different aptitudes for different occupations amongst different men." Robertson continues in support of his thesis:

> "The Jansenists .... reminded their flocks that the Christian life was 'a serious life, a life of toil and not of diversion, play or pleasure' so that one ought never to forget that it 'should be filled with some useful and sober occupation suitable for one's state of existence.' The Jesuits stressed almost the same beliefs. In France the Church went out of its way to welcome the honest bourgeois on the ground that he was the only type of man who followed God's commands and lived in a "calling." (Pierotti 2003)

It is precisely on the concept of Beruf that another of Weber's polemists focuses. Malcolm H. MacKinnon contends that Weber misinterpreted what the Calvinists understood by the concept of the calling and good works. He claims that:

> There are two fundamental theological flaws in Weber's line of reasoning, flaws that mean that Calvinism did not give a divine stamp of approval to earthly toil. [...] in Christianity generally and Calvinism in particular, works have nothing to do with mundane activities. As soteriologically conceived in relation to salvation, works are spiritual activities that call for obedience to the Law. MacKinnon goes on to explain that Weber's major failure is his misunderstanding of the Calvinist meaning of the calling. Using the Westminster Confession as his primary source, MacKinnon explains what the term "calling" meant to the Calvinists: There is a heavenly calling and an earthly calling or callings, the latter disqualified from making a positive contribution to our deliverance . . . Above all else, the devout must ensure that their mundane callings in no way impede the prosecution of the greatest good of all: their heavenly calling. Believers are sanctioned to "choose that employment or calling in which you may be most serviceable to God. Choose not that in which you may be most honorable in the world; but that which you may do most good and best escape sinning."

MacKinnon concludes by stating that it was Weber's misfortune to choose part of the Calvinist philosophy which, upon close examination, not only fails to support his fundamental thesis but in fact undermines it. "Again, the significant point here is that temporal obligations are at best indifferent and at worst sinful; they cannot make a contribution to the realization of celestial paradise. It is a grim twist of irony that Weber would choose such a spiritually worthless vehicle to realize his causal ambitions."

Amintore Fanfani, an economic historian in Rome in his article "Catholicism, Protestantism, and Capitalism" disagrees with Weber concerning the role that Protestantism played in the development of a capitalist spirit in Europe. At the very outset he states his argument:

> Europe was acquainted with capitalism before the Protestant revolt. For at least a century capitalism had been an ever growing collective force. Not only isolated individuals, but whole social groups, inspired with the new spirit, struggled with a society that was not yet permeated with it. Once we have ruled out that Protestantism could have produced a phenomenon that already existed, it still remains for us to enquire whether capitalism was encouraged or opposed by Protestantism." (Pierotti 2003)

He adds another sociological variable to the equation indicating that it was "not the Protestant Ethic which encouraged the growth of capitalism but the fact that many Protestants were forced to leave Catholic countries to escape persecution which 'fosters in the emigrants an internationalism that is no small element in capitalist mentality'. In fact, he says that many early Protestant leaders opposed capitalism, including Luther and Calvin: "Luther's conservatism in economic matters, to which his patriarchal ideas on trade and his decided aversion to interest bear witness. Even Calvin … condemns as unlawful all gain obtained at a neighbor's expense, and the amassing of wealth." The Huguenots and Dutch Reformers also preached against various aspects of capitalism: "… through the sixteenth and seventeenth centuries we find a continual repetition of the prohibitions of usury issued by the synods of the Huguenots and by those of the Dutch Reformers, whose ethical code also condemned even excessive labour, as robbing time and energy from the service of God, and held action born of desire for gain to be a sign of madness".

> [...] Fanfani argues that capitalism as we know it today was born in the Italian merchant states under the religious umbrella of Catholicism, but he discounts the effect that religion of any kind had on the growth of capitalism as the major world economic system. He concludes his article by stating, 'The creation of a new mentality in the economic field cannot therefore be considered as the work of Protestantism, or rather of any one religion, but it is a manifestation of that general revolution of thought' that characterizes the period of the Renaissance and the Reformation, by which in art, philosophy, morals, and economy, the individual emancipates … himself from the bonds imposed on him during the Middle Ages" (Pierotti 2003).

In addition, it should be pointed out that Weber's picture of Calvinism is one-sided. It has a communal emphasis (this apposite observation has in fact more general implications; both Weber and most supporters of his thesis downplay the role of(strange as it may seem) sociological, as opposed to religious, moral or ideological factors, in particular the specific character of closely knit communities in question by virtue of their strong social control over their members capable of enforcing desirable behaviour) as well as an individual one.

Covenant of the people with God. Work in the world to establish God's kingdom. This, as mentioned above, did not fit Weber's theories, so he played it down. Nevertheless, to be fair, it is Weber who was the first to treat seriously the idea that individual ethics (really group ethics practiced by the individual) could have unanticipated macrostructural consequences.

All in all, though, it must be admitted that Weber did not prove that the Protestant ethic was a necessary (albeit not sufficient) cause of capitalism. One of such unintended consequence of the popularity of Weber's work, which is in many cases superficially read, is the circumstance that most scholars (including many textbooks), think that "The Protestant Ethic" is "a disproof" of Marx. In Weber's eyes, it was no such thing.

It is not for me to speak on Marx's behalf, but what I can do is to present a very brief outline of the approach to the issue taken by socio-economic structuralism. As is repeatedly underlined in the book, this theoretical position has nothing in common with any view that would deny that ideas and forms of social consciousness inclusive of religion can powerfully influence individual and collective action. The thing is that for such relationships to be investigated scientifically one must take into consideration two sets of circumstances: firstly, to what degree an idea in question is itself conditioned by material, including economic conditions, and secondly how its influence on action is mediated by other societal structures and relations, not forgetting economic ones. It is only through such inquiry that one would be able to ultimately confirm or refute the famous Weberian thesis.

On the other hand, with the benefit of hindsight one can point to a lot of empirical cases of thriving capitalism on the grounds of non-Protestant religions, including those whose causal power in that regard were definitely rejected by Weber. Evidence casts doubt on Weber's (and other writers') association of managerial achievement motivation with the Protestant ethic of hard work. In their view, almost the exact opposite is true to the effect that managers and others with a high need for achievement seek to reduce their work by becoming more efficient, i.e. by obtaining the same result with less effort or in less time (McClelland & Burnham 1995). In this sense, the Protestant and any ethic of hard work, perhaps counter-intuitively, falls short of complete efficiency and rationality.

This seems in part ironic given the much-celebrated impact of Protestant doctrines on the spirit and practice of modern capitalism at least since Weber (1933).

Furthermore, notably in the Anglo-saxon variety of capitalism, it is instant gratification rather than deferred gratification that constitutes the governing principle, and this refers both to corporate managers who not without reason are accused of short-termism, which applies both to their conduct of business and personal orientation (e.g. executive bonuses and stock options) and consumers whose high rates of spending underlie the prosperity of the economies concerned and whose lowering plunges them, as a rule, into recession.

To be sure, Weber's thesis has its defenders as well. One of them holds that "History shows us that in fact those nations which were predominantly Protestant showed economic growth much greater than those which were predominantly Catholic. Even Jacob Viner's argument that the repressive nature of Scottish Calvinism does not damage Weber, since he acknowledged that once a religion becomes a creature of the state it then tends to oppress people rather than free them" (Pierotti 2003).

However, recent studies (Collins 1997) suggest that Protestantism was not the only factor in the historical emergence and expansion of capitalist production. In this view, such non-Protestant doctrines as Buddhism, especially its religious economy in the monasteries, played a significant historical role in the emergence as well as development of what is identified as the capitalist mode of production in Asia centuries ago. More frequently, researchers notice the strong effect of Confucianism on the nature and development of capitalist production in this region recently, with some attributing the rise of the East Asian economic tigers, including China, to this cultural pattern. For some of them, this East-Asian development model, just as that of Protestant Europe and America, re-actualizes the broader question as to what extent the economic and sociocultural features are causally linked (Berger and Hsiao 1993, 5). In comparative terms, the observed economic effect of Buddhism and Confucianism in Asia appears as an analogue to the much-celebrated impact of Protestantism on Western Europe and North America (Zafirovski 2002).

The above claim appears, however, to be too hastily constructed by analogy with Weber's famous thesis. Meanwhile, considering a bewildering gamut of varieties of religion (and political regime, for that matter) co-existing in this region of the world with economic progress (from the post-war Japanese economic miracle through rapid growth of Singapore, Indonesia, or South Korea to China and India's spectacular economic advancement), not to mention successful capitalisms of Ireland and Italy which are of course typical Catholic countries, the point attributing to them a causal power becomes highly doubtful.

I.2.5.1. Primitive Accumulation

While in his account of capitalism as a mature socio-economic system Weber, as we have seen notably in the section on formal and substantive rationality, offers a rich, multifaceted analysis, *The Protestant Ethic* suggests, conversely, a biased, stylised picture of the emergence of this economic order. And it is much more limited, too, in particular in its class focus. An alternative, wider view of the spectrum of social classes, those movers and shakers of history, is provided by Marx's theory of primitive accumulation,[14] subsequently developed and modified by a range of historians. To begin with, it is useful to consider a critique of a faithful follower of Weber:

> Max Weber has shown," the functioning of capitalism requires of the masses a completely new ascetic attitude to the labour process"," one which "cannot be achieved through a legal compulsion to labour in the form of serfdom". Accordingly, "it becomes necessary to supplement the legally established moral minimum with a religious or other form of normative moral maximum" (Borkenau, 152). This task is performed by Calvinism, which educates the masses in labour discipline. Which "masses" does Franz Borkenau mean when he speaks of the new "mass morality" and of a "completely new ascetic attitude of the masses towards the labour process?" The working masses come to mind. On occasion, Franz Borkenau states that "Calvinism (was) an instrument of mass domestication for the bourgeoisie" (169), that "religion is an indispensable means of mass domestication" (208). He speaks of the "compulsion for the labouring strata to adapt to capital" (161) and of the "new ascetic attitude" [...]

---

[14] The concept was initially named in different ways, and the expression of an "accumulation" which is at the origin of capitalism, began to appear with Adam Smith in book two of *Of the Nature, Accumulation, and Employment of Stock.* (1776): "... the accumulation of stock must, in the nature of things, be previous to the division of labour ...." Smith, in his English language *The Wealth of Nations* spoke of a "previous accumulation." Karl Marx, in the German language *Das Kapital*, reprised Smith's expression, translating it as *ursprünglich*, literally "original accumulation" or "primeval accumulation." Marx's translators rendered it back to English as "primitive," in German: *ursprüngliche Akkumulation*, literally "original accumulation" or "primeval."

He speaks of the development of a new "mass morality" and really means the emergence of a "capitalist morality" (160). Through its application to the working class, [Borkenau]'s characterization of Calvinism loses all meaning [as well of] the doctrine of "inner-worldly asceticism", which really means occupational asceticism. This characterization, however, focuses on the situation of the craftsmen who were-as Borkenau says-the chief bearers of Calvinism. Although Borkenau is speaking of the origins of capitalist morality, his whole section on Calvinism shows that he tailors the problem of the new morality to this craft stratum (153–70).

This problem of the new "mass" morality—totally borrowed by Borkenau from Weber—is only the logical and self-evident consequence of the theory, likewise taken from Max Weber, that capitalism originated among the craftsmen. The complete intellectual dependence of Borkenau on Weber is revealed in this formulation of the moral problem of the age, tailored to the craft stratum, as the fundamental problem of emerging capitalism. His opposition to Weber's thesis merely concerns details—Borkenau polemicises against Weber's attempt to formulate "a positive refutation of the materialist interpretation of history" (154) and against his idea "that capitalism was essentially conditioned by religion" (158). The Weberian interpretation, Borkenau shows, "is typical of the way in which the transformation of Marxist insights forces its way into non-Marxist science" (154). But, whatever the validity of the objections that Borkenau raises regarding Weber's methodology (158), the contents of his own employment of it are typical of the way in which Weber's petit-bourgeois ideology forces its way, unchanged, into Marxist science.

Wherein lies the difference between Weber and Borkenau? Both start from the taken-for-granted assumption that capitalism originated among the rising craftsmen, and that-together with the petty nobility-it was above all they who, "when their guild-life was shattered, became the chief bearers of the Calvinist religion in France, Holland and England (156) (Grossman 1934).

The term "stratum", middle or whatever, is out of place in the context under consideration Both Borkenau and his commentator seem to restrict the notion of class to capitalism, as though the feudal economic formation of society were devoid of its own class structure. Accordingly, the latter pertained also to the feudal guild mode of production, its principal mode of non-agricultural economic activity:

> The failure of the Weberian theory consists, according to B[orkenau], precisely in the fact that Weber thinks that he has refuted the materialist interpretation of history through the establishment of this "fact." According to the "mechanistic thinking" of Max Weber, "the bearers of a logically

> consistent capitalist religion" ought to have been "the capitalistically most progressive stratum of the time" (158). If that were not the case, then the materialist conception of history is refuted. As the unsettled small craftsmen adopted the Calvinist work ethic in order to ensure victory for themselves "in the competitive struggle, through rationalized, limitless effort," it is demonstrated that "this Calvinist work ethic preceded its application to that capitalist labour process," that, therefore, "capitalism is essentially conditioned by religion" (158).

Borkenau accepts Weber's claims about actual events: "M. Weber's thesis that the capitalistic way of thinking of these strata preceded their capitalist way of life is thus correct" (157). Weber has "for the first time provided concrete and irrefutable proof of the connection between religious doctrines and economic action" (154).

Nevertheless, Weber's conclusions are wrong. [...] the fact that non-capitalist strata are the bearers of capitalist ideology is no refutation of the Marxist conception of history. Rather, the problem consists precisely in the investigation of "why these not yet capitalist strata adopted a capitalist ideology" (157). Borkenau arrives at the following result: "The relationship between a religion and the class which bears it hardly ever takes the form of the religion expressing the true life-conditions of that class" (159). As a mere reflex, religion would indeed be meaningless. The function of new religions consists, as is the case with all ideological processes, of facilitating difficult social adaptations. "Calvinism is at first the denomination of non-capitalist groups which react to the capitalist process of decomposition with an adaptive shift" (157) and, by striving "to assert themselves in the context of a changing social totality, these groups direct their energy towards a way of life that is not yet at hand" (159). This means that they become "increasingly bourgeoisified" (157). Where the capitalist society does not yet function "automatically," [...] In such a society, "the norm of the capitalist labour-process can only be irrationalistic-religious" (162).

This summary of Borkenau's account is enough to show that there is [...] a whole chain of misunderstandings, inherent in it. However correct his polemic against Weber and the latter's supposed refutation of the materialist conception of history may be, it nevertheless shows that the issue here is not by a long chalk "the fundamental problem of emerging capitalism" and the latter's causation by religion, but concerns a remnant of earlier economic formations which stands outside the nexus of capitalism (capitalists/workers). It is a question, as Borkenau himself says elsewhere, of the "adaptation of the middle strata" (168) to the new mode of production. In other words, Calvinism is neither a question of the morality of the capitalists nor a mass morality, but a problem of petit bourgeois morality! It is only in this connection that Calvinism acquired a meaningful significance, as the religion of the threatened middle stratum and as its doctrine of self-justification, the effort to succeed in a changing society by means of "limitless effort." Only in this connection does it become understandable why these non-capitalist strata accepted the typically petit bourgeois (and not, as Borkenau has it, "capitalist") ideology of social ascent through limitless effort. (Grossman 1934)

Whilst his critical discussion has much to be said for it, it is clouded by Grossman's eclectic and inconsistent theoretical language. As repeatedly pointed out throughout the book, the concept of stratum is inconsistent with the analytical framework Grossman is keen to employ, and the adjective "middle" makes it only clearer.

> Calvinism had nothing at all to do with the origin and development of capitalism. Historically, this is apparent in the fact that the emergence of capitalism certainly lies much further back than Calvinism and the Reformation. [...] the bearers of the capitalist mode of production were neither the "aspiring Calvinist little people" (90), nor the "up-and-coming craftsmen" but those who accumulated large capital through trade and usury and who employed the proletarian elements that were being displaced by the decomposition of medieval organization in town and country. It was they who created in the putting-out system and later in manufacture what was, although on a craft basis, a superior economic form. Under pressure from this massive capitalist form of production, unhampered by guild regulations, backward, small-scale craft production, which suffered from lack of capital, could only be preserved "by unlimited effort," that is, by an unlimited exploitation of the workers employed, such as has since become typical of craft production. This had nothing to do with "rationalized" effort (1971, 161). One has rather to speak of an irrational, almost limitless waste of labour which is characteristic of petit-bourgeois morality. (Grossman 1934)

And again inconsistent with the theory of class, those "small producers" are not classified correctly as small capitalists, since the petty bourgeoisie comprises only those who are self-employed, i.e. do not employ other people's labour power.

That Calvinism or some related religious current did not form a necessary precondition for the origins of capitalism and that the "creation of a capitalist mass morality" can only "succeed on the basis of religious irrationalism" is refuted by the historical fact that capitalism emerged two centuries earlier in Italy without any help from religious irrationalism, without the help of Calvinism! Borkenau himself calls Italy the land "of religious indifference," "of the most radical break with religious tradition" (101). The clear, rational, sober-minded spirit of the Florentines [...] brings us to the second characteristic feature of Borkenau's theory. Following Weber, he places exaggerated stress on the significance of Calvinism for the education of the masses in labour discipline and describes the new mass morality as a necessary precondition (169) for the emergence of capitalism. He also asserts that the functioning of capitalism made necessary a 'new ascetic attitude of the masses towards the labour process' (152). [...] he follows directly in the footsteps of the petit bourgeois ideology of Max Weber, in which the history of emergent capitalism is an idyll. However, as Marx already showed, the "real history" of the educational methods used to instil labour discipline was "anything but idyllic." Rather, brutal, direct violence was the chief means used for compelling people to work.[...] The advance of capitalist production, [however, note: J.T.] develops a working class, which, by education, tradition and habit, looks upon the requirements of that mode of production as self-evident natural laws" (1976 [1867]: 899). The religious education of which Weber and Borkenau speak is only a part of the general capitalist education of which Marx speaks. (Grossman 1934)

The law of over-population that, according to Grossman, was an effective instrument of the aforementioned discipline should, to be sure, be understood in socio-economic rather than purely demographic terms- as "the reserve army of labour", or more precisely- labour force, whose size and the very presence result from the workings of capitalist economic system rather than some Malthusian population laws.

"The combined working of all these forces-and not just the religious education one-sidedly stressed by Weber and Borkenau-set the seal on the capitalist's domination of the worker" (Grossman 1934).

Grossman (1934) goes on to argue that:

> However, these "soft" means were insufficient in the period of capitalism's emergence, and the rising bourgeoisie still availed itself of "direct extra-economic force" to impose labour discipline (1976 [1867]: 899).
>
> It is not the case-as Borkenau believes-that, with the disappearance of the traditional order of social estates, "a space emptied of law" arose (Borkenau, 152), which had to be filled by the new religious morality.[...] It was not through 'inner-worldly asceticism', not through Calvinist morality but through "Bloody legislation against the expropriated at the end of the fifteenth and during the whole of the sixteenth century throughout Western Europe" that the outlawed proletarians who had been driven from their land and soil and turned into beggars and vagabonds were "educated" in labour discipline. "Legislation treated them as 'voluntary'

> criminals, and assumed that it was entirely within their powers to go on working under the old conditions which in fact no longer existed" (1976 [1867]: 896). Instead of outlining these real historical connections, Borkenau reproduces the children's storybook idyll invented by Max Weber.
>
> Seen in the light of historical facts, this petit-bourgeois idyll evaporates without a trace. Here as elsewhere, [...] he renounces "descriptive historical accounts" (xii). Precisely because he has devoted his chief attention to the French case, it is relevant in this context to present concrete historical material regarding France in order to show how far in reality religious education in mass morality was created by "inner-worldly asceticism."
>
> The bloody legislation in England has been known since Marx's *Capital*. However, in France, too, the mass of the agricultural population were dispossessed and condemned to "idleness" with the decomposition of the old feudal social order and the breakthrough of the money economy. [...]
>
> The edict of 1601 confirms the existence "of an incredible number of poor vagabonds" (Hauser 1927, 172). Fifteen … years later, Montchrestien (1615) speaks of the "million poor people," composed of "vagabonds, beggars, idlers, pickpockets, girls, women, children and unemployed workers who hang around all day and acquire the habits of all the vices of idleness"[...] As early as 1604, de Laffennas offered some suggestions for the "education" of the unemployed and youth to labour in public workhouses. "The means that he suggests to counter unemployment are not public assistance but the suppression of vagabondage. He [...] Laffennas's proposals are for the erection of two public workhouses in every city, one each for men and women. "This was forced labour, those dwelling in these charitable buildings were constrained to 'labour' by shackles and confinement" (Hauser 1927, 178).

This moving depiction of working conditions under this early capitalism highlights that the then workers differed from their counterparts under regular, fully-fledged capitalist conditions in that the former do not own their labour power, cannot freely dispose of it.

> Together with the unemployed, criminals and public prostitutes, "abandoned infants" should also be educated in these buildings. Following the already existing practice of the Grande Aumône of Lyons and the "red children" of Paris, Laffennas wants the workhouse to make its pupils available to masters as that precious and rare commodity, apprentices (Hauser 1927, 178). "He was already uttering that terrible phrase: take the children" (Hauser 1927, 12). [...] M[ontchrestien] sees clearly that the money economy has completely undermined the feudal society with its old class structure and traditional morality, and that "private profit" has become the driving force of the new society.[...] With regret, he asserts that "in matters of profit there are not many people who remain loyal" (1615,

> 90). Worried by the alarming increase in anarchy, he turns to the King with the request that he prevent the impending misfortune of the "corruption of our ancient discipline." [...] With pathetic brutality, he describes the "do-nothings" and suggests measures that would compel the poor to labour, without burdening the state: "slothful stomachs, useless burdens on the earth, people born into the world solely to consume without producing! ... It is rightly against you that the authority of the magistrate must be deployed! It is against you that he must aim his just severity; it is for you that there are whips and canes.[...] In relation to this sort of people, one may justly employ violence[...] in a certain building which they call the workhouse (*Werkhuis*) where labour makes some new miracle every day". [...] One should already begin this education through forced labour in childhood, which means that the children of the poor must be locked up in compulsory workhouses, too. [...]

The edict of 1662 demanded [that] in every city and town buildings bearing the revealing name "general manufacturing hospital" (*hôpital général de manufacture*) should be found. In fact, they had nothing at all to do with hospitals in the modern sense. "These sorts of establishments," says Cilleuls, "had as their immediate aim the curbing of vagrancy, correcting by enforced labour the habits of idleness." The operation of these methods was not to be confined to those compulsorily detained occupants of the institutions.

The rest of the "layabouts" were to be moved by the deterrent effect of these compulsory workhouses to take up labour voluntarily (Cilleuls 1898, 25).

> [...] Prison, compulsory labour in chains, the over-exploitation of child labour, the extremely brutal misuse and waste of human lives-these were the means which marked the road to "the strictest rationalization of labour" (Borkenau, 157) in the period of emergent manufacturing.
>
> There were similar "manufactories" in the cities of England, Holland and Belgium. The Copenhagen prison bore the revealing name of "Spinhuis."
>
> [...] Once it is demonstrated that Calvinism did not have the function in the emergence of capitalism that M. Weber and Borkenau attribute to it, [...] the question nevertheless still remains of whether it played an especially important role, not in the advance of capitalism but rather in making its operation possible by means of "the ascetic attitude of the masses towards the labour process." Even for this formulation of the thesis, however, Borkenau in his book neither offers historical documentation nor otherwise shows of what the "ascetic attitude of the masses to the labour process" consists. The doctrine of "ceaseless effort as a result of the lack of certainty of success in the capitalist competitive struggle" (176), tailored for the petite bourgeoisie, is not applicable to the working class. It was not

> even the specific doctrines of Calvinism which made it suitable for "keeping the masses obedient" (214) but rather the generally irrational presuppositions [...] Calvinism, just like every other religion, is an instrument for distracting the masses from the struggle for a rational structuring of their fate in life-an instrument of mass domestication. In the light of this conclusion, the Weberian thesis, which Borkenau accepts, of the special role of the Protestant Ethic in the origins and development of capitalism appears as the legend that it really is. Specific religious currents in Catholicism, not only Jesuitism in the form of Molinism, which was aimed directly at securing the obedience of the masses, but also Jansenism, were in principle better suited than Protestantism to become an instrument of mass domestication. (Grossman 1934)

Thus, despite some inconsistencies of the above account as regards the volatile use of such terms as "classes," "strata," "groups" and "masses," it is clear that an approach to the emergence of capitalism in terms of preceding it with original accumulation makes it possible to present a far wider panorama of social classes and class struggles than the narrow Weberian conception, which concentrated on an ideational rather than economic structure and viewing their relationship, as we have seen, as not being without mistakes. It is fair to say that the former approach, being more faithful to historical realities and much broader in scope than its alternative, considers not so much the economic efficacy of religion and work ethics as the economic function of the political structure, i.e. the state in relation to the economy at this early stage of capitalist development. Both those aspects are apparent in Marx's classic account of the process in question. In *Capital* (Vol. I, Chapter 26), Marx writes in his witty style, implicitly or indirectly pinpointing some weak points in Weberian theory:

> … a primitive accumulation (previous accumulation of Adam Smith) preceding capitalistic accumulation; an accumulation not the result of the capitalistic mode of production, but its starting point … plays in Political Economy about the same part as original sin in theology. Adam bit the apple, and thereupon sin fell on the human race. Its origin is supposed to be explained when it is told as an anecdote of the past. In times long gone by there were two sorts of people; one, the diligent, intelligent, and, above all, frugal elite; the other, lazy rascals, spending their substance, and more, in riotous living. The legend of theological original sin tells us certainly how man came to be condemned to eat his bread in the sweat of his brow; but the history of economic original sin reveals to us that there are people to whom this is by no means essential. Never mind! Thus it came to pass that the former sort accumulated wealth, and the latter sort had at last nothing to sell except their own skins. And from this original sin dates the poverty of the great majority that, despite all its labour, has up to now nothing to

sell but itself, and the wealth of the few that increases constantly although they have long ceased to work. Such insipid childishness is every day preached to us in the defence of property. M. Thiers, e.g. had the assurance to repeat it with all the solemnity of a statesman to the French people, once so *spirituel*. But as soon as the question of property crops up, it becomes a sacred duty to proclaim the intellectual food of the infant as the one thing fit for all ages and for all stages of development. In actual history it is notorious that conquest, enslavement, robbery, murder, briefly force, play the great part. In the tender annals of Political Economy, the idyllic reigns from time immemorial. Right and "labour" were from all time the sole means of enrichment, the present year of course always excepted. As a matter of fact, the methods of primitive accumulation are anything but idyllic.

It is useful to clarify the theoretical content of the concept under consideration:

In themselves money and commodities are no more capital than are the means of production and of subsistence. They want transforming into capital. But this transformation itself can only take place under certain circumstances that centre in this, viz., that two very different kinds of commodity-possessors must come face to face and into contact; on the one hand, the owners of money, means of production, means of subsistence, who are eager to increase the sum of values they possess, by buying other people's labour power; on the other hand, free labourers, the sellers of their own labour power[...] Free labourers, in the double sense that neither they themselves form part and parcel of the means of production, as in the case of slaves, bondsmen, etc., nor do the means of production belong to them, as in the case of peasant-proprietors; they are, therefore, free from, unencumbered by, any means of production of their own. With this polarization of the market for commodities, the fundamental conditions of capitalist production are given. The capitalist system presupposes the complete separation of the labourers from all property in the means by which they can realise their labour. As soon as capitalist production is once on its own legs, it not only maintains this separation, but reproduces it on a continually extending scale. The process, therefore, that clears the way for the capitalist system, can be none other than the process which takes away from the labourer the possession of his means of production; a process that transforms, on the one hand, the social means of subsistence and of production into capital, on the other, the immediate producers into wage labourers. The so-called primitive accumulation, therefore, is nothing else than the historical process of divorcing the producer from the means of production. It appears as primitive, because it forms the prehistoric stage of capital and of the mode of production corresponding with it.

> The economic structure of capitalist society has grown out of the economic structure of feudal society. The dissolution of the latter set free the elements of the former.
>
> The immediate producer, the labourer, could only dispose of his own person after he had ceased to be attached to the soil and ceased to be the slave, serf, or bondsman of another. To become a free seller of labour power, who carries his commodity wherever he finds a market, he must further have escaped from the regime of the guilds, their rules for apprentices and journeymen, and the impediments of their labour regulations. Hence, the historical movement which changes the producers into wage-workers, appears, on the one hand, as their emancipation from serfdom and from the fetters of the guilds, and this side alone exists for our bourgeois historians. But, on the other hand, these new freedmen became sellers of themselves only after they had been robbed of all their own means of production, and of all the guarantees of existence afforded by the old feudal arrangements. And the history of this, their expropriation, is written in the annals of mankind in letters of blood and fire.

Marx sketches out the background to this class war:

> The industrial capitalists, these new potentates, had on their part not only to displace the guild masters of handicrafts, but also the feudal lords, the possessors of the sources of wealth. In this respect, their conquest of social power appears as the fruit of a victorious struggle both against feudal lordship and its revolting prerogatives, and against the guilds and the fetters they laid on the free development of production and the free exploitation of man by man. (Marx 1977)

A recent supplement to Marx's theses has been contributed by Brenner (1996), who explains the transition from feudalism to capitalism in terms of:

> the rise of a "capitalist aristocracy" which was presiding over an agricultural revolution. While the peasants possessed the means of production—land—the feudal class could appropriate part of their production only by juridical and political power, backed by force. The weakening of that power, as a result of peasant resistance, caused a crisis from which the feudal class recovered by shifting from claims to power over people to claims to power over land. Smaller holdings were consolidated into larger farms, which were cultivated not for subsistence but for the market, by means of wage labour. Landlords entered into contractual relations with free, market-dependent commercial tenants (who increasingly hired wage workers) … [...]

> Capitalism developed in England from the end of the medieval period by means of the self-transformation of the old structure, specifically the self-transformation of the landed classes. (Manning 1993)

In contrast to Brenner's focus upon the aristocrats transforming themselves from feudal lords to capitalist landowners, Dobb's (1964) focus was on small producers rising to become capitalists. Dobb followed closely Marx's chapter on "Primary Accumulation" in Volume One of Capital, where the first stage of the development of capitalism was the emergence of richer peasants who expanded their holdings and employed wage labour, so that "… at the close of the 16th century, England had a class of capitalist farmers …." Also "… many small guild masters, and yet more independent petty artisans or even wage workers, developed into small capitalists; and later (extending by degrees the scale of the exploitation of wage labour, and thus extending accumulation) some of them developed into full-blown capitalists."

Dobb [...] pointed to "the rise of relatively well-to-do peasant-farmers in the village," who, by taking advantage of local trade and local markets, accumulated small amounts of capital, improved their lands and enlarged their holdings, and hired the services of their poorer neighbours. The 16th century "… saw a considerable growth of independent peasant farming by tenants [...] Dobb saw the point of transition as being when the "growth in the resources of the small man" became "sufficient to cause him to place greater reliance on the results of hired labour than on the work of himself and his family, and in his calculations to relate the gains of his enterprise to his capital rather than to his own exertions …" Thus a capitalist class was born "from the ranks of production itself."

This also occurred, according to Dobb, in industry, as the next and most vital stage of the transition to capitalism. " … This final stage generally seems, as Marx pointed out, to have been associated with the rise from the ranks of the producers themselves of a capitalist element, half-manufacturer, half-merchant, which began to subordinate and to organise those very ranks from which it had so recently risen." The opening of the 17th century witnessed the beginnings of an important shift in the centre of gravity …" "the rise among the craftsmen of a richer, capitalist element who wished to invest their capital in the employment of other craftsmen and themselves to assume the role of merchant-employers

[...] there had to be the developments such as Dobb described if there were to be the developments such as Brenner describes, for there had to have come into existence, before the aristocracy could be transformed, richer peasants who could afford to lease the larger farms, and who had the capital to invest in wage labour and improving production. "The breakthrough from below of the yeomanry on the basis of petty capitalist accumulation," as Colin Mooers says, "was a crucial intervening stage in the later development of large-scale capitalist farming." Landlords were responding to changes taking place within the peasantry. Patricia Croot and David Parker comment that Brenner's 'concept of capitalist relations is narrow and cannot do justice to the perhaps decisive role played by the small capitalist farmers at least from the early 16th to the mid-17th century. [...] Dobb thought that before the revolution the ruling class was still by and large feudal, maintaining that "the majority of small tenants, although they paid a money rent (which was, however, more often a customary payment than an economic rent), were still largely tied in various ways and subordinated to manorial authority" and that labourers still often had some land and common rights and were not solely dependent on wages: "Social relations in the countryside between producers and their lords and masters retained much of their medieval character, and much of the integument at least of the feudal order remained." In that earlier debate on the transition Hilton and Hill agreed with Dobb, Hilton saying that "... however important were the changes which gave free reign to the agricultural and industrial commodity producers, there was no transformation of the basic relationships constituting the feudal mode of production," and Hill saying that "... the partial emancipation of the petty mode of production does not in itself change the economic base of society (and still less the political superstructure), although it does prepare the conditions for the development of capitalism." Dobb added, however, that "... in many places the feudal integument was wearing very threadbare," and though the form of exploitation of the petty mode had not shed its feudal form, it was "a degenerate and rapidly disintegrating form." Those are bare assertions, and whether the focus is upon the aristocrats or the yeomen, there is a problem about how far capitalism had advanced by 1640, and whether the mode of production had changed. It is not just a question of how many peasants and artisans had become petty capitalists or how many landlords had become big capitalists, but also how far the poorer peasants and artisans had been reduced to a proletariat. "... Capitalism presupposes the existence of a proletariat," wrote Dobb, who stressed what Marx said on "Primary Accumulation":

> ... primary accumulation ... is nothing other than the historical process whereby the producer is divorced from the means of production. It assumes a 'primary' aspect because it belongs to the primary phase that is traversed immediately before the history of capitalism begins, immediately before the establishment of the method of production proper to capitalism.

[...] In his account of the transition Brenner leaves out industrial developments, but if agrarian developments were transforming economic and social structures in some areas, so were industrial developments in others. This is shown in two recent books, one by David Levine and Keith Wrightson on the impact of coal mining on an agricultural community, and the other by David Rollison on the impact of clothmaking on a rural district before the revolution. It is a one sided view to focus on agrarian changes in the 16th and early 17th centuries to the exclusion of the contemporaneous restructuring of rural societies in a number of regions—economically, socially and intellectually—by the development of clothmaking, metalworking and mining. Brenner's concentration on the landowners, and to a lesser extent his concentration on merchants, cuts him off from adequately explaining both the transition to capitalism and the English Revolution.

Although he maintains that the ruling class was already a capitalist class before the revolution, Brenner does not fall back on explaining the conflict in conventional terms as one within the ruling class over the constitution or religion or both[...]

His theory of the transition cannot explain the revolution whereas Dobb's can.

Dobb's thesis that capitalism in its revolutionary form developed from the ranks of the small producers led him to pose that the smaller gentry and rising yeomen 'were a most important driving force in the bourgeois revolution of the 17th century... His view of the transition helps to explain the crucial role of the 'middling sort' in the parliamentary party and in driving forward the revolution. Brenner's thesis ignores industrial development before 1640 and so cannot explain why industrial districts-not all of them-provided a main base for the parliamentarian and revolutionary parties. Dobb stressed the development of industrial capitalism before 1640 and the parliamentarianism of industrial districts in the civil war. This is supported by modern research and, for example, Rollison says that without the manufacturing districts there would have been no effective parliamentarian party in Gloucestershire.

Manufacturing, as Marx claimed, was the dynamic element in the field-of-force. It alone made the kind of civil war which took place in the 1640s possible. [...]

Brenner builds on Marx's stress on the role of colonisation in primary accumulation, but Marx also linked it to the proletarianisation of the masses: "... the veiled slavery of the European wage earners became the pedestal of unqualified slavery in the New World. (Manning 1993)

Thus, it is fair to conclude that post-Marxian scholarship, while here and there enriching the general picture and filling in some gaps in Marx's analytical framework, has left it essentially unscathed.

So we can safely return to further claims put forward within the said framework:

> The starting point of the development that gave rise to the wage labourer as well as to the capitalist, was the servitude of the labourer. The advance consisted in a change of form of this servitude, in the transformation of feudal exploitation into capitalist exploitation. To understand its march, we need not go back very far. Although we come across the first beginnings of capitalist production as early as the 14th or 15th century, sporadically, in certain towns of the Mediterranean, the capitalistic era dates from the 16th century. Wherever it appears, the abolition of serfdom has been long effected, and the highest development of the middle ages, the existence of sovereign towns, has been long on the wane.
>
> In the history of primitive accumulation, all revolutions are epoch-making that act as levers for the capital class in course of formation; but, above all, those moments when great masses of men are suddenly and forcibly torn from their means of subsistence, and hurled as free and "unattached" proletarians on the labour-market. The expropriation of the agricultural producer, of the peasant, from the soil, is the basis of the whole process. The history of this expropriation, in different countries, assumes different aspects, and runs through its various phases in different orders of succession, and at different periods. In England alone, which we take as our example, has it the classic form. (Marx 1976)

The above description of the class structure of the feudal economic formation of society shows, *inter alia*, its material classes in the form of agrarian holders of the means of production, including land, but deprived of ownership of their labour power (ascription to land in the classic case). Marx substantially enriches this picture as he continues his narrative in Chapter 27 supplementing, at the very outset, his outline of the feudal economic formation of society with an important peasant mode of production based on common property:

> In England, serfdom had practically disappeared in the last part of the 14th century. The immense majority of the population consisted then, and to a still larger extent, in the 15th century, of free peasant proprietors, whatever was the feudal title under which their right of property was hidden.[15] In the

[34] Marx states that "The petty proprietors who cultivated their own fields with their own hands, and enjoyed a modest competence … then formed a much more

larger seignorial domains, the old bailiff, himself a serf, was displaced by the free farmer. The wage labourers of agriculture consisted partly of peasants, who utilised their leisure time by working on the large estates, partly of an independent special class of wage labourers, relatively and absolutely few in numbers. The latter also were practically at the same time peasant farmers, since, besides their wages, they had allotted to them arable land to the extent of 4 or more acres, together with their cottages. Besides they, with the rest of the peasants, enjoyed the usufruct of the common land, which gave pasture to their cattle, furnished them with timber, fire-wood, turf, etc. In all countries of Europe, feudal production is characterised by division of the soil amongst the greatest possible number of subfeudatories. The might of the feudal lord, like that of the sovereign, depended not on the length of his rent roll, but on the number of his subjects, and the latter depended on the number of peasant proprietors. Although, therefore, the English land, after the Norman Conquest, was distributed in gigantic baronies, one of which often included some 900 of the old Anglo-Saxon lordships, it was bestrewn with small peasant properties, only here and there interspersed with great seignorial domains.[...] The prelude of the revolution that laid the foundation of the capitalist mode of production, was played in the last third of the 15th, and the first decade of the 16th century. A mass of free proletarians was hurled on the labour market by the breaking-up of the bands of feudal retainers, who, as Sir James Steuart well says, "everywhere uselessly filled house and castle." Although the royal power, itself a product of bourgeois development, in its strife after absolute sovereignty forcibly hastened on the dissolution of these bands of retainers, it was by no means the sole cause of it. [...] the great feudal lords created an incomparably larger proletariat by the forcible driving of the peasantry from the land, to which the latter had the same feudal right as the lord himself, and by the usurpation of the common lands. The rapid rise of the Flemish wool manufactures, and the corresponding rise in the price of wool in England, gave the direct impulse to these evictions. The old nobility had been devoured by the great feudal wars. The new nobility was the child of its time, for which money was the power of all powers. Transformation of arable land into sheep-walks was, therefore, its cry.[...] The process of forcible expropriation of the people received in the 16th century a new and frightful impulse from the

---

important part of the nation than at present. If we may trust the best statistical writers of that age, not less than 160,000 proprietors who, with their families, must have made up more than a seventh of the whole population, derived their subsistence from little freehold estates. [...] the number of persons who tilled their own land was greater than the number of those who farmed the land of others." Even in the last third of the 17th century, 4/5 of the English people were agricultural.[...] We must never forget that even the serf was not only the owner, if but a tribute-paying owner, of the piece of land attached to his house, but also a co-possessor of the common land.

Reformation, and from the consequent colossal spoliation of the church property. The Catholic church was, at the time of the Reformation, feudal proprietor of a great part of the English land.

Thus, Marx appreciates the role of the Reformation in the rise of capitalism, but views it in different class and ownership terms than Weber:

The suppression of the monasteries, etc., hurled their inmates into the proletariat. The estates of the church were to a large extent given away to rapacious royal favourites, or sold at a nominal price to speculating farmers and citizens, who drove out, en masse, the hereditary sub-tenants and threw their holdings into one. The legally guaranteed property of the poorer folk in a part of the church's tithes was tacitly confiscated. [...] The property of the church formed the religious bulwark of the traditional conditions of landed property. With its fall these were no longer tenable.

Even in the last decade of the 17th century, the yeomanry, the class of independent peasants, were more numerous than the class of farmers. [...] About 1750, the yeomanry had disappeared, and so had, in the last decade of the 18th century, the last trace of the common land of the agricultural labourer. We leave on one side here the purely economic causes of the agricultural revolution. We deal only with the forcible means employed.

After the restoration of the Stuarts, the landed proprietors carried, by legal means, an act of usurpation, effected everywhere on the Continent without any legal formality. They abolished the feudal tenure of land, i.e., they got rid of all its obligations to the State, "indemnified" the State by taxes on the peasantry and the rest of the mass of the people, vindicated for themselves the rights of modern private property in estates to which they had only a feudal title, and, finally, passed those laws of settlement, which, mutatis mutandis, had the same effect on the English agricultural labourer, as the edict of the Tartar Boris Godunof on the Russian peasantry.

The "glorious Revolution" brought into power, along with William of Orange, the landlord and capitalist appropriators of surplus-value. They inaugurated the new era by practising on a colossal scale thefts of state lands, thefts that had been hitherto managed more modestly. These estates were given away, sold at a ridiculous figure, or even annexed to private estates by direct seizure. All this happened without the slightest observation of legal etiquette. The Crown lands thus fraudulently appropriated, together with the robbery of the Church estates, as far as these had not been lost again during the republican revolution, form the basis of the today princely domains of the English oligarchy.

This class war of massive proportions aimed at the establishment of new private property relations:

The bourgeois capitalists favoured the operation with the view, among others, to promoting free trade in land, to extending the domain of modern

> agriculture on the large farm-system, and to increasing their supply of the free agricultural proletarians ready to hand. Besides, the new landed aristocracy was the natural ally of the new bankocracy, of the newly-hatched haute finance, and of the large manufacturers,[16] then depending on protective duties. [...] the law itself becomes now the instrument of the theft of the people's land, although the large farmers make use of their little independent methods as well. The parliamentary form of the robbery is that of Acts for enclosures of Commons, in other words, decrees by which the landlords grant themselves the people's land as private property, decrees of expropriation of the people. Sir F. M. Eden refutes his own crafty special pleading, in which he tries to represent communal property as the private property[17] of the great landlords who have taken the place of the feudal lords, when he, himself, demands a "general Act of Parliament for the enclosure of Commons" (admitting thereby that a parliamentary coup d'état is necessary for its transformation into private property), and moreover calls on the legislature for the indemnification for the expropriated poor.
>
> Whilst the place of the independent yeoman was taken by tenants at will, small farmers on yearly leases, a servile rabble dependent on the pleasure of the landlords, the systematic robbery of the Communal lands helped especially, next to the theft of the State domains, to swell those large farms, that were called in the 18th century capital farms or merchant farms, and to "set free" the agricultural population as proletarians for manufacturing industry
>
> [...] From little occupiers of land, they are reduced to the state of day-labourers. [...]
>
> The last process of wholesale expropriation of the agricultural population from the soil is, finally, the so-called clearing of estates, i.e. the sweeping men off them. [...] They conquered the field for capitalistic agriculture, made the soil part and parcel of capital, and created for the town industries the necessary supply of a "free" and outlawed proletariat. (Marx 1976)

The following paragraph may be viewed as a direct polemic with Weber's approach, and the "spirit" of Protestantism:

> In the south of England certain landed proprietors […] have proposed that we shall erect a prison in the parish, and then give notice to the

[16] Thus, the aforementioned Brenner's thesis, hailed by many as absolutely innovative, upon closer scrutiny loses this supposed merit.

[17] As an author of a four-volume study on Poland's privatisation, and another one devoted to the privatisation process in general, the similarity of the latter as a method of primitive capitalist accumulation to those characteristics pinned down by Marx is striking.

> neighbourhood, that if any persons are disposed to farm the poor of this parish, they do give in sealed proposals, on a certain day, of the lowest price at which they will take them off our hands; and that they will be authorised to refuse to any one unless he be shut up in the aforesaid prison." the abolition of the property of the agricultural labourer in the soil made him a proletarian, and eventually a pauper.[...]
>
> Professor Rogers, although formerly Professor of Political Economy in the University of Oxford, the hotbed of Protestant orthodoxy, in his preface to the "History of Agriculture" lays stress on the fact of *the pauperisation of the mass of the people by the Reformation* [author's emphasis] [...]
>
> Depopulation and transformation into sheep-walks were the most convenient means for getting an income without expenditure ... A deerforest in place of a sheep-walk was a common change in the Highlands. The landowners turned out the sheep as they once turned out the men from their estates, and welcomed the new tenants. (Marx 1976)

Effects of the political legislature on the human side of the capitalistic equation are shown in Chapter 28 of *Capital*, whose detailed account allows us to grasp those class links in the transformation chain that are still missing:

> The proletariat created by the breaking up of the bands of feudal retainers and by the forcible expropriation of the people from the soil[...] could not possibly be absorbed by the nascent[18] manufactures as fast as it was thrown upon the world. On the other hand, these men, suddenly dragged from their wonted mode of life, could not as suddenly adapt themselves to the discipline of their new condition. They were turned en masse into beggars, robbers, vagabonds, partly from inclination, in most cases from stress of circumstances. Hence at the end of the 15th and during the whole of the 16th century, throughout Western Europe a bloody legislation against vagabondage. The fathers of the present working class

---

[18] Marx notes that "When the steam-engine transplanted the factories from the country waterfalls to the middle of towns, the "abstemious" surplus-value maker found the child-material ready to his hand, without being forced to seek slaves from the workhouses. An intimate friend of Ricardo, said in the House of Commons: "It is notorious, that [...] a gang, if he might use the word, of these children had been put up to sale, and were advertised publicly as part of the property. [...] a number of these boys, apprenticed by a parish in London to one manufacturer, had been transferred to another, and had been found [...] in a state of absolute famine. Another case more horrible had come to his knowledge [...] that [...] an agreement had been made between a London parish and a Lancashire manufacturer, by which it was stipulated, that with every 20 sound children one idiot should be taken".

> were chastised for their enforced transformation into vagabonds and paupers. Legislation treated them as "voluntary" criminals [...]
>
> In England this legislation began under Henry VII.[...] A statute of 1547 ordains that if anyone refuses to work, he shall be condemned as a slave to the person who has denounced him as an idler. The master shall feed his slave on bread and water, weak broth and such refuse meat as he thinks fit. He has the right to force him to do any work, no matter how disgusting, with whip and chains. If the slave is absent a fortnight, he is condemned to slavery for life and is to be branded on forehead or back with the letter S; if he runs away thrice, he is to be executed as a felon. The master can sell him, bequeath him, let him out on hire as a slave, just as any other personal chattel or cattle. If the slaves attempt anything against the masters, they are also to be executed. Justices of the peace, on information, are to hunt the rascals down. If it happens that a vagabond has been idling about for three days, he is to be taken to his birthplace, branded with a red-hot iron with the letter V on the breast and be set to work, in chains, in the streets or at some other labour. If the vagabond gives a false birthplace, he is then to become the slave for life of this place, of its inhabitants, or its corporation, and to be branded with an S. All persons have the right to take away the children of the vagabonds and to keep them as apprentices, the young men until the 24th year, the girls until the 20th. If they run away, they are to become up to this age the slaves of their masters, who can put them in irons, whip them, etc., if they like. Every master may put an iron ring round the neck, arms or legs of his slave, by which to know him more easily and to be more certain of him. The last part of this statute provides, that certain poor people may be employed by a place or by persons, who are willing to give them food and drink and to find them work. This kind of parish slaves was kept up in England until far into the 19th century under the name of "roundsmen." [...]
>
> These statutes were legally binding until the beginning of the 18th century. [...] Thus were the agricultural people, first forcibly expropriated from the soil, driven from their homes, turned into vagabonds, and then whipped, branded, tortured by laws grotesquely terrible, into the discipline necessary for the wage system.

This dramatic class narrative of capitalism's origins extend its class lens to include not only lumpenclasses (beggars etc.) but also, as it turns out, slaves, i.e. persons deprived of ownership in their labour power.

> It is not enough that the conditions of labour are concentrated in a mass, in the shape of capital, at the one pole of society, while at the other are grouped masses of men, who have nothing to sell but their labour power. Neither is it enough that they are compelled to sell it voluntarily. The advance of capitalist production develops a working class, which by education, tradition, habit, looks upon the conditions of that mode of

> production as self-evident laws of Nature.[...] The dull compulsion of economic relations completes the subjection of the labourer to the capitalist. Direct force, outside economic conditions, is of course still used, but only exceptionally. In the ordinary run of things, the labourer can be left to the "natural laws of production," i.e., to his dependence on capital, a dependence springing from, and guaranteed in perpetuity by, the conditions of production themselves. It is otherwise during the historic genesis of capitalist production. The bourgeoisie, at its rise, wants and uses the power of the state to "regulate" wages, i.e., to force them within the limits suitable for surplus-value making, to lengthen the working-day and to keep the labourer himself in the normal degree of dependence. This is an essential element of the so-called primitive accumulation.

And further Marx takes full advantage of his dialectical historicism, far distant from formalism and universalism noticeable in a good deal, if not the majority of theories being advanced in social science:

> The class of wage labourers, which arose in the latter half of the 14th century, formed then and in the following century only a very small part of the population, well protected in its position by the independent peasant proprietary in the country and the guild-organisation in the town. In country and town master and workmen stood close together socially. The subordination of labour to capital was only formal—i.e., the mode of production itself had as yet no specific capitalistic character. Variable capital preponderated greatly over constant. The demand for wage labour grew, therefore, rapidly with every accumulation of capital, whilst the supply of wage labour followed but slowly. [...] Legislation on wage labour (from the first, aimed at the exploitation of the labourer, and always equally hostile to him. [...] aim at compulsory extension of the working-day.

Two points should be made at this juncture. Our class evolution is now complete—between post-feudal peasant classes and the capitalist working class stands the autocephalous[19] (petty bourgeois) lumpen class, since to it that the above-mentioned robbers, pickpockets, vagabonds etc. belong. Naturally, this general statement could be modified upon closer examination of particular cases, e.g. when gangs of criminals are concerned, individuals at the top may well occupy such a class position that is analogous to that of bourgeoisie rather than petty bourgeoisie, which implies that other, rank-and-file members of a gang are lumpenproletarians. Second, the guild mode of production ought to be described a little more precisely than it

[19] The term as well as the reasons for its use are clarified in the respective section of the book.

was by Marx. An important feature of that mode of production (or trade or services, for that matter) is that it has a built-in route of class advancement, i.e. those at the bottom of the hierarchy have a reasonable chance of reaching the status of a master. What is more, this blurring of class divisions was grounded in common ownership; an apprentice shared with his master the common fund of consumption or, in more plain terms, a table which commensalism means precisely common property. In contradistinction to Marx, Weber probably would not have overlooked this proprietary character of the said mode of production given that he repeatedly used the term "commensalism."

To return to the misfortunes of early-capitalist lumpen classes:

> A tariff of wages was fixed by law [...] It was forbidden, under pain of imprisonment, to pay higher wages than those fixed by the statute, but the taking of higher wages was more severely punished than the giving them. (So also in Sections 18 and 19 of the Statute of Apprentices of Elizabeth, ten days' imprisonment is decreed for him that pays the higher wages, but twenty-one days for him that receives them.) A statute of 1360 increased the penalties and authorised the masters to extort labour at the legal rate of wages by corporal punishment. All combinations, contracts, oaths, etc., by which masons and carpenters reciprocally bound themselves, were declared null and void. Coalition of the labourers is treated as a heinous crime from the 14th century to 1825, the year of the repeal of the laws against Trades' Unions. The spirit of the Statute of Labourers of 1349 and of its offshoots comes out clearly in the fact, that indeed a maximum of wages is dictated by the State, but on no account a minimum.
>
> In the manufacturing period par excellence, the capitalist mode of production had become sufficiently strong to render legal regulation of wages as impracticable as it was unnecessary; but the ruling classes were unwilling in case of necessity to be without the weapons of the old arsenal. [...] Only] in 1813, the laws for the regulation of wages were repealed. They were an absurd anomaly, since the capitalist regulated his factory by his private legislation.

With the whole uniqueness of its proud history in which the progressive Revolution played a prominent part, the developments in the land of Rousseau and Voltaire were strikingly similar:

> During the very first storms of the revolution, the French bourgeoisie dared to take away from the workers the right of association but just acquired. By a decree of June 14, 1791, they declared all coalition of the workers as "an attempt against liberty and the declaration of the rights of man," punishable by a fine of 500 livres, together with deprivation of the rights of an active citizen for one year. This law which, by means of State compulsion, confined the struggle between capital and labour within limits comfortable

for capital, has outlived revolutions and changes of dynasties. Even the Reign of Terror left it untouched. It was but quite recently struck out of the Penal Code. Nothing is more characteristic than the pretext for this bourgeois coup d'état. "Granting," says Chapelier, the reporter of the Select Committee on this law, "that wages ought to be a little higher than they are, … that they ought to be high enough for him that receives them, to be free from that state of absolute dependence due to the want of the necessaries of life, and which is almost that of slavery," yet the workers must not be allowed to come to any understanding about their own interests, nor to act in common and thereby lessen their "absolute dependence, which is almost that of slavery;" because, forsooth, in doing this they injure "the freedom of their cidevant masters, the present entrepreneurs," and because a coalition against the despotism of the quondam masters of the corporations is—guess what!—is a restoration of the corporations abolished by the French constitution. (Marx 1976)

The preceding "picturesque" account leads its author to a key question:

Now that we have considered the forcible creation of a class of outlawed proletarians, the bloody discipline that turned them into wage labourers, the disgraceful action of the State which employed the police to accelerate the accumulation of capital by increasing the degree of exploitation of labour, the question remains: whence came the capitalists originally? For the expropriation of the agricultural population creates, directly, none but the greatest landed proprietors. As far, however, as concerns the genesis of the farmer, we can, so to say, put our hand on it, because it is a slow process evolving through many centuries. The serfs, as well as the free small proprietors, held land under very different tenures, and were therefore emancipated under very different economic conditions. In England the first form of the farmer is the bailiff, himself a serf. His position is similar to that of the old Roman villicus, only in a more limited sphere of action. During the second half of the 14th century he is replaced by a farmer, whom the landlord provided with seed, cattle and implements. His condition is not very different from that of the peasant. Only he exploits more wage labour. Soon he becomes a metayer, a half-farmer. He advances one part of the agricultural stock, the landlord the other. The two divide the total product in proportions determined by contract. This form quickly disappears in England, to give the place to the farmer proper, who makes his own capital breed by employing wage labourers, and pays a part of the surplus-product [...] to the landlord as rent. So long, during the 15th century, as the independent peasant and the farm-labourer working for himself as well as for wages, enriched themselves by their own labour, the circumstances of the farmer, and his field of production, were equally mediocre. The agricultural revolution which commenced in the last third of the 15th century, and continued during almost the whole of the 16th

> (excepting, however, its last decade), enriched him just as speedily as it impoverished the mass of the agricultural people.
>
> The usurpation of the common lands allowed him to augment greatly his stock of cattle, almost without cost, whilst they yielded him a richer supply of manure[20] for the tillage of the soil. To this was added in the 16th century a very important element. At that time the contracts for farms ran for a long time, often for 99 years. The progressive fall in the value of the precious metals, and therefore of money, brought the farmers golden fruit.[21] Apart from all the other circumstances discussed above, it lowered wages. A portion of the latter was now added to the profits of the farm. The continuous rise in the price of [...] all agricultural produce, swelled the money capital of the farm without any action on his part, whilst the rent he paid (being calculated on the old value of money) diminished in reality. Thus they grew rich at the expense both of their labourers and their landlords. No wonder, therefore, that England, at the end of the 16th century, had a class of capitalist farmers, rich, considering the circumstances of the time.
>
> In France, the régisseur, steward, collector of dues for the feudal lords during the earlier part of the middle ages, soon became an homme d'affaires, who by extortion, cheating, etc., swindled himself into a capitalist. These régisseurs themselves were sometimes noblemen. [...] in all spheres of social life the lion's share falls to the middleman. In the economic domain, e.g., financiers, stock-exchange speculators, merchants, shopkeepers skim the cream.

A counterpart to the capitalist farmer within the industrial bourgeois mode of production is, of course, the industrial capitalist whose genesis Marx sheds light on in Chapter 31 of *Capital*. His initial comment explains that "industrial here is meant in contradistinction to agricultural. In the 'categoric' sense the farmer is an industrial capitalist as much as the manufacturer" is unclear. It may well be that Marx here refers to standard official classification according to which manufacturing, farming, education, health care and even government are all 'industries'." But another possibility remains, one that does not, to be sure, confound the economic with non-economic domain, but exposes Marx to a much more serious criticism. It appears as though he would not be able to take advantage of his own analytical framework in which, after all, the concept of property figures prominently. From the standpoint of economically conceived property, owners of agricultural, manufacturing and extractive means of production are by no means members of the same class. To be precise, they all belong to the capitalist megaclass but at the same time to three

[20] And again, note how well those two elements fit the rent theory of ownership.
[21] This colourful phrase refers, naturally, to economic ownership.

different capitalist classes owing to considerable differences in their respective objects of ownership. The full sense of this statement will not be made clear until we consider in a later chapter the very notion of economic ownership.

Marx says that:

> Many small guild-masters, and yet more independent small artisans, or even wage labourers, transformed themselves into small capitalists, and (by gradually extending exploitation of wage labour and corresponding accumulation) into full-lown capitalists. [...] The snail's pace of this method corresponded in no wise with the commercial requirements of the new world market that the great discoveries of the end of the 15th century created. But the middle ages had handed down two distinct forms of capital, which mature in the most different economic social formations, and which before the era of the capitalist mode of production, are considered as capital quand même (all the same)—usurer's capital and merchant's capital. The capitalist may now be said to be the first owner of all the wealth of the community, though no law has conferred on him the right to this property[22] … this change has been effected by the taking of interest on capital … and it is not a little curious that all the law-givers of Europe endeavoured to prevent this by statutes, viz., statutes against usury[23] … The power of the capitalist over all the wealth of the country is a complete change in the right of property, and by what law, or series of laws, was it effected?"[24]
>
> The money capital formed by means of usury and commerce was prevented from turning into industrial capital, in the country by the feudal constitution, in the towns by the guild organisation. These fetters vanished with the dissolution of feudal society, with the expropriation and partial eviction of the country population. The new manufactures were established at sea-ports, or at inland points beyond the control of the old municipalities and their guilds. Hence in England an embittered struggle of the corporate towns against these new industrial nurseries.
>
> The discovery of gold and silver in America, the extirpation, enslavement and entombment in mines of the aboriginal population, the beginning of the conquest and looting of the East Indies, the turning of Africa into a warren for the commercial hunting of black-skins, signalized

---

[22] And here, in contradistinction to the above-mentioned lapse, the author of *Capital* speaks truly economic-property language not conflating economic property relations with legal or moral rights.

[23] Marx adds that "even as late as 1794, the small cloth-makers of Leeds sent a deputation to Parliament, with a petition for a law to forbid any merchant from becoming a manufacturer."

[24] The author should have remembered that revolutions are not made by laws.

the rosy dawn of the era of capitalist production. These idyllic proceedings are the chief momenta of primitive accumulation. [...]

In England at the end of the 17th century, they arrive at a systematical combination, embracing the colonies, the national debt, the modern mode of taxation, and the protectionist system. These methods depend in part on brute force, e.g., the colonial system. But, they all employ the power of the State, the concentrated and organised force of society, to hasten, hot-house fashion, the process of transformation of the feudal mode of production into the capitalist mode, and to shorten the transition. Force is the midwife of every old society pregnant with a new one. It is itself an economic power. [...] The treasures captured outside Europe by undisguised looting, enslavement, and murder, floated back to the mother-country and were there turned into capital. [...]

The public debt becomes one of the most powerful levers of primitive accumulation. As with the stroke of an enchanter's wand, it endows barren money with the power of breeding and thus turns it into capital[…] . But further, apart from the class of lazy annuitants[25] thus created, and from the improvised wealth of the financiers, middlemen between the government and the nation – as also apart from the tax – farmers, merchants, private manufacturers, to whom a good part of every national loan renders the service of a capital fallen from heaven – the national debt has given rise to joint-stock companies, to dealings in negotiable effects of all kinds, and to agiotage, in a word to stock-exchange gambling and the modern bankocracy. [...] With the national debt arose an international credit system, which often conceals one of the sources of primitive accumulation in this or that people.

[...] Colonial system, public debts, heavy taxes, protection, commercial wars, etc., these children of the true manufacturing period, increase gigantically during the infancy of Modem Industry. The birth of the latter is heralded by a great slaughter of the innocents. Like the royal navy, the factories were recruited by means of the press-gang. […]the necessity of child-stealing and child-slavery for the transformation of manufacturing exploitation into factory exploitation, and the establishment of the "true relation" between capital and labour-power [… and the transformation of] conditions of labour, to transform, at one pole, the social means of production and subsistence into capital, at the opposite pole, the mass of the population into wage labourers, into "free labouring poor," that artificial product of modern society.[26] If money, according to Augier,

[25] In fact, as mentioned above, it is not as simple as that. Marx fails to make the necessary distinction between savings and capital (there are several socioeconomic criteria for differentiating between those, and only capital holders may be classified as a class).

[26] Thus, it turns out that the contemporary buzzword "working poor" is no conceptual novelty; on the contrary, it is several centuries old; "The phrase, "labouring poor," is found in English legislation from the moment when the class

"comes into the world with a congenital blood-stain on one cheek," capital comes dripping from head to foot, from every pore, with blood and dirt [...] Capital eschews no profit, or very small profit, just as Nature was formerly said to abhor a vacuum. With adequate profit, capital is very bold. A certain 10 per cent. will ensure its employment anywhere; 20 per cent. certain will produce eagerness; 50 per cent., positive audacity; 100 per cent. will make it ready to trample on all human laws; 300 per cent., and there is not a crime at which it will scruple, nor a risk it will not run, even to the chance of its owner being hanged. If turbulence and strife will bring a profit, it will freely encourage both. Smuggling and the slave-trade have amply proved all that is here stated. (Marx 1976)

1.2.5.1.1. Primitive Accumulation and Globalisation

We now take a break; our analysis of Weber's sociology of the economy will be continued in the next section. In the meantime, we must deal with some important ramifications of the central issue of the preceding section. Marx states that: "Expropriation is the starting-point of the capitalist mode of production, whose goal it is to carry it through to completion, and even in the last instance to expropriate all individuals (Marx 1981, 570–1). Indeed, contrary to what is commonly assumed, one ought not to relegate primitive accumulation to the pre-capitalistic past. As a matter of fact, referring to Edward Gibbon Wakefield, Marx does not qualify his appreciation of the father of modern colonial theory by limiting its relevance to the specific socio-historical time. Quite the contrary, he holds that Wakefield offered significant insights into the England where Marx lived and worked. (Marx 1977, 940).

No matter, though, what Marx's views on the question of temporal location of the process of primitive accumulation eventually were, what is crucial in this regard is not Marx's authority, undisputable as it is, but the historico-sociological facts. And the fact of the matter is that the separation of people from their traditional means of production occurred over time as capital gradually required additional workers to join the labour force. Furthermore, the process of primitive accumulation is a matter of degree. It can be argued that in modern conditions all out

---

of wage labourers becomes noticeable. This term is used in opposition, on the one hand, to the "idle poor," beggars, etc., on the other to those labourers, who, pigeons not yet plucked, are still possessors of their own means of labour. From the Statute Book it passed into Political Economy, and was handed down by Culpeper, J. Child, etc., to Adam Smith and Eden. After this, one can judge of the good faith of the "execrable political cant-monger," Edmund Burke, when he called the expression, "labouring poor,"—"execrable political cant." (Marx 1976).

primitive accumulation would not be in the best interest of capital. Instead, capital would manipulate the extent to which workers relied on self-provisioning in order to maximize its advantage. The same refers to the preservation even by late capitalism of autocephalous classes (with their agrarian counterparts), and taken globally- also many pre-capitalist ownership relations, such as slavery, bonded labour, people trafficking, etc.

The continuity[27] of primitive accumulation sharply contrasts with its usual image as the one-time destruction of the peasant economy, the immediate effect of which was to create a society with capitalists on the one pole and workers on the other. The typical perception is in fact misleading. Indeed, True,on the eve of capitalism, the majority of people were peasants or at least had some connection with farming, but primitive accumulation was not limited to agriculture. It extended across many, if not all, sectors of the economy. (Berg 1986, 70), occurring in the city as well as in the countryside. After all, urban people provide for themselves directly in a multitude of ways other than the growing of food. Depriving people of these means of provision forces a greater dependence on the market just as surely as restricting their access to the means of food production.

Take a relatively modern example. Packing people into crowded urban quarters leaves little space for doing the laundry, and as a result, people become dependent upon commercial laundries.[27] In post-World War II United States, the ability of the typical family to produce for its own needs continued to diminish, despite the widespread availability of household appliances such as washing machines that should make many types of self-provisioning easier. In our terms, this process should be interpreted as the shrinking of the area of quasi-work being squeezed out by Labour for wage taking place within the commercial sector of the economy.

Similarly, Paul Sweezy thinks that Japan's vast entertainment sector can be considered a partial result of living in such small quarters that people are unable to socialise in their homes (1980, 13). The need to purchase such services creates by the same token substantial pressures to lease more labour. The impact of such pressures has surfaced in the recent increase in numbers of women in the labour force. Relatedly, work has demanded a rapidly escalating share of the typical family's time.

---

[27] It has to be pointed out that from the standpoint of socio-economic structuralism, this example concerns indirectly material work rather than so-called services which term has its specific meaning in the analytical framework of the above-mentioned theory.

This process can feed on itself. Since people have to earn more wages to compensate for the increased difficulty of providing for their own needs, they have less time to do other sorts of what we call quasi-work on their own, inducing families to transfer still more activities from the household to the commercial sector. Child care centres are a case in point. The whole rationale of fast-food industry is the difficulty of working at a job and performing a multitude of other chores in the same day.

There are many modern-day examples of goods and services that were once produced within the household, which became commodities and are sold by commercial firms. This new arrangement is inextricably related to the pattern of ownership of the means of creating these goods and services in the household. The lack of ownership of a workspace for doing laundry may be likened to the lack of ownership of the parcel of land on which a household once grew its own food, insofar as the latter produced only for satisfaction of its members' needs. For goods produced for sale are private rather than personal property, as in the former case, which converts quasi-work from the former example into regular work. At any rate, in either case, the denial of ownership to a particular means of production creates a change in the mix of work and quasi-work or, in less technical language, wage and non-wage labour.

This restructuring of the life of a modern household could thus be read as a contemporary variant of the process of primitive accumulation.

According to an orthodox interpretation, primitive accumulation is primarily concerned with the creation of two stocks: (1) a substantial section of the population with no other means of livelihood but their labour power to be pushed out onto a nascent labour-power market and (2) an accumulation of money (and other forms of) capital that may be used to finance nascent industries. In this view, the adjective "primitive" refers to a clear-cut temporal dimension (the past).

However, there is also possible a different interpretation of notion under consideration the, arguably-not diverging from the spirit, and even letter of Marx's teachings. The latter, after all, repeatedly stressed that capital is to be viewed primarily as a social relation. Also, to put it in modern economics' terms, not from the standpoint of "resource" but "stream" or process Marx focused on "divorcing" of people from the means of production". Taking both those observations together, primitive accumulation can be redefined to mean a continuous process of capitalist accumulation rather than one confined to the rise of capitalist mode of production. Looked at in such terms, new light can be thrown on some key contemporary processes characterising the capitalist mode of economic activity.

Capital's drive to accumulate necessitates the commodification of larger and larger spheres of life. This implies the promotion of further separation between people and means of work, including quasi-work. Both the commodification of new spheres of life and its accompanying strategies aimed at dismantling barriers erected to protect society from the market can be conceived of as new enclosures. This is the case because they are bringing about a separation between people and their conditions of life. One key aspect of globalisation strategies takes this form. In the contemporary world new enclosures have no geographical and social limits.

In many countries in the South of the world, where the population is largely dependent on farming, imposing a tax in cash may be an instrument of expropriation by forcing mostly self-sufficient peasants into allocating part of their land to produce "cash crops" instead of food they can eat, thus transforming this portion of their personal property into private property. The same result can be reached by many of large development projects such as the construction of dams (as in Malaysia, India, China), or other means to promote cash crops (massive deforestation). Another form of new land enclosure is the result of environmental damages caused by multinationals. Likewise, the intense shrimp production occurring in some Indian and other East Asian regions makes the land of the local farmers unusable for subsistence crops.

In order to show the pervasiveness of the new enclosures, a few cases of urban enclosure may be mentioned.

Urban design in fact is an important attempt to enclose human and social behaviour in forms and patterns compatible with the accumulation process. For example, the lack of public benches in public sites such as the large main hall of Waterloo station in London can be puzzling, unless we understand it as aimed at the minimisation of vagrant behaviour (which takes us back to the rationale of the Tudor's "bloody legislation" following the early enclosures). Such efforts are aimed at the marginalisation of the homeless to "invisible sites" and also to give local businesses (cafes or restaurants) a monopoly on places to sit. [...] Similarly, what public benches are available are now constructed with a series of arms in London, or with convex surfaces as in Los Angeles (Davis 1990, 235). They are designed as instruments of social engineering to keep us on the move and to prevent our modern "vagrants" (especially the homeless) from sleeping off the ground. In the same spirit many businesses fill their window sills with metal uprights to prevent people from sitting on them. Even the satisfaction of primary physiological functions have become the subject of enclosure in train stations and other public spaces of the West where access to toilets require payment.

The term "social commons" means in plain language those commons that have been erected as a result of past social movements and later formalised by institutional practices. A classic example is the body of rights, provisions and entitlements universally guaranteed by the welfare state in spheres such as health, unemployment benefits, education, and pensions. Although these social commons served at the same time as a site for administrative regulation of social behaviour (Piven & Cloward 1972), they also allowed to a certain extent the access to public wealth without a correspondent expenditure of work (that is, to access it directly). At a deeper theoretical level, one should refer to such relations as common or fiscal property which, although administered by the state and its organs, belongs to the nation as a whole.

This characteristic has been under increasing attack by neoliberal policies of the last twenty years. In the North, enclosure of these social commons have gone through the transformation from welfare to workfare (as in the U.S. and in Britain), through the imposition of strict "convergence criteria" that limited social spending in countries wanting to join the European Union (thus hampering their efforts to liken themselves to more mature European nations subscribing, as they do, to stakeholder capitalism), and attempts to solve crises, such as the recent financial crisis and the Euro-zone monetary and debt crisis at the expense of poorer classes of society who bear the brunt of draconian austerity policies.

"Natural commons" is another instance of common property, as it refers to those commons that are given by nature and used directly by people. For example, the wilderness, to the extent that it is a means of recreation and of the reproduction of human energies (i.e. reproduction of labour- and quasi-work power that together make up human personality) conditions the very human biological existence. Deforestation and increasing carbon dioxide emissions or the process of massive road building and large infrastructure projects are not only destroying important natural sites but are threatening the biological conditions of life for all species, including our own. In the meantime, even the greenhouse effect can be turned into a profitable activity. Faced with governments' indecision regarding cuts in emissions and the tackling of the global environmental problems of our age, calls have started to be heard regarding the need to react to new global climatic trends, reaction which will allow for example to replace traditional crops suitable to standard climate with genetically engineered crops resistant to changes in temperature. By the term "reproduction commons" one can designate those commons based on women's ability to reproduce life. This also includes women's ability to breast feed their children, (those activities form a key part of what is termed within socio-economic structuralism the reproductive structure of society) and the shared knowledge communicated across generations and within communities on child-rearing techniques. These types of quasi-work are constitutive of what is termed in socio-economic structuralism the reproductive societal structure. Enclosure in this case occurs when advertisement campaigns and the massive promotion of "baby-milk" occurs in countries where hygienic conditions would make natural milk the most sensible choice for mothers, a choice that does not make them further dependent on the market.

One example of enclosures of cultural commons is the transformation of museums and areas of historical interest into "commodities" to be sold by the tourist industry. This commercialisation and monetisation limits the scope of common property freely accesible to each member of society and conditions one's ability to perform a given kind of quasi-work by one's possession of money. Finally, just as agricultural and farming methods and skills constitute the inalienable base of human society, without which it would not survive, so genes are the building blocks of biological life. Enclosure here is taking the form of large multinational corporation's seeking legislation that would turn knowledge and genes into private property. These forms of enclosures are known under the name of Intellectual Property Rights, the consequences of which are potentially devastating.

As can be seen, these few examples of new enclosures are either aimed at commodifying aspects of life that were not previously touched by the market, or cracking open social spheres which have been developed by society(tacitly following Polanyi's warnings) to protect itself from the market. The following text in this section draws heavily on De Angelis (1999).

I.2.6. Property

Weber reserves the term "property" for a particular class of appropriated rights, namely those which survive the individual lifetime, and are inheritable by a particular individual heir or other social unit, whether by testament, or by an automatic rule of succession. If alienable they constitute "free property."

From our theoretical standpoint, which will be elaborated in due course, Weberian definitions are marked by a degree of arbitrariness. The former property relation suggests some kind of group, family ownership, whilst the latter one, as will be later argued, refers to one of the two essential relations comprising property ownership. However, the adjective "free" does not contribute any new insight to the content of the concept.

What is more, Nonc of thc above cited sentences include any definition of the concept in question. What is relevant in this context is his claim to the effect that:

> it is essential to include the criterion of power of control and disposal (*Verfügungsgewalt*) in the sociological concept of economic action if for no other reason than that an exchange economy involves a complete network of contractual relationships, each of which originates in a deliberately planned process of acquisition of powers of control and disposal. This, in such an economy, is the principal source of the relation of economic action to the law. But any other typc of organization of economic activities would involve some kind of distribution of powers of control and disposal, however different its underlying principles might look like ...
>
> The term *Verfügungsgewalt*, of which Weber makes a great deal of use, is of legal origin, implying legally sanctioned powers of control and disposal. This, of course, has (in Henderson and Parsons' view no place in a purely economic conceptual scheme but is essential to a sociological treatment of economic systems. It is another way of saying that concretely economic action depends on a system of property relations. (Weber 1947)

Quite apart from any criticisms against Weber's treatment of property, the above assertion underscoring the role of property relations in the economy is very close to the present author's view.

Another merit of the Weberian approach, similar to that noted earlier in relation to his notion of utilities, is the fact that Weber does not couch the subject discussed in terms of a classification of objects or things. The concrete content of appropriated rights may be anything, tangible or intangible, for which the individual or unit has one or more "uses," which has "utility." Moreover, it is not the concrete object, the "thing" as such, tangible or intangible, which is the basis of the interest in appropriation, but the "use" to which it can be put. Correspondingly it is not the "things" which are appropriated, but rights[28] in them. It is by no means impossible for a number of different individuals or units to have appropriated rights in the same concrete thing, such as a certain tract of land, at the same time.

A functional classification of the content of appropriated rights is, however, essential to Weber's analysis. Thus, let us reiterate, it is this approach in terms of property objects' role in human activities that not

---

[28] Weber's view is in this regard strikingly similar to that of property rights theory.

only deserves a very positive evaluation, but confirms our earlier interpretation of the concept "subjective meaning," and, incidentally, parallels an approach particular to the theory of property rights, which is the subject of analysis in a subsequent chapters.

The foregoing does not imply, as has been hinted at above, that Weberian theory of property is flawless. Criticism should be especially levelled against its underlying contention according to which it is disposal, control, decision-making, etc. that constitute the essence of ownership. This is also evidenced by Weber's account of the socialist economy and, in particular, the condition of the working class under that economic system:

> Full socialization would not, ipso facto, destroy the "expropriation" of the workers unless one were to consider the socialistic state as one enormous producers' co-operative. But even if it were such in principle the average individual would be so remote from the points of controlling decision that he could hardly have a much greater sense of personal participation in the decisions than he does in those of his present "capitalistic" employers. (Weber 1947)

That this treatment is mistaken can be most easily shown on a number of specific examples. The circumstance that an executive of a public library makes a concrete decision on where, say, Russian literature should be stored, and which room should accumulate English fiction and poetry and so on and so forth does not, to be sure, transform them into an owner of these resources and the building itself. Similarly, while city authorities may take a decision that a definite street must be closed to traffic, it does not renders them private owners of the street involved. The list of such illustrations of our point might be multiplied. What ownership does consist of will be considered in a later chapter.

I.2.7. Theory of class

Whether, and if so to what extent, the drawbacks of property theory identified above have affected Weberian theory of class need to be explored.

Whilst in its most explicit form it is laid out in the chapter fragments assembled posthumously in *Economy and Society*, an additional proof of the importance of the concept for Weber is provided by his early empirical and historical studies in which the analysis of class figures very prominently, most notably his studies of East Elbian farming labourers, his exploration of the causes of the decline of the Roman Empire and his more general work on the agrarian sociology of ancient civilizations.

In his usual manner, Weber introduces an array of interelated concepts starting from "class status" which:

> applies to the typical probability that
> (a) given state of provision with goods,
> (b) external conditions of life, and
> (c) subjective satisfaction or frustration will be possessed by an individual or a group.
>
> These probabilities define class status in so far as they are dependent on the kind and extent of control or lack of it which the individual has over goods or services and existing possibilities of their exploitation for the attainment of income or receipts within a given economic order. (Weber 1947)

Thus, even as a point of departure, Weber refers to ownership of labour power and the means of production (as an ultimate source of goods mentioned in the definition). Small wonder that an implicit or explicit reference to property relations is found in the remaining definitions introduced by him. So for Weber, a "class" is any group of persons occupying the same class status. He goes on to say that

> the following types of classes may be distinguished:
> (a) a class is a "property class" when class status for its members is primarily determined by the differentiation of property holdings;
> (b) a class is an 'acquisition class' when the class situation of its members is primarily determined by their opportunity for the exploitation of services on the market. (Weber 1947)

In order to demonstrate to what extent his theory relies on ownership relations, Weber even declares, in non-ambiguous terms, that: "The possession of property defines the main class difference." According to Weber:

> The owners of property have a definite advantage, and in some cases a monopoly on, action in the market of commodities and, especially, labor. They have privileged access to the sources of wealth creation, by virtue of ownership and control of the markets. Weber identified a subdivision among property owners based on the means of their wealth creation. Entrepreneurs use wealth in commercial ventures. Rentiers profit by interest on their property, through investments or rent of land. Both forms of ownership yield advantages resulting from the ability to convert

> property to money. The property class is defined by the kinds of services individual workers provide in the labor market. (Shortell 2002)

That the identification of these classes is property-based is also shown by the examples indicated by Weber. Thus, amongst property classes there are landowners, owners of slaves, and other rentiers such as, among others, creditors, holders of securities, and at the opposite pole individuals owned by others, i.e. slaves and serfs which, in the theoretical language used in this work, translates into a lack of ownership of their own labour power. Similarly, among acquisition classes Weber distinguishes entrepreneurs including industrialists, merchants, but also labour aristocracy defined on the basis of monopolised skills, and on the bottom skilled manual semi and unskilled workers. It is evident that in the case of the latter group they have been stratified according to the quality of their labour power. Likewise, the term "monopolised skills" refers to nothing other than ownership of labour power.

The above-mentioned definition of class status or situation contains, however, one more interesting aspect connected with a dramatic question put forward by one author who asks:

if even social classes do not have boundaries, then what does? And if sociologists cannot even say what are the exact boundaries of a social class—one of the most fundamental of all sociological concepts—then what is the point of sociology?

He reckons, however, that

> one fairly obvious possibility seems to have been overlooked in traditional discussions of this question. This is the idea that sociology might do better, especially when it comes to the statistical analysis of social scientific data, to follow the lead of the natural sciences and try to develop a probability concept of social class. Boundary problems are common in the natural sciences but these can usually be overcome by making use of probability theory. For example, since 1926, when Erwin Schrodinger devised his famous equation, rather than trying to define the precise location of an electron at any particular point in time, modern physics has accepted that it can only know the probable location of any particular electron at a given point in space . [...] the solutions of his equation predict the probability that the electron will be found at each point of space, not, as in classical physics, the precise location of the electron at any instant (in time). (Smith 2007)

The author cited draws then an analogy, which is the most disputable aspect of his view, as it smacks of naturalism:

> If the position of the electron in a hydrogen atom can only be determined probabilistically, then why not the position of human individuals in social classes, too? And, if even physics cannot solve the problem of finding the exact location of an electron at any one point in time (and, of course, with a 90 per cent 'boundary' there must be a 10 per cent chance at any one time that the electron is not within the predicted area), why then should sociology be required to say exactly where particular human individuals stand in the class structure at any given point in time, especially when one considers that, with the relatively high degree of social mobility in late industrial society, the social space that many individuals occupy in the class structure is likely to change a number of times during their lifetime? And, of course, this objection to class boundaries also has much wider implications for the social sciences generally, since this problem is generic to all social boundaries. (Smith 2007)

And he goes on to say:

> Perhaps then sociology too might do better to develop some kind of probabilistic concept of social class?
>
> But if all this talk of probability sounds a little bit remote from sociology (why, after all, should sociology "follow the lead" of the natural sciences, even in the area of statistical analysis?) I would argue that this is not the case since there already exists within sociology a classical discussion of just such a probability concept of social class, and this in the work of none other than one of the founders of modern sociology, Max Weber.

While, by and large, Weber's theory of class is commendable, it is not the fact that he "defines class situation probabilistically" (Smith 2007) as betraying clear naturalistic leanings that deserves most praise. No such reference should release class theorists from the necessity of precise and unambiguous definitions.

In addition, it must be pointed out that Weber's theory of class includes yet another, much more controversial concept; his definition of "social class" as "composed of the plurality of class statuses between which an interchange of individuals on a personal basis or in the course of generations is readily possible and typically observable" (Weber 1947). One questionable aspect of this definition is its terminology: are there any grounds to assume that only social mobility is of social character, whilst this characteristic is for some undisclosed reason not to pertain to property relations, although their socio-economic nature can be denied only on the basis of jurisprudential approach which is, however, unacceptable within the social sciences?

More importantly, Weber identifies his social classes on a different basis than the ownership criteria used with reference to the property and commercial classes. This violates a principle of internal coherence and consistency as well as that of formal elegance, which both ought to characterise genuinely scientific theory. There is no denying that in the form of the concept in question Weber addresses an important issue of different levels of class analysis. His own solution is, for reasons given above, unsatisfactory, which would lead us, in due course, to present our own approach to the same question.

Some further Weberian comments are worthy of mention, since they refer, amongst others, to an important and controversial topic of class struggle, and not only for scholarly reasons. Weber argues that "different wages result in different qualities in terms of the standard of living":

> Weber did not believe that class interests necessarily led to uniformity in social action. Neither communal nor societal action is the inexorable result of class interest. Weber challenges, here, the Marxian notion of the primarily material basis of social action. He is not denying it outright, but rather introducing an element of unpredictability. Weber did not believe that proletarian revolutionary action would arise as a certain result of structural contradiction.
>
> Communal or societal action may develop from a common class situation in certain conditions. Weber believed that the general cultural conditions played a large role in this determination. Intellectuals, in his view, occupy a key position in this regard. Weber argued that the extent of the contrasts between the property owners and the property-less workers must become transparent to the workers in order for collective action around the issue of class to occur. Intellectuals function either to call attention to and explain these contrasts, or, to obscure them.
>
> For communal or societal action to take place, the workers must not only recognise the differences in wealth and opportunity, but these differences must be seen as the result of the distribution of property and economic power. If the differences are believed to be a natural characteristic of society, as a given fact, then only occasional and irrational action is possible. Very often, collective action centers on the labor market. Workers seek higher wages, and see this as the goal of their struggle. Most class antagonism, Weber noted, is directed at managers, rather than at owners—stockholders and bankers—because they appear to be have the power to set the price of labor power. (Shortell 2002)

Thus, class groups do not constitute communities, according to Weber. It seems, however, that the author of *Economy and Society* did not fully appreciate circumstances helping common action stemming from concentration of large masses of workers in a single workplace or in workplaces characterised by similar working and industrial conditions, including structural conflict with those who benefit from their toil, be it business owners or top executives. On the other hand, Weber's pointing out of the role of intellectuals relative to the working class recalls, paradoxically, one of the theses of so-called Marxism-Leninism about the class function of the intelligentsia lying in their mission to upgrade working class consciousness from the level of trade-unionist to the political, revolutionary dimension.

All those criticisms of Weber by no means imply that we concur with those who argue for the supposed superiority of the so-called "new economic sociology" over "old economic sociology." Well, any science, whether hard or social science, cannot, or at least should not, accept any "calendar theory of truth." The best examples are many "old" economic sociologists whose theories appear to be much more vital, timely and topical than an overwhelming bulk of their, in chronological terms, younger counterparts.

CHAPTER I.3.

TALCOTT PARSONS AND NEIL SMELSER'S "ECONOMY AND SOCIETY" AS AN EXAMPLE OF SOCIOLOGY OF THE ECONOMY

I.3.1. Basic principles

The procedure Talcott Parsons adopted to analyze both the general system of action and its subsystems is called "the AGIL scheme" or "AGIL paradigm":

> To survive or maintain equilibrium with respect to its environment, any system must to some degree adapt to that environment, attain its goals, integrate its components, and maintain its latent pattern, a cultural template of some sort. These are called the system's functional imperatives.
>
> In the case of the analysis of a societal action system, the AGIL Paradigm, according to Parsons, yields four interrelated and interpenetrating subsystems: the behavioral systems of its members (A), the personality systems of those members (G), the society as a system of social organization (I) and the cultural system of that society (L). To analyze a society as a social system (the I subsystem of action), it can be treated as a complex system of interrelated functional subsystems, namely:
>
> • The economy—societal adaptation to its action and non-action environmental systems
>
> • The polity—societal goal attainment
>
> • The societal community—the integration of its diverse social components
>
> • The fiduciary system - processes and units that function to reproduce societal culture (also called pattern maintenance and tension management).
>
> Parsons put forward the idea (to which we shall come back to analyse it in mor detail) that each of these systems also developed some specialized symbolic mechanisms of interaction analogous to money in the economy, e.g., influence in the societal community. Various processes of "interchange" among the subsystems of the societal system were postulated. One might add that the said theory of subsystem interchanges is at the same time an

attempt to incoporate the model of factors of production, i.e. capital, labour, land and organization.

His theory is similar to Weber's seminal work, in that it contains two strands of thought, i.e. both sociology of the economy and economic sociology- especially in "Economy and Society". One cannot agree more with a diagnosis presented in the foreword, where mutually damaging effects of the divorce of economics and sociology are stressed and, correspondingly, the need for the integration of the two disciplines is proposed. The above issue has been repeatedly considered earlier in this book, so at this point we limit ourselves to indicating some reasons for this sad state of affairs being the resignation of contemporary sociologists, with some exceptions (such as Bourdieu, Habermas and Luhmann, the latter two, significantly, drawing heavily on Parsons' achievements), from creating a general social theory. All the more interesting will be to see how Parsons and Smelser have succeeded in that regard. As has been said above, society is seen as composed of four basic functional subsystems. The first question that comes to mind concerns a problem of interest in the case of all theories explored here, i.e. conceiving the boundaries of the economy. Parsons answers this question by pointing to objectives of the economy as a functional subsystem of society at large, defining the economy's function as the production of consumer goods and services.

Two comments should be made about this. Firstly, the definition lacks any mention of the means of production or investment goods. How come? While they, of course, constitute an indispensable condition of reproduction of the economy, there has been no room for them within the Parsonian scheme, as they are not subject to any interchange with any other societal system. As a result, Parsons' notion is useless from the standpoint of economics (a discipline, let us remember, with which he is seeking integration) as being of no help in constructing national balance, tables of reproduction such as those found in Quesnay or Marx's writings for example, and adequate schemes of flows of economic outputs, which is the most striking in the face of the most probable source of Parsons' paradign, i.e. Leontief's input-output scheme. It is also the second component of the definition that at least needs more precise specification. "Services" is, after all, a notoriously ambiguous term and if, as Parsons appears to be promoting in the footsteps of most economists, they are to be understood as all actions that satisfy other persons' wants, there could be no reasons to not include in the economy such activities as that of the clergy in satisfying believers' need of peace of mind and clear conscience, or police in securing the need of order, or even, as Marx ironically noted: "The criminal [who] produces an impression, partly moral and partly tragic, as the case may be, and in this way renders a 'service' by arousing the moral and aesthetic feelings of the public" (1861–3), thus conflating economic and non-economic activities.

The task of delineating the economic structure's boundaries is not made any easier but, on the contrary, further complicated by Parsons' introduction of the notion of income as a purpose of functioning of the economy. Another claim of this sort states that a key attribute of internal economic processes is measurement and monetary calculation which must be charged with ahistoricism, an attempt of viewing all various historical economic structures from an angle of merely one of such systems, i.e. commodity-money, whose most perfect manifestation is capitalism.

In that regard Parsonian functional analysis does not produce any useful insights either. Application of its categories leads to a rather fuzzy contention to the effect that the economy is aimed at production of generalised facilities as means of a limitless number of uses or, to put it differently, physical, social and cultural objects instrumental in solving adaptive problems of social systems.

The concept of utilities having little relevance as regards our "demarcation" purpose stems from the fact that this concept includes everything which contributes to achieving any goals valued by a system or its subunits. It follows that the reader is almost completely free as far as recognition of a given object as a "generalised facility" is concerned.

The gravest flaw of Parsons' conception of the economy is in including only some relations of commodity-money circulation. As a consequence, Parsons takes the odd decision to classify banks, together with political parties and also insurance companies etc. as political units.

I.3.2. The Economy vs. The polity

The above-mentioned financial institutions are, along with any (even individual) creditors, part and parcel of the polity, because their function consists in providing capital which, according to Parsons, is no more and no less than political activity. Of course, these conceptual choices have no empirical grounds. To put it more precisely, despite the fact that the authors of the book are Americans, their view, paradoxically, is congruent not with an Anglo-Saxon model of capitalism, wherein corporate financing is based on the stock exchanges, but rather continental and Asiatic models where the financial role of banks is much more prominent. Anyway, financial institutions are, of course, to be treated as economic institutions.

It is to be noted that to exaggerate the significance of banks is to commit the so-called Hilferding fallacy. This economist's theory of financial capital has never, frankly speaking, strictly matched capitalism's reality, and is even more outdated in relation to the American economic system(mind you, investment banks and commercial ones are very different entities). The above considerations are closely associated with another misjudgement concerning the role of self-financing. Parsons, to be sure, perceives the existence of such source of corporate capital, but-- surprise, surprise!-- regards them as "special cases," definitely playing down their significance. When one supplements this position with an answer to the question about the causes of the Parsonian stance, clear methodological conclusions follow. In point of fact, they have to do with a weak spot in his deductive methodology, to which issue we shall return later. Namely, as an output of the polity, as couched in terms of Parsonian theory of system interchanges, is power, which term has something in common with "purchasing power," the whole conception gains, in Parsons' opinion, credibility. This account, it has to be pointed out, diverges from one presented in his earlier *The Structure of Social Action* where the political sphere has been associated with extra-economic violence. What has changed since that treatment is an adoption of the notion of interchanges, or an input-output analysis. In all probability it was precisely this view that has imposed the solution mentioned above. Simply put, in a given place within the scheme a specific input or output has to be found. Parsons's treatment of empirical phenomena comes to be derived from the categories of a scheme that is itself held to be non-empirical. Supposedly empirically-oriented categories are all generated by the logic of the *a priori* categorical scheme. The categories are not empirically derived and their "applications" have no consequence for the theory:

> In this way, it proves all too easy for Parsons to assimilate all arguments to his general theory, that is, to a general argument about the progressive differentiation of social structures around specialized functions. (Beckert 2006)

Parsons' methodological position could be described as formalism. According to this position, contact with empirical data does not lead to modification, improvement or enrichment of the conceptual constructs previously worked out; it is, as a matter of fact, superfluous, or even undesirable and harmful, as it can violate logical coherence of the theoretical system, constructed without any reference to empirical facts. It is this that accounts for the frequent use in Parsons' writings of safety hatches of which the aforementioned "special case" is a case in point. They help the American exponent of the so-called "Grand Theory" avoid uncomfortable confrontations with reality, whilst maintaining *prima facie* integrity of his aprioristic schema and models.

Fortunately, there is a silver lining to the Parsonian treatment of interrelations of the economy on one hand, and the polity on the other. Namely, Parsons' theory of interchanges distinguishes an input of the latter for the benefit of the former, which is termed "supporting productive enterprises." This general term involves such methods of state intervention in the economic structure as protective tariffs, import restrictions, direct subsidies aiding various industries and others. However, Parsons uses overly broad categories: he speaks in this context both of nationalisation and of calls directed at the collective "*Geist*" of enterprise, which make it difficult if not impossible to distinguish qualitatively different ways of government economic interventions. Thus, from the viewpoint of Parsons, both a single armaments order and determination of minimal wage or regulation of prices in specific industries will be classified on the same footing. Meanwhile, all activities belonging to the latter category, i.e. consisting of business management, including planning and targets determination at the macro-level, should be classed as inherently economic activities. Their economic nature is by no means erased with the transfer from the micro to the macro-scale.

> There is more to Parsons' view of the interchanges between the economy and the polity. Namely, the said theory makes it possible for the American sociologist to consider conditioning of the political system on part of the economic structure. He notes that each political system must have at its disposal physical facilities of power. In other words, for the political subsystem to function, it must possess tanks, batons, prisons, court and police premises, offices etc. In view of this dependence, the political system is, as Parsons points out, vitally interested in the size and productive potential of the industrial apparatus.

I.3.3. The economy and science

The authors of the book being discussed deal with the relationship of the economic structure to other non-economic substructures of society at large.

Writing about land as one of the factors of production, they distinguish within it another factor of science. The combination of these two factors should be regarded as fortunate and sound given the nature of the land, which in terms of ownership theory discussed in more detail later in the book provides its holder with free benefits. The same applies, as will be argued later, to science.

The cases of science's penetration into the sphere of the economy are by no means merely material components of production. Parsons mentions in this context such phenomena as an implementation of various technologies, purchases of know-how, but also points to the embodiment of science in the form of skills of labour power. It should be added that this kind of science's economic relevance refers exclusively to those elements of physics, geometry, chemistry and so on which are actually applied by a given worker in their operations, and not to his or her scientific knowledge in general. To put it another way, it is only that scientific knowledge that is a necessary condition of execution of this or that work task which is at stake here.

The above supplement is needed because of certain interpretations of the role of science with reference to the economic structure present, among others, in theories of "scientific-technological revolution," "knowledge-based society," and "information society" etc. What is meant at this juncture are that such views, which from the evidence on heightened economic power of the natural sciences draw the conclusion that science, supposedly occupying an ever larger space of the economy, broadens its scope as a substructure of society at the expense of the economic substructure whose size is, therefore, dwindling. This misinterpretation is based on the following misunderstanding: While science is in fact present in various forms within the economy, it does not follow, of course, that the types of activity in which definite elements of science are used are transformed into scientific activities. Thus, any talk about appropriation by science of even a small part of the economy relies on a complete misunderstanding. The situation here is analogous in certain respects to that considered above in relation to state activities, which in some instances are of economic nature. For example, if a given management activity is performed not by an chief executive officer, but by someone who bears the title of Trade Secretary or Energy Minister, it does not lose thereby its economic characteristics.

Parsons, however, does not commit the above error. He avoids this misplaced view by simply outlining a scheme showing the social journey of science all the way from creation to entering the economy. Especially relevant in the present context is a divide between those components of science that are potentially accessible to the purposes of economic use and those which are in fact used in productive consumption.

I.3.4. The economic microstructure

Pre-material or conceptual labour consists of the production of so-called ideal means and objects of work, and is an activity typical in modern conditions based on the application of science belonging to the economic structure, or to use Marx's term, productive forces of society. These problems are considered at length in *Economy and Society*.

What the authors do is an application of their functional scheme not only at the macro- but also micro-level. The economy, therefore, is divided into four familiar systems, which are further subdivided. Often, not entirely clear and convincing terminology hides fairly precise and detailed analysis of the inner structure of the economic system. It is conducted, to be sure, with reference to the unit division of labour, and it covers relationships within the all-societal division of labour to a much smaller degree which, however, does not detract from the cognitive worth of the particular observations that are to be found in this section of the book.

Thus, there emerges a hidden premise of placement within the "production subsystem" of the substructure called "co-ordination of production" showing the recognition of types of work performed within it, i.e. organisation of collective material work (the exact meaning of this term will be explained in a subsequent chapter), and assignment of particular workers to specific means of production as economic (in our terminology, indirectly material) labour.

Similarly, considering that within the production system the sector termed "provision with utilities" is included, it turns out that all the problems with qualifying such activities at the macro-level notwithstanding, at the micro-level it is much more difficult to deny evident facts. Despite previously analysed reservations, therefore, Parsons finally includes exchange, purchase of instruments and materials of work into the economy and admits that their continuous inflow is a necessary condition of the latter's functioning.

We have considered so far Parsons' views on the economic structure, including its microstructure. What this analysis has shown is that the economy is a complex network of interrelated social relations. This complexity as well as its social dimension exclude its reduction to a primitive labour process and, equally, its conceptualisation in terms of the means of work plus their operator.

Turning to the issue of mutual relations of particular societal structures, let us recall that in particular an analysis of how Parsons views the ties of science and the economy has allowed us to correct some erroneous, to our mind, treatments of the issue in question. Parsons, however, does not restrict himself to the above-mentioned substructure of society. Equally instructive, as will be seen, is his treatment of the so-called basic cell of society.

I.3.5. The economy and family

In the case of the family, one can observe similar problems as regards its relation to the economy as those considered above with reference to science, the difference being that in the present case the problems are in reverse, as it were. In the former instance, from the presence of numerous elements of science in the economy, the conclusion has been derived that those parts of the economic structure in which science has been applied are no longer economic but scientific in nature. In the present case, on the other hand, the reasoning, resting on a similar basis, goes in an opposite direction; just as it is argued that at a certain stage of its development the economy cannot exist without science, it is also pointed to the fact that it cannot also function without the family as a source of labour power which is, of course, an indispensable factor of production or, more generally, any economic action. From this undisputable circumstance it is concluded that this time round it is acts of reproduction and socialisation that have economic character.

Again, Parsons' position relative to the aforementioned issue is, in contradistinction to the supporters of the view mentioned above, singularly sound. He even labels the view according to which "socialisation is a form of economic production" as "naive." To substantiate his criticism, he builds, as in the above discussed case of science, a scheme showing an entire life career of an hypothetical individual and he argues that the fact that the individual enters at a certain moment into the labour force it does not turn all his or her previous life stages, including birth and socialisation, into a component of the economy.

I.3.6. Summary and theoretical-methodological conclusions

Summing up our discussion of *Economy and Society* thus far, it can be pointed out that it clearly, albeit indirectly, suggests that, firstly, the interrelations between the economic structure and non-economic structures are so complex and multifaceted that they cannot be reduced to any simple formulae, all the more that, secondly, they are variable in time, and, thirdly, that their scientific analysis requires, as its point of departure, the working out of precise concepts of both the economic and non-economic structures. Thus, from an analysis of Parsonian views one can draw not only negative but also positive lessons.

Amongst the former, a pivotal role is played by Parsons' methodological approach or, rather, "anti-approach," in that one should be warned against its use. One of its traits is the speculative approach to the issues considered, squeezing their real or imaginary solution into the straitjacket of a deductive model adopted *a priori*. Such an approach is also evident in the aforementioned theory of productive factors, as interpreted through the prism of the notion of subsystem interchanges. Take, for example, the "organization" factor treated as a contribution of the entrepreneur. First and foremost, *Economy and Society* leaves us essentially ignorant as regards the real content of that factor. One does not know whether, following in the footsteps of Schumpeter, one should understand that a given agent withdraws some of the resources existing in the static economy, and then proceeds to use them in a different manner, i.e. carrying out of new combinations. On the other hand, Parsons by no means rules out an interpretation according to which the concept under discussion would refer to day-by-day management, which does not necessarily imply any innovative activity in the above-mentioned sense.

Parsons associates entrepreneurial function with "co-ordination and planning of economic actions," but another page of the book shows "necessary co-ordination" as a distinct concept. Thus, one is not able to determine whether one has to do with an agent of creative construction as the moving force that carries out new combinations in the economy, or an ordinary manager, the driving force of the economic development or a common economic functionary.

One consequence to this lack of clarity is the obscuring of what is from our point of view an important distinction between co-ordination and supervision of work[1] which, though they may be carried out by the same person, remain analytically distinct.

In another context, Parsons himself points out that organizational activities can be performed by employees occupying various positions, e.g. members of managerial or administration staff, but also those employed in the technological division. This is a genuinely sociological approach, and as such deserving praise. Parsons implies here that for purposes of socio-economic research, knowledge of formal occupational titles is not enough, one should look at the empirical content of given types of work. There is more to that, however. Parsons construes the concept of organization as a

[1] In our view, this is distinguished by the use of sanctions, whilst from the viewpoint of Parsons' general theory, is characteristic of each and every action.

function of his subsystem whose aim is societal integration. His formalism is manifested in the fact that there is no independent substantiation of this decision apart from citation of the definition of the function in question alone.

I.3.7. Economics and Sociology from the Standpoint of *Economy and Society*

The above-mentioned theory of production factors may serve as an example of how Parsons approaches the issue of mutual relations between the two disciplines concerned. On the grounds of the theory just mentioned, particular factors of production represent more general categories of inputs and outputs. And indeed, more generally speaking, Parsons treats economics as a special case of his theory of social systems which, in turn, remains in the same position relative to the even more universal theory of general system of action. At the beginning of his book Parsons lists a number of examples, which are to corroborate the above view. Even giving the author the maximum benefit of the doubt, he is not in a position to convince the reader that it is really the case. Thus, in Parsons' view such economic categories as "demand" and "supply" represent special cases of more general concepts of "achievement" and "sanction," which, under his general theory, pertain to each action. This is hardly convincing, however. Note that along the same lines one could lay out an indefinite number of analogies between similar or complementary phenomena. Why not, for instance, juxtapose the above pair of economic concepts with "sea inflow" and "outflow." But does it follow from the above comparison that economics is a special case of hydrology? Or, possibly the opposite is the case. Furthermore, Parsons argues that what in economics is known as "goods" and "services" refers in fact to a sociological dichotomy of "physical objects" and "social objects." This view, again, is entirely useless in terms of both economics and sociology; one is not able to indicate any advantage that would stem from the substitution of the concepts in question.

On these grounds it could be claimed that Parsonian methodology is based on an underlying principle of "application" or "subsumption," which is also evident in his theory of the general system of action characterised by sweeping generalisation or universalism, as its categories, which according to the author are to refer to the entire bio-psycho-sociocultural world.

The term "subsumption" indicates the above-considered feature of Parsons' thought that consists in conceiving phenomena of a given realm as special cases of some more general one, thus establishing particular spheres of reality in a hierarchical order. In the case of economics, just as in other instances, the logic of reasoning should, though, lead the author in an opposite direction—after establishing that the economy constitutes a distinct subsystem of the broader societal system, the next logical step ought to consist of working out a set of categories and propositions that would highlight that specificity. Unfortunately, in *Economy and Society*, Parsons has gone in quite another direction, symbolised by his words: "At the most general, constitutive of the economic theory level, no specifically economic variables exist, they are categories of the general theory of action, as the economic categories can be derived from the general theory" (Parsons 1956).

Such a reductionist view cannot but affect proportions of pages of the book concerned, occupied by numerous attempts to place this or that category in a definite box within a certain scheme or diagram, and those devoted to a rather neglected, in comparison with the former preoccupation deemed as, it appears, less interesting, down-to-earth analysis of economic phenomena and processes. Such a hierarchy of priorities also leaves much less room for what, as suggests Parsonian theory of interchanges, should constitute the key focus of his interest: i.e. an investigation of interrelations between the economic structure and other societal structures, which are so complex and multisided that any attempt to reduce them to a pair of factors exchanged between every two structures is doomed to failure.

It has to be pointed out that the period used by Parsons, of what has been termed here a methodological approach, premised on subsumption has lasted long after the publication of *Economy and Society*. It would be no exaggeration to say that it dominated his work; Parsons, retaining the basic functional scheme, has focused in later years on its reformulation, adding new details and extension into previously neglected societal fields.

Looking at this development, one can observe an increasing tendency towards formalism. The strengthening of formalism manifests itself in pushing the boundaries of concepts used, so that they become devoid of any identifiable empirical reference, and eliminating categories possessing such a referent. Thus, as far as the relations between the economy and the polity go, Parsons ceases to talk about per cent drawn from loans and the factor of supporting industrial enterprises' vanishes as well. The concept of organisation which, despite it's ill definition, has allowed one to capture some real economic processes, gets substituted by an even more unclear notion of "patterns of allocation of resources," which allocation is to be carried out by means of influence. The connection of the two appears rather enigmatic, and in all probability is accounted for, in keeping with our earlier observations, by the circumstance that the medium termed "influence" has found itself at the intersection of certain subsystems, and not others. By the way, the term more in place would be industrial authority or power to command rather than Parsonian benign influence.

To do justice to Parsons' treatment of economic phenomena, though, one should draw attention to the fact that it can be interpreted from another perspective, namely as a more or less successful attempt to introduce a sociological point of view to an analysis of the economic structure. We cannot agree more with Parsons, therefore, when he criticises modern economists, not excluding Keynes, for explaining economic processes by individuals' psychological leanings or tendencies and motivations as well by specific traits of human nature. However, fully sharing Parsons' critique of psychologism and anthropology in economics, we cannot restrict ourselves to expressing this solidarity. It must be checked, however, what the real effects of this convincing rhetoric are or, to put it differently, to establish if his research practice is where his mouth is, so to speak.

We are sorry to say that the results of this practical test do not match Parsons' declarations. It is true, then, that Parsons aims at the sociological treatment of motives of economic action. He writes, for instance, that different stimuli of bankers on the one hand, and workers on the other are to be explained by their involvement in distinct situational contexts. The reader, however, does not receive any analysis of these respective objective conditions, but merely the statement , being another example of "application" procedure identified above according to which an analysis of motivations in occupational roles is a special case of a general theory of motivation in institutionalised roles and, with proper modifications, these broadest- unstated - categories will satisfactorily account for the behaviour of any economic agent.

The remaining illustrations of Parsons' sociological approach to economics are not consistent with his intentions either. Could one, for instance, agree without any reservations with the view that the main problem concerning the labour force in a capitalistic economy is their socialisation, such as the shaping of workers' motivation so that they would be willing to adopt as their own the goals of productivity?

One cannot leave this statement without criticism, given that this Parsonian account of workers' motivation and mechanisms of the labour power market does not take account of the fact that the workers, as owners of sole labour power, are subject to economic compulsion to work, it being for them the one and only chance of acquiring the means of subsistence.

In return, Parsons indulges in rather dubious formulae about "common value patterns" shared by the free partners of a contract which, after all, are the employee and the employer, on "comprehensive loyalty" and "trust" constituting, according to Parsonian theory, inputs of the worker for the benefit of the firm, which reciprocates in the form of "support" and "moral approbation."

Leaving aside an ideological bias of the above statement one should, once again, raise a question of its applicability to Parsons' fatherland rather than the European or Asiatic capitalisms, where indeed workers' rights are respected to a much greater extent than in the former type of capitalism.

Other exemplifications of Parsons' approach are not able to invalidate our doubts as to its inability to overcome psychologism on a practical basis. For instance, Parsons proposes to explain a decrease of labour force on the labour market by, for one thing, their deficit of "comprehensive loyalty," and, for another, by the fact that they ceased to value production. Not only does the above contention, contrary to, as he himself refers to them, anti-nominalistic and holistic methodological assumptions not transcend a vicious circle of individualistic subjectivism, but it is subject, as can be easily seen, to the criticism of tautology. It is of little if any use to criticise the Keynesian notion of "general propensities" if all that is meant to replace it are such quasi-explanatory factors, similar to Moliere's famous "explanation" of why one falls asleep after taking opium by the latter's hypnotic properties.

On similar grounds there is essentially no phenomenon that cannot be explained: "I wonder why Americans are fond of highly advanced high-technology sector"—"Because they value science and technology." "I wonder why Mr Smith does not love Ms Smith anymore"—"Well, it's crystal clear: because love is no longer any value to him." And so on, and so forth, the list can be practically endless. Thus, has not Keynes' low-grade psychology been substituted with an equally ill-conceived sociology? Values, their patterns and systems are, incidentally, Parsons' favourite explanatory factor. What remains as "specifically sociological" categories meant to fight psychologism is extremely limited. Is there, for example, any material difference as regards their cognitive worth between the concept of "propensities," which appears in Keynes, and its substitute from *Economy and Society*, i.e. "expectations"?

From the economist's standpoint, it turns out, the well-known set of functional imperatives is worthless. Morsey notes in this context that Parsons' assertion according to which different patterns of family expenditures reflect distinct solutions of those four functional problems does not contribute anything of value to economics.

The inability to successfully purge psychologism from economic sociology is also evident in Parsons' theory of change. What is relevant here is especially his claim accounting for the much discussed phenomenon of separation of ownership and control (Parsons 1975).

> … exchange with Gintis (1975) around the issue of ownership and control within the capitalist enterprise, was conducted by Parsons entirely as a matter of correct specification in terms of the theory of the social system, with no consideration that there may also be issues of empirical adequacy in their competing accounts. (Holmwood 2006)

Such an approach allows the author of *The Social System* to explain the said phenomenon in a rather idiosyncratic way, pointing to the dissatisfaction of prospective managers and other, as he calls them, dissident elements with the way in which corporations are run. In this odd account, the whole sphere of objective conditions is left out of the picture. Amongst these objective conditions are an increase in size of enterprises making it difficult, if not impossible, for an individual owner to single-handedly manage the firm, an increasing extension and complication of production and sales, necessitating the hiring of industrial engineers, marketing specialists, finance directors etc.

This lack of taking account of the aforementioned objective factors is not the sole drawback of Parsonian comments in the said context. One such problematic claim holds that the personal ownership of securities on the part of professional executives has only nominal significance. This assertion not only does not take consideration of objective data to the contrary, some of which will be cited in the chapter on the theory of property rights, but taking as his frame of reference jurisprudential rather than socio-economic property theory, it fails to consider in that context not only various equity-based forms of managerial compensation, but even salaries and bonuses, which are in many cases so astronomically high that they cannot be regarded as simply pay for work done. In fact, they are bound to contain a lesser or greater portion of the surplus value, which is also shown by their further destination: because of their size, they cannot be consumed, but are converted into some form of capital.

It is not only on the grounds of the above considerations that one must call into question Parsons' related assertion pointing out the demise of property in modern capitalism, which implies a shift of the focus of power into the hands of professional managers. The aforementioned lack of disposal of truly socio-economic theory of property makes it impossible for the author of *Economy and Society* to notice that the modern capitalist society is characterised, if anything, by an increase of the role of ownership. This is evidenced, in particular, by the fact that ownership of capital allows its holder to live without a necessity of any work (taken over by the hired managers).

By way of summary, it should be noted that *Economy and Society* contains two relatively independent layers, as it were. The first one consists of the application of the "subsumption" model to an account of interrelations of economics and Parsonian general theory of action. In lots of cases, as the alleged analogies between dyads of concepts pertaining to the two disciplines most clearly show, the said procedure produces manifestly figurative results. In the same field one should include all instances in which the functional paradigm reveals its arbitrary nature, most blatantly in the unsubstantiated association of given empirical phenomena and processes with specific functions. If, however, we describe the above discussed layer as epiphenomenal, it follows that it can be without any harm divorced from the second layer, whose worth is incomparably higher.

I.3.8. Modern Capitalism as Portrayed in *Economy and Society*

Parsons' paradigm of inputs and outputs has led him to successfully investigate the interrelationships between the economic structure and other societal structures. On the other hand, his approach to systems as consisting of a set of subsystems, strongly recalling a matryoshka doll, or babushka doll, i.e. a Russian nesting doll which is a set of dolls of decreasing sizes placed one inside the other, has made possible an in-depth analysis of the inner structure of the economy, with equally valuable results. As a consequence, *Economy and Society* contains a relatively adequate picture of contemporary capitalism.

It depicts its big corporations, underlines the role of science in the economy, highlighting, among others, the significance of a scientifically trained labour force, and takes account the economic functions of the state. To be sure, facts cited by Parsons do not always match their theoretical interpretations, and in many cases one has also to do with over-generalisations, treating as universal the phenomena specific to concrete nations. For example, the claim reducing trade unions' functions to their purely semi-ritual role as opposed to collective bargaining cannot be said to be generally true. Certainly not all unions, as Parsons would have it, have transformed themselves from an institution protecting employees as against employers into an organisation protecting employees in relation to the remaining citizens of society. Luckily, in *Economy and Society* one can find other, much more pertinent and apposite contentions.

In one of the above passages, Parsons' questionable account of relations between workers and capitalists has been discussed. There is, however, another, more felicitous side to it in which Parsons uses more realistic language. He writes, for example, that a worker taking a job in a firm entrusts the latter with his own and his family's security, pointing out that the firm, that representative of the collective capitalist acquires thereby rights of intervention into the life of the household whose head is its employee (its extreme form being his or her layoff or dismissal), which implies a capability to control the long-term fortunes of the household.

Acknowledgement of long-term dependence of a capitalistic employee and her or his family upon the laws governing the capitalist economy is, in Parsons' case, connected with recognition of the essentially antagonistic character of relations in bourgeois society. Parsons does not hesitate to speak of what he considers to be a hidden conflict of interests of employees and employers, not excluding its outbreak. He also points to the contradiction of value systems, attitudes and ideologies of the world of work and the world of business.

These statements have been cited also in order to show frequent misjudgments of Parsons' ideological position, often charged with conservatism,[2] right-wing bias, or even reactionism. Meanwhile, Parsons in *Economy and Society* seeks to avoid ideological commitments, striving to study the phenomena under discussion *sine ira et studio*.

I.3.9. Parsons' sociology of money

Parsons presents an interesting and valuable theory of money, which apparently draws on Weber, Simmel and Marx. Along with familiar economic functions of money, his deliberations contain fairly original notion of degrees of freedom made possible thanks to this medium.

---

[2] This conservatism may be also understood in a methodological sense—as a one-sided emphasis on the notion of equilibrium and stability and, correspondingly, an inability to conceptualise change. This charge must be rejected for two reasons. For one thing, Parsons deals extensively with societal change, including evolution. For another, the charge is misplaced because each and every structural theory, theory of statics etc. is, at least implicitly, a theory of dynamics and change. For instance, from the perspective of socio-economic structuralism, to identify the core of a given structure is at the same time to indicate those structural components whose change will entail the most far-reaching changes of the structure as a whole.

Parsons described money as a medium of exchange whose function consists in measuring value (Parsons 1963, 236). Money is thereby symbolic, "in that though measuring and thus 'standing for' economic value or utility, it does not itself possess utility in the primary consumption sense—it has no 'value in use' but only 'in exchange,' i.e. for possession of things having utility" (Parsons 1963, 236).

The offers to buy or sell goods or services are communicated through the medium of money. Parsons traced the development of money to its roots in precious metals, which have intrinsic value. This connection is fully lost in differentiated money economies, to the extent that money becomes worthless in regard to its use value. The theoretical problem arising from the worthlessness of money (why should ego be willing to exchange a good for worthless money in the exchange process?) is resolved by Parsons pointing to the four degrees of freedom that actors achieve through the medium of money: the buyer can spend money on any good or service available on the market; he or she can buy from any producer or service provider; the buyer can freely decide on the time of purchase; and he or she is free to accept or reject the terms of exchange. The disadvantage of the worthlessness of money is compensated by the gain in options and motivates acceptance of the medium in exchange.

However, the risk remains that money will not be accepted by third parties or that it will become worthless due to inflation. This risk remains because money is not tied to a product that has a use value. However, the disconnection of money from its historical origins in precious metals is, according to Parsons, a precondition for its functional efficiency as a medium of exchange, which is why this risk is part of the structure of differentiated economies. Only the actors' trust in the stability and acceptance of the symbolic medium can be supported through its institutionalization: "There must be an element of bindingness in the institutionalization of the medium itself—e.g. the fact that the money of a society is a 'legal tender' which must be accepted in the settlement of debts which have the status of contractual obligations under the law" (Parsons 1963, 240). The institutionalization of money allows also a separation of economic exchange processes from their anchoring in normatively sanctioned expectations of reciprocity.

> What, from whom, when, and for what price something is purchased is no longer culturally decided. The resulting uncertainty of economic decisions can no longer be normatively reduced "(Beckert 2006).

To put it from a slightly different angle,

money, as a generalised medium of exchange, can stand for a wide range of goods, allowing a sophisticated division of labour not available in barter economies.

Furthermore, it allows for large amounts of capital to be built up, and hence large scale production. [...] This example highlights the importance of input from the other subsystems. As money is symbolic it has no real use-value in itself;input from the value commitment and normative subsystems generates trust allowing us to accept that we can exchange the note for its promissory value on demand.

... Parsons sees the precondition for the functional differentiation of the economy in the development of a money economy. In an economy that is characterized by highly specialized production processes, the direct exchange between labor and consumer goods would not be practicable and, besides, would not take the diverging interests of families and companies into account. While a company's production decisions are oriented toward expected profits, [...] the medium of money [...] makes it possible to [...] speak of the development of lifestyles on the basis of consumer choices. The different needs of the economy and the family can be reconciled as consumer demand and labor demand become separated by the exchange medium of money from concrete producers and at the same time remain connected to each other on a generalized level. (Beckert 2006)

This presentation of Parsons' treatment of money allows one to refer to certain counterarguments that have been raised by its critics:

Ganssmann (1989, 293) argues that Parsons's theory of money has always assumed that an institutional trust in money exists without, however, explaining where this trust comes from. According to Ganssmann, the theory therefore describes a functioning economy but cannot explain its origins. The first point is simply untrue. It is one thing to accept Parsons' explanation, but the denial that he has put forward such an explanation based on his conception of subsystem interchanges is quite another. The second point, however, refers to some genuine weakness in Parsons' approach, but only indirectly. What should be expressly pointed to here is not any lack of purely theoretical argument but, rather, an in fact important gap that lies in its lack of historical dimension. Only in this way, as shown by Marx and many economic historians studying the process of transition from feudalism to capitalism or, more generally, the emergence of the commodity-money economy, can the problem indicated be solved. Even less justice to Parsons' approach is provided by the second main criticism made by his opponents (in this case, the aforementioned one): the obvious underestimation of money's societal relevance. By considering money merely as a symbol—which was already problematic (1963, 290ff)—Marx's and Weber's insight that the monetary economy enables an orientation toward profits as its own end was ignored. Money is the central instrument for the orientation toward the profit motive and makes possible

> the principally unlimited dynamics of capitalist economies, detached from concrete needs (1963, 292). Parsons's theory of money, however, completely in the tradition of the neoclassical theory of money, plays down the possible social implications of money by understanding it only as a neutral means to simplify exchange". Christoph Deutschmann's (1999, 44) criticism follows precisely these lines. He accuses Parsons's theory of money of not recognising wealth characteristics of money" and with this its potential to reach beyond the economic system and to attain social power. This suggests that money is not only a neutral means of exchange; it contains the "additional usefulness" of freedom of choice. Compared to the owner of a good, the owner of money can transfer his or her wealth easily from one use to the next and achieve social power by strategically exploiting this possibility.

All in all, this criticism of Parsons's theory of money from economic sociology basically amounts to the point that he underestimates the social-structural importance of money.

> "The reason for this is suspected to lie in Parsons's premise to acknowledge the neoclassical theory of money" (Beckert 2006).

This criticism is obviously biased in that it fails to recognise Parsons' discussion of precisely social functions of money, his notion of the degrees of freedom attainable thanks to money included. Second, while Parsons is, to be sure, not Marx, his sociology of money brings to light some genuine contradictions and conflicts peculiar to the capitalist economy, and the association of money with an orientation on profit of capitalist firms is, contrary to Parsons' critics, one of the cardinal arguments of the theory. The critics' blunder is made even more glaring by their failure to take account of Parsonian criticism of conventional economics. In point of fact:

> Parsons relied heavily on Keynesian economic theory. And for Keynes it holds true that 'money matters'! [...] Keynes [...] establishes a connection between money and the real economy, a connection that is largely refuted in neoclassical theory. [...] the integration of economic processes depends to a high degree on the creation of confidence (or trust) in processes of social interaction.
>
> Parsons's media theory follows this central characteristic of modern money economies by no longer primarily referring to mechanisms of normative integration for explaining the interpersonal generalization of meaning, but instead turning to the expressive-symbolic communication of affect. What matters is convincing alter in situations that are principally characterized by uncertainty, that is, to produce a "state of confidence." The result of Parsons and Smelser's analysis of financial markets was specifically that no general value orientations guide action, but rather that

> the contingent achievement to convince actors of the positive prospects of their investments is what really counts. The state of confidence can be created only through communication—the possibility of which is established by the very same differentiation processes, induced through the medium of money, that represent the expansion of the freedom of choice for the actor. With that, economic sociology is guided toward an interactionist theory of the communication of affect. None of the critiques from economic sociology on Parsons recognised this theoretical aspect that paves a way to a pragmatist understanding of action in economic contexts. (Beckert 2003).
>
> This commentator of Parsons reckons that "an important theoretical basis for the sociological understanding of the integration of market processes could lie in this because it offers an alternative to the less plausible assumption of primarily normative integration of modern economies" (Beckert 2006).

This is, in our opinion, necessary in doing justice to the Parsonian sociology of money but does not mean, however, that it is flawless.

Parsons' idea of money as a "symbolically generalized medium of communication" (1967) was taken up and modified in different respects by Habermas (1981) and Luhmann (1994). These differences notwistanding, the three theorists' shared starting point was an analogy between language and money. A second analogy was used to introduce other "symbolically generalized media of communication," first among them power. These media, one for each subsystem of society, were constructed in analogy to money.

Parsons himself says that:

> … the theory was developed as a generalization from the properties of money (Parsons 1977a: 198–201; 1977b: 205–8); the very name of the theory indicates a fundamental tension running through it. The idea of media, firstly, refers to the necessity of building links between social relations already differentiated. The idea of interchange, secondly, refers to money being paradigmatic for conceptualizing the "give-and-take" relationships between subsystems, and for measuring the equivalence of those relations as well. In the case of the concepts of symbolization and generalization, thirdly, the former refers to the exchange-value of money as well as the symbolic utility of language (Parsons 1977b, 206); whereas the latter means that every medium can represent several objects in different contexts of interaction. The references to generalization and symbolization are also related to the anthropological and sociological capacities of human beings to operate symbolically and to use these skills in a socially effective way. In that sense, language, as a set of generalized symbols, is the [...] source for the understanding of media. (Chernilo 2002)

Let us consider the basic premise of the theory in somewhat more detail.

It is true that language may be construed as a medium of communication of the aims of its given user. These functions of money (medium of exchange, store of value etc.) can be ascertained from the context of the act in question. In this respect money is indeed similar to language, which can also be deployed as a means of various ends. Thus, language may serve to describe the external world, or own feelings and evaluations; it can be also used as an instrument of singing, persuasion or command. The two last examples show the fallacy inherent in the juxtaposition of language and other media. To utter a command is in no way power itself, which can be conceived of as a capability of forcing other people's action, its modification or stopping, but merely an instrument of its implementation. Meanwhile, with reference to the view assigning power to the political system, it should be noted that it represents only one form of power, i.e. the monopoly of legitimate use of the means of coercion, thus not taking account of what is often termed economic power. Similarly, persuasion is not the same as influence, which can be understood as causing other people to take action, modify or stop within the voluntary social relation, but can be considered merely as a means of such influence.

Thus, in both these cases there occurs a confusion of levels of analysis; language cannot be treated as analogous to social relations mediated by it. However, the central analogy of language and money also suffers from inherent limitations. Despite a much trumpeted term "generalised symbolic medium," it is certainly language as indefinitely elastic medium, by means of which one can both swear and express with Proustian sophistication most subtle psychological tones that deserves the label "universal" or "general" than money, which reduces all qualities to quantities.

In addition, language contains within itself metalanguage; by means of language one can refer to or clarify particular utterances or pronouncements, which cannot be done in case of money. On the contrary, it is the use of money that is usually accompanied by language utterances as explaining the objective of action taken with its participation, or kind of function realised by it.

It happens sometimes, to be sure, as Ganszmann notes, albeit in a limited context, that money performs the role of language requiring, however, an additional use of the body language. Such cases can be observed with reference to tourists in an exotic country when purchasing goods from local inhabitants. Thus, both Habermas and Luhmann are right in defining money in terms of a special language. Indeed, language can exist without money, whilst money cannot function without language.

Exchange means transfer of property. Money as an object of ownership is exchanged in return of, say, some consumer good. Even more clearly this ownership linkage is brought out in the case of money as the foundation of money capital. Meanwhile, language constitutes public good; particular symbols are not, generally speaking, subject to appropriation. One can, however, speak of language as an object of non-economic ownership (professional codes, jargons used by specific groups etc.).

The aforementioned reductionism of money implies that on its basis one can generate communications of considerably poorer content than in the case of language. On the other hand, however, the conceptualisation of money as a means of influence implies that it, significantly more often than language, can serve as a cause of events it is oriented on, be it the selling of a dress by a shop assistant, or booking a hotel room through the internet, thus comprising both direct interaction and indirect socio-economic relation. This provides yet another argument undermining the "communication" metaphor. The use of money cannot be reduced to communication, because it is concerned with non-communication objects: material goods and services or labour power.

As regards transferring the characteristics of money as a model medium onto remaining media, one can note that power is not characterised by any symbolic system that could be conceived of as the direct and undisputable equivalent of money. As distinct from money, any quantification of power units is not feasible. Power is, to be sure, alienable, but it cannot circulate so freely as money. It also cannot be put into any bank account, and owing to the fact that in modern democracies it is election processes that determine the distribution of power, any talk of inflation or deflation of power, as analogous to respective monetary processes, is groundless. In addition, whilst an extension of credit or investment in the economy increases the inner complexity of the system (Plucinski 2006), the intensification of power is a double-edged sword, as it leads, sooner or later, to more or less strong countermeasures, the boomerang reaction of which precludes production of any greater complexity.

Even more questionable is the analogy between money and two remaining media: "Influence and value-commitments are extremely difficult, if not impossible to alienate, measure and accumulate" (Plucinski 2008). In this criticism we are not alone. Other scholars also point out that Parsonian:

analogies are somewhat misleading. Money has properties reaching beyond language. And other media, like power, do not share crucial properties of money (Ganszmann 1988 and 1996).

In abstracting from the differences between objects, institutions, social relations and concepts by lumping together money, power, influence, love, truth and more, in Luhmann's case, or money and power in Habermas' emphasis on the system/life-world distinction, the idea of symbolically generalized media of communication became too fuzzy to be useful … the analogy of language and money, the idea that money is a "special language" is misleading in picturing money merely as a harmless, beneficial social device. (Ganszmann 2007)

CHAPTER I.4.

THE PROPERTY RIGHTS THEORY

I.4.1. Ownership Structure and Performance

According to property rights theorists, there is no evidence to show, theoretically or empirically, that the wealth of the owner is less well protected in the publicly traded corporation with dispersed ownership than in the concentrated ownership or closely held firm. There are a number of economic forces countervailing the effects, if any, of a reduced ability of the owners of a modern corporation to control the corporation's' decision makers. It follows, *a contrario*, that if managers in manager-controlled firms pursued their own objectives at the expense of profit, then such firms should perform worse than owner-controlled firms, other conditions being equal. Is this contention borne out by the empirical evidence available?

I.4.1.1. Evidence on corporate performance

Monsen, Chiu and Cooley (1968) found for a sample of seventy-two corporations, selected from the five hundred largest industrial firms in the United States, that owner-controlled firms show a more efficient allocation of the shareholders' resources, as manifested in a much better return on shareholders' equity. Specifically, they reported that from 1952 to 1963 the ratio of net income to net worth was 75% higher for owner-controlled firms (12.8%) than management-controlled ones (7.3%). Holding the type of industry and the size of the firm constant, in a study published in about the same time, Kamerschen (1968) found a similar, albeit less pronounced, tendency toward higher profits in owner-dominated companies as compared with management-dominated ones, after controlling the effect of concentration, barriers to entry and a number of other variables. What appears at first sight to be a different conclusion emerges from Kamerschen's analysis of those firms which experienced a change in the type of control between 1929 and 1963. The change, which in most instances was from owner to manager dominance, turned out to have a favourable impact on profits. However, the conclusion that manager-controlled firms are more profitable would be too far-fetched, since it is not known what the firms' profitability before the change in control was: "These firms may well have been even more profitable in the past and dropped only after the managers came into power" (McEachern 1975, 40). Moreover, Kamerschen's findings are distorted by the inclusion in his sample of a great number of public utilities whose profits and prices are regulated by government agencies.

The same reservations apply to Jorgensen's research (1972), who used Kamerschen's sample but changed the period covered from 1959–1964 to 1958–1963. Oddly enough, he obtained results different from those of Kamerschen as in their light management-controlled firm they do not exhibit lower profit rates.

In turn, an inquiry carried out by Monsen et al. was, by and large, replicated by Boudreaux's study (1973), the only difference being a slightly altered sample. This study, like the original one, shows that owner-controlled corporations are more profitable. In his study of 187 corporations, Larner (1970) found but small influence of managerial control. According to his analysis, management-controlled firms showed a post-tax profit rate of 0.5% (compared with 5.5% in Monsen,Chiu and Cooley's sample) lower than owner-controlled firms. Radice (1971) examined the average rate of return of eighty-nine British companies between 1957 and 1966. His analysis indicated that the owner-controlled group was more profitable, although when the sample was broken into subsamples by industry, the results were less clear. Also according to other UK studies (Steer and Cable 1978, Cosh and Hughes 1989, Leech and Leahy 1991) profitability is higher with family control. Similarly, profitability is higher with family control in France (Jacquemin and de Ghellinck 1978).

Owner-controlled firms also appeared to earn higher rates of return according to Sorenson's study (1974) of 60 U.S. firms. In a study of 360 firms from the Fortune 500 Largest U.S. corporations, after attempting to control for size and structure, Holl found that MC firms were 4.53% less profitable than OC firms. He concluded that "although a market for corporate control exists, its discipline is imperfect and the imperfection probably increases with firm size" (Sorenson 1977). In Mikkelson & Partch, no significant decline in operating performance of firms that go public has been found. Insider ownership falls from 68% to 18% after ten years of the IPO.

In all these studies, sampling procedures leave something to be desired. In addition, they did not use the same definitions of types of control. Furthermore, in various studies different variables were held constant, which makes any direct comparison of their results difficult. That this factor can make a difference is shown by a replication of Larner's study in which the industry variable was held constant, as distinct from the original research, with the result that management-dominated firms turned out to be more profitable than owner-dominated enterprises, although only slightly so, with the difference not being statistically significant. Similarly, Andersen & Lee (1996) show that many of these studies used data from unreliable commercial sources and correcting for these measurement errors can flip the results. Other common econometric shortcomings of ownership-performance studies are reverse causality (endogeneity), sample selection, missing variables and measurement in variables. See Börsch-Supan & Köke (2002) for a survey of econometric issues.

Last but not least, many studies reported above do not strictly bear on the property rights theorists' thesis which refers to the relationship between the dispersion of shareholding and changes in the wealth of shareholders, as measured by both dividends and capital appreciation. And this is not the same thing as such financial ratios, based as they are on accounting data, as the relation of firms' net income to net worth. In addition, what shareholders are interested in is not the rate of return on their investment but the risk associated with this investment or the variability of returns. Even so, it is fair to say that the studies reviewed above do not lend support to the thesis that corporate managers pursue profit maximisation eagerly and vigorously, regardless of the structure of ownership and control of the firm.

The counterclaim against the property rights school's thesis gains an even greater force when some other studies, differing in certain respects from those referred to above, are considered. Thus, the defect of relying on the firm's rate of profits as a measure of the shareholders' return has been eliminated in McEachern's study of forty-eight large firms (1975, 90). His calculations showed that the combined rate of return, considering all dividends as reinvested, experienced on a share held from 1963 to 1972 inclusively, was significantly higher in the case of firms with a dominant shareholder than for those which were manager-controlled. Firms whose chief executive was also a major owner (holding 4% or more of the equity) showed a rate of return on shareholders' investment that was about twice the rate of firms having no single dominant interest (management-controlled).

That the aforementioned distinction is important, is shown for example by the following study. Leach & Leahy (1991), as reported in Mathiesen, in their research paper in *The Economic Journal* examined 470 large industrial UK firms in the period 1983–85, their main finding being that

OC firms are significantly more profitable than MC firms with regard to return on equity, return on sales, growth of sales and growth of net assets. However, more concentration caused significantly less performance in terms of historic market value/ ordinary share capital and return on sales.

Somewhat similarly, Thonet and Poensgen (1979) after Mathiesen, in their investigation of 62 of 297 large German industrial firms in *The Journal of Industrial Economics*, found no significant difference between MC and OC with regard to return on stocks, growth, variance on equity and beta risk, but that at the same time OC firms were significantly less profitable than MC firms in terms of return on equity and market value to book value. Ambiguous results were also produced by Elliot (1972) in the *Journal of Financial and Quantitative Analysis* study, wherein 88 of 840 firms observed from 1964 to 1967 demonstrated no significant effects between OC and MC except in regard to change in cash flow. Similarly, Ware (1975) after Mathiesen in the *Quarterly of Economics and Business*, in investigating seventy-four U.S. firms in the food and beverage industry found that OC firms were significantly less profitable than MC firms with regard to return on equity, but at the same time OC firms had significantly higher net sales of employees and retained earnings / net income.

Inconclusive results have also been found by other studies such as Holderness and Sheehan (1988), in their *Journal of Financial Economics* study which examined 101 majority held and 101 diffusely held large NYSE and AMEX listed firms in the period 1979–84.

Other relevant information is: 95%> MH >50.1%, ownership by any single individual or entity (other corporation, or fund). DH<20% ownership by any shareholder. Tobin's Q by firm's market value to replacement cost of plants and inventories. Return on equity: Each of the 101 majority held firms are paired with a diffusely held firm with approximately same (1) size by total assets, and
(2) two-digit SIC code. Standard t-tests are applied. The sample is further classified in order to control for identity of MH control: MH by individuals and OC by entities.

The study found no significant difference in performance between majority held (MH) and diffusely held (DH) firms. Much the same applies to Murali and Welch (1989) in their *Journal of Business Finance and Accounting* which investigated forty-three closely held and eighty-three widely held industry matched U.S. firms in the period 1977–81.

Closely held firms- > 50% by small group or individual. Widely held firms- all other firms. (Data from Value Line).

They were interested in adjusted stock market return, return on assets, return on equity, size by assets or equity and some other measures. They found no significant difference in performance between closely held and widely held firms.

Another study which has tried to take account of shareholder interests is that by Stano (1976) in the *Bell Journal of Economics*. It was concerned with 354 of the largest U.S. firms (in the Fortune 500) during 1963–72 and took into account stock return assuming dividends are reinvested, observed during 1965–72. Observed was growth of earnings per share, growth of sales, growth attributable to mergers & acquisitions, beta risk, equity/assets and size by assets. The study found that SOC firms were significantly more profitable than MC firms, but WOC were not.

Some of the above mentioned shortcomings (except the last two) were avoided in a more limited but better controlled study by Shelton (1967), who examined profit rates of identical restaurants of a large chain. He found for a sample of twenty-two restaurants that the same franchises were much more profitably when operated by owner-managers than by hired managers (9.5% compared with 1.5%), and that profits almost always increased with a change from hired manager to owner operation, while with a change in an opposite direction the reverse was the case. The results, however, might have been affected by the fact that the managers appointed by the parent company were not familiar with the local conditions.

However, a study of the food and beverage industry found that whereas OC firms tended to have a higher average product of labour than MC firms, MC firms had a higher rate of return than OC firms (Ware, 1975). Glassman & Rhoades's study (1980) also focuses on a single industry, specifically 1,406 banks. Upon examination the authors found that owner controlled banks tend to have higher profit rates that manager controlled ones. Their study is notable for including tests for nonlinearity to empirically determine at what percentage of ownership performance differences between owner and manager controlled firms become apparent. The tests showed that it was only at a relatively high level of ownership control that the effects of that control are evident. Moreover, Glassman & Rhoades, again unlike most other studies of the owner vs.manager issue, accounted for the market structure, their conclusion being that "the level of competition affects the level of managerial discretion" (1980, 269). The product market constraint was also taken account of in Palmer's study (1973). He showed that the control type mattered only when this constraint was relatively weak and thus firms had a considerable monopoly power (with an analogous tendency toward higher profitability of OC companies). Kamerschen found no statistically significant relationship between concentration ratios and firm profitability, but found a positive and significant association between barriers to entry and profitability.

These results are significant in so far as at least according to some claims made by the property rights theorists, their conclusions as to the efficiency with which different property right systems are used "do not depend on the degree of competitiveness" (Demsetz 1966, 64). This is by no means an exceptional statement; De Alessi also maintains that "the utility maximization hypothesis … seems to be independent of the degree of competition and of whether the market is open or closed" (1973, 843). On the other hand, elsewhere the same writer expresses a quite different opinion to the effect that "competition from other firms in the industry and from prospective entrants provides a check on performance, encourages the evolution of internal control devices, and ultimately eliminates higher cost firms unable or unwilling to adjust" (De Alessi 1983, 74).

I.4.2. Managerial rewards

If evidence tends to call into question the general thesis that the shareholders' wealth is protected in the dispersed ownership corporation equally well as in the concentrated ownership corporation, this may be due to the failure of internal and external control forces which are regarded in the property rights literature as diminishing managerial discretion.

According to the property rights literature, the identity of interest between the managers and shareholders is engendered by tying compensation of the former to the wealth of the latter. The proponents of this thesis are indeed able to point to several studies that appear to lend support to it. In his widely quoted study, Lewellen (1971) found that the role of equity-related income, including share options, capital gains and dividends occasioned by the top managers' shareholdings in their own companies in their total income outweighed that of the salary-plus-bonus portion of income. Specifically, for the sample of large manufacturing corporations, with extreme values deleted to exclude firms with still pronounced family ownership and control, the ratio of the former to the latter increased from about 0.8 in the early 1940s to 2.8 in the early 1960s (1971, 102). Lewellen concluded that "this does not seem the kind of circumstance which would lead one to believe that executives are apt to become indifferent to the legitimate interests of shareholders. Indeed, over time, the apparent tendency is toward a growing harmony of objectives" (1971, 92).

In a parallel study of a smaller sample of thirty-nine companies, Masson showed that "a significant number of firms do have stock market return as an important determinant of executive compensation" (1971, 1285). Thus, evidence would appear to confirm the contention that "a manager is paid to increase the wealth of stockholders" (Furubotn & Pejovich 1972, 1151).

Unfortunately, matters are not that simple. Shareholders may be more interested in dividends than in capital gains, and the share option, claimed to be the most effective mechanism for inducing the management to run the firm in the best interest of its owners, orients the managers on share appreciation above all. Another problem with share option schemes, profit-sharing systems and related mechanisms is that they cannot exclude free-riding (Williamson 1970, 93). That is to say, because, as is generally known, the performance of the firm is the resultant of a multitude of factors, some of them controlled by the management and some not, and, even more to the point, some of them related more to certain managers' actions and some affected more by the others' decisions, it cannot be insured that only those who are responsible for a given improvement in profits or an increase in share prices etc. will benefit from them, and those who have not contributed will be excluded from sharing in the gains available.

Perhaps more importantly, there is also much evidence to the contrary. First, a number of studies showed that executive compensation is primarily determined by sales, which would point to the power of managers to pursue their own objectives at the expense of shareholders' interests. Thus, for instance, McGuire, Chiu & Elbing (1962), building on the research of Patton (1961) and Roberts (1959), found that executive remuneration was causally related to sales volumes. Lewellen & Huntsman, drawing upon Lewellen's original sample and correcting for multicollinearity (correlation between sales and profits) and some other statistical or measurement problems, demonstrated, to be sure, that "both reported profits and equity market values are substantially more important in the determination of executive compensation than are sales," their inference being that "there is a greater incentive for management to shape its decision rules in a manner consonant with shareholder interest than to seek the alternative goal of revenue maximization" (1959, 718–9). The results of later research, however, have been more mixed. Larner's research (1970) generally confirmed Lewellen & Huntsman's findings about the relationship between compensation and profit. Ciscel (1974), however, found more evidence for the alternative position on executive remuneration. Smyth, Boyes & Peseau (1974) re-examined Lewellen & Huntsman's model and found both profits and sales had a positive effect on executive compensation.

Similarly, in what has been perhaps the most sophisticated attempt to eliminate all the econometric problems encountered in testing for executive compensation determinants, Ciscel & Carroll (1980) failed to resolve the controversy. On the other hand, two studies of the issue relating to Great Britain (Cosh 1975; Meeks & Whittington 1975) indicate that executive compensation is more highly influenced by sales than by profits.

Of course, the results of the above mentioned studies have to be interpreted with caution. Even abstracting, for the moment, from those findings which stress the link between compensation and sales, a positive relationship between profits and executive rewards does not necessarily imply that managerial objectives coincide with shareholders' goals. "profit maximisation" and "shareholder welfare maximisation" are not equivalent concepts. This is admitted by one of the leading exponents of the property rights school, who argues that:

> The accounting profits relevant to a manager's wealth would roughly be limited to those occurring during his tenure in office, and this time horizon would necessarily be shorter than a shareholder's to whom all future accounting periods matter. It follows that a manager would have the incentive to increase current accounting profits and the length of his tenure at the expense of the owners' wealth (market value of equity. (De Alessi 1973, 848)

More recent research based on a study of 459 major U.S. companies showed that executive compensation was almost completely unrelated to total returns to shareholders (defined as capital gains plus dividends). Specifically, according to these calculations, only a paltry 4% of the differences between the pay-packets of the chief executives of America's largest corporations can be accounted for by the performance of their companies. Likewise, Towers Perrin, a consultancy specialising in pay and benefits, calculated that in 1990 the median increase in the chief executive's pay at 350 of America's biggest corporations was 6.7%, even though shareholder value (share price plus dividends) fell by 9% (The Economist 199, 21). Another consultancy, Booz-Allen & Hamilton, in an earlier study obtained much the same results. Over ten years, on an inflation-discounted basis, chief executive pay increased about 40%, while shareholder value remained entirely flat. With dividends excluded, shareholder value would have dropped 31% (Thackray 1983, 64).

It may well be that Lewellen's and other analogous results were valid for a particular period of time. Stock options were popular when the stock market boomed in the 1960s, but largely declined in importance during the flat market in the 1970s. Lewellen himself, in a later survey, following the end of the stock market boom, noted the marked decline in the share of stock options in the compensation package from 36% in 1955–63 to only 12% in 1970–73 and a decline in equity-related rewards from 44% to 23% (1975, 161–4). Lewellen also noted that the decrease in the role of stock market-based rewards did not entail any slowdown in the growth of management earnings; it is only that for this equity-related compensation other forms of payment were substituted.

This leads to an important conclusion that "the 'incentive' effects of different kinds of income may be overrated if the determinants of income are under management control and management can rearrange them to achieve predetermined result" (Herman 1981, 96). The subsequent popularity of bonuses based formally on performance, such as earnings per share growth, is a case in point. These schemes "are fixed by the management or the board at levels of their own choosing" (Herman 1981, 96), and so appear to be simply one method of reaching income targets set by managers themselves. This, concludes Herman, "should give pause in thinking about both the equitable basis and incentive impacts of compensation systems" (1981, 96). Similarly, a management consultant observed in the early 1980s that "executive wealth and stockholder wealth no longer run in tandem, as they did in the 1960s" (Thackray 1983, 62).

According to *Management Today*: "In that decade the systems seem to have been basically equitable. Corporate performance was excellent by any measure ... Executive pay was not nearly as complex and multi-layered as it has since become. The subsequent proliferation of annual bonuses has often been only very loosely tied to annual performance" (Thackray 1983, 63). Bonuses based on the rise in earnings per share might appear to be performance-tied, but it would be a mistaken impression: "Bonuses became a colossal part of total anticipated compensation—amounting to 70% of chief executive salaries in 1982. What's more, earnings per share—apart from being easily manipulated—had the further disadvantage in inflationary times of being a poor indicator of success or failure. Even worse, truly talented managers have been shortchanged by the inequities[1] of performance measurement" (Thackray 1983, 64).

This is not an isolated opinion; according to *The Economist*: "America's experience suggests that rewards geared to corporate profits, sales or quarterly earnings per share often do more to enrich the managers than the

---

[1] It would be hard to argue, however, that an effective cure for these ills is the institution of guaranteed bonuses, so common in recent years, especially in the finance industry.

shareholders" (1985, 73). Seven years later, this judgement was echoed: "Ironically, bosses' pay has soared over the past decade because of the spread of incentive schemes designed to do the opposite: make bosses act less like bureaucrats and more like entrepreneurs. These schemes have gone badly wrong, loading American bosses with treasure no matter what happens to their companies" (*The Economist* 1992c, 15).

These reservations apply to share options as well. Advocates of share options argue that they give managers an incentive to increase the company's long-term prosperity, and so the wealth of its owners. The share option, which of course is the right to buy shares at a pre-determined price, irrespective of the market price, has many defects, however. One of these has been already touched on above; options are far from being an ideal measure of executive performance if only because many factors beyond the control of its managerial holder, such as bull markets, inflation, takeover bids and the like, can bring him unearned gains.

Interestingly enough, while top executives do reap such unearned benefits, they are at the same time protected from the adverse effects of other outside effects. That is to say, if the market price of a company's shares falls below the so-called strike price (at which shares can be purchased by exercising the option), making thereby the options worthless, senior executives are typically offered new options with a lower strike price.

Brenner, Sundaram & Yermack found that on average 1.3% of executives had options reset each year-average reduction in exercise price of 39%. The S&P 500 Index rose by about 50% during the period studied by the authors, with no significant downturns. The frequency of resetting is likely to be much higher in falling markets. When share prices plunged in the late summer of 1998, many firms re-priced their options just in time to enjoy massive gains when the market rebounded. James Record, an analyst with SNL Securities, a research firm, found that seventeen financial-services firms lowered their strike prices a previous Autumn by one-third on average; since then, their share prices have, on average, trebled. The fact that firms re-price managers' options reduces to nonsense the comparison of bosses with owners, who cannot write off downside risk so blithely.

Executive options open up a plethora of ways of gaining extra profits. Reloadable option plans are schemes under which an executive who exercises options pays the exercise price by handing over firm shares that he or she already owns, and receives a new option for each share tendered with the same expiration date as the old options being exercised. These plans allow executives to profit from share price volatility even if the long-term share performance is flat.

Erik Lie, a finance professor at the University of Iowa's College of Business, has analyzed 5,977 option grants between 1992 and 2002 and found that it was statistically improbable for them not to have been backdated at many companies. According to this financial expert, "backdating is the practice of marking a document with a date that precedes the actual date. The benefit of backdating ESO grants lies in the fact that CEOs are usually granted at-the-money, i.e. the exercise price of the options is set to equal the market price of the underlying stock on the grant date. Because the option value is higher if the exercise price is lower, executives prefer to be granted options when the stock price is at its lowest. Backdating allows executives to choose a past date when the market price was particularly low, thereby inflating the value of the options.

The *Wall Street Journal* pointed to a CEO option grant dated October 1998, illustrating the potential benefit of backdating to the recipient. The number of shares subject to option was 250,000 and the exercise price was \$30. Given a year-end price of \$85, the intrinsic value of the options at the end of the year was (\$85–\$30) x 250,000 = \$13,750,000. In comparison, had the options been granted at the year-end price when the decision to grant to options actually might have been made, the year-end intrinsic value would have been zero. In addition, The terms "spring-loading" and "bullet-dodging" refer to the practices of timing option grants to take place before expected good news or after expected bad news, respectively. The term "forward dating" has also been used to describe the practice of setting the grant date to occur after predicted future price declines and/or before predicted future price increases.

Thus, executive share options, unlike normal shares owned by ordinary shareholders, are a one-way street; their lucky holders can win but, for all practical purposes, cannot lose. This rule applies to incentive arrangements in general:

> The executive who was 'rewarded' for success on the upside is deemed not responsible for slippage and failure on the downside … In difficult times, the leadership of corporate America shows little inclination to share sacrifices along with shareholders. Indeed, when it proves impossible to play by the old rules, corporations simply junk their previous pay-for-performance incentive packages and rewrite new ones in management's favour. (Thackray 1983, 62 and 65)

The incentive value of option schemes is also doubtful in another respect. In most such plans, the strike price is the market price of the shares on the day of the grant which is usually valid for ten years. These are hardly demanding terms. Moreover, in most cases some of executive options can be exercised as early as six months after they are granted, and all of them within four years. This, understandably but contrary to its alleged merits as a long-term incentive, encourages the holder of such an option to act in ways that push up the share price in the short term, so than he or she can collect his windfall gains. And this conclusion has, again, a broader relevance: "according to many commentators of America's corporate scene, "the spread of performance-related pay has encouraged many executives to focus of short-run financial indicators at the expense of investments that will boost longer-term profitability" (*The Economist* 1988b, 50).

Thus, upon closer inspection, incentive, "performance-related" schemes do not assimilate the position of top managers as regards their exposure to risks and opportunities to that of normal shareholders; in terms of the property rights school, and contrary to its claims, they do not appear to face "the same mixture of rewards and penalties as other shareholders face" (*The Economist* 1992, 22).

This position is hardly altered by the managers' direct shareholdings. Arguably, when managers of large firms hold significant equity stakes the question of their remuneration may become less important since the majority of their income would come from their equity stakes (Mehran 1995, 173). However, the fact of the matter is that the fraction of his or her employer firm's shares that an American chief executive of a large public company owned was ten times smaller in 1980s than in the 1930s (Brownstein & Panner 1992, 35). Jensen & Murphy (1990) investigated 120 largest U.S. firms by market value and found that CEO mean (median) ownership declined from 1.7% (0.3%) in 1938 to 1.5% (0.05%) in 1974 to 1% (0.03%) in 1984. MBOs have increased from $1.2 billion in 1979 to $77 billion in 1987.

Holderness, Kroszner & Sheehan (1999), using a full sample, observed 1,419 listed U.S. firms in 1935 and 4,202 listed U.S. firms in 1995, and a limited sample of the 120 largest U.S. firms in 1935 and in 1995. They determined the percentage and monetary ownership by the firms officers and directors both directly and indirectly, and the percentage and monetary ownership by the CEO.

Combined shareholding by officers and directors in the ranges were (0-5%), (5-25%), and (25-100%). Tobin's Q by market value of stock, and book value of debt to book value of assets (1) size by total assets, (2) leverage by debt to assets, and (3) industry by one digit SIC codes. Full sample descriptive statistics were as follows: Mean (median) ownership by managers and directors increased from 13% (7%) in 1935 to 21% (14%) in 1995. In $ millions it increased from $18 ($3) to $73 ($16). For any given firm size ownership is higher in 1995 than in 1935. However, using the value-weighted mean, ownership increases insignificantly from 4.2% in 1935 to 5.9% in 1995, and median ownership of the 10% largest firms has fallen from 2.1% to 1.5%. In the full sample OLS, for the limited sample mean (median) ownership by CEO is 1.25% (0.09%) in 1935 and 1.25% (0.06%) in 1995. In $ millions the mean (median) ownership increased by $23.6 ($1.5) in 1935 to $386.5 ($11.9) in 1995.

According to the study, the reasons for such changes include factors such as lower volatility of stocks and greater hedging opportunities associated with the development of the financial markets that lower the risk of managers holding equity. Above all, however, the possibility of managerial ownership substituting for alternate corporate governance mechanisms did not find any empirical support (Holderness, Kroszner & Sheehan 1999). It should be also noted that from 1988 to 2003, the average change in managerial ownership is significantly negative every year for American firms (Fahlenbrach & Stulz 2007). Even more significantly, the absolute sensitivity of CEO wealth to performance remains small. For a $1,000 change in firm value, the wealth of the average CEO of large, public corporations currently changes only by about $10.62

All else being equal, then, a CEO who wrote themself a checque for an extra $1,000 would net about $990 after taking into account the impact of the change in firm value on his shares and options (Bebchuk, Fried & Walker 2001).

Nevertheless, to be fair, one should review other empirical studies bearing on the issue of the relationship between managerial ownership and corporate performance. A major study has examined the impact of managerial ownership on risk-taking and firm performance. The study utilized data from thirty randomly selected companies from four industries in four different sectors: Industries are oil and gas and field services from the energy sector; insurance, property, and casualty from the financial sector; drugs from the health sector; and computer and data processing from the technology sector. This yielded a total of 120 observations.

Accounting measures and correlation analysis were used to determine the relationship between managerial ownership, risk-taking, and firm performance in each industry and for the whole sample. However, the research found no significant relationship between these variables in different industries and for the whole sample.

According to the study, "managerial ownership seems to be merely a reflection of the way in which managers receive their benefits. Managerial ownership does not seem to have any incentive to work harder for improving the company's performance in the accounting sense" (Jahmani & Ansari 2006).

It is along the same lines that the insider-reward augmentations argument, according to which: "Other things being equal, managers may prefer equity compensation when they expect their firm to perform well and, consequently, the value of the firm to increase. As a result, higher levels of insider ownership are expected at firms with high corporate values" (Cho 1998, 115). It is also other researchers that argue that owner-managers are insiders who may capitalize on their insights by increasing their ownership when they expect the financial performance to improve and decrease their ownership when they expect the financial performance to deteriorate (Loderer & Martin 1997, 237).

Similarly, Himmelberg, Hubbard and Palia (1999), using Panel data from Compustat, observed small and large U.S. firms—398 in 1982, 425 in 1983 and 427 in 1984, and varius performance indices, such as Tobin's Q by market value of stock + estimated market value of preferred stock + book value of total liabilities to book value of total assets, and return on assets. They found no relation between managerial ownership and performance even for sub-samples of large and small firms.

It must be admitted that there are a number of studies that reach other conclusions. Mehran (1995) investigated 153 large and small industrial U.S. firms for the period 1979–80. Taking into account Tobin's Q by market value of all firm securities to replacement costs of all tangible assets and return on assets, he found that both performance measures increased significantly with CEO ownership. Other findings were the significant effect of ownership by all officers and directors or ownership by outside directors. Blockholder ownership is not significant in any sense. Morck, Shleifer & Vishny (1988a), in the *Journal of Financial Economics*, investigated 371 of the largest U.S. firms (from the Fortune 500) in 1980. They took into account the combined shareholding by all members of the board in the ranges: (0–5%), (5–25%) and (25–100%). With a combined shareholding by the top two officers, and a dummy for the presence of the founder on board, their finding being that profitability is significantly increasing for board ownership in the (0–5%) range and significantly decreasing in the (5–25%) range and if the founder is present on the board of old firms. Similar results for top two officers.

> It is possible, however, that these results are accounted for by certain neglected factors, as some other studies seem to suggest. One such study examines whether the relationship between equity ownership and firm value varies with the growth opportunities of firms. For high growth firms, it finds that equity ownership is only significant in three out of nine regressions while for low growth firms, it is significant in eight of the nine regressions. This provides some evidence that equity ownership may be more important for low growth firms because managers in these firms can only increase the size of the firm (see above), and consequently the magnitude of their utility, by taking negative present value projects. However, the fact that the coefficient on the equity ownership variable for high growth firms is significantly larger than the coefficient for low growth firms in two of the regressions is inconsistent with the argument (McConnell & Servaes 1995).

Another study has focussed on how UK companies compare to their U.S. counterparts because of institutional differences across the two markets. The authors find a strong U-shaped relationship between the level of managerial ownership and the probability that the roles of chairman and CEO are split, that a non-executive director is appointed as chairman, and the proportion of non-executive directors on the board. However, they report a generally weak relationship between firm value and managerial ownership, board structure and the combination of managerial ownership and board structure. These results cast doubt on the effectiveness of these internal corporate governance mechanisms (Faccio & Lasfer 1999, Cass Business School Research Paper).

Another investigation of the issue of whether managerial ownership is related to firm value found that data is consistent with firms facing agency problems of empire building and overvalued equity. Firm value is impacted by managerial ownership through specific managerial actions of higher labour expenses, accruals management and avoiding debt that are subject to agency problems (Khanna 2005). The agency approach, e.g. Jensen & Meckling (1976), Morck, Shleifer & Vishny (1988) and Stulz (1988), posits that greater managerial ownership benefits shareholders because it increases managers' incentives to increase firm value, but when managerial ownership becomes too large, it enables managers to entrench themselves, so that firm value falls as managerial ownership increases.

Meanwhile, property rights scholars such as Demsetz (1983) and Demsetz & Lehn (1985) represent what has been called the contracting theory approach to managerial ownership. The contracting approach posits that firms have an optimal level of managerial ownership that solves a principal-agent problem. Shareholders set the terms of a compensation contract for management which includes management's ownership in the firm. If actual managerial ownership is the solution to a contracting problem between management and shareholders and there are no adjustment costs, firm value would always be maximized given the constraints faced by shareholders (Fahlenbrach & Stulz 2007).The authors of that label argue that the relevant empirical evidence can be better explained by an alternative managerial ownership theory, which they call the managerial discretion theory of inside ownership. This theory emphasizes that managers own shares to maximize their welfare.

A more general approach to managerial compensation has been also proposed—under the "rent extraction" view, the executives, as part of the agency problem, influence pay levels to provide themselves with rent. Under rent extraction corporate managers are firmly in control. The outside directors are connected to the executives by bonds of interest, collegiality, or affinity (Bebchuk et al. 2001). And indeed, it is in this vein that one should interpret studies such as that by Cho (1998), who showed that managerial ownership had no impact on corporate value and investment but that corporate value had a significant impact on managerial ownership, or by McConnell & Servaes (1990) in the *Journal of Financial Economics* who investigated 173 firms in 1976 and 1,093 firms in 1986. They measured U.S. firms listed on NYSE or AMEX using such measures as (1) Tobin's Q by market value of stock, preferred stock and debt to replacement value of assets, and (2) return on assets by earnings before depreciation, interest and taxes divided by replacement value of assets.

It turns out that both measures of profitability are significantly increasing with ownership by managers and directors, and this relation is significantly roof-shaped with a performance peek for 69% ownership in 1976 and 41% in 1986. For the fact of the matter is that with such high stockholding, managers in question become blockholders themselves, which implies a necessity of changing their classification.

And indeed, in the next study, using the new 1988 sample reproduces the results from McConnell & Servaes (1990). The only difference is that Tobin's Q now is significantly increasing with blockholder ownership. For all sample periods the relation between Tobin's Q and all ownership variables is insignificant for high-growth firms and significantly positive and roof-shaped for low-growth firms (McConnell and Servaes 1995).

The same necessity of reclassification is shown by Denis & Denis (1994) (after Mathiesen) in the *Journal of Corporate Finance* who studied 72 U.S. firms with above 50% insider ownership by managers and directors finding no difference in performance between majority controlled firms and other firms. They also found that the likelihood of majority control increased significantly with family or founder involvement.

Indeed, 80% of majority controlled firms had substantial family or founder involvement, majority controlled firms had significantly less outside directors, less outside blockholdings, less institutional shareholdings, and paid less dividends and dual class shares.

Another study which shows that our comment is relevant is that by Wruck (1989) (after Mathiesen) in the *Journal of Financial Economics* who find that profitability is significantly increasing for changes in board voting stock in the (0–5%) range and significantly decreasing in the (5–25%) range. Considering the model using changes in combined voting stock by managers, directors and 35% block holders, profitability is significantly decreasing in the (5–25%) range and significantly increasing in the (25–100%) range.

Furthermore, even leaving for the moment these criticisms aside, there remains one fact inconsistent with the property rights position, because it suggests the ineffectiveness of corporate control mechanisms. But if one particular level of managerial ownership maximizes value, why would other combinations of managerial ownership and Q or any other corporate performance measure for that matter appear in the data?

There is, to be sure, one other possibility suggested by Coles, Lemmon & Meschke (2003). The authors, however, refute that argument:

> The point at which the maximum of the hump-shaped relationship between Q and ownership appears in our sample is 20.09%. Based on our estimates of the Q-performance relation, increasing CEO ownership by one standard deviation, from 14.41% to 20.06% implies an increase in firm value equal to $659 million on average. It seems implausible that the transaction costs of realigning CEO pay-performance sensitivity exceed that figure, much less the even greater amounts associated with larger departures of ownership from that which supports maximal Q. Based on this line of reasoning and plausible transaction costs, there is far more variation in observed ownership structure than one would expect. (Coles, Lemmon & Meschke 2003)

Related reservations as those put forward above, where it has been indicated that different categories of corporate stakeholders are being conflated, apply to studies which use data referring to directors rather than managers, while it is only insider executives who should be compared with non-executive stockholders (among whom board members can be found as well). After all, as Hanson explains, some directors should be:

> … classified as inside if they are current or past employees or are related to the firm's chief executive or part of the founding family. Directors fall into the gray area if they have a close but indirect relation with the firm such as

> consultants, lawyers, or executives of firms with a business relationship with the firm. Otherwise, directors are deemed independent outside directors such as executives of unrelated firms, private investors, or directors from outside the business community. (Hanson 1997).

This applies to, for example, Keasey, Short & Watson's (1994) research in *Small Business Economics* which studied seventy-two small and medium sized UK firms in 1986–88, their finding being that performance is significantly increasing with board ownership and this relation is significantly roof-shaped.

Similarly, the results of the following study can be interpreted in insider entrenchment terms: standard mechanisms of corporate control are ineffective and its functions are taken over by the insiders. Agrawal & Knoeber (1996) (after Mathiesen), in the *Journal of Financial and Quantitative Economics*, investigated 383 large U.S. firms (from the "Forbes 800") in 1987. According to his study, Tobin's Q by market value of stock, preferred stock and debt to book value of assets decreases significantly with board outsiders. It increases significantly with insider ownership.

As regards the relevance of the entrenchment argument, suffice to mention the following study by Boyle, Carter & Stover (1998) (after Mathiesen) from the *Journal of Financial and Quantitative Analysis*. They found that insider ownership is weakly (10% level) negatively related to the number of anti-takeover provisions at levels of ownership below 10.3%. This is evidence of substitution between two entrenchment mechanisms.

Even so, there are studies that contradict such results, for example Kole (1996) (after Mathiesen) in *Working Paper* investigated 371 of the largest U.S. firms (of the Fortune 500), finding that profitability is only significantly increasing for board ownership in the (0–5%) range.

By contrast, while in 1960 the average boss of a big American corporation earned about twenty times as much as the engineer who designed their products, in the late 1980s they made over forty times as much (*The Economist* 1989, 79). In 1981 the average chief executive was paid $315,000, about fifteen times as much as a factory worker ($21,300). Ten years later, a survey of the five hundred largest U.S. corporations showed that the total annual pay of chief executives (including the estimated value of stock options) averaged $2 million, about eighty-five times the pay of the average factory worker (*The Economist* 1992, 22).

Compensation for top executives has grown at an unprecedented rate resulting in a dramatic increase in the ratio between the compensation of executives and rank-and-file employees. The chief executive officers of large U.S. companies averaged $10.8 million in total compensation in 2006, more than 364 times the pay of the average U.S. worker, according to the latest survey by the United for a Fair Economy.

> According to a recent study by ERI Economic Research Institute and *The Wall Street Journal*, executive compensation grew substantially faster than corporate earnings in the former year. The study of forty-five randomly selected public companies found that executive compensation increased 20.5% from a year ago, while revenues grew just 2.8%.
>
> During the last twelve months, the study found that the overall total compensation of the highest-paid executive increased 20.5% while revenues increased 2.8%. As of February 2008, the average top executive received an overall total compensation of $18,813,697. In comparison, the median pay for workers rose only 3.5% to $36,140 in 2007, from $34,892 the previous year, according to the U.S. Bureau of Labor Statistics.
>
> Moreover, while (and this pattern is consistent with our earlier remarks) "performance-based" bonuses for chief executives of large public companies dropped in 2007, companies more than made up for that decline by giving out bigger discretionary bonuses and other payments not tied to a specific financial target, according to a recent study by Equilar, the executive compensation research firm.
>
> Equilar found that the median value of bonuses tied to performance fell 18.6% in 2007, from $949,249 to $772,717. Thanks, however, to sizable increases in discretionary awards and multi-year performance awards, overall CEO bonuses for 2007 inched up 1.4% to a median value of $1.41 million from $1.39 million in 2006. (AFL-CIO 2008).

An example of the degree of control over their pay that some CEOs may have is Angelo Mozilo, chairman and chief executive officer of Countrywide Financial Corp, who brought in a second compensation consultant to renegotiate his package in 2006 when the first one said his pay package was inflated. In an e-mail message, Mozilo complained to John England of Towers Perrin, who helped redo his pay package: "Boards have been placed under enormous pressure by the left-wing anti-business press and the envious leaders of unions and other so-called 'C.E.O. Comp Watchers'."

Mozilo's renegotiated contract with Countrywide included an annual salary of $1.9 million, an incentive bonus of between $4 million and $10 million, perks and fringe benefits, as well as $37.5 million in severance benefits. Under public pressure, Mozilo subsequently agreed to give up the severance package.

> 2010 was another good year to make lots of money—if you were a CEO. CEOs of the largest companies received, on average, $11.4 million

> in total compensation last year, according to the AFL-CIO analysis of 299 companies in the S&P 500 Index. Overall, CEOs of the 299 companies in the AFL-CIO Executive PayWatch database received a combined total of $3.4 billion in pay in 2010, enough to support 102,325 jobs paying the median wages for all workers.
>
> The Wall Street executives who helped create the financial crisis and economic recession also did well. While cash bonuses fell, in accord with the above-mentioned restructuring of executive pay packages, total compensation for Wall Street firms increased in 2010. The Wall Street Journal estimates that total compensation at large financial services companies rose 5.7 percent to a record $149 billion in 2010. (AFL-CIO 2011)

The average CEO pay of companies in the SP 500 Index rose to $12.94 million in 2011.[1] Overall, the average level of CEO pay in the SP 500 Index increased 13.9 percent in 2011, following a 22.8 percent increase in CEO pay in 2010.

Table 1: 2011 Average CEO Pay at SP 500 Index Companies

Salary	$1,091,182
Bonus	$268,110
Stock Awards	$5,279,828
Option Awards	$2,352,544
Non-Equity Incentive Plan Compensation	$2,382,529
Pension and Deferred Compensation Earnings	$1,308,625
All Other Compensation	$252,657
TOTAL	$12,935,475

The ratio of CEO-to-worker pay between CEOs of the SP 500 Index companies and U.S. workers widened to 380 times in 2011 from 343 times in 2010.[2] Back in 1980, the average large company CEO only received 42 times the average worker's pay.[3]

CEOs supposedly deserve all this money for increasing shareholder value. However, while the average CEO pay increased 13.9 percent at SP 500 Index companies in 2011, the SP 500 Index ended the year at the same level as it started.

This double-digit increase in average CEO pay for the second consecutive year shows just how disconnected the top 1 percent is from the 99 percent. In 2011, average wages increased just 2.8 percent and average worker pay totaled $34,053.[4]

Both workers and shareholders have suffered over the previous decade. On Dec. 31, 2010, the SP 500 Index closed 19 percent below its high on

March 24, 2000. U.S. median household income fell $3,719 between 2000 and 2010.[5]

Runaway CEO pay is one reason why income inequality is growing in the United States. A Congressional Budget Office report found that inequality has risen dramatically, with the top 1 percent receiving most of the income growth between 1979 and 2007.[6]

What's more, a new study by economist Emmanuel Saez at the University of California shows that in 2010—the first year of the economy's recovery from the Great Recession—the top 1 percent captured 93 percent of the growth in income. (AFL-CIO.ORG. 2012)

What about the standard arguments for executive skyrocketing compensation, if the latter word is proper at all. Firstly it may be surmised that these CEOs are being paid to expand their companies, grow the real economy and create good-paying jobs. However, this argument does not stand up to evidence. According to the Federal Reserve, U.S. corporations held a record $1.93 trillion in cash on their balance sheets. A lack of business investment is one reason that more than fourteen million Americans remain unemployed.[2]

During the past decade, CEOs of the largest American companies received more in compensation than ever before in U.S. history. They, secondly, supposedly deserved this money for increasing stock prices. But did they? On December 31, 2010 the S&P 500 Index closed 19% below its high on March 24, 2000.

Over the past decade, shareholders—including workers—lost trillions of dollars in retirement savings through the collapse of the internet stock bubble and the corporate accounting scandals at Enron and other companies. More recently, shareholders have suffered further declines from the bursting of the real estate bubble and the Wall Street financial crisis. CEO pay is often set based on peer group analysis rather than what is best for the company's own internal pay structure.

> Excessive CEO pay is fundamentally a corporate governance problem. The board of directors is supposed to protect shareholder interests and ensure that CEO pay reflects performance. However, at approximately two-thirds of companies, the chief executive officer also chairs the board.

---

[2] Joblessness in the U.S. remains stubbornly high; the unemployment rate in the United States was last reported at 9.1% in May of 2011 (it later dropped somewhat). From 1948 until 2010 the United States' Unemployment Rate averaged 5.70% reaching an historical high of 10.80% in November of 1982 and a record low of 2.50% in May of 1953.

> When the same person serves as both chairman and CEO, it is impossible to objectively monitor and evaluate his or her own performance.
>
> CEOs also dominate the election of directors. The vast majority of directors are hand-picked by incumbent management. Because of the proxy rules, it is prohibitively expensive for long-term shareholders to run their own director candidates. Moreover, even if a majority of shareholders withhold support from directors, they still are elected to the board at many companies. (AFL-CIO 2008) [3]

Small wonder that more and more critics are pointing out that aside from the issue of the relationship between compensation and performance (which is generally lacking), such huge pay rises are unavoidably subject to the law of diminishing returns and have less and less, if any, motivational impact. John Kotter, a professor at the Harvard Business School, has this to say: "I don't think you can encourage leadership with money. In fact, you can discourage it. The kind of people who make good leaders are not obsessed with money." W. Edwards Deming, the famous quality-control expert, adds that "incentive schemes have destroyed teamwork at many big American companies, setting worker against worker, manager against manager" (*The Economist* 1992b, 21).

That the above mentioned law is indeed at work has been shown by a study of 955 chief executives, which revealed the negative correlation between the number and value of incentive schemes and the company's performance. According to the study, each new plan offered to the chief executive lowered shareholders' ten-year compounded return by 1.4 percentage points (*The Economist* 1992b, 22).

To sum up our discussion in this section, it seems fair to state that the incentive systems fail to motivate managers to maximise the wealth of shareholders. If this is the case, then, the question is the probability of replacement of the management if its members behave in ways not acceptable to a majority of the stockholders (Alchian & Demsetz 1972, 788). The most important mechanism of such displacement is corporate takeover.

---

[3] To be sure, in the UK at least, there are some plans of limited reforms according to which companies will have to have binding votes on executive pay every three years. BBC business editor Robert Peston said executive pay rises may also be tempered by the new simplicity and clarity Mr Cable(Business Secretary) hopes to bring to the question of how much bosses actually pocket every year.

> "Right now it is very difficult to see the total amount that any executive takes home because the remuneration sections of annual reports are immensely long, complex and woolly, especially in regard to earnings from large and important long-term incentive plans."

I.4.3. Market for Corporate Control

The evidence on the relationship between turnover and performance is mixed. Huson, Parrino & Starks (1999) find that CEO turnover is more sensitive to changes in operating income from 1989 to 1994 than in earlier years. On the other hand, Murphy (1999) finds that CEO turnover is less sensitive to industry-adjusted stock performance from 1990 to 1995 than in earlier years. A study of the Forbes 500 firms in the 1980s determined that takeover bids were more common in industries in which CEO's were overpaid, but found no significant difference between the compensation of the CEO's of firms that were and were not targeted for takeover within these industries (Bebchuk et al. 2001).

In the light of the property rights literature, the principal means by which the capital market can exert pressure on managerial behaviour is the sanction of takeover. If corporations fail to make efficient use of their assets, takeovers enable inefficient managements to be removed by some outsider who believes that assets are being poorly managed and reckons they can do better.

Moreover, the beneficial impact of the market for corporate control as a corrective mechanism is independent of the character of the product market. According to the property rights theorists: "so long as free capital markets are available, the absence of competition in product markets does not imply a different quality of management in monopolistic as compared with competitive enterprises" (Alchian & Kessel 1962, 160). According to this argument, whether or not competition in the product market exists is irrelevant, for competition in the capital market enforces profit maximisation and optimal resource allocation.

It is not clear what is meant by "free capital market" in the above quotation. Free of restrictions? In most free-market countries, mergers and acquisitions are subject to antitrust laws and official bodies enforcing such laws. Free can also mean costless. But the real-world market for corporate control is anything but costless. According to Williamson: "two types of costs need to be recognised. First is the expected cost of making a successful displacement offer. Second is the transition cost of bringing the acquired firm under control" (1970, 90). In the case of the tender offer the first type of costs takes the form of a premium over the current market price of the target company's shares that must be offered to induce the existing shareholders to sell their holdings. According to Ernst & Young, the average premium for takeovers between 1996 and 2000 ranged between 40% and 50%. As a rule, the premium goes higher when management resistance is encountered.

Secondly, there are various side effects of hostile takeovers, such as the fact that "middle management may perceive the change at the top as a threat to its security, and dysfunctional behavior, with its attendant effects on performance, may develop" (Williamson 1970, 103).

In fact, as a theory propounded by Shleifer & Summers suggests (1988), these takeover costs should be conceived more broadly. According to the theory, a corporation should be viewed as a set of long-term contracts between it and "stakeholders" (i.e. all those whose welfare is dependent, in one way or another, on the company, be they employees, customers, suppliers, bondholders, members of its local community, etc.), both written and unwritten. Shareholders gain from these implicit contracts, as it would be difficult, if not impossible, to draw up a contract that would cover all details of such informal agreements. For instance, shareholders will benefit from workers' willingness to learn about their jobs and upgrade their skills. As, however, much of this knowledge is unique to a specific firm and difficult to use with other employers, the workers will obviously be willing to invest more time and energy in training, i.e. in augmenting one's own labour power if they can trust managers to carry on employing them. New managers, however, may fail to honour informal contracts made by their predecessors, the more so that by breaking these contracts they can reduce, in the short-term, the firm's costs. Cost savings, achieved by redundancies or wage cuts, can benefit shareholders, but breaches of implicit contracts have adverse longer-run effects because stakeholders are likely to become reluctant to enter into implicit contracts generally. For instance, work motivation and, consequently, work performance of employees can suffer, and they may demand more pay in return for their greater insecurity.

So even at this point of analysis it is evident that the costs of failing to honour trust-based agreements can be substantial. That such contracts may be vital to the long-term efficiency is shown by the example of the superior economic performance of companies in Japan and Germany, where hostile takeovers are virtually unknown. In addition, those who are able to do so (managers above all), will try to secure for themselves costly formal contract rights. Such lucrative severance packages have been aptly dubbed golden parachutes. French executives, for instance, receive roughly double their salary and bonus in their golden parachute.

More generally, to forestall hostile takeovers, incumbent managements can institute a variety of defensive measures that are apt to increase the cost of takeover substantially. While the proponents of hostile takeovers as disciplinary devices point out that the mere threat of takeover can impel managers to change their ways, the opponents argue that such changes may often boil down to panicky protective strategies which are detrimental to long-term profits and efficiency. Managers facing takeover threat, in other words, may become too profit oriented, focusing on "quick gains at the expense of risk-taking and longer-term investment that more stable tenure might allow" (Herman 1981, 100). And among longer-term strategies, growth, regardless of its profitability, to a size impeding, if not precluding, takeover is apt to become an attractive option.

Even more ironically, the prospect of takeover may have the perverse effect of the incumbent manager having an even greater interest in increasing his personal satisfaction at the expense of the shareholders while he or she is still in the control of the firm. In Demsetz's sweeping assertion that: "In a world in which self-interest plays a significant role in economic behavior, it is foolish to believe that owners of valuable resources systematically relinquish control to managers who are not guided to serve their interests" (1983, 390), property ownership is endowed with almost supernatural powers, while it is overlooked that self-interest pertains to managers as well. There is no denying that in the last analysis the takeover market can serve to discipline and replace bad managers, the evidence suggests that 'a manager can waste about 40 percent of the value of his firm before there is any serious risk of takeover" (Murphy 1989, 63). The threat of takeovers also causes a loss in management efficiency because "a management spending its days and nights with lawyers, public relations firms, and investment bankers is not spending enough time developing new products, manufacturing more efficiently, or improving its balance sheet. (In fact, a company would be foolhardy to improve its balance sheet and make itself a more tempting target for raiders.)" (Williams 1985, 136).

In addition, the theory discussed is not able to account for the periodical character of takeovers. In the U.S. in the twentieth century there occurred several such waves of takeover activity: in 1893–1904, in the 1920s, 1960s, 1981–1989 and the last one in 1995–2000.

For this evidence to be consistent with the property rights theory's treatment of takeovers as a disciplinary mechanism, it would be necessary to assume that poor management has a cyclical nature, as it intensifies every twenty years, which is of course totally non-credible. Takeover waves must be obviously brought about by some other factors. And, indeed, while the wave of the 1960s was one of conglomeration, that of the 1980s served instead as an effective way to break up inefficient conglomerates created during the former wave.

The final nail in the coffin of the theory under consideration was in the early 1990s through the essential collapse of the market for corporate control in the U.S. Indeed, following the wave of anti-takeover laws and charter amendments introduced at the end of the 1980s, most U.S. corporations are now extremely well protected against hostile takeovers. Their control is generally no longer contestable. In contrast, in the UK the City Code prevents post-bid action that might frustrate the bid and few companies have put in place pre-bid defences, thus making the UK the only OECD country with an active and open market for corporate control (Becht, Bolton & Röell 2002).

Even this claim can be called into question, though, by pointing for example to the empirical findings of a poor disciplinary takeover market in the UK by Franks & Mayer (1996) who, in contrast to the findings of Martin & McConnell (1991) for U.S. corporate firms, find no significant relation between poor company performance, hostile takeovers and top management turnover. These findings point to a similarity between the UK and Germany where Franks & Mayer (2000) discuss a lack of takeover market in which to provide management with incentives for maximising firm value.

To conclude, neither internal nor external mechanisms assumed by the property right theory to align managers' interests with those of shareholders are effective. Instead, the extensive empirical evidence is compatible with such approaches as the managerial discretion theory, the rent extraction view, or the entrenchment argument.

These theories can be interpreted to mean that corporate executives, rather than fulfil their fiduciary duty, expropriate other corporate stakeholders.

CHAPTER I.5.[1]

THE AUSTRIAN SCHOOL

I.5.1. Introduction

The Austrian School (also known as the "Vienna School" or the "Psychological School") is a heterodox school of economics that emphasizes the spontaneous organizing power of the price mechanism. It holds that the complexity of subjective human choices makes mathematical modelling of the evolving market extremely difficult (or undecideable) and advocates a laissez-faire approach to the economy. Although often controversial, the Austrian School was influential in the early twentieth century and was for a time considered by many to be part of mainstream economics.

Austrian School economists forewarnings' about the global financial crisis has led to renewed interest in the School's theories. More generally, however, with the re-emergence of Friedrich von Hayek's *The Road to Serfdom*, he and Ludwig von Mises have begun to attract attention among general readers. They wrote before, during, and in the years after World War II when capitalism was under heavy ideological assault by Marxism. Today, in their writings, one can find an articulate defence of capitalism and a rapier attack on socialism and collectivism in general. Both economists offer an alternative to Galbraith, and to current proponents of neo-Keynesian economics. Many of the hot topics such as "individual" or "choice" in today's economic discussions centre around ideas first popularized by the Austrian School. The Austrian School derives its name from its predominantly Austrian founders and early proponents, including Carl Menger, Eugen von Böhm-Bawerk and Ludwig von Mises. Despite this name, proponents of the Austrian School can be from any part of the world, and there are now only a few Austrian School economists of Austrian nationality.

---

[1] The chapter is an extended and amended version of "Between subjectivism and individualism: a critical appraisal of the Austrian case for private ownership," *Cultural Logic* (2009).

Vienna in the late 1800s was a site of incredible intellectual activity, producing an array of memorable figures whose work defined our current view of the world. Great advances in the fields of psychology (Sigmund Freud), art (Gustav Klimt), music (Arnold Schoenberg, Gustav Mahler), medicine (Theodor Billroth) and philosophy (Ludwig Wittgenstein) were all made in this one place. But Vienna was also the site of our modern view of economics. While Freud was revolutionizing psychology, a group of vanguard economists, led by Carl Menger, Eugen von Böhm-Bawerk , and Friedrich von Wieser were using similar principles to reinvent economics. Eventually called "The Austrian School," these men rejected the mechanical and deterministic approach of their colleagues, advocating instead a "pure" economics that attempted to account for the role of individuals and their desires.

The Austrian School took consideration of risk and uncertainty in their models. It emerged around one of the pioneers of the 1871 Marginalist Revolution, Carl Menger, at the University of Vienna. The first generation was composed of professors who, although not directly students of Menger, were nonetheless heavily influenced by him: Friedrich von Wieser and Eugen von Böhm-Bawerk. It was they who, for the most part, spread the Austrian School gospel throughout the Austro-Hungarian Empire and trained the next two generations. These later generations were dominated by the figures of Ludwig von Mises and Friedrich von Hayek.

The Austrian School maintained its base in Vienna until the 1930s, when most of its members moved or were exiled to Great Britain and the United States. Already in Wieser and Böhm-Bawerk we find many core ideas of Austrian economics, a lot of which became clearer and more distinctive in the hands of their students, notably Mises and Hayek. These can be generally enumerated as follows (with notes, in parentheses, on their main disputants):

A radically "subjectivist" strain of Neoclassical marginalist economics[2] (versus Classical School[3]).

A dedication to an aprioristic "pure" theory, with an emphasis on "methodological individualism" (versus the German Historical School[4]).

The theory of alternative cost[5] (the link uses the term "opportunity cost") which reduces all goods and factors, by "imputation," to the

[2] See http://homepage.newschool.edu/het/essays/margrev/margrev.htm.

[3] See http://homepage.newschool.edu/het/schools/ricardian.htm.

[4] See http://homepage.newschool.edu/het/schools/historic.htm.

[5] See http://homepage.newschool.edu/het/essays/margrev/oppcost.htm.

subjective valuation of consumer goods (versus Classical School and the Marshallian Neoclassicals[6]).
A time-theoretic approach to capital and interest (versus everybody else, especially Chicago[7]).
A monetary overinvestment theory[8] of the business cycle (versus Keynesians[9]).
Support for anti-cyclical monetary policy and, later, a free banking system (versus Monetarists[10]).
A general political, economic and philosophical defence of laissez-faire economic policy (versus) Keynesians and Marxians.

How come that the Austrian school has been able to ignore such empirical facts?

I.5.2. Methodology

Austrian economic methodology rests on the related tenets of methodological individualism and subjectivism. Among the implications of subjectivism for economic theory are the unpredictability of human action, the uncertainty that necessarily faces each market participant, the dynamic conception of time, and the conception of the market process and competition as a discovery or learning process involving entrepreneurship and private decentralised knowledge. These points illustrate the relevance of seemingly abstract epistemological and methodological considerations for theoretical and applied economics, including the issue of public versus private ownership.

> Rational economic choice or decision making requires a broad sweep of knowledge, including, but not limited to, the knowledge of prices. Prices require competitive markets if they are to be able to fulfil their informational function. As Mises puts it, "it is only by … the competition between entrepreneurs, trying to wrest from each other the material means of production and the services of labour, that the prices of the factors of production are formed" (1936, 520). In turn, competition necessarily requires private ownership of the means of production in order for it to serve its function as a discovery procedure, for it is only through the rivalrous bidding of independent owners of the means of production that

[6] See http://homepage.newschool.edu/het/schools/english.htm.
[7] See http://homepage.newschool.edu/het/schools/chicago.htm.
[8] See http://homepage.newschool.edu/het/essays/cycle/moneycycle.htm.
[9] See http://homepage.newschool.edu/het/schools/cambridge.htm.
[10] See http://homepage.newschool.edu/het/schools/monetar.htm.

> prices tend to have the coordinative meaning necessary for their function in economic calculation (Lavoie 1985, 181–83). Looking at the matter from a slightly different angle, "the continuous changes over time in tastes, techniques, available resources, prices, plans and expectations demand that individuals be free to act and dispose of their property while using their knowledge of their circumstances of time and place as they see fit, in order to gain access to more and better knowledge than would be possible with less freedom of action" (Moldofsky 1989, 18).

I.5.3. The Perils of Subjectivism

A line of criticism which will run like a thread throughout this section points to several major differences of opinion within the Austrian school. Let us state at the very outset that this kind of critique cannot be easily dismissed by describing them as merely differences of emphasis to be found in any developing discipline (Littlechild 1986, 85). For the Austrian school claims to constitute a system of thought and the deep differences between the members of the school call into question the integrity of the system. One of these differences consists in the fact that the Austrian thinkers differ in regard to the role of *a priori* (Littlechild 1986, 85). Some of them believe that the fundamental assumptions from which the rest of the theory can be deduced are *a priori* to all experience[11] (Mises 1949, 1960). Others, however, insist on the empirical nature of these assumptions (Hayek 1935; Rothbard 1976a). More specifically:

> Hayek thought that the main difference between him and Mises was that Mises regarded the market theory as *a priori* (genetically *a priori* and *a priori* valid), while for Hayek only the logic of individual action (rational action) was *a priori*. The interaction of people and the resulting network, the free-market economy, were for Hayek empirical phenomena, and hence, the topic of empirical research. (Radnitzky 1995, 190)

Worse still, even the thought of single writers can be marked by inconsistency. Hayek asserted that his proposition about a tendency toward equilibrium rests on an empirical basis (1952, 46). In another text, however, he stated that the validity of the theory of competition, of which the thesis about the tendency to coordination in the market is an integral part, can never be tested empirically (1984, 255). Assuming the former

---

[11] It is in this context that The Nobel prize winning economist Paul Samuelson wrote that, "I tremble for the reputation of my subject" after reading the "exaggerated claims that used to be made in economics for the power of deduction and *a priori* reasoning" (1964, 736).

proposition to be valid, some other doubts arise, however. While Hayek maintains that the co-ordinating tendency is in principle falsifiable, he never states under what conditions this could be so, which means that the failure of the market to co-ordinate can always be explained away in terms of some institutional impediment to this process (Barry 1984, 45). Kirzner, in turn, points out that the empirical proposition on which the equilibration thesis relies is inconsistent with a tenet fundamental to Austrian methodology. The former asserts that market participants learn from experience in a systematic manner so that their actions become increasingly coordinated. This, however, is incompatible with the basic Austrian insight that there is an inherent indeterminacy in the way by which human knowledge changes (Kirzner 1976b, 49).This indeterminacy view is consistent with Mises & Rothbard's rejection of many of the key elements of modern neoclassical economics. On the other hand, this very view is impossible to reconcile with opposite views of Hayek. That disagreement among the Austrian economists manifests itself in, for example, Mises & Rothbard's stringent rejection of mathematical economics as opposed to Hayek's desire to:

> … avoid giving the impression that I generally reject the mathematical method in economics. I regard it as indeed the great advantage of the mathematical technique that it allows us to describe, by algebraic equations, the general character of a pattern even where we are ignorant of the numerical values determining its particular manifestation. Without this algebraic technique we could scarcely have achieved that comprehensive picture of the mutual interdependencies of the different events in the market. (Hayek 1979)

There is another dimension to the aforementioned inconsistency, however. If Hayek's proposition that people learn to avoid mistakes is rejected, then the basis for viewing the market process as a coordination and equilibrating mechanism is undermined and, by the same token, the basic task of economic theory, which according to Hayek is the explanation of the unintended market consequences of human action, turns out to be unfeasible. This points out that the second task of economic explanation mentioned by Austrians, that of making the world intelligible in terms of human action, based on the recognition of human purposefulness, is in fact quite distinct from the above-mentioned task and should not be confused or even associated with it (Kirzner 1976b, 40–50).

It is clear from the foregoing that the existence of the tendency toward equilibrium is a subject of controversy among the Austrian scholars. Kirzner, generally following Hayek, has developed a conception of an equilibrating market process as based on his concept of entrepreneurship (1982). In his view, opportunities have a tendency to be discovered by entrepreneurs, and hence the market process is characterised by continuous discovery and increasing coordination. Other Austrians, however, have maintained that this view does not do justice to, if not totally ignores, the possibility of errors. If a market participant acts on the basis of a perceived opportunity that turns out not to exist, they may further discoordinate the market rather than increasing coordination in it (Littlechild 1989, 32). Lachmann (1976 and 1977) underscores the subjectivity of expectations and hence the importance of uncertainty to such an extreme so as to make it impossible to assert on theoretical grounds that the market will tend toward equilibrium. In this view, since expectations are no more than guesses about the future we cannot be sure they will be correct. Indeed, an expectation that turns out to be successful is already a past event and is therefore irrelevant to the prospects of future successful coordination (Barry 1984, 46).

Shackle (1972) takes an even more radical view, positing a kaleidic, or moving from one disequilibrium to another process. Shackle regards the economy as subject to sudden landslides of re-adjustment to a new, precarious and ephemeral pseudo-equilibrium, in which variables based on expectation, speculative hope, and conjecture are deliberately stacked in a card-house of momentary immobility, waiting for the news to upset everything again and start a new disequilibrium phase (1972, 433). By contrast, O'Driscoll & Rizzo maintain that:

> there is a place for the notion of equilibrium in the framework of Austrian economics. However, it must be revised so as to incorporate the possibility of error. In their opinion, it is only when equilibrium is conceived of as entailing the absence of not merely exogenous but also endogenous change that its idea is incompatible, as in Shackle (1972, 253–4), with the Austrian world of time and uncertainty. However, a looser idea of a pattern equilibrium allows for uncertainty and change. In this view, coordination can exist with respect to plans or the typical features of planned activities, but not with respect to the actual activities themselves. The latter are a complex of typical and unique features and are not stable in real time because the unique aspects of events are time-dependent and hence change from within the system as opposed to the relatively stable types or patterns which are, in the short run, affected only by exogenous shocks to the system. (O'Driscoll & Rizzo 1985, 86–7)

There is thus among the Austrian theorists an almost bewildering variety of positions on equilibrium or equilibration. The aforementioned requirement that economics should make the world intelligible in terms of human purposes, which according to Austrian methodologists is one of the two fundamental tasks of economic explanation, naturally refers to the subjectivist understanding of economic phenomena. Subjectivism involves the recognition that the real world is more than the external world; the real world includes a whole range of matters beyond the scope of the measuring instruments of the econometrician. The notion that economic science must be able to encompass this realm (Kirzner 1976b, 47) is a useful reminder of the narrow-mindedness of behaviourism and related doctrines.

But making reference to human plans and motivations (Kirzner 1976b, 47) is not the same thing as, to quote Lavoies definition of subjectivism, the approach that focuses on perceptions on reality by individual minds rather than directly on reality itself. It is one thing to look at the world from the point of view of thinking and acting subjects, but it is quite another thing to limit one's scientific interest to the contents of individual minds (Lavoies 1985, 101–2). It may be conceded that the latter alternative does not necessarily follow from the notion of subjectivism. Hayek, for instance, cannot be accused of reducing reality to human perceptions, etc. or of failing to see the relationship between consciousness and the external world. He writes, for instance, that the apparatus by means of which we learn about the external world is itself the product of a kind of experience. It is shaped by the conditions prevailing in the environment in which we live, and it represents a kind of generic reproduction of the relations between the elements of the environment which we have experienced in the past (1984, 225).

But matters are even more complex than that. Representatives of the Austrian school put the emphasis on the teleological nature of human action as an expression of its subjective nature. In contrast to events resulting from natural processes, occurring without participation of man, actions are conscious intervention in the natural course of events focused on the goals chosen by the operator. This kind of concept of action is difficult to accept for the neoclassical economics due to the non-observable nature of its main elements: the purpose and choice. Orthodox economics under the influence of positivism and behaviorism focuses primarily on observable phenomena and relationships that link them. Following the fact that human beings are here recognized not as genuinely teleological entities but as "mindless automata, responding in a completely programmed way to external stimuli, such as price signals, or quantitative" (Jackson 1982, 87).

There will be no exaggeration to say that the only trace of subjectivity in the orthodox economic thought are individual tastes and preferences manifested in the so-called, indifference curves. As Pareto wrote: "an individual may disappear, if only it leaves us a photograph of its preferences" (1971, 120). Interest of the standard economics in the awareness of the individual or the process of its decision-making is therefore limited to the aspect of preference, leaving outside the scope of interest such aspects as autonomy of choice. In the neoclassical model of human behaviour based upon the pattern of stimulus-response there is no place for an authentic, individual choice. However, subjectivism perceived by Austrian theorists, understood as a concept "claiming that the contents of human consciousness, and thus making decisions is not uniquely determined by external events" (O'Driscoll & Rizzo 1985, 1) assumes that individuals have the ability to make autonomous, sovereign choice, and therefore actions having such nature.

Putting aside all controversies around subjectivism and individualism of the Austrians, it should be pointed out that their understanding of economics as a theory of action rather than a decision is one of those characteristics which most clearly distinguish them from their neoclassical colleagues. Moreover, for the Austrian scholars, the most important factor is not the concept of decision itself, but doing so in action, or process (which might achieve a goal or not), which consists of a series of interaction and coordination processes. Examination of the latter is, according to the Austrians, the object of economic science.

Thus, economics being a very distant science from a mere theory of choice or decision, talks about the processes of social interaction, coordinated more or less depending on the precautionary principle of actors involved in any project. Subjectivity can also be understood as in the view of Rothbard taking up Mises' criticism and rejecting one of the foundations of neoclassical economics; the concept of indifference curves on the basis that indifference is something that cannot manifest itself in action, action can reveal preferences, but not indifference. Rothbard utters this view as follows: "The fundamental error is the misunderstanding that indifference cannot work as a basis of action. If man was truly indifferent to the two alternatives, he would not be able to make any choice between them, and his choice could not be disclosed in action" (1962, 265). Meanwhile, Mises stated in the same spirit: "the scale of values and needs manifests itself only in real action. These scales have no independent existence outside actual behavior of individuals. The only source of our knowledge concerning these scales is observation of human activities (1989, 105).

It seems that it is wrong to critically understand the "shared by Mises and Rothbard" assumption, according to which there are “no preferences apart from those that are disclosed in action" (Kaplan 1997) as a kind of letting behaviourism in through the window having just thrown it out the door.

It seems that one is allowed to assume also this interpretation of the position presented above according to which it does not mean vulgar-materialist denial of the existence of awareness, but proper assumption by the author of sociological concept of action and awareness of the distinction between two layers of the latter: epiphenomenal, i.e. not manifested in the actual behaviour of individuals; and (truly important for the sociologist) that manifested in this or other form in real action.

In contrast to neoclassical economics that preserves at its best slight traces of subjectivity, the Austrian thought makes far wider use of the subjectivist point of view. Among implications that has subjectivity to economic theory in the Austrian school there are the unpredictability of human actions, the uncertainty as an inherent feature of location of each market participant, a dynamic concept of time, the concept of market process and competition as a discovery processes of learning assuming entrepreneurship and private, decentralized knowledge.

One of the perils of extreme subjectivism is that it tends to undermine any policy conclusions drawn by Austrian economics, including those supporting privatisation and condemning nationalisation. Rothbard is thus consistent when he argues that Austrian economics does not enable the economist to make any value pronouncements or to advocate any public policy whatsoever; "the case for *laissez-faire* and the free-market economy" (1976b, 109) included. He, accordingly, criticises Mises for failing to see the contradiction between methodological subjectivism and making normative or policy statements.

Indeed, from the subjectivist point of view, a preference for this or another policy is a matter for the individual alone. Kirzner, while agreeing that it is "impossible to speak of efficiency in terms other than those of the purposes of specific individuals under discussion" (1976c, 81) tries to defend Mises by pointing out that for the latter: "professional approval by an economist of a specific policy proposal merely means that the economist believes the policy will enhance the fulfillment of the purposes of those interested in the economist's professional opinion" (1976c, 81). Rothbard, however, remains unconvinced by Kirzner's defence, for "how could Mises know what the advocates of the particular policy consider desirable? How could he know what their value scales are now or what they will be when the consequences of the measure appear?" (1976b, 101). Suppose that one wishes to show that nationalisation is a bad measure because it leads to impoverishment in contrast to privatization, which is shown to lead to affluence. This effect may still be favoured by advocates of nationalisation as consistent with their own individual preferences and values. They may, for instance, prefer public ownership as supposedly leading to a more equitable distribution of income and wealth as opposed to privatization, which is they believe increases wealth and income disparities. Other supporters of nationalisation may set a high value on it as a means of protecting jobs and reducing unemployment, and so on. And indeed, Mises concedes that:

> … if no other objections could be raised to the socialist plans than that socialism will lower the standard of living of all or at least of the immense majority, it would be impossible for praxeology to pronounce a final judgment. Men would have to decide the issue between capitalism and socialism on the ground of judgments of value and of judgments of relevance. They would have to choose between the two systems as they choose between many others things. (Mises 1963, 580)

Another problem with subjectivism is that it may lead to the neglect of the inherent social dimension of human consciousness and knowledge. This is the point made by Hodgson who, criticising what he calls the extreme subjectivism of the Austrians, writes of "the intrinsically non-autonomous character of preference and beliefs" (1988, 122–3). He goes on to add that:

> … we cannot hope to create a conceptual framework capable of handling vast quantities of information on our own. We have to rely on interactions with others to develop our cognitive skills, to form judgements about the world, and to acquire guidelines for action. Furthermore, for cognition we rely on a language and linguistic structure which is socially formed. (Hodgson 1988, 121)

It should be noted that in order to rebut this charge it is not enough to assert simply that "individuals are continually learning from and influencing each other" (Rothbard 1976a, 31), for it must be shown how these indeed commonplace points can be incorporated into the subjectivistic framework. One particularly significant implication of this criticism of the Austrians' over-subjectivism concerns economic knowledge. As Hodgson points out:

> Whilst the Austrian argument that it is impossible to centralise all argument is valid, it is wrong to assume that all knowledge is individual in character. Some information (often information about the location of other information) is necessarily centralized and institutionalized (e.g. in a telephone directory). It is thus doubtful that the decentralized market can

> provide an effective signaling device for all information and all activities in a complex economic system. (Hodgson 1988, 237)

Another tension, which has already been hinted at, arises between the subjectivistic programme and the Austrians' self-imposed question: "How can individuals acting in the world of everyday life unintentionally produce existing institutions or, more generally, the overall patterns of social interaction?" Given that there is a "complex chain of mutually reinforcing actions that produce results beyond those that can be individually apprehended or intended" (O'Driscoll & Rizzo 1985, 20) or that "the spontaneous collaboration of free men often creates things that are greater than their individual minds can ever fully comprehend" (Hayek 1984, 135), what place is there for the subjectivist assumption? This is another way of saying that social relations cannot be reduced to inter-subjective relations. Social, including economic, relations are in great part suprapersonal in nature. Such relations involve individuals, but these individuals are not necessarily aware of the nature and the very existence of the said relations.

In this sense, the Austrian view that "artifacts—tools and instruments or other products of human beings … cannot be interpreted to refer … to things irrespective of what people think about them" (Hayek, quoted in Kirzner 1976a, 46) does not go far enough. For such artifacts can be the media of the relations between people who do not know that they have entered into a given relation. For instance, consumers of given goods enter into a relation with their producers without knowing or seeing them. The former are dependent on the latter for the satisfaction they derive from the act of consuming, and bad products can have harmful consequences for the consumers' health. Thus the relation, which exists independently of its participants' awareness, has very real implications for their behaviour.

From that perspective, referring to our considerations on economic and social values, we beg to differ with Karl Marx, who in Part I in his *Critique of Political Economy* states:

> Different use-values have different measures appropriate to their physical characteristics; for example, a bushel of wheat, a quire of paper, a yard of linen.
>
> Whatever its social form may be, wealth always consists of use-values, which in the first instance are not affected by this form. From the taste of wheat it is not possible to tell who produced it, a Russian serf, a French peasant or an English capitalist. Although use-values serve social needs and therefore exist within the social framework, they do not express the social relations of production. For instance, let us take as a use-value a commodity such as a diamond. We cannot tell by looking at it that the

> diamond is a commodity. Where it serves as an aesthetic or mechanical use-value, on the neck of a courtesan or in the hand of a glass-cutter, it is a diamond and not a commodity. To be a use-value is evidently a necessary prerequisite of the commodity, but it is immaterial to the use-value whether it is a commodity. Use-value as such, since it is independent of the determinate economic form, lies outside the sphere of investigation of political economy. It belongs in this sphere only when it is itself a determinate form. Use-value is the immediate physical entity ... (Marx 1976)

Granted that Marx is correct, his statement goes some way toward accounting for the fact that perhaps the best saying rendering the state of mutual relations between economics and sociology is still "Mind the gap!" From the standpoint of sociology of the economy in the sense of socio-economic structuralism use values cannot be reduced to their physical qualities since the latter must be understood as an effect of given types of social labour (work, quasi-work or definite kinds of lumpenwork) which means that those "things" express determinate social relations.

I.5.4. The Perils of Methodological Individualism

The foregoing argument points to a further source of confusion present in the Austrian approach. Kirzner identifies the aforementioned realm of reality (with which economics is concerned) as one of human conduct, which in turn he describes as interests, motivation, and purpose (1976b, 44). But the concept of action cannot be reduced to that of the agent's purpose. Action involves not only ends but also means, and it takes place in concrete conditions. This remark points to a further deficiency in the Austrian approach.

In their over-reaction to mechanistic and deterministic models of behaviour in orthodox economics, the Austrian writers tend to assume either that action bears no significant influence of the environment within which the individual acts, or that the question of why particular ends and courses of action are adopted lies outside the confines of economic theory. The first assumption is simply false; the socio-economic and institutional environment has a significant effect "on the kind of information we receive, our cognition of it, or preferences, and thereby much of our behaviour" (Hodgson 1988, 71). These undeniable facts are admitted by some members of the Austrian school. Rothbard, for instance, calls "the assumption that each individual arrives at his values and choices in a vacuum, sealed off from human influence absurd" (1976a, 30). Rothbard, however, does not offer, as he indeed cannot if he wants to remain a consistent methodological individualist, any positive conception of the moulding or determination of men's goals and actions by social influences. Instead, he asserts that "economic theory does not need to investigate the origin of choices" (Rothbard 1976a, 31). But this boils down to evading the question at issue. Hayek, too, wants to exclude the explanation of individual purposes from economics and indeed from any social science. He accomplishes this goal by allotting the task of explaining the springs of human action to psychology. He writes: "If conscious action can be explained, this is the task for psychology but not for economics … or any other social science" (Hayek 1948, 67).

However, psychology conceived as a social science that views human behaviour in general, transhistorical terms is obviously too abstract to explain particular human actions taking place within, and conditioned by, concrete social structures. When, on the other hand, Hayek admits that "the tastes of man, as is also true of his opinions and beliefs and indeed much of his personality, are shaped in a great measure by his cultural environment" (1965, 40), then he clearly contradicts his own statement cited above. Moreover, if such cultural and social influences on individuals and their goals are conceded, then the whole methodological individualism label is called into question. Since the individual forms an indissoluble, interpenetrating unity with the social and the cultural, and their very individuality and personality are shaped by their socio-cultural environment, methodological individualism becomes clearly untenable. The individualist label can be saved only if one regards human action as totally spontaneous and indeterminate. Such a view provides a plausible excuse for refusing to investigate the formation of purposes. In some pronouncements Mises & Lachmann, for instance, come close to this position (Hodgson 1988, 63). The view in question is indefensible, however, as it undermines the very notion of choice, so dear to the Austrians. As two Austrian scholars rightly note, "unless an individual can expect a great deal of predictable decision-making on the part of others, he will find it impossible to make a meaningful choice" (O'Driscoll & Rizzo 1985, 29). Given this element of predictability in human behaviour, one is obliged to ask what the sources are. And with this the argument comes full circle since one arrives at social structures and institutions as well as culture, which all are excluded by strict methodological individualism.

The above remark by O'Driscoll & Rizzo inadvertently reveals a further weakness in the Austrian approach to human action. While on the one hand the Austrian view of individual purpose is too narrow in that it removes the question of its conditioning beyond the compass of investigation, on the other it is too broad as it regards all human action, including habitual, as purposeful. O'Driscoll & Rizzo try to make room for predictable or habitual actions in their version of Austrian theory by arguing that in the case of such actions the individual is actually "freely choosing to repeat his activity and hence it can be described as purposeful activity whose contents have been routinised" (1985, 29). But this begs a critical question: what causes habits to arise in the first place? And the point is that "people do not always acquire habits from conscious and rational choice" (Hodgson 1988, 125). More generally, by explicitly or implicitly assuming that all human action is conscious and deliberative, the Austrians fail to do justice to the Freudian discovery of the unconscious.

Of course one does not have to be a Freudian to recognise the role of subconscious and irrational factors in human behaviour. The Austrians' neglect of this role leads to distortions in their economic theory, as illustrated by their view of advertising. They regard advertising as an entrepreneurial device, an indispensable instrument whose function is to alert consumers to the opportunity for them to buy a given product (Kirzner 1976a, 121–3). In this model advertising does not "change tastes … it reveals tastes to the hitherto unsuspecting consumer. The agents real tastes are assumed to be given, though he or she may not properly appreciate them" (Littlechild 1989, 34). But it is an elementary truth, known to every student of business administration, that tastes and wants cannot be assumed to be given and immutable as they are often in fact created by advertising and related activities. Kirzner's picture of the producer who anticipates the wishes of consumers and the advertised product that satisfies consumer desires is at best only partially true since these desires and preferences of consumers can be significantly manipulated. This would be a case of making much ado about nothing only if the advertising industry limited itself to conveying information about the advantages and disadvantages of a given good, thus enabling the customer to make a rational choice. The employment by the advertising industry of elaborate techniques of non-rational sales persuasion is, however, a matter of common knowledge. In advertising the emphasis is more often than not on a product's image or symbolic significance. Advertising, like propaganda, the movies, theatre, and fiction, "work[s] on the level of emotional responsiveness" rather than reason; "The experience of advertising is … an emotional one" (Furst & Sherman 1969, 24) rather than that of rational choice or deliberate decision-making. It is not without good reason that the best-selling books about modern sales techniques are titled *The Hidden Persuaders*, *Subliminal Seduction* and *Media Sexploitation*. Indeed, in illegitimately assuming that all forms of action are equally purposive, the Austrians seem to ignore the implications of their own argument as to the fallacy of central planning. Just as the extensive economic information cannot be considered given to a single mind (or groups of minds of the central planners), neither can "the human mind fully and rationally process all the information relating to individual human action at the highest level of deliberation" (Hodgson 1988, 114). In other words, the problem of informational indigestion faces not only a central planning body but also any individual.

There are, to be sure, some attempts among the Austrians to accommodate the important notions of habit and routinisation in social and economic life to their theory. Let us discuss two such attempts. However interesting and plausible in other respects their view of habituations might be, O'Driscoll & Rizzo make out a singularly unconvincing case for the lack of incompatibility between their usual Austrian assumptions and the notions of institutions broadly understood as "patterns of routine behaviour" (1985, 39). They argue, namely, that their inclusion of institutions makes subjectivism even more, not less, important than before because "the nature of what is transmitted (through institutions) is subjective" (O'Driscoll & Rizzo 1985, 40). There is a clear difference in kind between the contents of the individual mind and a suprasubjective, objectified rule that exists independently of particular individuals and that, precisely due to this fact, can be—like all elements of culture—transmitted from one generation to another. The information created and distributed by social institutions has a social and not a purely subjective character. It is established by "the routinised behavior of a group of individuals … Its foundation is the social institution, even if the information given may be perceived differently from individual to individual" (Hodgson 1988, 133).

Hayek, in developing in his later writings a theory of cultural evolution based on the survival and adaptation of traditions and rules, has moved away from his earlier position. As Gray, among others, correctly notes: "it is at least not altogether obvious that this application of natural selection theory to social explanation is entirely consistent with methodological individualism" (1984, 53). The incongruity between the latter position, not relinquished by Hayek, and his theory of cultural evolution manifests itself in this theory's deficiency; while laying stress on the emergence of the various institutions of society from the interaction of individuals it does not extend to the individuals themselves. Although Hayek expressly rejects a simple conception of one-directional laws of cause and effect and appeals to what he calls, after Donald Campbell, downward causation, his approach is in fact one-directional in that it considers individuals purposes and preferences as given, not subject to the very evolution that generates a spontaneous social order. Viewing the sociocultural framework as the resultant of individual interests and actions is not enough, since the latter are shaped and structured by the former.

Once this point is admitted, moreover, Hayek's argument against intervention in the spontaneous order is open to criticism. Hayek asserts that "the particular results that will be determined by altering a particular action of the system will always be inconsistent with its overall order" (1989, 130). But once it is seen that the actions in question, and indeed the agents themselves, are subject to endogenous, and not only exogenous, change (or intervention), the argument loses its force.

I.5.5. Entrepreneurship and Ownership

The same methodological individualism is responsible for the one-sidedness of the Austrian view of entrepreneurship. Just as in the Austrian general view of the human agent the circumstances moulding his choices and decisions are not put into the picture, so entrepreneurial ability is portrayed as immaculately conceived. The following statement may be considered typical in that regard. Littlechild writes that "under public ownership projects that rely on imaginative vision or hunch will find it more difficult to gain acceptance" (1989, 37). Whatever shapes this imagination is left outside the picture. Obviously, however: "imagination and entrepreneurship require a variety of economic, social, and cultural conditions to flourish. Importantly, there is no obvious relationship between the pattern of private or public ownership, on the one hand, and the fertility of these conditions, on the other" (Hodgson 1988, 268).

Consequently, what matters more than the form of ownership is "the type and level of social culture, the level of technical and general education, and the material and institutional supports for entrepreneurial activity" (Hodgson 1988, 268). Hodgson's view on the relationship (or rather the lack of it) between ownership and entrepreneurship is shared by many other authors. For instance, Horvat points out that an entrepreneur, as was long ago pointed out by Joseph Schumpeter, is not an owner of capital: "Owning the capital is the function of the capitalist (who is not forbidden to be also an entrepreneur, but that is not necessary). All that is necessary for an entrepreneur to function efficiently is that he is legally free to engage in a business venture of his choosing and has an access to capital" (1991, 5). Even an author sympathizing with the Austrian approach concedes that "entrepreneurship does not require ownership to exist, though of course the exercise of it may be inhibited by limited access to necessary resources" (Barry 1984, 43).

These flaws in the view of the relationship between entrepreneurship and ownership taken by Austrian economics reflect its vagueness over the concept of ownership. For instance, in one of his polemics with market socialism, Hayek writes: "If the community is the owner of all material resources of production, somebody will have to exercise this right for it, at least in so far as the distribution and the control of the use of these resources is concerned" (1989, 135). But, a few sentences later, it turns out that this "central authority would simply have rights of ownership of all real resources" (Hayek 1989, 135). It is one thing, of course, to attribute ownership of the means of production to the community, and quite another to vest it in the state, the centre or some other institution. Moreover, although Hayek is not completely clear on this point, he seems to equate ownership with decision-making or power over the means of production. In the present writer's opinion, this notion is erroneous, as it refers to consequences or preconditions of what Berle and Means call beneficial ownership (1969, 8), and not to this ownership as such. To argue that ownership consists in either "the power to assign the means of production to given uses or in the power to dispose of the products obtained" (Poulantzas 1979, 18) is like staging *Hamlet* without Hamlet. Making decisions determining the use of the object is not the same thing as actually benefiting from that use. It is not the same thing also in the sense that those who exercise control over given assets need not be those who enjoy the fruits of these assets. The above argument applies even more explicitly to Mises, who expressly states that "ownership is the right of disposal" (1936, 517). If the present writer is right, the premise of Mises' further reasoning is thus erroneous. From this he argues that:

> it is impossible to reconcile socialism with a competitive exchange economy. Under socialism, ownership of the means of production, or the right of disposing of production, must be vested either in the central body, the commune, or in associations of producers. The former solution faces the insuperable contradiction between the inescapably fragmented and decentralised character of economic knowledge and centralised direction. The latter solution, for a change, lacks any coordination mechanism at all. (Mises 1936, 517–8)

The problem is that the latter argument is double-edged and can be directed against free-market capitalism as well. This is another way of saying that, owing to their simplified concept of ownership, the Austrians fail to notice that their criticism of common ownership really only applies to state ownership. Anyhow, even this point, as it turns out, may constitute a bone of contention within the Austrian school. Thus, Hayek accepted nearly all of Mises's criticism of socialism, but thought that Mises's criticism could not be effective, because Mises's view that man is strictly rational and can know the consequences of his actions opens the door to constructivist rationalism, which is one of the corner stones of socialism (Radnitzky 1996).

Be that as it may, common or social ownership can appear in many different forms, of which state ownership of the East or public enterprises of the West are only some. Even a writer sympathetic to the Austrian approach notes that "group ownership seems to be compatible with market economy as long as there are many groups, independent of each other, and individuals have the choice whether join them or not (i.e. whether to invest their resources in them or not, becoming in this way materially responsible for risks that they take)" (Jasinski 1991, 18). One can even go further and say that the Austrian argument about the dispersed nature of knowledge really reinforces the case for such workers' self-management as tapping into knowledge of many more individuals than is possible under private ownership. On the other hand, it should be noted that workers participation in the decision-making process is of course possible within the capitalist context. Efficiency requires constant information about both the external environment in which the firm functions and its internal operation. This insight underlies not only many individual experiments designed to involve workers in company decision making but also the whole system of industrial relations in Japan. Alas, the Austrian school, focusing as it does on the entrepreneur, has little to say about organizational structure, industrial relations, and other important features of real-world firms. As Hodgson correctly notes, "the analysis bypasses the shopfloor and there is silence about the real processes of production" (1989, 237).

Another deficiency in the Austrian treatment of the entrepreneur is that it fits best with early capitalism with its small firms whose owners combined simultaneously the functions of manager and entrepreneur. However, as Lukes observes, "there is the ever-growing gap between the economic individualist model and the corporate neo-capitalist reality" (1973, 153). In the large, modern corporation the entrepreneurial function may be differentiated among many salaried managers or it may be spread out to the entire workforce if some kind of group incentive can be developed to elicit the workers' participation. Some entrepreneurial functions are being shared by employers with unions, and some are disappearing altogether. In any event "the risks are not ordinarily borne by those who innovate since the professional managements which operate most large firms do not fire themselves for making wrong decisions" (Buckingham 1958, 215). The last sentence in particular undermines

Hayek's case for private and against public ownership to the effect that entrepreneurship is not possible without making those "who are responsible for the decisions pay for their mistakes" (1989, 138). Buckingham has referred in the above cited assertion to the disappearance of certain entrepreneurial functions. Schumpeter, as it is well known, went much further in arguing that under modern capitalism the whole entrepreneurial function is becoming obsolete. While his pessimistic view of capitalism as doomed to self-destruction is almost certainly overstated, his perceptive analysis of the routinisation of entrepreneurship and innovation (being, in his view, the main factor in this alleged self-destruction) has much to be said for it. In Schumpeter's view, the function of entrepreneurship is being taken over by a rationalised, bureaucratic form of management, and individual action tends to be replaced by bureau and committee work. Innovation is reduced to a mechanized routine carried out by teams of trained specialists who turn out what is required and make it work in predictable ways (1942, 133), and the personal effort formerly producing, to use his well-known phrase, gales of creative destruction loses its importance. One need not agree with all Schumpeter's conclusions to appreciate his effort to explain the real historical development of capitalism. This compares favourably with the work of the Austrian school as a whole.

Even Hayek, despite his otherwise laudable work in the theory of cultural evolution, makes little, if any, use of a historical perspective in his account of capitalism. Overall, the Austrians have very little to say about the real-world modern economic system whose main actors are not so much individuals as institutions, such as corporations whose actions also need to be coordinated, and if this system of internal nonmarket coordination does not work well, "the information conveyed by prices will be very imperfect, and the agents themselves will be unable to react properly to the cues provided by the price system" (Rapaczynski 1992, 62).

The efficiency of this system of corporate governance obviously cannot be taken for granted, as it seems to be in the Austrian theory. The Austrian argument about the difficulties of the centre with collecting, processing, and acting on the basis of microeconomic information can be easily extended to modern corporations, many of them being very large and highly diversified. It is not plausible to treat such a firm as a single entrepreneur since it is in fact a complex social system consisting of many organizations and individuals whose activities, based as they are on divergent and differently interpreted information, are by no means automatically mutually co-ordinated.

The point about the structure of the economic system is indicative of a further error in the Austrian argument in favour of private ownership. Namely, it is not necessary to assume that buyers and sellers cannot act rationally unless they own the means of production or own the firms they represent. It is the exceptional, rather than the usual, case where economic calculations are made by the legal owners of resources any more. The growth of the institutions of proxies, professional managements, holding companies, agencies, even the corporate device itself, have shown that "an economic system can operate without the direct owner-trader relationship" assumed by Mises and Hayek (Buckingham 1958, 345). This kind of argument is damaging to Mises' recasted concept of entrepreneur. This concept is a better approximation to reality of modern capitalism in that it takes account of the separation of ownership and management characteristic of large joint stock corporations. It does not go far enough, however. Mises emphasises the:

> … important function of owners … the speculators, promoters, investors and moneylenders … who buy and sell stocks and shares, who make loans and recover them, who make deposits in the banks and draw them out of the banks again, who speculate in all kinds of commodities … (and) in determining the structure of the stock and commodity exchanges and of the money market, circumscribe the orbit within which definite minor functions can be entrusted to the managers discretion. (Mises 1936, 139; 1949, 708; Lavoie 1985, 176)

This argument, however, underrates the role played in the capital and money markets by institutions such as banks, insurance companies, pension funds, investment trusts, etc. Accordingly, an ever-increasing proportion of decisions in these markets are made by professional executives and hired agents of these institutions. Mises' assertion that "The speculators and investors expose their own wealth, their own destiny" (1949, 709) does not apply to portfolio managers, trustees, proxies, and others who act on behalf of a plethora of financial intermediaries. One should also not exaggerate the actual importance of bankruptcy. Bankruptcy is a means of last resort; its threat, even when real, will only prevent management from letting the company fall too far beyond the other players in the field. But, "by itself, it provides no real incentive to excel in competing, and as long as the company is able to coast along the borders of profitability, the management can do quite well in the meantime" (Rapaczynski 1992, 63).

I.5.6. Market information and ecology

It follows from the foregoing that there is a fatal confusion in the central Austrian argument regarding information. Rowthorn points out that:

> … the view that privatisation will help to generate the information required for effective decision-making … is very misleading since the information provided by the market is normally the result of product market competition and not private ownership per se. Product market competition, if effective, will generate the same information regardless of ownership of the enterprise concerned. (Rowthorn 1991, 4–5)

On theoretical grounds, the issues of competition and decentralisation of economic decision-making are quite separate from that of public or private ownership. On these grounds at least, therefore, the argument in favour of increased competition does not necessarily entail a justification of privatisation. It is arguable that "the sheer technical problems of costing and pricing in state enterprises are minimized when they operate within a general environment of private enterprise since the market place resolves most difficulties. An ocean of private enterprise will determine the level of a bay of governmental enterprise." It is only, as Nutter argues, when the roles are reversed, when governmental enterprises become the ocean and the private ones the bay, that the problem becomes serious (1974, 223). Indeed, Lavoie concedes that "the classical Austrian case against public ownership is strictly applicable only to a socialist economy and that it is evidently possible for a few nationalized industries to calculate on the basis of the prices generated by the capitalist market in which they are embedded" (1985, 76–7). There arises another problem, however—that of drawing the line between what counts as a mere bay and what does not. Expressions such as to a certain degree found in Mises (1935, 77) are not terribly helpful since they do not preclude that the decision in question can be arbitrary.

Let us tackle an important issue of economic calculation and the (alleged) impossibility of socialism. Whatever the role of other arguments, Mises considered the "socialist calculation argument" to be a decisive objection to the economic feasibility of socialism. While he pointed out that "No judicious man can fail to conclude from the evidence of these considerations that in the market economy the productivity of labor is incomparable higher than under socialism" (1963, 678). However, for Mises the critical indictment is that "socialism is not a realizable system of society's economic organization because it lacks any method of economic calculation … Socialism cannot be realized because it is beyond human power to establish it as a social system (Mises 1963, 680).

However, as Caplan points out, this conclusion is inconsistent with Mises' view according to which economic theory gives only qualitative, not quantitative laws. For example, in *Human Action*, Mises states that:

> The impracticality of measurement is not due to the lack of technical methods for the establishment of measure. It is due to the absence of constant relations. If it were only caused by technical insufficiency, at least an approximate estimation would be possible in some cases. But the main fact is that there are no constant relations. Economics is not, as ignorant positivists repeat again and again, backward because it is not "quantitative." It is not quantitative because there are no constants. Statistical figures referring to economic events are historical data. They tell us what happened in a nonrepeatable historical case. (Mises 1963, 28)

If so then how could he, as Caplan aptly notes, possibly know by economic theory alone that the negative effect of the lack of economic calculation would be severe enough to make socialism infeasible? Even granted, the socialist economy would suffer due to the impossibility of economic calculation, one wonders how, on his own theory, could Mises know that this difficulty would be so severe that society would collapse?

The strength of this objection becomes even clearer when one considers the case of economic decision-making of Robinson Crusoe, alone on his island. As Mises puts it: "Isolated man can easily decide whether to extend his hunting or cultivation. The processes of production he has to take into account are relatively short. The expenditure they demand and the product they afford can easily be perceived as a whole" (1963, 28). Crusoe runs his one-man economy simply by using "calculation in kind"—mentally weighing his preferences and opportunities to make decisions. Mises concedes that this situation is conceivable, adding only that this method is unworkable for a larger economy. "To suppose that a socialist community could substitute calculations in kind for calculations in terms of money is an illusion. In an economy that does not practice exchange, calculations in kind can never cover more than consumption goods. They break down completely where goods of higher order are concerned" (1963, 102). But Mises' conclusions appear ill-considered. To see this, suffice it to ask whether Crusoe's one-man socialism become "impossible" when Friday shows up? Hardly. What if 100 people show up? 1,000?

Caplan rightly points out that:

> Mises' distinction between a modern economy and Crusoe's, and why the economic calculation argument applies only to the former, again shows that Mises has underlying quantitative assumptions in spite of his strictures against them. He is making a quantitative judgment that the lack of calculation would not greatly worsen Crusoe's economy, but would devastate a modern economy. Perhaps Mises was right, but pure economic theory did not give him the answer. (Caplan 1997)

However, ever since, Austrians have overused the economic calculation argument. In the absence of detailed empirical evidence showing that this particular problem is the crucial one, it is just another argument out of hundreds on the list of arguments against socialism. And indeed, one can easily argue that the problem of work motivation, or innovation, or the lumpen economy, or the role of the nomenclature in the management of the economy were far more important factors in the final collapse of "actually existing socialism" than the notorious calculation problem.

Thus, when in the late 1980s Austrians boasted that "Mises was right," this proclamation was ill-considered, because they were not able to show that economic calculation was the insuperable difficulty of socialist economies. Neither economic history nor pure economic theory supports the view that the economic calculation problem was a severe challenge for socialism and the chief cause of its demise.

However much truth is there in the Austrian view of the role of prices, and it certainly should not be dismissed entirely, it has some significant shortcomings. While many Austrian economists concede that price signals need not always be correct, they tend to limit their attention to such cases of this imperfection in which even incorrect (i.e. non-equilibrium) prices convey information by revealing "inconsistencies and plan discoordination" (O'Driscoll & Rizzo 1985, 39). But there is more to this than that. Markets are inherently incomplete; there are, for instance, many public goods which, because it is impossible to exclude non-payers from their consumption, cannot be provided by the market mechanism. The price of such natural resources as air or water is zero. By market logic, this conveys to consumers and producers the wrong information: that the resources in question are not scarce and their supply is infinite. Hence each individual, in deciding upon the scale and character of his own use of the resource, will fail to consider the effect this may have on the welfare of other users. The upshot is overutilisation, overexploitation, excessive pollution, and economic inefficiency.

The same argument applies more generally to all externalities, whether in production or consumption, imposing harmful (or beneficial, as the case may be) effects on the welfare of non-consenting (or nonpaying in the case of benefits) parties. These external costs and benefits are not reflected in market prices. The overexhaustion problem reveals the incurable "myopia of a price-market system, which only reflects the interests and needs of those now living but not that of future generations" (Blackburn 1991, 37). The long-term ecological and genetic effects on posterity have to be added to the damage incurred by existing populations. On these matters the Austrian theory is particularly deficient. In his Constitution of Liberty (1960, 367–75), Hayek attempts to brush aside what he calls, disparagingly, neighbourhood effects. Thus Hayek's own laudable emphasis on the unintended consequences of human action appears to be somewhat one-sided, to say the least.

For any particular individual, for instance, it may be perfectly rational to buy a car as a convenient means of personal transportation, but the overall effect of all these rational individual decisions is traffic congestion and air pollution, phenomena which probably none of the individuals concerned wanted and none of them would have chosen had they known, but they nevertheless emerge as a consequence of their small-scale decisions in the market. In point of fact, ecological arguments cannot be satisfactorily dealt with within the framework of the Austrian subjectivist theory, as Rothbard's discussion, for instance, amply shows. In the framework of subjectivism, argues Rothbard, "there is no way that one could assert the superiority of the long-run over the short-run" (1976b, 103). According to this logic, if a producer discharges effluent into a river and derives a short-term benefit from this (while necessarily inflicting injury on others and perhaps, in the long-run, even on himself), so be it; after all, it is not possible to criticize anyone's "rate of time preference, to say that A's was too high and B's too low" (Rothbard 1976b, 103).

Hayek's aforementioned argument about the unintentional nature of market outcomes is biased in another respect as well. Hayek holds that the outcomes of the market that adversely affect the position of an individual cannot be said to be unjust because such outcomes were not willed or intended by anyone: "In such a game in which the results for the individuals depend partly on chance and partly on their own skill, there is evidently no sense in calling the outcome either just or unjust" (Hayek 1989, 128). The fact of the matter, however, is that in many cases the outcome of the game of competition in the market is determined neither by skill nor by chance. It is clear that, by and large, those with the greatest initial property and income will derive the greatest benefits from markets and those "with least will derive least" (Hoover & Plant 1989, 215). The economic position of a billionaire's son is hardly a matter of chance, not to say skill. Inherited capital put into a banking account or invested in gilt-edged securities provides the income without any effort and with hardly any risk.

Hayek's own defence of inheritance is rather weak and related to a traditional conservatism based on such institutions as the family rather than to classic liberalism. He argues that the family's function of passing on standards and traditions is clearly tied up with "possibility of transmitting material goods" (1989, 337).

I.5.7.Conclusions

Although theoretically sophisticated and philosophically informed, the Austrian school failed to prove that entrepreneurship, innovation, and economic efficiency are associated with the private sector only. Entrepreneurship does not require private ownership to exist and the information needed for effective decision-making is the result of product market competition rather than private ownership as such. Finally, it should be borne in mind that this whole counterargument implies one crucial premise: "given a market economy." This is another way of saying that the issue of alternative economic systems and forms of common ownership, which has been hinted at above, deserves much more comprehensive attention that it could be given to in this chapter.

John Stuart Mill's statement, which seems to express well the central tenet of all supporters of private property, to the effect that "there is no one so fit to conduct any business or determine how it should be conducted as those who are personally interested in it" should by no means be regarded as a justification for private ownership of the means of production, since nobody is more 'personally interested' in a company than "the workers whose livelihood depends upon its commercial success" (Hattersley 1984, 117).

If our argument refers to ownership, it is not ownership of the means of production which is at stake; even granted that "private ownership of the factors of production results in more effective control of these assets. More effective control in turn implies more efficient use" (Gueltekin & Goldstein 1994, 94), one should bear in mind that among those factors of production there is also labour or labour power. Such considerations tend to support the contention (which is at the same time a criticism of the Austrin school, which overlooks such a possibility) that there may be "alternative mechanisms that provide accountability and yet do not involve private ownership in the traditional sense" (Aliber 1992, 57).

CHAPTER II.6.

THE THEORY OF SOCIAL EXCHANGE BY G. C. HOMANS AS AN EXAMPLE OF ECONOMIC SOCIOLOGY

Most theories developed in the framework of economic sociology, in the meaning adopted in this work, assume as their foundation the paradigm of rational choice. The precursor of this approach in sociology was George C. Homans, the creator of the so-called Social Exchange Theory. The author of the theory expounded its principles primarily in the book *Social Behaviour*: *Its Elementary Forms* (published twice, although the second version introduces some changes compared to the first), and the article "Social Behaviour as Exchange."

II.6.1. Basic principles

According to the theory of social exchange, the main variable in the social sciences that most easily lends itself to measurement in terms of order, frequency and duration, the variable that has been chosen, has been called interaction, it "being an event in which an action of one man was the stimulus for an action of another" (Homans 1962, 37). In fact, interaction is a whole class of variables that could be measured in regard to how often and how long a given person spoke in conversation; how often and how soon that person initiated talk or other action either at the beginning of a conversation or after a pause; how many persons within a given place or time that person interacted with and with how many he or she initiated the interaction (Homans 1983, 14). From then on Homans began to think of other classes of variable that could be added to interaction to account for, not its order, frequency, and duration, but its content. He came up with two others, which he referred to as "sentiment" and "activity." In classifying these three variables—interaction, sentiment, and activity—Homans began the construction of a conceptual scheme.

Sentiment is behaviour expressive of a person's attitudes toward other person's and includes the "liking and disliking for individuals, approval and disapproval of the things they do" (Homans 1947, 14).

In formulating his propositions he relied on the principles of behavioural psychology, with which to explain the "sub-institutional," or elementary forms of social behaviour in small groups. This new approach to the explanation of social behaviour first appeared in Homans's influential paper, "Social Behaviour as Exchange" (1958).

In *Social Behaviour: Its Elementary Forms*, Homans demonstrates further how various empirical findings in the field studies of small groups logically follow from a small number of general principles of behavioural psychology. In his view, both the individualistic and structural sociological approaches to social behaviour require, for their explanation, psychological propositions. Such propositions are not statements about the interrelations of institutions or about the conditions some society must meet in order to survive (as in structural functionalism), rather they are statements about the characteristics of the behaviour "of men as men." This meant, Homans insisted, that sociology had no general propositions of its own, and thus, from then on, he was branded a "psychological reductionist."

The general psychological principles that Homans could deductively apply in explaining the basic social situation—in which the actions of each of at least two persons reward or punish the actions of the other—were already available to him in the writings of his long-time friend and Harvard colleague, B.F. Skinner. Homans, therefore, adopted Skinner's behavioural psychology, along with a few basic ideas from marginal utility theory in microeconomics, and put forth a systematic set of five general propositions about elementary social behaviour grounded in notions of reward and punishment, deprivation and satiation, cost and profit, aggression and approval. This theory posits that all human relationships are formed by the use of a subjective cost-benefit analysis and the comparison of alternatives. For example, when a person thinks the costs of a relationship outweighs the perceived benefits, then the theory says that the person will choose to leave the relationship.

The interest of the social exchange theory, as it is recognised by Homans, is the "social behaviour of people in direct contact with one another" (Homans, 1961, 3). The specificity of the approach based on the concept of exchange is based in recognising this relationship of mutual interpersonal interaction as an exchange of "rewards" and "penalties." That "behaviour is social means that when a person acts in a way, it is rewarded or punished by the conduct of another person, although it may also be rewarded or punished by the non-human environment" (Homans 1961, 2), which, however, no longer is a part of the scope of the notion of interaction, by definition, limited to direct man to man relations.

Homans defines the concept of interaction as synonymous with the concept of "social behaviour" (1961, 35). He writes that "when an action (or sentiment) emitted by one man is rewarded (or punished) by the action issued by another man, then, regardless of the type of emitted behaviour, we say that these two people interact." Rewards can be either tangible or intangible, and Homans does not restrict in any way this concept (ie everything can be a reward), distinguishing only a special class among them: sentiments externalized in behaviour (sentiments) as signs of some internal psychological states, emotional attitudes towards others (e.g. approval). We should add that behaviour expressed within the scope of so understood interaction is called by Homans elementary social behaviour.

These initial assumptions are further developed by Homans. In a fairly systematic way, he introduces a number of categories and statements of his theory, referring to the findings of two branches of science: behavioural psychology, especially in its version proposed by B.F. Skinner, and the so-called microeconomics. As we shall see, in addition to the above two, recognised by the author, there is also another one equally important, though more hidden source of his ideas. This will be discussed later; for now let's focus on Skinner's experimental studies that provided the essential inspiration for Homans, whose object was a caged dove. The bird moves in its room and pecks, sometimes hitting a certain point. Then the experimenter as a reward feeds it with grain. It turns out that the pigeon will again peck at the target, namely, as Homans says, it will "emit behaviour" bringing it a coveted reward, the food. In the terminology used by Skinner and then by Homans, this behaviour has been reinforced, and the dove itself has been subjected to instrumental conditioning (in the more colloquial language: it learned this behaviour.) What patterns regarding manifestations of learned behaviour can be determined on the basis of Skinner's studies? Among other things, the following: a pigeon will peck the more it is hungry, i.e. the less food it has received lately. Conversely, increased, along with frequently repeated enhancement, saturation implies a reduction in its activity. Meanwhile, total lack of reinforcement in the long run will lead to the complete extinction of the behaviour. Finally, the dove also meets adverse conditions, or penalties (for example, the experimenter can pour a bucket of water on it.) The penalties, which the pigeon cannot avoid if it wants to turn on the behaviour leading to a prize, Homans calls "cost." The result of the existence of a cost is reduction of the frequency of relevant behaviours. Not only being in adversive conditions has punishing properties, but also the withdrawal of reinforcing properties; the direct result of interruption of feeding is, "in an animal emotional behaviour called aggression."

As it turns out, we already have in this way all the essential elements needed to formulate the theory of "social exchange, human exchange", according to Homans, it is enough to repeal the assumption of a one-way exchange, which it has in the case of the dove-experimenter relationship. When there are two human individuals facing each other, provided that "each of them shows behaviour to some extent reinforced by the other's behaviour, we do not need any new statements to describe and explain their social behaviour (Homans 1975, 106; 1961: 30). The outlined "laws of individual behaviour," binding for both a pigeon and the man, according to Homans, "result in laws of social behaviour." One only needs to "extrapolate" the results of observations of animals onto the regularity of behaviour of people introducing not more than a few additional terms, especially occurring in economics, and not used by Skinner. We will get to know them soon, in the course of discussing the five basic theorems of the theory of exchange formulated by Homans.

Of course, one could dismiss out of hand those claims "binding for the behaviour of all higher animals" (Homans 1974, 15), among which the author of *Social Behaviour* also counts humans. Homans, to be sure, admits that the human differs from a pigeon, bringing this specificity, unless you count the obvious anatomical differences, to the possession of a language, and in the second edition of his book he adds "exceptional intelligence" appropriate for the species. One can therefore ask, ignoring any other possible substantive evaluations of Homans' way of understanding the relationship between the animal and human world, can behaviour (which is the consequence of, among others, these differences) be explained by using statements describing what is common to man and beast?[1]

---

[1] See Sulek (1975; 1990–92), where we read that the results of experiments on animals are fundamentally inadequate to explain the areas of human-specific phenomena. The article also mentions a number of conditions that must be met in the animal experiment, if it is later to be used to draw any analogy with human behaviour; the assumptions of such an experiment "should define: the modeled phenomena area, i.e. the subject of an analogy;

(a) phylogenetic limits of analogy, and more precisely to positively prejudge the question of the existence of analogies between the used animal model and the human original

(b) phenomena that determine that the object under investigation is suitable for the model

(c) should also recognise the specific features of the original as irrelevant to the course of the mapped phenomena." The author's critical conclusion that "in

II.6.2. The propositions of the theory of exchange in the light of its own assumptions

Let's suppose, however, a sympathetic attitude towards Homans, giving the author of *Social Behaviour* the benefit of the doubt, and consider the statements of the theory of exchange, as suggested by the author, "as if they applied only to human behaviour" (Homans 1974a, 15). Within this, more "internal" point of view, let's try and look at those arguments of Homans' theory from the standpoint of, among others, their logical consistency, precision of concepts, explanatory power and similar attributes of science, which should be in place given the intentions of their creator.

Homans is characterised by high expectations about standards of research conduct in science. He is among others known for his violent reactions against his colleagues (especially Talcott Parsons), refusing to see their research as theoretical practice. Homans insisted that sociology had no general propositions of its own. To this alleged state of affairs Homans opposes the collection of his own "general statements" based on the achievements of behavioural psychology and having to distinguish themselves with the real explanatory power, allowing for the use of them for effective explanation of social life. They are also to go beyond the mere "quality, anatomical view of human behaviour" as Homans defines them with a hint of derogatory note; although not reaching the rank of statements such as "x = log y," stating however the regularities "x varies depending on the y" which say that the value of x increases with each increase in the value of "y," implying that x and y are quantitative variables. The mere explanation, or otherwise is according to Homans

fact these assumptions are rarely formulated, and if so, then in rudimentary form" also refers to Homans. In the general criticism—on the basis of psychology—behaviorist direction (especially in the Skinner version) which is the basis for theoretical concepts of Homans' approach. However, Stanislaw Ossowski draws attention to the unsuitability of concepts based on assumptions of behaviorism for understanding social life assessing the "research on the formation of conditioned reflexes, or, more broadly, on the mechanism of the formation of imperative habits and on the mechanism of their disappearance." In this way: "the most general laws (formation and decay of habits) can, as it seems, achieve a very high degree of generality, but they are not the laws regarding social phenomena: if a living creature of the same or distinct species acts as a stimulus in shaping the habits of other creatures, then, according to these general laws, it plays it in the same role as other stimuli" (1967, 334).

equivalent to the formulation of a "deductive system, i.e. such that explicandum (what is explained with a general form of "a claim that adjudicates the relationship between at least two features of the world") is a logical consequence can be logically derived from other, more general premises of the system" (Homans 1961, 51; 1974, 8).

Let us begin, therefore, in accordance with previous assumptions, our analysis of the theory of exchange by an attempt to measure it with its own, that is to say, acknowledged by the author himself measure. Proposition One: "If in the past, the occurrence of a particular stimulus situation (in the issue of Social Behaviour from 1974 this was simply called a "stimulus" or a set of "stimuli") was associated with a reward, then the more closely the stimulus situation resembles the situation from the past, the more likely it is that the same or similar action will occur" (Homans 1961, 53).

In the revised edition of the book it was called "The Stimulus Proposition": If in the past the occurrence of a particular stimulus, or set of stimuli, has been the occasion on which a person's action has been rewarded, then the more similar the present stimuli are to the past ones, the more likely the person is to perform the action, or some similar action, now (Homans 1974, 22–23).

The Value Proposition: The more valuable to a person is the result of their action, the more likely they are to perform the action (Homans 1974, 25).

One can see immediately that the key concept in the preceding sentence is the concept of the stimulus, or "stimulus situations," and the similarities existing between the two situations such that the observer must be able to determine if the Homans statement is to have postulated explanatory power. Homans gives no rules that may serve in determining the similarities between two teams of stimuli (i.e. typically associated with obtaining reward factors), and what's more, he does not say anything about how to distinguish a stimulus from what is not a stimulus. He admits himself that the problem of (isolating) distinguishing stimuli, determining the similarities and differences between them "can be extremely complicated" and the resulting lack of its clear solution on his part he considers a "great gap" in the whole notion. The way out that he suggests is highly unsatisfactory, and in a sense only worsens the situation, as it reveals some, as we shall see, general features of the theory of Homans as a whole. The author of *Social Behaviour* suggests that in the case when "the same kind of action is repeated, one should virtually accept stimuli as a resolved case and explain changes in behaviour through looking at the way in which it is enhanced" (Homans 1961, 54). If we called attention to this sentence, it is because it reveals circularity of the "first law of exchange theory." Without having criteria for the determination of the similarity between the two stimuli situations, as well as any definition of reward that is independent from the proposition, we are forced—when using this "law"—to reverse the order of parts occurring in it, and hence, to deprive it of the status of "general behaviour law." The "explanation" that we are able, using Homans' assertion, to provide, is a typical example of an *ex post facto* explanation: we observe the occurrence of a behaviour and we infer that in that case it must have been rewarded in the past in some respect under similar conditions (although the "law" would require us to do the opposite on the basis of the fact of "reward" to determine the likelihood of an occurrence of a behaviour). Not being able to say with confidence that the current situation "is similar" to the former, nor to distinguish what, in this situation is the reward from what is not we have to accept the faith that the behaviour "which is more likely in the situation" and behaviour, which is referred to in the first part of the theorem, involving the occurrence of "stimulus" and the reward is one and the same.

The above example provides evidence of the dangers linked with the direct takeover by a researcher of human behaviour of conclusions and methods of animal psychology. The experimenter from the study of the pigeon could in fact solve relatively easily all difficulties encountered by his findings having transferred them into human reality. In artificial conditions isolated from all external influences, one can actually get a similarity of "stimulus situations," for example, by extracting a bell as a stimulus, which resounds with each peck of the pigeon at the target. Similarly, knowing that the dove before the experiment was not fed for a long time, it can be easily inferred that nothing other than the "reduction of hunger" in obtaining food will be a reward for the animal. Of course, in real social life such situations, achievable in the laboratory, do not happen at all or very seldom which, naturally, undermines the value of reasoning, which is based precisely on the assumption of the possibility of identification, including under one universal "law."

The same criticisms can be addressed towards the second argument presented by Homans, Proposition Two: "The more frequently within a given time segment, human activity rewards an action of the other, the more frequently the other will emit rewarded action" (Homans 1961, 54). This contention is also known as "The Success Proposition": For all actions taken by persons, the more often a particular action of a person is rewarded, the more likely the person is to perform that action (Homans 1974, 16). Also here the only indicator of "rewarding" properties of behaviour of one person to another is the fact of taking actions by the latter which, as is assumed, are to be the result of this positive stimulation. Here, too, the order of reasoning is the opposite to that assumed by Homans' "law" and creates for the researcher a "vicious circle", it is said that the Person B manifests certain behaviours, those that met with the reward from the Person A, but wanting to show the fact of being actions of the Person A, a reward for the Person B, may be given as the only evidence that B "emits" these behaviours. Nowak has a similar opinion, writing that with relevant theories of learning "the meaning of the term reward, law with strengthening the role of rewards is a definition tautology … essentially empirically impossible to solve" (1970, 200–2). Irrespective of these drawbacks of the Homans position, different type of difficulties can occur in the case of the concept of "frequency." This concept has great importance in the theory of exchange, because "it constitutes a measure of amount of action."

The possibility of measurement carried out with it assumes however, which Homans recognises, the existence of "units of action, that can be counted" (Homans 1961, 36). Whereas in the case of the pigeon the indication of such a unit ("pecks") was not a complicated matter, the author admits that "in the case of human actions, the isolation of units, and hence calculation of frequency can not be so easy" (Homans 1974b, 18). Given Homans' explanatory and deductive ambitions, the solution that he proposes in this situation may surprise: "'methodological liberalism' tantamount to … the absence of rules in this area. Each method of choice of 'action units' is OK, on condition that it is suitable; one can recognise that it is suitable on the basis of Homans' understanding of the methodology probably only in one way … saying that it is OK. Opening an arbitrary way, no rules are provided of preference for one rather than the other way of defining units."

The next theorem is named in the revised version of the work as the Value Proposition: "The more valuable to a person is the result of his action, the more likely he is to perform the action" (Homans 1974, 25). In the first edition it is named Proposition Three, to the effect that: "The more valuable to the human the action unit, which is given to him by the second, the more often he will emit activity rewarded by the action of the other" (Homans 1961, 55) (e.g. the more someone needs help, the more often they will ask for it, and the more thanks, constituting a reward for the other, they will give upon its receipt). In Homans' view, this proposition reinforces very much the explanatory power of the whole theory, because in conjunction with Proposition Two it will allow for the measuring of the "rate of exchange" between the two activities (aiming to be an equivalent of price in the economy as defining the number of units of a particular product, which can be exchanged for a given number of units of other goods) and to determine the proportion in which amounts of "emited units of action" remain towards each other. "The rate of exchange" Homans defines as "the number of units of action that a person emits in each limited period of time in exchange for a certain number of units issued by the other person."

The author hastens to the practical demonstration of the merits of his law, argueing that "in pursuance thereof, the rate of exchange between the approval and help (sample enumerated "goods should be equal to the ratio between the value imparted by the person to help and the value that the other person gives to approval" (Homans 1961, 55).

First and foremost, this raises a problem of Homans' solution to the issue of isolation of "units of action" which are in question. In both cases, the author proposes to use "minutes": both in terms of approval and support; that "a minute of help" can mean something completely different than "a minute of approval," and that help can regard different issues, and thus help is unequal help, it is not an obstacle for him to bring both of these "actions" to one common denominator. The possibility to set any "equivalence, equality" and "proportionality" of which the statement talks, however, assumes as a prerequisite the possibility of an independent measurement, and thus determining units occurring therein. Meanwhile, the status of the concept of "value" is represented in the theory of Homans analogically to the definition (or rather lack thereof) of "reward": you cannot, contrary to the postulate of Homans, explain by this concept—understood by the author as "the degree of strengthening or punishment that man obtains from a given unit of action" (Homans 1961, 40)—the fact of taking such and such actions by the individual, because the sole proof that the value is a factor motivating them is the observation of these same behaviours that are to be explained by it and not be used as a basis for inference of its existence. Compare this with examples from Homans: "Our only way to measure the relative value of milk and tea for the Chinese is to observe whether he will perform more work to obtain one of these things than to have the other" (1964, 955). The way of measuring "factors in the law" is just another way of expressing the contents of the law.[2] The concept of value is on the basis of the theory of Homans among

---

[2] Homans postulates, in order to dodge the trap, the return to the "history" of an individual in order to know its value. But of course it only moves the problem on to a temporarily different level, without removing the difficulty—we do not exceed the vicious circle of the argument, "the greater value," for example. The more help one person has, the more they will take action rewarded by help (1943) either in a

the most ambiguous. In the quoted formulation, it still has behavioural connotation. Soon, however, “value” appears as the "psychological value" (62) and as noted by Ossowski, Homans "resigns from behaviourist purism" (1967, 346).

This same example is to be found in *Social Behaviour* in the form of a syllogism: the greater value the result of an action has for a person the more likely that he will perform this action. For the Chinese, tea has more value than milk. Therefore, it is more likely that the Chinese will take an action that results in getting tea rather than getting milk (the premise of this syllogism is a slightly modified form of our Proposition Three).

According to Homans, anything can have a value for the human, (1961, 45, 79, 287; 1944, 27, 270), as everything can be a reward (the value is always "the value of reward," or a negative reward, e.g. a penalty). Yet we know that if something is supposed to explain everything then, as a result, it explains nothing, and such a role the pseudo explanatory concepts is actually performed by these and other categories of his theory. Since the concept of value or the reward does not contain any concrete empirical content, then their incorporation in the theoretical proposition may not give it explanatory values or make it a seemingly explanatory statement, because you can always say that something is a "reward" or a "value" and there is no way that this sentence can be verified.

Here is one example of essentially tautological nature of the whole theory of exchange. Homans explains the phenomenon of a group conformism in the following way: "Suppose a Person A is a man who considers it valuable that his behaviour is subordinated to a group norm and that Person B's behaviour is also subordinated to it. If the Person B considers the same values as the Person A, so the conformity of each of them is the value for the other, then the Person A rewards the Person B and the Person B rewards the Person A to a more or less the same extent. The exchange between the two is in a state of equilibrium" (Homans 1961, 116).

In the second edition of *Social Behaviour*, Homans admits that the proposition in which there is the concept of value is a tautology (he motivates the persistence of this concept with its teaching usefulness), and also withdraws from the former thesis anticipating the possibility of

---

present, or its past version. Skidmore also draws attention to that fact (1975, 35) and Parsons writes that "history becomes for Homans a final residual category, escape to which can resolve every difficulty which arises due to shortcomings in the more specific parts of the conceptual scheme ... he makes history very extensive and very laden residual category, as history is not analyzed here, but taken as given" (Turk 1971, 34).

comparison of the values. But what if instead of Person B there will be a Person C, who will not want to submit to the norms prevailing in the group? Well, apparently, the theorist responds, the Person C "sufficiently strongly praises actions inconsistent with conformism." In other words, someone submits, which means the person appreciates the subordination, if someone does not comply he or she does not appreciate subordination.

The figurative sense of Homans' notion of value, based on the "third law of exchange," is also clearly shown by the case of their application, not to the phenomena of small groups, but to historical events. The author of *Social Behaviour* explains why William the Conqueror never conquered Scotland with the following inference schema: The greater value a reward has for an individual, the more likely it is that the individual will take an action to obtain the reward (this is a version of the proposition concerned). In the circumstances, William the Conqueror (a specific individual) did not consider the conquest of Scotland as something of value, thus it was unlikely that he would take action to Conquer Scotland (Homans 1967, 44).

Thanks to the fact that it includes the said "law," this pattern corresponds, according to Homans, to scientific standards and is a "real explanation," but the same standards of science do not consider as "real" the circular explanation, and this is what we are dealing with in this case . The author in fact has no evidence that William the Conqueror did not regard the conquest of Scotland as something of value, except only that he did not conquer Scotland (and therefore the fact that was to be explained itself), and using "law" as the main link of the explanation turns out to be nothing less than tautology, since the value of the reward and the associated action are in fact only verbally different conclusions from the same empirical state of affairs (lack of conquest of Scotland by William).

The same rules are applied, subject to the same criticism, by Homans in explaining the conduct of his hypothetical individual, the "interactor." He gives him or her a partner, a person liked by him or her, but at the same time a person whose views he disagrees with. How to explain in this situation our hero's choice of one of the two alternatives facing him: a change of partner or changes of beliefs? Homans responds with an assertion of nature, like that of Moliere, of accounting for the fact of creating a dream through opium by the circumstance that it has hypnotic properties: "probably the person who gives more value to getting consent form another person than to reward of original exchange, will take the first opportunity and will break the initial exchange … meanwhile the person for whom the value of the initial exchange outweighs the expense of giving up his opinion, is likely to adopt the second option and will change his mind in the direction of the consent with the partner." (Homans 1974b, 62)

However, even assuming the solution of all the difficulties inherent in the concept of "value" as a category empirically explanatory, does the law of Homans used in the above "deductive system" as "a condition for higher reasoning" add anything to the understanding of the proceedings of our ruler?

Homans' notion of scientific explanation comes from "these positivist traditions" described by Ossowski according to which "the explanation consists in indicating the general proposition, which is a logical premise for sentences claiming the occurrence of specific phenomena. In the plain language, explanation would consist in the conclusion that this always happens." One should also agree with Ossowski, when he states that "the relationship between the phenomena does not always become clearer when the general argument is given, which is the right logic for appropriate detailed sentences" (Ossowski 1967, 265). The programme of deductive explanation in Homans' version is an explicit opting on the side of ahistorical position, understood as "the explanation of certain social concretes by indication that they are merely a variation of some general universally applicable category or a universal ahistorical law" (Kozyr-Kowalski & Ladosz 1976, 191–2).

Marx has pointed out that:

> it is the fashion to preface a work of economics with a general part—and precisely this part figures under the title 'production' (see for example J. St. Mill)—treating of the general preconditions of all production. This general part consists or is alleged to consist of (1) the conditions without which production is not possible, i.e. in fact, to indicate nothing more than the essential moments of all production. But … see, this reduces itself in fact to a few very simple characteristics, which are hammered out into flat tautologies. (Marx 1939)

This is not the only moment in which Homans' ahistoric approach manifests itself. Further aspects of Homans' allegedly scientific strategy is revealed by the next of the "laws" of exchange, Proposition Four: "The more frequently in the recent past a man received rewarding actions from the other, the less valuable each subsequent unit of this action becomes for him and, therefore by the power of the Proposition [Three], the less he will emit an action that brings him the reward" (Homans 1961, 55).

It is enough to compare this sentence with Proposition Two to see that they state greatly conflicting dependencies: once the reward is to cause an increase in the frequency of behaviour (Proposition Two), once, on the contrary, its decrease (Proposition Four). Now truly the theory of exchange has gained an almost unprecedented universalism: there is simply no fact that could undermine it, and there is no phenomenon that it could not "explain." Homans, indeed, sees this contradiction, saying that the "proposition assertion [Four] may mask the truth of the proposition [Two] … this proposition is valid only when all other conditions are equal; among those other conditions is the effect of proposition [Four] that saturation reduces the degree of emission of action … in the case of a pigeon living in its natural state there lacks an experimental control to separate effects (judged by these two propositions) (Homans 1961, 55, 21). If you cannot do it in the case of a pigeon, then probably even more so in the case of a man living in a society; respectively, a social scientist is left free to choose a proposition "matching" the observed state of affairs, "explaining" transforms into an explanation constructed ad hoc. The theory of Homans is therefore subject to the full extent of Ossowski's remark: "that once fashionable phrase *ceteris paribus* deprives the general theory of empirical risk and the empirical utility" (Ossowski 1967, 328).

At the same time, thanks to the above remarks, we have arrived at a general and characteristic feature of Homans' manner of theorising: for almost every state of affairs, to which the theory of exchange refers, for each relationship stated by it, you can without much difficulty find a counterexample, an opposite state of affairs or opposite relationship (in many cases, moreover, the author himself helps the reader).

In the second part of his book, Homans cites various studies and experiments proving, in his view, the relevance of the assumptions of the theory of exchange and demonstrating their usefulness for understanding of such or other phenomena or social processes. This practical test turns out however to be the evidence of infertility of the conception. It shows that the theory of Homans does not meet the requirements imposed on it by the author himself, according to whom in explanation there "must be claims for which acceptance or rejection empirical facts, or figures are relevant as well as observations and evidence" (Homans 1974b, 8). These, as well as the previously quoted examples, illustrate, among others, the fact that the theory of exchange, contrary to a well-known Popper's criterion of scientificity, is virtually irrefutable, since, as confirming it, there are facts that are a direct negation of each other. The results of U.S. research on employee groups and youth groups are interpreted by Homans as consistent with the proposition which is a consequence of the fundamental axioms of the theory of exchange, according to which "the higher the esteem that a specific member of the group enjoys, the more frequent are interactions taken against him by other members" (Homans 1961, 188, 203). However, not only the reader's intuition, but the author himself shows that a reversed relationship is possible and probable; high esteem often creates between the esteemed person and the others barriers, and reduces the number of contacts. Homans will therefore say, dozens of pages later, and in accordance with the principles of the same theory, that the respected "leader of the group tends to be very often a lonely man … his followers are willing to hold away from him" (Homans 1961, 311). One of the theoretical conditions of the proposition describing the first of these situations is, according to Homans, an argument that "liking a person by another changes directly depending on the frequency of their interactions" (Homans 1961, 182). But everyone could easily give hundreds of well-known examples from everyday experience, when such frequent contact with others does not lead to an increase of positive feelings towards them, but results in indifference, boredom, or negative emotions. Treated in the tradition of positivism as a key differentiator and the value of scientific claims, "strict universality" in the case of the "law" above turns out to be illusory; depending on conditions, its inverse is met as often as itself. No greater is the predictive power of another Homans claim, which is to determine the relationship between the position of the individual and the type of interactions undertaken by the individual. According to him, a person demonstrates at the same time a "tendency to interact with people of higher status, as well as tendencies to interact with people of equal status." In order for the picture to be complete and the universality of the proposition boundless, we may also add interacting with people of lower status, because it is rewarding to give someone the feeling of one's superiority, to be confirmed in the sense of superiority by appropriate behaviour from others. Elsewhere Homans argues as follows: "explaining the behaviour of two people to each other, we need to know the relationship between the values and one and the values of the other. Sometimes what makes the exchange between them possible, is the difference between their values, but sometimes it is the similarity between the values of the two people that cements their relationship. As you can clearly see, this statement has roughly the same value as the following prediction: 'it is going to rain or it is not going to rain'."

II.6.3. The Theory of Social Exchange and the Common Sense Knowledge, or Every Stick Has Two Ends

There are probably enough examples to reveal another characteristic of the Theory of Social Exchange. Simply ask yourself where you might encounter a similar situation: the coexistence in perfect harmony of perfectly contradictory claims, and mutually exclusive theses? Of course, in the area of so-called common sense, whose characteristic feature is eclecticism, is the reconciliation of the conflicting views of fact and ideas. One of the truths of common sense will proclaim that "absence makes the heart grow fonder," a proverb stating the opposite will be found immediately in the area of the same colloquial reason: "out of sight, out of mind."

You can recommend as a mental puzzle—with a warning that the list would be a long one—to search for such proverbs and maxims of an entirely contrary sense, including those that are self-contradictory such as: "A change is as good as a rest," functioning on the basis of common thinking. This observation of a very intimate relationship of the propositions of the Theory of Social Exchange with common-sense wisdom should not surprise us, both in light of Homans' own statements, who concedes that his claims "are part of the traditional common-sense psychology," and that they would therefore "probably not be something completely unexpected, even to prehistoric man." According to Homans, it is precisely the advantage of his theory of exchange that, as he believes, "people have always explained their behaviour by pointing out what it gives them, what it costs them, on a daily basis using expressions such as: 'I found this and this is good' or 'I have obtained from him a lot' or even 'This conversation with him cost me a lot'" (Homans 1975, 69).

The program of sociology, brought down to the level of popular consciousness, from which it is supposed to be different only by the degree of systematization as can easily be seen, actually eliminates it as a science, for is there any need for a science that does not go beyond the horizons of knowledge available for each layman? Is the "discovery" by Homans, solemnly uttered, not in fact a commonplace cant, that "the rivalry between groups generally increases the hostility expressed by the members of one group against members of the other group" (Homans 1961, 144)? What, beyond a quasi-scientific method of expression, does represent another "theorem," according to which "after a break in their interactions, the man who will emit the first action of the new series will be the one who recognises the action of the other to be more valuable" (Homans 1961, 201).

Homans' book is full of similar commonplace truths, sometimes as trivial, as is this candidate to the title of the "law of science": "out of two people more or less similar in other respects, the person who receives more of some specific reward, is the person more pleased from both of them" (Homans 1961, 269). Or take another example: "A person with a low position does not have many friends, or a lot of enemies, whereas a person of high position has both many friends and many enemies" (Homans 1961, 307). Contrary to appearances, the above "word of wisdom" comes not from another book of folk proverbs but from a purportedly scientific work.

We therefore have every right to call Homans' sociology a "vulgar sociology" by analogy to the "vulgar economy" whose characteristic feature, according to Marx, was that it amounts to an exercise in thinking in which surface appearances are mistaken for underlying social reality. As clearly shown by the Theory of Social Exchange, its pseudo-theoretical content not only remains within the confines of pre-scientific, everyday thinking, but it is not even able to reproduce it in full form, to render the real scope of human knowledge about society, not limited to a few shallow statements elevated by the "vulgar sociologist" to the dignity of a science. As is apparent from the above quotations, and from what we shall document more fully now, the theory of exchange captures only a narrow aspect of experiences of human behaviour in society, associated with the interpretation of their cost-benefit considerations. A set of these "economic" terms is introduced by Homans on the occasion of his discussion of the fifth proposition of the theory, adapting for it the concepts developed previously in the analysis of the experiment with the pigeon. "Cost" is defined by Homans as the value of lost reward, which could be brought by the implementation of an alternative behaviour to the one already taken. The pigeon, pecking, is running the risk of fatigue and loses the reward (no penalty is, according to Homans also a reward), consisting in its avoidance; the decision to choose one of two offered propositions "costs" me losing the rewards associated with the position which I give up. The difference between the reward obtained and the cost of its receipt Homans calls "profit" and puts forth as a thesis of his theory a statement that "no exchange will last if both parties do not reach the profit in it" (Homans 1961, 61).

Finally, he advances the idea of "distributive justice," according to which in each exchange there must be a rule of proportionality of cost and rewards, i.e. the proportionality of investment to global profits. "Investments" are certain characteristics of an individual, authorizing her or him to a greater or lesser share in the total pool of rewards, both in her / his own eyes and in the eyes of the partner (for example, age or sex). Let us even dispense the very unlucky choice of the term "investment" wiping out the difference between, using the terminology of the long-term adversary of the author of the theory of exchange, the features ascribed and achieved, with which logic would rather order to combine the notion of investment.

It is more difficult to refrain from the comment that the fact of why such an "investment" as a specific skin colour is on an "interactive market" of a society valued higher or lower, based on the Homans assumptions is impossible to understand. The cause of this state of affairs we return to below. In essence, for Homans, social behaviour is an exchange of material and nonmaterial (for example, symbols of approval and prestige) goods. For a person engaged in exchange, what they give may be a cost to them, just as what they get may be a reward, and their behaviour is apt to change less as profit, that is, reward less cost, increases. In other words, the more they get, the less valuable any further unit of that value is to them, and the less often they will emit behaviour reinforced by it. The cost, or the reward foregone, and the value of what they give and of what they get varies with the quantity of what they give and get. But persons involved in an exchange relationship also expect to receive as much reward from the other as they give to the other. That is to say, they expect there to be a fairly equitable exchange of rewards and costs between persons. Homans calls this the rule of distributive justice and describes it as: "A man in an exchange relation with another will expect that the rewards of each man be proportional to his costs—the greater the rewards, the greater the costs—and that the net rewards, or profits, of each man be proportional to his investments—the greater the investments, the greater the profit (Homans 1961, 75).

From these five general propositions of the elementary forms of social behaviour, Homans endeavoured to explain a wide range of phenomena from conformity to competition, from status to satisfaction—and more generally, and for many sociologists more significantly, the emergence and maintenance of social structures.

A few years after the publication of *Social Behaviour*, Homans candidly admitted that he was not wholly satisfied with the clarity of the exposition of the book's thesis. Indeed, despite his uncommon ability for clear and lucid writing, his propositions in *Social Behaviour* are stated in a rather turgid prose that makes them ponderous reading. He also admitted that he had "handled rather clumsily" (1968, 5), the topics of status and power. So, in 1974 he produced a revised edition of *Social Behaviour* in which he keeps much of the substance of his main thesis but tightens up the argument to make it more lucid and logical. He also adds an entire chapter on power and uses payoff matrices of the sort developed by social psychologists John W. Thibaut and Harold H. Kelley in their *The Social Psychology of Groups* (1959) to illustrate how power works. Additionally, Homans restates his general propositions adding also The Aggression-Approval Proposition, Part a: When a person's action does not receive the reward they expected, or receives punishment they did not expect, they will be angry; they become more likely to perform aggressive behaviour, and the results of such behaviour become more valuable to them (Homans 1974, 37). Part b: When a person's action receives a reward they expected, especially a greater reward then they expected, or does not receive punishment they expected, they will be pleased; they become more likely to perform approving behaviour, and the results of such behaviour become more valuable to them (Homans 1974, 39).

The Rationality Proposition: In choosing between alternative actions, a person will choose that one for which, as perceived by them at the time, the value V of the result, multiplied by the probability p of getting the result, is the greater (Homans 1974, 43).

II.6.4. Sociology and economics

Before presenting the next and for that matter last of Homans' proposition associated with the aforementioned notion of distributive justice, let us put forward a couple of comments regarding a broader issue of his relation to economics.

The American sociologist boasts that his, as he himself calls it, "economic approach" is one which could bring closer the two social sciences in question, the key proof being this closeness of the fundamental premise of Homans' approach, with all its theoretical and methodological implications. Homans, namely, reckons that both disciplines deal with goods in terms of rewards, the difference being that economics focuses on material rewards, whereas "the general theory of exchange" lacks any such limitations.

The basic fact that the two disciplines have so much in common implies, amongst other things, a number of analogies between the economic laws and their equivalents formulated on the grounds of the theory of social exchange.

Thus, the Law Of Supply, a microeconomic law stating that, all other factors being equal, as the price of goods or services increases, the quantity of goods or services offered by suppliers increases and vice versa is, according to Homans, equivalent to the proposition that the greater the value of reward acquired thanks to a given action, the more frequently it will be performed. In turn, another microeconomic law that states that, all other factors being equal, as the price of goods or services increases, consumer demand for the goods or services will decrease and vice versa, i.e. Law Of Demand is allegedly analogous to the following thesis: the greater the cost implied by an action, the rarer it will be taken (Homans 1961, 69).

It appears that in a later period Homans has modified his view as to the interelations of his theory of exchange and economics, putting stronger emphasis on the greater generality, and thus superiority of the former. The above-mentioned laws of supply and demand are, according to this new approach, not to be treated as equivalents in the field of social sciences, (Homans 1974a, 77), but as "consequences of general laws of behavioural psychology, which constitute the general explanatory premises in the realm of human behaviour. That is another way of saying that all social sciences are provided with the most general propositions used in explaining their respective phenomena of interest by only one amongst these sciences, i.e. psychology" (Homans 1974b, 70).

This degradation of economics from the role of a theoretic source to that of science essentially reducible to others clearly brings out the spurious character of Homans' attempt to make the categories and claims of economics an integral part of any social research, thereby recognising the relevance of the economy as a factor shaping the social life. Even apart of any assessment of the value of the kind of economics which constitutes an inspiration for Homans,[3] it is difficult to imagine a worse way of establishing the relationships of the economic structure to the non-economic realm of social life. The thesis, which on the basis of socio-economic structuralism proclaims the role of the economy as conditioning the whole of social life, which economy, contrary to Homans, does not boil down to the market, the relations of exchange, but includes at the very least the relations of production and property relations, has nothing in common with any attempt to reduce these non-economic phenomena and processes to the economic ones, or with a mechanistic application of economic categories to non-economic structures. This deserves to be dubbed "economic imperialism" and obscures the boundaries between what constitutes the economic structure and what does not.

It is hard to imagine a more distorted proof of the primacy of the economy in social life. When one treats all social relations in the likeness of an exchange, one loses any possibility of an empirical investigation on the various ways in which the economic structure affects non-economic structures, and transforms the issue of the relationships of the two domains into a linguistic problem, one of applying to non-economic phenomena some kind of economic label. To the theory of social exchange the following criticism put forward by Lenin (1908) can therefore be applied:

[3] It is the subjectivistic direction whose connection with the vulgar economics is apparent, as Oscar Lange, among others, has remarked.

> It need hardly be said that all this play with biology and sociology contains not a grain of Marxism. Both in Spencer and Mikhailovsky one may find any number of definitions not a whit worse than this, defining nothing but the "good intentions" of the author and betraying a complete lack of understanding of "what is idealism" and what materialism.

The author begins Book III of Empirio-Monism, the article "Social Selection (Foundations of Method)," 1906, by refuting the "eclectic socio-biological attempts of Lange, Ferri, Woltmann and many others" (1), and on page 15 we find the following conclusion of the "enquiry": We can formulate the fundamental connection between energetics and social selection as follows:

> "Every act of social selection represents an increase or decrease of the energy of the social complex concerned. In the former case we have 'positive selection,' in the latter 'negative selection'."

And such unutterable trash is served out as Marxism! Can one imagine anything more sterile, lifeless and scholastic than this string of biological and energeticist terms that contribute nothing, and can contribute nothing, in the sphere of the social sciences? There is not a shadow of concrete economic enquiry here, not a hint of the Marxist method, the method of dialectics and the world outlook of materialism, only a mere invention of definitions and attempts to fit them into the ready-made conclusions of Marxism. "The rapid growth of the productive forces of capitalist society is undoubtedly an increase in the energy of the social whole ..." The second half of the phrase is undoubtedly a simple repetition of the first half expressed in meaningless terms which seem to lend "profundity" to the question, but which in reality in no way differ from the eclectic biologico-sociological attempts of Lange and Co.! "... but the disharmonious character of this process leads to its culmination in a crisis, in a vast waste of productive forces, in a sharp decrease of energy: positive selection is replaced by negative selection" (18).

In what way does this differ from Lange? A biologico-energeticist label is tacked on to ready-made conclusions on the subject of crises, without any concrete material whatever being added and without the nature of crises being elucidated. All this is done with the very best intentions, for the author wishes to corroborate and give greater depth to Marx's conclusions; but in point of fact he only dilutes them with an intolerably dreary and lifeless scholasticism. The only "Marxism" here is a repetition of an already known conclusion, and all the "new" proof of it, all this "social energetics" (34) and "social selection" is but a mere collection of words and a sheer mockery of Marxism. Bogdanov is not engaged in a Marxist enquiry at all; all he is doing is to re-clothe results already obtained by the Marxist enquiry in a biological and energeticist terminology. The whole attempt is worthless from beginning to end, for the concepts "selection," "assimilation and dissimilation" of energy, the energetic balance, and so forth are, when applied to the sphere of the social sciences, but empty phrases. In fact, an enquiry into social phenomena and an elucidation of the method of the social sciences cannot be undertaken with the aid of these concepts. Nothing is easier than to tack the labels of "energetics" or "biologico-sociology" on to such phenomena as crises, revolutions, the class struggle and so forth; but neither is there anything more sterile, more scholastic and lifeless than such an occupation. The important thing is not that Bogdanov tries to fit all his results and conclusions into the Marxist theory—or "nearly" all (we have seen the "correction" he made on the subject of the relation of social being to social consciousness)—but that the methods of fitting—this "social energetics,"—are thoroughly false and in no way differ from the methods of Lange. (Lenin 1908)

II.6.5. The utilitarian man

Let us, finally, cite Homans' Proposition Five, associated with his socio-economic rule of distributive justice. The proposition in question holds that the more to a man's disadvantage the rule of distributive justice fails of realization, the more likely he is to display the emotional behaviour we call anger (Homans 1961, 75).

Again, it is impossible to determine whether the rule of distributive justice holds in practice, or establish the point in which it is violated, since any proportions between rewards, punishments, costs, profits and investments cannot be, naturally, calculated. An even more important question concerns the genesis of this sentiment of distributive justice felt by any participants of any exchange, i.e. all interactions, since each one of these is, as has been noted, treated precisely as an exchange. Because any other answer to this question is not given, one must surmise that the rule in question is hard-wired, so to speak, is coded in genes, and constitutes an aspect of human nature. It is apparent that the set of propositions put forward by the author of the theory of social exchange must imply a conception in that matter. Even in the absence of an in-depth analysis of the content of the above-mentioned statements, one can easily ascertain that these are drawn on the well-known doctrines of utilitarianism and hedonism.

To convince oneself about that, suffice it to recall the basic assumptions of what constitutes the third amongst those mentioned at the beginning of the chapter, the source of the theory of social exchange. They state, firstly, that all people are by nature similar, and secondly that they all also by nature strive to achieve where their self-interest lies. And, indeed, the human being as conceived of by Homans is an egoistic creature, whose goals involve both maximisation of profit, and assuring that anyone in his or her peer group does not achieve profits greater than herself or himself (Homans1975, 119). In other words, he or she is oriented to maximising the balance of pleasure or profit, pain or cost, just as in utilitarianism and hedonism.

It is assumed that people are driven by an aim of maximizing utility and minimizing negative utility (utility can be defined as pleasure minus pain).

What is more, the content of Homans' concept of man leads to the conclusion that this, in Homans' intention, notion of human nature in general in fact refers to people of a definite historical period, i.e. the capitalist system as based on the most developed form of the commodity-money economy. This is yet another confirmation of Homans' ahistorism, to which we have referred already above.

In Homans' theory, the king of early feudalism is transformed into someone in the likeness of the modern capitalist entepreneur. Just as a contemporary "industrial baron" he has "capital" at his disposal, and makes various "investments" which can pay off or not (Homans 1961, 380–8). At the same time, the above criticism calls into question Homans' claims regarding the supposed universalism of the theory of social exchange, whose propositions "are valid everywhere, and in the relation to all people" (1961, 317).

This is the case, in his view, because "the features of elementary social behaviour are shared by all humanity" (Homans 1961, 6), which circumstance stems from the existence shared by all human beings; Homans, for instance, reckons that "human nature is the only true cultural universal" (Homans 1961, 317).

II.6.6. Interactions vs. Society at large

Homans is a committed supporter of methodological individualism. As regards his laws of social exchange, he says: "they are propositions about the behavior of individual human beings, rather than propositions about groups or societies." It is for this reason, for instance, that Homans disagreed with some key ingredients of Emilie Durkheim's work. For example, Durkheim believed that although individuals are clearly the component parts of society, society is more than the individuals who constitute it. He believed that society could be studied without reducing it to individuals and their motivations. However, Homans, through his Exchange Theory, believed that individual beings and behaviour are relevant to understanding society.

While being confident that it is direct interpersonal relationships that constitute the basic building blocks of society, Homans was, of course, aware of the fact that in society more than just these relations exist. Is it, however, possible to consider and explain these macrostructural, as opposed to microstructural phenomena on the basis of the theory of social exchange? So far, we have dealt with what Homans calls elementary or subinstitutional social behaviour. He distinguishes it from types of behaviour taking place at an institutional level, for example determined by various official norms, formal rules and any socially fixed and transferred historically patterns (an institution in Homans' view is both "bureaucracy" and the "role of the physician").

What precisely differs between the two level of behaviour isn't entirely clear. As two basic criteria Homans mentions the fact that at the formal level rewards and punishments have a more complex and indirect character (for example, a worker in a firm obtains her or his wages not from their direct overseer, i.e. a foreman, but from the hands of an official such as a cashier), and secondly that the said rewards are so-called "generalised reinforcements" such as money or social approval, which are applicable in a host of variegated social situations, as distinct from primitive reinforcements referring to certain kinds of behaviour. Let us put aside any self-evident question of whether all extrainteractional relationships can be covered by the concept of "institutional" behaviour, and let us deal rather with the question of how the interrelations of the two fields distinguished are conceived.

Let us remind ourselves that in the theory of social exchange elementary social behaviour signifies *ipso facto* one which is primal and primary. By the same token Homans reckons that "one (institutional) type of behaviour always stems from the other (substitutional)," and the differences between them are merely differences of degree" (Homans 1961, 380).

The above cited claims are in keeping with Homans' general position, which the American sociologist himself describes as "psychological reductionism." In his own words it consists in the belief that "as the ultimate elements of social behaviour are humans and their activities, the general propositions used for an explanation of social behaviour must refer to individuals and their behaviour, and thus they must be psychological propositions," meaning that "sociology is derivative of psychology at least in the sense that social phenomena require for their explanation psychological propositions." (Homans, 1974a, 80–1).

Homans' argument is a typical example of paralogism; the fact that society is composed of individuals and their actions by no means entails that the patterns and regularities of its functioning and development are laws of individual behaviour or, rather, a dyadic one since, as has been outlined above, the fundamental building block of society is for Homans an interaction of two persons.

Small wonder, therefore, that Homans' attempts at the derivation of these or other macrostructures or phenomena must end in failure.

II.6.6.1. Social stratification

The principles of the Theory of Exchange are extended by their author to include, among others, social differentiation. Homans introduces to that end the concept of social status: "as a general rule, it seems that people will perceive a given person as one of higher status than another one, if in the course of an exchange she or he gives more of a good, which is scarce relative to demand, and can be perceived as such, obtains, however, more of a good, which is relatively abundant. And on the reverse, they perceive a given person as one of lower status, if he/she obtains more of a scarce good, and gives greater quantity of an abundant good."

It is, then, basically a subjective theory of social differentiation; objective considerations, which are mentioned in Homans' definition, are relevant as a determinant of a position only when they are seen are such. That it is awareness that underlies the notion of social status is still more apparent in its definition given in the first edition of the book as: "this, which people perceive about one of their peers. Stimuli comprising a status of an individual involve kinds of rewards received … kinds of behaviour emitted … granted that these stimuli are recognised and distinguished by other people … Status is a matter of awareness, which stimuli will be crucial as defining an individual's status, depends on what relationships between various forms of her / his behaviour her or his partners has become aware of."

For example, says Homans, the fact that someone receives a higher salary than someone else, does not *per se* give him or her a higher status; it will happen only as far this fact will be registered in the consciousness of the members of a group to which a given individual belongs. Homans reckons that the category of status so construed serves as an instrument of studying not only small groups, but also as a source of an analysis of stratification of broader society, for if: "status of individuals in every stratified society, regardless of the fact whether it is inherited or achieved, is chiefly determined by their occupation in the broadest sense of the word, and an income earned thanks to this occupation," In his opinion it means that status in society as a whole, like in small groups, is "earned or recognised by what people give and get in social exchange … the phenomena of stratification in small groups are so similar to this how these phenomena look like in global societies, that in both cases they must have been generated by the same processes" (Homans 1974b, 307–8).

The consequence of this theory of social stratification, and at the same time proof of its subjectivist nature, is an inability of an identification of particular strata or, as Homans himself calls them, "classes." He uses, in order to outline the character of social divisions as viewed by his theory, the telling metaphor of the spectrum of colours within which are higher bands such as purple, then the next one a little lower, e.g. red, and so on. A difference can be discerned, but the interstice between the colours is continual, and "only an arbitrary line of partition can determine where crimson has ended, and where redness has begun" (Homans 1974b, 309).

In another statement, this time not based on metaphors, Homans maintains that from the standpoint of his conception, the "attribution of individuals to particular classes cannot be an arbitrary thing; it would be perfectly right to call a member of the upper clas a member of the middle class" (Homans 1974b, 310). It is thus evident that any sociologist, who would be interested in an objective investigation of social structures, should not look to Homans for inspiration. "Classes" as conceived by Homans have little in common with the classic theories of social differentiation, such as those by Marx or Weber. In one of the subsequent chapters we are going to put forward the theory of class of our own, which draws, among others, on these classics, while being construed in terms entirely independent of any consciousness criteria. This is thanks to the conceptual basis of the theory, which lies in socio-economic property relations. On the other hand, social activities determined by property are beyond the confines of the theory of social exchange; treating as two main determinants of "status" occupation (as what is given), and income (as what is received), it leaves out of picture the phenomena which, like private ownership of the means of production, make it possible to acquire the means of subsistence without an equivalent in the form of one's own work, which do not enter, say, an exchange of the labour power in return of wages, but constitute its underlying premise.

In line with his subjective viewpoint, Homans also takes issue with Marxian political economy. For instance, he considers Marx's theory of surplus value to be a groundless speculation, treating its recognition as a "matter of taste … when someone says that one group exploits another, all that his / her words mean is that he or she does not personally accept the way in which the rewards are distributed between these two groups" (Homans 1974b, 251). Well, the only positive thing that can be said as regards this statement is that it is consistent with the author's subjectivism which, however, apparently rules out any substantive consideration of the theory involved. Later in the book the reader will be able to judge for themself what, if any, scientific status pertains to the said theory.

Homans' "interactional reductionism," as it can be termed, is also apparent in his theory of power. He defines power as follows: "when the total reward of a Person A, associated with taking action which rewards the Person B is lower—at least in B's perception—than the total reward of B linked to the performance of action, which rewards A, and as a result B alters his / her behaviour in a way advantages to A, then A exercises power over B" (Homans 1974b, 83). This definition, in Homans' opinion, involves both cases of power not based on coercion, "where no penalties are deployed," a person who cares about the reward provided by another less than vice versa has, thanks to this, power over them. It also involves instances of power dependent on the means of violence, and it is in this context that the above principle of "smaller interest" holds a universal, in Homans' view, base of power. A bandit, for example, enjoys a unique capability of rewarding actions, as they are able to mete out capital punishment, and punishment is simply, as is well-known, a negative reward. They have the power of forcing their victim to give them all their money, but their profit is relatively less compared to the benefit enjoyed by their partner in this peculiar exchange.

Homans, for better or worse, goes even further than that. He juxtaposes two situations: "We can watch the case of power exercised by the leader of a small group over his supporters. We can also observe power exercised by the president of the U.S., who commands his soldiers to fight in Vietnam" (Homans 1971, 371). Homans' assumption that "mechanisms of behaviour of people at the level of interpersonal relations and in big organisations are the same, are identical," is concretised in the form of the contention that "psychological mechanisms, which produce power in both cases are the same." From the foregoing he concludes that power does not rely on specific rewards and punishments pertaining to human activities, but is based on the fact of functioning of rewards and punishments alone (Homans 1971, 371).

On the grounds of Homans' approach, the same kind and degree of power is exercised by the father over his children, by the teacher over their pupils, by the capitalist over the workers, and the state over its citizens. What is alleged here is an identity of processes relevant for entire nations with some played out at the level of interpersonal relations only, and relevant exclusively for participants of these relations. State power is at the same footing as parental authority, and the power of the army commander is equated with a transient power exercised by the leader of a peer group waging a "war" against another. Such an approach, of course, effectively blocks any understanding of the real roots of power as a macrosocial phenomenon. This is a consequence of the more general fact: an inability to grasp macrostructures by means of the conceptual tools worked out at the level of direct interpersonal relations.

One cannot agree more with Talcott Parsons' opinion, according to which as yet "Homans has not shown how his principles can account for the basic structural features of large social systems" (1971, 34). This inability is written into the fundamental premises of Homans' theoretical position; psychological propositions advanced by him as a universal explanatory tool refer to "what people have in common, they cannot illuminate the differences between societies" (Blau 1970, 337), those various forms and products of social life that humanity has generated throughout its history.

The above discussed partial and unsuccessful attempts to go beyond the vicious circle of face-to-face relationships by means of the categories of the theory of exchange indirectly point to the untenability of its starting point, which, therefore, must be turned on its head: to comprehend society through the microscopic prism of "elementary relations" is not possible, but much of what happens inside small groups cannot be understood without taking account of the broader societal context. This, of course, applies also to such phenomena the theory of exchange is dealing with. Can, for instance, the presence in the social life of even many highly developed nations of a host of informal exchanges of various services, not excluding goods be explained on the basis of the individual traits of the participants of those transactions or, rather, the concrete socio-economic, but also political and legal situation of a given society should be taken into account.

II.6.7. rational action and structure

Several of the currently popular sociological theories, namely, structural exchange theory, rational choice theory, and network exchange theory, have their roots in Homans' work. His ideas, to be sure, had a profound influence, positively or negatively, on the thinking of major sociologists like Richard M. Emerson (1972a; 1972b), Peter M. Blau (1964) and James S. Coleman (1990). Additionally, Homans has also impacted the research of scholars such as Linda D. Molm (1997), Karen S. Cook (2003), and Edward J. Lawler (2001) who are currently working in the social exchange tradition. Moreover, Homans' famous plea for, as the title of his important article has it, "Bringing Men Back In" (1964), led sociology away from an overly abstract focus on society and toward the earnest consideration of human activity, be that in the form of symbolic interactionism, Goffmanian sociology, ethnomethodology, or economic sociology Homans did not and would not endorse, but which nevertheless have a "micro" focus of analysis.

Homans' major works, particularly the two books discussed above, have had an indelible influence on contemporary contributions of social exchange that focus on trust, commitment, affective bonds, power relations, and distributive justice. Yet, if his poem, "Just Like the Rest," which appears that he wrote later in his life, is an accurate indication of just how he felt about his works, Homans did not believe they had made much of an impact. The poem reads in part:

> I never thought that I should fail:
> Failure was not for men like me.
> Others would eye the floor and see
> That all their works would not prevail …
> In what respect had I been blind?
> My books were sound, but lacked the spell,
> The confident presence, to compel
> Their judgments on another mind.
> (Homans 1988, 83–84)

However, "Homans was largely mistaken about his lack of lasting influence. While many rational choice theorists, network theorists, justice scholars, and small group researchers have failed to explicitly acknowledge his sway on them, many others continue to point to Homans' works as worthy of being read and reread" (Treviño & Javier 2009).

This is not to say that all these readers and followers of Homans have approached his theory uncritically. The weakest and most critically vulnerable aspect of Homans' theory of social exchange has been its psychologism, and especially its dependence upon one particular version of psychology. The followers of Homans' ideas, therefore, whilst starting from similar premises, modified or even eliminated that most controversial aspect of the theory of exchange. Authors such as Blau (1964), Coleman

(1973), Cook (1987) and others extended or changed his conceptual system. These developments occurred under the serious influence and with a growing closeness to microeconomics, which manifested themselves in both the growing formalisation and mathematisation and the construction of "undersocialised" theoretical model, that is to say, its departure from the former conception, which with all its drawbacks, grasped certain real aspects of social relations, despite the fact of their limitation to the interactions, and moreover reducing them all to a narrow and deformed exchange. In return, a "generalised" model of rational action was put forth, whose introduction, to be sure, allowed the avoidance of the above-mentioned criticism, but did not exempt their approach from a related charge, referring to methodological individualism. The difference with Homans' theory is its adoption in a non-psychological version. Critical comments addressed against this approach appear in various places of the book, but despite this we may at this juncture put forward a brief commentary concerned with the above-mentioned case.

When Homans says that "the secret of society consists in the circumstance that it is a human creation," he formulates undisputable truth, which could be called into question perhaps only by the believers in a certain form of sociological deism. There is more to that, however. The author of *Social Behavior* puts forward the related claim, which is only seemingly true, that "there is nothing in society, which has not been contributed by humans" (Homans 1961, 385), for it negates the autonomy of society or, more broadly, any supraindividual structures. Following in his footsteps other representatives of the strand of rational choice reject an autonomy or the fact of "restraints imposed on human action by the social structures" (Scott 2000). Meanwhile, the fact that social structures consist mostly, albeit not exclusively of human individuals does not mean that the former could be reduced to the latter, for structures are not simply aggregates or collections of elements, but precisely structures, i.e. sets of not only elements *per se*, but also relationships between them, a fact which gives rise to various, to use a popular buzzword, synergies or, more simply, emergent structural effects that underlie the relative autonomy of the social wholes in relation to their components, which can also be rendered as referring to some novel characteristics that are not present at the level of the ingredients. This fact cannot be recognised by the proponents of methodological individualism who, like those proverbial bourgeois in the Polish poet Tuwim's poem, cannot see the wood behind the trees.

Part and parcel of society whose relation to its constituent individuals proves so difficult to comprehend, are also social norms. In their case, as it turns out, the above-mentioned problem returns with a vengeance. The theory of rational choice finds it difficult to account for both the nature of social norms and the question of why they are obeyed by the members of society. The first reason for these difficulties is the lack of distinguishing various types of norms: legal, religious etc. It is associated with its lacking an adequate theory of society at large, and of its particular substructures in which given norms function. Furthermore, even abstracting from the question of social location of norms, one should admit that people's compliance is often inconsistent with their rationally conceived interest. How do the theorists of rational choice handle this problem? They lean to the view considering norms to be merely arbitrary preferences. Thus, if "individuals help others [in accordance with the moral norm obliging to such assistance] and drive derive satisfaction from that, then such help is a rational act, consistent with self-interest" (Scott 2000). It is easy to see that this kind of argument leads to inadmissible sophistry. Looking at the matter this way would force us to classify heroic acts of nurses at the front line, or of Mother Theresa, as consistent with the model of rational choice and self-interest. Another solution to the problem being discussed provided by the supporters of the theory of rational choice is equally unsatisfactory. Ridley looks for that solution in genetically programmed, natural predispositions for cooperation and reciprocity. Referring to instincts, drives and other similar factors can always be taken as a proof of the theorist's incapability to face a given problem, constituting instead an example of the escapist strategy—it is easy to postulate the existence of this or that instinct, it is much more difficult, however, to prove its real existence. Even granted the existence of such instincts, they would have to be really potent in order to produce a whole gamut of cooperative and altruistic behaviours present in human societies.

Furthermore, positing instinct and, more broadly, the entire category of rational choice, the theory under consideration is not in a position to account for the fact that humans frequently perform given actions as normative, out of duty, obligation or commitment. Blau attempted to address this problem, stating that people are willing to bear costs in the course of exchange relations, insofar as they are included in a longer chain of activities. They then count on the fact that any loss will be compensated by an equivalent profit in the future. People expect reciprocity in the long run, and since it is in the interest of everyone, it gets accepted as a norm. This approach does, however, suffer from the basic logical error: it assumes what should be yet proved, mutual trust. A must have trust in B, and similarly B must give C the benefit of the doubt, C must have confidence as to the next links in the chain, and so on and so forth. Thus, we are back at the square one, because we still do not know what the source of that trust is, an indispensable component of Blau's explanation.

The flaw of the theory of rational choice is not only unacceptable from the standpoint of psychology rationalistic monism or reductionism, rooted in the rejection of specificity of standards of behaviour derived from habits, morality etc, their reduction to the cost-benefit calculus, but, first and foremost, asociologism and ahistorism, taking its objects out of the sociohistorical network in which they are embedded. In terms of the sociology of the economy, for the notion of trust to be of any real value, it must be referred to specific types of the economy.

On the grounds of the model of rational behaviour one cannot, as has been argued earlier, account for actions such as paying taxes, or participation in green or other non-governmental organisations, which all have in common the fact that an individual taking an action in question contributes much more for the welfare of others than his or her own benefit amounts to. The taxpayer parts with often a significant portion of their income, whereas she may not even use roads, bridges etc. built from, among others, their taxes. An analogous challenge for the theory of rational choice are such organisations as trade unions and professional associations. A prospective unionist is aware that his or her membership will strengthen the bargaining power of organisation to a relatively small degree, whereas it will defend their interests anyway. Similarly, any professional will think twice before joining their respective association, because of the minimal personal benefit, which will be drawn from the activities of the institution anyway. Some representatives of the stream of thought being considered, for example Olson or Hechter, mention statute restrictions to cope with the problem, for example regarding pay hikes, or delivery of special legal advice exclusively to the members of a given organisation. Regardless of the general soundness of that idea it remains undisputable and uncomfortable in terms of the adherents of the theory under consideration in the fact that many organisations both act and attract new members on other grounds, which calls into question the idea discussed.

Finally, let us cite an extensive excerpt from an article which refers to the theory just considered, but is also a critique of the main character of the present chapter, i.e. social exchange theory:

> The exchange paradigm entertains high aspirations concerning its place within social psychology and generally in sociology and psychology. This is epitomized[…] by its fundamental premise that all social life can be treated as an exchange of rewards or resources between actors. […] exchange paradigm features equivalent generality and relevance for sociological theory … The examination does not provide prima facie

support for the claims of social exchange theory, especially its economic-behavioural formulations … actors in exchange can be not only individuals but also groups, and that in-group processes and intergroup relations are more complex than being sets of market transactions. [...]

[…] Typically social exchange theory […] explains non-economic exchange processes by the operation of *homo economicus* and other economic laws, especially marginal utility, supply and demand and related market principles. […]

Some of its prominent advocates (Emerson 1976; Homans 1990) regard exchange theory's main assumptions as derived from or isomorphic to those in conventional economics (utility seeking) and behaviorist psychology (reward-punishment). In this view, these do not represent macro-sociological or structural assumptions in that they eschew the structure and functioning of whole societies (Homans 1971). [...]

Rational choice models are bivariate (or causally univariate. Such bivariate rational choice models appear overly simplistic, mono-factorial, uni-dimensional and mis-spelled in the light of the actual multiplicity of explanatory variables in social exchange. Since they commit the fallacy of mono-causality, reductionism, and mis-specification, this greatly diminishes their methodological-empirical adequacy. Likewise, by positing a single class of explanatory psychological variables—e.g. mutual reinforcement, reward, stimuli, reciprocal gratification, etc.—behavioral models of social exchange also appear bivariate, thus committing the same fallacy as their rational choice counterparts. To the extent that they explain social exchange by a single set of explanatory variables, rational choice and behaviorist models look like causally univariate explanations of a multivariate phenomenon. […] they are methodologically deficient […], they are unable to provide substantively plausible explanations of social exchange. A sensible alternative to such methodologically-theoretically untenable models is a multivariate model of social exchange. [...] A considerable number of empirical results do not support, and some even falsify. [the theory under consideration ...] Some of its advocates claim that a single, rational choice model can explain exchange and other social processes, including group cohesion, in both traditional community or *Gesellschaft* and modern society or *Gemeinschaft* (Hechter & Kanazawa 1997). *Prima facie*, it seems questionable to subsume both types of society under a single overarching rational or utilitarian principle, given the essential differences between the two, as Marx, Tönnies, Durkheim, Weber, Simmel and others classically argue and demonstrate.[...]

Extra-economic criteria like cultural or symbolic "capital" play a greater role than economic ones in assortative mating, as a presumed hallmark of marriage "markets",[...] rational choice models fail to establish micro-macro links in that they center on individual action cum optimizing in exchange and de-center on social structure, which requires a different framework as a corrective.

> One may expect that the rational choice model will be validated in market exchange as its original realm of application and validation. However, even in this realm the model is not necessarily superior to a multilevel sociological theory of market exchange based in economic sociology, including that of markets (Lie 1997); [...] A key [...] principle regulating economic exchange and other social relations in traditional societies is the norm of reciprocity or mutualism.
>
> Contrary to the standard economic axiom of a natural propensity to exchange for profit, including "self-seeking with guile," moral norms of reciprocity reportedly govern economic exchange and all social life in today's primitive societies. [...] also [...] people establish and sustain exchange relationships based on reciprocity (gift exchanges) rather than markets in some modern developing societies (e.g. Oriental bazaar economies. [...]
>
> Empirical studies also suggest that multiple non-economic variables have strong influences on rational choices in market exchanges. [...] market exchange cannot always be accounted for by strictly rational variables like profit or efficiency because these produce narrow explanations, thus supporting a broader multivariate model. […] a more broadly conceived alternative [...] draws upon the classical insights of […] sociologists or anthropologists, combined as primary elements with, not displaced by, those of traditional economists and behaviorists as secondary ingredients.
>
> Overall, various types of in-group processes and between-group relations, as a collective form of social exchange, can be mediated by certain generalized media. In addition to wealth (economic capital) and power ("political capital") as the media of market and political exchange respectively, prestige, influence and ties ("social capital") as well as symbols and knowledge of culture (symbolic-cultural "capital") mediate extra-market processes within groups and relations between groups. [...] […] exchange and related concepts borrowed from orthodox economics-viz., non-economic (marriage, political, religious, intellectual) markets, social capital, psychic income, profit, costbenefit, investments-are metaphors or analogies at best.[...] just as an overarching mono-utility function (Etzioni 1999) or cost-benefit model (Elster 1998) spuriously homogenizes diverse human goals, preferences and affects into a single measure or unit ("utility") that is content-empty. (Zafirovski 2003)

The above-cited excerpt, to be sure, contains many sound points; in the opposite case its citation would be largely pointless. But even though essentially sound, the above passage includes also some doubtful claims. We have in mind the author's constructive proposal in the form of "… a multivariate model of social exchange, which includes economic and noneconomic, behavioral and cultural, individual and structural variables alike. For the sake of outlining a multivariate model of social exchanges, several classes of explanatory factors can be considered to exhaust or approximate these variables. For terminological convenience, these classes may be called economic, political, social and cultural capital, respectively."

We take issue not with the use of the term "capital," since Zafirovski takes a position close to that which will be argued in the next chapter and has already been in the Bourdieu section. He rightly states that "the term 'capital' is not appropriate for non-economic variables because of its original and prevalent economic-financial connotation ... insofar as in social exchange (and rational choice) theory the capital concept becomes a weak figure of speech rather than potent and precise tool ... it should be avoided or used as a metaphor at best."

For brevity, let us abstract here from an otherwise necessary polemic with the notion of capital deployed in the passage cited above. As has been argued before, capital is a social relation in the first place. The disputable point is the methodological character of the approach proposed by the economist concerned. Zafirovski fails to see that if a unidimensional or mono-factorial approach, as he himself has argued, is wrong, a multidimensional or multi-factorial approach simply multiplies the flaws of the former approach as long as it remains simply a juxtaposition of several perspectives without changing their foundations and mutual relationships. What is first and foremost at issue is how to distinguish particular "variables" and view their relationship to one another. Because Zafirovski does not dispose of a comprehensive theory of society writ large and a dialectical methodology, both of which are part and parcel of socio-economic structuralism, his variables are a mix of several factors selected at random rather than guided by some explicit theoretical perspective. Political, cultural, economic, social—this list could be much longer but as long as no theoretical criteria of their identification and methodological principles of conceiving their interrelations are not in place, this supposedly alternative approach replicates rather than overcomes all the shortcomings of the standpoint rejected by him. The fact that his variables' isolation leaves much to be desired is shown, amongst others, by his own contention to the effect that "economy is an 'instituted process' in virtue of being 'embedded and enmeshed in a variety of (social) institutions'". In conjunction with his another assertion including one of the most important concept present in the above critical argument to the effect that "Simple economic models of labor markets are incomplete and misspecified relative to a multivariate model in that they overemphasize only one aspect of market exchange while neglecting its manifold sociological dimensions [...] social structure, notably embeddedness in interpersonal networks", which exposes the researcher under consideration to the criticism of interactionist reductionist levied, inter alia, against,

Granovetter, but in his connection paradoxical insofar his critique is focused on theories grounded in the very interactionist paradigm.

It is for this very reason that his rhetorically sound claim that "combined micro-macro properties underlie a multivariate model of social exchange" lacks theoretical and hence empirical grounding in a concrete sociological perspective.

Many threads of thought outlined in this chapter will be continued in later ones, including the next chapter, devoted to an outstanding economic sociologist.

CHAPTER II.7.

ECONOMIC SOCIOLOGY OR ECONOMIC IMPERIALISM? THE CASE OF GARY S. BECKER

"Economics must be the handmaid of sociology."
—Wicksteed, The Common Sense of Political Economy

II.7.1. The Scope of Becker's Economic Approach

More than one of the features displayed by the theory of social exchange are also shared by Gary C. Becker's economic sociology. His fundamental axiom—that all actors in the social game are economic persons who maximize their advantages in different cost situations—allows Becker to study so many different social phenomena that their sheer variety is mind-boggling: racial and sexual discrimination, human capital, social capital, crime and punishment, marriage and divorce, the family, drug addiction, and other in his eyes only apparently non-economic dimensions of society.

Thus, Becker does not restrict himself only to analyzing market behaviour; rather he expands the domain of economics by applying an economic approach in understanding problems beyond those characterized by market transactions. The orthodox economist's way of thinking about behaviour is one where economic agents, both as individuals as well as parts of a larger community, face resource limitations that force them to make choices. At an individual level they make rational choices that are co-ordinated through the market or some other mechanism. In other words, economists apply an optimization principle subject to resource constraint and use equilibrium conditions for coordination of individuals' actions.

This notion refers to an abstract market, whose "extreme abstraction" (Slater & Tonkiss 2001, 16) or ontological indeterminateness allows for its putatively universal application to all social domains. Since neoclassical economics taken over by Becker construes society as Bastiat's "great market place," it becomes a set of ordinary or explicit and social or implicit “markets” (Becker & Murphy 2000). An adversary of Becker in his statement to the effect that:

> The economic approach [...] assumes that individuals maximize their utility from basic preferences that do not change rapidly over time and that the behavior of different individuals is coordinated by explicit or implicit markets ... The economic approach is not restricted to material goods and wants or to markets with monetary transactions, and conceptually does not distinguish between major or minor decisions or between "emotional" and other decisions. Indeed, the economic approach provides a framework applicable to all human behavior—to all types of decisions and to persons from all walks of life. (Bourdieu 2005, 210)

comments that:

> nothing now escapes explanation in terms of the maximizing agent—structural organizations, firms or contracts, parliaments and municipal authorities, marriage (conceived as the economic exchange of services of production and reproduction) or the household, and relations between parents and children or the state. This mode of universal explanation by an explanatory principle that is itself universal (individual preferences are exogenous, ordered and stable and hence without contingent genesis or evolution) no longer knows any bounds. Gary Becker does not even recognize those bounds Pareto himself was forced to assume in the founding text in which, identifying the rationality of economic behaviour with rationality as such, he distinguished between strictly economic behaviour, which is the outcome of “a series of logical reasonings” based on experience, and behaviour determined by “custom [...] (thus acknowledging another principle of action—usage, tradition or custom—unlike methodological individualism. (Bourdieu 2005:210)

II.7.2. Fixed preferences

The neoclassical analytical framework takes individual preferences as given and stable (Stigler & Becker 1977), assuming that persons have a particular and constant set of "tastes," "values," or "aspirations." Changes in behaviour are assumed to result from changes in "constraints" or income, but not in preferences. Thus, for example, a neoclassical analyst investigating the reasons that American consumption of alcohol has declined since 1980 will ask if the price of alcohol has increased or if the age of drinking has been raised and so on, but not whether the desire to consume alcohol has been reduced due to changes in the valuation of "drinking", which on its part may be due to such factors as [...] the health-and-fitness movement and a neo-temperance movement.

> Neoclassicists argue that incorporating preference changes in the explanation of behavior precludes useful analysis, because whenever behavior changes, presumably we shall state that preferences have changed. There is, however, a satisfactory rebuttal for this argument. If we have several-or, preferably, numerous—observations over time, we can test hypotheses about changes in constraints and in preferences (including value changes that often cause preference changes). For instance, tax compliance has been shown to be affected both by the level of taxation (basically, the higher the tax rates, the lower the level of compliance) and by whether or not taxes are viewed as fairly imposed (Lewis, 1982). Thus, if an increase in compliance follows a period in which tax rates have not been reduced, all things being(...) equal, we would expect that the change is due, in fact, to an enhanced sense of fairness. The argument of some neoclassicists—that they need not study preference changes, or the value changes that drive them, because these phenomena belong to "different" disciplines (namely psychology and sociology)-may, indeed, be correct. Yet this argument demonstrates precisely the necessity of a broader paradigm, one that encompasses both social and economic factors. (Etzioni 1990)

There is, as a matter of fact, "much evidence that preferences are subject to modification under the impact of psychological and social processes, and that they often reflect the dissonance (or conflicts) that arise when emotions, values, cognition are not all well aligned" (Janis & Mann 1977). In addition, referring to our earlier criticism of methodological individualism, the following questions need consideration:

> What range of economic behavior is group determined vs. subject to individual decision-making? Under what conditions do group factors dominate, under what conditions are individuals relatively freer (e.g., some see individuals relatively freer when the group forces clash; others—as anxiety-ridden under these circumstances)? Which groups are the Significant Others, and what are the relations among them? (Etzioni 1990).

II.7.3. Human capital

Becker's name figures prominently among those who have contributed to the popularity of an idea of the augmentability of human capital. His approach posits that individuals make choices of investing in human capital based on rational benefits and cost that include a return on investment as well as a cultural aspect. Becker's research included the impact of positive and negative habits such as punctuality and alcoholism on human capital. He explored the different rates of return for different people and the resulting macroeconomic implications. He also distinguished between general to specific education and their influence on job-lock and promotions.

Pierre Bourdieu begins his statement on the theory under consideration on a kind note, so the reader may be forgiven for being taken by surprise by what follows—namely, an assault on human capital from the perspective, paradoxically, of other forms of capital to which Bourdieu himself[1] subscribes:

> Economists might seem to deserve credit for explicitly raising the question of the relationship between the rates of profit on educational investment and on economic investment (and its evolution). But their measurement of the yield from scholastic investment takes account only of monetary investments and profits, or those directly convertible into money, such as the costs of schooling and the cash equivalent of time devoted to study; they are unable to explain the different proportions of their resources which different agents or different social classes allocate to economic investment and cultural investment because they fail to take systematic account of the structure of the differential chances of profit which the various markets offer these agents or classes as a function of the volume and the composition of their assets (see esp. Becker 1964b). Furthermore, because they neglect to relate scholastic investment strategies to the whole set of educational strategies and to the system of reproduction strategies, they inevitably, by a necessary paradox, let slip the best hidden and socially most determinant educational investment, namely, the domestic transmission of cultural capital. Their studies of the relationship between academic ability and academic investment show that they are unaware that ability or talent is itself the product of an investment of time and cultural capital (Becker 1964a, 63–66). Not surprisingly, when endeavoring to evaluate the profits of scholastic investment, they can only consider the profitability of educational expenditure for society as a whole, the "social rate of return," or the "social gain of education as measured by its effects on national productivity" (Becker 1964b, 121 and 155). This typically functionalist definition of the functions of education ignores the contribution which the educational system makes to the reproduction of the social structure by sanctioning the hereditary transmission of cultural capital. From the very beginning, a definition of human capital, despite its humanistic connotations, does not move beyond economism and ignores, inter alia, the fact that the scholastic yield from educational action depends on the cultural capital previously invested by the family. Moreover, the economic and social yield of the educational qualification depends on the social capital, again inherited, which can be used to back it up. (Bourdieu 1986)

---

[1] This critique should then be conceived of as a competitive strategy.

Our Criticism of Becker's and others' abuse of the concept of capital does not mean denying the importance of the reality of the issues hiding behind all these buzzwords. For their exploration it is essential to carefully separate what was hastily combined as a result of often imperfect economic knowledge regarding the relationship between such categories as capital, rent, quasi rent and most of all property. It is on the latter —in economic respect—we focus later in the text.

W. Petty, in the late seventeenth century, attempted to estimate the conversion of the monetary value of the entire population of England at that time, into, including human, capital. Humans incur expenditure which are the source of the ability to provide services. With sales of services expenditure is paid back at a profit. Petty estimated the value of labour resources as over 70% the value of fixed assets.

Similarly, for Adam Smith knowledge embodied in man and his learned skills were one of the forms which manifests itself in the fixed capital. The employee earns their qualifications and skills while studying or training. At the same time they must receive funds for maintenance. Skills lead to greater efficiency and productivity of the worker, which in turn depend on the division of labour. According to our formerly mentioned socio-economic approach we are actually dealing here with the economic ownership effect.

Further development of the concept of accumulation of knowledge and skills of human beings is associated with the name of J. B. Say. According to Say, work may be either productive or not productive. This second type can bring intangible effects, such as a lecture which is used by the student. Processing such effects by its consumption, increases the production fund. However, this fund is a form of capital, from which its owner may derive income or profit. In other words, the "capital" which one has in the form of knowledge, skills, was transformed into an intangible result. In the process of accumulation and consumption, this effect was turned into a "capital" of another person. In *The Treatise of Political Economy*, Say also alluded to other aspects that currently form the human capital theory. He suggested a method for estimating the value of "human capital" according to the achieved income in the period of earning. He also touched the problems of emigration of human resources from the point of view of losses for the left country.

More theoretically reasonable, however, is the approach to this issue from the point of view of the socio-economic theory of property which turns the attention to the national nature of expenditure and training of labour power, whose holders' emigration leaves the nation without the possibility of benefiting from the results of education and, taking in the form of their private labour power, the effects of this education transfer them to the other nation, including its specific classes. Thus, an accurate picture of the socio-economic nature of the relationship concerned cannot be drawn by any theory of human capital.

Observations on the quality of human resources may be encountered in a pragmatic approach to business processes by A. Marshall. He lists the characteristics of labour as a production factor, to which he particularly includes: lack of the existence of the capital market for labour and integral bond of employee with the work done by them. Marshall also argued, touching implicitly on the economic issues of ownership, that during training of workforce from the initiative of the employer external benefits arise from which effects the employer cannot fully benefit.

Arthur Cecil Pigou said: "Equally with investment in material capital, there are investments in human capital. Upon recognition of this fact the difference between saving in the consumption and savings in production is blurred. To some extent, consumption is an investment in an individual production capacity." And again, this claim touches on the economic and sociological issues of the property theory, but since it does so in a cryptic way, it hides more than it discloses.

As far as modern neoclassical economics is concerned, the pioneer of the use of the term was Jacob Mincer in the article "Investment in Human Capital and Personal Income Distribution," published in *The Journal of Political Economy* in 1958. Apart from this economist, among the best-known works regarding human capital are those by T. Schultz and, naturally, G. Becker, particularly the book titled *Human Capital*, published in 1964.

In terms of economic and sociological forms of ownership one should also consider the following condition, often cited as explaining and justifying the introduction of the concept of human capital, and consisting of the special characteristics of knowledge:

> Unlike manual labour and other production factors, the use of knowledge leads to its expansion and self-development, as far as physicians acquire more experience, their knowledge base grows, similarly to their equipment in human capital. Economics of scarcity is replaced by spontaneous generation.[2] Portable knowledge can be shared and transferred. This

---

[2] It is easy, however, to overplay the peculiarities concerned. The thesis that "information, unlike material goods, needs to be produced only once and can then be copied and transferred" overlooks, as Carchedi (2010, Ch. 3) points out that "information too has costs associated with its reproduction even though they might be less than the costs for the reproduction of material commodities."

> transfer does not prevent the use of the given knowledge by its original holder. (Wikipedia.org).
>
> The intimate relationship of the concept of human capital to one of the key objects of economic and socio biological ownership, i.e. labour power is demonstrated by the concise definition of the former: "human capital is embodied knowledge and skills. (Becker et al. 1990)

This similarity is also shown by the otherwise surprising and rarely quoted use of the term "human capital" by non-other than Karl Marx (1859) who wrote in relation to one of the modes of production of feudal economic formation of society:

> One of the ways in which the nobility disposed of its human capital was letting them [the carriers] or allowing for an annual fee (fodder) per journey and earn a living in a random way" (Marx 1859).This type of serfdom of the feudal peasant was expressed in the necessity for donations to the owner of labour rent, although they, as a partial holder of its own labour power, to some extent freely disposed of it.

Viewing the working class and other employee classes as owning their own labour power points to the most fundamental, in our view, flaw of human capital theory which, contrariwise, treats them in effect not as employees but as their own employers! From its perspective, after all, the classes concerned own their own human capital, hence should be treated as capitalists. And indeed, on the basis of the theory under consideration both the workers and their class opponents earn "rates of return" on their respective capitals. By the same token, the theory accomplishes a genuine feat—it in one go erases out of existence the crucial class cleavage in the capitalist economic formation of society. All the above-mentioned classes own capital, after all, albeit it does not directly detracts from the cognitive merits of the theory, which must be demonstrated or called into question separately, the ideological nature of the just mentioned conclusion is crystal clear.

Returning to the former scientific focus, it may be noted that the fundamental theory of G. Becker has been undermined by the microeconomic approach to information theory. Among others, as Fine points out, in its framework "the category of information asymmetry was applied to completely disregarded by Becker's financial markets," and similarly, the application of this approach to the labour market revealed its shortcomings, calling into question the notion of efficient wages and with it the whole concept of human capital, especially its empirical conclusions about rates of return on investments for education which, as noted by Fine, was enough to ensure that the theory of human capital was renounced by one of its most ardent supporters (2001, 20 and 46).

It is, on the other hand, another rather harsh criticism of the theory under consideration which condemns its ideological function manifested in its capacity: "to justify inequalities … with reference to … two people working a similar number of hours at the same company, one of which earns 10, 100 or 1000 times more than the other. The concept of human capital justifies this glaring inequality, as well as any other, which can always be said to result from the 'non observed' and 'non observable' differences in human capital in both people" (Hyde 2007). According to the researcher, the human capital theory plays equally apologetic functions under the legal doctrine, not adding an ounce of explanatory power. The discussed theory has not become part of the accounting practice, for example, when AT&T Corporation reduces employment by forty thousand employees that we will call conceptual, it "does not write down any share capital; it only subtracts their salaries from the amount of corporate spending."

Hyde goes on to say that "the theory of human capital plays no role in the tax law or accounting practice, and its absence facilitates preference of lay-offs and reduction over other methods of cutting corporate costs." The theory is also absent in employment discrimination, nineteen cases in which requirements of education regarding individual positions are pushed aside because of their "divergent effect" on different racial groups. Such educational requirements cannot be maintained as a stimulus for further individual investment in human capital.

On the other hand, human capital theory hides behind the justification of otherwise non defensible features of the labour law, such as "competition limitation, the obligation of employees to pay back employers for training costs and trade secrets. The theory of human capital is a fundamental obstacle on the road towards the realization of our most urgent legal and economic needs: to understand the economics of information, particularly ownership of the information when it is nobody's property "(Hyde 2007).

Without challenging the validity of the argument of the author, one has to accuse him, in turn, of legal formalism of the concept of property, showing in the use of the above-mentioned notion of nobody's property behind which most likely some sort of common property is hiding.

Going beneath this kind of juridical or common sense fiction adopted in this socio-economic theory of property also permits, as we shall see, the consideration of some phenomena neglected by the concept of human capital, such as discrimination. Discrimination based on gender, ethnicity, connections, networking, personal credentials etc. can be incorporated into our theoretical framework. It does not negate the importance of phenomena dealt with under the slogan of human capital or certain achievements of the theory such as drawing attention to diversity, in our categories, of labour power, unlike the unidimensional concept of the factor "labour" or extension of the field of study onto long-term (or even lifetime) earnings, as opposed to only the current wage. On the other hand, due to the fundamental theoretical reasons we cannot remain uncritical to it.

According to the theory under investigation the rational worker invests in training which will maximize the economic return (earnings) on investments while free competition among firms for labour skills guarantees a price for that labour power. The theory's focus on individuals means that explanatory variables are personal properties while taking structure largely for granted. As a result, socio-economic success or failure hinges upon the characteristics brought into the marketplace by the individual workers. This model of earnings determination, however, is unsustainable. Beck et al. (1979) focus on the issue of fixed returns, the assumption by human capital theorists that economic returns to worker characteristics are uniform. In order to do this, they rely on sectoral economic differentiation models based on theories of economic dualism. These models[3] divide the industrial structure into distinctive sectors within which employers and workers face fundamentally different conditions and operate according to fundamentally different rules. Beck et al. distinguish two sectors:

(1) **The core industrial sector**. This is dominated by large corporate enterprises which came to constitute an oligopolistic system of production. It includes those industries that comprise the muscle of American economic and political power. The firms are noted for high productivity, high wages, high profits, intensive utilization of capital, high incidence of monopoly, and high degree of unionization. For example, automobile, steel, and rubber industries.

(2) **The peripheral sector**. This is characterized by small firms, operating in a more or less open, competitive capitalistic environment. They are concentrated in agriculture, nondurable manufacturing, retail trade, and sub-professional services. The peripheral industries are noted for their small size, labour intensity, low profits, low productivity, intensive productivity, intensive product market competition, lack of unionisation, and low wages. Unlike the core sector industries, the periphery lacks the assets, size

[3] They are similar to that by Galbraith.

and political power to take advantage of economies of scale or to spend large sums on research and development.

Theories of dual economy suggest that these sectoral differences have important implications for the opportunity structures and work experiences faced by individual employees. Moreover, even ethnic and racial group differences may be the outcome of differential assignments of group members within the sectoral structure of the economic system.

There are three questions that the authors seek to answer:

(1) Are there differences in the labour force composition of the core and periphery sectors?
(2) Can differences in individual earnings between sectors be accounted for in terms of the individuals located within those sectors?
(3) How similar are the processes of earnings determination for core and periphery sectors?

In order to answer these questions, Beck et al. perform empirical analyses on data from the 1975 and 1976 General Social Surveys. The sample consisted of 1,683 members of the experienced civilian labour force. The independent variables were: (a) Human Capital Variables, parental education and occupational prestige, age, respondent's education (investment); (b) Demographic Variables, gender and race (from the perspective of socio-economic structuralist theory of ownership of labour power and ascribed characteristics of labour power); (c) Occupational Variables, occupational prestige, union membership, employment status, work stability, and industrial sector (core vs. periphery).
The dependent variables were the natural logarithm of annual earnings and a binary variable coded for earnings below the poverty threshold.

The answers to the above questions are:

(1) There are important differences in the labour force composition, work experiences, and earnings of the sectors. Core workers have larger, more homogeneous annual earnings than do periphery workers. They also have, on the average, more schooling, better educational credentials, parents with better education and higher occupational status, and they are more likely to be male and white than female and non-white. Also, core members are more likely to be in higher prestige occupations, to be employed full time, to work more hours per week, and to belong to a union.

(2) There are persistent sectoral differences in economic outcomes which cannot be explained by the racial, sexual, human capital, or occupational characteristics of their respective labour forces (Baron 1994).

This interesting analysis leads to the conclusion that the divergence discovered is in fact class differentiation, as classes are distinguished, as will be explained in one of the later chapters, according to their ownership of not only means of economic activity but also labour power.

The early twentieth century Polish methodologist Leon Petrazycki (working, incidentally, at the same Poznan University as the present author) coined the term "the leaping concept" as one which is over-inclusive, too broad in scope, thereby obliterating the qualitative differences between the phenomena in question. This notion applies equally to the concept of human capital and the concept of social capital.

As regards the notion of human capital, one cannot but overlook its ambiguity. Becker, in the entry written for the *Small Encyclopaedia of Economics*, writes that the material forms of capital are not the only ones; education, computer courses, spending on health care, lectures on the virtues of punctuality and honesty are also capital. However, because they raise earnings, improve health or develop a person's good habits over the majority of the person's life, economists therefore claim spending on education, training, health care, etc. to be investment in capital. These are called human capital: The ambiguity here lies in the inability to determine whether the author refers the concept of equity to education, health, etc. or to the efforts to gain or improve these." This definitional vagueness is not eliminated by the fact that Becker further claims that education and training are the most important investments in human capital. Such a dual approach also applies to certain concepts related by substance to the Becker theory of human capital, in particular the notion of the family or household.

II.7.4. Households

On the basis of his own questionable (as will be clarified) assumptions, Gary Becker stated that 80% of the resources of rich countries is human capital. Material resources, facilities and natural resources make up only 20%. In his *Treatise on the Family*, the U.S. economist and sociologist emphasized the role of the so-called basic cell of society in the creation of human capital. According to Becker, it is in the family that young children acquire these basic characteristics that make society function properly—

characteristics such as solidarity between siblings, solidarity between parents and children, respect for others, punctuality, love of order, etc.—all these basic features are acquired in the family. As a standard, these tasks and many others fall on the shoulders of women (Becker stresses that the mother is a cook, seamstress, teacher, nurse, an economist, judge etc.). Becker claims that he was able to even give a number that indicates the importance of the mother: according to him through their work they produce at least 30% of national income.

These statements are a part of Becker's theory of the household according to which "households" are no longer treated as passive consumers of goods and services purchased in the market sector, but as active producers of such non-market goods as health or prestige. These goods are the result of a combination of market goods, the time available to household members and the variable "environmental," such as education, capacity and others (Becker 1990 162).

These statements touch on a number of problems. While what has been called Becker's economic imperialism has been often criticized, we also have to admit the undeniable merit of his analysis in its extension onto activities in the household. Leaving the answer to the question primarily to economists, as to what extent such activities should be counted towards national income, and similar economic indicators, we cannot leave without a comment on many specific characteristics of their recognition by Becker. In the above part of the book, the Polish translator used the term "commodity." In that same book there is talk about commodities, which are "a direct source of utility" (Becker 1990, 236). The English equivalent of the term "goods" is "goods" (*dobro*) rather than "commodity" (*towar*), the latter term means commodity, and if we apply it to "goods" it means to mass produce goods on a large scale, which, as is easy to notice, does not apply to households, however we recognise their creations. Classic examples of the products described in the language of economists as commodities are the products of agriculture or extractive industries: wheat or oil, for example, units of which are indistinguishable from each other and therefore exchangeable for others that are natural candidates for the role of the object of trade in the markets of futures and other derivative instruments.

The fact that the author himself had doubts about his own terminology is evidenced by the *Treatise on the Family*, in which the term "commodities" is indeed consistent, but always in inverted commas, which naturally causes more problems than solves them. Becker writes, for example: "Time and goods are contributions to the production of 'commodities', which are a direct source of utility. These goods can not be purchased on the market, but they are produced and consumed by households using market purchases" (Becker 1990, 31).

Becker, therefore, on the one hand distinguishes market goods or non-market goods, but blurs the distinction by introducing the ambiguous term "commodities" or quasi-goods. However, goods and services produced and consumed within families or households are not any goods, because they are devoid of their basic feature, which is exchange value, production for profit. The goods and services in question are an element of natural economy, not market economy, a sector of the economy of real fundamental economic and social significance.[4] From this point of view, it's good that Becker paid analytical attention to it, though of course he was not the only nor the first. However, the theoretical categories through which he considers this sector are neither adequate nor fortunate. Later in this book we will suggest our own categories whose task will be to highlight both the similarity of economic activities undertaken within the framework of a household and the regular economy while avoiding obscuring of fundamental socio economic differences between them. From this point of view, the notions used by Becker to describe mainly women's tasks in a household, which include, in this or any other version, the word "work," "housework," and "the division of household labour" violate this last principle.

---

[4] Data from twelve OECD countries from different years in the period between 1985–1992 shows that the average time for an adult's paid job was twenty-four hours per week, while the average duration of "work" in the household was more at twenty-six hours per week (Goldschmidt-Clermont and Pagnossin-Aligisakis 1995; Ironmonger 1995). Becker has therefore the basis to claim (even if the statement contains questionable parts) that "in the entire history the volume of expenditure of time assigned to paid work never permanently exceeded the volumes of time spent on other types of human activity. Even if the working week was six days 14 hours a day, still half of the global time was devoted to sleeping, eating and other activities. Economic development led to the great secular shortening of the work week, so that now in most countries it is not more than fifty hours, i.e. is less than one third of total disposable time. As a consequence issues of allocation of time not used for commercial activity and efficiency of this use may be at present more important for economic welfare than the issues of working time itself; interest of economists in the issues of working time is, however, still uncomparably greater. Fortunately, there can be observed some turn in the direction of restoring appropriate proportions. A longtime time tendency of shifts in the volume of time devoted to earnings-oriented work is decreasing—in part because the young come late to the labour market due to longer periods of education. (Becker 1990, 161).

Activity, whether a man's or woman's or a child's, within the family is not work nor labour unless it has the nature of commercial activity, and is used to get the basic means of subsistence.

This theoretical and conceptual confusion has its source equally in the dogmatism of our awardee. In seeking to expand what he posits as the extension of the principles of economic theory onto non-economic fabric of society, this materializes in reality not as much in an expansion but in a narrowing of the point of view and forcing phenomena and processes within these structures into too tight frames of these initial ones, which reveals a lack of clarity in the understanding of the concept of economy and its relationship to the concept of production of material goods. One of the consequences of a lack of having an adequate theory of society as a whole is a conflation in Becker's description of "production" of a household of real economic activities with the activities which by no means belong to economy, which is seen in this hodgepodge: "Goods produced in the household are numerous and include, for example, quality of meals, offspring quality, prestige, recreation, companionship, love, health … 'good health,' the offspring, marriage or 'interurban visits'" (Becker 1991, 257 and 353). Glossing over the socio-economic distinction between economic activity and, as we shall call it, quasi-economic, leads to false analogies: "Great companies are much more common than large households because scale benefits from specialized investments and division of labour are more important for companies" (Becker 1991, 301).

II.7.5. Families

Closely connected with the theory of household production remains, linked to the concept of human capital, Becker's theory of the family. This notion, with its central thesis on the distribution of "work" between the spouses, according to which one (in a typical situation the husband) may specialize in commercial activities, while the second in the household activities. This allows both to focus on that in which they show comparative advantages which serves to explain the phenomenon of higher wages that men achieve compared with women. In contrast, no one bachelor is able to establish such a division of activities and from the nature of things is loaded with both paid work and household duties, which must limit his investments in his own human capital. Because of the relative impairment of unmarried men compared to married men, the latter according to Becker's model should be more productive and hence earn more (Loh 1996).

Becker's family theory does not work, however, when confronted with empirical data. According to this theory, working men with non-working wives should receive higher salaries compared with those who also work, but whose wives also work. They have greater opportunities for human capital accumulation through greater specialization. However, in a situation when both spouses work, the possibilities of specialization are decreased, and the excess wages earned by such men compared to unmarried men should accordingly also be reduced (Gray 1997).

The results of multiple regression, however, have not confirmed the existence of such interdependencies between the size of the premium and the number of hours devoted by the wives to the household. It was assumed that more educated wives are more likely to specialize in paid work, thus forcing their husbands to take on more household duties reducing the size of this premium. It was found that compared with single men, married men whose wives did not complete secondary education earn 11.8% , and those with secondary education earn 4.3%. Those with incomplete higher education earn 7.1% more and those with completed higher education earn 11.5% more (Cornwell & Rupert 1997).

It is clear that, contrary to Becker's notion, married men gain from marriage with educated women. But how to explain these results, contrary to the implications of Becker's theory according to which the work of wives means the transfer of most of the domestic yoke onto the shoulders of men, which reduces their commercial focus preference? First, families with higher income, which is often associated with higher education, usually employ nannies and other domestic servants and, secondly, which is even compatible with more general assumptions of Becker's approach, families with higher education realize the existence of higher costs of abstaining implied by time spent on household activities, therefore choosing to have fewer children. Both factors make the yoke of domestic toil in the better-educated families actually smaller (Loh 1996).

Attention is also drawn to another factor that may act in the same direction—better career opportunities for men who have educated wives thanks to the help (advice on transfers, tasks etc.) which the wives are able to give them in this field (Korenman & Neumark 1994).

In another study testing Becker's theory, it was taken into account the class differences based on comparing with each other the differences of salaries of married men and single men on the basis of, on the one hand, the so-called self-employed (i.e. the representatives of the autocephalous class), and on the other hand employees. According to Becker's theory, if married men are actually more productive than the unmarried men, then this higher productivity should be revealed with higher earnings regardless of where and how much they earn for a living. Meanwhile, regressions showed that there is a significant difference in this respect, to the detriment of the self-employed. Whatever the reasons for this state of affairs (among the possible reasons the following were hinted at: later marriages of businessmen arising from the time they have to devote to the establishment and operation of their businesses, which means reduction of benefits from marriage, lowering revenue by business people for tax reasons, which reflects the specific socio-economic situation of this class, and their earnings from work, both incomes and losses from economic activity) it does not correspond to the Becker thesis of the family theory.

Finally, the third large study focused on the comparison of the salaries of men who lived with their subsequent spouses before the wedding and those who did not go through such cohabitation. According to Becker's theory, wages should be higher in the first case due to the longer period of investment in human capital. Even if in the period of cohabitation there was no formation of any division of labour, the knowledge accumulated during this period by both partners on their strengths and weaknesses gives them a privileged starting point for developing such a specialisation at the beginning of the formal period of cohabitation (Loh 1996.) Meanwhile, empirical data suggest that both groups receive remuneration with the same difference compared to unmarried men, which undermines Becker's concept of specialization.

It is worth citing the results of a test of identical twins which, while not necessarily upholding the theory formulated by Becker, however confirms the thesis of higher salaries earned by married men compared to unmarried men. This type of twins were selected for the study due to their identical genetic equipment and the environment in which they grew up, which means having identical physical and mental capacity and thus, which can be reasonably assumed, productivity. This allows for the conclusion that if between these brothers there is a difference in earnings, the reason is marriage.

As the study of 136 pairs of monozygotic twins showed (85% of them were married and in 23% of the cases one of the twins was married) married men with these characteristics controlling the impact of education have 26% higher wages than their unmarried brothers. Similar results were obtained, taking into account other factors whose impact on the studied phenomenon was neutralized, such as the status of divorcee, a widower, spouse's work experience, the career, and number of children (Antonovics & Town 2004).

Gary Becker was, as is well known, both an economist and sociologist. It is strange, therefore, that he did not pay attention to common property (in the socio-economic sense) as the basis of the family in the sense defined by him. He stated that:

> The family is an organization with a very high level of internal, mutual, connections. It has the following characteristics: any redistribution of income within it does not impact on consumption or on the welfare of any of its members because it immediately entails compensatory transfers from the head of the family. Both the head of the family and its other members act as if all "loved" each other (even if they were selfish) in the sense that they maximize not their individual "own" income, but income of the family. (Becker 1990, 436)

In the above definition a formulation appeared suggesting that "even the selfish family members are sometimes willing to do, as if their attitude towards others was altruistic."

This tendency to simulate altruism Becker termed the "rotten kid" theorem. This theorem, according to the naturalistic trend detectable in Becker, was used by the American economist and sociologist to, among other things, "explain why biological selection can in the course of time work in favour of altruistic behaviour" (Becker 1990, 432). Interestingly enough, in another work the author challenged the validity of his theorem, showing that it does not apply:

> when parents do not provide children with gifts or inheritances. This may be because their altruism is weak, but even parents with strong altruistic tendencies may not give gifts or inheritances, if they expect that their children will be much richer than themselves. Children are more affluent than their parents, when economic growth is fast and if their equipment in the skills and other characteristics is higher than that of their parents.
>
> Inheritances are large in rich families, quite common in middle-class families and irrelevant to the poor. One of the reasons is the fact that children's equipment is usually greater than their parents' in poor families, but are often lower in rich families. (Becker 1991, 364)

Empirical evidence for the concept of altruistically motivated transfers and altruistic ties having an impact on consumption in families are at best mixed (Cox 1987; Cox 1990; Cox & Rank 1992; Altonji et al. 1992; Altonji et al. 1997).

The "rotten kid" theorem itself was negatively verified in research. Although in the above formulation Becker used the term "as if," in the *Treatise* he calls altruism the same behaviour without any adjectives, which blurs the qualitative differences between different types of actions and may be accepted only on the basis of extreme type of behaviourism: "Because the altruist maximizes his own utility , he may be from the perspective of utility called selfish, not altruist … I give a definition of altruism, which concerns the behaviour—choices of production and consumption, rather than a philosophical discussion about what really motivates people" (Becker 1991, 279).

II.7.6. Marriage

As has been indicated above, Becker's research on human capital has had many implications for the family such as the marriage market, divorce, and fertility. Becker argued that such decisions are made in a marginal cost and marginal benefit framework. For example, he found that wealthier couples had a higher cost to divorce and thus a lower divorce rate. A major focus of Becker's research was the impact of higher real wages in increasing the value of time and therefore the cost of home production such as childrearing. As women increase investment in human capital and enter the work force, the opportunity cost of childcare rises. Additionally, the increased rate of return to education raises the desire to provide children with formal and costly education. Coupled together, the impact is to lower fertility rates. A more controversial issue was Becker's conclusion that parents often act altruistically towards selfish children by heavily investing in a child in an effort to indirectly save for old age. Becker believed that the rate of return from investing in children was often greater than normal retirement savings. However, parents cannot know for sure that the child will take care of them. Since they cannot legally bind a child to care for them they often resort to manipulation through instilling a sense of "guilt, obligation, duty and filial love that indirectly, but still very effectively … commits children to helping them out." Becker even went so far as to say that social security can cause families to be less interdependent by removing the motivation of parents to use altruistic behaviours in incentivizing their children to care for them.

> The content of this chapter provides ample evidence that many writers are not comfortable with Becker's approach. One such insightful commentator asserts that (and her comments deserve attention both for their descriptive and critical merits) analysis of the family places considerable explicit or implicit reliance on rational choice theory) [...]: William Landes and Richard Posner, collaborators of Becker, conceptualize the altruistic rescuer as someone who recognises that their utility is affected by the utility of an endangered person, and who is motivated to act in order to preserve the value of their own "wealth."

> It also may be economically rational for an individual to make commitments that lead them to eschew opportunities for immediate gains, if pursuing those gains might be inconsistent with their long-term interests. [...] A stable marriage may be in a person's long-term interest because it maximizes expected utility over their lifetime. [...] proponents of economic analysis do not regard the viability of their approach as undermined by the fact that many, perhaps most, people do not engage in the kind of deliberation that the economic model describes. As Richard Posner puts it, "Economics is not a theory about consciousness. Behavior is rational when it conforms to the model of rational choice, whatever the state of mind of the chooser" (1986). Even if persons as a phenomenological matter do not regard themselves as engaging in rational cost-benefit assessment, theorists argue that the model is vindicated to the extent that their actions can be reconstructed as if they do. (Regan 1999).

Irrespective of how one assesses the overall framework under consideration, the methodological, or rather epistemological, point mentioned above is praiseworthy, and even more so in light of the latest neuroscience research which indicates, *inter alia*, that the notion of free will, so dear to theologians and certain philosophers, is untenable; our unconscious brain or mind takes decisions faster than and prior to its conscious department. To return to Regan's both descriptive and evaluative argument, she goes on to say that:

> Gary Becker's work reflects the most comprehensive attempt to fashion a theory of the family based on economic principles. [...] Becker and his colleagues Elisabeth Landes and Robert Michael have used an economic model to analyze some of the factors influencing the probability of divorce. They suggest that the probability of divorce may rise the higher the search costs of finding a marital partner and the less that spouses invest in marriage-specific capital. High search costs tend to increase the probability of divorce because they limit the ability to explore many alternatives before selecting a marriage partner. The less the amount of market information before making a choice, the greater the chance that there will be surprise about marital outcomes—that is, a discrepancy between one's expected and actual marital experience. The more likely this discrepancy, the more the net benefits from marriage will seem unsatisfactory compared to alternatives.
>
> Marriage-specific capital reflects the ability to produce things of value for a particular marriage. [...] The fact that this capital is tailored to his or her needs and interests tends to increase the amount of utility from staying in the marriage compared to that available from alternatives. Conversely, the less the investment in such particularized capital, the weaker the incentives for either party to remain married. Economic analysts observe that the relatively high contemporary rate of divorce may make individuals

> reluctant to invest in marriage-specific capital because of the risk of economic disadvantage in the event of divorce.
>
> According to the Becker, Landes and Michael model, this in turn will increase the probability of divorce, creating even greater incentives to invest in labour market skills than in household capital, in a self-reinforcing cycle. (Regan 1999)

And Regan identifies then a key property of Becker's approach that should not surprise the reader:

> Economic analysis [...] represents a "subjectivist and individualist" theory of value. [...]
>
> By taking as fundamental the discrete and separate character of individuals *qua* individuals, an economic approach mirrors the insistence of the external stance that each individual has a distinct set of interests that distinguishes them as a unique human being.[...] regardless of whatever diverse and distinctive characteristics any two options may have, one can extract from them the common feature that each offers a certain amount of utility. This approach reflects what philosophers call "monism": the view that the only relevant difference between or among options is their differing amount of a single value.[...] On this view, "the difference between pleasures such as that of sunning oneself on the beach and of discussing philosophy are differences simply of the source of the same thing.". (Regan 1999).

The other side of this individualistic coin is a glaring asociologism:

> In the context of marriage and divorce, for instance, the perspective of the external stance insists that an individual should not succumb to social pressures to marry if they are not convinced that marriage will offer more utility than remaining single. They should not stay married because of guilt or concern about the reactions of others if they are convinced that divorce would offer greater utility than remaining married. [...] This critical distance is reflected, for instance, in Becker, Landes and Michael's criticism of the "common belief that marital dissolutions are evidence of marital failure that should be avoided if at all possible."
>
> Instead, they argue, divorce should be seen simply as a response to new information about the gains from marriage compared to other alternatives.
>
> Similarly, economic theorists emphasize that marriage is not unique but is governed by the same principles that apply to any other long-term contract. [...]
>
> Viewing an actual or potential spouse as a source of utility that can be compared with other sources is not a particularly romantic perspective. (Regan 1999)

Regan then points to methodological, and even epistemological consequences of the kind of subjectivistic-individualist framework pertinent to becker's theory of family as based on human capital. Her conclusions, to be sure, are not surprising to us, as we have drawn attention to, inter alia, Homans' practice of ex post explanation flowing from a similar framework:

> To the extent that utility is defined as an individual's inner state of satisfaction, we have no way of ascertaining which arrangements are actually utility-maximizing for them. [...] As a result, we have no firm basis for concluding that any given social practice is valuable to the individuals who participate in it beyond their own genuine consent to such participation. Rather than attempting from some privileged standpoint to determine the effect of each option on each individual, we need to rely only on the individuals' own judgments of whether they are worse or better off in making assessments about alternative courses of action.
>
> Depicting marriage as a series of transactions over time in which spouses implicitly exchange resources of various kinds therefore can be seen as a way of keeping in focus the fact that marriage is comprised of two separate individuals, each with distinctive interests. (Regan 1999)

Arguably, though:

> The external stance is a partial perspective. It neglects a different but also important dimension of marriage: the internal stance. [...] The internal stance would seem to offer an account of marriage that is at odds with economic theory. This moment of marriage is characterized by the understanding that one is part of a collective unit to whose welfare one may be committed quite apart from a calculation of individual costs and benefits. Such an orientation is associated with "prosocial" attitudes and behaviour such as empathy and cooperation, which appear to prompt one person to forgo private advantage for the sake of another. Ordinary language, for instance, distinguishes between self-interested and other-regarding attitudes and commonly draws a distinction between selfish and unselfish behaviour. Herbert Margolis' description of the way in which altruism seems to diverge from individual rationality serves also as a general description of the common understanding of a prosocial orientation: a person "could have done better for himself had he chosen to ignore the effect of his choice on others."
>
> Such behaviour would appear to be inconsistent with a portrait of persons as individuals inexorably devoted to maximizing their own utility. (Regan 1999)

And again, Regan's reply to that question is consistent with our earlier comments on semantic manipulations by means of stretching given concepts to the point of vacuity thus immunising them against empirical falsification.

> Economic theory purports to accommodate such behaviour by emphasizing the ways in which prosocial or other-regarding conduct in fact provides individual rewards. One approach maintains the assumption of independent utility functions and narrowly egoistic benefits. It emphasizes the subtle and often intangible rewards that accrue to an individual as a result of altruism or cooperation, such as social approval, avoidance of guilt, or the satisfaction that comes from doing one's duty. In addition, prosocial conduct may simply reflect enlightened self-interest, in the sense that an individual may anticipate reciprocal assistance and consideration from others in the future. In each instance, the action is self-interested because the discrete individual gains or expects an increase in their own consumption of goods independent of the consumption of any other person. (Regan 1999).

However, a compelling case may be made for the fact that:

> neoclassical economists try to explain why people–most people–with spouses who have Alzheimer's disease stay with them. These economists treat marriage as an economic contract, in which an exchange of services takes place for income and services. But with Alzheimer's disease, there is no payback because there's no reasonable hope that the person who is afflicted will recover and take care of the other person. One may say that the treating spouse does so because of the kudos he or she will receive from members of their extended family and neighbours and friends. (Regan 1999)
>
> However, tending to an Alzheimer's patient day in and day out is so taxing that all the kudos in the world could not make up for it. And finally, economists use the notion of psychic income. But again, that explanation fails because the afflicted person does not respond with a warm appreciation for the service; indeed, they become ever more abusive as time goes on. So why do most spouses not walk out on their afflicted husband or wife? When one interviews these people, one repeatedly hears the statement that "this is the right thing to do"; [...] there is a continual conflict and tension between self-interest and the pleasure principle on one hand, and powerful moral commitments on the other. (Etzioni 2003)

> Recent empirical and theoretical work [...] calls into question the contention that economic theory entirely captures the phenomenon of others- regarding behaviour. Several experiments in social psychology profess to refute the claim that cooperation and altruism depend on incentives for some form of egoistic gain, and to establish that individuals are not uniformly attentive to private costs and benefits in all kinds of

> relationships. These studies suggest that persons sometimes act on the basis of a social identity that goes beyond the discrete individual to include other persons as part of the self. Furthermore, refinement of public goods theory suggests that the concept of interdependent utility functions may not adequately capture what occurs when individuals forgo personal advantage for the sake of a larger collective good. (Regan 1999).

We shall return later to the issue of co-operation because it is relevant not only to Becker's theory. Thus, it is worth bearing in mind the argument laid out in the present chapter as it constitutes a useful supplement to those later deliberations. Regan adds that :

> One body of research on close personal relationships that is consistent with the model of an expanded sense of self is the work of Arthur Aron and his colleagues on the cognitive processes involved in falling in love. They suggest that a particularly useful way to characterize these processes is that they blur the distinction between oneself and another, so that the other is included in a person's sense of self. [...] people in a close relationship make less of a distinction between self and other in allocating resources. This appears to result from a perception that resources are communal, rather than from an expectation that generosity will be directly reciprocated. (Regan 1999)

This point is worth emphasising: the researcher implicitly shows that the types of behaviour depicted are grounded in common ownership.

> People who desire a communal relationship with another are more likely to keep track of the other's needs than are persons who desire an exchange relationship, even when there is no opportunity for the other to reciprocate, or when the person is actually unable to offer any assistance to the other. Similarly, persons oriented to a communal relationship with a person are less likely to keep track of that person's inputs into a joint task for which a reward will be provided than are persons who seek an exchange relationship with that person.
>
> [...] intimates, through identification with and empathy for their partners, come to define themselves as a unit; as one couple. They see themselves not merely as individuals interacting with others, but also as part of a partnership, interacting with other individuals, partnerships, and groups. This characteristic may have a dramatic impact on intimates's perceptions of what is and is not equitable. (Regan 1999)

By analogy, one might render the distinction between the two perspectives and relationships involved by comparing it to the distinction between two different principles of fair pay postulated for socialism and communism, respectively: "according to one's work" and "according to one's needs":

> Studies indicate that spouses in happy marriages avoid a "book-keeping" perspective that emphasizes conceptions of equity and equality that are associated with exchange. [...] they are quite willing to ignore the relative allocation of benefits between partners. Such couples seem instead to use a "bank account" approach that focuses more generally on whether there are more "deposits" than "withdrawals," rather than on whether benefits given are reciprocated by benefits received. Partners are more likely to respond to each other's needs as they occur, rather than to emphasize equal exchange. Indeed, the problems associated with an exchange orientation have led many marital therapists to abandon earlier *quid pro quo* models of marriage and to stress a concept of generalized reciprocity that encourages unilateral initiatives that do not include explicit penalties or rewards. (Regan 1999)

Regan deals with another expedient by means of which economists, or should we say economic imperialists and semantic abusers try to take on board evidence that is inconsistent with their very narrow perspective on reality.

> As an alternative to the egoistic reward thesis, one might claim that economic theory can fully account for prosocial orientation by expanding the concept of self-interest to include satisfaction of prosocial preferences. One could posit, for instance, that a person has an interdependent utility function, which reflects the fact that they gain utility from the welfare of others. One may also argue that some individuals have a taste for identification with others. Such persons are willing to sacrifice some amount of narrow egoistic benefits in order to enhance the welfare of others because doing so increases their own satisfaction. [...] By expanding the concept of self-interest to incorporate prosocial preferences, one might argue, economic theory is able to capture the underlying essence of behaviour and attitudes that characterize the internal stance. (Regan 1999)

Having read her previous argument, Regan's reaction should not come as a surprise to us:

> This argument [...] takes as the relevant unit of analysis the separate individual and attributes to their cognitive and motivational processes characteristic of individual rationality. This neglects the insight of social identity theory that persons may be changed psychologically through identification with others, so that collectively oriented behaviour cannot be treated simply as the aggregation of individual actions. [...] Social co-operation reflects not an interdependence of separate, personal self-interests, but a cognitive redefinition of self and self-interest, (which) hence has a strong element of altruism. [...] Margolis notes the persistent difficulty of rational choice theory in providing a non-tautological account

> of why persons contribute to the acquisition of public goods, given that the marginal individual costs of such contributions typically exceed the expected marginal individual benefits.

As Margolis observes: "(E)mpirically, it is obvious that people do have preferences about budgets for public goods which turn on social judgments of costs and benefits to society as a whole. (Regan 1999)

This unwillingness to face the facts, one might add, seems to have something to do with the generally non-dialectical character of conventional economics for which the concept of contradiction is an alien body. Anyway, one may subscribe to Regan's conclusion that "in short, expansion of the concept of self-interest to include interdependent utility functions or a taste for group identification ultimately seeks to subsume the internal within the external stance and thus doesn't do justice to the former's distinctive character".

Further comments by Regan are fully in line with our repeated critical remarks on the "leaping" logic of over-inclusiveness:

> A second, broader, problem with extensive expansion of the concept of self-interest is that at some point economic theory runs the risk of becoming tautological and non-falsifiable. This danger in large measure is a function of the elasticity of the rational choice paradigm. That paradigm does not specify preferences in advance, so any behaviour in hindsight theoretically can be seen as rational. Furthermore, given a lack of consensus about what it means to be a rational actor, it is not clear precisely what kind of behaviour in theory could fail to be explained by some variant of rational choice theory.
>
> Too often the result, as eminent game theorist Anatol Rapaport observes, is that those who subscribe to a theory of egoistic incentives "are always ready to retreat to previously prepared positions by extending the concept of 'selfishness' to include any demonstrable source of motivation not previously subsumed under the concept." Thus, for instance, rational choice theory can explain why a person does not vote as a natural response to the relative insignificance of their single ballot, but can also explain why a person does vote by referring to the utility that they gain from doing their duty or appearing to be a good citizen.
>
> In instances such as these, the theory becomes "trivially true, and never disconfirmable". (Regan 1999)

Regan deals also with another methodological issue characteristic of neopositivism:

> One may assert that it is misguided to criticize economic theory on the grounds that its assumptions are unrealistic, that its model does not

> comport with how people actually understand themselves when they engage in much prosocial behaviour. For instance, the influential approach known as "predictionism," most closely associated with Milton Friedman, argues that the criterion for identifying a fruitful theory is the accuracy of its predictions, not the realism of its assumptions. Friedman observes that a completely realistic theory would have to be so complex and encompass so many variables that it would be utterly useless as a tool of analysis. Any valuable theory necessarily abstracts from experience and in that sense is unrealistic.
>
> The real question is whether it is "realistic enough,'" and this must depend on whether it "yields predictions that are good enough for the purpose in hand or that are better than predictions from alternative theories." If it does, we can treat phenomena "as if they occurred in a hypothetical and highly simplified world containing only the forces that the hypothesis asserts to be important," without worrying about whether there is a discrepancy between the model's assumptions and the real world. Indeed, Friedman argues, the most productive hypotheses are those that are "wildly inaccurate descriptive representations of reality," because they explain much by using a small number of variables that have been abstracted from complex phenomena. [...] we can predict [...] the actions of a businessman as if he engaged in complex computations based on perfect information about market conditions. The fact that the businessman understand[s his] own behaviour in such terms is irrelevant. (Regan 1999)

Before passing to Regan's commentary to the aforementioned conception, let us themselves indicate a few points. First and foremost, Friedman does not recognise any qualitative difference between the social and natural. But even within the natural realm one is reminded of the Ptolemaic astronomy which in fact quite well accounted for and hence predicted the motions of planets. There is only one problem: the theory was, as we know since Copernicus, entirely false. But most importantly, Friedman's criterion of scientifity in social science is based on a total misunderstanding of the nature of the social world. The latter is much more complex than biological or physical structures, the key reason being a myriad of human actions and relationships between those actions and relationships between the former that compose it. As a result, "the Revolutions of the Heavenly Spheres" are small beer in comparison to the complexity of the inter-relations of a variety of social structures and substructures. Regan is also critical of those methodological simplifications:

> The premise of Friedman's argument is that a social science such as economics must conform to the methodology of the physical sciences if it is to be truly scientific. His view that predictive accuracy is the sole test of

a theory, and that the realism of assumptions is irrelevant, is contestable even as an account of physical science.

Nonetheless, even if we accept *agruendo* the claim that prediction is the sole aim of physical science, it is far less plausible to assert that predictive accuracy in social science is unaffected by the realism of one's theory. In the physical sciences, one need not be concerned about the mental states of the inanimate phenomena under study because they have none. [...] the assumption of mental phenomena is taken to distinguish behaviour, which is common to all organisms, from action, which is distinctive to humans: "Human beings do not just behave. They act, and their actions occur with an understanding of their significance in a wider social context."

Mental states such as motive, purpose, and intentionality thus are essential features of human events. [...]

Without appreciation of these mental states, observers may have a poor sense of what is actually occurring in marital interaction. As a result, recent work has emphasized the need to focus on "the symbolic aspects of exchange," how parties themselves actually experience marital interaction, as the basis for their description of the situation. A sense of actors' mental states is therefore necessary in order to engage in the fundamental scientific act of observation. [...] In short, it is perilous to regard the realism of a theory's assumptions as irrelevant to social science, even if we regard predictive accuracy as the criterion for evaluating social science theory. [...] If prediction has its problems, however, so does insistence that a theory is valid only if it captures the actors' own understandings of their action.

As Alfred Schutz once suggested "We should certainly be surprised if we found a cartographer in mapping a town restricting himself to collecting information from natives" (1978). One of the most significant consequences of Freud's work, for instance, is to make us question whether an individual's explanation of their own motives is a complete account of the sources of a given instance of human action. Individuals have the capacity to delude themselves in a variety of ways, and observers may have a clearer perspective on underlying grounds of action than persons directly involved in events. Furthermore, individual action takes place within a dense field of social practices that are not reducible to individual mental states. Such practices "are neither subjective nor objective but what ties behind both." They exert subtle influence of which an individual may be only dimly aware, creating patterns of interaction that may be best discerned by "outsiders." (Regan 1999)

Whilst many of her observations and claims are sound, Regan's reference to "economic behaviour" in the above context is extremely problematic; recall, inter alia, the debate between formalism and substantivism reported in the first chapter—the said account can hardly be regarded as an adequate reflection of the scope and diversity of economic action. Thus, in our view at least, the following Regan's argument should be read with a pinch of salt:

> One may concede that economic theory doesn't accurately capture all of social life, but argue that nonetheless it is realistic enough to serve as our basic model of human behaviour. The human being that it depicts is an ideal type. Treating people as if they pursued only self-interest is a useful simplification that enables us to make reasonably accurate predictions about both egoistic and prosocial behaviour. Why bother with two theories when one will do the job? (Regan 1999)

This is rather uncontroversial and even banal, but what seems more interesting, and unfortunately not explored by the aforementioned researcher, is what social conditions are likely to produce the predominance of such instrumental motives. She, by and large, does not go beyond the sphere of microstructures:

> To the extent that a person internalizes the economic theory of behaviour as a complete account of human experience, they may ironically proceed on the basis of motives that undercut their ability to maximize utility in a domain of life that most would regard as a source of profound gratification. The plausibility of economic theory rests in part on its common-sense assertion that we can model individual behaviour on the assumption that human beings seek happiness. (Regan 1999)

This assumption, however, is contradicted by her own earlier valid stress on the autonomic status of behaviour oriented on the welfare of others. Therefore, Regan's conclusion is somewhat disappointing:

> We can accept this assumption, however, while recognising that directly seeking personal happiness in an economically rational way may be counterproductive in some circumstances. If we are to avoid this pitfall, we need a richer account of human motivation and experience that recognises the limits of economic analysis. Despite claims by some scholars that economic analysis offers the framework for a comprehensive account of marriage and divorce, I have argued that this school of thought in fact is an expression of an external stance toward marriage. As such, it offers an insightful but partial perspective on spousal behaviour.
>
> Its emphasis on critical reflection on attachments, the importance of individual welfare, consent as a prerequisite for the assumption of obligation, and distributive justice place it squarely within the mainstream of traditional liberal thought and its normative commitments. Situating law and economics within this tradition also illuminates its limitations. It is

> unable to fully account for all instances in which individuals act for the benefit of others. In particular, it does not capture the expansive sense of self that characterizes an internal stance toward marriage. This suggests that our choice of an economic perspective on marriage and divorce in a given instance is particularly appropriate when we wish to underscore concerns about the welfare of spouses as discrete individuals. This approach will be less successful, however, when we seek to understand and to reinforce the sense of communal attachment that marriage can involve. Any adequate account of marriage ultimately must speak to both sides of our ambivalence. (Regan 1999)

The preceding offers a lot of food for thought. At this juncture, to Regan's excellent analysis we may add just a brief remark. Firstly, one's point of departure in research of the family or indeed any other social structure ought to be a comprehensive and accurate theory of society writ large with its accompanying assumption on the mutual irreducibility and, correspondingly, specificity of particular societal structures whose content and functions are different. From this perspective, which is one of socio-economic structuralism, it is no brainer that, for example, families as units of the reproductive structure are to be explained by other tools than firms, i.e. units of the economic structure. This, of course, does not preclude certain similarities, but it is important to keep in mind what the starting point is—the recognition of relative autonomy of specific societal structures. It is no big surprise that approaches which do not rely on such a theory may, wittingly or not, obliterate that autonomy.

II.7.7. Social capital

Turning to the second of the two concepts classed earlier as examples of methodological notion of a pejorative connotation created by Petrazycki , to cite Fine:

> Becker has also been in the vanguard in deploying the notion of social capital. Why is this? The answer is that social capital allows Becker to accommodate an even wider range of economic and social phenomena whilst retaining a continuing commitment to methodological individualism or economic rationality. In effect, social capital becomes a catch-all for anything that improves life but that has not already been covered by those elements of personal capital that provide the starting point for understanding capital. (Fine 2001)

Fine passes a scornful judgment on this all-embracing notion:

> gargantuan appetite, [...] with its application having encompassed everything from individuals to societies. [...] A partial list of its scope of topics includes explanation for the sick, the poor, the criminal, the corrupt, the (dys)functional family, schooling, community life, work and organisation, democracy and governance, collective action, transitional societies, intangible assets or, indeed, any aspect of social, cultural and economic performance, and equally across time and place. On the other hand, social capital has been deployed across theories and methodologies as diverse as postmodernist Marxism and mainstream neoclassical economics. Everything can be interpreted through or as social capital. It is truly the academic's Third Way! (Fine 1999)

And indeed, while in the work of authors such as Pierre Bourdieu and James Coleman the concept of social capital related, more or less strictly, to the benefits or, in the language of Weber, economic chances of others arising from the participation of an individual in a certain type of relationship or social collectivities, through Robert Putnam social capital became more of a characteristic of whole groups and even nations. However, as aptly noted by Alejandro Portes and Patricia Landolt (1996), "collective social capital cannot simply be the sum of individual social capitals". Long before Schumpeter talked about creative destruction, Marx emphasized with awe the achievements of the modern bourgeois, while not ignoring the negative aspects of the overwhelming power of capital. Meanwhile, modern proponents of the category of social capital do not remain faithful to this dialectical approach, emphasizing only the positive results of social ties, whose inclusiveness for some means exclusiveness for others.

Another weakness of the concept, related to the lack of clarity as to what in reality is capital is the conflation of sources of social capital with its alleged benefits. This leads to circular reasoning, as the presence of social capital is often inferred on the basis of existence of benefits gained by an individual or a group. And so for instance, in the example suggested by Portes & Landolt, a student who earns money for school fees thanks to parents or relatives is regarded as the holder of social capital. Such a conclusion does not include, however, the existence of less fortunate classmates that can also count on support from sympathetic family, although not having sufficient means to make such expenditures.

Some other logical and methodological errors can be detected in several quantitative studies on social capital. These, *inter alia*, claim to show that social capital (trust, civic norms, etc. in civil society) is associated positively with income and income equality; see Knack & Keefer's (1997) study of a sample of twenty-nine market economies, and with poverty reduction in Indian states in Morris (1998). Social capital is associated negatively with infant mortality and income inequality in thirty-nine U.S. states (Kawachi et al. 1997). World Bank researchers assert that the social capital of rural households—social capital understood as networks and associations—is positively and causally associated with household expenditures and welfare in African and Latin American countries (Grootaert et al. 2002; Grootaert & Narayan 2004). The aforementioned studies, however:

> tend to equate correlation with causation. It is also possible that when social capital is treated as one factor operating along with many others-and especially with class related factors such as the strength of working-class power-it may have weak association with its purported social outcomes. A study of health and social capital in sixteen wealthy countries suggests this to be the case (Muntaner et al. 2002). Besides, there is also the possibility that both social capital and its supposed effects (e.g. economic growth) are a result of a third factor, such as state intervention or specific class relations. (Das 2006).

This fallacy is not accidental—social capital writers almost unanimously tend to overlook or marginalise the class societal structure. More specifically, they refer to it but in their own perverted way since, as the exponents of other purported, excluding economic, forms of capital, they by definition endow with it all social classes, a possible difference laying only in its size in particular class cases. It is rather boring to reiterate that the owners of sole labour power in no way cannot be compared or, worse still, identified with the owners of industrial, financial, commercial, transportation, service or money capital, that is the only genuine forms of capital. Of course, it is theoretically possible for a worker to inherit a large sum of money which, put in the bank, brings them income so substantial that it becomes for them an important source of the means of subsistence, equally important than his or her wages. In such cases, however, we are dealing with a mixed class: both capitalist and employee.

It might seem that the above-mentioned "class gap" in the literature on social capital is somewhat mitigated by the fact that in it there is a discussion of poor people. But even in this discussion, in which social capital is said to be the "capital" of the poor (World Bank 2001), the class character of social capital is not examined. "There are at least two reasons for this neglect. For one thing, the class character of the poor themselves is usually left out: the fact that the poor generally belong to wage-earning classes and semi-proletarian classes whose material interests are in conflict with the classes having ownership / control over resources" (Wright 1995) is usually not considered. "In addition, social-capital scholars often assume that as the social capital of society develops, the poor will benefit and, indeed, that they benefit from social capital more than the non-poor. This assumption is arguably the social-capital version of the neoclassical trickle-down theory of poverty" (Das 2006)

If one points out that in such and such approach the notion of class is missing, it might be expected that such a criticism is grounded in a robust theory of class. Unfortunately, in this instance this is not the case. Das (2006) refers to "a discussion on the social capital of peasants (semiproletarians)." The term: "semiproletarians" with reference to peasants may underline their debt dependence on landowners and financial capitalists, but it is firstly an unstated assumption, and even so creates a rather weak basis for comparing their class situation to one of industrial proletariat, if, again, this is what is meant by the term "proletarians" proper since it is also unstated.

Das goes on to state that:

> the working class is defined here as the class that is excluded from the ownership of, and control over, means of production, and whose main source of income is the sale of labour power. The working class thus defined can include labourers with small properties, as long as the main class contradiction the working class faces is with capitalists rather than with any other class/group. (Das 2006)

This concept of class is most likely borrowed from E. O. Wright (although the author himself indicates Weber as his source of inspiration) and is faulty due to putting ownership and control on the same footing. As is argued elsewhere the equation is erroneous. Further, Das announces that for some again unstated, reason he is "specifically dealing with a subset of the working class: poorly paid, unskilled / semi-skilled labourers with limited security of employment, and a very low level of autonomy at work:

I use 'working-class social capital' primarily as an investigative category with which to look at the ways in which the working class (re)makes and lives its life." Das goes on to clarify that:

> … micro-level working-class social capital is the social capital of the working class inhering in civil society. It refers to norms of trust and reciprocity, and to networks and organisations among working-class people. Working-class micro social capital has class-specific effects.
>
> Norms of trust and reciprocity can discourage free-rider behaviour and facilitate collective actions such as the building of physical and social infrastructure in working-class communities (e.g. community centres, roads, library, reading groups), which can enhance their social

connectedness; launching political action against employers paying low wages; or monitoring corrupt officials implementing antipoverty policies. Norms of trust and reciprocity can lead to informal mechanisms of support within working-class communities.

These can take such forms as the informal borrowing of food and other items of necessity, worker-managed eating places, micro-credit groups, and the sharing of information or tacit knowledge between (propertied) labourers-those whose income comes mainly from wages, but who supplement their wage income through petty entrepreneurial activities. Working-class people also use relations based around family and kinship as survival strategies (Argyle 1994, 79). Self-help (e.g. food sharing; informal credit) is particularly important during strikes, since it can increase workers' staying power ....

E. P. Thompson ... commenting on the influence of religion on class struggle ... referred to processes that arguably connote social capital: the working class community injected into the chapels its own values of mutual aid, neighbourliness and solidarity (1963: 392).

Indeed, mutual aid and neighbourliness are important forms of social capital. If, as Marx says in his famous preface to *A Contribution to the Critique of Political Economy*, the material conditions under which people live generally structure their 'social consciousness' and political organisation, then it is not difficult to argue that the common, class-specific ways of life of working-class families can create a specific type of bond between them-what is known as “bonding social capital” in the social-capital literature, i.e. social relations and norms of reciprocity among people of similar socio-economic status (Putnam 2000, 22–23).

As Marx says in *The Eighteenth Brumaire*, in order to be a politically organised class, workers must have a community, a national bond, and a political organisation. Community, bond and organisation are also keywords in the literature on social capital. Portes develops a four-fold typology of sources of social capital. One is “bounded solidarity” (Portes & Sensenbrenner 1993, 1325). This concept is exemplified by Marx's analysis of the rise of working-class consciousness: “The weapon of the working class in this struggle is precisely its internal solidarity born out of a common awareness of capitalist exploitation” (Das 2006)

The above passage contains, no doubt, many apposite observations, but still no proof that the concept of social capital has been needed or is indispensable for their presentation. Conversely, it could be eliminated without any harm to Das’ substantive discourse. After all, Das himself draws attention to the fact that:

Social-capital enthusiasts’s” uneasiness with class is very well expressed in the following quote: “If a community is riven by conflicting interests, the nature and meaning of social capital becomes more complicated” (Evans

> 1997b, 196; also see Duncan 2001, 75). If this is so, why not take conflict and its underlying theoretical underpinnings, including class, as the starting point rather than social capital, and why not discard social capital altogether? (Das 2006)

Precisely so. The contents of the social capital concept appears in this book in three places, but in each without even mentioning the term. These are: the following section; the next chapter, especially its parts concerning stakeholder capitalism; and in the section of social estates where some of the ingredients of what passes as "social capital" are construed as objects of non-economic ownership. And the term of social capital is incredibly misleading, as Das' deliberations indicate as well. His intention has been perhaps quite different, but his argument transforms workers into (social) capitalists, which leads to further complications when a given worker, as in Das' own example, is herself a small capitalist.

7.7.8. Human capital, social capital and ownership of labour power

It is our contention that the substantive scope of the two categories criticised above is covered by theory of ownership of labour power. Whilst the use of the category of labour power is widespread, notably in Marxian and Marxist writings, the fact remains that neither the former nor the latter unambiguously defines what ownership of it consists in. The following set of about a dozen statements is an attempt toward this goal. From a certain point of view we might say that this theory aims to reflect the circulation or circuit (albeit not comprising its production and reproduction) of the labour power or otherwise its history from the moment of entering the plant until leaving it.

7.7.8.1. Leasing Universalism and Particularism Versus Lumpen Ownership and Employee Co-ownership

With regard to the first of the possible stages, the theory is interested in what recruitment criteria are used: general principles (for example, tests based on science) vs. particular criteria: network of contacts, nepotism, corruption, role of characteristics associated with labour power, sex, age, etc. as the basis for negative and positive discrimination. On that basis, one can distinguish universalist and particularistic labour power.

Related to this is the first Proposition of the theory submitted here:

Proposition 1: The greater the role of universalism in lease relations of the labour power, the smaller the range of lumpen ownership relations, worker co-ownership of resources and work time in the enterprise.

Universalist (unlike particularistic) labour power is not involved in the relationship of lumpen ownership (co-ownership). Here the issue is the use of work resources for one's own needs (lumpen-personal property) and / or monetary gain (lumpen-private). Lumpen ownership is distinguished not by its external material characteristics but by the fact that it is not endorsed by the owner or the management, unlike the relation accepted by the owner of the company—employee co-ownership.

7.7.8.2. Leasing Collectivism and Ownership of Jobs

Going back to the stage of entering the employee to the company, the theory draws attention to the way contracts are entered into, individually or collectively (collective bargaining, the role of trade unions). The greater the role of factors of the second type, the greater the degree of socialization (collectivization) of labour power we are dealing with.

Proposition 2: the greater the scope of socialization of labour power, the stronger the ownership of jobs on the part of employees, revealed in, among others, guarantees of employment, conditions of lay-offs (severance, outplacement), etc.

How important not only in practical (for the persons involved and the policy-makers) but also in theoretical terms is the category of ownership of labour power and its corollary in the form of the above-mentioned notion of ownership of jobs is shown, amongst others, by some claims put forward by Ulrich Beck believing that it is the notion of risk that is constitutive of modern society. Arguably:

> an increase in patterns of flexible working has intensified the degree of risk involved in acquiring and maintaining employment. In modern society, employees are required to be adaptable and receptive to change in a fluctuating labour market. In support of the risk society perspective, flexibilization has eaten away at standardized full-time contracts and facilitated the diversification of employment practices. In Britain, over six million people are currently employed on a part-time basis, with self-employment becoming an entrenched trend.
>
> Although predominantly located within manual and service industries, 'self-employment' has also seeped into the professions, with employment agencies supplying lecturers, accountants, and computer analysts on demand. Again, at a surface level we can agree with Beck's line of reasoning. It is probable that employment risks are impacting upon a wider section of society than in previous eras. However, from this axiom, Beck

> superinduces that risk and insecurity are becoming universal features of employment. It is at this deeper structural level that the risk society thesis comes unstuck. (Mythen 2005)

According to Beck, the overarching purpose of the Fordist system was to eliminate scarcity by producing sufficient goods to meet the collective needs of society. Hence, the central dynamic (or logic) of the Fordist regime revolved around the concept of class. Beck argues that the distributional patterns of the class society were noticeably interrupted in the 1970s, when the distribution of social goods became augmented by a cachet of "social bads," such as endemic unemployment, mass pollution and nuclear hazards. Underlying the division between "goods" and "bads" is a rudimentary distinction between social priorities under the two modes of organisation: class societies are bound up with issues of scarcity, risk societies are preoccupied with the problem of insecurity (Beck 1992, 49).

In the risk society perspective, labour market insecurity is emblematic of a new fleet of risks which undermine social structures and threaten established cultural practices. The most obvious manifestation of employment risk is the social diversification of joblessness. With the emergence of cyclical global recessions,[5] unemployment and job insecurity no longer blight only the poorest and least academically qualified groups in society. In times of economic uncertainty, labour market fluctuations universalise the threat of redundancy: "you can run into anyone down at the unemployment office" (Beck 1998, 55). Not only does employment insecurity undercut established class and gender divides, the new logic of risk produces a circular motion of "boomerang effects," as risks return to haunt their original generators. For example, high-status business elites well-schooled in dispensing with labour, themselves become dispensable. In this way, the sectoral effects of the class society are juxtaposed with the universalising effects of the risk society: "poverty is hierarchic, smog is democratic" (Beck 1992, 36). The social diffusion of unemployment, combined with the flexibilization and casualization of labour, leads Beck to postulate that the traditional logic of the wealth distributing society is being replaced by a burgeoning logic of risk. In the risk society, new inequalities and unions emerge as "class positions" and become superseded by "risk positions." As risk and insecurity become routine features of the employment system, the distributive motor of the

---

[5] Of course, this claim of Beck expresses merely the historical fact that the Keynesian era of relative calming of inherently cyclical and crisis-prone nature of the capitalist economy cannot last forever, thus betraying his theoretical and historical ignorance.

class society misfires, leading to widespread uncertainty. The relative rise in cross-class unemployment in Europe leads Beck to the apocalyptic conclusion that post-industrial nations are headed towards "capitalism without work": "Insecurity on the labour market has long since spread beyond the lower classes. It has become the mark of our times. The old 'lifetime profession' is threatened with extinction. No one wants to admit that with it an entire value system, a society based on gainful employment, will disappear." (Beck 1998, 55)

From the viewpoint of socio-economic structuralism, the key weakness of Beck's argument lies in its lack of the category of ownership of labour power. From this perspective, it is clear that the phenomena depicted by Beck refer to various degrees of expropriation from that ownership, its extreme form being an employee's long-term unemployment leading to deskilling and eventually to elimination from the labour power market. Similar considerations apply to Manuel Castells' approach which addresses the issue under consideration and would greatly benefit from the notion of ownership of labour power. Castells' labour is divided into networked labour, which serves the goals of the network, and switched-off labour, which has nothing to offer the network and in the context of the network economy is non-labour. On the other hand, short-term contracts, casual labour practices and other processes considered under the rubric named "individualisation" express depriving a given worker of his or her property or of his or her job. Even granted the wide incidence of such practices, Beck's far-fetched conclusion about his "risk society" as replacing "class society" is unfounded. Essentially, the crux of the matter revolves around whether there has been a discernible shift from a sectoral logic of class to a universal logic of risk. Of course, this question can be approached in any number of ways. If we approach the issue with reference to "objective" empirical criteria, the logic of class demonstrates remarkable continuity (Goldthorpe and McKnight 2003; Mackintosh and Mooney 2004, 93). Despite being aware of the resilience of economic inequalities (1992, 35), Beck is adamant that risk positions are steadily supplanting class positions as principal markers of identity and experience. Granted, at a "subjective" level class may well be losing its purchase as a social glue that binds individuals and communities together (see Furlong and Cartmel 1997; Saunders 1984). Yet while class identities may be receding, class location remains a key determinant of employment opportunities and, at a broader level, life chances (Nolan and Whelan 1999). Since the diffusion of employment risk is strikingly uneven, labour market insecurity is universal in a strictly hypothetical sense. Whilst it may be possible to "run into anyone down at the unemployment office," in reality, it is the most impoverished, least qualified members of society that remain routinely dependent on social security. Class position remains a fundamental indicator of vulnerability to unemployment (see Gallie et al. 1998; Goldthorpe 2002). Bluntly put, the critical issue is not one of risk perception, but risk impact. In a changeable economic climate, we may all sense labour market insecurity, but it does not sequentially follow that we will share the consequences. Indeed, in Britain, empirical evidence suggests that the socio-economic divide is expanding, rather than contracting:

> Between 1979 and 1996, while average income increased by 44%, the income of the lowest decile fell by 9% and that of the top decile increased by 70% … the growing inequalities are evident in the falling life expectancy for the lowest two social classes, the first time a fall has been recorded since Victorian times (Perrons 2000, 290). Moreover, Beck's claim that long-term stable employment is a relic of the past is not born out by empirical research. As a case in point, Doogan (2001) on the basis of EUROSTAT data demonstrates that average job tenure in Britain remained relatively constant between 1992 and 1999, with long-term employment showing a significant increase from 7.4 million in 1992, to 9 million in 1999. Thus, the British case shows that the general trend toward downsizing (taking place in the 1990s) can co-exist with an extension of long-term employment. It would be extremely hard to find any evidence pointing to the emergence of a "universalising logic of risk".
>
> A fortunate group of employees remain insulated against risk, whilst the unlucky numbers find themselves episodically out in the cold. From a theoretical point of view, the distinction between class and risk positions is far from drum tight. At best, the risk society thesis makes an unclean separation between class and risk effects. At worst, Beck's presentation of distributional logics is internally inconsistent, with his vista obscured by an unrelenting fixation with risk. (Mythen 2005)

Devilishly twisting the oft-cited maxim, Scott matches up the social effects of each logic: "The wealthy were protected from scarcity and remain protected from risk; 'protection' here being understood as 'relative protection'. Smog is just as hierarchical as poverty so long as some places are less smoggy than others." (Scott 2000, 36)

One may wonder how such highly regarded sociologists can commit such empirical blunders. It appears we know the answer. At a deeper structural level, the risk theory stems from the same intellectual roots as, for example, Parsons' general value system theory or Lukacs' notion of alienation or reification as an overriding principle of capitalist society. All these conceptions, and our list could be easily extended, conceive the relationship to society of their selected idea just as Hegel conceptualised his "spirits." Well, the term itself may be outdated, but this by no means applies to the underlying notion. All conceptions establishing one key principle permeating the entire social world bear thus strong resemblance to Hegelian explanations. Hegel's philosophy of history is termed objective idealism, belonging to one family with, for example, Platonism. The Platonic cage is not, to put it mildly, the best vantage point from which to observe and describe the empirical reality. From this standpoint, the above-mentioned errors are not accidental, which of course constitutes no justification.

We ought to explain why, instead of the concept of sale more generally used by Marxist economists and sociologists, the lease of labour power is used. Marx, underlining that in the case of labour power we are dealing with a commodity, always emphasizes that this is a peculiar commodity. And in actuality, the peculiarities of that commodity, related to the fact that it is an inseparable part of human personality, are very significant. Any other commodity, for example consumer goods purchased in a store, are wholly owned by the purchaser, who may deal with it at will (and, let us add, according to the popular legal notion of property), including for example, destruction, donation, etc.

Meanwhile, there is no such thing in relation to labour which is supposed to be also the object of sales. It can be utilized only in a certain way: consumed by the owner in the production process or providing services, or more generally by servicing a given type of operating conditions. However, a capitalist cannot, for example, sell his or her worker or otherwise dispose of them. It results from the fact that the latter remains the owner of their labour power, which is reflected among other things in the possibility of its withdrawal, for example by a strike, or changes in the workplace. The relationship between the worker and the owner of the working conditions resembles, in my opinion, the relationship between the owner of the land and the farmer leasing it from the owner who uses the land under cultivation. In addition, the term "lease" rather than "rent" or "hire" has been chosen for important theoretical reasons; the latter concepts refer, in our view, to personal property, e.g. renting a house from someone for her / his own use, as opposed to its use in the character of business premises.

7.7.8.3. Horizontal and Vertical Socialization Versus Diffuse, Detail and Combined Labour Power

Meanwhile, translating into the socio-economic terms the above-mentioned concept of social capital, we can point out that it is about synergies or the so-called effects of structure arising thanks to mutual relationships, in which participants of given work processes and production come into an investment-free surplus of efficiency gains due to specialisation, division of labour, proper chains of communication, etc. Related to this is the definition of the scope of ownership of horizontally socialized labour power (in the work process) included in the relations of developed cooperation (based on the division of labour) and a description of the property relations of vertically socialized labour power (incorporated in the vertical hierarchy of command). The use in this double context of the term "sociation"[6] is justified by the essential meaning of the term, which is based on the interdependence of given individuals and other people. We are social beings, because our very existence, behaviour and thinking is dependent on the actions and hence the existence of other people.

Proposition 3: lower horizontal socialization of the labour power (technical autonomy in the work process) is combined with a smaller vertical sociation (authority autonomy, independent place in the hierarchy of command).

Proposition 4: more functionally autonomous (technologically) labour power coexists with a combined labour power that is encompassing qualitatively different types of work—for example, apart from the machine operator's job, a job in providing materials for a work place, cleaning the factory floor, etc.

Proposition 5: Poorly socialized horizontally (functionally), although strongly vertically, hierarchically (involved in the processes of simple heterogeneous co-operation) labour implies the labour power in real terms (at the level of practical competence), including mono-skills.

7.7.8.4. Types of cooperation

An inherent component of the theory under discussion is the description of cooperation relationships and the division of labour within the plant, which involves types of the means (tools, machines, automatic machines) and objects of work; relations of organic cooperation and heterogeneous cooperation as conditioned by the characteristics of objects and means of

---

[6] According to Simmel, "sociation" refers to the particular patterns and forms in which people associate and interact with one another. Sociation (*Vergesellschaftung*) is a crucial concept in Simmel's formal sociology and constitutes the process that ties the parts to the whole, individuals to one another and society. "Sociation is the form (realized in innumerably different ways) in which individuals grow together into a unity and within which their interests are realized."

labour. Conditioning of material work by the structure of its means is reflected, among others, in the necessity of a certain number of people to perform a specific job. A single person cannot cope with a huge log; it can only be lifted in a collective effort of a group of people. Those employed at such a task therefore enter a certain relationship, called a simple cooperation.

Thus, a simple cooperation is a combination of the same type of work for the achievement of a specific result in the work process (production, such as for example while digging ditches, picking potatoes, etc.). Thanks to cooperation there is created a new production force which exceeds the arithmetic sum of production capacities of individual labour powers. The unification of efforts of a lot of people enables the implementation of actions unattainable for a single man, such as lifting a significant weight, or such that could be done only in a much longer time. Bricklayers arranged in a series of twenty will transmit a brick on top of scaffolding much faster than it would be done by a single worker running back and forth. Collective work also stimulates the spirit of competition, contributing to the intensification of activity and the capacity of individual participants.

In many types of production and work without the cooperation it could be impossible to achieve the desired result or achieve it only partly, for example sheep shearing requires that work starts and finishes at a certain time. Achieving this result in this time depends on the simultaneous use of a numerous labour force. A grower cannot wait indefinitely to gather fruit from trees, and if he or she cannot find a certain number of hands in the specified time, they will have to come to terms with the loss of a substantial portion of his or her crop.

Referring to the terminology and category, not necessarily used in the same sense, of Weber, Durkheim and Marx, we can distinguish between simple cooperation (heterogeneous) and simple organic cooperation. Simple heterogeneous cooperation occurs when those working exercise their qualitatively homogeneous activities independently. Therefore, the same result can be achieved here in whole or in part by an individual labourer or by a few individual direct producers engaged in the job not next to each other, but consecutively. Employment of only one worker to lay the parquet in the flat will extend the period of completion of works, but it will still be done. However, in the case of simple organic cooperation, the expected outcome may not occur at all without the simultaneous operation of a number of people. Simple organic cooperation is a necessary condition for the creation of a particular product or useful effect. Time will not compensate for joint collaborative work here. Neither within a minute nor within an hour will a single worker be able to lift a heavy log, which can be handled easily by twenty people.

Simple cooperation may be, however, not only cooperation in space (synchronic or simultaneous) denoting the simultaneous execution of the same work by a group of individuals working together, but also in time (successive or diachronic), comprising a sequence of consecutive, equal actions of a number of individuals. Such a relay, for instance, is the way the Australian natives hunt the kangaroo. Members of the group replace one another in the activity of hunting the animal, until it is completely exhausted. If a simple cooperation creates a social productive force, the greater production force is created thanks to complex or developed cooperation, i.e. based on the division of labour. It differs from a simple cooperation in which the units perform not the same, but qualitatively different work. In complex cooperation the division of individual operations between various units allows their simultaneous execution, thus shortening the time required to produce the final product, and in many cases, the mere production of this product. The difference between these two types of cooperation reflects the distinction, analogous to the above, between heterogeneously developed cooperation (complex) and organic cooperation.

Heterogeneous developed cooperation is based on the performance of various technically and directly independent jobs, setting up a certain result. This work could take place simultaneously or consecutively. The first of these cases is called syncronic or simultaneous cooperation (spatial), the second successive or diachronic (temporal). An example of cooperation in space may be the production of watches: the body, clock face, hands, etc. are manufactured by separate workers, and only then all the parts are assembled together into the finished product. Whilst cooperation in time indicates that the result of one worker is the starting point of the second, these works are carried out independently. Plasterers, for instance, can start their job only after the walls are erected by the masons.

Meanwhile, complex organic cooperation requires the simultaneous performance of various different but mutually supporting activities. To use an example borrowed from Marx, when one person is paddling, the other is steering, and the third is casting a net or is harpooning a fish. The fishing therefore yields results that would be impossible without this cooperation. Developed cooperation or, in other words, work combined by distributing the production process into small components, gives specialisation to workers in performing the same actions, which increases the efficiency of their work. Increased operating efficiency, in turn, reduces the time consumed to perform each operation. Saving time is also created by the elimination of loss of time associated with moving from one operation to another. Relations of cooperation and division of labour are not limited to one type of manual labour associated with handling the principal means of work in order to process the object of labour. The division of labour also takes place between different categories of material workers. The complex relationship of cooperation, mostly heterogeneous, are entered into by workers carrying out the basic production processes and workers carrying out repairs of work resources, as well as workers supporting auxiliary work resources (plumbers etc.). The work of these two categories of workers ensures efficiency and continuity of the functioning of means of production. On the basis of division of labour, activities such as maintaining cleanliness in the premises, administration, and delivery of work resources on directly material workplaces become independent and are assigned to separate workers. Thanks to this exemption of the executor of directly material work from executing activities of loading and transportation of parts, tools and finished products may be realised, which increases the relative amount of time that they can devote to direct the exercise of their own work. Cooperated jobs require adequate supervision and management. Allocation of tasks scheduled between direct producers, organizing, controlling and coordinating the conduct of their current implementation is a task of a special category of employees (masters, foremen). Managerial and organizational work is also performed by mid-level managers (e.g. heads of departments) and highest level managers (e.g. chief executive officers and chief operating officers). The division of labour also leads to a separation of functions of development of resources, processes and production methods performed by the staff of scientific and technical backgrounds.

Relations of cooperation and division of the above-mentioned types of material work are not only between each of these types of work and work directly material, but also between individual types of indirectly material work. Description of cooperation and division of labour within the workplace leads us inevitably outside[7] its framework in the field of supra-plant division of labour. For example: analyzing the work of services providing technology and materials we go inevitably beyond the walls of the undertaking, even taking into consideration the "external" transport cooperating with it. Cooperation of individual companies includes the relationship of both temporal and spatial character. Just as the division of

[7] This is an example of what has been referred to above as the interdependence of micro- and higher-level analysis.

labour within the enterprise is subject to dismemberment of the production process into separate stages carried out by different workers, so the process of production of a particular product may be distributed among a number of factories, which carry out particular phases of the process. Cooperation and division of labour on a supra-plant scale includes also the relationship between individuals performing directly material and conceptual work (e.g. laboratories and research and development centres belonging and not belonging to the company), managerial work (e.g. holding companies etc.), or the material and technological sale and supply (e.g. wholesale centrals), etc. The appropriate relations of cooperation are also entered into by agents of specific areas of the supra-plant division of indirectly material labour.

7.7.8.5. Real and Formal Labour Power

The analysis of these types of relationships brings to light many aspects of, as is termed by sociologists, “social capital.” To use another widespread in sociology term, the analysis below leads to identifying the traditional accounting forms of “human capital.” It assumes that description of: (1) qualifications (education, training) and (2) skills (not formal, certified as having the relevant certificates, but real competences of) employees.

7.7.8.6. Detail and Diffuse Labour Power

This piece of analysis is used to distinguish types of ownership of the labour power located along a continuum: detail-diffuse or comprehensive. The holder of detail, in the terms of Talcott Parsons, is functionally specific in contrast to the diffuse labour power, characterized by the fact that he or she performs only a part of the activities and operations necessary for the formation of the final product. This type of labour power tied to routinized work is best exemplified by Fordism. As Marx writes:

> The implements of labour, in the form of machinery, necessitate the substitution of natural forces for human force, and the conscious application of science, instead of rule of thumb. In Manufacture, the organisation of the social labour-process is purely subjective; it is a combination of detail labourers; in its machinery system, modern industry has a productive organism that is purely objective, in which the labourer becomes a mere appendage to an already existing material condition of production. In simple co-operation, and even in that founded on division of labour, the suppression of the isolated, by the collective, workman still appears to be more or less accidental. Machinery, with a few exceptions,

> operates only by means of associated labour, or labour in common. Hence the co-operative character of the labour-process is, in the latter case, a technical necessity dictated by the instrument of labour itself. (Marx 1976)

The product is converted from direct product of the individual producer into social product of a combined worker, i.e. combined production personnel work turned into a series of individual operations in a number of social activities, and products from the products of individuals transformed into products of society. Yarn, textiles and metal products coming from the factory is the joint product of many workers, through whose hands it had successively pass before it became final products. However, no one man can say of them: “I did it, it's my product”[8]: "In a manufacture and crafts a worker uses a tool used in a factory a machine. There, he set in motion the means of production, here he must follow their movement."

For a worker functioning as an operator of the craft or artisan means of production, diffuse labour power is more characteristic, i.e. an ability to perform all the different technical activities and actions that are necessary to achieve the final outcome of this type of work. More broadly, holders of diffuse, multi-skilled labour power prevail in flexible, small-batch production pertinent to post-Fordism with its multipurpose equipment as opposed to the specialised production machinery in Fordist industries characterised by mass production.

7.7.8.7. Combined labour power

The combination of advantages associated with both the concept of social capital and human capital pertains to the category of combined labour power; that is to say, apart from the main activities making up the actual content of work are included some activities outside direct material labour such as maintenance of equipment or cleaning rooms, for example. For many workers functioning as a member of socialized labour relations are entailed certain features of labour power. If a worker functions in practice in the work process only as part of the collective, diffuse workforce, that fact implies that the labour power receives some features of socialization, or more precisely, collectivization.

---

[8] A version of this statement included in *Grundrisse*: “the product ceases to be the product of isolated direct labour, and the *combination* of social activity appears, rather, as the producer. ‘As soon as the division of labour is developed, almost every piece of work done by a single individual is a part of a whole, having no value or utility of itself. There is nothing on which the labourer can seize: this is my produce, this I will keep to myself’.”

Other forms of collectivization of ownership of the labour power of industrial workers are collective forms of remuneration such as a brigade or team. The fundamental unit of distribution here is a definite work collective and only secondarily the indirectly individual workers. The dependence of wages on other workers' performance may relate to the results of work of the brigade, division, and the whole plant, or take the form of plans at the branch level etc. Other types of work are characterized by a lower degree of concentration of work resources than the industry, and greater autonomy of the individual work process and its reduced dependence on the work of the work collective.

7.7.8.8. Operationally Particularistic and Universalist Labour Power

Another axis of the analysis of ownership of the labour power refers the operationally particularistic ownership to the universalistic, based on a formal basis. At one extreme is a situation that can be expressed through the saying: "do what the procedure requires," or do what you want, just to reach the desired effect.

7.7.8.9. Labour Power Receiving Achievement-Based Wage and Labour Power Obtaining Ascription-Based Salary

Proposition 6: In terms of remuneration, the higher the practical skills related to the real, as opposed to the formal, property of the labour power, the more often it coincides with achievement-based, as opposed to ascriptive, labour power.

From a formal perspective (manifested by credentials) we should distinguish substantive labour power that manifests itself through practical skills. Systems of remuneration of individual categories of employees can be attributed to two major types leading to a separation of two related types of ownership of the labour power: achievement-based (remuneration dependent on performance), or ascriptive (salary based on the characteristics of the labour power: Its qualifications, work experience, etc.).

Proposition 7: The higher the formal qualifications of the labour power, the more often it coincides with the ascription-based pay.

I.7.8.10. Collectivity-Based Wage of Labour Power and Ascriptive Labour Power

Proposition 8: The weaker the socialization of the labour power (colloquially: unionisation), the less Proposition 7 is fulfilled.

I.7.8.11. Ownership of Labour Power and Labour Market

Proposition 9: the direction of occupational mobility is determined by the type of operational labour power.

Operational labour power can be divided into three types: intellectual, affective and manual. Each task, and thus occupation is characterised by a particular mix of the above-mentioned three types, e.g. they are jobs where analytical tasks predominate, and others in which interactive, communicative skills are prominent. Generally, people move to such jobs in which their skills can be used. For instance, it is far easier, and thus more likely, to move from sales to advertising in both of which an affective (interactive) labour power is required, than for a construction labourer to find a job in the latter, since his labour power is completely different. As for each job a specific type of operational labour power pertaining to it can be determined, the above-mentioned proposition should possess a substantial explanatory and predictive power.

Proposition 10: Both the horizontal sociation and vertical sociation are greater in industry than in transport, trade and services. When performing tasks requires the involvement of machines and humans, then the hierarchy increases, because very strict coordination of the work of people and machines is necessary.

When the company's task is services, and not production of material goods, the hierarchy is significantly reduced because there is no need to control almost every move. Supervision is, rather, viewing the documents and verifying information to ensure that the work has been done properly; workers have a much greater autonomy both in functional and authority terms.

I.7.8.13. Theory of Ownership of Labour Power and the Conventional Theory of the Firm

The set of propositions presented above leads to conclusions that undermine the dominant, not only in the so-called mainstream economics, company image, and thus a paradigm of thought on which the majority of sciences involved in one way or another in the economy.

The intellectual basis for this paradigm lies in the theory of rational choice derived from liberal political philosophy and the doctrine of utilitarianism, which is the core method used by neoclassical economics. It assumes that agents make such a choice, from among the available alternatives, which will allow them to maximize their benefit (utility, satisfaction). Although it is based on methodological individualism (concentration on an individual), thus excluding the possibility of collective action taken under the influence of social environment, it is not a theory applied only to analyze the behaviour of individuals. It is also applied to the debate about companies and countries, and it is often used in other social sciences.

It applies also to sociologists, from whom the largest legion of critics of this paradigm is recruited. On the other hand, it is sociology, classic sociology at that, which has contributed significantly to the preservation of essential conditions for this one-sided (in the categories of the theory of property introduced here) universalist concept of the company. Karl Marx should be counted among this group with his notion of capitalist enterprise as a machine for the production of surplus value and its accompanying assumption, that when removed from its context may well reinforce the stylised and idealized (in terms of theoretical and methodological, not normative) account of relationships governing it, according to which, as the author declares in the preface to the *Capital*:

> I paint the capitalist and the landlord in no sense *couleur de rose* (i.e. seen through rose-tainted glasses). But here individuals are dealt with only in so far as they are the personifications of economic categories, embodiments of particular class-relations and class-interests. My standpoint, from which the evolution of the economic formation of society is viewed as a process of natural history, can less than any other make the individual responsible for relations whose creature he socially remains, however much he may subjectively raise himself above them. (Marx 1976)

Max Weber, in turn, considered "rational enterprise, division of labour and fixed capital" to be the basis of modern capitalism. Features of this enterprise as a rational organisation are best expressed by a model comprised of the following elements: First, a clearly defined division of labour, and each position with a fixed range of responsibility. Second, the norms governing the behaviour within the scope of a given position, and the relationships between positions are bright and clear, and formulated in writing. Third, various positions are arranged hierarchically, with those higher controlling and managing those that take lower places. Fourth, the people occupying the positions perform their assigned roles in an emotionally neutral and impassive way, suppressing all their emotions and passions. Fifth, the people are assigned individual positions because of their professional competence, not for personal reasons. Sixth, the positions and offices are not the property of the people involved in them, but the larger organization. And seventh, career lies in the fact that individual people climb up the hierarchy through a combination of these features, such as their qualifications and achievements, as well as seniority.

It has been pointed out that perhaps the best example of formal rationality in Weber's thought is found in his theory of modern bureaucracy. For Weber, bureaucracy is characterized by increasing formalization, technical efficiency and specialized technical expertise. When fully developed, it is dominated by pervasive impersonality, operating sine *ira et studio*, without hatred or passion, increasingly resistant to substantive moralizing about compassion, fraternity, equality or *caritas*. Formal rationality is increasingly characterized by abstraction, impersonality and quantification, even to the extent of "quantifying even the unquantifiable." Weber argued that: "Bureaucracy develops the more perfectly, the more it is 'dehumanized,' the more completely it succeeds in eliminating from official business love, hatred, and all purely personal, irrational, and emotional elements which escape calculation" (Weber 1947).

Meanwhile, our research has shown an inalienable presence in enterprises of numerous elements of an alternative to rationalist universalism particularistic model of socio-economic relations, starting from the recruitment stage, where the existence of several deviations from Weber's model of selection according to ability and merit was observed , through a variety of relationships within the company, including the diverse nature, as opposed to optimal performance-based[9] pay system, and especially the putting out of the picture, or at best marginalisation by orthodox approach of lumpen ownership of the labour power, resources and working time.

Meanwhile, treatment of such relationships as only the pathological deviations from the major reality and in accordance with the ideal model is becoming increasingly untenable in the face of overwhelming empirical

---

[9] In this respect as well in others our evidence-based theory is in conflict with all those approaches in which the move from ascription to achievement as a primary basis of social selection is seen to be one of the defining characteristics of modern societies (Parsons & Bales 1956; Blau & Duncan 1967; Kerr, et al. 1960). Ascriptive characteristics are deemed irrelevant to the judgment of an individual's merit, and are necessarily superseded by achievement criteria designed to allow for the efficient allocation of occupational positions.

evidence. According to the report from Price Waterhouse Coopers on economic crime, victims of economic crime within two years (2004–05) were 45% of companies in the world, and 54% in Poland.

This percentage is growing steadily—in 2003 46% of companies showed abuse. In Central and Eastern Europe in 2005 the index amounted to 47%, said the experts. The average cost incurred by a single company for financial losses caused by, among others misappropriation of assets, frauds and forgery, was USD 1.7 million. In Poland, a company in connection with abuse lost an average of USD 0.5 million dollars. According to the experts, economic crimes did not spare any sector. Important cases of abuse were reported by—depending on the industry—between 38 to 60% of companies surveyed in the world. In Poland, the most common abuse is the misappropriation of assets or theft of inventory and fixed assets from the employer (indicated by 80% of surveyed companies). Another common crime is fraud (56%) and corruption (19%). Around the world these proportions were, respectively: 22%, 19% and 19%. Worldwide, 50% of the offenders were employees of the companies and 25% belonged to senior management. In Poland, approx. 30% of those responsible for this were employees. 45% of them are members of top management, while in Central Europe and Eastern Europe it was 37%. The study was carried out in thirty-four countries between May and September 2005 at 3,634 companies, selected randomly with particular emphasis on the 1,000 biggest companies in the country. The survey was executed by Price Waterhouse Cooper in cooperation with the German Martin Luther University in Halle-Wittenberg.

The consulting firm Price Waterhouse Cooper is conducting an overall survey on fraud in companies. In Poland, the survey took place among one hundred companies, and the country fared slightly worse than the world average. In Poland, 54% of companies were the victims of abuse. The percentage of fraud in Poland, in comparison with the previous survey conducted in 2003, increased by 8 percentage points.

The most common crime committed is misappropriation of assets (80% of responses). Second is fraud, and the third corruption. As much as one third of the companies "owe" the crimes to their employees, as much as 45% among them are members of the highest management. This is not the best of Polish managers, especially since worldwide the percentage is much lower, at about 20% of such employees. The remaining two-thirds of people who cheat the company, are usually contractors, customers and their friends (*Gazeta Wyborcza* 2005).

Another common type of (mostly personal) lumpenownership of the labour power is revealed by other studies. U.S. analytical companies calculated losses caused by "killing time" on the internet in 2005 at USD 12.5 billion, the British estimate losses for 2005 for the cause in the UK even higher, at GBP 10 billion. In turn, the French television TV5 argues that the French are leaders in the private use of corporate internet access. Indeed, studies by a U.S. study group Websense show that the French and Italians are able to devote 50% of working time on the internet shopping, sending e-mails etc. On the other hand, studies of a group of analysts in South Korea have shown that the employees from that region handle so many private affairs, using the company's internet access, that they are wasting an average of 2.5 working days each week. In all the research it is claimed that leaders in the use of the corporate internet for private purposes are employees of small and medium enterprises. In large companies and multinational corporations prevention from such use of the company's network is so developed that staff are afraid to get caught and any possible unpleasant consequences.

"Cyberslacking" or abuse of the internet at work for personal or private reasons has not been spared for the small and medium-sized domestic companies either, whose employees willingly use the company for access to unofficial purposes. This was proved by a study conducted at the end of last year by e-Marketing. They were executed among 300 workers (35%), independent workers (28%) and the managerial staff and representatives of the boards (37%) from government research institutions, medical and administrative (21%.), IT companies and telecommunications services (31%), media and cultural institutions (10%), banking and finance (7%), and trade and services (15%). The majority of the respondents came from companies and establishments of small and medium sized offices (57% companies and public offices to 50 employees; the next 12% of such employees up to 100 employees).

In the study, it was found there was a surprising discrepancy between the officially declared use of the internet and the real use of the network. Officially, the internet was used solely to contact with customers or contractors (87%), trade information search (79%), as a source of expertise (75%), and posting commercial offer (62%). Its use was to improve communications (91%), improve employee productivity (57%), and contribute positively to financial performance (35%). If the internet is the cause of negligence in work, it means, according to a survey, that the worker is unsuitable (54%), because the internet is only provided to improve efficiency (53%).

If this was the real attitude of employees to the network, Poland would be unique in the world. However, further questions of the survey show a completely different picture. 69% of employees claim that in their company the internet is used for private purposes, and a further 17% is done in secret from superiors. Only 6% do it with the consent of a supervisor. In Polish companies and offices the internet is used often, and the interval from two hours to full-time was indicated by 50% of the respondents, and from one to two hours a day by the next 18%. Quite a large part of time spent on the internet is for private matters. A total of 70% of subjects indicated that their settling in takes several minutes to an hour a day, and the next 16% of such employees indicated one to three hours.

According to the comparison of Polish and British tests, Polish staff treat the private use of company internet access in a more utilitarian way. They gather specialist information and information about a hobby and exchange (often used when playing the stock market; this is particularly true of managers), read news, use e-banking, check on online auctions and read advertisements. The British treat private use of the web as entertainment, as evidenced by the prevalence of erotic services in the private surfing of employees from this country. According to e-Marketing.pl, "cyberslacking" has many direct risks for companies where employees use work time on the internet for private purposes. These are the loss of productivity of employees, undermining the company's image, overloading of the network, the threat of viruses, worms, spam and spyware, and deteriorating financial results.

Decline in employee productivity is a simple function of the use of official access to the internet for private purposes. With such use of the internet they may in fact hamper their work, not doing tasks entrusted to him on time or delaying projects. A given employee's work is often a key link in the working chain of the entire department, and in a company where responsibility is diffuse (e.g. the boss decides everything), such workers contribute effectively to the emergence of chaos and missing deadlines. Making up of lost time by the employee does not compensate for the deficiencies. Work for twelve to fourteen hours daily in the long run induces a state of permanent fatigue, reduces creativity and creates a false picture of a workaholic, with a passion for working after hours. These workers contribute also to a deterioration in the company's image among customers and clients. The result may be a bad reputation in the market or even the loss of important orders.

Surfing without limitation can also cause technical disturbances in the operation of corporate networks, caused by downloading MP3 files, movies or video trailers. Meanwhile, opening various websites creates the threat of downloading and installing spyware on computers which is dangerous for the company, because some types of such software, such as keyloggers, are used to detect passwords and logins to web services and internet services such as e-banking. Those who often visit favourite web sites sign up for newsletters, giving the company's e-mail. This means a danger of flooding corporate mailboxes with spam. This threat may be proved by the fact that an email account of an employee of a medium-sized company in Warsaw, not secured by anti-spam software, may receive during a weekend up to six hundred spam messages. On the other hand, worms and viruses, in the event of anti-virus software defects, can create havoc in the software of the company and its databases. It is also obvious that all these hazards can cause a drop in business results, not least because of the downtime necessary to restore the infected network to a satisfactory condition or to clean a mail server of spam.

In addition, the losses caused by "cyberslacking" are real. According to e-Marketing.pl, a person who surfs the internet for private purposes spends more than an hour a day doing so, and can lose during the week as much as one day. It is likely that there are over 15% of such employees. The weekly average for Poland reaches 2.5 hours, which means a loss of a day's work over three weeks (*Rzeczpospolita* 2006).

Naturally, it would be an exaggeration to say that the propositions presented here bring about a radically new understanding of reality. At least some of this knowledge is already available in the field of social sciences, albeit not in such a theorised form of interrelated concepts and theorems. For example, it is noted that "people usually find a way to make even in the bureaucratic structures life more bearable and enjoyable" (Maryanski & Turner 1992). Sociologists know that bureaucracies do not always operate in a precise, formal and impersonal manner. Between members of the organization personal relationships are often formed, which sometimes leads to channels other than formal authority. The rules are sometimes bent and even broken. Informal ways of taking action can alleviate the existing formal machinery.

The formal structure of the organization is only an outline, a general frame that provides guidance for actions of employees. In their daily activities members of the organization try to act in order to, in their view, discharge their duties, with many attemptting to do so in the easiest way. Sometimes, personal goals make members of the organization behave differently than required by the rules and regulations. It happens that relatives and friends of employees use personal relationships, the importance of which cannot be ignored, and demand such actions, which are not allowed by the formal structure of the organization. In short, people adapt to the situation in spite of the formal requirements of their work, giving the bureaucracy a "human face" (Goodman 1980). Similarly:

> According to symbolic interaction theory, people form social bonds, even when they are imposed significant bureaucratic restrictions, because they are not robots or small cogs in a cold, impersonal bureaucratic machine; they form social bonds in parallel, and often in spite of the formal structures of the position rules and authority. This process of producing more personal and informal ties is often called the informal system. (Roethlisberger & Dickson 1939)

Sometimes the system works for the benefit of the organization, as in the case where employees avoid uncomfortable regulations that inhibit productivity. At other times, on the other hand, it impedes the functioning of the organization in that it establishes a network of informal links that distract people from work. For example, we have sometimes met people in some organizations that were so busy chatting or gossiping, that they neglected duties, but just as often we met employees who used their informal networks to help us break through the red tape: “The structure of the organization is so much more than a set of positions and sources of power. This formal structure is overlapped by informal relationships that complement, and sometimes even replace the formal system of positions, norms and authority" (Perrow 2002).

II.7.9. Economic sociology of politics

The power of the ideological beliefs of Becker is proved by the characteristic example of his economic sociology, which is its applicability to the political sphere contained in the sketch "Competition and Democracy."

This approach is based on an analogy between the market and the political system, called—its name can be a cause of serious reservations, which will be discussed further—representative democracy. Becker takes as his starting point the definition of the ideal political democracy as "some institutional setting serving policy decisions in which individuals compete for offices by perfectly free competition—competition for the votes of broad electoral masses” (1970, 70). The latter means that a country can lay claim to the title of “political democracy” only under the condition that in the vote there may be a high percentage of its population. Although the "high percentage" is a relative concept, it is clear that the situation in individual countries was in this respect very different, for example in seventeenth-century England, the electoral base was far too small for the country to be able to pretend to be a political democracy (Becker 1970, 71).

Meanwhile, the above-mentioned competition "is free" in the sense that there are no major barriers of costs or other artificial barriers that hinder an individual to run for an electorate office or submit their own position to the voters.

Moving activity from the market into the state sphere of the political democracy does not necessarily have to lead to reduction in competition, however it changes its form, and competition between businesses is replaced by competition between the parties. You could even say that the excellence of the competition is in the same way indispensable for the ideal political democracy as for an ideal system of free enterprise. This suggests that in order to understand the functioning of political democracy one can apply the analysis of a functioning system of free enterprise.

The immediate objective of any political party is to raise the voters, and similarly the immediate purpose of any business is to attract consumers. The immediate goal of the enterprise is compatible with the entire set of final goals, as the desire to help consumers (altruism) or the desire to gain economic power the aim best fitting the available data and the most common is the desire to maximize income or profit. Similarly, the direct objective of the action of a political party is in line with numerous final goals, such as the desire to help its country (altruism) or a desire to gain prestige or income; the most common goal is the strive for power, which can be defined as the possibility of exercising impact on the behaviour of others. This definition implies further among others the freedom of expression of views as well as the freedom of criticism of platforms proposed by others (Becker 1970, 72). In terms of Becker, the ideal political democracy should be fully sensitive to the "will of the people," and respond well to it.

The problem remains that certain assumptions take us from the sphere of real problems and social conflicts, where rarely we have to do with volumes that can be quantified as eagerly as the U.S. economist would wish into the domain of mathematical Platonic pure ideas. Even if there are differences in the preferences of voters, ideal democracy could still be perfectly sensitive to its "will of the people." Suppose that a political decision consists in selecting a particular value of a constantly changing numerical variable (the minimum wage, allowed rate of income of a public benefit company, the coefficient of discrimination, etc.).

The measure of preference for each of the voters is a value of this variable, the situation is the better, the closer to this value political choice turns out to be. The frequency distribution of these values would provide then a full description of the distribution of preferences among all voters. It seems that you can take the median as an expression of "will" of the total electorate, as this value is a "democratic" compromise between the preferences of different voters.

It is easy to prove, in any event, assuming the existence of two political parties and majority rule that political choice in equilibrium corresponds to a, defined in this way, "will" of voters. For example, if a program of party A promises a value at a level corresponding to the twenty-fifth percentile, while party B programme at the level of forty-fifth percentile, then the party B will win as it will get at least 55% of votes (all those for whom the data values lie in the range of the forty-fifth percentile). In the same way, it can be proved that the value equal to the median would win with all other propositions, as it would win at least 50% of the votes. Thus, the choice of the median value would be a political choice in balance (Becker 1970, 73).

The ultimate goal of each party may be gaining power, but in equilibrium no one, even those "in power," has any political power. There is no place for the choices made by politicians, because the decisions are completely determined by the preferences of the total electorate. This claim sheds some light on the controversy as to whether an electable member of the representative organs should vote according to his or her belief or in accordance with the will of their voters. In an ideal democracy they will not retain their position for long if they do not apply the "will" of voters. Thirdly, in a perfectly competitive system of free enterprise, only the fittest enterprises "survive." If the level of costs in the enterprise did not depend on the volume of production and was different for individual companies, only the company with the lowest costs would "survive." In a perfect democracy, only the most efficient parties "survive," if the costs incurred by the state in relation to the management of a branch of industry were independent of production volume:

> … the power would be yielded always by the party having the lowest costs. A particular branch could be equally effectively managed both by the state and the market, where costs are guaranteed by the most efficient party and the most efficient firm would be the same. This theorem says nothing but that , as stated by Oscar Lange, political sector could, in theory, restore free competition balance, but the costs of the most efficient party and the most efficient company may differ. Private entrepreneurship would manage industry more effectively than the State only if the most efficient company would have costs lower than the most efficient party—and vice versa. (Becker 1970, 74)

Before we present the conclusion of Becker's argument we need to criticize the basic premise that sees the parliamentary system or representative system as democratic in the sense of expressing the will of the people. As rightly pointed out by J. Sowa, democracy may indeed assume:

> … the use of agents, representing the citizens in decision-making process. However, in order for it to remain a democracy in the strict sense of the word, the representative must be bound by the citizens to vote in certain ways. If he does not, citizens have the opportunity to cancel him immediately and send their new delegate. Only then can we conclude that the representative expresses their will ….
>
> [In the parliamentary system, we] choose our representatives, but later they govern at their own discretion. Therefore, representative democracy is not any democracy in any sense of the formula. Indian political scientist Bhikhu Parekh believes that, with regard to parliamentary democracy one can speak at most about representative government. In the words of one of contemporary theorists of democracy, "representatives draw their authority from the will of the people, but they are not joined by common interest and therefore they do not represent it." (Sowa 2008)

The nature of the system defined by Becker as a democracy is portrayed better by the term developed by the well-known American political scientist Robert Dahl—polyarchy. As noted by Sowa, "it is defined as a system in which liberal civil rights are given to a relatively large population and there is a possibility of change of power in regular, universal and free elections."[10]

Dahl lists seven characteristics of polyarchic regimes. They are as follows:

(1) The choice of representatives
(2) Free and fair elections
(3) Universal election right
(4) Passive election right
(5) Freedom of speech
(6) Access to independent information
(7) Freedom of association.

As aptly underlined by Sowa:

> this approach is very close to Schumpeter's approach, under which different groups compete for power in the state and share it. The word

[10] See R.A. Dahl, *Democracy and its Critics*.

> "polyarchy" means the same as 'multi-governance'. In such a perspective parliamentary democracy can be described as a mixed system in which representative government must reckon with the other centers of power of an oligarchic or aristocratic nature [to which belong] groups and organizations that are not constituted, formed and managed in a democratic way, but have real power, i.e. have the opportunity to influence specific decisions of the government or parliament. These are, for example, multinational corporations, military, religious organizations (such as the Catholic Church in Poland or Ireland), international institutions (World Bank, International Monetary Fund, World Trade Organization, NATO), lobby groups, foreign countries, etc. (Sowa 2008)

When, in the 1940s, Joseph Schumpeter argued that ordinary citizens should limit their participation in a democracy to electing its leaders, he was effectively arguing for polyarchy. This contrasts with the view presented in the eighteenth century by Rousseau that the health of a polity depended on active citizen involvement in all aspects of governance. According to Schumpeter, massive political participation is regarded as undesirable and even dangerous. Schumpeter thought that the electoral masses are incapable of political participation other than voting for their leaders. He claimed most political issues are so remote from the daily lives of ordinary people, that they cannot make sound judgements about opinions, policies and ideologies.

In *Preface to Democratic Theory* (1956), Dahl argues that an increase in citizen political involvement may not always be beneficial for polyarchy. An increase in the political participation of members of "lower" socio-economic classes, for example, could reduce the support for the basic norms of polyarchy, because members of those classes are more pre-disposed to be authoritarian-minded.

In a discussion of contemporary British foreign policy, Mark Curtis stated that "Polyarchy is generally what British leaders mean when they speak of promoting 'democracy' abroad. This is a system in which a small group actually rules and mass participation is confined to choosing leaders in elections managed by competing elites" (Curtis 2003, 147). This provides a rather powerful counterpoint to Becker's idyllic model. The same is true of Public Choice theory discussed in the next chapter which portrays politicians and government officials as manipulators rather than followers of the will of the people. Similar conclusions emerge from the "selectorate" theory which emphasises that "all political leaders must satisfy a winning coalition to remain in power, this need to please backers affecting, *inter alia*, how leaders fight wars and which wars they choose to fight" (Bueno de Mesquita et al. 2011).

If the reader of the American economic sociologist could take even a modest conviction of his impartiality and objectivity, the above mentioned conclusion, based on the contested assumption, reveals his ideological nature, pointing out that what was to be the conclusion was in fact its presupposed condition compatible with the free market and anti-interventionist views of the author.

Becker writes that the ideal system of free enterprise and the ideal political democracy are relatively similar, both being effective and responsive to the preferences of voters. Those who advocate the transfer of business from the market to the sphere of the state must prove that the actually existing enterprise system is far from ideal, because it contains a number of monopolies and other imperfections. Those who call for minimization of the activities of the state must prove that the real political system differs more from the ideal. Becker assumes that these "market imperfections" are known, so that "we can focus on some important shortcomings in the political system," which is one of the moments in which Becker's idea comes close to the approach analyzed in the next chapter.

Because each person has a certain number of votes (either 1 or 0) regardless of the amount of information that the person disposes of, and the intelligence used in the operation based on this information, and because minorities generally are not represented, the acquisition of good information and wise pondering over the political problems, and even participation in the vote does not "pay off." An efficient party may prove to be unable to convince enough voters that is more efficient than the other parties. In the market, minorities have their own "representation" and the number of votes that a person has depends on its "relative productivity,"[11] so incentives for prudent conduct here are stronger than in the political sphere. Therefore, a company's survival is relatively easy, because for this purpose it must only gain the support of lenders and consumers, who are directly and have a vested interest in making wise decisions. Political competition is reduced by the "grand scale" of activities of political organizations. Candidates for various offices—the president or governor of the state—must have sufficient means to "reach out" to a large number of voters. Although the companies must sometimes organize on the scale of the entire state or the whole country, it is clear that on the market it is much less important than in the political sector. Scale of political activity is also huge because many of the offices combine various activities. A

[11] This neoclassical axiom shows how far orthodox economics overlaps ideology-disguising rather than revealing the sources of incomes in the capitalist economy.

candidate with the knowledge in, for example, the efficient management of state mail must convince their voters that they know a little something on the issue of immigration, the legal framework for public utilities and a whole host of other problems in addition to postal management. The need for discernment in these different activities may hinder the application for the office by the proper persons in the exercise only one of them. These different types of activities are also on the market, but regard relatively few types of activities (Becker 1970, 76).

On the basis of his argument, Becker contends that the "monopoly, and other imperfections in the political sector are at least as important—and perhaps more important—than on the market":

> If this notion is only approximately correct, then it has important consequences for the whole problem, [...] namely: Does the existence of market imperfections justify state intervention? The answer is "no" if the imperfections of behaviour of the government are greater than the market. It might, however, prove that uncontrolled economic monopolies and elimination of their negative effects of their existence is better than regulating them, and suffering from political imperfections. (Becker 1970, 77)

The above discussion creates the natural point of transition to the next chapter, devoted to one particular version of economic sociology applied to the political structure.

Before, however, turning to these considerations, a brief summary of the chapter on Becker is needed. It is commonly believed that his main accomplishment lies in the extension of the scope of an economic analysis to include numerous, traditionally considered as non-economic, phenomena. This extension, however, is only feasible at the expense of another extension, this time of the scope of the concepts used. This over-inclusiveness, in turn, makes his theories impossible to falsify, thus calling into question their scientific quality. In the process of considering Becker's particular conceptions, i.e. human and social capital, the family, marriage and household, a host of other specific drawbacks of Becker's economic approach to social processes have been indicated. It is not Becker's most general intention, i.e. investigating economic conditioning of social structures that is questionable; on the contrary, this is, in our view, a key task of economic sociology. What is unacceptable about his approach, however, is the easiest possible way of looking for such relationships—a mechanical forceful application of economic notions to intrinsically non-economic structures yielding cognitive pain rather than gain. Becker's economic reductionism over-simplifies the interrelations between the economy and its social setting. Their thorough examination, totally missing in Becker's "economic approach," requires, however, the disposal of an adequate theory of the economy which Becker, unfortunately, cannot be accused of.

CHAPTER II.8.

PUBLIC CHOICE THEORY AS AN ECONOMIC SOCIOLOGY OF POLITICS

Also contributing to an understanding of economic sociology is Public Choice theory, which has many features in common with Becker's approach analysed in the previous chapter.

II.8.1. Historical Background

The modern literature in *Public Choice* began with Duncan Black who in 1948 identified the underlying concepts of what would become median voter theory. He also wrote "The Theory of Committees and Elections" in 1958. Gordon Tullock refers to him as the "father of Public Choice theory." James N. Buchanan and Godon Tullock co-authored *The Calculus of Consent* (1962), considered one of the landmark works that founded the discipline of Public Choice theory. In particular, the book is about the political organization of a free society, but its method, conceptual apparatus, and analytics "are derived, essentially, from the discipline that has as its subject the economic organization of such a society." The book focuses on the positive-economic organisation of constitutional democracy, but in the ethical context of consent. Kenneth Arrow's *Social Choice and Individual Values* (1951) further influenced the formulation of the theory. Among other important Public Choice theorists are Anthony Downs and Mancur Olson. Not only economists and political scientists, but also scholars in related fields, such as philosophy, public administration and sociology contributed to the development of the discipline.

Public choice deals with topics that lie at the intersection of economics and political science. It emerged as a distinct field of study in the 1960s when a small group of economists at the University of Virginia under the intellectual leadership of James Buchanan and Gordon Tullock became interested in the application of essentially economic methods to problems traditionally studied by political scientists. Public choice has retained strong traces of economic methodology, but new and fruitful analytical techniques have been developed which are not recognisable by economists.

> Public choice can best be described as the study of non-market decision making, or the study of decision making by groups of individuals in settings where the decision makers are not guided by explicit price and profit signals. The topics addressed by Public Choice scholars range across the breadth of issues of interest to traditional political scientists, including the impact of alternative voting rules on political outcomes in a representative democracy, legislative processes, bureaucracies and other complex organizations, the provision of public goods, the design of constitutions, the politics and economics of regulation, and the growth of government. (Shughart II & Razzolini 2001)

II.8.2. KEY principles

Public choice theory can be defined as a branch of economics that studies the decision-making behaviour of voters, politicians and government officials from the perspective of economic theory, namely game theory and decision theory. Public choice theory may also be referred to as rational choice theory, social choice theory and political economic theory. It may thus be considered as an application of economic models to politics. According to this approach, "political and governmental decisions can be understood as rational choices of persons and institutions seeking to maximize their self-interest" (Dunleavy 1981). In other words, Choice The theory under consideration is about the analysis of governmental behaviour, and the behaviour of individuals who interact with government.

The theory came about when economists looked at some apparent contradictions in human behaviour. Think about it in this way—what do governments exist for? One might argue that they are there to act in the public interest. Acting in the public interest might be defined as a case where decision making is based on a principle where the maximum benefit is gained by the largest number of people. To be sure, in the real-world conditions any decision will involve some sort of cost, so there will be some people that will be affected adversely by those decisions. If those people are in the minority and the benefits to the majority outweigh those costs, a decision might then be regarded as acting in the public interest.

An example could be road congestion.

> One solution for road congestion is to make people pay for the use of the roads. If this results in a reduction in road usage, or a more efficient use of the roads, there will not only be widespread benefits for road users, but also for the environment as a whole. [...] However, there is a vocal group

that are very much against road pricing. They are backed by some newspapers, for example, which have decided to champion the cause of the road user, going so far as to provide car stickers showing support for the abandonment of road pricing. On the Downing Street website [of the UK government], there was consternation when a person called Peter Roberts posted an online petition calling for the abandonment of road pricing. Would road pricing succeed in helping to reduce the costs imposed by congestion? Could an individual politician ever put themselves in a position were they see the public interest beyond self-interest? (Alexander Abolinsh, from stock.xchng)

The petition gained over 1.8 million signatures, which received high-profile media coverage. Each of those individuals who signed the petition is acting in their own self-interest. The chances are they see the impact of road pricing on them personally and feel it is grossly unfair. This is where the contradiction in human behaviour comes in. If a person felt so strongly about road pricing that they decided to go into politics as a result, would they suddenly become an individual consumed with the desire to promote and maximise the public interest? (biz/ed. 2009)

II.8.2.1. Methodological individualism

Public choice approach, like Becker's "economic approach," draws on the conventional orthodox neoclassical microeconomics, which is applied within its analytical framework to an investigation of the state, law and polity. This accounts for its numerous theoretical and methodological features. Thus, for example Ostrom & Ostrom (1971, 205) note: "Work in Public Choice begins with methodological individualism where the perspective of a representative individual is used for analytical purposes. Since the individual is the basic unit of analysis, the assumptions made about individual behavior become critical in building a coherent theory." The Ostroms cite four Public Choice assumptions about individuals:

- Self-interest: Individuals are assumed to be motivated by self-interest, which, unlike selfishness, can be perceived in short or long term and in personal or collective aspects differing by individual.

- Rationality: Individuals are assumed to be rational, preferring superior alternatives to inferior ones. If A is preferred over B, and B is preferred over C, then A will be preferred over C.

- Benefit-maximizing: Individuals adopt strategies to maximize benefits of their choices. [...]

- Uncertainty-minimizing: Individuals adopt strategies to reduce the uncertainty of outcomes of their choices. Strategies may include obtaining more information about more alternatives.

II.8.2.2. The invisible hand versus public interest

Public choice theory developed out of an economics tradition that stems from Adam Smith. Smith famously referred to a state where individuals pursued their own interest and in doing so, would through an 'invisible hand' promote the interest of the state as a whole. However, despite this seemingly unreserved support for self-interest, Smith did spend a good deal of time discussing government in The Wealth of Nations.

"The basis of Public Choice theory, therefore, centres on the behaviour of people as individuals in comparison to the behaviour of those individuals when they become political animals. [...] The invisible hand, it is argued, may act to guide resources in a manner that leads to an efficient allocation of those resources. However, government will always have some role—do they allocate resources efficiently?" (Semacc, from stock.xchng).

> "Public choice theory likens politicians to a business. Imagine that a business produces a good which does not meet customer needs. It is very likely to fail. Politicians are like products: if they do not meet the customer's needs, they fail—they are not re-elected at the next election! The obvious behaviour, therefore, is to do what the consumer (the electorate) wants. What the electorate wants is not always clear. What is clear is that those who make the most noise are likely to be the ones that attract the most media attention (the moral panic) and these may be the people who politicians listen to" (Biz/ed. 2007).
>
> An obvious implication of the Public Choice idea that politicians exchange legislation for political support is the prediction that "legislators seek assignment to those committees that have the greatest marginal impact over their electoral fortunes." In other words, legislators use their committee memberships to maximize political support. This simple observation yields a number of empirical insights. Members of committees are disproportionately successful in bringing to their own jurisdictions the pork barrel projects generated by legislation in their committees. For example, John Ferejohn found that each member of the Public Works Committee in Congress obtained 0.63 additional projects for his state over nonmembers. Similarly, R. Douglas Arnold found that if a member of Congress wants a water and sewage grant for his or her home state, the chances for success are 80% higher if the member sits on the relevant appropriations subcommittee and 60% higher if he or she is a member of the relevant authorizing committee. [...] members of the Armed Services Committees received a statistically significantly greater share of defense

> spending than nonmembers, and [...] businesses in congressional districts with oversight responsibility over the Federal Trade Commission (FTC) get investigated less frequently by the FTC when compared with their less well-connected rivals. (White 1988)

II.8.2.2.1. Back of the "Invisible Hand"

> In The Wealth of Nations Adam Smith postulated the concept of an "invisible hand" that would lead individuals to further the common interest through the pursuit of their own self-interest. The success of the free market of private goods, compared to the failure of socialism's controlled distribution of private goods, is a strong demonstration of this concept. [...] many at the universities and in the news media deny the success of the free market concept!
>
> [...] Public Choice scholars argue, the pursuit of self interest magically promotes the common interest when we are dealing with private goods, but it usually does not when we are dealing with public goods. One example will suffice here to illustrate the phenomenon.
>
> Consider the fisheries and the ocean and assume that the collection of fish in the ocean is a "public good." What is the economic motivation for each fisherman? To take all he can, right? For, if a conseeintious fisherman says to himself, "This is no good, grabbing all we can. I will limit my fishing, which I hope others will do the same, so as to preserve the fishery for the long term," he will just lose for the other fishermen will continue with the over-fishing. So, to maximize his own return, he grabs all he can and so do the others. The fishery collapses from over fishing.
>
> That this does not happen in the market of private goods is routinely demonstrated, as Public Choice scholars argue, at the university in courses on Economics or, better yet, the local shopping mall. (Felkins 1997)

Well, it is not so simple as that; what we consider to be the real source of the problem involved is disclosed in another context of the present work.

II.8.2.3. Asymmetric Information

> At the heart of the theory is the principle of asymmetric information. Individuals have specific knowledge about certain issues that are closely related to them. As a result of this information, special interest groups that represent these views tend to develop and politicians may be more inclined to listen to these groups and base their decisions on what these groups are saying. (Biz/ed. 2007)

There are a number of key ideas that form the basis of Public Choice theory. We will discuss each in turn.

II.8.2.4. Logrolling

"Logrolling" is a term used to describe vote trading in government. A voting member of the government [...] will vote for something which she or he does not really support or believe in on the understanding that another member will vote in support on something that she or he does feel passionate about and want to support.

The activities of the 600-plus Members of Parliament in the UK government system might all be centred on dealing with case of self interest that have beneficial effects on some but might represent a net loss to society as a whole.

[...] The problem with logrolling comes when the benefits to the group are negligible. In a complex web of agreements and deals over voting, it is quite possible that the net gain to society is less than the costs imposed in achieving those net gains. In other words, resources are allocated inefficiently and the public interest is not maximised.

One excellent example of where this might occur in reality is the whole issue of agricultural support—subsidies. The vast majority of the public know that subsidies exist but do not really understand the complexities of the issue or the effect it has on them.

For farmers, the issue is a very real one and there are plenty of lobbying groups that have particular self-interests—be it in dairy farming, arable farming, livestock and so on. The net effect of this web of agricultural support mechanisms in place throughout the world on society as a whole represents a significant misallocation of resources. The costs of agricultural support are less than the benefits. The benefits to those who receive them, however, are very important.

"The costs to society of the Common Agricultural Policy (CAP) are huge and are likely to far outweigh the benefits to society as a whole" (Stephanie Bretherton, from stock.xchng). (Biz/ed. 2007)

II.8.2.4.1. Special interests

Public choice theory is often used to explain how political decision-making results in outcomes that conflict with the preferences of the general public. For example, many advocacy groups and pork barrel projects are not the desire of the overall democracy. However, it makes sense for politicians to support these projects. It may make them feel powerful and important. It can also benefit them financially by opening the door to future wealth as lobbyists. The project may be of interest to the politician's' local constituency, increasing district votes or campaign contributions. The politician pays little or no cost to gain these benefits, as he or she is spending public money. Special-interest lobbyists are also behaving rationally. They can gain government favours worth millions or billions for relatively small investments. They face a risk of losing out to their competitors if they don't seek these favours. The taxpayer is also behaving

> rationally. The cost of defeating any one government give-away is very high, while the benefits to the individual taxpayer are very small. Each citizen pays only a few pennies or a few dollars for any given government favour, while the costs of ending that favour would be many times higher. Everyone involved has rational incentives to do exactly what they're doing, even though the desire of the general constituency is opposite. (It is notable that the political system considered here is very much that of the United States, with "pork" as a main aim of individual legislators; in countries such as Britain with strong party systems the issues would differ somewhat.) Costs are diffused, while benefits are concentrated. The voices of vocal minorities with much to gain are heard over those of indifferent majorities with little to lose. (Wikipedia—"Public Choice Theory")

II.8.2.5. Rent-Seeking

"Rent-seeking" is the act of obtaining special treatment by the government at the expense of the rest of the population. A specific and major case of rent-seeking is the transfer of land to private organizations. "Rent" in this context refers to the income some individual or group receives from an activity. The rents concerned are likely to have a negative social impact.

"Rent seeking" refers to cases where resources are allocated to provide rents for individuals or groups and where those rents have negative social value. Wikipedia adds that:

> … much political activity is a form of rent-seeking which wastes resources. In a parallel line of research Fred McChesney claims that rent extraction causes considerable waste, especially in the developing world. As the term implies, rent extraction happens when officials use threats to extort payments from private parties. (Wikipedia—"Public Choice Theory")

II.8.2.6. Tax Issues

"Taxes are a reality in most people's lives. However, some people or groups are in a position to know enough about the system or have the resources to be able to legitimately avoid paying tax. There are plenty of loopholes in the tax system that individuals can exploit. [...]

There are also plenty of people who live and work in the so-called 'black economy' or 'informal economy'. In such cases, these people will earn income which is not declared for tax purposes. That earned income might be legitimate or it might be from criminal activity" (Steve Woods, from stock.xchng). These issues are captured by our notion of lumpen economy which is discussed elsewhere in the book.

"The cost to society of the combined activities of tax avoidance[1] and tax evasion is substantial. Because of the very nature of the two, estimates vary, but figures of Ł75 billion and above have been mentioned. That represents about 15% of the total tax receipts of the government in the UK." (Steve Woods, from stock.xchng).

There are plenty of adverts in the UK at the time of writing, which suggest that benefit fraud is wrong, but also highlights that many people do not see it as wrong. There are few individuals in society who have not contributed to the informal economy in some way. Most would not see themselves as criminals.

One of the reasons for the existence of tax avoidance and tax evasion might be the design of the tax system. [...] if people perceive that the system is unfair, there is a greater incentive to find ways around the system or live outside it. In such circumstances, there is a clear case of government failure. (Biz/Ed 2007)

II.8.2.7. The Drugs Problem

Public choice scholars argue as follows:

If we take a rational look at the drugs issue, as suggested by Professor King, we see that drugs impose a huge social cost on both individuals and society. Those involved in selling drugs do so because the returns can be considerable. The risk to them of getting caught is deemed to be less than the size of the benefits they receive from being involved—profits are high.

In any economic analysis, we can see that when profits exist, there is an incentive for new firms' to join the industry attracted by the profits that exist. Attempts by government to restrict supply serve to force up the price of drugs and make the returns, and therefore the attractiveness, even greater. [...] Have governments around the world got drugs policies right, or do Professor King and his colleagues have a point? (Josh Klute, from stock.xchnG).

He proposes a radical rethink in how we approach the drugs issue and wants to see drugs classed alongside tobacco, alcohol, over the counter and prescription drugs and solvents. The major focus of policy should be to reduce harm and treat users as requiring health treatment rather than focus on seizing drugs and prosecuting offenders. In shifting the emphasis in this way, there is an implication that treating drugs such as tobacco and

---

[1] A grotesque example of which has been recently provided by one of the wealthiest people on the planet who had the guts to announce that he is taxed at a lower rate than his secretary!

alcohol could lead to the opportunity for the government to tax non-medicinal drug use. In so doing, the attractiveness of the drugs industry dims, because the profits are not as great. The long-term effect might be to reduce the incidence of harm as a result. (http://www.rsa.org.uk/acrobat/rsa_drugs _report.pdf).

> The important issue is the idea that current government legislation might serve to meet the self-interests of some groups who believe that a strong response is needed against drug users. Whether such a policy is ultimately in the public interest is not necessarily the case. Professor King would argue, I suspect, that current drugs policy was a clear case of government failure an example of Public Choice theory in action. (Biz/Ed. 2007)

Well, one may like public choice or not, but it must be recognised that their field of study is public also in the sense of dealing with important public policy problems. Regarding the above case, it is a pity that the abstract theorising presented to us has not been replaced by some evidence-based investigation of such countries as Portugal, Spain, or Italy that have decriminalised the use of all drugs.

II.8.2.8. Social Dilemmas

> Public Choice scholars examine the options involved with solving the many social dilemmas resulting from living in groups or collectives. [...] Private enterprise is not a good solution to the problem of the distribution of public goods. From that one cannot conclude that government can do the job better [...] Public Choice scholars address the challenge of determining what is the best "of the imperfect solutions." (Felkins 1997)
>
> The social phenomena discussed ... centre around the problem of individuals in groups faced with the choice of doing what is best for themselves or what is best for the group. Instances of the phenomena are called by many different names: "Volunteer's Dilemma", "Prisoner's Dilemma", "Collective Choice", "Rational Choice", "Social Choice", and "Voter's Paradox" to list just a few....
>
> Public Choice Theory is directed toward the study of politics based on economic principles. (Felkins 1997)

II.8.2.9. Sugar daddy or nanny state?

In the eyes of the theory's adherents, the most important contribution of Public Choice approach is that it recognises that politicians are motivated by self-interest just like other ordinary mortals. In fact, more so! From this it immediately follows that the fact that we are having so much trouble with our government today results from our losing sight of the reality that politicians are self-interested.

Arguably, this crucial aspect of Public Choice Theory is captured in a paragraph from an essay by Paul Starr:

> Public choice [reveals within the political sphere] pathological patterns [which] represent different kinds of "free-riding" and "rent-seeking" by voters, bureaucrats, politicians, and recipients of public funds. Coalitions of voters seeking special advantage from the state join together to get favorable legislation enacted. Rather than being particularly needy, these groups are likely to be those whose big stake in a benefit arouses them to more effective action than is taken by the taxpayers at large over whom the costs are spread. In general, individuals with "concentrated" interests in increased expenditure take a "free ride" on those with "diffuse" interests in lower taxes. Similarly, the managers of the "bureaucratic firms" seek to maximize budgets, and thereby to obtain greater power, larger salaries, and other perquisites. Budget maximization results in higher government spending overall, inefficient allocation among government agencies, and inefficient production within them. In addition, when government agencies give out grants, the potential grantees expend resources in lobbying up to the value of the grantsan instance of the more general "political dissipation of value" resulting from the scramble for political favors and jobs.

An author of the respective article in the popular web encyclopedia writes:

> Prior to the emergence of Public Choice theory, many economists tended to consider the state as an agent outside the scope of economic theory, whose actions depend on different considerations than those driving economic agents. (The many other economists who did place the state and its agents within such theory include Vilfredo Pareto).
>
> Public choice theory attempts to look at governments from the perspective of the bureaucrats and politicians who compose them, and makes the assumption that they act based on budget-maximizing model in a self-interested way for the purpose of maximizing their own economic benefits (e.g. their personal wealth). The theory aims to apply economic principles to the political decision-making process in order to reveal certain systematic trends towards inefficient government policies. There are also Austrian variants of Public Choice theory in which it is assumed that bureaucrats and politicians may be benevolent but have access to limited information. The assumption that such benevolent political agents possess limited information for making decisions often results in conclusions similar to those generated separately by means of the rational self-interest assumptions. Randall Holcorn and Richard E. Wagner have also developed

the notion of "Political Entrepreneurship." (Wikipedia—"Public Choice Theory")

A Public Choice writer recapitulates:

At the heart of all Public Choice theories then is the notion that an official at any level, be they in the public or private sector, "acts at least partly in his own self- interest, and some officials are motivated solely by their own self-interest" … For Niskanen, for instance, self-interest is the sole motivator.

The realisation that politicians and government employees are driven by self interest is an extremely serious conclusion. The question immediately comes to mind, "How far will they go?" The answer to that is profound and extremely disturbing, for history shows us that they will to advance their own careers subject thousands of citizens to abuse, torture, starvation, confinement, and yes, death.[...] A good case can be made that most of the wars that the U.S. has found an excuse to be the dominant force in since World War II was to further various politician's lust for power and wealth. This also applies to the bureaucrats, contractors, and military leaders that promote war in order to advance their own career and to sell merchandise. Bureaucrats and others in the "Military/Industrial Complex" make no apologies about promoting in any way they can their war machines in order to further their own careers. As a former military officer, assigned to the procurement business, I personally observed these actions first hand. It was not a pleasant business to be involved in!

Yes, Public Choice Theory exposes some really nasty aspects of governance … (Felkins 1997)

And indeed, irrespective of any criticism that might be levelled toward it, this down-to-earth approach to politics for the reader of many political science textbooks can be truly eye-opening.

II.8.2.10. Voting

Much attention has been devoted in the Public Choice field to the problem of voting. The simple approaches currently used have been shown to be defective as they do not always achieve the desired results.

A surprising conclusion of Public Choice theory is that it is rational to not concern yourself with the issues or to bother to vote. I quote Jane S. Shaw from her article "Public Choice Theory":

One of the chief underpinnings of Public Choice theory is the lack of incentives for voters to monitor government effectively. Anthony Downs, in one of the earliest Public Choice books, "An Economic Theory of

> Democracy", pointed out that the voter is largely ignorant of political issues and that this ignorance is rational. Even though the result of an election may be very important for political, economic, or other social reasons, an individual's vote rarely decides an election. Thus, the direct impact of casting a well-informed vote is almost nil; the voter has virtually no chance to determine the outcome of the election. So spending time following the issues is not personally worthwhile for the voter. Evidence for this claim is found in the fact that public opinion polls consistently find that less than half of all voting-age Americans can name their own congressional representative. (Felkins 1997)

The Wikipedia entry on Public Choice Theory states that:

> One of the basic claims that results from Public Choice theory is that good government policies in a democracy are an underprovided public good, because of the rational ignorance of the voters. Each voter is faced with a tiny probability that his vote will change the result of the elections, while gathering the relevant information necessary for a well-informed voting decision requires substantial time and effort. Therefore, the rational decision for each voter is to be generally ignorant of politics and perhaps even abstain from voting. Rational choice theorists claim that this explains the gross ignorance of most citizens in modern democracies as well as low voter turnout. Rational abstention does, however, create the "paradox of voting" whereby strict costs benefit analysis implies that nobody should vote. (Wikipedia—"Public Choice Theory")

II.8.2.10.1. The Median Voter Theory

The above-mentioned view has been, however, called into question. Geoffrey Brennan and Loren Lomasky's *Democracy and Decision* (1993) challenges the Public Choice analysis by arguing that people do not vote by calculating whether the benefits of doing so outweigh the costs. To the contrary, they vote from what these authors call "expressive" motives. Voting, and more generally[2] participating in politics, is a way they can show their commitment to a set of beliefs. The fact, stressed by the earlier Public Choice analysis, that a single choice will have a minuscule effect on the outcome, retreats to at best secondary significance. The act of voting is deemed valuable in itself, not just for its "instrumental" results.

---

[2] While voting in a large scale election is the prime example of expressive behaviour, it is not the only area in which the expressive idea might carry implications: expressive issues in the formation of political groups, and in the role of political leaders.

In *Free Riding* (2008), Richard Tuck challenges the Public Choice model at its fundamental premise. True enough, he says, your vote will not affect the outcome in an election with millions of voters, but why is this the criterion of rationality? What if you just want to be part of the winning coalition? If so, you have a good chance of achieving this by voting, depending on how close the election turns out to be. Before Olson's book appeared in 1965, Tuck claims, voting with this goal was considered perfectly rational.

The Wikipedia entry on Public Choice Theory puts it slightly differently:

> Brennan and Lomsky claim that democratic policy is biased to favor "expressive interests" and neglect practical and utilitarian considerations. Brennan and Lomasky differentiate between instrumental interests (any kind of practical benefit, both monetary and non-monetary) and expressive interests (forms of expression like applause). According to Brennan and Lomasky, the voting paradox can be resolved by differentiating between expressive and instrumental interests. While voters have virtually no instrumental incentive to vote, they do have an expressive interest in voting. Since voters vote for expressive reasons, politicians win by targeting the median expressive preferences. (Wikipedia—"Public Choice Theory")

It is owing to this crucial difference that the following attempts at defending the theory under consideration must be deemed unsatisfactory, since it is based both on ignoring the aforementioned distinction and on unduly stretching meaning of the notion of self-interest:

> To a large extent, voters vote because they enjoy voting. And there is every indication that people who vote do so according to their own private interests. Because everyone belongs to or identifies with some special interest group or another, there is nothing inconsistent between the practice of voting and Public Choice theory. (Macey 1998)

> There is no more difficulty reconciling voting with private interest than there is with reconciling attendance at sporting events with private interest. (White 1988)

This claim overlooks the fact that a policy Bias in favour of expressive interests means that public policy often ignores important practical considerations. For instance, there are instrumental costs to restricting international trade. Yet many people favour protectionism as an expression of nationalism, despite its economic costs.

This argument has led some Public Choice scholars to claim that politics is plagued by irrationality. Brian Caplan contended that voter choices and government economic decisions are inherently irrational. [...] He claims that politics is biased in favor of irrational beliefs; democracy effectively subsidizes irrational beliefs. Anyone who derives utility from potentially irrational policies (such as protectionism) can receive private benefits while imposing the costs of such beliefs on the general public. Were people to bear the full costs of their "irrational beliefs," they would lobby for them optimally, taking into account both their instrumental consequences and their expressive appeal. Instead, democracy oversupplies policies based on irrational beliefs. Caplan defines rationality mainly in terms of mainstream price theory, pointing out that mainstream economists tend to oppose protectionism and government regulation more than the general population, and that more educated people are closer to economists on this score, even after controlling for confounding factors such as income, or political affiliation. (Wikipedia entry—"Public Choice Theory")

To return to the main topic of this subchapter, one model here holds that if parties A and B want to catch the median voters, they should move towards the centre. The median voter theory is also known as the median voter theorem or Black's theorem, It posits that in a majority election, if voter policy preferences can be represented as a point along a single dimension, if all voters vote deterministically for the politician who commits to a policy position closest to their own preference, and if there are only two politicians, then a politician maximises their number of votes by committing to the policy position preferred by the median voter.

Political commentator Micky Kaus of Slate Magazine wrote in 2004 that the U.S. presidential elections of 2000 and 2004, in addition to local elections in those years, provide evidence that this phenomenon is taking place in the United States.

The theorem was first articulated in Blacks's 1948 article, "On the Rationale of Group Decision-making" and popularized by Downs' 1957 book *An Economic Theory of Bureaucracy*. The theorem is central to moderation theory that delineates the processes through which radical political groups are incorporated into the existing political system:

If the distribution of preferences in a given policy area is single-peaked (ex. a normal curve), then the most popular policy position will be the median one. (Black 1958)

Majority voting reflects collective preferences under conditions of single-peakedness since most preferences cluster around the median. However, when preferences are bipolar or multi-peaked, majority voting may not reflect collective preferences. With bipolar preferences, the most popular policy position is the larger of the two peaks, but fewer than half the individual preferences may cluster around it.

Since public agencies deal with different policies having different preference distributions, therefore different agencies will require different constitutional choice and voting rules (cf. Black 1958).

In other words, there are many situations in which the Median Voter Theorem may not be applied:

Among the most common is the case of preferences which are not single-peaked (multimodal preferences) or order-restricted. Consider the case where several voters are voting on the budget of a public school, for instance, and there are three options: low, medium and high. If one of the voters prefers both low and high to medium, then the preferences will not be single-peaked (they form a "valley", instead of a "mountain", if represented in a unidimensional diagram).

The non-verification of single-peaked preferences may lead to the Condorcet paradox, in which the agenda-maker who chooses in which order propositions are voted on may have the power to choose any outcome. (Mas-Collel et al. 1995, 802–3).

"When preferences are not single-peaked or the policy space is multi-dimensional (e.g., individuals vote on both taxation and public expenditure), the median voter theorem yields no prediction. This has led some political economists to increasingly adopt the newer probabilistic voting theory, which has a unique equilibrium in a multi-dimensional spaces as well" (Wikipedia entry—"Medium Voter Theorum").

In 1970 the median voter theory was accepted without question in Public Choice, but by 1980 it had been assaulted on so many fronts that it was almost abandoned. Works by Romer and Rosenthal (1979) and McKelvey (1976) showed that, when political issues are considered multidimensional rather than single dimensional, an agenda setter could start at any point in the issue space and, by strategically selecting issues, end up at any other point in the issue space, so that there is no unique and stable majority rule outcome.

During the same decade, the probabilistic voting theory started to replace the median voter theory, since it clearly showed how it was able to find Nash Equilibria also in multidimensional space. The theory was later completely formalized by Peter Coughlin. (Wikipedia entry—"Public Choice Theory")

II.8.2.11. Constitutional, Democratic Government

> Public Choice theorists attempt to examine the system of government in which the people governed define their government by means of a constitution. The successes and failures of this concept are examined in detail. (Felkins 1997)

Indeed:

> One way to organize the subject matter studied by Public Choice theorists is to begin with the foundations of the state itself. (Black 1958)

This indicates, and will be further corrorobated below that notwithstanding protestations on the part of public choice theorists, their approach is not empirical, but deductive or axiomatic in character. Moreover, despite their pretense to modernity, their framework bears in fact resemblance to old theories of social contract and the like, wherein the institution of the state or government was accounted for on the same basis of agreements between human beings, conceived of as generally and abstractly as in the above-mentioned account.

> [...] the bulk of the study in this area has concerned the fundamental problem of collectively choosing constitutional rules. This work assumes a group of individuals who aim to form a government. Then it focuses on the problem of hiring the agents required to carry out government functions agreed upon by the members. (Black 1958)

The reader surely has come across some logical puzzles. They may be more or less difficult, of course, but as a rule they require some, ant sometimes a good deal of intellectual work,but on top on that, the latter, regregtfully, is often without avail. So, small wonder that public choice writers admit (overlooking, though, that this failure may have something to do with their type of highly stylised approach, in this instance to the genesis of state) that:

> These are difficult assessments to make. In practice, most work in the field of Public Choice has dealt with more limited issues. (Black 1958)

II.8.2.11.1. Politics without romance

It is worthwhile to cite a statement by one of the founding fathers of the theory, and without any doubt one of its most prominent exponents:

Public choice should be understood as a research program rather than a discipline or even a subdiscipline of economics. Its origins date to the mid-20th century, and viewed retrospectively, the theoretical "gap" in political economy that it emerged to fill seems so large that its development seems to have been inevitable. Nations emerging from World War II, including the Western democracies, were allocating between one-third and one-half of their total product through political institutions rather than through markets. Economists, however, were devoting their efforts almost exclusively to understanding and explaining the market sector. [...]

Initially, the work of economists in this area raised serious doubts about the political process. Working simultaneously, but independently, Kenneth Arrow and Duncan Black proved that democracy, interpreted as majority rule, could not work to promote any general or public interest. [...] The suggestion of this analysis was that majoritarian democracy is inherently unstable. [...] Tullock and I commenced to work on what was to become The Calculus of Consent. The central contribution of this book was to identify a two-level structure of collective decision-making.

We distinguished between "ordinary politics," consisting of decisions made in legislative assemblies, and "constitutional politics," consisting of decisions made about the rules for ordinary politics. [...]

The analysis in our book [...] offered a substantive criticism of the then-dominant elevation of unfettered majority rule to sacrosanct status in political science. Our book was widely well received, which prompted Tullock and me, who were then at the University of Virginia, to initiate and organize a small research conference in April 1963. We brought together economists, political scientists, sociologists and scholars from other disciplines, all of whom were engaged in research outside the boundaries of their disciplines. The discussion was sufficiently stimulating to motivate the formation of an organization which we first called the Committee on Non-Market Decision-Making, and to initiate plans for a journal to be called Papers on Non-Market Decision-Making. We were unhappy with these awkward labels, and after several meetings there emerged the new name "Public Choice," both for the organization and the journal. In this way the Public Choice Society and the journal Public Choice came into being. [...] In some of their implicit modeling of political behavior aimed at furthering special group or class interests, the Marxists seemed to be close associates of Public Choice, even as they rejected methodological individualism. But how was the basic Marxist critique of politics, as observed, to be transformed into the idealized politics of the benevolent and omniscient superstate? This question was simply left glaringly unanswered. [...]

Public choice, in its basic insights into the workings of politics, incorporates an understanding of human nature[3] that differs little, if at all,

[3] This shows that despite the aforementioned protestations to the contrary, public choice theory in fact accepts, just as conventional economics, a definite model of

> from that of James Madison and his colleagues at the time of the American Founding. The essential wisdom of the 18th century, of Adam Smith and classical political economy and of the American Founders, was lost through two centuries of intellectual folly. Public choice does little more than incorporate a rediscovery of this wisdom and its implications into economic analyses of modern politics. (Buchanan 2008)

In Buchanan's view, "Public Choice theory demonstrates why looking to government to fix things can often lead to more harm than good." James M. Buchanan, winner of the 1986 Alfred Nobel Memorial Prize in Economic Sciences has published in *Imprimis* (March 2003) his national speech digest of Hillsdale College in which he, among other things, stated:

> In summary this theory models the realities rather than the romance of political institutions. My primary title for this lecture, "Politics without Romance," was chosen for its descriptive accuracy. Public choice theory has been the avenue through which a romantic and illusory set of notions about the workings of governments and the behavior of persons who govern has been replaced by a set of notions that embody more skepticism about what governments can do and what governors will do, notions that are surely more consistent with the political reality that we may all observe about us. I have often said that Public Choice offers a "theory of governmental failure" that is fully comparable to the "theory of market failure" that emerged from the theoretical welfare economics of the 1930's and 1940's. [...] Public choice almost literally forces the critic to be pragmatic in comparing alternative constitutional arrangements, disallowing any presumption that bureaucratic corrections for market failures will accomplish the desired objectives. (Buchanan 2003b)

Regardless of any above-mentioned criticisms and those put forward below, upon our discussion of Public Choice theory one must admit that it offers a healthy cynicism about the role of government and its insights into the political arena certainly should not be dismissed out of hand. But, of course, although a wide range of criticisms against the theory being discussed will be considered below, it is rather difficult to refrain himself from a brief comment addressing a few issues treated fairly superficially, or misleadingly by Buchanan. To treat, as he does, the notorious human nature as the purported empirical umderpinning of public choice is to beg the question, for, as we shall see later, not only the notion per se but the way it is conceived of within public choice framework is untenable. It follows that Buchanan's bold claim regarding the original sin of the

---

man which is bound to be that of economic man.

government is uncredible, as it lacks –at least on the basis of the argument outlined above—any, theoretical, logical, or empirical ground.

II.8.3. Public Choice Theory Criticised

While our earlier discussion of Public Choice theory contained a number of rumblings, it is in the present section that the bulk of the in-depth critical arguments are concentrated. One thing it is perhaps necessary to note: the order of presentation is not any ranking of the value of particular contributions to the debate.

II.8.3.1. Marshaw's Criticism

Let us begin with a brief review of Mashaw's argument who, amongst others, believes that "much legislation, particularly antipoverty programs, appears inconsistent with Public Choice theory, because such legislation apparently does not involve wealth transfers from the politically weak to the politically powerful (as Public Choice theory would predict" (1997). Furthermore, the author criticises what he considers the "vagueness of public choice." Mashaw complains, namely, that in his view Public Choice theory is not sufficiently well specified.

II.8.3.2. Ahistoricity

The above argument about the lack of clarity of Public Choice theory can also be understood in terms of a tendency to formulate transhistorical, universal propositions, rather than ones embedded in a concrete socio-historical context. Thus, even such an ardent proponent of the said theory as Buchanan admits that while "in a constitutional democracy, persons owe loyalty to the constitution rather than to the government … that on precisely this point, American public attitudes are quite different from those in Europe" (1997).

II.8.3.3. An ideological bias

Buchanan also acknowledges that "there is a familiar criticism of Public Choice theory to the effect that it is ideologically biased" (2003b). His reply to the question that he puts to himself to the effect: "In comparing and analyzing alternative sets of constitutional rules, both those in existence and those that might be introduced prospectively, how does Public Choice theory, as such, remain neutral in the scientific sense?"

remains unconvincing, however, because it lumps together essentially distinct elements: welfare economics, welfare state, scientific socialism or Marxism both as an ideal notion and as its practical embodiment, which refer to entirely different realms. After all, Stalin or Jaruzelski, for that matter, cannot be equated with Marx and Engels, whatever ideas to the contrary can be found in writings of right-wing scholars and commentators. *Realpolitik* of politicians in "real socialism," while paying lip service to Marxism, had in actual fact little in common with the supposed founding fathers' ideas. Any claim to the contrary would require a much more elaborate examination than the one, or rather a lack of one, offered by Buchanan:

> Here it is necessary to appreciate the prevailing mindset of social scientists and philosophers at the midpoint of the 20th century when Public Choice arose. The socialist ideology was pervasive, and was supported by the allegedly neutral research programme called "theoretical welfare economics," which concentrated on identifying the failures of observed markets to meet idealized standards. In sum, this branch of inquiry offered theories of market failure. But failure in comparison with what? The implicit presumption was always that politicised corrections for market failures would work perfectly. In other words, market failures were set against an idealised politics: "Public choice then came along and provided analyses of the behavior of persons acting politically, whether voters, politicians or bureaucrats. These analyses exposed the essentially false comparisons that were then informing so much of both scientific and public opinion. [...] Public Choice became a set of theories of governmental failures, as an offset to the theories of market failures. (Buchanan 2003)

In Buchanan's view, Public Choice theory deals with "modeling of political behavior aimed at furthering special group or class interests, the Marxists seemed to be close associates of Public Choice" (2003). In our opinion we are not alone. Brennan, for instance, writes:

> Public choice is often associated with the normative project of analysing "political failure"—in the spirit of that strand of welfare economics in which the category of "market failure" is central. That particular project is sometimes seen as being ideologically motivated. The search for a different term ("rational choice political theory," "positive political theory," "modern political economy" are all in play) possibly reflects a desire to distance the project from any ideological connotation. Our view is that although the various terms may have different connotations the analytic core of the project remains the same. (Buchanan 2004)

In the essay "The Meaning of Privatization" Paul Starr states:

> "Public choice," ill-named because the only choices it recognises are essentially private, is both a branch of microeconomics and an ideologically-laden view of democratic politics. Analysts of the school apply the logic of microeconomics to politics and generally find that whereas self-interest leads to benign results in the marketplace, it produces nothing but pathology in political decisions. These pathological patterns represent different kinds of "free-riding" and "rent-seeking" by voters, bureaucrats, politicians, and recipients of public funds. (Starr 1988)

II.8.3.4. Bureaucracy

As it is well-known:

> The early Public Choice literature on bureaucracy, launched by William Niskanen, assumed that these agencies would use the information and expertise they gained in administering specific legislative programs to extract the largest budget possible from relatively uninformed, inexpert legislators. Budget maximization was assumed to be the bureaucracy's goal because more agency funding translates into broader administrative discretion, more opportunities for promotion, and greater prestige for the agency's bureaucrats. (Shughart 2008)

Tullock (1965) developed a model of the civil servant as an "economic man," motivated by the goal of career-advancement. Career advancement is best served by pleasing one's superiors. Pleasing superiors creates an incentive to forward favourable information up the chain of command and to suppress unfavourable information. This distortion of information accounts for the error-prone nature of large bureaucracies.

> Superiors may respond by tightening controls, but this only creates more incentives for distortion. This argues that there are limits to economies of scale as bureaucratic size increases.
>
> This critique, however, is one-sided inasmuch as it neglects the following considerations:
>
> Legal rights to acquire information, participate in the rulemaking process, and obtain extensive judicial review guarantee accountability and interest representation in the United States' system of separation of powers and pluralist interest group politics. As argued above, these elements of American rulemaking allow Congress to monitor and control the administrative process even though the executive branch is independent. In addition, legal rights to information, participation, and judicial review enable the many interest groups that influence the legislative process -

> through the Senate, House of Representatives, and the President—to also influence the administrative process, notwithstanding the President's control of the executive branch.
>
> These features of notice and comment rulemaking, however, also have negative consequences for the administrative process. Critics claim that notice and comment leads administrators to make too many concessions to "special" interests. They also point to the slow pace of American rulemaking and argue that it is a product of the numerous legally guaranteed rights that individuals enjoy in the process. (Bignami 1994)

The book reviewed takes on the critics of government regulation. Providing the first major alternative to conventional arguments grounded in Public Choice theory, it demonstrates that regulatory government can, and on important occasions does, advance general interests. Unlike previous accounts, regulation and public interests takes agencies' decision-making rules rather than legislative incentives as a central determinant of regulatory outcomes. Drawing from both political science and law, Steven Croley (2008) argues that such rules, together with agencies' larger decision-making environments, enhance agency autonomy. Agency personnel inclined to undertake regulatory initiatives that generate large but diffuse benefits (while imposing smaller but more concentrated costs) can use decision-making rules to develop socially beneficial regulations even over the objections of Congress and influential interest groups. This book thus provides a qualified defense of regulatory government. Its illustrative case studies include the development of tobacco rulemaking by the Food and Drug Administration, ozone and particulate matter rules by the Environmental Protection Agency, the Forest Service's "roadless" policy for national forests, and regulatory initiatives by the Securities and Exchange Commission and the Federal Trade Commission.

It is argued that:

> "Public Choice theory," rests on a seriously incomplete and under-theorised understanding of regulatory government, and furthermore that its empirical predictions are not supported by careful consideration of the evidence about how regulatory agencies operate or what they do". The book then offers an alternative vision of regulatory government that emphasizes the legal-procedural mechanisms by which administrative bodies actually regulate. It shows how those mechanisms can be—and on important recent occasions have been—employed to produce regulatory outcomes that promote public interests, that is to say, outcomes that vindicate an uneasy faith in regulatory government.
>
> The central thesis advanced here is that the cynical view of regulation shows far too little attention to the actual processes through which administrative agencies regulate, and that such inattention is largely

> responsible for the dominant, jaundiced view of regulation. [...] the ingredients of a complete understanding of regulation that are missing from the Public Choice account are largely legal-institutional. That is to say, they concern the legal vehicles—such as the Administrative Procedure Act—through which regulatory agencies translate legislative requirements and commands into particularized regulatory decisions. Most critics of regulatory government skip over, or downplay, administrative law.[...] The thesis of this book is not that regulatory government works well all or even most of the time. [...] The more modest ambition of this effort, rather, is to show that cynical but commonplace accounts of the regulatory state have enjoyed an influence that far exceeds their conceptual rigor and empirical support: Regulatory failure is not inevitable. Under certain conditions—conditions that are plausible given the real-world legal-institutional environment in which federal administrative agencies operate— regulatory outcomes can and sometimes do advance broad social interests and increase social welfare. While caution towards regulatory government is to some extent surely healthy, at the same time reliance upon regulatory institutions as the least-worst solution to pressing social problems in an ever-complex world is not misplaced. (Croley 2008)

Returning to Public Choice theorists in the role of critics of the school of thought of their own:

> At the heart of all Public Choice theories is the notion that an official at any level, be they in the public or private sector, "acts at least partly in his own self- interest, and some officials are motivated solely by their own self-interest" (Downs 1967). For Downs, broader motivations such as pride in performance, loyalty to a programme, department or government, and a wish to best serve their fellow citizens may also affect a bureaucrat's behaviour, and the level to which self-interest plays a role in decisions is different for each of five bureaucratic personality types that he identifies …. [In addition,]
>
> Coalitions of voters seeking special advantage from the state join together to get favorable legislation enacted. Rather than being particularly needy, these groups are likely to be those whose big stake in a benefit arouses them to more effective action than is taken by the taxpayers at large over whom the costs are spread … For Niskanen, self- interest is the sole motivator. (Felkins 1997)

II.8.3.5. Special Interests

The alleged Special Interest Capture constitutes one of the favourite objects of Public Choice critique.

> American rulemaking has been criticized for giving too much power to interest groups, in particular special interest groups. This claim is related to the vociferous opposition wet kiln operators mounted to the BIF Rule. Although both industry and environmental protection groups took part in the EPA proceeding, business interests proved most difficult to accommodate and occupied a disproportionate share of the Agency's and the court's time. [...] Fewer than fifty-seven furnace operators and within that set a particularly obstinate group of six to ten wet kiln operators caused the bulk of the EPA's worries. And the extra time spent trying to find a regulatory solution that would placate wet kiln operators (i.e., the third toxic organic compound emissions standard) was very likely meant to fend off a successful challenge in court. In other words, where the costs of regulation were especially concentrated, interests mobilized against it.
>
> Public choice scholars argue that interest groups such as the furnace operators appropriate public resources for private ends through their involvement in policymaking and are thus ultimately destructive of public welfare. The [...]
>
> The exceedingly dark view Public Choice takes of interest participation is unwarranted. Notwithstanding its predictions, legislative politics and administrative procedure are used by public interest groups as well as "special" ones. Further, Public Choice theory rests on the assumption that the public welfare, what special interests tend to thwart, may be determined absent reference to politics by summing up individual preferences and utilities and arriving at an optimal policy outcome. Such preferences and utilities, however, are themselves the product of a political process in which interest groups are vital participants. They represent their constituencies, which indeed may be broader than they appear (e.g., coalitions between firms that produce environmental technologies and the environmental lobby), and galvanize public opinion.
>
> Administrative law scholars [...] argue that all lawmaking, even, say, detailed rules on the disposal of hazardous waste, should occur in the light of day of the legislature because although special interest deals will still occur, they will be visible to the electorate and legislators will have to take responsibility for them. If legislators are at all concerned about reelection, according to this view, they will think twice before supporting a law that sacrifices the public good for private welfare. On the opposite end of the spectrum, Jerry Mashaw argues that administrators are more likely than legislators to protect the common good because they are directly responsible to the President who in turn is elected by a national constituency in which single interest groups, unable to deliver a sizable chunk of the vote, have little influence. (Bignami 1999)

Green and Shapiro object that given their ceteris paribus clauses, rational choice theories may be dealing with only one percent of the causes. How can one apportion causal responsibility between rational choice causes and other causal factors? How do causal factors other than rationality itself enter into rational choice theories? Do other causal factors play any role? (Green & Shapiro 1994).

II.8.3.6. *Homo Economicus*

The following is another instance of defending the position of Public Choice theory by means of what in another context we refer to, after Petrazycki, as a logically mistaken, over-stretched concept. Notwithstanding their intentions, as will be apparent, the authors end up calling into question one of the central tenets of Public Choice theory:

> We believe that the choice between "rational choice political theory" and "Public Choice theory" is more a matter of identifying the audience than it is identifying either methodological or substantive distinctions. A central point of relevance in relation to Public Choice theory concerns the specification of the content of the idea of rationality … mainstream rational choice theory … adheres strictly to the thesis of *homo economicus*. In other words, it explains the operation of institutions and justifies the reform of those institutions under the assumption that individuals normally maximise their own utility in every action they undertake …
>
> The identification of utility maximisation with *homo economicus* conflates two distinguishable aspects of the *homo economicus* notion – one referring to the idea of utility maximisation (or the broader structure of rationality) and the other to the precise content of utility functions (or the specific content of rationality). Nevertheless, we broadly accept the charge that the mainstream Public Choice position is one that emphasises a relatively narrow conception of self-interest as motivating choice in the political as well as the economic domain. [...] While taking the broad idea of "utility maximisation" to be a defining feature of the motivational structure of individuals engaged in either private or Public Choices, we want to argue for a rather broader concept of "utility" than is typically assumed in the mainstream approach to Public Choice theory, where utility is often taken to be restricted to a relatively narrow concept of self-interest … we introduce the idea of what we there termed "somewhat moral motivations." These motivations are directly responsive to normative considerations; that is, to considerations that are taken to have normative status by the individual concerned.[...] there is no logical or formal difficulty in incorporating these somewhat moral motivations within the standard framework of utility maximisation. We make no strong or specific claims about the precise content of these moral or normative motivations;[...] moral or normative motivations sit alongside other motivations within any individual - they do not pre-empt or otherwise dominate those other motivations but, we argue, their presence will at least sometimes make a difference to action.

> To the general idea of somewhat moral or normative motivations, we add the further idea of esteem as a motivational force. We place this idea as providing one possible link between self-interest and more normative concerns. On the one hand, my quest for esteem is clearly self-interested to the extent that it relates to my quest for others' good opinion of me as a sort of positional consumption good.[...]
>
> the expressive argument recognises that there may be benefits (generalised utility) from speech acts [...] that merely express an opinion or view or preference [...]The seeds of ... revisionism lie deep in the traditions of Public Choice theory itself.
>
> The strong family resemblance is in part the result of a shared commitment to analytic modelling that takes the structure of individual rationality as one of its foundations. Our concern is to extend the range of explanation that the rationality approach admits. It would be absurd to construe this aim as abandoning our commitment to that approach. [...]
>
> [...] the normative criterion underlying Public Choice theory might be crudely categorised as a form of normative individualism. [...] a hallmark of normative rational choice theory is that it adopts an essentially individualistic approach to value, so that social or collective value supervenes on individual value. (Brennan & Hamlin 2007)

The positive argument of the aforementioned old-fashioned utilitirians is very weak; it rests on the extension of the meaning of the word utility so that the principle of utility maximisation were equally relevant to an egoist and altruist. Therefore, more interesting lessons can be derived from their critical diagnosis of Public Choice.

This is by no means the only case of what one can call an insider critique of Public Choice. In the first instance, it is the case of a dissident. Linda McQuaeg writes in *All You Can Eat*:

> The absurdity of public-choice theory is captured by Nobel prize-winning economist Amartya Sen in the following little scenario: "Can you direct me to the railway station?" asks the stranger. "Certainly," says the local, pointing in the opposite direction, towards the post office, "and would you post this letter for me on your way?" "Certainly," says the stranger, resolving to open it to see if it contains anything worth stealing. (McQuaeg 2001)

It should be noted that scenarios of this sort contain an implicit assumption of zero probability of the two strangers ever interacting again. With a positive probability of future interactions and the propensity of humans to use tit-for-tat type strategies (someone harms or helps you, you return the favour in kind), the optimal totally self-interested decision may be to point to the train station. Furthermore, as David S. Friedman observes, the benefit of cheating the stranger on one occasion may not be worth the mental effort of conceiving a way to do so and weighing the odds of suffering the consequences. Sen, as a matter of fact, has participated in the development of Public Choice theory, in such works as *Collective Choice* and *Social Welfare*.

The following case, however, concerns two, no doubt, top representatives of the current theory being explored. James Buchanan and Gordon Tullock outline the limitations of their methodology:

> … even if the model (with its rational self-interest assumptions) proves to be useful in explaining an important element of politics, it does not imply that all individuals act in accordance with the behavioral assumption made or that any one individual acts in this way at all times … the theory of collective choice can explain only some undetermined fraction of collective action. However, so long as some part of all individual behavior… is, in fact, motivated by utility maximization, and so long as the identification of the individual with the group does not extend to the point of making all individual utility functions identical, an economic-individualist model of political activity should be of some positive worth. (Buchanon and Tullock 1962)

It is no surprise that Public Choice theorists have been criticized for failure to explain human actions motivated by non-rational or non-economic considerations. They respond, however, that the theory explains a broad variety of actions since humanitarian or even a madman's actions are also rational. This is once more an example of what Petrazycki termed "skipping," i.e. an over-reaching concept.

Similarly, it is claimed that:

> McChesney and the Public Choice theorists in general have a view of human nature (their "economic man") which is grotesquely narrow. Ask yourself why some political actors -judges, for example-are generally viewed as making decisions that are not driven by maximization of personal gain. There is no single, agreed upon answer, but many observers are impressed by the role of specialized legal training, a highly developed institutional structure, ethical and legal strictures against conflicts of interest and corruption, and the culturally instilled drive to please peers and specialized critics. In varying degrees, similar pressures apply to politicians and bureaucrats, and this makes for a far more complex model than we are offered. (Foer 1998)

It is worth presenting the viewpoint of a sociologist, who in his book explores the limits of Public Choice. In the reviewer's opinion:

> … practitioners may find that Lars Udehn's is not the right book for them. As its subtitle suggests, it is written from a decidedly sociological viewpoint … Critics of Public Choice looking for an erudite discussion of the limitations of economic methodological orthodoxy argued from a sociological perspective that scorns economic imperialism will no doubt find this book much to their liking …
>
> [...] Udehn alerts readers to empirical shortcomings stemming from the selfishness assumption. [...]
>
> "The point I wish to make is that some use of economic policy to increase the probability of re-election does not prove that politicians are all selfish. It only proves that they are human, perhaps all too human" (p. 69).[...] Udehn is correct that the task of explaining manifestations of altruism poses a special challenge to economists. Perhaps economists can develop better ways of dealing with other-regarding behavior … political man can be so much more than merely selfish; he can be socialized to care about his group interest and the public interest, too (p. 60) … He is concerned that the Public Choice movement has been about more market and less democracy (p. 188), especially as the movement has accompanied the rise of the New Right in politics, a deplorable development in Udehn's opinion (p. 8).
>
> Most economists (of the Public Choice stripe) revel in the self-regulating and social-harmonizing attributes of markets, attributes that transcend the character of the participants. It is quite natural for such economists to advocate political institutions that will work in some sense independent of the personal character (or lack thereof) of political actors ….If economists in the Public Choice movement wish to encourage a larger role for markets, I submit they do so because they have studied extensively human behavior in the context of markets and are enamored of the consequences in a way few sociologists are. Fine art is necessarily less appreciated by the untrained eye. Economists, by virtue of their understanding of human action in markets, do indeed have privileged insights into nonmarket behavior. (Schap 1997)

His claim, however, begs the question, since it is precisely economists' understanding of "human behaviour in markets" that is at issue, and in that regard it is fair to say that, as follows from our analyses throughout the book, the economy is too important to be left merely to economists, all the more that they do not handle their subject well.

It is with this issue of economics vs. sociology that the following comments are concerned:

> *For homo economicus*, each social act is a considered choice, an exercise in naked self-interest. For *homo sociologicus* there is no choice.

> Man is a boat without rudder, drifting at the mercy of the powerful tides of social forces. [...]
>
> The answer to the question of when and why individuals feel and act upon social obligations, or act in altruistic ways, is contested by these two explanatory traditions. Some rational choice theorists argue that obedience to norms is a direct expression of self-interest. Norm obedience directly generates utility. For example, Riker and Ordeshook (1968) and Tullock (1967) eliminate the paradox of voting by having the act of voting itself generate utility beyond its (negligible) instrumental effect on the outcome. Others, such as Ellison (1994) and Kandori (1992), view social norms as implicit long-term contracts. When social interaction is recurrent, reciprocity is rational. [...] Making norm obedience an argument of a utility function simply pushes back the explanatory problem. How did norms get there? Why do some social prescriptions become normative while others do not? The long-term contracting explanations are based on what some might regard as a weakness of dynamic game theory. When social interaction is recurrent, reciprocity is rational if individuals are sufficiently patient.[...] Nearly every outcome is rational if individuals are sufficiently patient. [...] Now the problem is pushed back to equilibrium selection. Why (or when) do we observe those equilibria which are norm-respecting and not some others?
>
> *Homo sociologicus* offers a different set of answers. Much effort has been expended demonstrating that commitment to norms is complementary to, rather than consequent of, instrumental behavior. As put succinctly by Durkheim, "it is therefore in the nature of society itself that we must seek the explanation of social life." [...] what is being rejected by this tradition is not rational action per se, but methodological individualism. [...] The methodological holist position does not preclude understanding the functionality of social norms, and thus, to some degree, their persistence, for any truly dysfunctional norm would adversely affect the future of any society that took it up. [...] Durkheim writes: [...] no collective entity can be produced if there are no individual consciousnesses: this is a necessary but not a sufficient condition. In addition, these consciousnesses must be associated and combined, but combined in a certain way. It is from this combination that social life arises and consequently it is this combination which explains it. By aggregating together, by interpenetrating, by fusing together, individuals give birth to a being, psychical if you will, but one which constitutes a psychical individuality of a new kind.
>
> For Durkheim, social life, and in particular, the "collective consciousness," is an emergent property of a system of interacting individuals. (Blume & Easley 2008)

The aforementioned scholars are highly selective as regards the said holist tradition; while their account is a fair enough depiction of Durkheim's approach, the starting point does not have to be "individual consciousnesses", and thus the end result- some kind of psychic collective entity; the notion of emergent structural properties has a much wider scope.

It is also, without doubt, interesting to see how our economic man fares in the context of field ethnographic studies: "research in experimental economics has emphatically falsified the textbook representation of *Homo Economicus*, with hundreds of experiments that have suggested that people care not only about their own material payoffs but also about such things as fairness, equity, and reciprocity."[4] [5] [6] The following thinker writes in the same vein:

> In the 20th century, rational choice theory replaced what was once a substantive concept of utility with purely formal requirements: the axiomatic framework of rationality. Action was henceforth conceived of as the product of the agent's beliefs and desires directed to securing what he or

---

[4] Consider just one example of such studies: "The ultimatum game could not be simpler. Two players are allotted a sum of money. The first player, now often called the Proposer, offers some portion of the money to the second player, called the Responder. If the Responder accepts, she gets what was offered, and the Proposer gets the rest. If the Responder rejects the offer, both players get nothing. This game first attracted attention because the empirical results differed so dramatically from the predictions of game theory, which assumes self-interest. If both players are income maximizers, and Proposers know this, then the Proposer should offer a penny (or the smallest unit of currency available), and the Responder should accept. Instead, offers typically average about 30-40 percent of the total, with a 50-50 split often the mode. Offers of less than 20 percent are frequently rejected. These facts are not now in question" (Cammerer 2004).

[5] Regarding other similar experimental results, we learn that they "all posit some form of nonselfish behaviour, since contributing to a public good is an action against self-interest" (Bardsley 2000).

[6] Yet another proof of the fallacy pertinent to the central building block of public choice and other theories based on neoclassical economics is provided by other experimenters' data by virtue of which:

> "The behaviours displayed by our subjects provide considerable evidence, consistent with many others in the literature, in support of the proposition that most people are not simple maximizers of their own monetary payoffs.[...] the possibility of 'self-committing' to agreements are at least as interesting. In traditional economics, a promise is of no account unless backed by external penalties, as for instance may happen through reputation. Yet the large majority of our subjects appeared capable of self-commitment[...] Most people seem to feel at least somewhat bound by their promises, an observation that offers considerable reassurance for the possibility of co-operation within organizations, fulfillment of obligations by trusted agents, etc. (Putterman 2009).

> she most wants, and the issue of the motives for action was ruled out of the core of the theory. [...] There is now (a substantial body) of experimental results showing that, contrary to the predictions of standard rational choice theory, most individuals do not solely try to maximize their self-interest but instead behave as if they were guided by social or moral motives … the explanation of the "puzzling facts" that experimental findings have brought into light calls for theoretical elements that are deeply alien to standard game and rational choice theory. If morally driven behavior is to be seriously taken into account in economics, the ontology of the individual is to be revised to encompass the social nature of the constitution of human identity and the communicative dimension of action. (Lopes 2008)

> However, this research has left fundamental questions unanswered: are such social preferences stable components of human nature; or, are they modulated by economic, social, and cultural environments? Until now, experimental research could not address this question because virtually all subjects had been university students, and while there are cultural differences among student populations throughout the world, these differences are small compared with the full range of human social and cultural environments. A vast amount of ethnographic and historical research suggests that people's motives are influenced by economic, social, and cultural environments, yet such methods can only yield circumstantial evidence about human motives. In combining ethnographic and experimental approaches to fill this gap, in reporting the results of a large cross-cultural study aimed at determining the sources of social (non-selfish) preferences that underlie the diversity of human sociality. The same experiments that provided evidence for social preferences among university students were performed in fifteen small-scale societies exhibiting a wide variety of social, economic, and cultural conditions by experienced field researchers who had also done long-term ethnographic field work in these societies. The results … demonstrated no society in which experimental behaviour is consistent with the ecanonical model of self-interest, and showed that variation in behaviour is far greater than previously thought, and that the differences between societies in market integration and the importance of co-operation explain a substantial portion of the variation found (which individual-level economic and demographic variables could not). (Henrich et al. 2004)

Behavioural economics in an important way contributed to the weakening of the pillar of its senior discipline:

> Empirical and experimental evidence mounted against the stark predictions of unbounded rationality.
>
> [...] Many economists have argued that a combination of market forces (competition and arbitrage) [...] should produce a world similar to that

described in an economics textbook. [...] the early impressions of many economists that markets would wipe out irrationality were, well, optimistic.

Consider a specific example: human capital formation. Suppose that young economist, call him Sam, decides to become a behavioral economist, perhaps because Sam mistakenly thinks this will lead to riches, or because he thinks it is going to be the next fad, or because he finds it interesting and lacks the willpower to study "real" economics.

Whatever the reason for the choice, let's assume for the sake of argument that this decision was a mistake for Sam by any rational calculation. So, what will market forces do? Well, Sam may be poorer because of this choice than if he had sensibly chosen to study corporate finance, but he will not be destitute. Sam might even realize he could switch to corporate finance and make tons more money but is simply unable to resist the temptation to continue wasting his time on behavioral economics. So, markets per se do not necessarily solve the problem: they provide an incentive to switch, but they cannot force Sam's hand.

What about arbitrage? In this case, like most we study in economics outside the realm of financial markets, there is simply no arbitrage opportunity available. Suppose a wise arbitrageur is watching Sam's choices, what bet can she place? None. The same can be said if Sam saves too little for retirement, picks the wrong wife, or buys the wrong car. None of these irrational acts generates an arbitrage opportunity for anyone else.

Indeed, economists now realize that even in financial markets there are important limits to the workings of arbitrage. First, in the face of irrational traders, the arbitrageur may privately benefit more from trading that helps push prices in the wrong direction than from trading that pushes prices in the right direction. Put another way, it may often pay "smart money" to follow "dumb money" rather than to lean against it[...] So, markets per se cannot be relied upon to make economic agents rational. [...] the standard economic model of human behavior includes (at least) three unrealistic traits: unbounded rationality, unbounded willpower, and unbounded selfishness. [...] *Homo Economicus* is next assumed to choose the optimum. Real humans, even when they know what is best, sometimes fail to choose it for self-control reasons. Most of us at some point have eaten, drank, or spent too much, and exercised, saved, or worked too little. (Mullainathan & Taylor 2001)

II.8.3.6.1. Cooperation

The connection of the heading of this subchapter with the topic of the previous one is readily apparent:

Economic analysis—and virtually all game theory—starts with the assumption that people are both rational and selfish. For example, predictions that players will defect in the prisoner's dilemma game and free ride in

> public goods environments are based on both assumptions. People are assumed to be clever enough to figure out that defection or free riding is the dominant strategy, and are assumed to care nothing for outcomes to other players; moreover, people are assumed to have no qualms about their failure to do "the right thing."

The reader may be forgiven for being surprised that:

> The predictions derived from the assumption of rational selfishness are violated in many familiar contexts. Public television successfully raises enough money from viewers to continue to broadcast. The United Way and other charities receive contributions from many if not most citizens. Even when dining at a restaurant away from home in a place never likely to be visited again, most clients tip the server. And people vote in presidential elections where the chance that a single vote will alter the outcome is vanishingly small.

As summarized by Jack Hirshleifer (1985, 55):

> " ... the analytically uncomfortable (though humanly gratifying) fact remains: from the most primitive to the most advanced societies, a higher degree of cooperation takes place than can be explained as a merely pragmatic strategy for egoistic man." (Dawes & Taylor 1988)
>
> A curious thing about the human animal is that he is prone to sacrifice himself for non relatives who are unlikely to return the favour. This phenomenon, which we term gratuitous cooperation, eludes traditional evolutionary explanations. [...] The adjective "gratuitous" derives from the Latin word *gratuitus*, meaning free, freely given, spontaneous. [...] The main conclusions of our work are as follows.
>
> First: conformism (the tendency to imitate the most frequent behaviour), altruistic punishment (the tendency to punish free riders at a cost to oneself) and gratuitous cooperation coevolve. Group selection, the natural selection of competing groups, is a necessary ingredient in this evolutionary soup.
>
> Second: [...] people don't cooperate by mistake. [...]
>
> Third: conformism [...] should be understood as a learned preference. [...]
>
> Fourth: within groups, cooperation is a cycle of sudden rise, long lasting prosperity, and abrupt decadence. Occasional "group mutations" are needed to stabilise cooperation in the system as a whole; for example, the emergence of a charismatic leader who brings order to a group and leads it to war against other groups. Our simulations show that even if group mutations occur very infrequently, every 500 years or so, a culture of conformism, altruistic punishment, and gratuitous co-operation can persist in the long-run [...] we simulated our model for conditions that approximate those in which early humans lived, and found that the mixture

formed by altruistic punishment, conformism, and group selection was capable of sustaining gratuitous cooperation in groups of thousands. [...]

In 1986, six hundred thousand liquidators—firemen, soldiers, workers, medics, and many volunteers—entered the exploded Chernobyl Nuclear Plant. Exposing themselves to deadly radiation, they extinguished the fire, cleaned the area of radioactive debris, and built the concrete sarcophagus that now seals the reactor. Of the 40 firemen who were the first to deal with the disaster, the majority died within the first three months. The remaining ones are all dead today.

About 60 thousand of the liquidators have died since 1986. Amongst the survivors, some 165 thousand are now chronically ill or disabled [...] If everyone else stays and helps with the exploded plant, the family of the liquidator is saved: he obtains a benefit of B > 0. The cost for a liquidator of staying and helping is C > 0 ... If everyone else stays and helps with the exploded plant, the liquidator's family will be saved: better for him to run with his family and enjoy life than to expose himself to the radiation (B > B C). And if everyone else flees the site of the disaster, the liquidator's family is doomed no matter what; there is nothing the liquidator can do about it. Run, and he and his family will have a better chance of surviving (0 > –C). Thus, a selfish liquidator will conclude it is best for him to flee regardless of what his fellow liquidators do. And if all liquidators are selfish, then all liquidators will flee. And yet they stayed. And by staying, they averted a catastrophe of undreamed consequences.

The heroism of the liquidators is hard to explain from a biological point of view. Why should anyone kill himself (i.e., remove himself from the gene pool) for the sake of mankind? A gene that predisposed us to such an act should have gone extinct millennia ago. Kin selection, the evolution of selfish genes that move you to sacrifice yourself for blood relatives, is clearly not the answer to the conundrum. The liquidators would have done their families a much better service by fleeing with them. Reciprocal altruism, the exchange of favours in the course of time, neither is the answer. When you are due to die within three months, there is not much time to get repaid for any favour. The explanation must lie elsewhere.

The Chernobyl dilemma is an example of what is known as a cooperative dilemma, a situation in which a person must decide whether or not to subordinate his own interests to those of the group. And the behaviour of the liquidators represents an extreme example of gratuitous ... cooperation: the sacrifice of oneself for others to whom one is not genetically related, and who will have little or no chance of returning the favour.

[...] The behaviour of our ancestors can only be described as gratuitous co-operation. Hunting is costly in reproductive terms: it consumes thousands of calories which are precious when one lives on the edge of starvation. A selfish hunter may plausibly blame bad luck if he returns to the campsite with empty hands. Fighting is also costly since there is a risk of death or serious injury. Nevertheless, our ancestors did their share of

> hunting and risked their lives fighting for the band. (Rowthorn et al. 2009:1–16)

II.8.3.6.2. Common-Pool Resources

Public goods are indivisible (not in discrete units) goods and services distributed under non-competitive market conditions to consumers who, as individuals, cannot easily be excluded from enjoyment of the benefits (for example roads). Private goods, in contrast, are goods and services which can be allotted in discrete units and distributed under competitive market conditions to consumers based on ability to pay (for example automobiles).

Public and private goods form a continuum, not a dichotomy. In between are goods and services which spill over into the other sector in positive or negative directions. Air pollution produced by a paper mill is a public good illustrative—in economists' jargon-- of a negative externality. Improved quality of life provided by a public park[7] is a public good which illustrates a positive externality for the nearby real estate market.

Public goods such as environmental expenses benefit all people within the jurisdiction of the country, regardless of the amount (if any) they pay for it in the form of taxes. A self-interested, rational, benefit-maximizing individual cannot purchase more of the public good than already received and has no incentive to try to do so. But rational individuals also have no incentive to conserve public goods held in common - hence the "tragedy of the commons" described by Hardin (1968), in which benefit-maximizing rational individuals intensively graze their own sheep in the common pasture, harming it and leaving everyone worse off). Note that the aforementioned account implies that only egoism is rational, and that only the maintenance of private property can be rational. Below we shall see whether this picture of "doom and gloom" and its implications for collective action are indeed true.

II.8.3.6.2.1. Excludability and the Free-Rider Problem

When it is difficult or costly to exclude beneficiaries from a good once it is produced, it is frequently assumed that such a good must be provided publicly, rather than privately. When the benefits of a good are available to a group, whether or not members of the group contribute to the provision of the good, that good is characterized by problems with excludability. Where exclusion is costly, those wishing to provide a good or service face a potential free-rider or collective-action problem (Olson 1965). A strong

---

[7] The conception being discussed is a valuable contribution to the theory of, especially common, property.

incentive exists to be a free-rider in all situations where potential beneficiaries cannot easily be excluded for failing to contribute to the provision of a good or service.

Public sector provision of common-pool resources or infrastructure facilities raises additional problems in determining preferences and organizing finances. When exclusion is low-cost to the supplier, producers learn about preferences through the consumers' willingness to pay for various goods offered for sale. Where exclusion is difficult, designing mechanisms that honestly reflect beneficiaries' preferences and their willingness to pay is complex, regardless of whether the providing unit is organized in the public or the private sphere. In very small groups, those affected are usually able to discuss their preferences and constraints on a face-to-face basis and to reach a rough consensus. In larger groups, decisions about infrastructure are apt to be made through mechanisms such as voting or the delegation of authority to public officials "where the difficulties of translating preferences into collective choices that adequately reflect individual views are present" (Arrow 1951; Shepsle 1979).

> "In the early 1980s, the National Academy of Sciences organized a research panel on the study of common property. [...] We have consequently developed a theory of how boundedly rational individuals use heuristics such as 'measured responses' to stabilize agreements achieved in settings where there are no external enforcers to impose rules on participants" (E. Ostrom, Gardner & Walker 1994).
>
> We have been able to challenge many of the empirical assumptions used by development scholars who have presumed that farmers are unable to self-organize and engage in costly collective action without the imposition of rules from external authorities. We have found that farmer-managed irrigation systems in Nepal are able to outperform agency-managed systems in regard to agricultural productivity when we have controlled for factors such as size of group, length of canal, and type of terrain.[...] the only forests where deforestation is not extensive are where local institutional arrangements are viewed by local residents as legitimate and are monitored extensively.
>
> [The study] provides an empirical challenge to the presumption of many scholars that collective action becomes progressively more difficult as the size of the group increases from a very small face-to-face group. He shows that moderately sized villages are better able to generate the labor needed to protect local forests than are very small villages. [...] theoretical work in the Public Choice tradition focuses only on one arena and takes the variables specifying the situation and the motivational and cognitive structure of an actor as givens. The task of analysis is then to predict the behavior of individuals, assuming that some kind of equilibrium is likely in

> a fixed situation. [...] Many of the situations of interest in understanding Public Choices about common-pool resources, however, are uncertain, complex, and lack the selective pressure and information-generating capabilities of a competitive market. [...] With incomplete information and imperfect information-processing capabilities, all individuals may make mistakes in choosing strategies designed to realize a set of goals (V. Ostrom 1986). Over time, however, they can acquire a greater understanding of their situation and adopt strategies that result in higher returns. Reciprocity may develop, rather than strictly narrow, short-term pursuit of self-interest (Oakerson 1993; E. Ostrom 1998). [...]
>
> [...] Instead of completely independent decision making, individuals may be embedded in communities where initial norms of fairness and conservation may change the structure of the situation dramatically. [...] In field settings, multiple studies have shown that individuals have far more capabilities to change rules to reduce the incentives to overproduce and in many cases achieve sustainable use of renewable resources. (Ostrom & Ostrom 2004)

II.8.3.7. Olson's Theories

This part of the book is devoted to the researcher who, like a number of others considered previously, ended up refuting his own earlier theses. Mancur Lloyd Olson Jr.'s first major book, *The Logic of Collective Action*, has been perhaps more theoretically innovative; however, it was his next main book, *The Rise and Decline of Nations* (henceforth *RADON*) that made him famous and indeed can be regarded as the grand application of his earlier ideas to the world and history at large. In The earlier work, as writes Rosser whose fine account is used here, Olson suggested that groups have goals in their collective as they become larger, with a greater disjuncture between the interests of the individual and of the collective group. Such groups could damage the broader economy, especially groups unable to organize themselves that would then have to "suffer in silence."

While he rarely used the term, this argument can be regarded as foreshadowing the later theory of rent seeking, and in his later works he more openly recognised the affinity of his ideas with the Public Choice school of thought.

Two main ideas underlie Olson's central thesis. One is the distinction between distributional coalitions, which are seen as leading to outcomes inimical to economic growth, and encompassing coalitions, which are looked at as potentially aiding economic growth in a society. Because of their greater size, the latter are viewed as having trouble organizing themselves and achieving influence, although they may have a better chance of doing so in a smaller and more homogeneous society.

Olson's other novel argument states that over time a stable democracy will tend to accumulate more and more distributional coalitions whose political power will accumulate, thus gradually impeding the economic growth of the society. This becomes the key to his most famous thesis in *RADON*. He especially focused on the post-World War II performance of Germany and Japan as compared with the United Kingdom, arguing that the defeat of Germany and Japan in the war had led to the overthrow of the power of narrow particularistic interest groups that impeded growth whereas in the UK such groups reached a peak of power that was responsible for the relatively weak performance of the British economy. this was the book's model case. Meanwhile, even as *RADON* was being published, the UK began to undergo a substantial political and economic transformation during the period of rule by Margaret Thatcher that triggered a global movement to privatization and marketization, even though Britain was not invaded and did not experience a violently revolutionary upheaval. Thus his central example undermined his thesis about the inevitability of stagnation in a stable democracy. It turns out, therefore, that, contrary to Olson, The power of special interest groups could be broken, and a stagnant economy could regain growth and dynamism through peaceful democratic means.

"Whilst Britain was the primary inspiration, the case that provided the data for the econometric support of his argument in *RADON* came from comparing the states of the United States. Pulling the states of the Confederacy aside, he found a strong negative relationship between how long a state had been in the Union and its rate of economic growth. He identified this also with the presence of older industries in the older states along with some evidence of more entrenched and numerous special interest groups. [...] Olson argued that the extremes of laissez-faire and a command socialist economy would avoid rent-seeking, while a mixed economy would be subject to it.[...]

Given Olson's general argument was that defeat led to economic growth as entrenched groups were overthrown or undercut, the question arises as to why the South did not grow after its stunning defeat in the American Civil War. Furthermore, the question arises as to why it then later took off into dramatic growth after World War II" (Rosser 2007).

It should be pointed out that Olson also emphasizes a factor that has nothing to do with distributional coalitions or their power: transportation costs.

He argues that before the twentieth century, railroad costs were too high to justify northern manufacturers taking advantage of the low wages in the South (although the wage differential was not as great as it would be after unionization took hold later in the North). However, costs of railroads steadily declined over the first half of the twentieth century, undoing this disadvantage. The emergence of alternative modes of transport, the automobile and the airplane, and ultimately the construction of the interstate highway system, would eventually alter this situation such that the South would no longer suffer a transportation cost disadvantage and thus could take advantage of its lower wage rates to attract industrial development. So, Olson recognises other factors at work besides his distributional coalitions.

Olson concludes his discussion by forecasting that "the South will fall again" (ibid., 932) as it becomes like the rest of the U.S. and begins to accumulate its own collection of distributional coalitions, and "the same level of cartelization as the Northeast and the older Middle West." He goes so far as to say that it will "even fall out of sight," as it loses its distinctiveness along with its "old evils and the old romance." It will become "one with the nation as a whole." This view is rather problematic from today's perspective. To sum up, Olson is able to fit the American South into the framework of *RADON*, only at the expense of the introduction of some additional explanatory factors.

The serious challenge for Olson and his existing framework of analysis was to explain how it was that after the defeat of fascism there had been this outburst of economic growth in West Germany and Japan, whereas in the aftermath of the defeat of (we reluctantly use the following term, which is an incorrect lable, but nevertheless employed by many, including—most importantly in the present case--Olson) communism (which was, to be sure, an internal collapse rather than an externally imposed military defeat) there occurred this massive decline in material output and other indices of economic activity in most of these countries.

Attempting to maintain consistency with his arguments from *RADON* he claimed that during the communist years powerful distributional coalitions had arisen in the state-owned industries in particular, with an important sign of this phenomenon being the emergence of the soft budget constraint in the more market-oriented of these economies. These groups were not necessarily overthrown after the fall of communism, but rather asserted themselves in corrupt privatizations and the rise of the underground economy. They began to participate in private predation, whereas previously they had participated in public sector predation.

Whilst there is certainly a grain of truth in Olson's argument, it at the same time betrays his ignorance regarding the economies concerned. Matters were not as simple as Olson's superficial diagnosis would have it. Such an analysis requires more subtle conceptual tools, e.g. a precise theory of class, without which it is difficult, if not impossible, to identify true beneficiaries of privatisation in the post-socialist countries. Besides, contrary to Olson, privatisation is a glaring example of predation by private interests, to be sure, but of public sector assets. Secondly, it is risky on Olson's part to condemn the socialist and post-socialist nomenklatura (as it is this megaclass that had constituted the main driving force and beneficiary of denationalisation), since without them privatisation, and thus restoration of capitalism with its corollary in the form of multi-party, parliamentary democracy would not have been possible.

This kind of ambiguous assessment also applies to Olson's other contention referring specifically to China. Olson contended, namely, that for China in particular, the Maoist Cultural Revolution destroyed the old elites and coalitions, thereby laying the foundation for more rapid growth later (Olson 2000, 166–167), even though communism remains in political control there. Leaving aside the matter of the nomenclature (with reference to the body that collectively promotes capitalism, the word "Communist" is inappropriate, to say the least), and not negating, of course, China's impressive economic growth, it remains highly doubtful whether one can pronounce oneself on this growth without mentioning its effects in the form of environmental pollution, often inhumane working conditions, huge socio-economic disparities and, last but not least, rampant corruption which, in Olson's view, should have been rooted out thanks to the slow pace of privatisation.

Whereas in *RADON* he would highlight the potential for democracies to lead to economic stagnation, in his final work he would affirm their fundamental importance in guaranteeing long-term economic growth. Thus Mancur Olson, at the endpoint of his intellectual career, embraced a position that described an optimal state as being one of middle-of-the-road balance between laissez-faire and autocracy. The self-contradiction consists here in the circumstance that the above-mentioned statement is exactly the opposite of the argument that he made in the mid-1970s that set him off on the road to write *RADON*, the argument that there would be no rent-seeking in either pure laissez-faire or pure command socialism.

Inner contradictions are present even within a single work. Olson, namely, became concerned with the problem of negative externalities and how rapid economic growth could be socially destabilizing because of these problems. He would express these ideas in several publications, including a quite lengthy discussion in a footnote in *RADON* (249–250) in which he noted the possibility that economic growth may not always be a good thing, just the opposite of what he was assuming throughout the rest of that particular work. In this footnote he submitted the motto "Beyond the Measuring Rod of Money."

II.8.3.8. Around Methodological Naturalism

Last but not least, Schram & Caterino (2006) contains a fundamental methodological criticism of Public Choice theory for promoting the view that the natural science model is the only appropriate methodology in social science and that political science should follow this model, with its emphasis on quantification and mathematization. Schram & Caterino argue instead for methodological pluralism, which –they overlook—is far from a satisfactory approach, since on such a baisis, one may perfectly remain a methodological naturalist, only combining it with, say, an interpretive approach, which, of course, is an absurdity .

Further methodological counterarguments against Public Choice have been put forth in *Pathologies of Rational Choice Theory* by Donald Green and Ian Shapiro. Criticism of Rational Choice theory is, in a sense, nothing new; early rumblings can be heard in Stigler's 1950 commentary on the marginalist economists of the late 1800s, in Herbert Simon's writings on administrative behaviour and bounded rationality in the 1940s and 1950s. Empirical questions about the fundamental assumptions of rational choice theory have been raised by Allais, Ellsberg, Tversky and Kahneman, and numerous behavioral researchers; while questions about the logical consistency of the foundations were raised in the papers by Shafer and Sugden … More strident forms of rational choice bashing can be found in Mirowski's More Heat than Light, which portrays all of neoclassical economics as a product of misguided "physics envy," and in the papers of Kadane and Larkey, who refer to game theory as "cumulatively useless." But the 1994 book by Green and Shapiro created a new quality. Their book is ostensibly about applications of rational choice theory in American politics, but insofar as it addresses "characteristic methodological pathologies," it can be interpreted to apply to rational choice applications more generally. Their claim is that rational choice theory has not yielded empirically useful results to date, and the reasons why it has not done so are systematic: applications are "theory driven" rather than "problem driven." The following passage (6–7) summarizes their argument:

> "We contend that much of the fanfare with which the rational choice approach has been heralded in political science must be seen as premature once the question is asked: What has this literature contributed to our understanding of politics? We do not dispute that theoretical models of immense and increasing sophistication have been produced by practitioners

of rational choice theory, but in our view the case has yet to be made that these models have advanced our understanding of how politics works in the real world. To date, a large proportion of the theoretical conjectures of rational choice theorists have not been tested empirically. Those tests that have been undertaken have either failed on their own terns or garnered theoretical support for propositions that, on reflection, can only be characterized as banal: they do little more than restate existing knowledge in rational choice terminology.

The discrepancy between the faith that practitioners place in rational choice theory and its failure to deliver empirically warrants closer inspection of rational choice theorizing as a scientific enterprise. In our view, the weaknesses of rational choice scholarship are rooted in the characteristic aspiration of rational choice theorists to come up with universal theories of politics. This aspiration leads many rational choice theorists to pursue ever more subtle forms of theory elaboration, with little attention to how these theories might be operationalized and tested—even in principle. When systematic empirical work is attempted by rational choice theorists, it is typically marred by a series of characteristic lapses that are traceable to the universalist ambitions that rational choice theorists mistakenly regard as the hallmark of good scientific practice. These pathologies manifest themselves at each stage of theory elaboration and empirical testing. Hypotheses are formulated in empirically intractable ways; evidence is selected and tested in a biased fashion; conclusions are drawn without serious attention to competing explanations; empirical anomalies and discordant facts are often either ignored or circumvented by way of post hoc alterations to deductive arguments. Collectively, the methodological defects of rational choice theorizing that we discuss in this books generate and reinforce a debilitating syndrome in which theories are elaborated and modified in order to save their universal character, rather than by reference to the requirements of viable empirical testing. When this syndrome is at work, data no longer test theories; instead, theories continually impeach and elude data. In short, empirical research becomes theory driven rather than problem driven, designed more to save or vindicate some variant of rational choice theory than to account for any specific set of political phenomena.

The upshot is that, valid as the rational choice criticisms of other perspectives in political science might be, rational choice scholarship has yet to get off the ground as a rigorous empirical enterprise".

Green and Shapiro go on to enumerate the cardinal sins of which they find rational choice theorists to be guilty: post hoc theory development ("a thought experiment designed to generate an explanation of a given phenomenon that is consistent with rational choice assumptions, somehow specified"), slippery or vaguely operationalized predictions (introducing unmeasurable latent constructs to explain aberrations, shifting from point predictions to marginal predictions, etc.), fishing for confirming evidence (while ignoring disconfirming evidence), projecting evidence from theory ("imagining a datum consistent with economic logic"), and arbitrary domain restrictions ("draining lakes that contain problematic data").

Later chapters in the book deal with particular kinds of political phenomena to which rational choice models have been applied. Chapter 4, for instance, deals with the above-mentioned paradox of voting. Rational choice models of the voting problem predict that voter turnout should converge to (almost) zero, whereas voter turnout is usually significant. (Indeed, it appears that about half the population consists of habitual voters and the other half consists of habitual non-voters, just as subjects in prisoner's-dilemma experiments tend to be either habitual cooperators or habitual defectors.) Friedman (in the follow-up book) summarizes this chapter as follows: "In Green and Shapiro's estimation … rational choice theory only avoids falsification by the phenomenon of voting by being either arbitrarily restricted to other domains (where stakes are higher) or modified beyond recognition (by bolstering utility functions with attributes of civic obligation)". Chapter 5 is concerned with more general kinds of social dilemma problems, including the 2-person and n-person prisoner's dilemma. Again, the obvious empirical fact is that economic agents are more civic-minded (they are more likely to cooperate and less likely to free-ride) than rational choice models say they ought to be. Friedman notes: "According to Green and Shapiro, rational choice scholars avoid this problem by discussing only confirming evidence for their theory or by comparing it only to unchallenging null hypotheses."

do Green and Shapiro suggest that, rather than engaging in armchair speculation and the post hoc development of models that explain stylized facts winnowed from aggregate survey data, researchers should engage in closer-to-the-ground empirical research that tracks the behavior of real individuals and which systematically tests for the effects of different costs and benefits on the decision making behavior of those individuals. Furthermore, such studies should test rational choice models against credible null hypotheses, based on the best alternative explanations—including "normative, cultural, psychological, and institutional" theories—rather than straw men such as "random" behavior. They admit that "Designing and conducting this sort of research is likely to be arduous."

"The Rational Choice Controversy: Economic Models of Politics Reconsidered," edited by Jeffrey Friedman, contains a series of comments and rebuttals by 13 other scholars that were originally published as a double issue of the journal Critical Review in 1995, together with an introduction by the editor of the journal.

Ferejohn and Satz defend the "universalist" aspirations of public choice theory ... natural scientists are often guilty of the same sins of post hoc theorizing, selective interpretation of evidence, etc. ...

Murphy argues that Green and Shapiro do not go far enough in attacking the common "pathologies of equilibrium analysis" that also pervade other branches of "social physics" such as economics and biology as well as political science. He states: "What strikes Green and Shapiro as an overweening aspiration for a universal theory of politics seems more understandable if the enterprise is really social physics. Seeing rational choice theory as social physics helps account for the paradox that the prestige of equilibrium models in political science does not depend on the empirical success in political science (nor even in economics). Rational choice theory borrows its prestige from the theoretical, empirical, and technological successes of classical mechanics. When rational choice theorists appeal to explanatory success in evolutionary biology or in microeconomics to defend equilibrium analysis, what they are really appealing to is no biological theory or economic theory per se, but rather the deployment of physics by those disciplines". He points out that these equilibrium theories based on pre-entropic physics seem to have as their objective the elimination of history from the explanation of the phenomena under consideration. Instead, everything that is observed is imagined to be the inevitable solution to a problem of optimal design. This approach has been strongly criticized in evolutionary biology by Stephen Jay Gould, among others. Later, Murphy observes, consistent with our earlier remarks: "Attempts to modify equilibrium analysis in rational choice theories have been largely comic: if we find that people are ignorant, then ignorance is optimally rational, given the costs of information; if we find that people are impulsive and passionate, then passion and impulse are optimally rational, given the costs of deliberation; if we find that people act out of habit, then habits are optimal decision strategies given the costs of thought; and so on. The auxiliary theorems modify rational choice theory in the sense that a cat is modified by the mouse it eats". Ordeshook's paper argues that rational choice theory should be viewed as a "science" for which the "engineering" remains to be worked out".

"Green and Shapiro's critique, though sometimes incomplete and inaccurate, nevertheless seems to be largely correct: the substantive relevance of much formal rational choice analysis is tenuous, and its empirical content lacks coherence. Even the treatment of such basic matters as voting, committee agendas, and spatial conceptualizations of preferences are confounded by dubious assumptions and often wholly irrelevant analyses. [...] Green and Shapiro, rational choice analysts, and most other political scientists fail to

> distinguish between science and engineering—that is, between the discovery of first principles and the identification of the empirical generalities to which they pertain on the one hand; and, on the other, the resolution of practical issues. Too many rational choice researchers try to do science when engineering better describes their goal. The failure to make this distinction leads to research that does not identify first principles, isolate empirical phenomena that warrant empirical generalization, delineate phenomena that are manifestations of complex interdependent processes, develop expertise that has practical relevance, or refine our ability to predict something other than gross or trivial events" (Nau 1970).

Rational choice theory searches for first principles, and "it is incorrect to insist that our analytical explorations should have an immediate empirical payoff." Ordeshook goes on to contrast the work of an engineer who must build a bridge with that of a natural scientist who develops basic theory. Later he re-examines the problem of the voting decision, arguing that rational choice models do provide non-trivial insights in races with 3 or more candidates. His concluding section on "disincentives to learning" is remarkably candid, providing a rational choice explanation of why rational choice theory (and much academic activity in general) is characteristically method-driven rather than problem-driven:

> "… Green and Shapiro's demand for 'relevance' will fall on deaf ears until incentives change. Indeed, rational choice theory itself tells us that behavior does not change unless incentives change, which requires that the basis of our professional rewards—tenure, salary, and prestige—must change first. This is a tall order, and requires among other things that journal editors become less tolerant of manuscripts that merely mimic some naive view of scientific inquiry and more tolerant of those that propose solutions to specific problems." (Nau 1970)

CHAPTER I.9.

CAPITALISM IN PLURAL

I.9.1. Definition of capitalism

Any discussion of alleged varieties of capitalism presupposes a definition of this socio-economic system. From the theoretical standpoint of the present writer capitalism can be defined as this type of mode of production (leaving aside, for sake of simplicity, the difference between what Marxists refer to as an economic formation and a mode of production[1]) or, more loosely, a socio-economic system that is based on private ownership of all factors of production, i.e. capital, land and labour power, with the caveat that it is the bearer of his / her labour power that is its owner. It is important, since in earlier economic formations this was not the case. In antiquity slaves were owned by their masters. In feudalism, too, peasants were ascribed to land and as such did not own their labour power, i.e. could not dispose freely of it, or defect to the bidder or employer of their choice as workers under capitalism can.

The definition of capitalism in ownership terms is important not only because it allows one to distinguish it from other socio-economic systems or modes of production. It is in these terms, as we shall see, that the differences between various types of modern capitalism can be couched.

I.9.2. VC literature discussed

> In 1776, Adam Smith suggested that economic laws dictate that there is one best way to organize economic life. Trial and error would, he argued, reveal the details to nations. This suggested that modern societies would converge on one optimal set of economic institutions and behavior patterns. That assumption is now part of modern common sense, but comparative studies of capitalism do not bear it out. (Dobbin 2004)

---

[1] The former term refers to all modes of production that are present in a given society. For instance, as American history shows, capitalism is perfectly compatible with the slave mode of production.

Indeed, an overview of the existing academic literature shows that it is now increasingly recognised that capitalism manifests itself in more than one variety (Aoki 1984; Dore 2000; Hall & Soskice 2001; Allen 2004). This, naturally, does not prejudge how these particular capitalisms are to be conceived of and where the differences between them should be sought.

At one extreme there is a "nominalist" stance according to which, in the last analysis, there are as many capitalisms as capitalist countries. It is indeed the case that each industrial nation (leaving aside, for sake of purity of analysis, developing countries) exhibits some specific features and on his basis could be classified as a separate entity. It is in this direction that La Porta et al. (1998) go when they lay out a single ranking of countries' corporate governance systems according to the extent of minority shareholder protections as measured by an "anti-director rights index" based on six elements of corporate law.

In the comparative capitalism literature more frequent are approaches based on some kind of collective classifications, however. For example, various capitalisms can and are distinguished on a regional basis (Mediterranean, Scandinavian, Asian or Southeast Asian etc.) More widespread though is a two-class treatment.

I.9.2.1. Two capitalisms

Although there is as yet no agreement on the number of distinct types of capitalism or the "dimensions used to characterize the various types of capitalism" (Jackson & Deeg 2006, 6), typically, the comparative capitalism literature has tended to contrast two polarized varieties: the Liberal Market Economy (LME) or the Anglo-Saxon model (epitomised by the UK and the U.S.) and the Coordinated Market Economy (CME) variety exemplified by Germany, France and Japan (Hall & Soskice 2001). Other scholars have put the same basic dichotomy in slightly other terms, using such categories as "bank oriented" and "market oriented" systems (e.g. Berglöf 1990) and "insider" versus "outsider" systems (e.g. Franks & Mayer 1995).

I.9.2.2. Shareholder capitalism and stakeholder capitalism

While all the above names are useful, the most adequate pair of concepts seems to be that of "shareholder capitalism" vs. "stakeholder capitalism." I do not, of course, claim originality in this regard; there are numerous social scientists who use these terms, albeit some of them as an element of a wider typology.

Amongst them are Hansman & Kraakman (2000) who call the U.S. model the "standard shareholder oriented model." In the shareholder model:

> ultimate control over the corporation should be in the hands of the shareholder class; ... managers ... should be charged with the obligation to manage the corporation in the interests of its shareholders; ... other corporate constituencies, such as creditors, employees, suppliers, and customers should have their interests protected by contractual and regulatory means rather than through participation in corporate governance; ... non-controlling shareholders should receive strong protection from exploitation at the hands of controlling shareholders; ... the principle measure of the interests of the public corporation's shareholders is the market value of their shares in their firm." (Hansman & Kraakman 2000)

They contrast this "standard model" with the "manager oriented model," the "labour oriented model," the "state-oriented model" and the "stakeholder model." Where the present approach may be original is in underpinning the dichotomy outlined above by what may be called its property foundation. This constitutes at the same time a justification for choosing the pair of terms mentioned above.

I.9.3. Economic ownership

The above argument, however, is premised upon a specific, i.e. economic or, more precisely, socio-economic concept of ownership. It is particularly important to distinguish this meaning of ownership from the legal one, due to, among others, fictitiousness of juridical concepts of "legal persons"[2] and "things." In analysing property relations to concentrate on purely legal forms is insufficient, since it is possible for the forms of legal ownership not to coincide with economic ownership. Study of law must be related to its concrete economic and social context. The above argument begs the question, however, how his economic or socio-economic ownership is to be understood. Broadly speaking there exist two possible approaches to the definition of ownership, leaving aside casus of hybrid definitions.

---

[2] When it is forgotten and the concept in question is treated as referring to a real person, very weird consequences may follow, as in the following telling example. Murray Hill is a public relations firm with liberal tendencies. So when the U.S. Supreme Court ruled recently that companies had the same rights as individuals when it came to financing political campaigns, the people at Murray Hill decided to go one step further. They put up the company as a candidate for election. "Why not, under the newly clarified law, a company for president?" campaign manager William Klein explained to the BBC's Steve Evans.

The issue has already been alluded to in the chapter on Weber and, more importantly, will be considered in more detail in the next chapter, so that here we may confine ourselves to indicating that these two approaches consist in, respectively, conceiving of property as control or decision-making, and as benefit rather than use alone, which is the notion subscribed to by the present author. In this regard it follows in the footsteps of such thinkers as Simmel or Hegel.

I.9.4. The distinction between shareholder capitalism and stakeholder capitalism in ownership terms

It remains to demonstrate that the socio-economic concept of ownership outlined above makes it possible to throw some new light on the varieties of capitalism in question. Let us take into consideration a typical argument according to which the "basic distinction between two modes of capitalism is based on a range of characteristics of governance and financial systems, such as the importance of long-term bank lending relations, share ownership concentration, stock market capitalisation and regulatory restrictions on shareholder power" (Becht et al. 2002).

The share ownership concentration factor is related to ownership in a self-evident way, which is illustrated by Figure 1, based on La Porta et al. (1999), who contrast the ownership of large and medium sized companies across countries. The study lists several large German and Japanese firms as having no controlling shareholder. However, because German banks typically vote the shares of small investors, Baums (1995) shows that these firms are actually controlled by banks. All the large Japanese firms La Porta et al. (1999) list as having no controlling shareholder are members of corporate groups called keiretsu, in which each firm is controlled collectively by other firms in the group. Although each group firm's stake in every other group firm can be small, these stakes accumulate to control blocks. In contrast, all the largest British companies get by with no controlling shareholders at all (Morck & Steyer 2005).

Figure 1. Who Controls the World's Great Corporations?
Fraction of top ten firms with different types of controlling shareholders is shown for each country. Control is assumed if any shareholder or group of shareholders believed to work in consort controls 20% of the votes in a company's annual shareholder meeting.

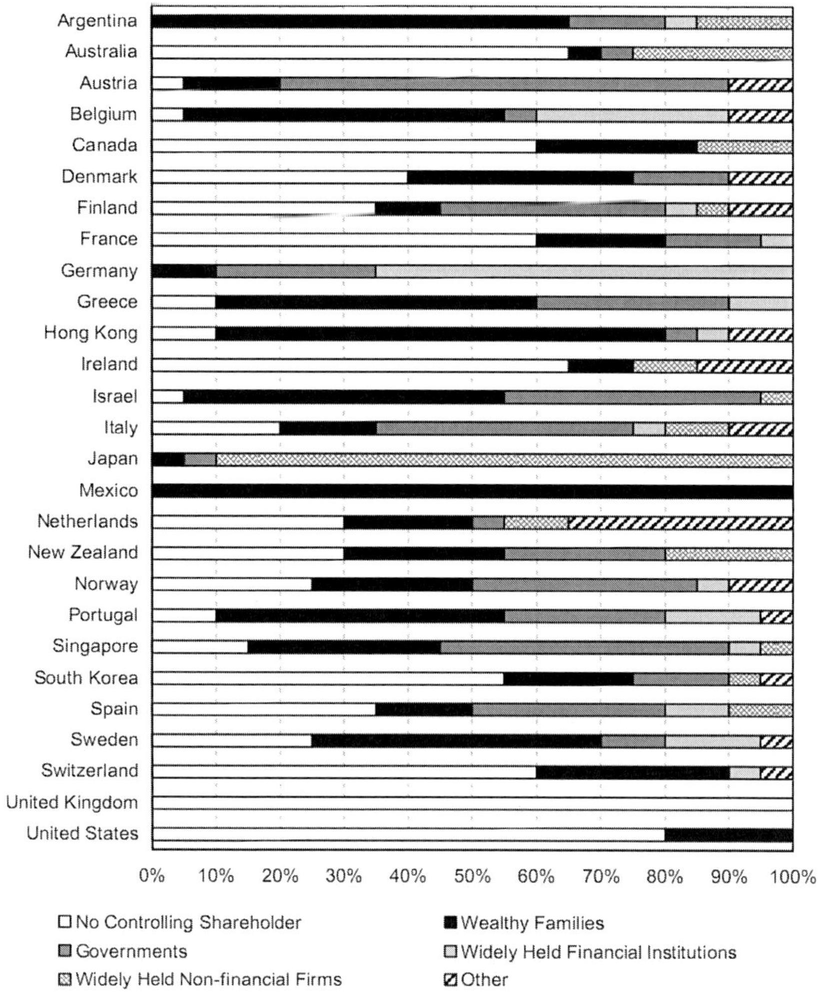

Source. *La Porta et al. (1999) with Japanese data augmented by Morck and Nakamura (1999) to account for combined keiretsu stakes and German data augmented with information from Baums (1995) to account for bank proxy voting.*

Our deliberations so far allow us to establish that the dichotomy under consideration expresses in fact a difference between two distinct capitalist modes of economic activity. In other words, they both belong to the bourgeois economic formation of society rather than represent a distinct formation themselves. This is shown by the fact that despite their predominantly geographic connotation both modes may, and indeed appear in more limited extent (a larger or lesser number of firms representing an "alien body") within an alternative geographical region of the world; e.g. some employee-, trust- or foundation-owned corporations in the U.S. We have used above the term "mode of economic activity" rather than sheer "mode of production" because in our view, as will be also argued later, the economic structure is composed of not only directly material production but also such modes of economic activity as transportation, commerce, finance and services.

I.9.5. Debt relations as economic ownership relations

For reasons of space, the fascinating topic of differences in class composition within an overall capitalist class structure generated by those two modes of economic activity cannot be, sadly, considered. Even a skin-deep knowledge suffices to notice, however, that for example: "The overall class structure in the UK in the early 1990s bears a closer resemblance to the USA than it does to Sweden with a smaller percentage of employers and self-employed groups and more skilled workers" (Hass & Leiulfsrud 2002).

The relationship mentioned in the headline may not be so evident but in point of fact is equally prominent owing to another central feature of differentiation:

> The preference of one system for equity credit, and the preference of the other for bank credit. The degree of importance given to one or the other of these two forms of financial structure defines the degree of differentiation between the two models. In this context, the evolution of financial markets is caught between forces that maintain a national character, and forces that push it to become international.
>
> To the former category belongs retail banking with its complex network of interrelated local and regional services. To the latter category belongs corporate finance as a way of insertion in global bond and equity markets. In the United States and Britain the model based on equity capital, with capital and money markets widely unregulated, has had a greater acceptance than in Germany and other European countries. In those countries, corporate financing has been dominated by bank lending. A

> fundamental element of the network-oriented European type of corporate governance comes from the long-term relationship between firms and the sources of finance: "Often with board representation (as in the German supervisory board system) banks will, at least in theory, be well informed about managerial behavior and performance and provide a more constructive form of control than the Anglo-Saxon market for corporate control —i.e., the threat of take over and dismissal. (Rhodes & van Apeldoorn, 8; Rozo 2002)

Table 2 below shows that bank's assets as a percentage of bank and non-banks financial institutions is much higher in any continental European country, with an average of 74.1%, than in the United States where this ratio is just 26%. It follows that Europe has been built on debt rather than on equity. The fact is that equity based investment and geographical spread of portfolios has been slow to develop in most EU members, except the UK and Netherlands.

Table 2. Assets of Banks

Austria	85
France	70
Germany	76
Italy	77
Netherlands	57
Spain	75
Switzerland	79
Average	74.1
United Kingdom	53
United States	26

Source: [Rozo, p. 11].

The thing is that from the viewpoint of socio-economic theory of property, creditor-debtor relations are in fact property relations, as creditors by virtue of receiving economic benefits, i.e. part of the firm's revenues become its economic co-owners, the extent of their ownership being dependent on the magnitude of the benefits involved.

An illustration is:

> … the crucial position of German banks in the ownership and operational structure of German capital. The main German banks still have a major influence on most of the large German companies through their own shares or —even more importantly—through the shares they hold in deposit. As a

> result, representatives from the major banks are very often members of the supervisory boards of big German companies. For example, the largest German bank, Deutsche Bank, holds shares in German companies with a total value of DEM 27.1 billion, while the 12 representatives on the executive board of Deutsche Bank are at the same time members of more than 70 supervisory boards of major German companies. (Schulten 1997)

Germany is not an exception as far as stakeholder capitalism is concerned. One of the main criticisms of Anglo-American market-based corporate governance has been that managers tend to be obsessed with quarterly performance measures and have an excessively short-termist perspective. Thus, Narayanan (1985), Shleifer & Vishny (1989), Porter (1992) and Stein (1988, 1989), among others, have argued that U.S. managers are myopically "short-termist"[3] and pay too much attention to potential takeover threats. Porter, in particular, contrasts U.S. corporate governance with the governance in German and Japanese corporations, where the long-term involvement of investors, especially banks, allowed managers to invest for the long run while, at the same time, monitoring their performance.

Long-term relationships are ubiquitous in Japan. Another example is the country's web of interlocking shareholdings:

> An implicit agreement is made between two companies to hold ownership in the other partners' stock, usually around one percent by nonfinancial firms and up to five percent by banks. Each company makes the same type of implicit agreements with, for example, twenty companies (Maitland & Umezu 2006). Consequently, a spider web of mutual stockholding among inside shareholders is created, thereby stabilizing majority stock ownership." (Shishido 2000 210–11)

Similar ties of mutual obligation bind companies to their "main banks" and their suppliers and vice versa. The resulting stability of supplier relations is suggested by the fact that of 60 or so members of Toyota's first-line suppliers' club in 1990, only two or three had not been members

---

[3] Characteristically, at a recent conference in Paris on the future of capitalism, the then French president Sarkozy called for a "new world, new capitalism" during his speech, as he commented: "In capitalism of the 21st century, there is room for the state." Meanwhile, Former UK Prime Minister Tony Blair called for a new financial order which he said should be constructed upon "values other than the maximum short-term profit."
(http://www.infowars.net/articles/march2009/170309AIG.htm).

in 1970, and only two or three of the names that figured in the earlier list had disappeared (Dore 2000, 36).

I.9.6. Transaction costs as the core issue of stakeholder capitalism

Japanese keiretsu have also been praised for their superior ability to resolve financial distress or achieve corporate diversification (see for example Aoki 1990 and Hoshi, Kashyap & Scharfstein 1990). This points to what can be viewed, in neoinstitutionalist terms, as the central axis of the model of capitalism just discussed. This type of capitalism effectively tackles the problem of transaction costs, as it encourages a better transfer of information between the various elements of the firm. Often the competitiveness of a firm will be affected by whether stakeholders (such as banks, sub-contractors, or workers) can reach agreements with managers which require the sharing of information and the generation of mutual commitment. A governance structure which encourages information disclosure will obviously be vital in generating these types of long-term relationships, or "implicit contracts," between stakeholders (Aoki 1988).

Putting it another way, banks form long-run relationships with firms to ease asymmetric information distortions. Stiglitz (1985) argues that well developed markets quickly and publicly reveal information, which reduces the incentives for individual investors to acquire information. Banks, on the other hand, mitigate this problem since they form long-run relationships with firms and do not reveal information immediately in public markets (Boot, Greenbaum & Thakor 1993). Kaplan (1994) and others argue that bankers can be sophisticated monitors of corporate insiders, and thus reliable guarantors of good corporate governance. Boot & Thakor (1997), for instance, argue that banks—as coordinated coalitions of investors—are better than uncoordinated markets at monitoring firms and reducing post-lending moral hazard (asset substitution).

Of course, the other side of the coin is that the insider role of banks may create an information gap for possible external investors. Powerful banks can stymie innovation by extracting informational rents and protecting established firms with close bank-firm ties from competition (Hellwig 1991; Rajan 1992). In addition, this arrangement may open the door to what Rhodes and van Apeldoorn called a "degree of collusive complacency" that leads to inefficiencies and even corruption. On their part, Morck & Nakamura (1999), Morck et al. (2000), and others point out that the bankers' aim in governance oversight is to make sure corporate borrowers repay their debts. This could induce excessive risk aversion and excessive investment in tangible collateralizable assets, rather than knowledge-based assets. Banks and other financial firms are also biased as monitors of corporate governance because they treat firms as potential or actual customers.

Before considering the question of relative merits of the two systems, however, let us bring to light some further aspects of the system being currently discussed.

I.9.7. Some further features of stakeholder capitalism

CME model views shareholders as just one among many important stakeholders (such as employees and customers) in whose interests firms should be run. The stakeholder model was developed initially to identify the various groups in society that were directly affected by business decisions, and in turn could influence the success or failure of a business enterprise.

A stakeholder is any individual or group that can affect or is affected by the activities of the firm. On the basis of this definition, the stakeholders of the business firms are not only the investors, shareholders and others whose claim denotes a share of financial ownership, but also managers and employees, suppliers and customers. The local community where the firm's facilities are located are also stakeholders. Some theorists indeed concluded that a firm or enterprise therefore in an economic and moral sense "belonged" not only to the shareholders of the firm, but also to the other stakeholders who had an economic link with the firm. One should not, however, indulge in such all-inclusive generalisations.

As argued above, economic ownership can be attributed to creditors. Other obvious candidates are corporate executives, not only through their financial ownership stakes and equity-based compensation, but also because their huge, if not stratopheric salaries and bonuses cannot be, in fact, socio-economically speaking, treated on the same footing as wages of hired hands, as they actually express ownership of corporate capital.[4]

The workforce can also be economic co-owners, owing to employee stock ownership plans, some forms of incentive pay etc. There is more to the ownership status of employees under stakeholder capitalism, however:

> An important characteristic of the Japanese system is lifetime employment and an inflexible labor market With Anglo-Saxon capitalism these are undesirable but with stakeholder capitalism they are an advantage and

[4] See Tittenbrun 1991.

> make consensus easier to achieve. What happens if there is a bad shock to a J-mode firm? In order to maintain cooperation it may be necessary to keep wages and employment high even if this means cutting returns to shareholders such as dividends.This is the opposite of what happens in an H-mode firm. (Alan & Gale 2003)

In the former system there is more security for labour force given that there are more constraints on employers in their relationship with workers, especially in their ability to hire and to fire. Labour power markets are thus less flexible than those generally found in the Anglo-Saxon model. This means that employees can be said to be socio-economic owners of their jobs. Their ownership of their conditions of work manifests itself in various social benefits and privileges they enjoy. A related factor of differentiation in the structure of corporate governance is the weight assigned to shareholder interests.

While shareholder interest is not a high priority in corporate governance in continental Europe and Japan, it is of core importance in the Anglo-Saxon model. This priority militates against labour-management relations and affects the return to labour; the result in Anglo-Saxon countries is "employee remuneration as a proportion of net value added is much lower" (Rhodes & Van Apeldoorn 1997).

Stakeholder capitalism possesses legal mechanisms that explicitly provide that firms do not have a sole duty to pursue the interests of shareholders. In the German system of codetermination (*Mitbestimmung*) for example, employees have an equal number of seats in the supervisory boards of large corporations (*Aufsichtsrat*) or all the seats in the factory councils (*Betriebsrat*) of most companies. Some firms even have both, in which case employees are twice represented. The supervisory boards are responsible for the strategic decisions of firms—investment, financial, operational and other strategic decisions—but through a process which gives employees both a voice and a stake, ensuring that firms are run in a manner that is socially acceptable to employees and that employees' actions and demands do not jeopardize the efficiency of firms (Allen 2005).

Wymeersch (1998) documents several other countries that have some form of co-determination. Austria has a system of co-determination similar to that in Germany. Under the Japanese system, managers have no fiduciary responsibility to shareholders (Allen & Gale 2003). It is widely accepted that they pursue the interests of a wide variety of stakeholders. This is well illustrated by a report of the annual meeting of the International Corporate Governance Network in Tokyo from the *Financial Times* of August 1, 2001. Hiroshi Okuda, chairman of Toyota Motor

Corporation and of the Japan Federation of Employers' associations, told the assembled money managers that it would be irresponsible to run Japanese companies primarily in the interests of shareholders. Mr. Okuda made his point by telling guests what Japanese junior high school textbooks say about corporate social responsibility. Under Japanese company law, they explain, shareholders are the owners of the corporation. But if corporations are run exclusively in the interests of shareholders, the business will be driven to pursue short-term profit at the expense of employment and spending on research and development (Alan et al. 2007).

I.9.8. Shareholder capitalism vs. stakeholder capitalism

By contrast, The Anglo-American markets assume that a firm's objective should follow the shareholder wealth maximization (SWM) model. More specifically, the firm should strive to maximize the return to shareholders, as measured by the sum of capital gains and dividends, for a given level of risk. Alternatively, the firm should minimize the risk to shareholders for a given rate of return.

The SWM model assumes as a universal truth that the stock market is efficient. The share price is always correct because it captures all the expectations of return and risk as perceived by investors. It quickly incorporates new information into the share price. Share prices, in turn, are deemed the best allocators of capital in the macro economy. The SWM model also treats its definition of risk as a universal truth. Risk is defined as the added risk that the firm's shares bring to a diversified portfolio. The total operational risk of the firm can be eliminated through portfolio diversification by the investors. Therefore, this unsystematic risk, the risk of the individual security, should not be a prime concern for management unless it increases the prospect of bankruptcy. Systematic risk, the risk of the market in general, cannot be eliminated. This reflects risk that the share price will be a function of the stock market.

I.9.9. Maximisation of corporate wealth vs. Maximisation of shareholder value

In contradistinction to the SWM model, Continental European and Japanese markets assume:

> … that a corporation's objective should be to maximize corporate wealth. Thus a firm should treat shareholders on a par with other corporate

interest groups, such as management, labor, the local community, suppliers, creditors, and even the government. The goal is to earn as much as possible in the long run, but to retain enough to increase the corporate wealth for the benefit of all interest groups. This model has also been labeled the stakeholder capitalism model.

The definition of corporate wealth is much broader than just financial wealth, such as cash, marketable securities and unused credit lines. It includes the firm's technical, market, and human resources. "Consequently, it goes beyond the wealth measured by conventional financial reports to include the firm's market position as well as the knowledge and skills of its employees in technology, manufacturing processes, marketing and administration of the enterprise."

The corporate wealth maximization (CWM) model does not assume that equity markets are either efficient or inefficient. It does not really matter because the firm's financial goals are not exclusively shareholder-oriented. In any case, the model assumes that long-term "loyal" shareholders should influence corporate strategy, not the transient portfolio investor.

The CWM model assumes that total risk, that is, operating and financial risk, does count. It is a specific-corporate objective to generate growing earnings and dividends over the long run with as much certainty as possible, given the firm's mission statement and goals. Risk is measured more by product market variability than by short term variation in earnings and share price. (Goswami 1988)

I.9.10. Theoretical grounds

To continue these theoretical deliberations, the LME's model is premised on Adam Smith's notion of the organization of the economy through the "invisible hand" and its modern refinement, the first and second fundamental theorems of welfare economics (the above-mentioned Arrow-Debreu Model—see Allen 2005).

The first theorem states that if the objective of firms is to maximize the wealth of their shareholders, and individuals pursue their own interests, then the allocation is Pareto efficient. The second theorem states that any Pareto-efficient allocation can be implemented as a competitive equilibrium, given appropriate lump-sum taxes. In this view, the role of the firm in society is precisely to create wealth for shareholders and this is embodied in the legal framework (Allen 2005, 165). The problem of the interests of other stakeholders in the economy (i.e. equitable income distribution, including inter-generational income distribution) is relegated to policies relating to redistribution through lump-sum taxes and/or charity. The Arrow-Debreu Model assumes the existence of economies with perfect competition, complete markets and symmetric information.

The CME model, on the other hand, recognises the reality of imperfect conditions and is concerned to ensure that firms are run in a way that efficiently utilizes societal resources. "For example, if there are externalities such as pollution, then maximizing the value of the firm is well known to cause a misallocation of resources" (Allen 2005, 165). Allen argues that in the case of such externalities, firms concerned with the interests of a wider range of stakeholders are more likely to change their behaviour and produce the socially optimal level of pollution so that although it may not be possible to obtain efficiency, it may be possible to achieve a better allocation of societal resources in the interests of a broad category of stakeholders.

This is equally true in the case of economic activities that have the potential to degrade the environment or natural resources (i.e. mining, oil and bioprospecting, commercial agriculture and fishing). In these instances, models of capitalism that put emphasis on the management of firms in the interests of shareholders are likely to generate more socially inefficient outcomes than ones concerned with the interests of a broader variety of stakeholders. Instead of the firm treating as many of its costs as possible as externalities and disclaiming responsibility for them, which leads to conflict in the shape of strikes, lawsuits, and government-imposed controls and regulation, the stakeholder firm seeks to handle these costs through internal negotiation with its stakeholders.

This is not to say that proponents of stockholder capitalism are not able to present an, at least seemingly equally persuasive case for their favourite model of socio-economic system. Since the purpose of the firm is to maximise profits, it is pointed out, only those stakeholders who bear financial risk directly, the shareholders, should have the right to determine policy (the right of voice). Other key stakeholders have the right of exit. Consumers can stop buying the product, workers can leave employment, banks can cancel loans. The key concept that is used in support of this position is the notion of "sunk costs," or "asset specificity" as Williamson (1985) calls it.

All stakeholders who have some sunk costs in the firm (such as a worker who has invested in skills which are specific to that firm) require some form of insurance against the firm acting opportunistically against their interests. The key issue is whether the stakeholder group should receive this protection through the conditions of its contract with the firm, or through having some say in the operations of the firm, that is the right of voice.

So far so good; further argument becomes somewhat convoluted, however. Shareholders are special, it is argued, as:

> … they are the only stakeholder whose relationship with the firm does not come up for periodic renewal, and because it would be particularly difficult for each shareholder to agree to a contract with the firm before investing in equity. Moreover, giving voting rights over company decisions to other stakeholders would impose additional costs, reduce the drive to maximise profits, and therefore lead to muddled objectives and deteriorating performance. (Gamble & Kelly 1997)

On this view, which Stoney & Aylott (1994) seem to share, capitalist firms should be left to do what capitalist firms do best—maximize profits. But many economists have criticised this orthodox view because it does not accurately describe the way in which modern firms operate. The divorce of ownership and control means that risk bearing by shareholders often occurs in a highly diversified manner (Gamble & Kelly 1997).

On the other hand, how does an even undiversified risk borne by a shareholder compare to the risk of losing his or her job, and thus livelihood by a worker? Along similar lines, both Freeman (1990) and Stiglitz (1986) have persuasively argued that the sunk costs faced by other stakeholders (such as employees or local communities) can be far greater than those born by individual shareholders, especially in countries with developed security markets. Admittedly, individuals who hold a significant share of a company's stock do face sunk costs if they try and sell their shares (i.e. the price of the shares they are selling will tend to fall). This is an argument in favour of large blockholders having a strong voice in a company; but it does not imply that shareholders are in some sense special in the risks that they face. The corollary of arguing that certain stakeholders, such as employees or suppliers, face firm- specific costs is that these groups have a strong incentive to strive and ensure that the firm is successful.

This incentive, combined with an often detailed knowledge of the firms operations, ensures that these stakeholders would have the information and motivation required to effectively monitor and shape the firms behaviour. It is the absence of precisely these qualities that have led many to argue that dispersed shareholders act as poor controllers of management (Gamble & Kelly 1997).

Another corollary of dispersed share ownership is what in terms of new institutional economics constitutes the main problem of shareholder capitalism. Whereas, as argued above, in the case of its alternative this role is played by the transaction costs issue, the shareholder system is focused on the agency problem, also known as the principal-agent problem. The problem arises because the separation of ownership and control creates opportunities and incentives for corporate managers-as-agents to deviate from the preferences of their principals, i.e. stockholders.

Dispersed ownership magnifies the problem by giving rise to conflicts of interest between the various corporate claimholders and by creating a collective action problem among investors. It is in this connection that some writers challenge the conventional idea that the corporation is a globally superior form of business organization, and by the same token:

> cast doubt on the related notion that Anglo-American legal institutions are superior to French and German ones—that is, that common-law regimes provide an inherently better environment for business than the code-based legal regimes of the European continent. If one looks at history from the vantage point of the PLLC rather than the corporation, then Germany, a code-based country, was the key legal pioneer, with Britain, a common-law country, following a decade and a half later. France, a code-based country, was a distant third, but if rapidity of diffusion is a good indicator of a form's ability to satisfy businesses' contracting needs, then France may have been the most successful innovator. (Guinnane et al. 2007)

The concept of a stakeholder firm changes the idea of what is efficient for the firm and for society. Takeovers for example are often argued to be economically efficient if the joint share value of both the acquiring and acquired firm rises. But many takeovers will impose severe costs on other non-shareholding stakeholders. Economists such as Shleifer & Summers (1988) have shown how takeovers that apparently create value in the form of higher share prices (and thereby increase overall social welfare) are often nothing more than an (anti-egalitarian) redistribution of existing value between stakeholders. Moreover the threat of takeover can act as an important deterrent on the formation of long-term stakeholder relationships, or on R&D spending, which many argue are vital to firm competitiveness. Hence takeovers which are privately beneficial to the shareholders involved may actually impose a cost on the rest of society.

I.9.11. Taxation as a form of economic ownership

The above mention of "the Rest of society" serves to reveal another ownership dimension of stakeholder capitalism. In terms of socio-economic ownership, taxes represent nothing other than property relations. Corporate income taxes represent society's share, realised by the medium of state taxation, in ownership of the means of production, while payroll taxes signify a similar share in the ownership of labour power; similar considerations apply in relation to property taxes etc. This is the case because members of society have free access and in fact use parks, roads, libraries, museums and other objects built by the state. With appropriate modifications the same rule applies in the case of local taxes and facilities accessible to local communities.

The relevant fact is, as tables 2 and 3 show, that there is a determinate difference in respect of the share of taxes in GDP as well of transfer payments and social spending between countries belonging to both alternative capitalist systems. Stakeholder capitalism differs from a "free market model" or LME in that it places significant limits on the way markets operate in order to reduce their tendency to either polarize society or to marginalize some groups within society (Cosmas 2008).

Suffice it to point out that according to the Organization for Economic Cooperation and Development, in the United States the tax burden is 25.6% of G.D.P. This ranks 17% among developed countries. The global average for the group is 36%.

Notes on Table 3 (over):

n.a indicates not available.

Note: EU 15 area countries are: Austria, Belgium, Denmark, Finland, France, Germany, Greece, Ireland, Italy, Luxembourg, Netherlands, Portugal, Spain, Sweden and United Kingdom.

EU 19 area countries are: EU 15 countries plus Czech Republic, Hungary, Poland and Slovak Republic.

1. The total tax revenue has been reduced by the amount of the capital transfer that represents uncollected taxes.

2. Unified Germany beginning in 1991. Starting 2001, Germany has revised its treatment of non-wastable tax credits in the reporting of revenues to bring it into line with the OECD guidelines. The impact of this change is shown in Table D in Part I of this report.

3. Secretariat estimate, including expected revenues collected by state and local governments.

Table 3. Total Tax Revenue as Percentage of GDP

	1975	1985	1990	1995	2000	2004	2005	2006 Provis-ional
Canada	32.0	32.5	35.9	35.6	35.6	33.6	33.4	33.4
Mexico		17.0	17.3	16.7	18.5	19.0	19.9	20.6 [3]
United States	25.6	25.6	27.3	27.9	29.9	26.0	27.3	28.2
Australia	25.8	28.3	28.5	28.8	31.1	31.1	30.9	n.a
Japan	20.9	27.4	29.1	26.8	27.0	26.3	27.4	n.a
Korea	15.1	16.4	18.9	19.4	23.6	24.6	25.5	26.8
New Zealand	28.5	31.1	37.4	36.6	33.6	35.5	37.8	36.5
Austria	36.7	40.9	39.6	41.1	42.6	42.8	42.1	41.9
Belgium	39.5	44.4	42.0	43.6	44.9	44.8	45.4	44.8
Czech Republic				37.5	35.3	38.3	37.8	36.7
Denmark [1]	38.4	46.1	46.5	48.8	49.4	49.3	50.3	49.0
Finland	36.5	39.7	43.5	45.7	47.2	43.4	44.0	43.5
France [1]	35.4	42.8	42.0	42.9	44.4	43.5	44.1	44.5
Germany [2]	34.3	36.1	34.8	37.2	37.2	34.8	34.8	35.7
Greece	16.9	22.2	22.8	25.2	29.7	27.1	27.3	27.4
Hungary				41.3	38.0	37.6	37.2	37.1
Iceland	30.0	28.2	30.9	31.2	38.1	38.3	41.4	n.a
Ireland	28.7	34.6	33.1	32.0	31.7	30.2	30.6	31.7
Italy	25.4	33.6	37.8	40.1	42.3	41.1	41.0	42.7
Luxembourg	32.8	39.5	35.7	37.1	39.1	37.9	38.6	36.3
Netherlands	41.2	42.6	42.9	41.5	39.7	37.4	39.1	39.5
Norway	39.2	42.6	41.0	40.9	42.6	43.3	43.7	43.6
Poland				36.2	31.6	33.4	34.3	n.a
Portugal	19.7	25.2	27.7	31.7	34.1	33.8	34.8	35.4
Slovak Republic [1]					32.9	31.6	31.6	29.6
Spain [1]	18.4	27.2	32.5	32.1	34.2	34.7	35.8	36.7
Sweden	41.6	47.8	52.7	48.1	52.6	49.9	50.7	50.1
Switzerland	24.5	26.1	26.0	27.8	30.5	29.1	29.7	30.1
Turkey	16.0	15.4	20.0	22.6	32.3	31.3	32.3	32.5
United Kingdom	35.3	37.6	36.3	34.7	37.3	35.6	36.5	37.4
Unweighted average:								
OECD Total	29.5	32.7	33.9	34.9	36.2	35.5	36.2	n.a
OECD America	28.8	25.0	26.8	26.7	28.0	26.2	26.9	27.4
OECD Pacific	22.6	25.8	28.5	27.9	28.8	29.4	30.4	n.a
OECD Europe	31.1	35.4	36.2	37.2	38.6	37.8	38.4	n.a
EU 19	32.1	37.4	38.0	38.7	39.2	38.3	38.7	n.a
EU 15	32.1	37.4	38.0	38.8	40.4	39.1	39.7	39.8

Source: OECD http://www.oecd.org/dataoecd/44/41/39494985.pdf

Table 4. Tax **Structures in the OECD-area**

	2005	1965	1975	1985	1995
Personal income tax	26	30	30	27	25
Corporate income tax	9	8	8	8	10
Social security contributions	18	22	22	25	26
Payroll taxes	1	1	1	1	1
Property taxes	8	6	5	6	6
General consumption taxes	14	15	16	18	19
Specific consumption taxes	24	18	16	13	11
Other taxes	1	1	1	3	3
Total	100	100	100	100	100

Source: http://www.39495035.pdf

I.9.12. Conclusion

From the foregoing it can be seen that none of the systems are clearly superior to their rivals, as both have their inherent weaknesses. The East Asia crisis of the late 1990s has demonstrated, for example, how cronyism and connected lending can be a source of major corporate governance failures throughout the economy. Meanwhile, where banks are sound and well-managed, as for instance in Germany, there is evidence of their effectiveness in disciplining management (Becht et al. 2002). The superiority of their style of corporate governance has been vividly demonstrated in the recent wave of financial crises from which German banks went out relatively unscathed.

On the other hand, there is no evidence that the cost of capital is lower in the U.S. or the UK It is commonly argued that the Anglo-Saxon market-based setting provides a better environment for startups, new technologies and the redeployment of resources into new, more profitable lines of business, while bank-based systems are perhaps more suitable for effective management of existing technologies. It turns out, however, that no convincing evidence on these points is available (Becht et al. 2002).

Open questions also arise in the context of findings that better legal enforcement of minority shareholder rights is associated with greater reliance on stock market financing. How important is this finding for the availability of suitable financing? And which way does the causality run? More generally, according to a comprehensive study, there is no cross-country empirical support for either the market based or bank-based views. Neither bank-based nor market-based financial systems are particularly effective at promoting economic growth (Levine 2002).

As a matter of fact, the system most favoured by commentators has varied over time as a function of the relative success of each country's underlying economy (not losing sight of various management fads): "with two broad phases: the 1980s—when the Japanese and German long-term investor corporate governance perspective were seen as strengths relative to the Anglo-American market based short-termist perspective—and the 1990s—when greater minority shareholder protections and the greater reliance on equity financing in the Anglo-American systems were seen as major advantages (Becht et al. 2002)."

Japanese and German corporate governance looked good in the 1980s when Japan and Germany were growing faster than the U.S. In contrast, in the late 1990s, following nearly a decade of economic recession in Japan, a decade of costly post-unification economic adjustments in Germany, and an unprecedented economic and stock market boom in the U.S., the American corporate governance model has been hailed as the model for all to follow (see Hansmann & Kraakman 2001). Yet later sentiment has turned again owing to the stock market excesses on Nasdaq, which have resulted in massive overinvestment in the technology sector, leading to some of the largest bankruptcies in corporate history, often accompanied by corporate governance scandals.

Dissatisfaction with U.S. corporate governance has re-emerged in full swing. There can be no doubt that the Enron collapse, the then largest corporate bankruptcy in U.S. history to date, was caused by corporate governance problems. Yet Enron had all the characteristics of an exemplary "Anglo-American" corporation. The later and most powerful crisis since the Great Depression could only aggravate the situation, since it is in the U.S. and UK that the housing boom which initiated the slump had reached the highest proportions, showing all the pitfalls of the short-term nature of the compensation systems in mortgage institutions and other financial organisations that came to be universally regarded as the culprit of the financial and economic malaise. It is also no accident that it is in those leading nations of stockholder capitalism that class anger against sky-high earnings, and bonuses in particular of the notably financial executive class was concentrated.

I.9.13. Prediction

This prompts one to turn to the question of the future of the two models discussed here. This is a controversial issue, since there are here a number of contradictory tendencies at work. Some commentators have predicted a world-wide convergence of corporate governance practice to the U.S. model (see for example Hansmann & Kraakman 2000).

In a variant of this view, world-wide competition to attract corporate headquarters and investment is seen like the corporate law competition between U.S. states portrayed by Romano (1993). Such competition is predicted to eventually bring about a single standard resembling the current law in Delaware or, at least, securities regulation standards as set by the U.S. SEC (see Coffee 1999).

It is in light of this that one should note a fundamental element in the trend of European transformation in contractual labour relations; there is an underlying weakening of labour union power plus a shareholder demand for a larger portion of the added net value that has traditionally gone to the workers. In this dispute, a central issue is the so-called "locational threat"; that is the way companies extract concessions from labour under the threat of moving to cheaper labour cost locations (Reich 2002). The result is a diminution of organized labour as a social force, what Martin denominates as "the Americanization of the European labour market" (1998).

A case in point is Alcatel, a mostly French-owned telecommunications company. When it announced that its annual profit would be less than had been forecast, its management was driven to the distinctly un-French solution of restoring profits by laying off some twelve thousand employees. CalPERS, the $175-billion health and retirement fund for California state employees, was not the sole instigator, although French President Jacques Chirac testily noted in his Bastille Day address that the layoff was triggered when "California retirees suddenly decided to sell Alcatel" (Reich 2002). Reich also observes that:

> Europe's much-vaunted stakeholder capitalism makes European companies sensitive to multiple constituencies, which is precisely why it doesn't sit well with shareholders intent on making companies attentive only to them—and why stakeholder capitalism is under attack. CalPERS recently complained that a German utility gave the cities it served too

> much control over its board, thereby diminishing the value of the utility's shares owned by CalPERS.
>
> Utility executives explained that its system of city representation maintained a bond with the utility's customers, but when CalPERS then threatened to dump its shares, the utility promptly scrapped the system. As power shifts away from governments to global investors, political rhetoric about corporate social responsibility is meaningless. Companies won't voluntarily become socially responsible if that means sacrificing earnings and share values; investors can easily punish them by putting their money elsewhere. So laws and regulations are needed to back up such rhetoric.
>
> But even government's power to regulate is weakening as highly mobile capital can find better deals elsewhere around the world, where profits are higher because regulations are meeker. (Reich 2002)

This view is not universally held, however. Some writers hold that in spite of increasing globalization, industrial countries are not converging towards a single model of capitalism or form of corporate governance (Fligstein 1996 and 2001). This is explained by the fact that national economies are characterized by distinct institutional constellations that engender particular systemic "logics" for economic action (Jackson & Deeg 2006) or "distinct institutional arrangements that outline the relations among investment, ownership, control and economic growth" (Fligstein 2001, 189).

It is argued that the aforementioned features of the transformation occurring in stakeholder capitalism under the impact of globalisation of stockholder capitalism are significant, but they are not yet prevalent and widespread. Not all companies or all countries are being transformed. These changes have taken hold in Europe, but their speed and diffusion are far from supersonic, as exemplified by the lack of a vibrant public corporate-bond market. Certainly, the ways and objectives of the financial and credit structure have been modified towards a tendency to lose the "particularly stable and compassionate lending through cross-shareholdings between banks and industry" (Rhodes & van Apeldoorn, 11).

However, as is argued further, this cannot be taken as a total renunciation of the social market model. In fact:

> … it could be argued that there is a "new social course" enclosed in the search for an option of development between the model of the United States and the more traditional European one. The central challenge in this design has been the correct placing of this inevitable transformation between two extremes. On one extreme there was the Anglo-Saxon type deregulation, with a perspective of short-run profitability that produces low unemployment, minimum social benefits, and job insecurity. On the other extreme was the preferred European option of greater official regulation with firms that make long-term planning a consequence of their attitude

> towards continuity, consensus, and the improvement of workers' capacities, resulting in generous labor benefits and workers' protection. It may be hypothesised that the step to implement monetary union(despite its current grave problems)[5] goes in the direction of finding a point of convergence between the two models.
>
> In the latter example, monetary union facilitates common economic policies, and is more conducive to the objectives of efficiency and stability needed for the economic and monetary development, in harmony and congruency with the social objectives postulated for Europe since the Treatise of Rome. The challenge for Europeans is solving the unemployment problem without recurring to an extreme degree of flexibility in labor markets demanded by stockholder globalization standards … there is an implicit acceptance to achieve a higher degree of efficiency, as postulated by the stockholder model of globalization. It does not seem to mean, however, an utter renunciation of the European social market model of a mixed economy with generous welfare benefits and high minimum wages that makes possible an ordering of the market with freedom for wage negotiations, but without eliminating social legislation. Economic efficiency is a must, but under the premise that it does not become social dumping. In this context, the new labor market structure should stand in between present European inflexibility and the cheap labor without social security of the Anglo-Saxon model. The underlying premise is that the market functions when competition between firms is correctly regulated, thereby fostering both competitive business and social consensus. Without doubt, the transformation taking place implies a degree of convergence in corporate governance that necessarily brings a weakening in traditional relations, as is happening in the German consensual industrial relations system. Neither the stakeholder model nor the shareholder model can remain unscathed under the impetus of globalization. (Rozo 2002)

The case for this kind of intermediate system does not take account, however, of another form of convergence between two capitalisms. After all, both Europe and Japan or Korea have not been below the U.S. as far as the number and size of financial and corruption scandals are concerned.

The Enron and other scandals have raised some serious doubts about the American shareholder-capital market-centric model. Even Paul Volcker, former chairman of the Federal Reserve ("The Fed") from August 1979 to August 1987, who was shocked by the explosion of corporate greed that occurred in the 1990s, has been quoted as saying:

---

[5] After all, the structural contradictions present in the U.S. military-financial complex are manifested in this state's piling mountain of debt and deficit. On the other hand, it may well be that the financial crisis in the Euro Zone will prompt an even greater integration, in the form of fiscal union, or even a super-state structure, which in our terms means transnational common property.

"Traditional norms didn't exist. You had this whole culture where the only sign of worth was how much money you made" (Rozo 2002). But greed alone does not explain what happened in America. Corporate governance is critical in that regard. It includes accountability, transparency, and disclosure—the sum of accounting standards and practices and legal rules and regulations that allow investors to feel that it is safe to part with their money. The relative lack of this factor in the past in Japan accounts for many corporate scandals, the low profitability of its companies and the lack of high levels of investment in new businesses.

Through the "Big Bang" financial reforms, the updating of accounting standards and amendment of the Commercial Code, Japan has recently made tremendous progress in the field of corporate governance. For example, the Commercial Code has been amended to provide an opportunity for large corporations to adopt a corporate governance system that will permit and encourage the appointment of independent directors and the establishment of audit, nominating and compensation committees of the board (Mitchell 2003). However, one of the lessons of the Enron-type scandals is that independent directors and audit committees by themselves will not ensure that there is good corporate governance. The Sarbanes-Oxley Act passed by The U.S. Congress expands criminal and civil liability in the securities area and creates a new regulatory regime for public accountants. The Sarbanes-Oxley Act enacted in 2002 has three major requirements: CEOs must vouch for the veracity of financial statements; Audit committees of board consist of independent director; Companies cannot make loans to directors; Companies must test their internal controls against fraud. Penalties have been spelled out for various levels of failure.

Recently, Japan has earnestly reformed its legal and regulatory system by introducing amendments or new legislation that permit holding companies (1997), stock-for-stock exchanges (1999), a Chapter 11-type Civil Rehabilitation Law (2000), a corporate spin-off law (2001), a broader range of corporate stock options (2002) and a new emphasis on the protection of intellectual property.

However, the condition of the Japanese economy and the state of its banks and corporations are not better than it was before these reforms. Proper rules and regulations alone will not suffice. The rules and traditional norms that Mr. Volcker mentioned did not prevent Enron from happening. In reality, Enron and the other American corporate scandals represent a perversion of the shareholder value model. While paying lip service to the goal of satisfying stockholder interests, these managers merely enriched themselves, committed fraud or simply stole corporate assets. In turn, the recent Japanese corporate scandals represent a kind of perversion of the stakeholder model, where management, in the name of protecting employees and other stakeholders, diverted corporate assets to pet projects, hid losses in subsidiaries and destroyed corporate value (the most recent example of this kind of malfeasance is Japan's Olympus).

Thus, it can be argued that at the extreme side of both ends of the spectrum—in a very perverted way both the American and the Japanese systems of corporate governance converged into a kind of managerial capitalism—or capitalism for the benefit of those who control the Corporation (Mitchell 2003).

CHAPTER I.10.

AN INTRODUCTION TO THE SOCIOLOGY OF THE ECONOMY FROM THE PERSPECTIVE OF SOCIO-ECONOMIC STRUCTURALISM

I.10.1. Introductory remarks

A critical analysis of writings of great (and not so great) forebears has been important not only per se, but also as a source of fruitful material and building blocks for our own theoretical framework.[1] This remark is relevant, as it sheds light on the nature of this approach. Indeed, while Marx's influence on our own thinking is undeniable, our approach could hardly be classified as Marxist, neo-Marxist or post-Marxist. It is the case because the scope of our inspiration is much wider; it comprises such thinkers as Weber, Durkheim, Parsons, Polish-American social scientist Florian Znaniecki and, last but not least, Polish contemporary sociologist Stanislaw Kozyr-Kowalski, to mention but a few.

From Max Weber one can learn, amongst other things, that any study of the economy must be embedded within a broader theory of society, an idea that the title of the present book tries to highlight. And indeed, one would like to consider such a multi-level approach as a distinctive feature of socio-economic structuralism. The first element of the label expresses an idea that whatever social phenomenon or process is investigated, its scientific investigation cannot take place without taking into consideration its relationship to the economy, which, however, does not entail any economic determinism or reductionism. The second part of the term chosen as a name for our theoretic and methodological approach signifies

[1] In this respect our approach is somewhat similar to that of Parsonian "The Structure of Social Action" but in another respect it is dissimilar, though since, unlike Parsons, we have not confined ourselves to looking for what appears to be consistent with the perspective of our own in a given theory, but we have attempted to give a broader critical analysis of the theories involved, to be sure, from this very author's perspective.

that society is viewed in terms of structures. The simplest definition of structure refers to it as a set of interrelated elements and, importantly, relationships between those structural components are more numerous and / or strong than any ties associating a given structure with its setting, thanks to which structure functions as a whole relatively isolated from its setting.

I.10.2. Society as a set of structures

Society at large consists of four structures: economic, political, ideational and reproductive, which allows us to label the theory as EPIR, by analogy with the famous Parsonian AGIL system. Before proceeding to clarify the content of these concepts, an additional remark is in order.

I.10.3. Activist versus contemplativ approach to structures

Marx's claim from *Grundrisse* that "Society does not consist of individuals, but expresses the sum of interrelations, the relations within which these individuals stand" can be, on the basis of certain interpretations, understood incorrectly. While without a doubt it renders such characteristic of socio-economic structuralism as holism, in another respect it may lead to misleading conclusions. What we mean here is the fact that actually society does not simply consist of mutual relationships of individuals to each other, as the building blocks of structures properly understood are not individual persons, but their actions and their inter-relations.

Thus, the reproductive structure involves all types of work and / or labour[2] as well as quasi-work serving the reproduction of the labour power. In plain language, this societal substructure comprises such smaller structures as the family, health service, sports and entertainment. The concept of quasi-work requires clarification. In reality, given kinds of quasi-work may not differ from their counterparts among regular work as regards their sensual and material shape. The distinction between them also does not imply any moral evaluation. Quasi-work may require greater effort, may produce quantitively larger and qualitatively better results, but still not transcend the limits of the notion, as it still does not lose its crucial characteristic, which is non-commercial orientation. In contradistinction to

---

[2] See the following comment by Marx: "the English language has two different expressions for these two different aspects of labour: in the Simple Labour-process, the process of producing Use-Values, it is *Work;* in the process of creation of Value, it is *Labour,* taking the term in its strictly economic sense."

quasi-work, labour can be conceived of as such an activity owing to which its agent earns the means of subsistence. Rearing children by their parents, cooking or small-scale repairs carried out within the household are examples of quasi-work. Again, the circumstance that these and other cases of quasi-work may be very socially and economically useful does not change their non-commercial nature, and thus does not remove them from the box named "quasi-work." Apart from both these categories, one should also distinguish what we shall call "para-labour," which is transitory, temporary work.

The ideational structure, in turn, comprises all those activities that consist in the production or dissemination of knowledge, information, or other ideas. Such activities are performed by scientists and lecturers, journalists, librarians, artists and the clergy. One can easily point to a number of examples of quasi-work in this field, such as acts of amateur painters, so-called citizen journalists, believers in some denominations who themselves execute what is in other churches done by professional clergy, writing a diary for one's own pleasure etc.

The political structure involves all activities linked to an application of the means of coercion. What is important to point out in this context is the fact that the state and all its organs: police, courts, prisons etc. use legitimate, public violence. The state may, however, cede some of its powers on behalf of families, as in the notion of "parental authority." In this familial situation one has to do with quasi-work in the sense specified above. In other situations of the use or rather abuse of violence one has to do with what will be dubbed here "lumpenwork." In this case no state powers are transferred—in fact the activities in question are outlawed, and hence the state uses its means of public coercion in order to defend its citizens who are harmed by pickpockets, mobsters and the like. To be sure, lumpenwork is present also within other societal structures, including the economy, as fairly widely spread expressions such as "informal economy," "unofficial economy," "underground economy," "shadow economy" and other synonymous terms indicate. The distinctive feature of the activities belonging to that peculiar economic substructure is, ironically, the fact that they represent pure private property. This is the case because, as has been explained in the chapter on various capitalist modes of economic activity, taxes represent the share of society at large or the nation as a whole in the property in the means of economic action and in the labour power. It follows that all economic lumpenwork, which avoids or, rather, evades taxation, constitutes private property pure and simple, devoid of any unwanted public or all-national additions. An additional comment should be made regarding the basis of differentiating between, respectively, the "grey" and "black" economy, the difference being that the former provides personally desirable use-values, which is not the case as far as the activities of narcotics producers or dealers, thieves and the like, generators of what should be called, rather, anti- or counteruse-values, as the products and services in question are harmful for individuals' health and often life itself. Hence, prostitution or, in more modern parlance, services provided by sex workers belong, barring relatively rare cases of female or male prostitutes infected with AIDS or other sexually transmitted diseases, to the grey zone of the lumpeneconomy. In the same category belong beggars, and buskers who are performing in public places for gratuities, which are generally in the form of money and edibles, etc.

In order to demonstrate how the aforementioned terms "quasi-work" "lumpenwork" and "parawork" may be helpful and, conversely, how much can any lack of such adequate notions harm an otherwise sound statement, let us quote the following passage:

> The more recent prophets of the "end of work" have focused their foreseeing on the relative growth rates of jobs and labour force and concluded, with the latter outstripping the former, that work was decreasingly able to play its former role as homogenising force in society. In both their Marxist and non-Marxist variants these prophets have focused on the displacement of waged workers by automation and computers—a process highlighted by recent epidemics of "down-sizing" through mass layoffs. The most serious objections to this vision derive from two sources: the narrowness of their understanding of "a job" and the successes of the current capitalist offensive to impose ever more work.
>
> The narrowness of their vision of dwindling jobs derives from the way they largely ignore unwaged work and the way its growth must be taken into account in any contemplation of the evolution of work. In the developed world high rates of unemployment are generally accompanied by increasing unwaged work. What can no longer be paid for must be done at home on what is usually dramatically reduced income. Meals out are replaced by home cooking, medical consultations by home care, storebought books by trips to the library, purchased food by home grown, working on the job by the work of looking for a job and so on. In this way what a one-sided representation of high unemployment portrays as a reduction in jobs available, a more comprehensive view must understand as a redistribution of work between waged and unwaged sites. (Cleaver 2002)

This solution to the problem posed above is unsatisfactory; whilst capturing some real trends, it frames these in misleading terms, suggesting that the two types of work distinguished should be treated on the equal footing, whereas in reality work and quasi-work are dissimilar in key socio-economic respects.

> In the South where high rates of formal unemployment and underemployment have persisted for much longer, the kinds of redistribution of work from waged to unwaged has crystallised into shifting work patterns of the so-called "informal sector" where very large percentages of many countries' labour forces are employed in various kinds of work necessary to the functioning of capital and to their own survival. The unavailability of fulltime waged jobs has not meant a reduction in work, on the contrary.
>
> The second objection to this line of argumentation is that it fails to recognise, or to take seriously, the central thrust of capitalist policy in this period which is focused on the imposition of work, sometimes of waged work, sometimes of unwaged work, but always of work. Just as capital renews its commitment to keeping the world organised around work, these social critics think it is disappearing—someone has serious illusions, and I'm inclined to think it is the critics.
>
> Even without retracing all the metamorphoses of capitalist policy in the last two decades it is not hard to see how policy has been oriented toward the renewed imposition of work. The basic elements of the counteroffensive in this period have been a direct assault on working class income aimed at inducing a greater willingness to work (in ways more profitable to capital) and, at the same time, a multi-dimensional restructuring designed to break the power of workers to resist the imposition of work and increased exploitation. The attack on working class income can be seen in everything from inflation to lower real wages through assaults via high interest rates and high unemployment to systematic attempts to eliminate the Welfare State whose unwaged income guarantees undergirded the wage hierarchy as a whole. The restructuring has come in everything from a recomposition of industrial sectors through technological reorganisation of what and how things are produced to the International Monetary Fund and World Bank's "structural adjustment" programmes designed not only to impose massive austerity, but to break the power of worker organisations and police-military-paramilitary measures where such "economic" programmes fail.
>
> The results of such policies, to the degree that resistance has been overcome and they have been successfully imposed, has been to weaken many workers' unwillingness to work. So for example we find waged workers fighting for longer hours to make up for wage reductions. We find the unwaged looking for waged jobs to add to their unwaged ones, or waged workers looking for second jobs. We find the unwaged working harder to survive on even less access to money than before. We find students willing to take "practical" courses and programmes of study in a search for waged work. And so on. (Cleaver 2002)

To be sure, as hinted above, the notion of lumpenwork has substantially broader reference, as it applies to other social structures as well. For the sake of illustration, just a few examples: illegal downloading of music or films through the internet, attendance at or organisation of illegal dog fights, production and propagation of pornographic films belong to the lumpeneconomy or, in the case it is done not for profit, to the ideational one, but watching them is an element of the lumpen reproductive structure.

The lumpeneconomy normally, i.e. excepting so-called rogue or failed states, falls short of accounting for the majority of the economy. A case in point is Greece which, as far as advanced industrial countries go, is characterised by one of the highest percentages in question, which still amounts to 25%. Hence, the general definition of the economic structure must be sufficiently broad to include such cases. This fairly strict criterion is met by the following definition: the economy is the totality of all kinds of substantive work and para-labour, i.e. generating use value and exchange value, including all types of material work and material quasi-work, as well as, to return to previously considered instances of the economic fringes, respective types of lumpenwork. The terminology introduced above refers to propagated especially by Polanyi distinction between two ways of viewing the economy. This brings us to the second concept as yet unknown.

I.10.4. Material work

To begin with, one specific comment is needed. Namely, we have decided to use the term "material work" in return of the better known "productive labour" in order to avoid engaging ourselves in the persistent and, to our taste, drawn-out dispute over the meaning of the notion of productive labour, as well a corresponding debate over which types of work deserve this proud name, as distinct from others, which must limit themselves to much less honourable label: "unproductive." Such disputes become increasingly sterile and scholastic, so it is better to keep away from them as far as possible.

In order to characterise the form of work under consideration, it is best to borrow the following statement from *Capital* in which its author proposes:

> To consider the labour-process independently of the particular form it assumes under given social conditions.
>
> Labour is, in the first place, a process in which both man and Nature participate, and in which man of his own accord starts, regulates, and controls the material re-actions between himself and Nature. He opposes

> himself to Nature as one of her own forces, setting in motion arms and legs, head and hands, the natural forces of his body, in order to appropriate Nature's productions in a form adapted to his own wants. By thus acting on the external world and changing it, he at the same time changes his own nature. He develops his slumbering powers and compels them to act in obedience to his sway. We are not now dealing with those primitive instinctive forms of labour that remind us of the mere animal. An immeasurable interval of time separates the state of things in which a man brings his labour-power to market for sale as a commodity, from that state in which human labour was still in its first instinctive stage. We presuppose labour in a form that stamps it as exclusively human. (Marx 1976)

I.10.4.1. Material and manual work

It is a notorious error to confuse this simple process of work with so-called manual or physical work. This may stem from a superficial interpretation of the word appearing in the Marx's text such as "bodily organs." Marx, however, stresses the indispensable mental character of human work. He writes, for instance:

> A spider conducts operations that resemble those of a weaver, and a bee puts to shame many an architect in the construction of her cells. But what distinguishes the worst architect from the best of bees is this, that the architect raises his structure in imagination before he erects it in reality. At the end of every labour-process, we get a result that already existed in the imagination of the labourer at its commencement. He not only effects a change of form in the material on which he works, but he also realises a purpose of his own that gives the law to his modus operandi, and to which he must subordinate his will. And this subordination is no mere momentary act. Besides the exertion of the bodily organs, the process demands that, during the whole operation, the workman's will be steadily in consonance with his purpose. This means close attention. The less he is attracted by the nature of the work, and the mode in which it is carried on, and the less, therefore, he enjoys it as something which gives play to his bodily and mental powers, the more close his attention is forced to be.
>
> The elementary factors of the labour-process are (1) the personal activity of man, i.e., work itself, (2) the subject of that work, and (3) its instruments .... [...]
>
> Tailoring and weaving, though qualitatively different productive activities, are each a productive expenditure of human brains, nerves, and muscles, and in this sense are human labour. They are but two different modes of expending human labour power. (Marx 1976)

To round off this discussion, consider one simple example: equating material with physical work would automatically qualify as the former e.g. rock drumming involving on average an expenditure of 600 calories an hour, often reaching even 900 calories.

I.10.4.2. Directly and indirectly material work

As a subtype of material work one can distinguish repairs of both investment and consumption goods. To repair, say, a chair (it may then, as in other cases, take the form of quasi-work) or a shoe is to produce them anew, albeit only in part. However, if one would like on that basis to reject our thesis of the material character of such activities, one would have to do the same with reference to the production of semi-finished goods or subassemblies which, by definition, are not final products themselves. To put it differently, partial manufacturing is still manufacturing.

Another related, albeit at the same time distinct form of material work consists in conservation or maintenance, i.e. preservation of use-value of the means of production or consumption. However, as distinct from both previously listed types of work, this one should be called indirectly, rather than directly, material, as is the case with regard to the two instances previously discussed. The same characteristic applies to further forms of material work discussed below.

For example, transportation can be classified as a type of material work, owing both to its role as an indispensable intermediary in production processes and as a necessary link in the process of delivering commodities to customers,that is, in the realisation of their exchange value, implying change in location, which is, of course, material in nature, and by the same token affects the use value of given commodities.

Let us emphasise that this characteristic of transportation concerns transport of goods only, as opposed to transportation of people which, however, may too constitute an element of the economy, even if the rational for this is different than ones specified above.

In all processes of collective work there must appear another type of indirectly material work, i.e. executive work which, by and large, consists of organisation and coordination of their subordinates. It can be analytically distinguished (as these functions are frequently fulfilled by one person) the work of supervision, whose defining feature is the ability of applying sanctions or, to be more precise, negative sanctions or punishment, which in modern conditions have chiefly the nature of monetary or moral stimuli.

I.10.4.2.1. Pre-material work

The above-mentioned form of indirectly material work has been chosen as a subject of a separate subsection on account of its extraordinary relevance in modern conditions, which are so often described as the "knowledge economy," "knowledge-based economy," "information society" etc. These phrases refer in actual fact to the activities of performers of conceptual or pre-material work. Scientists, engineers, technologists, computer programmers, designers and architects produce what may be called ideal means of economic activity, including material labour. Computer software, models, technical drawings, written or computer-generated instructions and manuals all constitute a necessary moment of many types of work, including above all material labour.

I.10.5. Substantive work

First and foremost, belonging and here very relevant under the capitalist mode of economic activity is work in the sphere of circulation, or commodity-money exchange. As such, this kind of labour does not add new value, or act on the use-value of a given good. However, some activities carried on in this domain are of indirectly material nature, as they meet the above condition. This applies to measuring, weighing, and packing done by shop assistants and their fellow employees. The wider the scope of such activities in commercial employees' work, the wider an extent in which they are engaged in (indirectly) material labour.

The sphere of circulation includes, too, a sphere of circulation of this peculiar form of commodity, which is money. Accordingly, Marx emphasised the role of credit for the capitalist system of economic activity, material production included. Regarding this, he stated, amongst others, in his ground-breaking work:

> The credit system, which in its first stages furtively creeps in as the humble assistant of accumulation, drawing into the hands of individual or associated capitalists, by invisible threads, the money resources which lie scattered, over the surface of society, in larger or smaller amounts; but it soon becomes a new and terrible weapon in the battle of competition and is finally transformed into an enormous social mechanism for the centralisation of capitals.
>
> Commensurately with the development of capitalist production and accumulation there develop the two most powerful levers of centralisation—competition and credit. (Marx 1976)

Thus, work associated with credit-financial operations should be undoubtedly included in the economic structure, as constituting in modern conditions an indispensable condition of the occurrence of economic processes. In this category one should also include work oriented on the realisation of use-values as exchange values, i.e. consumer credit. Still, financial work cannot be considered as either directly or indirectly material work, because what is missing in its case is the fulfilment of the criterion of empirically influencing use-value, which characterises each type of work considered in the previous subsection.

To sum up, the prime category of material labour is composed of not only work which directly produces material goods, but also all types of labour that is constitutive of the collective worker, i.e. constitutes one of his or her organs, under which guise both executive and pre-material work hide.

I.10.5.1. Work associated with private property of the means of economic activity and labour power as a substantive work

Whilst the place within the economy of all types of work considered so far raises no doubt even from the standard standpoint, an economic character of the activities which form the topic of the present subsection is, for what the eminent Canadian-American economist John Kenneth Galbraith used to call "the conventional wisdom," by no means so clear. Marx used the notion of productive labour as that which produces profit for the owner of the means of work. Thus, in his *Theories of Surplus Value* (often, and not without reason, called "Volume IV of *Capital*) he makes it clear that:

> An actor, for example, or even a clown, according to this definition, is a productive labourer if he works in the service of a capitalist (an entrepreneur) to whom he returns more labour than he receives from him in the form of wages; while a jobbing tailor who comes to the capitalist's house and patches his trousers for him, producing a mere use-value for him, is an unproductive labourer. The former's labour is exchanged with capital, the latter's with revenue. The former's labour produces a surplus-value; in the latter's, revenue is consumed.
>
> Productive and unproductive labour is here throughout conceived from the standpoint of the possessor of money, from the standpoint of the capitalist, not from that of the workman; hence the nonsense written by Ganilh, etc., who have so little understanding of the matter that they raise the question whether the labour or service or function of the prostitute, flunkey, etc., brings in returns.

> A writer is a productive labourer not in so far as he produces ideas, but in so far as he enriches the publisher who publishes his works, or if he is a wage-labourer for a capitalist.
>
> The use-value of the commodity in which the labour of a productive worker is embodied may be of the most futile kind. The material characteristics are in no way linked with its nature which on the contrary is only the expression of a definite social relation of production. It is a definition of labour which is derived not from its content or its result, but from its particular social form.
>
> On the other hand, on the assumption that capital has conquered the whole of production—and that therefore a commodity (as distinct from a mere use-value) is no longer produced by any labourer who is himself the owner of the conditions of production for producing this commodity—that therefore only the capitalist is the producer of commodities (the sole commodity excepted being labour-power)—then revenue must be exchanged either against commodities which capital alone produces and sells, or against labour, which just like those commodities is bought in order to be consumed; that is, only for the sake of its particular material characteristics, its use-value—for the sake of the services which, through its particular material characteristics, it renders to its buyer and consumer. For the producer of these services the services rendered are commodities. They have a definite use-value (imaginary or real) and a definite exchange-value. For the buyer, however, these services are mere use-values, objects in which hhe consumes his revenue. These unproductive labourers do not receive their share of revenue (of wages and profits), their co-partnership in the commodities produced by productive labour, gratis: they must buy their share in them; but they have nothing to do with their production. (Marx 1861)

However, the matter is not so clear-cut, as the above claim would suggest, for a member of the class in question may both render services and produce material goods (e.g. cooks). Marx's argument flows from his particular point of view, which is one of the capitalist. Be that as it may, it shows that the word "productive" can be ambiguous.

> It is, however, in any case clear: the greater the part of the revenue (wages and profit) that is spent on commodities produced by capital, the less the part that can be spent on the services of unproductive labourers, and vice versa.
>
> The determinate material form of the labour, and therefore of its product, in itself has nothing to do with this distinction between productive and unproductive labour. For example, the cooks and waiters in a public hotel are productive labourers, in so far as their labour is transformed into capital for the proprietor of the hotel. These same persons are unproductive labourers as menial servants, inasmuch as I do not make capital out of their

> services, but spend revenue on them. In fact, however, these same persons are also for me, the consumer, unproductive labourers in the hotel. (Marx 1861–3)

Meanwhile, from our viewpoint there is a definite difference between those exemplary embodiments of the Marxian category: "productive worker" who are, respectively, a cook employed in a privately-owned restaurant, and an artist, for example a singer, employed in the entertainment industry. The former performs in fact directly material labour, as he or she produces specific consumer goods in the form of particular dishes. Their fellow employee such as a waiter, however, just as the above-mentioned singer, does merely substantive labour, since he or she in no way acts upon the use-value of a specific good. To an even greater extent, to be sure, the above characteristics refer to the aforementioned tailor who works for a private client.

Thus, from the standpoint of socio-economic structuralism, any mechanical translation of Marxian categories of productive and unproductive labour into, respectively, material and substantive is ruled out. Our position departs from that of Marx also insofar as domestic servants, etc. are still viewed as performers of substantive work, since their activities bring in the means of subsistence. The fact that they do not bring in profit in any sense is irrelevant here. Another difference relative to Marx's position is concerned with the fact that while socio-economic structuralism pays lumpenwork its due, the author of *Capital* theoretically dismisses prostitutes, beggars and other participants of, in our terms, the lumpeneconomy. Even more importantly, it is to be noted that Marx constructed his concept of productive labour analysing the capitalist, based on exploitation, mode of production. Meanwhile, within the capitalist economic formation of society, there function also numerous representatives of the mode of economic activity who do not employ any wage-labour, and thus are not, by definition, exploiters of other people's labour power. One can mention here such work as that of owners of artisan workshops, self-employed agents, including individual suppliers of various services, including professionals such as lawyers, physicians, advisers and consultants.

I.10.6. The definition of services

Even a superficial glance at the relevant literature leads to the conclusion that the headline question is indeed a thorny issue. Let us, therefore, clear up at least some if not all misunderstandings which one encounters in this field. Often as a defining feature of services the point is raised that they vanish in the process of their consumption. However, it is not a primary, but rather secondary trait of services, since by any means each of them possesses this characteristic. What is distinctive about services is, rather, the fact that they come up as not objectified, but living labour, or work, for that matter. This kind of activity may be defined as a useful action of the labour power which directly satisfies wants of a given individual. That is to say, services satisfy personal needs in the form of an action itself, as opposed to a good or commodity.

We must deal with one more fairly common mistake as well. As indicated above, services are rendered in relation to individual persons. It follows that the activities of the policemen, government or local officials or the military etc. are not classified under that rubric. All these people satisfy by virtue of their activities some needs and interests of society as a whole, which is not the case of typical services, such as education, health services, private eyes, pop musicians, clergymen and so on and so forth.

I.10.7. Non-substantive work

The above listing of some characteristic services must be supplemented by an elucidation of the relation of the services to the category of substantive work. This leads us in a natural way to the concept correlative of the notion of substantive work. Put simply, under the category of non-substantive work one should place all these activities that bring in the means of material and spiritual existence, but are not identical to any types of substantive work which are, it should be kept in mind, part and parcel of the economy. It follows that non-substantive work should be located in the non-economic sphere. And indeed, this applies to all types of work, as opposed to quasi-work, which support respective varieties of non-economic structures. Let us briefly, as the very topic has been taken up above, indicate that in the case of the reproductive structure one has to do with physicians, nurses, sportsmen, film and theatrical actors, circus acrobats, jugglers etc. Insofar as the ideational structure is concerned, its primary constituents are scholars, university lecturers, librarians, journalists etc. The political structure, in turn, is composed primarily of work done by the central government members and officials, as well their equivalents at the level of local authorities, judges, prosecutors, prison guards, the military and the police.

What must be kept in mind here is that the categorisation of the above-mentioned types of work is not fixed once for all, as it is dependent not on their exterior, observable characteristics by themselves, but on their in-depth socio-economic reading. Thus, whilst a physician employed in a public hospital belongs in the substructure under consideration, her or his fellow doctor working in a private clinic is in a totally different situation, as they do substantive labour. Equally, teachers of public schools are in a different position than those employed in private schools. Working as a BBC journalist is one thing, and to be employed as a broadcaster in privately-owned media quite another. That said, we may, finally, restrict ourselves to reminding the reader that, as it is the case in all societal structures generally, those aformentioned also include para-work, quasi-work, and lumpenwork.

I.10.8. Social consciousness

This broad category comprises such ideal substructures as law, morality, religion, science, art, philosophy and social customs. This is not to say, as the above listing might imply, that these are kind of free-floating items. Nothing can be further from the truth. It is only upon careful investigation that one is able to determine their ultimate location in society. What we mean is the fact that this place is variable, depending on whether given moral, legal or customary norms become necessary premises of executing definite types of work. For example, if a legal ruling concerning the maximum working hours or minimum wage plays the role of a stimulus of action of industrial managers, then such rules become integral components of the economy. The parallel situation may repeat itself in the case of other societal substructures. In the case of social consciousness considerable caution is needed, since in many instances it is only upon careful investigation that the role of a given element can be established. For example, some political slogans, which appear to be merely spin, epiphenomenal ideology or a publicity stunt, may upon an analysis in more detail play a certain actual social role such as ideas attracting new party members or helping to win elections, even if the winning party has never seriously intended to implement them.

In conclusion, we may refer the reader to an explicit or hidden role that in the foregoing has been played by the notion of property. Ownership is, as a matter of fact, something whose importance in the economy cannot be over-estimated. This question has been, at least in part, addressed previously in the chapter on Becker, where a positive theory of ownership of the labour power has been laid out. However, there is, of course, much more to the issue of property, far too frequently in our opinion glossed over or put on the back burner by many scholars considered to be economic sociologists, than that. In particular, numerous misunderstandings over the notion in question require an analysis at more length. In addition this analysis, carried out in the next chapter, is the basis for a further discourse, concerning in actual fact not only social groups which are rooted in the economic property relations, but also, as it will be seen, groups functioning as social cells of the non-economic sphere.

I.10.9. Structure and Agency

Property as well other issues referred to at the end of the previous section will be analysed at length in the next chapter. Meanwhile, the final section of the present chapter, that is to say, where the reader's knowledge of the socio-economic structuralist theory of society can be taken for granted, is a proper place to take up an important but often misconstrued problem of human agency vs. structure.

The theory of structuration, proposed by Anthony Giddens (1984) in *The Constitution of Society* (mentioned also in *Central Problems of Social Theory* 1979), is an attempt to reconcile theoretical dichotomies of social systems such as agency/structure, subjective/objective, and micro/macro perspectives. The approach does not focus on the individual actor or societal totality "but social practices ordered across space and time" (1984, 2). Its proponents adopt this purportedly balanced position, attempting to treat influences of structure (which inherently includes culture) and agency equally.

To put it in a nutshell, the theory of structuration[3] holds that all human action is performed within the context of a pre-existing social structure which is governed by a set of norms and / or laws which are distinct from those of other social structures. Therefore, all human action is at least partly predetermined based on the varying contextual rules under which it occurs. However, the structure and rules are not permanent and external, but sustained and modified by human action in a textbook example of reflexive feedback. The theory under consideration posits, and rightly so (just recall our critique of, *inter alia*, Homans), that social life is not the sum of all micro-level activity (e.g. dyads). On the other hand, and this point is equally undisputable, social activity cannot be completely explained from a macro perspective.

What then is the relationship of the two to each other? The repetition of the acts of individual agents reproduce the structure. Social structures are neither inviolable nor permanent. The social structures constrain the

---

[3] This paragraph draws on information retrieved from http://en.wikipedia.org/wiki/Structuration.

actions of individual agents. Thus structure and action constrain each other in an evolving way. Structuration theory aims to avoid extremes of both structural (attributed to structural functionalism and Marxism) or agent (supposedly displayed by so-called interpretive sociologists) determinism. The balancing of agency and structure is referred to as the duality of structure: social structures make social action possible, and at the same time that social action creates those very structures.

For Giddens, structures are rules and resources (sets of transformation relations) organized as properties of social systems. Rules are patterns people may follow in social life. Resources relate to what is created by human action; they are not given by nature (explained further below). Here one comes across the first limitation of the theory under examination. As was apparent from the above discussed notion of material work, and will be also evident from the section on economic property below, natural phenomena and processes are part and parcel of society. Raw materials are objects of work already transformed by human work, but for them to exist one must assume also the pre-existence of, for example, mineral resources from which such raw materials can arise. In short, neither the concept of society nor that of social structure is reducible to human action, even including its product. Theories that overlook this essential fact could be dubbed pan-humanist (anthropic) or over-antinaturalist.

The structuration theory employs a recursive notion of actions constrained and enabled by structures which are produced and reproduced by those actions. These features caused that Giddens' approach has been adopted by those with structuralist inclinations, but who wish to situate such structures in human practice rather than reify them as an ideal type or material property. Some of our earlier suspicions are corroborated when we learn that the theory under investigation is different, for example, from Actor-Network Theory which grants a certain autonomy to technical artifacts. In turn, that the distinction between discursive and practical knowledge made by the theory of structuration is again irrefutable, but hardly eye-opening. Similarly, on the basis of mainstream sociology, it is commonplace to recognize actors as having knowledge is reflexive and situated, and that habitual use becomes institutionalized. According to the theory, a social system can be understood by its structure, modality, and interaction. Structure is constituted by rules and resources governing and available to agents (authoritative resources control persons, whereas allocative resources control material objects). This definition of "resources" is rather unfortunate; one can detect here the trace of property rights theory but, to an even greater extent, influences of a position that can be described as pan-dominationalism, i.e. a kind of reductionism where different social relations are treated as merely different varieties of the same essential core, i.e. power, control or authority.

Going further, the modality of a structural system is the means by which structures are translated into action. Interaction is the activity instantiated by the agent acting within the social system. It is murky, to say the least. Why should an act of a single agent be termed interaction given that the latter concept, by definition, refers to actions of at least two actors influencing one another?

Social systems have patterns of social relations that exist over time; the changing nature of space and time will determine the interaction of social relations and therefore structure. For example, nineteenth century Britain set out certain rules for that time and space. Those rules affected the action which determines structure and the structure was upheld as long as it was reproduced in action. It is a sign of an excessive self-confidence and over-estimation to claim that hitherto social structures or "models of society" were taken to be beyond the realm of human control—the positivistic approach; the other social theory would be that of action creating society—the interpretivist approach. Accordingly, we had to wait many years for a sociological saviour to come. It comes as no surprise that immersed in such euphoric proponents of the structure approach one can reach the conclusion that that they are one and the same—different sides to the coin of a similar problem of order.

Agency, as Giddens calls it, is human action. To be human is to be an agent, although not all agents are human beings. Advocates of animal rights would certainly welcome that proclamation. Less so, we are afraid, any reader of Giddens capable of logical thinking. How to reconcile the latter claim with the definition of action as necessarily reflexive? Agents' knowledge of their society informs their actions, which reproduce social structures, which in turn enforce and maintain the dynamics of action. Giddens defines "ontological security" as the trust people have in social structure; everyday actions have some degree of predictability, thus ensuring social stability. This observation is, again, a textbook commonplace. This stable predictability or predictable stability does not always maintain, though, as the possession of agency allows one to break away from normative actions, and depending on the sum of social factors at work, they may instigate shifts in the social structure. The dynamic between agency and structure makes such generative action possible.

Thus agency can lead to both the reproduction and the transformation of society. Another way to explain this concept is by what Giddens calls the "reflexive monitoring of actions" (1991, 36). Reflexive monitoring looks at the ability judge actions' effectiveness in achieving their objectives:

if agents can reproduce structure through action, they can also transform it. The creator of structuration theory should be praised for distinguishing those two types of change, but otherwise this approach remains vague. To state that agents are able to act in such a way so as to transform social structures is one thing, to determine on what conditions and in what situations they are able to do so is quite another. Without this indispensable supplement, the theory hangs in the air, remaining an unsuccessful attempt to integrate action and structure, failing to split those proverbial two sides of the coin. Merely to pass such a judgment is hardly sufficient, though, as it is rather sterile. A fruitful approach is, instead, to look for the reasons of the project's failure. They seem to lie in poor conceptual armoury. In particular, in the theory of structuration the notion of structural contradiction is missing. Contradiction is that link bridging statics and dynamics, reproduction and transformation or generation (a qualitatively new state of a given structure or a new structure). Before turning to an explication of the concept concerned, a comment regarding grounds on which to distinguish a birth of a new structure from qualitative changes remaining, however, within the framework of the structure concerned is required. In order to make this distinction an additional concept is needed, that of "structural core." This comprises a subset of those structural components that endow a given structure with its identity. For example, one can drive a car with broken glasses (non-core element) but without an engine any chance of a ride evaporates. So long as ongoing changes do not infringe the core, we are still dealing with the same structure, whatever secondary changes it has been subject to. The merit of the concept of contradiction stems from its dialectical character; contradiction may be defined as such relationships between components of a structure that the same phenomena that are responsible for its reproduction (simple or extended which refers to a quantitative change) cause its qualitative change or transformation. Such an approach forces one to search for, first of all, internal sources of change before trying to identify external ones. Moreover, the impact of the latter must always be investigated as mediated by the internal condition of a given structure, including its contradictions above all.

Our criticism levied at the existence of "black holes" in Giddens' analytical framework appears to be an adequate metaphor considering the fact that damage to other areas of structuration theory, by those absent concepts, is aggravated by its next part. Giddens distinguishes three types of structures in social systems: those of signification, legitimation, and domination. These are analytical distinctions, rather than distinct ideal types, that mobilize and reinforce one another.

Signification produces meaning through organized webs of language (semantic codes, interpretive schemes and discursive practices).

Legitimation produces a moral order via naturalization in societal norms, values and standards.

Domination produces (and is an exercise of) power, originating from the control of resources.

To understand how they work together, consider how the signification of a concept (e.g. the use of the word "patriot" in political speech) borrows from and contributes to legitimization (e.g. nationalistic norms) and coordinates forms of domination (e.g. a police state) from which it in turn gains further force.

Whatever merits there are to the above threefold taxonomy, it is miles away from constituting a fully blown theory of society. For this very reason an ambitious attempt was made by one of Giddens' supporters, Sewell (1992), to specify what has remained an underspecified aspect of the theory: the question "Why are structural changes possible?" is unsatisfactory. He argues that changes arises from: "The multiplicity of structures—societies are based on practices that derived from many distinct structures, which exist at different levels, operate in different modalities, and are themselves based on widely varying types and quantities of resources." The transposability of rules can be "applied to a wide and not fully predictable range of cases outside the context in which they were initially learned." This also takes account of the unpredictability of resource accumulation (e.g. investment, military tactics, or a comedian's repertoire), the polysemy of resources (e.g. to what should success in resource accumulation be attributed?), and the intersection of structures (e.g. in the structure of capitalist society there are both the modes of production based on private property and profit, as well as the mode of labor organization based on worker solidarity) (Sewel 1992, 16–19).

It is our contention that for the issue of causes of structural change to be effectively resolved, one has to dispose of a social theory worthy its name, inclusive of a rich set of conceptual tools that might serve to identify specific societal structures and the state of their internal and external relationships. That Giddens, sorry to say, fails to comprehend certain concepts which he himself uses, as the example of the "mode of production" clearly shows. Otherwise, Giddens would not compare the concept in question with one concerning a mode of workers' organisation; the latter, at first glance, is not concerned with relations of production.

The fact of the matter, however, is that the situation is even worse. Giddens unwittingly uses two related concepts, but remains blithely unaware of their intimate relationship. For this to come to his knowledge he would have to, firstly, understand the role of property relations as a foundation of the capitalist mode of economic activity and, secondly, conceive of the latter in economic terms. Nothing betrays that Giddens really has such knowledge. The affinity mentioned above stems from the fact that whilst the former of the two concepts refers, of course, to private property of the means of production, the latter may in some situations, refer also to the relations of ownership, but this time it is collective ownership of labour power which is at stake. A defender of Giddens might at this juncture object on the grounds that he is not obliged to be acquainted with the content of the above concepts, and he / she would be absolutely right were it not for one tiny detail. What is the point of using such concepts, the meaning of which one does not understand?

As it turns out, other scholars also find structuration theory implausible. Notably, Margaret Archer raises a similar point to our own observation put forward above. She, namely, draws attention to centralization as reducible to the exercise of power by determinate actors.
She charges Giddens with:

> The voluntaristic bias [which] means that institutions are what people produce, not what they confront—and have to grapple with in ways which are themselves conditioned by the structural features involved.
>
> For Giddens institutional recursiveness never reflects the durability of constraint: it always represents the continuity of reproduction. Only at this level does Giddens concede that "unintended consequences of action" stretch beyond the recursive effects of the duality of structure … producing what others would term "emergent properties," but which he calls "self-regulating properties." Immediately and categorically he asserts that it is their facilitating effects upon which theory should centre—"the self-regulating properties of social systems must be grasped via a theory of system contradiction" … The reason for this one-sidedness is that to Giddens contradictions represent cracks through which radical change can be forced by social conflict—"ceteris paribus, conflict and contradiction have a tendency to coincide" (1979, 144). (Archer 2010)

Thus, from Archer's analysis, it follows that the so-called duality structure is not the only dualism written into his approach. Contradiction is to account for transformation but has nothing to do with reproduction, so that the dualism of two types of change reasserts itself.

CHAPTER I.11.

OWNERSHIP, CLASS AND ESTATE

I.11.1. The two faces of ownership

The recent exchange between Demsetz & Frischmann (2007) has been focused on one particular (albeit significant) problem of copyright. This section of the book sets out to tackle an underlying question of how the flagship term of the whole approach representted by Harold Demsetz, and many other scholars for that matter, is to be understood.

Ownership is of more than merely academic interest. In particular, the recent worldwide privatization drive put the issue of ownership high on the agenda. Since it is also one of the most contentious theoretical issues and a focus of a whole host of pressing social problems, it is worth discussing in rather more detail. Despite, or perhaps because of, the fact that the concept in question appears to be self-evident, there is clearly no consensus among social scientists on its precise meaning. Some writers use the terms "ownership" and "property" interchangeably, while others distinguish ownership from property. More importantly, by no means all sociologists and economists are aware of a distinction between legal ownership (or property, for that matter) and economic ownership. It is not only that certain distinctions drawn by property lawyers such as those between "property" and "property rights" are irrelevant to economic analysis and can be ignored.

I.11.1.1. Legal vs. Economic ownership

Let us, therefore, enumerate more systematically at least some of the reasons for the inadequacy of this more common legal approach. This criticism is not towards the jurisprudential theory of property as such (which, of course, retains its relevance within its proper domain), as its indiscriminate use in positive or empirically grounded, as opposed to normative or dogmatic, realms of discourse lies at the heart of all the socio-economic analyses worthy their name. By the same token the scholars who subscribe to, as well as draw on the intellectual tradition represented by Karl Marx, Max Weber, Georg Simmel, Eugen von Böhm-Bawerk and other members of the Austrian school of political economy, who all have in common a tendency to distrust overgeneralized or reified concepts and step beyond formalistic fetishized legal notions to those relations that form the economic and social background of law, are by definition committed to this socio-economic perspective.

As has been implied above, ownership has a dual mode of existence, so to speak; economic ownership (to be defined later) is to be distinguished from legal ownership, which belongs to what Marxists call the superstructure, as opposed to the economic base of society. While the law generally sanctions the economic relations of ownership, the latter rarely correspond to the prevailing legal forms. Public or state ownership has varying economic and sociological contents or meanings depending on its concrete historical context. Compare, for instance, the ancient East, where the state, personified by the king, was the owner of immense land property, artisans' workshops etc., with the modern West with its often quite high degree of public ownership, or with the "socialist" nations of Eastern Europe, where government ownership was dominant. On the other hand, one and the same economic relation of ownership may find its expression in a variety of legal forms. For instance, legal arrangements concerning property in land differed greatly in the former Soviet Union, Czechoslovakia and Eastern Germany, yet real economic relations of ownership were very similar in all those countries. Furthermore, many legal concepts operate at too high a level of abstraction to be suitable for economic (and sociological) analysis. This applies, among others, to the crucial concept of the "corporation." The emergence of the joint-stock company as a major method of business organization involves legal recognition of the corporation itself as the owner of its assets. But economic ownership can be an attribute of only private or "natural," as opposed to legal, persons (or their groups). To recognise a corporation as the owner of its capital does not answer any of the following questions, which are relevant for economic or sociological analysis. Does the corporation belong to the body of shareholders as a whole or a portion of them? What is the corporation's managers" ownership status? Is economic ownership wielded by the company's employees as well? Does the concept of indirect ownership through employee pension funds apply here? What is the extent of foreign ownership? and so on. Standard jurisprudential thought fails to penetrate beneath this "corporate veil." It is not only with respect to the subject of ownership that jurisprudential analysis of property is found wanting. The same applies to its object. Property can be not only in physical "things" such as machines or land, or in incorporeal or intangible objects such as patents, but also in the labour power or, in Max Weber's terms, *Arbeitsqualifikationen*. More generally, there are many economic property relations that are not taken account of by the law. To own some object is not necessarily to have a legal title to it. The legal approach to property, by focusing on the holder of a legal document containing provisions enforceable through the courts, disregards, among other things, a host of illegal relations composing the black or hidden economy. Putting it another way, economic relations of ownership can rest not only on legal provisions but also on informal agreements, social customs or conventions, etc.

I.11.1.2. Property rights theory critically considered

With all its sophisticated analytic approach to ownership, the property rights theory retains, unfortunately, many essential features of jurisprudential doctrine of property. Thus, for instance, Furubotn & Pejovich state that "at any moment of time there is a legally sanctioned structure of property rights in existence" (1972, 1142). Elsewhere they write that "to argue for a change in the content of the right of ownership is to argue for a change in the allocation of resources to which legal support is given" (1972, 1140). They also maintain that the right to ownership "... is limited only by these restrictions that are explicitly stated in the law" (1972:1140). It is only from the narrow legal perspective, however, that ownership is subject to none but "legal restrictions" (Pejovich 1990, 28). In reality, ownership is also conditioned by current conventions, attitudes, group habits etc. In addition, the property rights writers sometimes fail to penetrate beneath the formal-legal surface insofar as they continue to consider the state and other legal persons as owners. Alchian & Demsetz, for instance, speak about "corporate, school and church owners of property" (1973, 19). In fairness to the property rights school, however, it should be noted that no such legal treatment of ownership is inherent in its theoretical framework. This is shown, for example, by the following statement:

> the (property) rights we have may be the product of the legislative process and may be enforced by a third party: usually the third party is the government ... rules which establish rights may not have third-party enforcement. In this case they carry weight in the decisions of individuals simply because individuals recognise and respect behavioral limits for themselves and others. (McKenzie & Tullock 1978, 78)

In the words of another pair of authors, "the attenuation of the stockholders' property rights in the firm and the 'rule of management' result not from legal restraints on private property rights, but from the costs to the owners of detecting and policing managerial decisions and of enforcing wealth maximising behaviour" (Furubotn & Pejovich 1972, 1149). Alchian notes that "the rights of individuals to the use of resources (i.e. property rights) in any society are to be construed as supported by the force of etiquette, social custom, ostracism, and formal legally enacted laws supported by the state's "power of violence and punishment" (1977, 129). Granted that all vestiges of the legal view of property would be removed, there remains a problem of how that economic ownership is to be understood. The property rights school draws its definition of ownership from Roman law. According to this classic definition, "the right of ownership in an asset consists of three elements: (a) the right to use the asset (*usus*), (b) the right to appropriate returns from the asset (*usus fructus*), and (c) the right to change the asset's form and/or substance (*abusus*) (Furubotn and Pejovich 1974, 4).

One of the inconveniences of such a broad concept is the difficulty of identifying the owner when property rights in a given asset are partitioned between two or more persons. The property rights writers handle such problematic cases in a not quite satisfactory and rather ambiguous way. Alchian, for instance, admits that a lease or rental agreement "does contain transfers of some of the rights that are included in ownership" (1977, 133). So is the lease holder the owner (or perhaps a part-owner)? No, answers Alchian, because in this case the rights are divided on a temporary basis, and therefore the right of ownership rests essentially with the leaser. But what if the ownership rights are partitioned on a permanent rather than temporary basis?

A case in point is the business corporation. The innovation of the corporation was a startling change in property rights as traditionally conceived. The corporation scattered among many persons the rights of ownership. Under it, those who supply capital in both equity or debt forms and enjoy the income generated by that capital may be quite different from those who direct the use of the capital. This much is acknowledged by Alchian & Demsetz who write that:

> instead of thinking of shareholders as joint owners, we can think of them as investors, like bondholders … If we treat bondholders, preferred and convertible preferred stockholders, and common stockholders and warrant holders as simply different classes of investors … why should stockholders be regarded as "owners" in any sense distinct from the other financial investors? (Alchian & Demsetz 1972, 789)

They go on to note that "the entrepreneur-organizer, who let us assume is the chief operating officer and sole repository of control of the corporation, does not find his authority residing in common stockholders" (Alchian & Demsetz 1972, 789). Does it mean that it is this "chief operating officer" who should be called the owner of the firm? In another paper one can find an even more unequivocal statement to the effect that in the case of the publicly-held corporation:

> a small management group becomes the *de facto* owners. Effective ownership, i.e. effective control of property, is thus legally concentrated in management's hands … shareholders are essentially lenders of equity capital and not owners … What shareholders really own are their shares and not the corporation. Ownership in the sense of control again becomes a largely individual affair. The shareholders own their shares, and the president of the corporation and possibly a few other top executives control the corporation. (Demsetz 1967, 358–9)

The problem with such contentions is that they are inconsistent with the property rights writers' own definition of ownership and that they undermine the whole logic of their arguments about the need for monitoring managers or the principal-agent problem, etc. It does not help much when "ownership of capital" is distinguished from "ownership of the firm" (Rowley 1982, 40) since such "escape hatches" do not sit well with the property rights writers' statements more in line with the conventional conception of the structure of ownership of the corporation, such as: "the manager need not be an owner or even part owner in the firm" (Alchian & Woodward 1988, 72).

Similar ambiguity pertains to the property rights scholars' treatment of public ownership. On the one hand, it is asserted that, according with its label, this kind of property is owned by the public at large. Alchian even stresses that "public ownership must be borne by all members of the public" (1977, 139). More nuances, but at the same time ambiguities, are found in Nutter, who argues as follows:

> If an abstract entity such as the state is to be called the owner, then government must be the concrete agency charged with trusteeship. Government will be … responsible to some group of persons for whom it is acting as agent, and it will presumably be responsive at least indirectly to their interests. Ultimately, then, the persons controlling government are the effective owners of state-owned enterprises, while government or some part of it serves as manager. (Nutter 1974, 222)

Note a shift in the criteria used to identify the owner of public enterprises.

To put it in a nutshell, beneficiaries have been replaced by controllers. and with that probably the locus of ownership has shifted as well; it is not the community at large, as in the former case, but probably some narrower group of people, not specified by Nutter, that is to be regarded as the owner of state enterprises. Pejovich is more specific in naming "the ruling group" as the owners of the means of production (1974, 351–2). In another paper, written with Furubotn, he speaks of "the state's ownership of the firm" (Furubotn & Pejovich 1972, 1154).

Picot & Kaulmann take a compromise position in describing the structure of property rights in government-owned enterprises in the following way: "the right to coordinate (to acquire and to allocate) resources is mainly in the hands of the managers of these corporations; the right to appropriation of profits (and losses) and the right to capitalization (to transfer all property rights to new owners) is in the hands of the government" (1989, 300).

This claim is not satisfactory, however, if for no other reason because government "appropriates" revenues from public enterprises not on its own account but on behalf of the citizenry. While the pinpointing of those who benefit from the expenditures of government (or tax reductions) may be difficult, nothing alters the fact that these benefits, however allocated, are real.

I.11.1.3. The rent theory of economic ownership

In other words, according to the present writer, ownership should be looked at as a benefit. And, incidentally, the authors seem to notice this as they write about "the citizens that are represented by the government" (Picot & Kaulmann 1989, 300). Be that as it may, it is difficult to escape the judgment that all in all we are presented with a plethora of views on the question of ownership of so-called state-owned enterprises.

It follows from the above discussion that the relationship between control and what Berle & Means term "beneficial ownership" may constitute a matter of dispute. According to the present writer it is, as indicated above, precisely this ability to benefit, as distinct from the ability to control, that constitutes the substance of ownership. In many cases these two aspects coincide with each other, but this is not necessarily the case and those who benefit need not be those who control or make decisions concerning the use of given objects. Because the users themselves do not decide on the admission hours to a botanical garden or because there is a state institution that manages public forests, the objects in question do no cease to be common property (because everyone can enjoy them). The fact that the state grants access to fish in rivers and lakes does not turn the fish into government property.

This conceived distinction between legal and economic ownership has nothing in common with the conception, quite popular in certain circles, according to which:

> Legal ownership is simple enough. It constitutes the various forms of legal title to property in the means of production. The usual form of such ownership in advanced capitalism is stock ownership ... economic ownership is the most complex ... Bettelheim (1975) defines it as "the power to assign the objects on which it bears (especially the means of production) to specific uses and to dispose of the products obtained through these means of production (p. 58)." Less abstractly, this means control over the flow of resources into production (i.e., investment and accumulation). (Wright 1979, 33)

The above-mentioned notion of legal ownership as something distinct from economic ownership is both common sense and superficial; to own a legal title to a portion of equity capital may or may not express economic ownership of capital or, to be more specific, real, as opposed to nominal, economic ownership of capital. There are a number of specific criteria by which to determine whichever is the case. Firstly, a given shareholding expresses real economic ownership of share capital if it could be transformed into ownership of a factory or other production unit. Secondly, if it yields income permitting its recipient to live without working. In the case of employee shareholders, they are to be classified as owners of capital rather than labour power when (1) their shareholdings are worth more than their labour power, and (2) their packages of stock are for them a more important source of the means of subsistence than their wages. Thus, as is easy to see, our view as to what is simple and what is complex is somewhat different from that of Wright.

His false (in our view) notion of ownership underlies his misplaced fights against various conceptual straw men, as in the following example: "For the managerial revolution proponents to prove their case, therefore, it is not enough to show that stock is widely dispersed. They must show that real economic ownership is in the hands of nonowning, professional managers, i.e., that they actually control the accumulation process as a whole" (Wright 1979, 35). Freiherr von Munchhausen, famous for his book of incredible adventures, told the readers how he pulled himself out of a swamp by tugging on his own hair. Wright's manner of escaping a self-created conceptual trap bears strong resemblance to Munchhausen's trick:

> Class structures may … differ not simply in terms of the relative magnitudes of contradictory locations, but also in the ambiguous locations that exist at the boundaries of the basic class locations.
>
> The existence of such ambiguous locations indicates the theoretical limits of a purely structural analysis of classes. Classes are not simply slots within a social structure; they are also organised social forces. The decisive question, then, is how these ambiguous class locations (as well as contradictory locations) become formed into classes; this, in turn, depends on class struggle, not just class structure. (Wright 1979, 49)

This escape hatch is rather awkward, to say the least. The whole point of any class theory worthy of its name is to provide a complete map of a given socio-economic dimension of social life and we hope that our own theory matches such expectations.

In addition, it must be pointed out that the benefits inherent in the ownership of the factors of economic activity always are, to a lesser or larger extent, gratuitous. It is precisely for that reason that, referring to the economic notion of rent as an unearned income, our whole approach to property may be called: "the rent theory."

It is in these terms that Marx proceeds in *Capital* (Vol. I, ch. 7), using a number of examples from modern capitalism, though it has to be stressed that the basic nature of economic ownership is universal, i.e. present in other economic formations of society as well. This is, incidentally, emphasised by Marx in, amongst others, the following statement:

> The soil (and this, economically speaking, includes water) in the virgin state in which it supplies man with necessaries or the means of subsistence ready to hand, exists independently of him, and is the universal subject of human labour. All those things which labour merely separates from immediate connexion with their environment, are subjects of labour spontaneously provided by Nature. Such are fish which we catch and take from their element, water, timber which we fell in the virgin forest, and ores which we extract from their veins. (Marx 1976)

It is true that this extraction of ores, coal, crude oil and other mineral deposits always requires some expenditure of human labour power. But can even the greatest effort of a worker equate with millions of years required for the natural processes to produce these forms of wealth? If the crucial aspect of economic property is apparent in the case of even transhistorically understood work, the more this is the case in the most developed system of production and labour, including exploitation of nature itself, as Marx points out:

> … that the productive forces resulting from co-operation and division of labour cost capital nothing. They are natural forces of social labour. So also physical forces, like steam, water, etc., when appropriated to productive processes, cost nothing. But just as a man requires lungs to breathe with, so he requires something that is work of man's hand, in order to consume physical forces productively. A water-wheel is necessary to exploit the force of water, and a steam-engine to exploit the elasticity of steam. Once discovered, the law of the deviation of the magnetic needle in the field of an electric current, or the law of the magnetisation of iron, around which an electric current circulates, cost never a penny. But the exploitation of these laws for the purposes of telegraphy, etc., necessitates a costly and extensive apparatus. The tool, as we have seen, is not exterminated by the machine. From being a dwarf implement of the human organism, it expands and multiplies into the implement of a mechanism created by man. Capital now sets the labourer to work, not with a manual tool, but with a machine which itself handles the tools. Although, therefore, it is clear at the first glance that, by incorporating both stupendous physical forces, and the natural sciences, with the process of production, modern industry raises the productiveness of labour to an extraordinary degree, it is by no means equally clear, that this increased productive force is not, on the other hand, purchased by an increased expenditure of labour. (Marx 1976)

As if proceeding on the basis of the definition given above, Marx illuminates this ownership effect:

> Machinery, like every other component of constant capital, creates no new value, but yields up its own value to the product that it serves to beget. In so far as the machine has value, and, in consequence, parts with value to the product, it forms an element in the value of that product. Instead of being cheapened, the product is made dearer in proportion to the value of the machine. And it is clear as noon-day, that machines and systems of machinery, the characteristic instruments of labour of Modern Industry, are incomparably more loaded with value than the implements used in handicrafts and manufactures.
>
> [...] the machinery, while always entering as a whole into the labour-process, enters into the value-begetting process only by bits. It never adds more value than it loses, on an average, by wear and tear. Hence there is a great difference between the value of a machine, and the value transferred in a given time by that machine to the product. The longer the life of the

> machine in the labour-process, the greater is that difference. It is true, no doubt, as we have already seen, that every instrument of labour enters as a whole into the labour-process, and only piece-meal, proportionally to its average daily loss by wear and tear, into the value-begetting process. But this difference between the instrument as a whole and its daily wear and tear, is much greater in a machine than in a tool, because the machine, being made from more durable material, has a longer life; because its employment, being regulated by strictly scientific laws, allows of greater economy in the wear and tear of its parts, and in the materials it consumes; and lastly, because its field of production is incomparably larger than that of a tool. After making allowance, both in the case of the machine and of the tool, for their average daily cost, that is for the value they transmit to the product by their average daily wear and tear, and for their consumption of auxiliary substance, such as oil, coal, and so on, they each do their work gratuitously, just like the forces furnished by Nature without the help of man. The greater the productive power of the machinery compared with that of the tool, the greater is the extent of its gratuitous service compared with that of the tool. In modern industry man succeeded for the first time in making the product of his past labour work on a large scale gratuitously, like the forces of Nature. (Marx 1976)

In another part of his work, Marx reveals an analoguous nature of what will be in the present book termed "material labour":

> While productive labour is changing the means of production into constituent elements of a new product, their value undergoes a metempsychosis. It deserts the consumed body, to occupy the newly created one. But this transmigration takes place, as it were, behind the back of the labourer. He is unable to add new labour, to create new value, without at the same time preserving old values, and this, because the labour he adds must be of a specific useful kind; and he cannot do work of a useful kind, without employing products as the means of production of a new product, and thereby transferring their value to the new product. The property therefore which labour-power in action, living labour, possesses of preserving value, at the same time that it adds it, is a gift of Nature which costs the labourer nothing, but which is very advantageous to the capitalist inasmuch as it preserves the existing value of his capital. So long as trade is good, the capitalist is too much absorbed in money-grubbing to take notice of this gratuitous gift of labour. A violent interruption of the labour-process by a crisis, makes him sensitively aware of it. (Marx 1976)

Elsewhere in *Capital*, Marx draws attention to the socio-economic nature of the relation: capital-labour power, which, as it turns out, brings about similar consequences and which extend far beyond the production of the surplus value, as his best known notion has it:

> I assume [...] that the capitalist advances the whole expenses, including the entire remuneration of the labourer" …
>
> Though the manufacturer" (i.e., the labourer) "has his wages advanced to him by his master, he in reality costs him no expense, the value of these wages being generally reserved, together with a profit, in the improved value of the subject upon which his labour is bestowed …
>
> The labourer is often compelled to make his individual consumption a mere incident of production. In such a case, he supplies himself with necessaries in order to maintain his labour-power, just as coal and water are supplied to the steam-engine and oil to the wheel. His means of consumption, in that case, are the mere means of consumption required by a means of production; his individual consumption is directly productive consumption. This, however, appears to be an abuse not essentially appertaining to capitalist production.
>
> The matter takes quite another aspect, when we contemplate, not the single capitalist, and the single labourer, but the capitalist class and the labouring class, not an isolated process of production, but capitalist production in full swing, and on its actual social scale. By converting part of his capital into labour-power, the capitalist augments the value of his entire capital. He kills two birds with one stone. He profits, not only by what he receives from, but by what he gives to, the labourer. The capital given in exchange for labour-power is converted into necessaries, by the consumption of which the muscles, nerves, bones, and brains of existing labourers are reproduced, and new labourers are begotten. Within the limits of what is strictly necessary, the individual consumption of the working class is, therefore, the reconversion of the means of subsistence given by capital in exchange for labour-power, into fresh labour-power at the disposal of capital for exploitation. It is the production and reproduction of that means of production so indispensable to the capitalist: the labourer himself. The individual consumption of the labourer, whether it proceed within the workshop or outside it, whether it be part of the process of production or not, forms therefore a factor of the production and reproduction of capital; just as cleaning machinery does, whether it be done while the machinery is working or while it is standing. The fact that the labourer consumes his means of subsistence for his own purposes, and not to please the capitalist, has no bearing on the matter. The consumption of food by a beast of burden is none the less a necessary factor in the process of production, because the beast enjoys what it eats. The maintenance and reproduction of the working class is, and must ever be, a necessary condition to the reproduction of capital. But the capitalist may safely leave its fulfilment to the labourer's instincts of self-preservation and of propagation. All the capitalist cares for, is to reduce the labourer's individual consumption as far as possible to what is strictly necessary.[...]

> Hence both the capitalist and his ideological representative, the political economist, consider that part alone of the labourer's individual consumption to be productive, which is requisite for the perpetuation of the class, and which therefore must take place in order that the capitalist may have labour-power to consume; what the labourer consumes for his own pleasure beyond that part, is unproductive consumption. If the accumulation of capital were to cause a rise of wages and an increase in the labourer's consumption, unaccompanied by increase in the consumption of labour-power by capital, the additional capital would be consumed unproductively. In reality, the individual consumption of the labourer is unproductive as regards himself, for it reproduces nothing but the needy individual; it is productive to the capitalist and to the State, since it is the production of the power that creates their wealth. (Marx 1976)

Of course, drawing attention to some less frequently discussed aspects of the capitalistic ownership of the means of production does not imply any underestimation of its key dimension, i.e. exploitation. As, however, the theory of exploitation hinges upon the labour theory of value, the latter should also be thoroughly examined.

I.11.1.3.1. The Labour Theory of Value

The sum total of objects available for appropriation in a given society or, in plain language, its wealth is anything useful produced by human labour from materials found in nature. In capitalist society, Marx stated, wealth takes the form of an immense accumulation of commodities. In modern conventional business parlance the term "commodity" refers to merely one class of them in terms of the theory under consideration, i.e. mass-produced goods, most notably products of extractive industries and agriculture. Meanwhile, from the perspective of the theory being discussed a commodity is an article of wealth produced for the purpose of being exchanged for other articles of wealth. Thus commodity production is an economic system where wealth is produced for sale, for the market. In its primitive forms it exists only on the outskirts of non-commodity producing societies where wealth is produced directly for use, either by the producers for themselves or by a subject class for their masters or, to put it in terms more congruent with socio-economic structuralism, in the form of material quasi-work, material work performed by domestic servants and by prisoners, i.e. persons deprived for a longer or shorter time of ownership of their labour power.

> The Labour Theory of Value is central to an understanding of the economics of capitalism because capitalism is commodity production par

excellence, and the Labour Theory of Value explains what determines the value of a commodity. Wondering what determines the proportions in which commodities exchange one for the other, Marx contrasts the role of money in simple commodity production with its role in the formula M-C-M. Here one finds the transformation of money into commodities, and the change of commodities back again into money; or buying in order to sell. Money that circulates in the latter manner (M-C-M) thereby becomes capital, and is already potentially capital (Marx 1976, Chapter IV).

The merchant who buys a commodity in order to sell it again is trying to obtain more money than with which they began. Money, or more generally the accumulation of capital, has become a motive in itself. But what a trader gains in monetary value in a trade another trader loses. So gains from trade cannot be generalized to the world as a whole as an explanation for the source of surplus value. Yet capitalism is a system in which capitalists systematically make profits from the buying and selling of commodities, including the buying of inputs into production and the selling of produced goods. How, in principle, is this possible? Marx's theory of exploitation answers this question,

Marx later expands M-C-M to M-C ... P ... C'-M' where money is used to purchase commodities consisting of the means of production and labour power. The capitalist removes these commodities from the market and they enter the production process P. The products re-enter the market as commodities which sell for money. (World Socialist Movement 2006)

To return for a moment to the indispensable foundation of surplus value, one may ask what all commodities have in common.

One conclusion we can draw from the fact that commodities consistently exchange for one another in fixed ratios is that all commodities must share some common characteristic to a greater or lesser degree. What? As articles of wealth, all commodities share two characteristics: they are useful and they are products of human labour. Which of these could provide a standard? Some have suggested usefulness (or utility), but the trouble here is that the same article can be useful to a greater or lesser degree to a different person. Usefulness is a personal matter: a personal relation between the commodity and its consumer. So utility would be a changing, subjective standard and could not explain why commodities consistently exchange at stable ratios. We are thus left with commodities as products of human labour.

Unlike usefulness, the amount of labour embodied in a commodity can be objectively measured—by how long it took to make it, for instance. However, all wealth, not just commodities, shares this characteristic of being a product of human labour. What we want to know is how do commodities differ from other forms of wealth. Wealth, we know, only takes the form of commodities under certain social conditions, specifically when it is produced for sale. Similarly with labour (used-up humanenergy):

under the same social conditions it becomes "value." Thus value is [...] a social property, a social relation. However, as value only expresses itself in exchange, as exchange value, this social relation appears as a relation between things. This is what is behind Marx's writing about the "fetishism of commodities." [...] Since the producers do not come into social contact with each other until they exchange their products, the specific social character of each producer's labour does not show itself except in the act of exchange.[1] [...]. (Marx 1967)

Commodity fetishism prevents socially necessary abstract labour from being perceived as the substance of value. Price is the monetary expression of value. Labour, holds the Labour Theory of Value, is the basis of value. But how does labour determine the value of a commodity? The value of a commodity, said Marx, is determined by the amount of socially necessary labour contained in it or, being the same thing, by the amount of socially necessary labour-time spent in producing it from start to finish. It is important to note that the Labour Theory of Value does not say that the value of a commodity is determined by the actual amount of labour contained in it. That would mean that an inefficient worker would create more value than an efficient worker. By socially necessary is meant the amount needed to produce, and reproduce, a commodity under average working conditions, e.g. average productivity, average intensity of labour. Under capitalism nearly everything is a commodity, or takes the form of a commodity, and is bought and sold. This qualification is necessary to counter the argument often advanced against the Labour Theory of Value—that some things that are bought and sold are either not products of labour or sell at prices quite out of proportion to the amount of labour embodied in them, e.g. land and objects of art. Land, under capitalism, has a price which, in its pure form, is merely the capitalisation of its rent. Land has no value as it is not the product of human labour. Paintings and antiques are indeed products of human labour but are not really commodities because they cannot be reproduced; the concept of "socially necessary labour" therefore has no meaning with reference to such articles. One silly objection is: why is a lump of gold from a meteorite valuable, when there is no labour embodied in it? Actually, this is a confirmation of the Labour Theory of Value since its value is the same as that of gold produced under normal conditions. If gold were to regularly fall from the skies then its value would drop to what is needed to collect it. Another thing that under capitalism takes the form of a commodity is labour power, i.e. the ability of human beings to work, human energy. Indeed this fact is the basis of capitalism since it presupposes the separation of the producers from the ownership and control of the means and instruments for producing wealth. But there is one very important difference between

[1] This is of course an excellent example of a suprapersonal social relation referred to earlier.

> labour power and other commodities: labour power is embodied in human beings who can think, act and struggle to get the best price for what they are selling (or rather, as opposed to this standard Marxist rendition, leasing out). Otherwise its value is fixed in the same way as that of other commodities: by the amount of socially necessary labour spent on creating it and recreating it. The labour spent on creating a person's labour power is that spent in producing the food, clothing, shelter and the other things needed to keep them in a fit state to work. Thus the value of an unskilled person's labour power is equal to about enough to keep them and their family alive and working. Skilled people get more because it costs more labour to produce and maintain their skills. When the worker finds an employer they are paid a wage, which is the price they are paid for allowing the employer to use their labour power for, say, eight hours. Wages, then, are a special kind of price; they are the monetary expression of the value of labour power.
>
> Labour power has a peculiar characteristic by means of which the author of *Capital* solved the conundrum of the existence and socioeconomic nature of capitalists' profits. […] labour power has the property of being able to produce and create new value […] […] So the source of all Rent, Interest and Profit is the unpaid labour of the working class.

To reiterate this crucial point: "labour power or capacity for labour is to be understood as the aggregate of those mental and physical capabilities existing in a human being, which they exercise whenever they produce a use-value of any description" (Marx 1967, Chapter VI).

> […] Capital can be divided into categories: […]
>
> Constant capital is that invested in the buildings, machinery and raw materials. In the process of production their value, or a part of their value, is only transferred to the finished product. Variable capital is that invested in labour power and is so called because this is the part of capital that expands. Labour power not only transfers its own value and is instrumental in transferring that of the constant capital, but it also creates new value. Thus, machines do not create value. All they do, and this only when set in motion by human beings, is transfer part of their own value (itself of course a past creation of the work of human beings) to the finished product. Even capitalist accountants recognise this: the part of the cost of a commodity they put down to depreciation is to cover the value transferred from the buildings and machinery.
>
> [...] The value of a commodity is fixed by the amount of socially necessary labour embodied in it from start to finish, not just in the final stage of its production. Thus it is inaccurate to say that agricultural workers produce food or that car workers produce cars. Production under capitalism is a social process in which all workers take part. An important corollary of this is: "the capitalist class as a whole exploits the working class as a

whole. The worker is not exploited just by their particular employer, but by the whole class of capitalists" (World Socialist Movement 2006).

And it is this genuinely socio-economic perspective that makes Marx's theory so useful for sociology of the economy.

But there arises another question: Why does price not always equal value?

Having been told that fixed proportions rule commodity exchanges, the reader may be forgiven if the fact that under capitalism commodities do not sell at their values takes her by surprise. The truth of the matter is, the Labour Theory of Value cannot be boiled down to a mere theory of prices. There are two simple reasons why price and value can differ: prices fluctuate with supply and demand, and with monopoly, a commodity will sell at above its value (or, with subsidies, below its value). The third reason is more complicated [...] the tendency is rather for capital to get more or less the same rate of profit wherever it is invested.

How to reconcile a labour theory of value with the averaging of profits was a problem that baffled Adam Smith and David Ricardo. But Marx solved it in the only way possible: by abandoning the assumption that all commodities sell at their values. [...] capitalist production and circulation is a social process: each individual capitalist does not exploit only his own employees but the whole capitalist class exploits the whole working class. Each capitalist employs so many workers who produce so much surplus value. Instead of going to the individual capitalist this surplus value goes, as it were, into a pool from which it is shared along with the rest of the surplus value amongst all the capitalists in accordance with how much capital they have invested. (This explains why, incidentally, a fully automated factory would still make a profit.) Consider the consequences of this on prices. Say s/v is 100 per cent and that there are three sectors with different organic compositions:

C V S value rate of profit A B C

With no averaging of profits B is the most profitable sector, but with an averaging we get:

C V S profit value price A 140 above value B 140 below value C 140 at value

Marx called this selling price, which is made up of cost plus average rate of profit, the price of production. This, in fact, is how businesses do operate and is regarded by academic economics (who, as Marx pointed out, merely take a businessman's view of economic events) as enough. But it is not. It is all very well talking airily about price being set at cost plus "normal profit". But what is normal profit? Something fixed by custom! This is only what it appears to be. Only the Labour Theory of Value, with its concept of value and surplus value, based on labour, can adequately explain why the "normal" rate of profit is, say, 10 per cent rather than 15 per cent. (World Socialist Movement 2006)

Whilst one can speak of rival theories of value, it is, though, largely thing of the past; now academic economics tends to deny the need for such a theory. All one needs, they say, is a theory of price. We shall see, however, that prices cannot be explained without recourse to the concept of value.

> Marginal utility modified labor theories of value in mainstream economics by adding the concepts of marginality (the tendency of the consumer to substitute one product for another in the marketplace and for producers to substitute one commodity for another in the production of goods and services) and diminishing utility to the original labor theory. Thus, under marginal utility, the first unit of production of a good or service yields more than the second or subsequent units. This may cause a reduction of the price of the subsequent units, but the units continue to reflect the total value of the labor that was used to produce the subsequent units. (Wikipedia entry—"Labor Theory of Value")

And indeed, it can be proved that there is no contradiction between those, usually treated as alternative, approaches.

> the name of labour theory of value must not be interpreted to mean that the theory reduces the entire costs of a commodity to labour costs. In Marxian terms, labor costs constitute merely the value of the respective labour power. Still, the value of the labour power and the labour value of a commodity are by no means the same thing. The distinction involved has been made by Marx himself but also by non-Marxist economists.
>
> A worker sells his labour power against wages. The labour value, however, depends on the production conditions and is not the subject of the labour contract. The analytical problem consists in showing that the cost of a unit of a commodity, its marginal cost, dC/dQ, is equal to its labour value converted into monetary units. (Hagendorf 2009)

How does one arrive at such a proof?

> Now according to the LTV the labour value of a commodity, thus a certain quantity of labour units, multiplied by the wage rate, w, is equal to the marginal cost of the commodity. The multiplication with the wage rate is necessary, in order to ensure the equality of the dimensions. The labour value of a unit of a commodity has the dimension labour units per piece whereas the marginal cost has the dimension money per piece. The dimension of the wage rate is money per labour unit. So the product of labour value with the wage rate has the dimension money per piece.
>
> w * labour value = marginal cost
>
> At this point it is already possible to find a solution intuitively. If marginal cost, dC/dQ, is the adequate expression for the costs of a unit of a commodity, then this means that dC is the cost, which result from the

additional production of a unit of the commodity, dQ. In analogy to this we can conclude that δL represents the quantity of additional labour units, which are needed for the production of an additional unit of the commodity δQ. [...] The marginal labour value, $\delta L/\delta Q$, represents the socially necessary labour for the production of a commodity. (Hagendorf 2009)

The subsequent stages of the proof are too technical, so we turn immediately to its final conclusion:

"The proof for the validity of the labour theory of value results immediately, since we receive the desired solution now by substitution:

δL dC

w —=—

δ0 dO" (Hagendorf 2009).

Having addressed this, allegedly damaging to the LTV, case of its purported theoretical alternative, we must deal with other criticisms to which the former is subject.

One such critic begins with an issue which has been just dealt with, but later he presents a number of other charges.

There are two fundamentally different answers to the question of where economic value originates. According to intrinsic theories of value, value is inherent in objects; remains constant despite changing demand, the passage of time, and other factors; and can be "objectively determined" by calculations based upon some fundamental scientific principle. The labor theory of value is clearly an intrinsic-value theory.

The other approach is the market-exchange theory. According to this theory, value is not inherent in objects, but is a product of many different consumer judgments. According to market-exchange theories, value depends upon people's desires: the more they esteem an object and are willing to trade for it, the more it is worth. This theory is the basis of free-market capitalism, which Marx bitterly opposed.

At first glance, both theories seem to make sense. It is generally true that the more labor invested in an object, the more it is worth; but it is also true that the more people want something regardless of how much or how little labor went into it—the more it is worth.

[...] We will argue that the labor theory of value is fundamentally wrong and the market theory of value is correct.

The assertion that labor is the sole determinant of value is hard to accept just based upon common sense and experience.[2] The assertion that

---

[2] Well, different people have different experiences which is only one reason why their "practical reason" may be also different. Besides, and most importantly, science would restrict itself to replicating knowledge available to all bearers, however common sense would lose its right to exist; why bother with science, social science included, if all what it purports to say is known anyway?

> only labor gives an object value ignores the fact that many natural objects in which no labor has been invested—such as scenic views, pure water, gems and minerals, and wild fruits and vegetables—have economic value. Also the labor theory cannot by its nature account for the fact that people value some natural objects, such as diamonds, tremendously more than other natural objects, such as leaves.
>
> The labor theory of value also fails to take into account changing consumer desires and the contextual nature of value. In a horse-and-buggy culture, horse-shoes are tremendously valuable commodities, but in a society without horses they are virtually useless. Similarly in a society with much leisure time, games and recreational facilities become important, but in a subsistence economy in which people must work nearly continuously just to stay alive, such things may actually have negative value. (Ernsberger 1988)

The critic, wittingly or not, creates a lot of confusion. He does not distinguish values from prices and ignores the cardinal fact that the LTV applies only to the commodity-money, as distinct from natural or subsistence economy. Most of his other objections have already been addressed above. This, in conjunction with what follows suggest unequivocally that the critic under consideration commits the Straw Man fallacy, for he chooses to ignore the vast literature on LTV and, last but not least, the content of Marx's theory , substituting its partial and arbitrary misrepresentation instead. He continues:

> For workers to be paid now, rather than later, someone must advance their wages, and clearly this service has a value. But proponents of the labor theory would have it both ways: workers are to receive the full future value of their product now.
>
> The final theoretical failure of the labor theory of value is the value-effort fallacy. It is folly to assume that all effort produces value. Every day each of us wastes time on fruitless efforts. To equate labor with the automatic creation of value is to fallaciously imply that all human effort is infallible and constantly productive. (Ernsberger 1988)

Of course, the critic commits here another blunder. He happens to overlook an socio-economic dimension of the LTV—it is not each individual case of time and labour power expenditure but only socially necessary one. In addition, the LTV by any means proclaims that the whole product must belong to its direct producers; it is rather its marginalist rival that posits that workers are paid according to their marginal product—which has little in common with the value of labour power that underlies wages according to the LTV. The critic concerned goes on to say:

> The labor theory is even more absurd in practice. If all value is derived from labor, and entrepreneurial effort is "parasitic," who would bother to invest the time and money necessary to build factories, plan product development or organize a production process? If all profits are "exploitation," what incentive does anyone have to risk money on a new and untried product or service? Where will the money come from to finance new investment in tools? (Ernsberger 1988)

The polemist quoted conflates moral and economic considerations and commits the fallacy of contradiction in terms. Firstly, moral condemnation of profits as "parasitic," as he would have it, does not undermine their existence as economic magnitudes, which is more than adequate to attract prospective capitalists. Secondly, his specific charge is based on the recognition of soundness of the labour theory of value which is in conflict with his own earlier claims.

That the critic does not understand the subject about which he writes is made blatantly clear by the next passage in which he "forgets" that the LTV does not, as is stressed in this section, negate the role of supply and demand, it is only that it views those market forces in its own way, way apparently not grasped by this opponent of it:

> The labor theory of value is violently anti-consumer by its nature. Under this theory, sellers are compelled to price all goods by the amount of labor that goes into them, rather than how much they are demanded by consumers. Thus stores could charge no more for an aged foreign wine than for a local cheapwine (given equal labor input) or more for the work hacked out by a beginner. This inevitably produces a surplus of unskilled and shoddy work, and a shortage of skilled work—which is exactly the situation that exists in communist countries.
>
> The labor theory also means the end of all economic freedom. Engels, Marx's disciple, wrote: "For a pure Marxist society to long endure, voluntary exchange between individuals must be abolished." In a communist society you produce what the rulers tell you and consume what scraps they allow you. If you don't like this, you are of course free to relocate—to a slave labor camp. (Ernsberger 1988)

The place of this piece of political speech is perhaps at this or that right-wing political rally but its scientific status is simply non-existent. Our brave anti-communist fighter did not bother to acquaint himself with either Marxian views on socialist and communist society or to distinguish them from Stalinist practices, which constitutes a perfect example of Whitehead's fallacy of misplaced concreteness. Even more relevantly, he fails to see that the LTV as applied to the market economy, by no means restrict "all economic freedom". Quite the contrary, it is well-known that Marx repeatedly acknowledged the progressive role of the bourgeoisie and market capitalism in general. In addition:

> This objection seems to miss the point of Marx's account of exploitation. Marx acknowledged that market exchanges are freely made:
>
> "This sphere ... within whose boundaries the sale and purchase of labour power goes on, is in fact a very Eden of the innate rights of man. There alone rule Freedom, Equality, Property, and Bentham. Freedom, because both buyer and seller of a commodity, say of labour power, are constrained only by their own free will. They contract as free agents, and the agreement they come to, is but the form in which they give expression to their common will. Equality, because each enters into relation with the other, as with a simple owner of commodities, and they exchange equivalent for equivalent. Property, because each disposes only of what is his own. And Bentham, because each looks only to himself. The only force that brings them together and puts them in relation with each other, is the selfishness, the gain and the private interests of each. Each looks to himself only, and no one troubles himself about the rest, and just because they do so, do they all, in accordance with the pre-established harmony of things, or under the auspices of an all-shrewd providence, work together to their mutual advantage, for the common weal and in the interest of all."
>
> Perhaps Marx intended that last sentence ironically. But consider the following quote, in which Marx describes the gains from trade:
>
> "So far as regards use-values, it is clear that both parties may gain some advantage. Both part with goods that, as use-values, are of no service to them, and receive others that they can make use of. And there may also be a further gain. A, who sells wine and buys corn, possibly produces more wine, with given labour time than farmer B could, and B, on the other hand, more corn than wine-grower A could. A, therefore, may get, for the same exchange value, more corn, and B more wine, than each would respectively get without any exchange by producing his own corn and wine. With reference, therefore, to use-value, there is good ground for saying that 'exchange is a transaction by which both sides gain."
>
> So it would seem that proponents of the objection to the Marxist account of exploitation need to consider how Marx could have found these ideas consistent with his theory. Note that these quotes describe only the exchange of use-values. They do not characterize the unity of production and circulation under capitalist institutions. (Vienneau 2001)

In the following passage the critic stubbornly reiterates his charge regarding the place of demand within the LTV and later he again shows either his ignorance or ill will (which is true, we don't know), by disregarding Marx's entirely clear justification of his choice of labour as a common substance of commodities:

The most interesting fallacies of the labor theory of value are methodological. Labor theory arose from two extremely poor methods of economic research. First it attempted to establish economic laws of exchange by examining only supply—ignoring demand entirely.

Even worse, the entire labor theory is unproven. In the entire first volume of Das Capital, where Marx proposed the labor theory, there is not one"positive proof". Rather Marx offers a fallacious "negative proof" in which he argues:

Premise 1: Some factor in the production of a good gives it value. TRUE;

Premise 2: Only those goods to which man has applied labor have value. FALSE;

Procedure: Examine all the factors producing a good by discarding those which did not create equal value in equal quantity, and end up with one factor—Labor. ARBITRARY;

Conclusion: Labor must be the source of value. FALSE.

Marx promised to provide a positive proof in the Volume 3 of Das Capital. However, that book does not offer a positive proof, and implicitly refutes one. Marx proclaims that two types of capital exist in production, only one of which can produce "surplus value". Thus exchange of items of equal value can have uneven mixtures of these two types of capital, implying that labor alone is not the sole determinant of value. (Ernsberger 1988)

Then the critic asks what in his view is surely just a rhetorical question: Does Capital = Exploitation? The labor theory of value is nonsense both in theory and practice [...,and leads to economic chaos and political slavery.

The free market, in contrast, rests upon voluntary trade. If workers choose to contract for employment in factories rather than work their own farms or produce handicrafts, it is because they prefer the wages and conditions in factories.

An entrepreneur contributes the great value of his organizational ability, foresight, and management skills. Because value is not solely a product of labor, these abilities are extremely valuable. Profits are his just reward for risking capital in an uncertain and changing world. (Ernsberger 1988)

Recall that Marx by no means ignores the role of the capitalist entepreneur. Suffice it to mention his notion of extra surplus value which constitutes precisely such a financial reward for risky investment in new unproven technologies and means of production.

The claim that free labour power market rules out exploitation is dealt with in this section. But the robust rebuttal of Ensberger's key claim denying Marxian theory's scientific status is provided by Cockshott and Cottrell (1997), who first formulate a couple of criteria by which to judge whether a theory is scientific such as testability, predictive power, and formal elegance, and next on that basis assess the relative merits of three variant formulae for predicting observed prices, namely "standard" Marxian values (or vertically integrated labour coefficients), Sraffian prices of production, and prices of production as interpreted by the "Temporal Single System" (TSS) school (e.g. McGlone & Kliman 1996:.

> The calculation of prices of production (whether in the Sraffian or the TSS variant) in effect assumes a pure circulating capital system, which suppresses the distinction between capital stocks (on which, presumably, the rate of profit "ought" to be equalized) and the flow consumption of capital (as measured in the "A" matrix of an input-output table). When this simplifying assumption is dropped, it becomes apparent that the price of production calculation requires additional data—namely the stocks of capital in each industry—while the vertically integrated labour coefficients emerge as distinctly the most parsimonious predictor.
>
> The second question demands a fuller discussion since it goes to the heart of the project of predicting prices using empirical labour values. In the standard presentation of the principle of calculation of Marxian values one starts from data on (a) intersectoral flows of product in natura and (b) direct labour-hours performed in each sector of the economy. Given the statistics that are available for capitalist economies, however, one has no choice but to use data that are expressed in monetary terms. Instead of in-kind figures for, say, the quantity of coal used by the steel industry or the quantity of aluminium used by the aircraft industry, we have figures for the money value of the purchases of each industry from each other industry. And instead of a vector of hours of direct labour performed in each industry we have a vector of wage bills.
>
> This raises a concern: if prices are written into the data we are using to calculate labour values in the first place, is there not something circular about turning around and claiming to predict or explain prices on the basis of these values?
>
> In fact this objection is mistaken. (Cockshott & Cottrell 1997)

As regards Marx's position in economics, Michio Morishima in his *Introduction to Marx's Economics* also has strong views. But he begins by addressing the just mentioned criticism:

> Walras' [theory of general equilibrium] is more detailed than Marx's in the analysis of consumer demand for commodities. This last point has often been reckoned as one of the defects of Marx's theory, but it must be remembered that only by drastically simplifying the aspect of consumers' choice was he able successfully to derive definite dynamic laws concerning the working of his system through time. It was a very practical bargain, which has become popular among us since Keynes' General Theory. Hicks

> accepted the same exchange in his Theory of the Trade Cycle. Leontief in his short-run theory, even regarded consumption as constant. Thus many contemporary economists believe that it is more important to obtain a theory which can describe dynamic movements of the economy, rather than one which can elaborate consumers' preference. This is exactly the choice which Marx made.
>
> Moreover, Marx's theory of reproduction is very similar to Leontief's input—output analysis. (Or more correctly, we should say conversely that Leontief reproduced Marx as well as Walras in a pragmatic way) … Marx's theory contains in itself a way to the von Neumann Revolution; although he will have lost some of his properties during the Revolution, after it he will be honoured as one of the authors of the Marx—von Neumann model, in which, if we wish, we can allow consumers' choice. [...] Thus Marx is still active on the frontier of our science. One of his tools has recently been rediscovered and named the factor-price frontier—one of the most fundamental concepts of present-day growth theory … The concept of the value-composition of capital, which Marx utilized in aggregating industries and in constructing his breakdown thesis, is no more than the Marxian counterpart of the capital-labour ratio, which has been found most useful in the analysis of growth. These would be enough examples to recommend Marx as a purely academic economist for one of the very few chairs with the highest authority. (Morishima 1977)

Often the following question is asked:

> It is apparent that workers' abilities and skills are different. How this is to be reconciled with the LTV? […]
>
> Does labour time, as the measure of value, suppose at least that the days are equivalent, and that one man's day is worth as much as another's? No.
>
> Let us suppose for a moment that a jeweller's day is equivalent to three days of a weaver; the fact remains that any change in the value of jewels relative to that of woven materials, unless it be the transitory result of the fluctuation of demand and supply, must have as its cause a reduction or an increase in the labour time expended in the production of one or the other. If three working days of different workers be related to one another in the ratio 1:2:3, then a change in the relative value of their products will be a change in the same proportion of 1:2:3. Thus values can be measured by labour time, in spite of the inequality of value of different working days; but to apply such a measure we must have a comparative scale of the different working days: it is competition that sets up this scale. "Is your hour's labour worth mine? That is a question which is decided by competition". [...] Anyway, Ian Steedman has shown that the fundamental theorem of Marxism is consistent with heterogeneous labor activities not reduced to a single measure of homogeneous labor. (Vienneau 2001)

Now the above-mentioned scholar turns to a more concrete and practical, but still theoretical issue:

> What the worker is being paid for is not the work he or she does. It is his/her keep. (Vienneau 2001)

The matter is not that simple. For the sake of theoretical argument Marx indeed assumes the labour power is paid according to its value. This does not mean this condition is met in each particular case. In terms of concrete wages and salaries the above-mentioned assumption is too genral, has no discrimatory power. In reality, holders of ascritptive labour power are paid according to its definite attributes, such as qualifications, seniority, and so on, while the alternative system of employee compensation is based on effects, or performance.

Finally, let us consider a vexed problem of the demonstration of the relation between commodities' unit values and their respective prices which is known in Marxian terms as the transformation problem or the transformation of values into prices of production. The transformation problem has probably generated the greatest bulk of debate about the LTV. The problem with transformation is to find an algorithm where the magnitude of value added by labour, in proportion to its duration and intensity, is sufficiently accounted for after this value is distributed through prices that reflect an equal rate of return on capital advanced. If there is an additional magnitude of value or a loss of value after transformation compared with before then the relation between values (proportional to labour) and prices (proportional to total capital advanced) is incomplete.

This very problem, amongst other questions, was tackled by Ernest Mandel. His point of departure is an observation repeatedly underlined earlier in the present book:

> As an economist, Marx is generally situated in the continuity of the great classical school of Adam Smith and Ricardo. He obviously owes a lot to Ricardo, and conducts a running dialogue with that master in most of his mature economic writings.
>
> Marx inherited the labour theory of value from the classical school. Here the continuity is even more pronounced; but there is also a radical break, For Ricardo, labour is essentially a numeraire, which enables a common computation of labour and capital as basic elements of production costs. For Marx, labour is value. Value is nothing but that fragment of the total labour potential existing in a given society in a certain period (e.g. a year or a month) which is used for the output of a given commodity, at the average social productivity of labour existing then and there, divided by

> the total number of these commodities produced and expressed in hours (or minutes), days, weeks, months of labour. (Mandel 1990)

An account given by Mandel is so valuable because it is socio-economic in nature rather than purely economic. Thus, Mandel emphasises that:

> Value is therefore essentially a social, objective and historically relative category, it is social because it is determined by the overall result of the fluctuating efforts of each individual producer (under capitalism: of each individual firm or factory). It is objective because it is given, once the production of a given commodity is finished, and is thus independent from personal (or collective) valuations of customers on the market place; and it is historically relative because it changes with each important change (progress or regression) of the average productivity of labour in a given branch of output, including in agriculture and transportation.
>
> This does not imply that Marx's concept of value is in any way completely detached from consumption. It only means that the feedback of consumers' behaviour and wishes upon value is always mediated through changes in the allocation of labour inputs in production, labour being seen as subdivided into living labour and dead (dated) labour, i.e. tools and raw materials. The market emits signals to which the producing units react. Value changes after these reactions, not before them. Market price changes can of course occur prior to changes in value. In fact, changes in market prices are among the key signals which can lead to changes in labour allocation between different branches of production, i.e. to changes in labour quantities necessary to produce given commodities. But then, for Marx, values determine prices only basically and in the medium-term sense of the word. This determination only appears clearly as an explication of medium and long-term price movements. In the shorter run, prices fluctuate around values as axes. Marx never intended to negate the operation of market laws, of the law of supply and demand, in determining these short-term fluctuations …. (Mandel 1990)

Mandel again puts his finger on the problem:

> The LTV does not deny the role of supply and demand influencing price since the price of a commodity is something other than its value. In Value, Price and Profit (1865), Marx quotes Adam Smith and sums up:
>
> "It suffices to say that if supply and demand equilibrate each other, the market prices of commodities will correspond with their natural prices, that is to say, with their values as determined by the respective quantities of labor required for their production."
>
> It is the level of this equilibrium which the LTV seeks to explain. This could be explained by a "cost of production" argument, pointing out that all costs are ultimately labor costs, but this does not account for profit, and it

is vulnerable to the charge of tautology in that it explains prices by prices. Marx later called this "Smith's adding up theory of value." (Mandel 1990)

Mandel sees the relationship of Marx to Smith in yet another respect:

The "law of value" is but Marx's version of Adam Smith's "invisible hand." In a society dominated by private labour, private producers and private ownership of productive inputs, it is this "law of value," an objective economic law operating behind the backs of all people, all "agents" involved in production and consumption, which, in the final analysis, regulates the economy, determines what is produced and how it is produced (and therefore also what can be consumed). The "law of value" regulates the exchange between commodities, according to the quantities of socially necessary abstract labour they embody (the quantity of such labour spent in their production). Through regulating the exchange between commodities, the "law of value" also regulates, after some interval, the distribution of society's labour potential and of society's non-living productive resources between different branches of production. Again, the analogy with Smith's "invisible hand" is striking.

Marx's critique of the "invisible hand" concept does not dwell essentially on the analysis of how a market economy actually operates. It would above all insist that this operation is not eternal, not immanent in "human nature," but created by specific historical circumstances, a product of a special way of social organisation, and due to disappear at some stage of historical evolution as it appeared during a previous stage. And it would also stress that this "invisible hand" leads neither to the maximum of economic growth nor to the optimum of human wellbeing for the greatest number of individuals, i.e. it would stress the heavy economic and social price humankind had to pay, and is still currently paying, for the undeniable progress the market economy produced at a given stage of historical evolution.

The formula "quantities of abstract human labour" refers to labour seen strictly as a fraction of the total labour potential of a given society at a given time, say a labour potential of 2 billion hours a year (1 million potential producers, each supposedly capable of working 2000 hours a year). It therefore implies making an abstraction of the specific trade or occupation of a given male or female producer, the product of a day's work of a weaver not being worth less or more than that of a peasant, a miner, a house-builder, a milliner or a seamstress. At the basis of that concept of "abstract human labour" lies a social condition, a specific set of social relations of production, in which small independent producers are essentially equal. Without that equality, social division of labour, and therefore satisfaction of basic consumers' needs, would be seriously endangered under that specific organisational set-up of the economy. Such an equality between small commodity owners and producers is later transformed into an equality between owners of capital under the capitalist mode of production. (Mandel 1990)

The next part of this socio-economic analysis touches on another frequent objection to the LTV:

> But the concept of the homogeneity of productive human labour, underlying that of "abstract human labour" as the essence of value, does not imply a negation of the difference between skilled and unskilled labour. Again: a negation of that difference would lead to the breakdown of the necessary division of labour, as would any basic heterogeneity of labour inputs in different branches of output. It would then not pay to acquire skills: most of them would disappear. So Marx's labour theory of value, in an entirely coherent way, leads to the conclusion that one hour of skilled labour represents more value than one hour of unskilled labour, say represents the equivalent of 1.5 hours of unskilled labour. The difference would result from the imputation of the labour it costs to acquire the given skill, while an unskilled labourer would have a labour potential of 120,000 hours during his adult life, a skilled labourer would only have a labour potential of 80,000 hours, 40,000 being used for acquiring, maintaining and developing his skill. Only if one hour of skilled labour embodies the same value of 1.5 hours of unskilled labour, will the equality of all "economic agents" be maintained under these circumstances, i.e. will it "pay" economically to acquire a skill.
>
> Marx himself never extensively dwelled on this solution of the so-called reduction problem. This remains indeed one of the most obscure parts of his general economic theory. It has led to some, generally rather mild, controversy. Much more heat has been generated by another facet of Marx's labour theory of value, the so-called transformation problem. Indeed, from Böhm-Bawerk writing a century ago till the recent contributions of Sraffa (1960) and Steedman (1977), the way Marx dealt with the transformation of values into "prices of production" in *Capital* Vol. III has been considered by many of his critics as the main problem of his "system," as well as being a reason to reject the labour theory of value out of hand.
>
> The problem arises out of the obvious modification in the functioning of a market economy when capitalist commodity production substitutes Itself for simple commodity production. In simple commodity production, with generally stable technology and stable (or easily reproducible) tools, living labour is the only variable of the quantity and subdivision of social production. The mobility of labour is the only dynamic factor in the economy. As Engels pointed out in his Addendum to *Capital* Vol. III (Marx, 1034–7), in such an economy, commodities would be exchanged at prices which would be immediately proportional to values, to the labour inputs they embody.

> But under the capitalist mode of production, this is no longer the case. Economic decision-taking is not in the hands of the direct producers. It is in the hands of the capitalist entrepreneurs in the wider sense of the word (bankers—distributors of credit—playing a key role in that decision-taking, besides entrepreneurs in the productive sector properly speaking). Investment decisions, i.e. decisions for creating, expanding, reducing or closing enterprises, determine economic life. It is the mobility of capital and not the mobility of labour which becomes the motive force of the economy. Mobility of labour becomes essentially an epiphenomenon of the mobility of capital.
>
> Capitalist production is production for profit. Mobility of capital is determined by existing or expected profit differentials. Capital leaves branches (countries, regions) with lower profits (or profit expectations) and flows towards branches (countries, regions) with higher ones. These movements lead to an equalisation of the rate of profit between different branches of production. But approximately equal returns on all invested capital (at least under conditions of prevailing "free competition") coexist with unequal proportions of inputs of labour in these different branches. So there is a disparity between the direct value of a commodity and its "price of production," that "price of production" being defined by Marx as the sum of production costs (costs of fixed capital and raw materials plus wages) and the average rate of profit multiplied with the capital spent in the given production.
>
> The so-called "transformation problem" relates to the question of whether a relation can nevertheless be established between value and these "prices of production," what is the degree of coherence (or incoherence) of the relation with the "law of value" (the labour theory of value in general), and what is the correct quantitative way to express that relation, if it exists.
>
> We shall leave aside here the last aspect of the problem, to which extensive analysis has recently been devoted (Mandel & Freeman 1984). From Marx's point of view, there is no incoherence between the formation of 'prices of production' and the labour theory of value. Nor is it true that he came upon that alleged difficulty when he started to prepare *Capital* Vol.III, i.e. to deal with capitalist competition, as several critics have argued (see e.g. Joan Robinson, 1942). In fact, his solution of the transformation problem is already present in the *Grundrisse*, before he even started to draft *Capital* Vol. I. (Mandel 1990)

Thus, Mandel has strong views regarding this purportedly insurmountable problem. It must conceded, though, he delivers on his promise:

> The sum total of value produced in a given country during a given span of time (e.g. one year) is determined by the sum total of labour-inputs. Competition and movements of capital cannot change that quantity, the sum total of values equals the sum total of "prices of production." The only effect of capital competition and capital mobility is to redistribute that

> given sum—and this through a redistribution of surplus value (see below)—between different capitals, to the benefit of some and at the expense of others.
>
> Now the redistribution does not occur in a haphazard or arbitrary way. Essentially value (surplus-value) is transferred from technically less advanced branches to technologically more advanced branches. And here the concept of "quantities of socially necessary labour" comes into its own, under the conditions of constant revolutions of productive technology that characterise the capital mode of production. Branches with lower than average technology (organic composition of capital, see below) can be considered as wasting socially necessary labour. Part of the labour spent in production in their realm is therefore not compensated by society. Branches with higher than average technology (organic composition of capital) can be considered to be economising social labour; their labour inputs can therefore be considered as more intensive than average, embodying more value. In this way, the transfer of value (surplus-value) between different branches, far from being in contradiction with the law of value, is precisely the way it operates and should operate under conditions of "capitalist equality," given the pressure of rapid technological change.
>
> As to the logical inconsistency supposedly to be found in Marx's method of solving the "transformation problem"—first advanced by von Bortkiewicz (1907)—it is based upon a misunderstanding in our opinion. It is alleged that in his "transformation schemas" (or tables) Marx calculates inputs in "values" and outputs in "prices of production," thereby omitting the feedback effect of the latter on the former. But that feedback eject is unrealistic and unnecessary, once one recognises that inputs are essentially data. Movements of capital posterior to the purchase of machinery or raw materials, including the ups and downs of prices of finished products produced with these raw materials, cannot lead to a change in prices and therefore of profits of the said machinery and raw materials, on sales which have already occurred. What critics present as an inconsistency between "values" and "prices of production" is simply a recognition of two different time-frameworks (cycles) in which the equalisation of the rate of profit has been achieved, a first one for inputs, and a second, later one for outputs. (Mandel 1990)

To return to the theory of economic ownership(as a matter of fact, implicit in the above discussion), concentration on what property rights scholars, as well as many other theorists, view as only one aspect of property, by no means leads to any oversimplification of the concept. On the contrary, ownership is here conceived of as an internally complex and multifaceted relation. Consider the most typical form of ownership of modern capitalism. Stock ownership has two basic aspects to it. Namely, it could be said that to own shares means to hold them and / or to dispose of them. Put differently, shareowners benefit from corporate activities in the form of dividends and capital gains. The two relations in question could be described in this context as, first, the relation of direct ownership of the means of production and, second, the relation of indirect ownership of the corporate means of production. Of course, the former relation can be classified as direct only in comparison to capital appreciation and its subsequent realization. From another standpoint, it itself is mediated by the ownership of shares. Thus the former relation could also be designated as ownership of industrial capital mediated by share ownership and exchange, and the latter as ownership of other people's money capital (or savings) mediated by stock ownership and exchange. In the first case, by means of exchange, dividend income is converted into consumer goods and services available in the market, whereas in the second case not only money is turned into goods and services but the shares are converted into money through the mechanism of the securities markets. In still other terms, a shareowner can benefit from, first, industrial capital as mediated by fictitious capital and, second, from sole fictitious capital.

I.11.1.4. Theory of open access property critically considered

The socio-economic approach to ownership adopted here allows one to also critically discuss the theory of open access property, which heavily draws from and is closely related to the property right approach. Its argument that "a resource, such as a road, a fishery, or a pasture, will generally be used inefficiently if access is free" (De Meza & Gould 1987, 1317) is deficient in that it fails to identify the real underlying cause of the "common pool" problem, which is not the form of ownership but the indivisibility of the source of supply. Even more importantly, the theory is indeed directed not against social or common ownership as such, but only, at best, against some types of it. Its target, namely, is the form of ownership called communal, whereby "neither the state nor individual citizens can exclude others from using the resource except by prior and continuing use of the resource" (Demsetz 1973, 19). Demsetz notes that communal ownership may or, may not be "technically associated with state ownership" (1973, 19). A closer look at the "tragedy of the commons" argument reveals, however, that it is misleading in other respects as well.

The argument fails to distinguish between situations in which a resource is used for personal purposes only and those in which it is used for the purposes of obtaining income. These two situations sharply differ in respect of incentives they create. It is only when the resource is used for producing goods from which profit can be extracted that there exists an incentive to overexploit the resource. Can one observe any tendency to overuse a city pavement? One comes to a public park when one feels a need to. It is one thing when one hunts for satisfying one's, and one's family's personal needs, and it is quite another thing when animals are hunted for sale and profit. The point is, individual needs of any particular user (and part-owner) of common property are, in most cases, limited and do not stimulate overutilisation. It is only when the motive of private profit appears, that the consequences described by the property rights theorists follow. From the theoretical point of view, the property rights literature errs in viewing exclusivity as the necessary feature of private ownership. For the private ownership to exist, it is sufficient that benefits are privately appropriated. Thus, a fishery exploited by one firm which holds an exclusive right of access and another which is exploited by many firms, also profit-oriented, are both objects of private ownership. On the other hand, in the case of using the fishery only for personal purposes and not for income, it would constitute (assuming open access) common property. Even though the literature of property rights ignores the above mentioned distinction, it quite clearly shows that its argument really applies to competitive, individual, private ownership rights. From the viewpoint of the nature of ownership, the fact that, to use an example of crude oil, "property rights are assigned to oil only upon extraction" (Libecap 1989, 19) makes little difference. Libecap means here exclusive rights, but the real point is that oil reservoirs are privately, i.e. for private profit, exploited. After all, the property rights scholars write about "decentralised competitive exploitation" and "decentralized competitive firms" contrasted with "the appropriation of a resource by a sole owner, or its legal equivalent" (Smith 1969, 189–90).This turns the argument of private vs. public ownership into one of competition vs. monopoly, and the two arguments are quite different. Indeed, from the latter argument one can derive conclusions about the superiority of public, or in legal terms, state ownership.

The theory of open access property "fails to give any credit to the democratic process or to professional management in raising the time horizons of voters, politicians, and bureaucrats to a level higher than that prevailing in the marketplace" (Starr 1989, 31). "A national government (for example) may well place a higher value on the welfare of future generations than would a private company" (National Consumer Council 1989, 33). Although differences between the property rights approach and one represented by the present writer are quite substantial, they have a lot in common with each other. Their differences notwithstanding, the two approaches are characterized by a common emphasis on the relationship between economy and society. This line of analysis investigates the impact of property relations on the character of not only economic life but also non-economic structures. It is this widening of the view of the relations between economy and society beyond the horizon of orthodox economics on the one hand and that of mainstream sociology (which has, just as orthodox economics, implicitly assumed that property has little influence on the functioning of the economy and, by and large, neglected the concept) on the other which constitutes in my opinion a key feature of the socio-economic approach.

I.11.2. Theory of class

Their theoretical and methodological differences notwithstanding, all sociologists would probably agree that there are only two dominant approaches in the theory of class, i.e. those by, respectively, Karl Marx and Max Weber. In point of fact, a strong case can be made for the assertion that all other accounts of class could be reduced to the above-mentioned classic ones. Put differently, among the multitude of social scientists who deal with the class issue, one could hardly find anyone who could not be described as neo- or post-Marxian or Weberian, be it Erik Olin Wright, Guglielmo Carchedi, Pierre Bourdieu, Jogn Goldthorpe or dozens of other scholars. One caveat and exception at the same time is in order. Namely, the aforementioned claim does by any means apply to all scholars who use the term "class." A case in point is above all stratification theory, whose numerous proponents are fond of using of the term in question.[3] This fact by itself, however, does not of course transform Warner or Parsons into class theorists in the proper sense of the word. What, then, are the most crucial differences between strata and classes?

Differentia specific of a class is the fact that classes are social groups rooted in the economic structure whereas, by definition, it is not necessarily the case as regards social strata. There are, broadly speaking, two basic types of stratification systems: one-dimensional and multi-dimensional. In the former case there is only one criterion of distinguishing particular social strata, be it prestige, access to power, income, wealth, education level, occupation etc., whereas the latter structure is based on a mixture of

[3] A typical example is provided by an author who wants "to make clear the limitations, for the investigation of normative issues, of the kind of class analysis primarily associated with Erikson and Goldthorpe but widely practised throughout European social stratification research" (Swift 2003). Irrespective of any assessment of this task, it will certainly be made no easier by his, at the very outset, conflation of class with stratification.

criteria. In both instances it is possible to discern such groups throughout the entire society. Thus, what, according to Wright, is "the contrast between unidiniensional and multidimensional perspectives on class and stratification" (1979) in actuality refers exclusively to stratification as opposed to class. This is associated with the second important, but oftentimes neglected difference between the two notions being discussed.

Social stratification refers to a system by which categories of people in society are ranked in a hierarchy. The rankings apply to social categories of people who share a common characteristic without necessarily interacting or identifying with each other. From this view it is concluded that in modern Western nations, stratification is broadly organised into three main layers: upper class, middle class, and lower class. Each class may be further subdivided into smaller categories (e.g. occupational).This approach closely follows that of W. Lloyd Warner, who made his name by the well-known definition of three social classes: upper, middle, and lower, with each level further divided into upper and lower. These categories are particular to state-based societies as distinct from, for instance, feudal societies composed mainly of nobility and peasantry. Stratification may also be defined by kinship ties or caste.

This statement contains a frequently committed mistake according to which social stratification is a general concept, of which class and caste are subtypes. Meanwhile, it is inconsistent with the position put forward here, by virtue of which all these three concepts refer to distinct social categories, which may be at most subsumed within the category of social differentiation that, from our standpoint, is broader than one of social stratification, as well as the class and estate systems.

Considering the distinction between the notions of class and stratum, one should point out that, in contradistinction to the latter, the former one, contrary to common wisdom, does not imply any hierarchy of rank or position. On the contrary, the notion of class structure refers to something more complex and interelated, and thus irreducible to any simple ladder-like system. The relevance of this point cannot be over-emphasised since even many authors of books on class theory are apparently not aware of it, as the example of Erik Olin Wright shows. He reckons, namely, that:

> the diverse definitions of class can be analyzed in terms of three nested theoretical dimensions: (1) Whether class is fundamentally understood in gradational or in relational terms; (2) if class is understood in relational terms, whether the pivotal aspect of class relations is seen as located in the market or in production; (3) if class relations are primarily located within production, whether production is analyzed above all in terms of the

> technical division of labour, authority relations, or exploitation. (Wright 1979)

We do not dwell here, as this question will be clarified below, on Wright's[4] reductionist approach to an issue of economic foundations of class relations which by no means cannot be brought down to the three factors mentioned by him. Wright asks "what it is about the organization of production that forms the basis for the determination of class," replying that "three different ways of understanding the structure of production relations have dominated the analysis of classes within production: production is defined primarily as a system of technical divisions of labor: production is analysed above all as a system of authority relations: and, production, insofar as it determines classes, is seen fundamentally as a system of exploitation" (Wright 1979), yet in his answer, strangely enough, the notion of property (not to be conflated with exploitation) is missing and, additionally, classes are situated not only within the system of production but also within other economic substructures, as we shall see below.

There is yet another kind of by-product in the way of determining strata. To be sure, it cannot be maintained that all class theories are consistent and built on well specified foundations, but in the case of stratification conceptions, arbitrariness and discreteness is written into their very foundations. When one lays out a scale of income, for instance, it may be divided in almost innumerable ways and such scales are never definitive in the sense that one can always shift particular income boundaries because in the nature of a given theory there is nothing to ban it. Much the same could be said about other approaches to stratification,

A high-profile theorist provides a vivid illustration of what consequences may follow if one does not dispose of precise criteria of class identification and as a result presents a whole gamut of positions which amount to nothing less than a horrible mishmash:

> … the opposition between the "elite" of the dominant and the "mass" of the dominated, a contingent, disorganized multiplicity, interchangeable and innumerable, existing only statistically … the dominant fraction of the dominant class … the major relations of order (high/low, strong/weak etc.) reappear in all class-divided societies.
>
> And the recurrence of the triadic structure … the relations between dominated fractions and dominant fractions within the dominant class; the

---

4 A more extensive analysis of Wright's conception can be found in Tittenbrun (2011).

> relationship between the dominant and the dominated, can also, by means of a first transformation, designate the relations between dominated fractions and dominant fractions within the dominant class.
>
> The intersection of the two principles of division which are at work in all class-divided societies—the division between the dominant and the dominated, and the division between the different fractions competing for dominance in the name of different principles, bellatores (warriors) and oratores (scholars) in feudal society, businessmen and intellectuals now. (Bourdieu 1984, 466–484)

Another writer, author of the book heralded as a new *Capital* pertinent to the modern age, presents a version of the obsolescence of old class divisions thesis which are allegedly replaced by some novel cleavages is Manuel Castells who in his theory of network society (2000a; 2000b) claims that we are passing from the industrial age into the information age. This historical breakthrough is brought about by the advent of new information technologies, particularly those for communication and biological technologies. Society remains capitalist, but the basis of the technological means by which it acts has changed from energy to information.

This information is of central importance in determining economic productivity. However, this central to an economic justification of the purported new era claim is hardly supported by any hard data. According to Garnham, there is little evidence of such productivity increases. Furthermore, as he aptly notes, the "lack of a stable calculable relationship between the value of outputs … lies behind the historical difficulties in commodifying information" (Garnham 2004, 191). In other words, even if information output is increasing productivity, this activity is difficult for capitalists to measure and commodify, therefore it is difficult to integrate into a capitalist economy. Granting this to be the case, the aforementioned claim that the wide incidence of information technologies does not cause any qualitative socio-economic innovations to lose credibility and must be regarded as resulting from its author's lack of disposing a cognitively valuable notion of economic property as underlying particular economic formations of society, capitalism included. From this ownership perspective the so-called commons-peer mode of production , described in another context in this book, constitutes , without any doubt, some novel quality within capitalism, as being based on voluntary work and making its product available free of charge. This, of course, is at odds with the capitalist, profit-oriented logic. The creator of the term adds a number of arguments for the above contention, as the advantages listed by him in what follows constitute in fact nothing less than ownership benefits. Benkler argues that:

> this mode has systematic advantages over markets and managerial hierarchies when the object of production is information or culture, and where the capital investment necessary for production—computers and communications capabilities—is widely distributed instead of concentrated. In particular, this mode of production is better than firms and markets for two reasons. First, it is better at identifying and assigning human capital to information and cultural production processes. In this regard, peer-production has an advantage in what I call "information opportunity cost." That is, it loses less information about who the best person for a given job might be than do either of the other two organizational modes. Second, there are substantial increasing returns to allow very larger clusters of potential contributors to interact with very large clusters of information resources in search of new projects and collaboration enterprises. Removing property and contract as the organizing principles of collaboration substantially reduces transaction costs involved in allowing these large clusters of potential contributors to review and select which resources to work on, for which projects, and with which collaborators. This results in allocation gains, that increase more than proportionately with the increase in the number of individuals and resources that are part of the system. (Benkler 2002)

Castells, much like other theorists of "post-industrial society," "information society," knowledge society," "post-modernity" and so forth claims that communication technologies, such as the internet, allow for decentralization of operations and focusing of control, increasing the effectiveness of networks relative to hierarchical structures. Of business he writes, "(t)he main shift can be characterized as the shift from vertical bureaucracies to the horizontal corporation" (2000b, 176).

The above two claims show how misty and nebulous the concept of network can become. Castells commits a rather grave methodological blunder identifying the general notion of structure with its certain historically specific variant in the form of a hierarchically organised capitalist business firm, so vividly depicted by, for example, Williamson. In point of fact, of course, the notion of structure does not entail any specific definition of how its internal relationships are structured, it only recognises their existence. That Castells is not far from endowing his "networks" with superhuman qualities is shown by, for example, his claim to the effect that:

"the logic of the network is more powerful than the powers of the network" (quoted in Weber 2002, 104). Some networks, such as that of financial capital, are global in scale. Networks also exist within and between businesses, where the organizational unit has shifted from being capability-oriented (e.g. accounting, human resources, etc.) to being project-oriented. Resources, including employees, consultants, and other businesses, are brought together to work on a particular project, then dispersed and reallocated when the task is complete. The ability of an actor in the network, be it a company, individual, government, or other organization, to participate in the network is determined by the degree to which the node can contribute to the goals of the network. This new environment requires skilled flexible workers: the organization man gives way to the flexible woman (Castells 2000a, 12). This leads to a binary process of inclusion and exclusion from the network. The people at the bottom are those who, with nothing to offer the network, are excluded.

Castells distinguishes the terms "information" and "informational". He says that information has been an essential component of all societies, whether capitalist or not. In the new "network economy," information becomes a key factor in economic productivity. Today, for example, the flow of capital into currencies, commodities, and stocks is based upon access to information about relevant topics, from international politics to climate change, weather predictions, and social trends. In that sense, the importance of information in contemporary society is not new. What is new, he claims, is the informational shift to the manipulation of information itself: the "action of knowledge upon knowledge itself" (Castells 2000b, 17) is now the basis to increased productivity.

Castells argues that the operation of networks, particularly their ability to include or exclude actors on the basis of their ability to contribute to the goals of the network, has individualized labor: "the work process is globally integrated, but labor tends to be locally fragmented" (2000a: 18). The constantly-shifting "variable geometry" of networks individualizes labor. In consequence, the era of industrial-age conflict between production-based classes ends: individual workers no longer comprise classes, much of the power of the capitalists has shifted to those who manage the networks (for example, the fund manager has greater control than the investors whose money s/he manages), and the class of human capitalists has been replaced by the collective faceless capitalist of the network.

Despite the disappearance of capitalists and the proletariat, exploitation and differentiation remain. In Castells' analysis, labor is fundamentally divided into networked labor, which serves the goals of the network, and switched-off labor, which has nothing to offer the network and in the context of the network economy is non-labor (that is not to say their labor has no value – the realm of discarded labor is also the realm of criminal organizations outside the networks; Castells mentions that the networks can make "perverse" use of these masses of people).If Castells approached

> the latter issue in similar terms as those proposed in the present book, i.e. lumpenwork and lumpenclass, then he would have more difficulty integrating his claim into his overall notion of societal differentiation as allegedly not class-based. His apparent lack of any precise criteria of class identification leads to other highly problematic claims. According to Castells, networked labor is itself divided into two groups. Self-programmable labor—such as financial analysts, company officers, journalists—manages information; it is flexible and skilled. Its interests coincide with the goals of the network. Generic labor (including many workers in natural resource, manufacturing, and service industries, also minimum wage and sweatshop labor) is deskilled, interchangeable and disposable; for these people, the goal is simple survival so as not to be relegated to the class of switch-off irrelevant labor. (Glass 2005)

Whether the Spanish sociologist rightly or not attributes the above-mentioned characteristics to his "generic" workers is another matter but what is relevant for the present purposes is that he, out of the blue, recognised the existence of the working class (formerly written off as non-existent) which tends to turn his whole scheme of societal differentiation in the information age upside down. As to the central category of that scheme:

> Castells includes such a wide diversity of tasks under the rubric of informational labor that it is difficult to accept the interests and values of these workers as a group. Webster provides the examples of journalists, stockbrokers, and surgeons. The relations between these occupations and the information they deal with is anything but consistent, and the group as a whole anything but homogeneous. (Is it level of education? Communication? Influence?) In fact, it seems that the other groups he mentions—commodity labor, surplus labor, etc. are far more homogeneous —in their work and in their common interests – than is informational labor. (Glass 2005)

It is difficult to ascertain how to reconcile the position discussed above with a rather different perspective, more akin to the elite theory, according to which: "The fundamental form of domination in our society is based on the organizational capacity of the dominant elite that goes hand in hand with the capacity to disorganize those groups in society which, while constituting a numerical majority, see their interests partially (if ever) represented only within the framework of the fulfilment of dominant interests" (Castells 1996, 415).

Our suspicion as to Castells' lack of theoretical coherence is in no way dispelled by the remaining parts of his lengthy work. As a matter of fact, Castells limits himself to a couple of truisms for pronouncing which sociological research is hardly needed. We learn, for instance, that elites live in global cities and help to define certain kinds of new urban space (Castells 1996, 415–7), and they hang around with each other in exclusive resorts such as Davos (Castells 1998, 55–356) but we are never told who exactly they are, what roles they have, what characteristics they display, how they gain access to elite positions, etc.

> These are far from being just academic issues. Similar views rejecting class analysis had a harmful effect[5] on the anti-globalist movement that was in awe of spontaneity. Movement ideas tend to echo the hype of the globalisers that economics reigned supreme. The revival of autonomist ideas led by Michael Hardt, Tony Negri and John Holloway downgraded politics. For Hardt and Negri globalisation produces opposition by creating a "smooth space" in which the multitude becomes a counterpower because of the erosion of mediating structures like nation states, representative institutions and trade unions (2001, 269).

Although the concept of multitude was first used long time ago by Machiavelli and later by Spinoza, it is Hardt and Negri's recent influential *Empire* that it draws its popularity from. Prominent or not, the concept suffers from serious shortcomings as it subscribes to an over-simplified polar conception of social differentiation.

To extricate this meaning of the concept in question from rather vague formulations we are offered is not an easy task. Negri describes the multitude in his *The Savage Anomaly* as an "unmediated, revolutionary, immanent, and positive collective social subject which can found a 'nonmystified' form of democracy" (1991). In his more recent writings with Michael Hardt, however, he still does not offer a clear definition, but presents the concept through a series of mediations. In *Empire* it is mediated by the concept of empire (the new global constitution that Negri

---

[5] "The emphasis on spontaneity led to an in-principle opposition to any kind of political leadership. The spontaneity hype was ironic considering the Herculean feats of organisation by often small networks of individuals that co-ordinated the great protests. It led to a string of problems. Naomi Klein, herself an admirer of horizontal, non-hierarchical methods of organisation, was sharp enough to point out their tactical downsides early on. She describes how a blockade of the IMF in Washington in 2001 ran into problems because the group at each intersection declared autonomy and there was no central plan. "This was impeccably fair and democratic, but there was just one problem—it made absolutely no sense.[...] They assume that militant unity is something that just happens in the right circumstances, rather than something that needs to be consciously fought and argued for. As Gramsci famously argued there is no such thing as a purely spontaneous movement." (Nineham 2001).

and Hardt describe as a copy of Polybius's description of Roman government):

> New figures of struggle and new subjectivities are produced in the conjecture of events, in the universal nomadism … They are not posed merely against the imperial system—they are not simply negative forces. They also express, nourish, and develop positively their own constituent projects … This constituent aspect of the movement of the multitude in its myriad faces, is really the positive terrain of the historical construction of Empire … an antagonistic and creative positivity. The deterritorializing power of the multitude is the productive force that sustains Empire and at the same time the force that calls for and makes necessary its destruction. (Hardt & Negri 2000)

Unambiguous language was not amongst the greatest merits of Hegelian dialectics.

Negri, like many other ex-Marxists, rejects class and invokes instead a seemingly altogether different image of social differentiation. However, his intellectual background haunts him and finally his Marxist chickens come home to roost. Among other arguments, Albert's following criticism, based on a simplistic view of class structure, clearly shows this:

> Class concepts focus us on the difference between owning factories and selling one's ability to do work. This difference produces capitalists versus everyone else. The source of this difference has to be eliminated if we are to transcend capitalism ….
>
> Being one word, multitude presumably refers to essentially one thing. What?
>
> Perhaps multitude refers to anyone who could conceivably become a revolutionary in revolutionary times. But since that could be anyone at all, the word population would do equally well as a label for that concept. I doubt the whole population is the intended meaning of the concept multitude, though I have heard people use the term that way. (Albert 2005)

The following discussion shows that Albert's search for an unambiguous definition of the concept in question may well produce no conclusive results:

> Perhaps multitude refers instead to everyone who is a very good prospect to become revolutionary in revolutionary times. But then the word multitude just replaces the two word label, likely revolutionary, and that does not seem very innovative or essential either. I also doubt that that is the intended meaning of the concept multitude, though again, I have heard people use the term that way.

Perhaps multitude means, instead, those who by virtue of their economic position are very good prospects to become revolutionary in revolutionary times. Taken in that sense, the concept multitude would replace the old concept proletariat, or even working class. As Michael Hardt himself put it in an interview back in January, (this) is one way in which you might think of our notion of multitude as being very close to a traditional notion of proletariat, that is, the class of all those who produce, once the notion of production itself has been sufficiently revised and expanded. This, I think, is the intended usage. Regretably, I also think it is the most counter productive usage.

If the term multitude means likely agents of economic and social change, and includes those who produce, I think there is a high likelihood emphasizing it would crowd out giving equal attention to kinship, race, and power based dynamics as to economy based dynamics.

I think emphasising multitude would tend to hide that procreation, sexuality, socialization, celebration, identification, adjudication, legislation, and implementation count just as much as production (and for that matter consumption and allocation) in people's conditions and consciousnesses, and also in igniting or thwarting revolutionary inclinations.

Advocates of multitude correctly want to highlight that production affects and is affected by culture, gender, and power - so far, so good. But if our method for incorporating that insight impedes our also using central concepts that are specifically rooted in those other domains and not just in thinking about production, not to mention if they impede our using more detailed economic concepts of class and of consumption and allocation, then despite our good intentions our adopting the concept multitude will narrow rather than broaden our focus.

To see what I mean, I hope it is sufficient to note that using multitude this way would mirror the impact on the left of the old use of the term proletariat, also meaning revolutionary agent based on being a producer.

For example, many activists who used the term proletariat as agent of change, took race very seriously, even considering it of paramount social importance. Nonetheless, the proletariat-based framework led them to understand and think about race in overwhelmingly economic terms. And using proletariat as an organizing principle had the same predictable delimiting effect on people's approach to gender and political power, as well, of course.

Despite multitude being defined more broadly than proletariat was defined, nonetheless, like the word proletariat, the word multitude identifies a revolutionary agent based on examining economic foundations. That approach will, I fear, cause people to think that the only or at least the most important way to become revolutionary is by way of economic concerns and attitudes. I thought we transcended that approach thirty years ago.

Moreover, even if the above danger was avoided, I think elevating the concept multitude would certainly enforce a bi-polar view of economic change. Regarding economy, with multitude guiding our thoughts there

> will be potential bad guys - maybe we will call them capitalists, or emperors, or whatever - and there will be potential good guys, the multitude. This is quite like when the conceptualization of economic struggle was capitalists versus the proletariat or versus the working class, with no other economic agents operating.
>
> The trouble with a two constituency approach to agents of economic change is that it covers over the existence of the coordinator class and makes it seem that beyond bad capitalist economics there can only follow either more of the same or, instead, good multitude economics.
>
> This is quite like orthodox Marxism Leninism's mentality that there is capitalism and then there is socialism. An economy simply must be one or the other. (Albert 2005)

In a similar vein, Adams states:

> The authors actually seek to move back to a time in which Marxist ideology ruled the vast majority of social movements, when it was still generally believed that economics was the fundamental driving force of world order. The way in which they accomplish this, it seems, is through an often rather imperceptible slippage between the nonlinear, existentialist and subsistentialist concept of the multitude and the linear, progressivist and productivist concept of the proletariat; as a result, the authors reinforce yet another version of the very particularity/universality nexus they claim to oppose as the concept of the proletariat finally comes to overdetermine the concept of the multitude. (Adams 2003)

Choonara concentrates in his pointed critique also on those aspects of Negri and Hardt's approach that are akin to ones criticised by us in another "informational" prophet, Manuel Castells:

> Michael Hardt and Antonio Negri's first collaboration, *Empire*, exerted a powerful influence on the anti-capitalist movement, especially on those sections describing themselves as autonomist. In it they argued that capitalism has entered a new historical stage in which the sovereignty of nation-states is withering away in the face of globalisation. A new, global form of sovereignty—Empire—is rising up in its place composed of a series of national and supranational organisms united under a single logic of rule. Multinational corporations and global institutions like the International Monetary Fund or World Trade Organisation preside over this system alongside nation-states. Empire is not based on fixed boundaries or territorial centres of power. Instead power lies "both everywhere and nowhere." Accompanying this process, they argued, a new form of production, based on "immaterial labour" is become dominant. Instead of producing things, immaterial labour produces "a service, a cultural product, knowledge or communication." Such labour is not

> confined to the workplace. Just as capital spreads smoothly across the globe, so it spreads across the whole of society, seeking to absorb our creative powers: "As labour moves outside the factory walls ... the proletariat produces in all its generality everywhere all day long." This new proletariat includes all those subject to the rule of Empire, not just wage labourers directly employed by capital.
>
> Hardt and Negri's description of Empire was attractive to anyone who accepted the most extreme versions of globalisation theory, without sharing the reactionary conclusions of those who preached them. But the main appeal of the book lay in the claim that a new counterpower to Empire was emerging. This counterpower—multitude—is a collection of distinct individuals acting in common. It seemed to offer a way of describing the forms of resistance on the streets of Seattle in 1999 and at subsequent anti-capitalist mobilisations, while avoiding the language of an old left, which was discredited or irrelevant in the eyes of many activists. (Choonara 2005)

This is a fairly convincing explanation, which, however, does not affect the author's overall critical stance:

> The concept of the multitude outlined by Hardt and Negri is equally problematic. The authors use the term in two senses: to describe all those subject to the power of capital and to describe the counterpower capable of overcoming Empire. In the first sense multitude is counterposed to Marx's idea of the working class: "Working class is fundamentally a restricted concept based on exclusions ... The working class is thought to be the primary productive class and directly under the rule of capital, and thus the only subject that can act effectively against capital. The other exploited classes might also struggle against capital but only subordinated to the leadership of the working class. Whether or not this was the case in the past, the concept of the multitude rests of the fact that it is not true today...all forms of labour are today socially productive." (Choonara 2005)

As suggested above, the concept "productive (labour)" despite its long history, and perhaps because of it is ambiguous , which is also evident in the above passage. Productive of what? Exploited on what basis? Such questions could be multiplied. To at least some of them we shall return above. But before reverting to the article quoted above, let us draw the readers attention to yet again source of the said ambiguity in this instance- our concern is with the phrase "socially productive". Does it mean the same as economically productive, which would be permissible insofar as the economy is ingrained into social relations. Equally, however(and below we will have an opportunity to test our supposition), the phrase can possess some special sense, closer to what one associates with an idea of "producing society" literally, whatever this might mean.

> Hardt and Negri [...] claim that "in the final decades of the 20th century, industrial labour lost its hegemony and in its stead emerged 'immaterial labour.' Immaterial labour produces symbols, codes, texts or ideas, or it takes the form of 'affective labour' producing and manipulating emotions or feelings. The first form of immaterial labour seems to fit most readily for media or IT workers, while 'affective labour' can be applied to 'flight attendants and fast food workers'." The authors[...] argue that [immaterial labour] is hegemonic in the sense that other forms of labour tend to become more like it, and they claim that immaterial labour does not obey the laws of motion of capitalist society developed by Karl Marx n his economic writing. Put crudely, for Marx the value of commodities—regardless of whether they are material goods or 'immaterial' services—reflects the average labour time required to produce them. But for Hardt and Negri the concept of the working day as the basic measure of value no longer makes sense: "If production is aimed at solving a problem ... or creating an idea or a relationship, work time tends to expand to the entire time of life." (Choonara 2005)

First and formost, one might say not without malice that the authors' leadership of the so-called autonomous movement has, nomen omen, led them too far to the extent that the above argument is grounded in autonomous, unorthodox, or more crudely- incorrect logic. They've commited the fallacy of contradiction in terms. If, as Hardt and Negri maintain, all other forms of labour become increasingly like their discovery, i.e. "immaterial labour", how come that between the latter and material labour there are so huge differences as regards what determines their respective values. In the history of economics, and more broadly-social science, many well-known and less known scholars attempted to refute Marx's LTV as well his particular conceptions. We are afraid, Negri and Hardt are not amongst those likely to success in that enterprise True, even in Marx's writings (more in his juvenile works) one may encounter some speculative arguments, mostly reflecting his Hegelian fascinations but nowhere the author of "Capital" comes near to Negri and Hardt's truly perplexing idea of lifetime of work as determining the value of their immaterial labour. Well, it is true, and by the way was also clear as day to Marx (of which the aforementioned authors are apparently unaware) that intellectual work, including one designated within our framework as "pre-material labour" is scarcely measurable , time is evidently not applicable in this instance. Well, Negri and Hardt's fame is in our humble opinion something of a puzzle (although below we attempt an explanation). The critic cited above is not very fond of the idea just mentioned either:

> Applying this to an example of an immaterial labourer they use, it implies that workers at McDonald's spend their leisure time obsessing over how to improve customer satisfaction. (Choonara 2005)

Highly ironic as it is, this remark shows the absurdity of the conception under consideration. And there is even more to the matter than that:

> The authors also discuss the increasing casualisation of jobs, and in doing so they massively overstate the trends that they discuss. There is a tension between the desire of capitalists to force workers into badly paid, less secure work and their need for a stable, skilled and healthy workforce.
>
> The core of workers in secure jobs in the developed world has proved remarkably resilient. There are other problems with their analysis. There is evidence that industrial workers are not just growing numerically, but that they also play an increasingly important role in world production as their productivity grows. The question of developing an industrial base continues to be a central concern of governments and capitalist elites around the world, not least as a prerequisite for them to wage war upon each other. In some areas of the world the service sector has grown. But these jobs are not part of a free-floating weightless economy based simply on ideas and concepts. The service sector involves workers like airport baggage handlers, postal workers and call centre workers, who all utilise large amounts of capital in their work and experience the same stresses and strains of work as industrial workers.
>
> I will consider the sector of the economy that seems to conform most closely to Hardt and Negri's vision. […] the bazaar method of software development […] is supposedly based on individual but cooperating programmers forming networks very similar to Hardt and Negri's model of the multitude. But the reality is rather different to the one they suggest. The most successful open-source product is the Linux computer operating system. Far from being developed by a network or swarm, its development is centralised through a "core-development team" to whom suggested changes to the source code must be submitted. According to one analyst, only 1,000 people contribute changes to Linux on a regular basis. An even smaller group of 100 programmers contributed 37,000 out of 38,000 recent changes, all of whom were paid by their employers to work on the operating system. The main employers willing to release staff to work on Linux include Intel, IBM, Hewlett Packard and other giants. They have a vested interest in competition with Microsoft's Windows operating system, and have accumulated vast amounts of capital, allowing them to dominate the world market. Nor is it clear that open-source programming produces better software. […] Even in this sector, capitalists are still driven to

> extract profits from their workers, to compete with their market rivals and then to accumulate capital in order to increase their competitive edge.
>
> Hardt and Negri's final argument is that "material production … creates the means of life [but] immaterial production, by contrast, including the production of ideas, images, knowledge, communication, cooperation, and affective relations, tends to create not the means of social life but social life itself." This is an extreme form of idealism turning Marx's view that "social being determines social consciousness" on its head. It reflects Hardt and Negri's real aim—to replace concrete analysis of the capitalist system with a theory of pure subjectivity in which Empire equals power and the multitude equals creativity.
>
> The weakness of the authors' economic theory means they cannot explain how capitalists are motivated, how capital is divided between different units or the uneven way in which it accumulates. So they offer no analysis of the weak points in the capitalist system or how best to strike at them. If Empire is "smooth" then all points are equally vulnerable. If a homeless or unemployed person is as critical to the capitalist system as an industrial worker, simply by virtue of their "extraordinary resourcefulness and creativity," then there is no need to assess the relative power of different classes in society. In short, there is no need for any kind of strategy to challenge Empire. […] Hardt and Negri argue that the commonalities between different members of the multitude will allow it to come to political conclusions spontaneously in the same way as it comes together to produce "cooperation, communication, forms of life and social relationships." […] the concept of multitude is more than a metaphor for the movement. It is a fundamental attack […] upon the need for political organisations to fight for a strategy to overthrow our rulers. (Choonara 2005)

Abstracting from extra-substantive, political issues, let us comment briefly on Negri's central notion of immaterial labour, that is, of:

> the informationalisation or computerisation of labour practices in industrial production as well as the analytical, symbolic functions and affective forms of labour in the tertiary (or service) sectors of the economy. Suffice it to say, here, that when the computer becomes the central tool of production, whether of immaterial or material goods, it becomes the "universal tool" that homogenizes labouring processes. In this way, "labour tends toward the position of abstract labour. (Hardt & Negri 2000, 292)

Hardt & Negri do not dispose of not only adequate economic but also social theory. Such notions as ownership or ownership of labour power are striking by their absence. From the perspective of socio-economic structuralism, the concept of immaterial labour should be dissected to mean pre-material, conceptual labour and work performed by holders of particularistically instrumental labour power, as those terms are explained in subsequent chapters. In short, no big deal, which also refers to the notion of multitude which invokes old divisions rather than constitutes any breakthrough, as its loud proponents would have it.

To return to Castells, he also claims that the information age is still a capitalist age (although he suggests the informational mode of development could survive the end of capitalism) it is post-capitalist. Castells' power of persuasion is apparently insufficient as many commentators remain unconvinced. For instance, May, considering work in the information society, covers the familiar ground of the growth of the service sector and focuses on the purported expansion of knowledge work as alleged by commentators such as Handy. The quantitative and qualitative dimensions of this thesis are assessed and found unconvincing due to the persistence, indeed intensification suggests May, of capitalism. The key continuity is that of property relations, which in the information society mainly concern intellectual property rights. As in the case of earlier forms of capitalism, May argues that the institution of private property operates in the same way for intellectual property as it does for other types of property. May reckons that the class nature of inequality in the information society has been neglected in "mainstream comment."

In Castells' model, capitalists are no longer the ruling class: their power has been usurped by the networks. The true logic of the system is the logic of the networks. Despite the Spanish internet guru's fans probable protestations to the contrary, this claim of the prophet of the "information revolution" is anything but revolutionary. Castells himself, as his Marxist background should prompt him, should know that Marx long ago wrote: "The function fulfilled by the capitalist is no more than the function of capital—viz. the valorization of value by absorbing living labor—executed consciously and willingly. The capitalist functions only as personified capital, capital as a person, just as the worker is no more than labor personified" (quoted in Garnham 2004, 240). Both Garnham and Webster point out that the capitalists remain in control. The propertied class has better access to education, and its members are dominant in the top managerial positions which Castells claims are in control of the networks (Webster 2002, 118). This criticism, however, is not precise enough; in actual fact there is hardly any class contradiction between capitalist managers and proprietors as the former, as is argued in the book, cannot be treated as simply gainfully employed professionals owing to the sheer size of their pay which in fact is composed also, and in many cases primarily, of surplus value.

His depiction of the contemporary world is so familiar, even derivative (Webster 2002, 115). Its propositions about the character of contemporary society seem commonplace: the increasing importance of information and knowledge, the increasing speed and of financial and other transactions and the consequent destabilization, the growing gap between the knowledge-rich and the knowledge-poor, the sense that we are indeed in a time of social and technological discontinuity. However, this can also be seen as a success in capturing contemporary life.

More serious criticisms target Castells' analysis of the role of information, of production, and of the relationship between informational labour and capitalism. These critiques call into question his claim that the present economic and social situation is a new age, rather than a continuation of industrial capitalism. Because Weber's treatment of class was extensively discussed in the chapter devoted to the German sociologist's theories, let us concentrate in the present chapter on Marxian or, more broadly, Marxist views. At the very outset, one common error should be corrected. We have in mind a widely held view according to which in Marx the class structure was conceived of as consisting of two polar classes. This view most likely stems from an interpretation of Marx and Engels' most influential work *The Communist Manifesto*.[6] We have in mind the following passage:

> The history of all hitherto existing society is the history of class struggles.
>
> Freeman and slave, patrician and plebian, lord and serf, guild-masterand journeyman, in a word, oppressor and oppressed, stood in constant opposition to one another, carried on an uninterrupted, now hidden, now open fight, a fight that each time ended, either in a revolutionary reconstitution of society at large, or in the common ruin of the contending classes.
>
> In the earlier epochs of history, we find almost everywhere a complicated arrangement of society into various orders, a manifold gradation of social rank. In ancient Rome we have patricians, knights, plebians, slaves; in the Middle Ages, feudal lords, vassals, guild-masters, journeymen, apprentices, serfs; in almost all of these classes, again, subordinate gradations.

[6] It would be difficult to find an opponent of the view according to which "Although it at first had little or no impact on the widespread and varied revolutionary movements of the mid-19th century Europe, the Communist Manifesto was to become one of the most widely read and discussed documents of the 20th century." We could add that there is no indication that the situation will be any different in the twenty-first century.

> The modern bourgeois society that has sprouted from the ruins of feudal society has not done away with class antagonisms. It has but established new classes, new conditions of oppression, new forms of struggle in place of the old ones.
>
> Our epoch, the epoch of the bourgeoisie, possesses, however, this distinct feature: it has simplified class antagonisms. Society as a whole is more and more splitting up into two great hostile camps, into two great classes directly facing each other—bourgeoisie and proletariat.
>
> From the serfs of the Middle Ages sprang the chartered burghers of the earliest towns. From these burgesses the first elements of the bourgeoisie were developed.
>
> [...] the demand ever rising. Even manufacturers no longer sufficed. Thereupon, steam and machinery revolutionized industrial production. The place of manufacture was taken by the giant, modern industry; the place of the industrial middle class by industrial millionaires, the leaders of the whole industrial armies, the modern bourgeois. (Marx & Engels 1848)

While it should be emphasised that even the above famous sentences involve a more complex view of the societal class structure than is commonly thought, let us, for the sake of simplification, accept that this contains a grain of truth. Such an interpretation, however, abstracts from the primarily political and ideological, as distinct from scientific, nature of the document under consideration. Even leaving this circumstance aside, though, the above-mentioned view is extremely difficult to reconcile with, for example, the historical writings of Marx. In *The 18th Brumaire of Louis Bonaparte* he writes, for example, about "aristocracy of finance, the industrial bourgeoisie, the middle class, the petty bourgeoisie." Thus, according to this statement the bourgeois class should be further subdivided. Let us keep in mind this idea, since it will be taken advantage of in our own scheme of the class structure. Nevertheless, there is no denying that Marx did not leave any systematic definition of class. It is perhaps due to a too big workload that the scholar of such calibre has left so much of his business unfinished. Unfortunately, this applies, too, to the theory of class.

The relevant, *nomen omen* last chapter of *Capital* (its third volume) is, as is well-known, similar to Schubert's famous symphony. Still, Marx's claims give rich material for thought. Consider this:

> The owners merely of labour-power, owners of capital, and land-owners, whose respective sources of income are wages, profit and ground-rent, in other words, wage-labourers, capitalists and land-owners, constitute then three big classes of modern society based upon the capitalist mode of production.

> In England, modern society is indisputably most highly and classically developed in economic structure. Nevertheless, even here the stratification of classes does not appear in its pure form. Middle and intermediate strata even here obliterate lines of demarcation everywhere (although incomparably less in rural districts than in the cities). However, this is immaterial for our analysis. We have seen that the continual tendency and law of development of the capitalist mode of production is more and more to divorce the means of production from labour, and more and more to concentrate the scattered means of production into large groups, thereby transforming labour into wage-labour and the means of production into capital. And to this tendency, on the other hand, corresponds the independent separation of landed property from capital and labour, or the transformation of all landed property into the form of landed property corresponding to the capitalist mode of production.
>
> The first question to be answered is this: What constitutes a class?—and the reply to this follows naturally from the reply to another question, namely: What makes wage-labourers, capitalists and landlords constitute the three great social classes?
>
> At first glance—the identity of revenues and sources of revenue. There are three great social groups whose members, the individuals forming them, live on wages, profit and ground-rent respectively, on the realisation of their labour-power, their capital, and their landed property.
>
> However, from this standpoint, physicians and officials, e.g., would also constitute two classes, for they belong to two distinct social groups, the members of each of these groups receiving their revenue from one and the same source. The same would also be true of the infinite fragmentation of interest and rank into which the division of social labour splits labourers as well as capitalists and landlords-the latter, e.g., into owners of vineyards, farm owners, owners of forests, mine owners and owners of fisheries. (Marx 1894)

Let us, however, put ourselves in Marx's shoes and attempt to answer the question which he put to himself. In our view, there can be any doubt that the classes distinguished by the author of *Capital* are based on economically understood property relations. Now let's return for a while to our deliberations on Weber. It was our conclusion that the author of *Economy and Society* looked at what he called economic classes in very similar way, again contrary to common wisdom, which, as a rule, counterposes Weber to Marx. This claim holds up, we hasten to add, in spite of an array of reservations towards Weberian approach, which were listed in the chapter in question.

Let us verify our interpretation on one of Marx's most prominent followers who, as opposed to his master, left the precise definition of class. We are speaking, naturally, about Vladimir Lenin according to whom:

> Classes are large groups of people which differ from each other by the place they occupy in a historically determined system of social production, by their relation (in most cases fixed and formulated in law) to the means of production, by their role in the social organization of labour and, consequently, by the dimensions and method of acquiring the share of social wealth of which they dispose. Classes are groups of people one of which can appropriate the labour of another owing to the different places they occupy in a definite system of social economy. (Lenin 1947, 4921)

Again, much like as in the case of *The Communist Manifesto*, the concrete shape of Lenin's definition was impacted by the fact that it was formulated in the midst of the Russian revolution, and thus the greater body of the text containing it was bound to possess political rather than academic nature. Nevertheless, it contains many valuable ingredients. First and foremost, there can be no denying that for Lenin social classes are grounded in the relations of ownership (which, of course, hide behind otherwise rather ambiguous term: "the relation to the means of production"), not only clearly distinguished from their legal expression, but also including, which is most important, the ownership of the labour power. This clearly follows both from other, historical and socio-economic works by Lenin, but also from the context of the definition under discussion. Namely, Lenin stresses that for the total abolition of classes to happen, it does not suffice to abolish merely private property in the means of production, as he writes:

> It is clear that, in order to achieve the total abolition of classes, not only must the power of the landlord and the capitalist be broken, and their rights of property taken from them, but that EVERY private interest in the means of wealth production must be destroyed. The contrast between hand and brain worker [i.e. the owners of different types of the labour power] must also be ended. (Lenin 1947)

How important it is to acknowledge a class-determining character of ownership of not only the means of economic activity but also labour power is shown by the following, rather odd statement from the perspective of socio-economic structuralism by E. O. Wright:

> Giddens (1973) emphasizes Weber's argument that "market capacity" is defined not simply by the possession of capital or labor power, but also by the possession of market-relevant skills (see also Parkin 1971, 18–23).

> Giddens defines market capacity as "all forms of relevant attributes which individuals may bring to the bargaining encounter (in the market; p. 103)." He then discusses the specific capacities which shape classes in capitalist society … When market capacity is extended explicitly to include skills, then the market definitions of class may closely coincide with definitions based on occupational categories, since skill level is one of the basic ways in which occupations are differentiated within the technical division of labor. (Wright 1979)

Both theorists singularly fail to see that economic ownership is not opposed to market skills, market-relevant skills etc. since skills constitute one of the basic dimensions of labour power which in its part is a key object of economic property.

Lenin's definition has more merits, however. The fact, for example, that he uses the term "social economy" is, of course, fully consistent with the approach of such classics of the sociology of the economy as Maximilian Weber, which in turn, lets us insert our more modest observation, has been also adopted in the present work. Even more valuable is Lenin's focus on "the system of social production" as it suggests that classes exist also outside the sphere of production itself, although not outside the bounds of the economy.

We do not, however, dwell on what seems more controversial in Lenin's definition, do not wonder whether class exploitation has been conceived of by the author as a necessary or merely secondary and conditional element of the concept of class. This is the case because whatever Lenin's eventual position was, we reject any attempt at the reduction of the notion of the class structure to antagonistic classes. As has been discussed in the previous chapter, and will be further clarified below, each class structure, including that of capitalism, includes classes whose status cannot be couched in these bipolar terms. And yet, it is this simplistic reading of Lenin's definition that is by many identified with the position of the whole current to which Lenin subscribed. To take but one example, E. O. Wright, recognised by many as an expert on class, reckons that "The hallmark of Marxist discussions of class is the emphasis on the concept of exploitation" (1979, 14).

That said, the reader's attention may be drawn to the fact that the implication of Lenin's definition, including his remark about social classes as "large groups," is taken up below. That is to say, the question of two levels of the conceptualisation of class is addressed. Now, though, following our earlier observation regarding what we consider fruitful components of the definition being discussed, we may define classes as groups of people which differ from each other by the place they occupy in a historically determined system of economic activity (i.e. production, exchange, transport, finance and services).

I.11.2.1. Classes in the capitalist economic formation of society

The definition of classes as based on economic property relations could be, naturally, applied within the framework of pre-capitalist or, as vulgar social science would have it, pre-industrial societies. This task, however, goes beyond the confines of the present chapter, as it would entail a description of all economic formation of society and modes of economic activity and, on this basis, would extend our already very lengthy book.

The relation of capital to wage-labour or, to put it more in accord with socio-economic structuralism, labour power, which in the earlier economic formations of society appeared, if anything, in an underdeveloped, primitive shape, in capitalism, on the contrary forms its cornerstone constitutive of the whole formation which permeates it. As noted above, common wisdom that the capitalist formation includes as its ruling and, more important in the present context, unitary class, the bourgeoisie, is not substantiated on theoretical grounds upon a more solid analysis. This does not mean, as we shall see, any abolition or elimination of the notion of the capitalist class as a whole. This view, however, must be reconciled with an analysis at a more detailed level.

It is our contention that what is termed here "the capitalist megaclass" is composed of a number of different capitalist classes, pure and simple.

Thus, firstly, one should distinguish the industrial capitalists, i.e. owners of the industrial means of production, be it in manufacturing or mining, and, on the other side, the working class, i.e. owners of the sole labour power who lease it to the former proprietary class. Marx refers to their interrelation in the following terms:

> The Proletarian, by selling his labour for a definite quantity of the necessaries of life, renounces all claim to a share in the product. The mode of appropriation of the products remains the same as before; it is in no way altered by the bargain we have mentioned. The product belongs exclusively to the capitalist, who supplied the raw material and the necessaries of life; and this is a rigorous consequence of the law of appropriation, a law whose fundamental principle was the very opposite, namely, that every labourer has an exclusive right to the ownership of what he produces … When the labourers receive wages for their labour ... the capitalist is then the owner not of the capital only" (he means the means of production) "but of the labour also. If what is paid as wages is included, as it commonly is, in the term capital, it is absurd to talk of labour separately

> from capital. The word capital as thus employed includes labour and capital both." (James Mill: "Elements of Pol. Econ.," 1821, 70, 71.) (Marx 1976)

Put differently, the industrial capitalist is the prime owner of the product manufactured by the worker, According to Marx's labour theory of value, this product contains the surplus product or, in value terms, the surplus value. It goes without saying that this approach to ownership viewing it, as it does, as benefit is diametrically opposed to E. O. Wright and other Marxist scholars' popular interpretation according to which:

> Capitalist social relations of production can be broken down into three interdependent dimensions or processes:
>
> (1) Social relations of control over money capital, i.e., control over the flow of investments and the accumulation process, or alternatively, control over how much is produced and what is produced.
>
> (2) Social relations of control over physical capital, i.e., control over the use of the physical means of production, or control over how things are produced.
>
> (3) Social relations of authority, i.e., control over supervision and discipline within the labor process.
>
> The first of these is often referred to as "real economic ownership"; the second and third are often grouped together under the rubric "possession."
>
> The term control within each of these dimensions of social relations needs some explanation. As I shall use the term, control does not primarily refer to an aspect of the relationship of people to things, but rather an aspect of the social relations among people. In everyday language, control implies a capacity to make some kind of decision, and thus a capacity to dispose of some kind of resource. A social relation of control thus implies that this capacity is an attribute of a relation. Individuals per se, in these terms, do not "have" control over money capital, physical capital, or labor; that control is lodged in the social relation into which the individual enters. To say that "capitalists" control the means of production, for example, is to say that the social relationship between capital and labor simultaneously confers on the capitalist position the capacity to dispose of the means of production and deprives the working-class position of that capacity. In a sense, the social relation between capital and labor defines a relationship between these positions and things and thus between the incumbents of these positions (individuals) and things.
>
> This distinction between "positions" and "individuals" cannot be overemphasised. It becomes clearest when the actual decision-making process is lodged in a collectivity of positions, so that even in behavioural terms individuals qua individuals are not "making" decisions. But even when a single capitalist makes all of the decisions about investments, use of physical capital, deployment of labor, etc.

> This way of breaking down class relations has been developed in different ways by a number of European Marxists, in particular Balibar (1970), Poulantzas (1973a, 1975), and Bettelheim (1975). A related, but rather different treatment can be found in Carchedi (1977). (Wright 1979, 24)

As has been repeatedly argued on the pages of this book, this approach to ownership conflates it with either its preconditions or consequences. In addition, another arbitrary conceptual decision is to class one relation of the above set as "ownership" and another as "possession." Is the latter an aspect of economic ownership or a wholly independent relation? You can argue both ways, but the point is that it is not your duty to secure those key concepts' lack of ambiguity. Ironically, Wright does not follow his own theoretical guidelines according to which "Abstractions are thus not merely arbitrary, analytical conventions used to formulate generalizations about the world; they are conceptual tools necessary to construct real explanations of the world" (1979, 26).

The primeval property relation mentioned above entails that the class of industrial capitalists also have a potential ability, not always implemented in reality, of appropriation of several specific varieties of surplus-value. Firstly, as Marx explains in *Capital*, the capitalistic owner of the means of production may seek to prolong the duration of the working day.

> By that means alone can the value of labour-power be made to sink, and the portion of the working day necessary for the reproduction of that value, be shortened.
>
> The surplus-value produced by prolongation of the working day, I call absolute surplus-value. On the other hand, the surplus-value arising from the curtailment of the necessary labour-time, and from the corresponding alteration in the respective lengths of the two components of the working day, I call relative surplus-value. (Marx 1976)

The other way to increase the ratio of surplus labour to necessary labour is to reduce the necessary labour. The crudest way to do this is to reduce the workers' standard of living by reducing wages, which of course the employer will always do if he can. However, the same result, of reducing the proportion of necessary labour, will occur if productivity is increased so that, for example, the labour time necessary for the production of the articles the worker needs is reduced and their prices fall, with the consequent reduction of the value of labour-power without reducing the worker's standard of living.

The discussion reported clearly refers at this moment to what we have learned above about property. Marx highlights the social dimension of property, the fact that that the industrial capitalist takes advantage of merits of the social division of labour:

> In order to effect a fall in the value of labour-power, the increase in the productiveness of labour must seize upon those branches of industry whose products determine the value of labour-power, and consequently either belong to the class of customary means of subsistence, or are capable of supplying the place of those means. But the value of a commodity is determined, not only by the quantity of labour which the labourer directly bestows upon that commodity, but also by the labour contained in the means of production.

An additional variety of surplus-value corresponds to the notion of creative construction realised by a capitalistic entrepreneur:

> There is a motive for each individual capitalist to cheapen his commodities, by increasing the productiveness of labour. [...]
>
> On the other hand, however, this extra surplus-value vanishes, so soon as the new method of production has become general, and has consequently caused the difference between the individual value of the cheapened commodity and its social value to vanish.

It is even more to the concept of capitalist ownership than that. One can enumerate a number of additional sources of free benefits accrued to the class of industrial bourgeoisie. They appropriate the products of a spontaneous activity of, firstly, (we are referring here to the results of our earlier discussion of economic property) natural agents of labour, as Marx himself called them or, our own terminological proposal, natural assistants of work, that is, forces and processes of nature taking part in the process of production. Secondly, the same applies to an outcome of the activities of socio-natural assistants of labour, i.e. machines and automata. Thirdly, they also take advantage of the results of ideal or intellectual work of not only present, but also previous generations, which manifests itself in benefiting from the contemporary and older science. Fourthly, the class under consideration benefit from the merits of cooperation and division of labour at the plant level, which generate definite synergies and emerging effects, and the thing is that the capitalist pays wages of individual workers only, but not those of the joint, collective labourer. Thus, what they produce additionally, the owner of the industrial means of production gets free of charge.

Other savings-on transaction costs are possible, as we have learned, thanks to the very existence of the capitalistic firm.

The Marxian account of variants of surplus-value makes it possible to distinguish a special subcategory of the industrial capitalist, i.e. the monopoly bourgeoisie, whose members benefit economically from extraordinary profits of usually, in modern conditions, oligopolies or, more rarely, monopolies in the true sense of the word. The background to these profits may be described, after Marx, as extra surplus-value, the difference being that in the monopoly case the profits achieved are more stable and long-term, as the corporations in question are able to fix above-average prices. The socio-economic substance of the benefits acquired by monopolists is composed of an outflow of value from other sectors of the economy (buyers of their products), which may refer also to foreign firms, and this source of extra income is paralleled by another in the form of savings and, occasionally, money capital of individual customers. This special position of the monopoly capitalist (treated here as a distinctive capitalist class) does not need to translate itself into privileged position of the workers employed in such companies, who may share in those extra profits in the form of higher wages, special fringe benefits etc. One may add that monopolies can also be found in other sectors of the economy, to a discussion of which we now proceed.

Before taking this step, however, an outline of the class position of a specific and very important cluster of classes is needed. Resting, as we do, on the theory of socio-economic ownership, that identification may be effected without any recourse to such terminological inventions as Wright's "contradictory class locations." He explains his "conception of the middle class" as follows:

> (1) Managers and supervisors occupy a contradictory location between the bourgeoisie and the proletariat.
>
> (2) Semiautonomous employees who retain relatively high levels of control over their immediate labor process occupy a contradictory location between the working class and the petty bourgeoisie.
>
> (3) Small employers occupy a contradictory location between the bourgeoisie and the petty bourgeoisie.
>
> (Wright 1979, 27)

Our notions of ownership of capital and labour power permit as precise a class identification of those categories as you can get. Wright's term suggests, and rightly so, that a foreman is close to a worker in class terms. Our rendering of this affinity, though, is completely different. Insofar as he or she performs material labour, he or she is subject to capitalist exploitation since his or her labour produces surplus value. On the other hand, more complex and thus higher valued labour power entails a distinct class position. The latter consideration to an even greater extent applies to the mid-level managers. Special qualifications pertain also to the conceptual class, i.e. performers of pre-material labour. Top managers, on the other hand, to be sure, are holders of complex labour power as well. However, these performers of indirectly material labour are, for all practical purposes, members of the capitalist class. As has been pointed out in other contexts, even irrespective of their, usually held shareholdings, their earnings cannot be placed at a par with wage-labour as they consist, in large proportion, of surplus value. This can be easily demonstrated by comparing what is erroneously termed "executive pay" with remuneration of, say, military commanders of battalions of roughly equal size than that of the group of subordinates of an executive in question. As to Wright's "small employers," they should be classed not in those abstract class terms but as small capitalists, their class distinction lying in the size of the means of production held not releasing them from performing in person an indirectly material work.

Another pair of capitalist classes are composed of the owners of the means of transport and their employees. The term "workers" is in the present book reserved for the just discussed members of the industrial working class.

These, just like other operators of the respective means of economic activity can be grouped into a broader notion of mega-employee class. In point of fact, particular employee classes are far from identical. The transportation employees' class position shows, however, many features in common with the industrial proletariat. Members of both classes are owners of material labour power (as they are involved in material labour), and, secondly, they both possess abstract labour power, i.e. are capable of producing surplus-value. Marx elucidates this question in *Grundrisse* asking himself the following question:

> … can a surplus value be extracted from the transport costs? Let us deduct the constant part of the capital consumed in transport, ship, vehicle etc. and everything which falls under the heading of their application, since this element contributes nothing to the question, and it is irrelevant whether this is posited as = 0 or = x. Is it possible, then, that there is surplus labour in these transport costs, and that capital can therefore squeeze a surplus value out of them? The question is simple to answer if we ask a further question, where and which is the necessary labour or the value in which it objectifies itself? The product must pay (1) its own exchange value, the labour objectified in itself; (2) the surplus time, which the shipper, carter etc. employs on its transportation. Whether he can or cannot extract the surplus value depends on the wealth of the country into which he brings the product and on its needs etc., on the use value of the product for this land.

> In direct production, it is clear that all the surplus labour which the manufacturer makes the worker do is surplus value for him, in that it is labour objectified in new use values, which costs him nothing. But he can obviously not employ him during transport for a longer time than is required for the transporting. Otherwise he would throw labour time away instead of realizing it, i.e. he would not objectify it in a use value. If the sailor, the carter etc. require only half a year of labour time to live a full year (if this is generally the proportion of labour necessary for subsistence), then the capitalist employs him for a whole year and pays him a half. By adding a whole years labour time to the value of the transported products, but paying only ½, he gains a surplus value of 100% on necessary labour. The case is entirely the same as indirect production, and the original surplus value of the transported product can come about only because the workers are not paid for a part of the transportation time, because it is surplus time, time over and above the labour necessary for them to live. That an individual product might be made so much more expensive, owing to the transport costs, that it could not be sold—on account of the disproportion between the value of the product and its surplus value as a transported product, a quality which becomes extinguished in it as soon as it has arrived at its destination-does not affect the matter. (Marx 1939)

The situation is different, though, in the case of other employees under the capitalist mode of economic activity which is, of course, tied to the socio-economic and property situation of their employers.

Thus, the commercial capitalist, owning the means of exchange, acquires, owing to her or his employees' labour, not surplus-value produced by them, as their concrete labour power is incapable of it, but merely participates, thanks to the very labour, in the general pool of surplus-value generated in these branches of economy, which have such a capability. Indeed, Marx's *Capital* (Vol. III, Ch. 17) says that:

> The commercial worker produces no surplus-value directly. But the price of his labour is determined by the value of his labour-power, hence by its costs of production, while the application of this labour-power, its exertion, expenditure of energy, and wear and tear, is as in the ease of every other wage-labourer by no means limited by its value. His wage, therefore, is not necessarily proportionate to the mass of profit which he helps the capitalist to realise. What he costs the capitalist and what he brings in for him, are two different things. He creates no direct surplus-value, but adds to the capitalist's income by helping him to reduce the cost of realising surplus-value, inasmuch as he performs partly unpaid labour. The commercial worker, in the strict sense of the term, belongs to the better-paid class of wage-workers—to those whose labour is classed as skilled and stands above average labour. Yet the wage tends to fall, even in relation to

> average labour, with the advance of the capitalist mode of production. This is due partly to the division of labour in the office, implying a one-sided development of the labour capacity, the cost of which does not fall entirely on the capitalist, since the labourer's skill develops by itself through the exercise of his function, and all the more rapidly as division of labour makes it more one-sided. Secondly, because the necessary training, knowledge of commercial practices, languages, etc., is more and more rapidly, easily, universally and cheaply reproduced with the progress of science and public education the more the capitalist mode of production directs teaching methods, etc., towards practical purposes. The universality of public education enables capitalists to recruit such labourers from classes that formerly had no access to such trades and were accustomed to a lower standard of living. Moreover, this increases supply, and hence competition. With few exceptions, the labour-power of these people is therefore devaluated with the progress of capitalist production. Their wage falls, while their labour capacity increases. The capitalist increases the number of these labourers whenever he has more value and profits to realise. (Marx 1894)

The same characteristics apply to, respectively, the capitalist financial class, i.e. the owners of the means of money circulation, and their financial employees, working in banks, insurance companies, etc.

It is also the class of employees working in the services sector that do not generate directly for their employers surplus value, but merely ensure them an access to such value generated elsewhere. Therefore, there should be no misunderstanding over the use by Marx in the following quotation of the term "productive." From the standpoint of socio-economic structuralism this term should in fact be referred to as "substantive." These are Marx's words from *Capital* (Vol. I, Ch. 15):

> … our notion of productive labour becomes narrowed. Capitalist production is not merely the production of commodities, it is essentially the production of surplus-value. The labourer produces, not for himself, but for capital. It no longer suffices, therefore, that he should simply produce. He must produce surplus-value. That labourer alone is productive, who produces surplus-value for the capitalist, and thus works for the self-expansion of capital. If we may take an example from outside the sphere of production of material objects, a schoolmaster is a productive labourer when, in addition to belabouring the heads of his scholars, he works like a horse to enrich the school proprietor. That the latter has laid out his capital in a teaching factory, instead of in a sausage factory, does not alter the relation. Hence the notion of a productive labourer implies not merely a relation between work and useful effect, between labourer and product of labour, but also a specific, social relation of production, a relation that has

> sprung up historically and stamps the labourer as the direct means of creating surplus-value. To be a productive labourer is, therefore, not a piece of luck, but a misfortune. (Marx 1976)

It is also the class of domestic servants who hold merely concrete labour power, i.e. the effect of this labour, be they services, or consumer goods, are purchased on account of their specific use-value, and not as a source of surplus-value and profit. Their work does not bring in their principal any income; on the contrary, the latter purchases the useful effects of the activity of their labour power from her or his personal income. Marx points out in *Capital* (Vol. I, Ch. 24) that:

> Just as little as the commodities that the capitalist buys with a part of the surplus-value for his own consumption, serve the purpose of production and of creation of value, so little is the labour that he buys for the satisfaction of his natural and social requirements, productive labour. Instead of converting surplus-value into capital, he, on the contrary, by the purchase of those commodities and that labour, consumes or expends it as revenue. (Marx 1976)

As has been suggested above, the most crucial reason for which any definition of class in polar terms is inadequate is the circumstance that there exist a number of social classes that do not fit into the simplified notion of class antagonism in that they remain outside the exploitative relations. Even in capitalist farming, there are to be found not only large landowners who, as appropriators of the ground rent constitute a special class, or large farmers, employing hired labour, but also smallholders, or peasants, who own or lease their parcels of land, and also own the agricultural means of production. Their essentially urban (although they may be also present in the countryside) equivalent are, commonly so-called in Marxist circles (the sociologist of another stripe would probably use the term the "middle class") "petty bourgeoisie." The term appears highly emotionally and ideologically laden, and is often conceived of as pejorative, although, frankly speaking, such a moral evaluation has no historical grounds. Each social class has its pluses and minuses, and amongst members of each of them there are both heroes and rogues. However, given this persistent historical tradition, it seems that the best way to avoid such dilemmas would be to propose an alternative term used, amongst others, by Weber: "autocephalous," which means (of an Eastern Christian Church) governed by its own national synods and appointing its own patriarchs or prelates (of a bishop) independent of any higher governing body.

The above term appears to render this crucial feature of the given class' socio-economic position that they own their means of economic activity, but set them in motion themselves, i.e. without employing any alien labour power.

Anyway, the existence of such classes is of course incompatible with Wright's sweeping generalisation that "all class positions are contradictory, in that class relations are intrinsically antagonistic social relations" (1979, 26). It remains a mystery how this acclaimed theorist reconciles this claim with his own observation that:

> simple commodity production (i.e. production organized for the market by independent, self-employed producers who employ no workers) has always existed within capitalist societies. Within simple commodity production, the petty bourgeoisie is defined as having economic ownership and possession of the means of production, but having no control over labor power (since no labor power is employed). (Wright 1979, 26)

To round off our discussion of class, let us mention two more sets of classes.

The first one is composed of lumpenclasses, i.e. functioning within the framework of the lumpeneconomy. Whereas the term "lumpenproletariat" is widely known, it should be considered too narrow, if it were to serve as a comprehensive notion describing the lumpenstructure for, in actual fact, this peculiar class structure is considerably more complex, and can be conceived of as a reflection of the class relations obtaining in the regular economy. The name "lumpenproletariat" should be applied to the individuals whose position in the lumpeneconomy is analoguous to that occupied by the industrial proletariat and other substantive wage employees. The case in point is supplied by the so-called "gang soldiers," whose class position cannot, however, be compared with that of drug barons, mafia bosses and other members of what certainly deserves to be called the lumpenbourgeoisie. Another distinct lumpenclass is the lumpenpetty bourgeoisie or, to use our terminological invention, the autocephalous class. An illustration is provided by independent drug dealers, also independent beggars, or self-employed prostitutes.

Finally, something which should be music to feminists' ears. In most sociological theories that, which is still rare rather than frequent, take account of the question of the class position of housewives, they are ascribed to the same class where the so-called head of the family, which still under the traditional family model, albeit slowly changing in modern conditions, is usually her husband. Of course, as suggested above, fully possible is the reverse situation, i.e. that it is the wife who works for pay, is the breadwinner, while her spouse is rearing their kids, and is cooking and so forth. This in no way alters our question, which is: how is the class position of those housewives or househusbands to be defined? Given the fact that the persons in question perform a lot of socially and economically important quasi-work, it becomes implausible to attribute to then only a secondary class position. From the perspective of socio-economic structuralism these persons should be classified as relatively independent quasi-classes. The word "relatively" refers to an undisputable distinction between quasi-work and regular labour, due to which it is only those members of the household who are engaged in the latter that bring in the means of subsistence. This circumstance is tied to the fact that particular quasi-classes take their prefixes from the kind of work performed by their life partners. Thus, if the basic means of subsistence are earned by the factory worker, then his non-working wife would be classed as a member of worker quasi-class.

I.11.3. The estate structure

The final part of this chapter must concern the groups whose societal position has so far not been taken into consideration. To make the long story short, it is the issue of agents of work executed in the particular non-economic structures. Polish economist Oskar Lange and, following him, sociologist Stanislaw Kozyr-Kowalski have chosen as a tool of description of these groups' social position the term "strata," adding that so understood strata are engaged in various types of non-productive work. Even leaving aside all the controversies that historically accrued to the said notion, the more serious criticism brings to light the fact of the impossibility of eliminating the arbitrary meaning of the concept, shared with the theory of stratification which uses the same term, defining the whole approach. In order to convince oneself that the approach being discussed is flawed, suffice it to ask whether the judge and the prosecutor, or the grammar school teacher and university lecturer are engaged in the same kind of unproductive work or not. Any answer goes, because there are no precise, or indeed any criteria for outlining the lines of demarcation between the different types of the said form of work.

Fortunately, some cues in that respect may be found (where else?) with Karl Marx. In his various writings (many of them posthumuously published manuscripts) he uses the term "nononproductive classes" with reference to social groups, whose livelihood rests on government taxes, such as the clergy, the law occupations, the state bureaucrats etc. These get to be called "social estates," and there's the rub. The term "*Soziale*

Stünde," which also figures prominently in Weber's theory of social differentiation is, as a rule, translated into English erroneously, as "status groups," or even "status classes." Meanwhile, the term has an altogether different connotation, and its association with feudalism or the old epoch of the Middle Ages is, rather than a drawback, the merit of the concept, as it allows us to pinpoint such contemporary social groups that bear similarity to their conceptual forebears in important respects. What conclusions, then, may be drawn from Marxian research practice? If the groups in question are called "unproductive classes" as distinct from "productive," i.e. economic classes, then the implication is that the, termed elsewhere and adopted here, social estates may be conceived of as based on the relations of non-economic property, as opposed to the relations of economic ownership the socio-economic classes are grounded in.[7]

Thus, non-economic property is manifested in various aspects of the social situation of military officers, clergymen, police officers, lawyers, judges, professional politicians etc. Namely and more specifically, the relations of non-economic property appear as definite material and immaterial goods enjoyed by the representatives of particular estates. As will be seen, in plain language our key concept has much in common with such phrases as privileges, perks, special advantages etc. In order to better comprehend the content of the term "non-economic ownership" a list of respective relations is presented below:

(1) Appropriation, on a monopolistic basis, of certain lucrative positions in the social division of labour, and thereby the benefits tied to them. The monopoly in question is most frequently secured by the regulation of supply of prospective candidates to privileged occupations. A case in point is a variety of professional associations or corporations, acting, as a rule, to stop or limit the inflow of new lawyers, or physicians, to mention but a few. These professional associations play, in fact, a role of old-time guilds, just as their historical antecedents influence, too, professional practice of their members, including its moral side.

What these and many other estate positions often give is:

---

[7] Thus, from this point of view the following statement, along usual anti-Marxian lines, is then misguided: "Weber's theory of stratification differs from that of Marx in that he introduced an additional structural category, that of 'status group.' Classification of men into such groups is based on their consumption patterns rather than on their place in the market or in the process of production. Weber thought Marx had overlooked the relevance of such categorization because of his exclusive attention to the productive sphere" (http://www. bodlinger.com).

(2) Special social connections, which are transferable into economic advantages.[8]

(3) Access to insider, privileged information. This refers, among others, to the police. Their occupational position gives them a higher salary, social benefits, and some other advantages, which are named below but, frankly speaking, often the chief appeal of the occupation lies in the fact that it creates many opportunities of extra earnings. These, in turn, are linked to the ability to take advantage of the spy ring and information they collect. This information has often very high monetary value, and can be sold to, for example, private detectives, parents of lost children, journalists,[9] owners of vehicles that have been stolen from them by professional thieves, acting, as a rule, on behalf of car dealers, mechanics or smugglers with whom the police often co-operate, as they do with other criminals.

(4) The ability to enter into short-term relations of lumpenproperty. This applies in particular to bribes received in many countries, notably those of immature capitalism by police officers, and bribes and kickbacks obtained by government officials.

(5) Appropriation of advantages listed under the previous two items can be facilitated and strengthened by the use of exclusive professional languages, jargons or codes. Among the social estates there are a lot of examples of the use of language or speech in order to create appearances of high knowledge seemingly enjoyed by this or that member of the social estate, whereas put in the plain language it would in all likelihood turn out to be quite comprehensible for the laymen, but it is precisely their ignorance that is the point.

(6) Privileged access to various consumer goods, new auto models and brands tried by journalists, mobile telephones and notebooks given to the journalists and politicians, special policy offers submitted by insurance companies.

(7) Special, often exclusive participation in various cultural or sport events.

---

[8] See Bourdieu who writes about "material profits, such as all the types of services accruing from useful relationships," and, elsewhere, about the "effect of social capital, 'a helping hand,' 'string-pulling,' the 'old boy network'" (1986).

[9] As the so-called hacking scandal connected with Murdoch's News Corp. clearly shows.

(8) The right to live in official, often luxurious apartments.

(9) The ability to take advantage of special recreational centres and facilities.

(10) An access to special, exclusive medical services of high standard.

(11) The ability to a shorter occupational expenditure of own labour power, be it in the form of longer holidays, or earlier retirement.
Items 8 to 11 express, in fact, the privileged capacity of reproduction and renewal of one's own labour power.

(12) The ability to take advantage of various reliefs and reductions, e.g. in transportation and communication, such as lower internet or cell telephone charges.

(13) Distinctive attire available to given social estates: police officers, firemen and customs officials' uniforms, professorial togas, gowns of clergymen.

(14) The right to hold definite official titles which refer to professorships, police officers, military officers, lawyers or doctors.

(15) The right to exercise power and control over the behaviour of other people. This applies, naturally, not only to the police, but also to, for example, the confessor who, within the mechanism of expiation is able to mete out punishments to the believers.

(16) The right to command special esteem or respect, which pertains to military officers, court judges, teachers and the academia. It follows that social respect is here understood as necessarily manifested in concrete behaviours.

(17) Diplomatic immunity which may take the form of an agreement between sovereign governments to exclude diplomats from local laws, immunity from prosecution (international law), exclusion of governments or their officials from prosecution under international law, judicial immunity, i.e. immunity of a judge or magistrate in the course of their official duties, parliamentary immunity or immunity granted to elected officials during their tenure and in the course of their duties, qualified immunity in the United States, immunity of individuals performing tasks

as part of the government's actions, sovereign immunity, the prevention of lawsuits or prosecution against rulers or governments without their given consent.

(18) Copyright or intellectual property relations (scholars, columnists, etc). Particular social estates are characterised by peculiar configurations of the relations of non-economic property listed above.

CHAPTER II.12.

ECONOMIC SOCIOLOGY OR THE ECONOMIC STRUCTURE AND THE NON-ECONOMIC SOCIETAL STRUCTURES AS CONCEIVED BY SOCIO-ECONOMIC STRUCTURALISM

II.12.1. The fundamental thesis of economic sociology as a theoretical-empirical proposition

A motto of economic sociology can be considered as what Marx in the Preface to "A Contribution to the Critique of Political Economy" calls "the guiding principle of" his studies which can be summarised as follows.

> In the social production of their life, men enter into definite relations that are indispensable and independent of their will, relations of production which correspond to a definite stage of development of their productive forces. The sum total of these relations of production constitutes the economic structure of society, the real foundation, on which rises a legal and political superstructure and to which correspond definite forms of social consciousness.
>
> The mode of production of material life conditions the social, political and intellectual life process in general. It is not the consciousness of men that determines their being, but, on the contrary, their social being that determines their consciousness. (Marx 1976)

Let us expand on the above contention and lay out some basic relations of dependence of non-economic structures upon, to use Marx's phrase, their economic foundation. In the course of this presentation we will try to obey the guidance given in "The German Ideology," according to which empirical observation must in every case demonstrate the relationship between the social and political structures on the one hand, and production without any speculation or mystification.

II.12.1.1. The economic structure as an existential basis of non-economic structures

The elementary, but at the same time vital mechanism of the dependence of non-economic structures from the economic structure has been nicely described by Friedrich Engels as the fact that people have to, first and foremost, eat, drink, have a shelter and, hence, work, before they are able to fight over power, deal with politics, religion, philosophy etc. By the same token, Engels maintains that those members of society that are members of non-economic structures and those who are engaged in the processes of production and exchange of material goods thanks to which politicians, artists, clergymen and others are in a position to do their respective kinds of non-economic work. This thesis implies another, according to which the means of material work must reach a definite level of development allowing their operators to produce more than is necessary for their functioning in that character, i.e. manufacture the surplus product, which provides the indispensable means of subsistence for the agents of non-economic structures.

II.12.1.2. Material work, immaterial work, and quasi-work as actions performed in the course of definite periods of time

The above-mentioned claim entails the next one, which suggests that the magnitude of the surplus product conditions the number of people which can be released from the economic activity, as well as, more generally, the quantity of time that society can devote to scholarly, governmental, religious, sport and other non-material activities.

The more developed are the means of material work, i.e. the shorter the period of time needed for the production of the necessary means of subsistence, the more societal resources, including time, can be assigned to the non-economic structures. This relationship, however, manifests itself not only at the global, societal level, but also at the nanostructural, i.e. individual level. Economic growth can be, amongst other things, taken advantage of in order to shorten the working time which, in turn, lengthens, proportionately, the quantity of time the individuals concerned can reserve for any kind of non-material work and, particularly, quasi-work such as theatre attendance, book reading, internet browsing, walking the dog or whatever. The opposite is true as well, that is to say employment restricts the quantity of time in which a person can engage in quasi-work. This concerns particularly, but not exclusively, working mothers who often have less time for their children and families in general due to difficulties in reconciling professional and household duties.

This relationship however, as hinted above, is broader than this. Everyone can in his or her everyday experience easily find examples of how lengthy working time negatively influences the opportunities for leisure, participation in culture etc. The length of working time influences the ability to engage in most extra-substantive activities. Upon coming back from one's job, when one is very tired, one's leisure is, as a rule, restricted to the most passive forms of rest like watching television or listening to pop music, as opposed to the activities which require more active engagement, be it opera or theatre attendance, or reading of books. Non-substantive activities also, naturally, take certain determinate time. This concerns for example political activity or self-education. A worker or employee whose wage or salary underprices her or his value of labour power has to take up some extra work in order to maintain their standard of living. This, as a rule, excludes any participation in the activities of political parties as well as self-development.

Work on shifts hugely limits one's capacity to rear children and access to many cultural or sporting events which take place at a certain time of a day or week, unsuitable from the point of view of a given individual. It restricts, if not rules out, any common time spent with the family. A more complete picture of how the work schedule affects individual and collective rhythms and patterns of life is obtained when its extended week scale is taken into consideration. An introduction of an additional day free of work enables material or substantive employees concentration on the book being read or on the lectures or talks attended, and it widens one's ability of, for example, tourist activity or physical exercise. The five-day working week also greatly exerts a positive influence on the organisation of time within the family. Now, for example, a working woman can do her chores in one holiday day, which leaves still one weekend day which can be devoted to the entire family. The said work schedule influences, too, the organisation of collective life, e.g. working hours of people employed in retail or services, as well in educational outfits, the entertainment industry, etc. It is also the work rhythm on a yearly basis that is relevant to the worker. When one's holiday is partitioned into short sections, it makes it difficult, if not impossible, to regenerate one's physical and psychic forces, or, in other words, one's own the labour power.

II.12.1.3. The economic structure as a source of the means of activity of non-economic structures

Our analysis of the influence that the economic structure exerts on non-economic structures began by pointing to its form which consisting in providing the latter the necessary means of subsistence. Material work processes, however, produce not only consumer goods, but also such goods that serve as indispensable means of non-substantive work and quasi-work.

For the political structure to function efficiently, for instance, lots of the means of respective work processes are needed: from police baton to an extramodern aircraft carrier. Engels points out that "This public force exists in every state; it consists not merely of armed men, but also of material appendages, prisons and coercive institutions of all kinds." However, it is much more to this than that. Engels may certainly be considered an expert on war; see the following account by Leon Trotsky:

> The old idea of the Pythagoreans, that the world is ruled by numbers—in the realistic and not the mystical sense of the word—may be especially well applied to war. First of all—the number of battalions. Then the number of guns, the number of ordnance pieces are expressed quantitatively: through the range of the firearm, through its accuracy. The moral qualities of the soldiers are expressed in the capacity to endure long marches, to hold out for a long time under enemy fire, etc. However, the further we penetrate into this field, the more complicated the question becomes. The amount and character of the equipment depends upon the condition of the forces of production of the country. The composition of the army and the personnel of its command is conditioned by the social structure of society. The administrative supply apparatus depends upon the general-state apparatus, which is determined by the nature of the ruling class. The morale of the army depends upon the mutual relations of the classes, upon the ability of the ruling class to make the tasks of the war the subjective aims of the army. The degree of the ability and talent of the commanding personnel depends in turn upon the historical role of the ruling class, upon its ability to concentrate the best creative forces of the land upon their aims, and this ability depends again in turn upon whether the ruling class plays a progressive historical role or has outlived itself and is only fighting for its existence.
>
> [...] In reality, the dependence of the various fields of war conduct upon each other, and of all of them taken together upon the various aspects of the social order, are much more complex and detailed. On the battlefield, this is all summed up in the last analysis in the number of ordinary soldiers, the commander, the dead and wounded, prisoners and deserters, in the size of the conquered territory and in the number of

> trophies. [...] Only the most immediate material elements of war may be expressed in numbers.
>
> In so far, however, as it is a question of the dependence of the material elements of the army upon the economy of the country as a whole, any appraisal, and therefore also any foresight, will have a much more conditional value.[...] In his military newspaper chronicle, so modest in the task it sets itself, Engels [...] brings to his work the sharp eye of a military analyst.[...] "Let us now compare the forces," says Engels, "that are being got ready for mutual destruction; and to simplify matters, we will take the infantry only. The infantry is the arm which decides battles; any trifling balance of strength in cavalry and artillery, including mitrailleurs and other miracle-working engines, will not count for much on either side" (Notes on the War, Note I, page 1.)
>
> What was right, by and large, for France and Germany in 1870, would undoubtedly no longer hold for our time. It is now impossible to determine the relationship of military forces only by the number of battalions. It is true that the infantry remains even today the main factor in battle. But the role of the technical coefficients in the infantry has grown extraordinarily, although in very unequal measure in the different armies: we have in mind not only the machine guns which were still "miracle-working" in 1870; not only the artillery, which has increased in number and importance; but also perfectly new auxiliaries: the motor truck for war as well as for transportation purposes, aviation, and war chemistry. Any statistics that do not take these "coefficients" into consideration and deal only with the number of battalions, would now be completely unreal. (Trotsky 1944)

In contemporary conditions, apart from the traditional armaments industry, there developed a whole sector of high-technology material work which produces the supermodern means of coercion, for example riot police. The use of these means has, it must be conceded, some humanitarian consequences for the participants of mass demonstrations or manifestations, as they allow for police interventions without any bloodshed.

Science, to be sure, itself impacts upon the economy, even to the extent that many scientific outputs become part and parcel of the process of material work. On the other hand, however, it is this process, whether in its handicraft or modern industrial shape that supplies for the development of the natural sciences fundamental means by which to carry observations and experiments, from microscopes and telescopes to lasers and spacecraft. More generally, it could be said, borrowing from Wikipedia, that:

> Scientific instruments are part of laboratory equipment, but are considered more sophisticated and more specialized than other measuring

instruments. They are increasingly based upon the integration of computers to improve and simplify control, enhance and extend instrumental functions, conditions, parameter adjustments and data sampling, collection, resolution, analysis (both during and post-process), storage and retrieval. Individual instruments can also be connected as a local area network (LAN) and can be further integrated as part of a laboratory information management system (LIMS) ….

Some scientific instruments can be quite large in size, like *particle colliders* that can be several miles in circumference or radio-telescope antennas and antenna arrays used in astrophysics. As you might expect, the converse or nanoscale also has been added to the list of the realm of scientific instrument applications and research, with much of the activity centered around the use of miniaturization in the field of medicine, particularly as non-invasive imaging has exploded on the diagnostic arts and minimally invasive tools and robotics have extended the reach of surgeons of every stripe. In fact, instruments on the scale of a single molecule may soon interact with our bodies at the cellular and biochemical level to collect diagnostic information and provide highly precise medication delivery mechanisms.

Scientific instruments can be found on board sounding rockets, satellites or planetary rovers and controlled by radiotelecommunication. (Wikipedia entry—"Scientific Instruments")

To illustrate the dependence being discussed in still more specific terms, the following are some of the current products of only one firm, Scientific Instruments Inc.:

- Liquid level, temperature and density tank gauging systems
- Cryogenic temperature sensors
- Cryogenic temperature monitors and controllers
- Industrial liquid level and temperature probes
- Aerospace liquid level and temperature probes and transducers
- Commercial aircraft temperature probes

Temperature sensors include Silicon Diode, Ruthenium Oxide, and Platinum RTD sensors. These sensors are used in petrochemical, aerospace, laboratory and research, high energy physics devices and industrial applications.

As some of the previous examples show, the dependence under consideration concerns, too, medicine which is certainly tied to science, but which in our terms is to be located within the framework of the reproductive structure.

It is also the educational substructure that uses to increasingly greater extent many products of material work. To be sure, the said dependence manifests itself equally in the case of the chalk, board, or desk, which all have to be manufactured by material work. Nowadays, however, the dependence being discussed manifests itself not only in the form of these relatively ancient instruments, but also in modern computers, video equipment, language labs etc.

The same holds in the case of art. The existence of the huge industry of musical instruments may be mentioned here. Film and Modern recording studios, CDs, DVDs, amplifiers, microphones etc. are all, of course, effects of material work.

Some strands of modern art provide an even more apparent manifestation of the artists' reliance upon technology and material work, using the means of material production to manufacture installations or other modern artistic forms, whereas the creator herself often confines themself to the role of a designer.

One specific example is Bob Campbell, also known as Stig, who is as much a metal sculptor as he is an industrial artist or furniture designer. Using scrap metal parts from cogs and wheels to chains and treads, he crafts recycled one-off pieces and furniture sets that use a creative combination of manufactured pieces and built-from-scratch shapes. He incorporates leather, wood and other industrial materials as needed but metal is always at the core of his work. He has sold his unique metal furniture pieces to all kinds of people through various venues, ranging from high-end luxury retail stores to music festivals, street markets and his own personal private gallery. His work itself is open to interpretation but his unique style and curious material choices certainly set him up to be seen as existing somewhere between traditional arts and crafts and modern mechanical engineering (www.stig-art.co.uk).

A similar relationship can be detected with reference to the remaining forms of non-substantive work and quasi-work. Industrialised sports of today is a case in point. Or take any contemporary household. Could one imagine oneself its effective functioning without such industrial goods as freezers, washing machines or, last but not least, garden lawns?

II.12.1.4. Socio-economic conditioning of language

The distinctiveness of the present subsection lies primarily in its focus on an ideal object, as opposed to the previous part of the text. The relevance of what follows to the broader topic of this chapter lies in the fact that language constitutes an indispensable instrument of work performed by the writer, the scholar, the journalist, the clergyman, the official, the military officer and the police officer alike. Now it turns out that the social sciences have collected a lot of evidence regarding socio-economic determinants of language. Language usage varies among social classes, and it is these "sociolects" that sociolinguistics studies.

Sociolinguistics, as a field distinct from dialectology, was pioneered through the study of language variation in urban areas. Whereas dialectology studies the geographic distribution of language variation, sociolinguistics focuses on other sources of variation, among them class. Class and occupation are among the most important linguistic markers found in society. One of the fundamental findings of sociolinguistics, which has been hard to disprove, is that class and language variety are closely related. In what follows it is, of course, only such studies as are available and can be used, and it would be rather pointless to criticise their theoretical framework (which, to be sure, leaves much to be desired in many cases) post hoc as we have no other option than to take their results as given anyway.

Members of the working class tend to speak less standard language, while the lower, middle, and upper middle class will in turn speak closer to the standard. However, the upper class, even members of the upper middle class, may often speak "less" standard than the middle class. This is because not only class, but class aspirations, are important. Class aspiration studies, such as those by William Labov in the 1960s, have shown that social aspirations influence speech patterns. This is also true of class aspirations. In the process of wishing to be associated with a certain class (usually the upper class and upper middle class), people who are moving in that direction socio-economically will adjust their speech patterns to sound like them.[1] However, not being native upper class speakers, they often hypercorrect, which involves overcorrecting their speech to the point of introducing new errors. The same is true for individuals moving down in socio-economic status:

> Basil Bernstein, a well-known British socio-linguist, devised in his book, *Elaborated and Restricted Codes: Their Social Origins and Some Consequences*, a social code system which he used to classify the various speech patterns for different social classes. He claimed that members of the

---

[1] Matters are not that simple, though; as opposed to this ladder-like, or elevator-like image, the working-class members may in certain contexts look down on someone who talks posh. In this area, as in many others, times change; BBC, for example, now makes more room for a variety of sociolects, whereas not long ago only one standard version of accepted English was used by its presenters.

middle class[2] have ways of organizing their speech which are fundamentally very different from the ways adopted by the working class. In Basil Bernstein's theory, the restricted code was an example of the speech patterns used by the working class. He stated that this type of code allows strong bonds between group members, who tend to behave largely on the basis of distinctions such as "male," "female," "older," and "younger." This social group also uses language in a way which brings unity between people, and members often do not need to be explicit about meaning, as their shared knowledge and common understanding often bring them together in a way which other social language groups do not experience. The distinctive feature of the restricted code is the emphasis on "we" as a social group, which fosters greater solidarity than an emphasis on "I."

Bernstein also studied what he named the "elaborated code," explaining that in this type of speech pattern the middle and upper classes use this language style to gain access to education and career advancement. Bonds within this social group are not as well defined and people achieve their social identity largely on the basis of individual disposition and temperament. There is no obvious division of tasks according to sex or age and generally within this social formation members negotiate and achieve their roles, rather than have them there ready-made in advance. Due to the lack of solidarity, the elaborated social language code requires individual intentions and viewpoints to be made explicit as the "I" has a greater emphasis with this social group than the working class.

The differences in grammar between the two examples of speech can be referred to as differences between social class dialects or sociolects.

It is generally assumed that non-standard language is low-prestige language. However, in certain groups, such as traditional working class neighbourhoods, standard language may be considered undesirable in many contexts. This is because the working class dialect is a powerful in-group marker, and especially for non-mobile individuals, the use of non-standard varieties (even exaggeratedly so) expresses neighbourhood pride, and group and class solidarity. There will thus be a considerable difference in use of non-standard varieties when going to the pub or having a neighbourhood barbecue (high), and going to the bank (lower) for the same individual.

(Wikipedia entry—"sociolinguistics")

---

[2] It may be relevant to note that from the viewpoint of the theory of class peculiar to socio-economic structuralism, the term in question does not refer to any class at all, but at best to a social stratum or a cluster of them, as only those refer to a ladder-like image of the social structure, while the class structure does not, contrary to accepted wisdom, constitute any simple hierarchy.

II.12.1.5. Social consciousness as a reflection of material work

This subsection is similar to the previous one in that it also deals with ideal structures. Illustrations of the title mechanism abound. Engels notices, for instance, that "the theory of heat did not develop from pure thought, but from a study of the economic working of steam engines," and comes to the conclusion that: "Until now they have only boasted of what production owes to science, but science itself owes infinitely more to production" (Engels 1894). Alternatively, take the history of painting. From its earliest, prehistoric examples where the most common themes in cave paintings are large wild animals, such as bison, wild horses, aurochs and deer in relation to which Henri Breuil interpreted the paintings as being hunting magic, meant to increase the number of animals through ancient Egypt and, a big leap forward, in many paintings of the Dutch school to the modern times[3] painters commonly depicted various objects and means of material work, as well as its subjects, be it peasants toiling in the field, or factory workers. Themes related both to material work and quasi-work are to be found, for example, within the broad spectrum of works by one of the most-loved artists, Vincent Van Gogh such as *Peasant Woman Laundering*, *Potato Digging (Five Figures)* or *Auvers Wheat Harvest*.

In relation to another substructure of social consciousness "Anti-Duehring" reads:

> … men, consciously or unconsciously, derive their ethical ideas in the last resort from the practical relations on which their class position is based—from the economic relations in which they carry on production and exchange.
>
> But nevertheless there is great deal which the three moral theories mentioned above have in common—is this not at least a portion of a morality which is fixed once and for all?—These moral theories represent three different stages of the same historical development, have therefore a common historical background, and for that reason alone they necessarily have much in common. Even more. At similar or approximately similar stages of economic development moral theories must of necessity be more

[3] To illustrate, Fernard Leger, "upon his return to France in 1945, his work became less abstract, and he produced many monumental figure compositions depicting scenes of popular life featuring acrobats, builders, divers etc. Art historian Charlotta Kotik has written that Leger's 'determination to depict the common man, as well as to create for him, was a result of socialist theories widespread among the avant-garde both before and after World War II.' However, Léger's social conscience was not that of a fierce Marxist, but of a passionate humanist."

> or less in agreement. From the moment when private ownership of movable property developed, all societies in which this private ownership existed had to have this moral injunction in common: Thou shalt not steal (Exodus 20:15; Deuteronomy 5:19). Does this injunction thereby become an eternal moral injunction? By no means. In a society in which all motives for stealing have been done away with, in which therefore at the very most only lunatics would ever steal, how the preacher of morals would be laughed at who tried solemnly to proclaim the eternal truth: Thou shalt not steal!
>
> We therefore reject every attempt to impose on us any moral dogma whatsoever as an eternal, ultimate and for ever immutable ethical law on the pretext that the moral world, too, has its permanent principles which stand above history and the differences between nations. We maintain on the contrary that all moral theories have been hitherto the product, in the last analysis, of the economic conditions of society obtaining at the time. And as society has hitherto moved in class antagonisms, morality has always been class morality; it has either justified the domination and the interests of the ruling class, or ever since the oppressed class became powerful enough, it has represented its indignation against this domination and the future interests of the oppressed. That in this process there has on the whole been progress in morality, as in all other branches of human knowledge, no one will doubt. But we have not yet passed beyond class morality. (Engels 1894)

This fairly brief sketch of the manifestations of dependence of various departments of social consciousness upon the economic structure is, of course, not meant as an exhaustive one. The same caveat applies to the whole section which is surely to be conceived of as an outline of some of the relevant processes and relationships in which further research is clearly both needed and desirable rather than as a comprehensive depiction of the topic.

II.12.1.6. Quasi-Work as Conditioned by Ownership of Capital and Labour Power

While language may be considered as a means of many types of work, including quasi-work, and various forms of social consciousness can perform that role as well, quasi-work is dependent on the economic structure in another important respect as well. Here, social classes as groupings of people of similar position relative to ownership of capital and labour power comes up as a mediating mechanism.

> … in many of the areas central to sociological endeavour there is little evidence that the influence of class is declining and, indeed, some evidence that its influence is Growing. Shavit and Blossfeld's (1993) edited collection shows that the influence of class origins on children's educational attainment showed no decline over the course of the twentieth century in thirteen developed nations. The papers in Evans (2000) demonstrate that the much vaunted 'general decline of class voting' is an inaccurate description of the rather complex and cross-nationally varying trends in this phenomenon. Class voting seems to have weakened in Scandinavia, but in Germany, France and elsewhere no such temporal change is evident. Lastly, in the area of social mobility, Breen and Goldthorpe (2001) show that in Britain, during the last quarter of the twentieth century, there has been no change in the extent to which class origins help shape class destinations. This holds true even controlling for educational attainment and measures of individual ability. This result may then be added to the evidence of longer-term temporal stability in patterns of class mobility in Europe reported by Erikson and Goldthorpe (1992). (Savage et al. 2006)

There are a number of studies showing classes vis-a-vis dependent outcomes, such as educational attainment (Halsey, Heath & Ridge 1980), social mobility prospects (Erikson & Goldthorpe 1992), voting behaviour (Evans 1999), and health outcomes (Bartley 2004; Savage et al. 2006). Another such study shows how work, position, life, social situation, etc. interact and combine. This analysis allows one to:

> … nail the myth that top managers are prone to more heart attacks because of "pressure." They are not and we now know why. With responsibility comes status, power, control, and the means to relieve stress (membership of the gym, a night at the opera, a holiday villa) is often arranged by your secretary and so on. As you move lower down, so people's lives become more bound up with lower status, less control and the need to battle and juggle a host of other commitments. It is the harassed worker on the shop floor or in the office who is more at risk of a heart attack and, beneath them, the cleaner doing two jobs on minimum wage. This also explains negative health behaviours and why these should give rise to different incidences of disease when the same immediate causal factors, e.g. smoking, appear to be present. But some readers may be puzzling about a theoretical problem in the link between social class and the health gradient. Those who insist that we live in a class society have to defend themselves not only against those who deny the reality of class but also those who want to define it simply in terms of hierarchy. It is here that we run up against the fundamental weakness of the argument about social gradients in health. It is clear that they exist, but what causes them? What is the "cause of the cause"? To solve this problem we have to look behind the gradients and explore what determines the different incomes, jobs and

> degree of control that people have over their lives. This means that the central thing has to be class analysis and showing how any gradient is structured by ownership and control and not least, in capitalism, by ownership and control of the means of production.
>
> Here several related concepts are absolutely central—alienation, exploitation, class and class conflict. Inequalities are a consequence of how these interact and it is from this that social gradients and gradients of ill health flow. Marmot makes occasional gestures towards this but they are weak and inconsistent. The same is true of Wilkinson even though he has a more systematic grasp of the social side. To insist on the importance of this is not just about adding an additional layer of possibly superfluous explanation. It makes the argument stronger in terms of its logic and explanatory power, and it gives it a clearer political thrust because it also forces us to consistently address the political economy of both health causation and the limits of reform within the system.
>
> Alienation, for example, is fundamental to explaining both our loss of control of social processes and the way that they are turned against us, and our resulting inability to relate to one another as proper human beings. Exploitation gives us the possibility of understanding how and why the rewards go to the few who make so little contribution to our real wealth. And class and class conflict help us to understand the resulting texture of social relationships and their antagonisms.
>
> We can make these arguments work in a more precise fashion too. As organisations have become more powerful the argument arises about who has effective disposition of capital and labour within them. The key social argument here is that the more your position gives you control over capital and labour, control over yourself, your work, the work and lives of others, the lower the levels of ill health. The more your life is controlled by others the less the level of health. The social gradient is not simply about "who has what" but the capacity to command people and resources—the very issue that is at the centre of class analysis. (Haynes 2009)

The same class approach fully confirmed its utility in my own research, as reported in Tittenbrun (2010), proving that class and estate positions significantly influence voting, political and high-culture participation, religious behaviour, the extent of exposition to occupational diseases, hazards and accidents.

The weight of the topic under investigation is clearly shown by the fact that it attracted the attention of a leading U.S. broadsheet. Reporters of *The New York Times* spent more than a year studying the conditions of life in contemporary America. The result of their field studies was a series of articles under the telling title "Class Matters" showing how class position affects religion, marriage, culture, mobility, education and health chances. As far as the latter field is concerned, the article in question reads:

Class is a potent force in health and longevity in the United States. The more education and income people have, the less likely they are to have and die of heart disease, strokes, diabetes and many types of cancer. Upper-middle-class Americans live longer and in better health than middle-class Americans, who live longer and better than those at the bottom. And the gaps are widening, say people who have researched social factors in health.

As advances in medicine and disease prevention have increased life expectancy in the United States, the benefits have disproportionately gone to people with education, money, good jobs and connections. They are almost invariably in the best position to learn new information early, modify their behavior, take advantage of the latest treatments and have the cost covered by insurance.

Many risk factors for chronic diseases are now more common among the less educated than the better educated. Smoking has dropped sharply among the better educated, but not among the less. Physical inactivity is more than twice as common among high school dropouts as among college graduates. Lower-income women are more likely than other women to be overweight, though the pattern among men may be the opposite.

There may also be subtler differences. Some researchers now believe that the stress involved in so-called high-demand, low-control jobs further down the occupational scale is more harmful than the stress of professional jobs that come with greater autonomy and control. Others are studying the health impact of job insecurity, lack of support on the job, and employment that makes it difficult to balance work and family obligations.

Then there is the issue of [...] differences in the knowledge, time and attention that a person's family and friends are in a position to offer. What is the effect of social isolation? Neighborhood differences have also been studied: How stressful is a neighborhood? Are there safe places to exercise? What are the health effects of discrimination? Heart attack is a window on the effects of class on health. The risk factors—smoking, poor diet, inactivity, obesity, hypertension, high cholesterol and stress - are all more common among the less educated and less affluent, the same group that research has shown is less likely to receive cardiopulmonary resuscitation, to get emergency room care or to adhere to lifestyle changes after heart attacks.

"In the last 20 years, there have been enormous advances in rescuing patients with heart attack and in knowledge about how to prevent heart attack," said Ichiro Kawachi, a professor of social epidemiology at the Harvard School of Public Health. "It's like diffusion of innovation: whenever innovation comes along, the well-to-do are much quicker at adopting it. On the lower end, various disadvantages have piled onto the poor. Diet has gotten worse. There's a lot more work stress. People have less time, if they're poor, to devote to health maintenance behaviors when they are juggling two jobs. Mortality rates even among the poor are

> coming down, but the rate is not anywhere near as fast as for the well-to-do. So the gap has increased."
>
> Bruce G. Link, a professor of epidemiology and sociomedical sciences at Columbia University, said of the double-edged consequences of progress: "We're creating disparities. It's almost as if it's transforming health, which used to be like fate, into a commodity. Like the distribution of BMW's or goat cheese." (Scott 2005)

As to the relationship between class position and education, a *New York Times* columnist has the following story to tell:

> Since high school, Caleb has had six jobs, none very promising. Now 28, he may never reach the middle class, he said. But for his father and others of a generation that could count on a comfortable life without a degree, the fall out of the middle class has come as a shock. They had been frozen in another age, a time when Kaiser factory workers could buy new cars, take decent vacations and enjoy full health care benefits.
>
> They have seen factory gates close and not reopen. They have taken retraining classes for jobs that pay half their old wages. And as they hustle around for work, they have been constantly reminded of the one thing that stands out on their résumés: the education that ended with a high school diploma.
>
> It is not just that the American economy has shed six million manufacturing jobs over the last three decades; it is that the market value of those put out of work, people like Jeff Martinelli, has declined considerably over their lifetimes, opening a gap that has left millions of blue-collar workers at the margins of the middle class.
>
> And the changes go beyond the factory floor. Mark McClellan worked his way up from the Kaiser furnaces to management. He did it by taking extra shifts and learning everything he could about the aluminum business.
>
> Still, in 2001, when Kaiser closed, Mr. McClellan discovered that the job market did not value his factory skills nearly as much as it did four years of college. He had the experience, built over a lifetime, but no degree. And for that, he said, he was marked. [...]
>
> By the time these two Kaiser men were forced out of work, a man in his 50's with a college degree could expect to earn 81 percent more than a man of the same age with just a high school diploma. When they had started work, the gap was only 52 percent. Other studies show different numbers, but the same trend—a big disparity that opened over their lifetimes. (Egan 2005).

Choices made in another field were investigated by the author of the next article:

> Marriages that cross class boundaries may not present as obvious a set of challenges as those that cross the lines of race or nationality. But in a quiet way, people who marry across class lines are also moving outside their comfort zones, into the uncharted territory of partners with a different level of wealth and education, and often, a different set of assumptions about things like manners, food, child-rearing, gift-giving and how to spend vacations. In cross-class marriages, one partner will usually have more money, more options and, almost inevitably, more power in the relationship.
>
> It is not possible to say how many cross-class marriages there are. But to the extent that education serves as a proxy for class, they seem to be declining. Even as more people marry across racial and religious lines, often to partners who match them closely in other respects, fewer are choosing partners with a different level of education. While most of those marriages used to involve men marrying women with less education, studies have found, lately that pattern has flipped, so that by 2000, the majority involved women, like Ms. Woolner, marrying men with less schooling—the combination most likely to end in divorce. (Lewin 2005)

Equally valuable as the case studies very sketchily outlined above are the general remarks made by the way of summary of the series:

> There was a time when Americans thought they understood class. The upper crust vacationed in Europe and worshiped an Episcopal God. The middle class drove Ford Fairlanes, settled the San Fernando Valley and enlisted as company men. The working class belonged to the A.F.L.-C.I.O., voted Democratic and did not take cruises to the Caribbean.
>
> Today, the country has gone a long way toward an appearance of classlessness. Americans of all sorts are awash in luxuries that would have dazzled their grandparents. Social diversity has erased many of the old markers. It has become harder to read people's status in the clothes they wear, the cars they drive, the votes they cast, the god they worship, the color of their skin. The contours of class have blurred; some say they have disappeared.
>
> But class is still a powerful force in American life. Over the past three decades, it has come to play a greater, not lesser, role in important ways. At a time when education matters more than ever, success in school remains linked tightly to class. At a time when the country is increasingly integrated racially, the rich are isolating themselves more and more. At a time of extraordinary advances in medicine, class differences in health and lifespan are wide and appear to be widening. [...] class as Americans encounter it: indistinct, ambiguous, the half-seen hand that upon closer examination holds some Americans down while giving others a boost [...] it appears that while it is easier for a few high achievers to scale the summits of wealth, for many others it has become harder to move up from

one economic class to another. Americans are arguably more likely than they were 30 years ago to end up in the class into which they were born.

A paradox lies at the heart of this new American meritocracy. Merit has replaced the old system of inherited privilege, in which parents to the manner born handed down the manor to their children. But merit, it turns out, is at least partly class-based. Parents with money, education and connections cultivate in their children the habits that the meritocracy rewards. When their children then succeed, their success is seen as earned.[...]

One study, by the Federal Reserve Bank of Boston, found that fewer families moved from one quintile, or fifth, of the income ladder to another during the 1980's than during the 1970's and that still fewer moved in the 90's than in the 80's. A study by the Bureau of Labor Statistics also found that mobility declined from the 80's to the 90's.

The incomes of brothers born around 1960 have followed a more similar path than the incomes of brothers born in the late 1940's, researchers at the Chicago Federal Reserve and the University of California, Berkeley, have found. Whatever children inherit from their parents—habits, skills, genes, contacts, money—seems to matter more today.[...]

One surprising finding about mobility is that it is not higher in the United States than in Britain or France. It is lower here than in Canada and some Scandinavian countries but not as low as in developing countries like Brazil, where escape from poverty is so difficult that the lower class is all but frozen in place.

Those comparisons may seem hard to believe. Britain and France had hereditary nobilities; Britain still has a queen. The founding document of the United States proclaims all men to be created equal. The American economy has also grown more quickly than Europe's in recent decades, leaving an impression of boundless opportunity. (Scott, Leonhardt 2005)

The facts reported above are actually not that surprising; they may come as a surprise merely to someone who remains a believer in some cherished American mythswhich picture the society concerned in a very selective way, to say the least. Certain vestiges of feudalism can be found also in many other societies; after all, although the phenomena concerned have entirely modern origins, the authors themselves point to many ascriptive, hereditary aspects of their own society. Finally, they do not identify the underlying source of those American peculiarities as compared to Europe, which lies in the distinction between the two socio-economic models analysed in the separate chapter.

But the United States differs from Europe in ways that can gum up the mobility machine. Because income inequality is greater here, there is a wider disparity between what rich and poor parents can invest in their children. Perhaps as a result, a child's economic background is a better predictor of school performance in the United States than in Denmark, the Netherlands or France, one recent study found.

"Being born in the elite in the U.S. gives you a constellation of privileges that very few people in the world have ever experienced," Professor Levine said. "Being born poor in the U.S. gives you disadvantages unlike anything in Western Europe and Japan and Canada."

This has helped produce the extraordinary jump in income inequality. The after-tax income of the top 1 percent of American households jumped 139 percent, to more than $700,000, from 1979 to 2001, according to the Congressional Budget Office, which adjusted its numbers to account for inflation. The income of the middle fifth rose by just 17 percent, to $43,700, and the income of the poorest fifth rose only 9 percent.

For most workers, the only time in the last three decades when the rise in hourly pay beat inflation was during the speculative bubble of the 90's. Reduced pensions have made retirement less secure.

Clearly, a degree from a four-year college makes even more difference than it once did. More people are getting those degrees than did a generation ago, but class still plays a big role in determining who does or does not. At 250 of the most selective colleges in the country, the proportion of students from upper-income families has grown, not shrunk.

[...] According to the data of Economic Policy Institute, In 1980, those with the highest socio-economic status had a life expectancy 2.8 years higher than those with the lowest status (75.8 versus 73.0 years, respectively). By 2000, that gap had grown: those in the top decile had attained a life expectancy of 79.2 years—4.5 years more than those in the bottom decile. Disparities in life expectancy also increased between the top and the middle decile and between the middle and the bottom.

Class plays an increased role, too, in determining where and with whom affluent Americans live. More than in the past, they tend to live apart from everyone else, cocooned in their exurban chateaus. Researchers who have studied data from the 1980, 1990 and 2000 censuses say the isolation of the affluent has increased.

Family structure, too, differs increasingly along class lines. (Scott, Leonhardt 2005)

The material presented or referred to in this section, of course, makes nonsense of fairly widespread claims of those thinkers who dub social class a “zombie variable” or “shell institution” (Beck 2002; Giddens 1999). Now, unlike the most eminent exponent of the concept, class itself has been buried many times. However, in all those cases rumours about its death have turned out to be premature, to say the least.

Given that all empirical evidence on the persistent relevance of class is widely available, all the prophets of its death should be ashamed, to say the truth. Gentlemen, it really is a no brainer!

AFTERWORD

"I hope I haven't bored you."
—The final words of Elvis Presley

The theoretical-methodological position underlying the book, whose reading you have just finished my dear reader, has been termed socio-economic structuralism as it is this name that appears to clearly point to what may be considered the two pillars of the author's approach: a sociological account of the economy on the one hand, and an investigation of various ways in which the economic structure affects the entire non-economic realm. Both these tasks are not viable, unless one disposes of a solid and accurate theory of society writ large which, in our view, is composed, to return to the title term of the approach, of a number of structures that themselves may be conceived of as consisting of a further sets of substructures.

It remains to clarify the character of what may be considered the third, as yet unmentioned pillar of our theory. Our epistemological (methodological) perspective in the strict sense of the word should be termed "dialectical realism." The role of dialectics is manifested especially in our stressing of contradiction as an analytical category forming, an intrinsic component of the concept of structure. The other side of this ontological coin is epistemological in nature, in the form of stressing the role of contradiction as an explanatory variable, notably accounting for change. It is also in dialectical terms that the cognitive relation is treated, which underscores the distinction between the said position and naive realism. In what ways the notion of dialectical realism is similar to, or distinct from that of critical realism, goes beyond the confines of the present study. The use of "realism" is at the same time our reason why, for example, the term "materialism" has not been chosen. From our standpoint, it is precisely our terminological choice, and not materialism as such, that is referred to in this account by Engels: "The basic premise of materialism is that there is an objective world which exists independently of and predates human beings, human ideas and consciousness." It is, therefore, also for these substantive as opposed to ideological reasons that we prefer our term "socio-economic structuralism" rather than "historical materialism." In addition, while Marx's influence on our thinking is undeniable, our approach, somewhat like *The Structure Of Social Action*, draws much from other theorists that have been discussed in the book, such as Weber, Durkheim or Parsons, to mention but a few.

To what extent our theoretical and methodological ideas have proved to be fruitful it is not for us to judge, of course. By way of summary, therefore, a statement reflecting to a considerable degree our own views will be cited:

> Although sociology and economics have ignored one another for decades, developments in both disciplines during the past twenty years suggest that cautious rapprochements are beginning to crack the solid lines that have separated them. [...] Ever since the early 1970s, starting from criticism of the restrictive assumptions of the general equilibrium theory and developments in game theory, economics has clearly been opened to problems and subjects that had previously been ascribed essentially to the domain of sociology. These include developments in the economics of information, the transaction cost theory, principal-agent approaches, the new historical economy, and the incorporation of bounded rationality into game theory.[...] Meanwhile, in the 1960s and 1970s, sociology moved away from functionalist and structuralist theoretical approaches and became increasingly devoted to approaches based on theories of action. Criticism of functionalism led especially to projects intended to make social structures and processes intelligible in reference to social action, without being tied to the rational-actor model for its behavioral typology. On this background, a renewed interest in socio-economic problems has developed since the 1980s. In the 1950s and 1960s, economic sociology dealt with problems that were marginalized by economics. But the "new economic sociology" claims to be able to demonstrate on the ground of the substantial core areas of economic theory how economic functions can be understood better through sociological conceptualizations. (Beckert 1996)

This appears to be a rather simplistic and overly optimistic judgment; on the one hand, many sociologists still cling to the rational choice paradigm, and on the other, the hype around the so-called new economic sociology is not matched by its accomplishments- and conversely, many "old economic sociologists", such as Parsons, dealt with problems that wer far from marginal.

> While these developments in economics and the new economic sociology indicate an entente between the disciplines, they still remain separated from one another at the demarcation line of the rational-actor model. (Beckert 1996)

Whilst Beckert's thesis is generally correct, his caveats laid out below are less so, especially as regards economists' treatment of altruism, which in most cases, as pointed out above, on both logical and substantive grounds leaves much to be desired.

> The central assumption of the maximization of utility has been both criticized and expanded by the theory of bounded rationality and by attempts to integrate altruistic behavioral motivations, yet the paradigmatic core of economics is defined by the action-theoretical notion of an individualized, universal maximizer of utility. Ever since the establishment of modern economics in the eighteenth century, the moral-philosophical justification for the behavioral model of *homo economicus* has consisted of the expectation, expressed in the metaphor of the invisible hand, that action directed at self-interest leads to a desirable allocation of economic goods, both collectively and individually. Pursuit of private interest is the basis for the emergence of the common welfare. This link between behavioral expectations and institutional structure is also the basis of liberal economic policy: the demand for unlimited markets by removing trade barriers and restraining government regulation is justified normatively by the expected increase of wealth.
>
> The new economic approaches developed as criticism of equilibrium theory with respect to its assumptions about market structures and the supply of information of market participants. They show that, often, under realistic premises, either no unequivocal equilibria exist or that stable equilibria with inefficient resource allocation develop. This results in market failure. But market failure calls into question the central link of economic theory between rational individual action, unlimited markets, and optimal distribution of economic goods; the claim of the superiority of rational individual action cannot be generally maintained under the more realistic assumptions. The close connection between self-interested action and economic efficiency becomes precarious ….
>
> … sociology can contribute to understanding the bases of economic efficiency. The decisive consideration here is that the discrepancy of the connection between rational action and efficient results asserted by economic theory forces the revision of the action theory that underlies the understanding of economic action. To substantiate this hypothesis … the emergence of efficient equilibria cannot be generally explained from the behavioral model of economic theory and, thus … removing limits on markets does not per se lead to the increase of economic efficiency. [...]
>
> A proper understanding of the significance of cultural, social, and cognitive structures for the efficiency of market economies can be achieved only when we go beyond the market as a universal institution for the allocation of economic goods and supersede the rational-actor model.[1] (Beckert 1996)

[1] There are some, though still rare, signs of hope; "a modification of these (rational choice) assumptions is essential to further progress in the social sciences. The

The last sentence of the above pronouncement is perfectly correct but it would be a mistake to think that the only impediments to overcoming the cognitive barrier indicated lie within the bounds of pure science. As Bourdieu aptly recalls:

> It is perhaps by recalling the arbitrary nature of the founding distinction (a distinction still present today in the minds of economists, who leave the curiosa or failings of economic operations to sociologists) between the economic order, governed by the effective logic of the market and a place of logical behaviours, and the uncertain "social" order, shot through with the 'non-logical' arbitrariness of custom, passions and powers, that we can best contribute to the integration, or 'hybridization', of the two disciplines of sociology and economics—disciplines which have undergone a dramatic separation, in spite of the efforts to the contrary on the part of some of their great founders (Pareto and Schumpeter, for example, in the direction of sociology, and Durkheim, Mauss, Halbwachs, and, above all, Weber, in the direction of economics). One can reunify an artificially divided social science only by becoming aware of the fact that economic structures and economic agents or, more exactly, their dispositions, are social constructs, indissociable from the totality of social constructs constitutive of a social order. But this reunified social science, capable of constructing models that cannot easily be assigned to either of the two disciplines alone, will undoubtedly find it very hard to win acceptance, both for political reasons and reasons relating to the specific logic of scientific worlds. There are undoubtedly many who have an interest in obscuring the connections between economic policies and their social consequences or, more precisely, between so-called economic policies (the political character of which asserts itself in the very fact of their refusing to take account of the social) and the social, and economic, costs—which would not be so difficult to calculate if there were any will to do so—of their short- and long-term effects (I have in mind, for example, the increase in e"conomic and social inequalities resulting from the implementation of neoliberal policies, and the negative effects of those inequalities on health, delinquency, crime, etc.). But if strong reasons exist for the cognitive hemiplegia currently afflicting sociologists and economists to perpetuate itself, in spite of the increasing efforts to overcome it, this is also because the social forces that weigh on the supposedly pure and perfect worlds of science, particularly through the systems of penalties and rewards embodied in scholarly publications, caste hierarchies, etc., promote the reproduction of separate spaces, associated with different, if not indeed

motivation of the actors is more complicated (and their preferences less stable) than assumed in received theory" (North 1990, 17).

> irreconcilable dispositions and structures of opportunity, which are the product of the initial separation. (Bourdieu 2005, 110)

The above concluding remarks would, however, remain incomplete without a summary, however brief it may be, of what we consider to be the innovative outcomes of our general approach. We shall confine ourselves to what we believe to be the most important accomplishments.

Abstracting from criticism of a host of other social scientists relevant to our discipline, which certainly contained many non-trivial arguments and insights, one should point to our, in many ways, revolutionary theory of social differentiation, where both in relation to its class part, and all the more to the estate structure, we present much in the way of fresh thoughts.

The same is true of the theory of ownership (including its human object) presented in the book, i.e. the concept that is frequently marginalised, and even where it is not we have tried to prove that it is misapprehended. Whilst following in the footsteps of the conceptualisations of the societal system as a whole worked out by Parsons, above all, our own general theory of society shows a number of distinctive traits.

Last but not least, referring to the idea already alluded to in this afterword, our distinction between two fields of what is generally understood as a unitary area of economic sociology, as well the principle of their division, certainly deserves the reader's attention.

BIBLIOGRAPHY

Abdolkarim, S. *The Alternating Double Auction Market*. Berlin: Springer, 1998.

Abolafia, M. *Making Markets: Opportunism and Restraint on Wall Street*. Cambridge: Harvard University Press, 1996.

Adams, J. Proletariat or Multitude? A Postanarchist Critique of Empire, 1994. www.infoshop.org (accessed December 20, 2010).

Ackerman, F. "Consumed in Theory: Alternative Perspectives on the Economics of Consumption." *Journal of Economic Issues* 31 (1997): 651–664.

Adams, J. S. "Toward an Understanding of Inequity." *Journal of Abnormal and Social Psychology* 67 (1963): 422–436.

Aiello, L.C. & P. Wheeler. "The Expensive Tissue Hypothesis: The Brain and the Digestive System in Human and Primate Evolution." *Current Anthropology* 36 (2) (1995): 199–221.

AFL-CIO. "Trends in CEO Pay"," 2007. <http://www.aflcio.org (accessed December 30, 2008).

—. "Trends in CEO Pay"," 2010 (accessed August 11, 2011).

—. "Trends in CEO Pay", 2011 (accessed June 10, 2012).

Agell, J. & P.Lundberg "Theories of Pay and Unemployment: Survey Evidence from Swedish Manufacturing Firms." *Scandinavian Journal of Economics* 97 (1995): 295–308.

Allen, F. "Corporate Governance in Emerging Economies." *Oxford Review of Economic Policy* 21(2) (2005): 164–177.

Allen, F., E. Carletti & R. Marque. "Stakeholder Capitalism, Corporate Governance and Firm Value." *Journal of Private Enterprise* 3 (2007).

Allen, F. & D. Gale. "A Comparative Theory of Corporate Governance." Wharton Financial Institutions Center, Working Paper 03–27. University of Pennsylvania, 2003.

Allen, M. "Not Enough Variety? The Varieties of Capitalism Paradigm." *Socio-Economic Review* 2 (2004): 87–108.

Albert, M. "Class or Multitude?" April 14, 2005, http://www.zcommunications.org/class-or-multitude-by-michael-albert-1 (accessed December 20, 2010)

Alchian A. A. *Economic Forces at Work*. Indianapolis: Liberty Press, 1977.

—. "Production, Information Costs, and Economic Organization." *Journal of Political Economy* 58 (3) (1950): 211–221.

Alchian A. A. & H. Demsetz. "Production, Information Cost and Economic Organization." *American Economic Review* 52 (1972).

Alchian A. A. & H. Demsetz, "The Property Rights Paradigm." *The Journal of Economic History* 33 (1) (1973).

Alchian A. A. & R.A. "Kessel Competition, Monopoly, and the Pursuit of Pecuniary Gain." In *National Bureau of Economic Research*, 1962.

Alchian A. A. & S. Woodward. "The Firm Is Dead, Long Live the Firm: A Review of Oliver E. Williamson's 'The Economic Institutions of Capitalism'." *Journal of Economic Literature* 26 (1988).

Alexander, J. "Structure, Value, Action." *American Sociological Review* 55 (1990): 339–345.

—. *Neofunctionalism and After*. Oxford: Blackwell Publishers, 1998.

Alphons J., C. van de Kragt, J. M. Orbell & R. M. Dawes. "The Provision of a Sanctioning System in the United States and Japan." *The American Political Science Review* 77 (1) (1983): 112–122.

Amin, Samir. "What's Modern About the Modern World-System?" *Review of International Political Economy* 3 (2) (1996).

Anderson, S. P., J. K. Goeree & C. H. Holt. "Stochastic Game Theory—Adjustment to Equilibrium Under Bounded Rationality." University of Virginia,Working Paper No. 304, 1997.

Andreoni, J. "Why free ride? Strategies and learning in public goods experiments." *Journal of Public Economics* 37 (1988): 291–304.

—. "Warm-glow versus cold-prickle: the effects of positive and negative framing on cooperation in experiments." *Quarterly Journal of Economics* 110 (1995):1–22.

—. "Cooperation in Public-Goods Experiments: Kindness or Confusion." *American Economic Review* 85 (1989): 891–904.

Andreoni, J. & J.H. Miller. "Giving According to GARP: An Experimental Study of Rationality and Altruism." SSRI Working Paper, University of Wisconsin, Madison, 1996.

Antoni, C. *From History to Sociology: The Transition in German Historical Thinking* (trans. Hayden V. White). Detroit: Wayne State University Press, 1959.

Antonovics, K. and R. Town. "Are All the Good Men Married? Uncovering the Sources of the Marital Wage Premium." *The American Economic Review* (2004).

Aoki, M. *The Economic Analysis of the Japanese Firm*. North Holland, Amsterdam, 1984.

Archer, M. "Morphogenesis versus structuration: on combining structure and action." *British Journal of Sociology* 61 (1) (2010): 225–252.

Arnseberg, C. M. & D. McGregor. "Determination of Morale in an Industrial Company." *Applied Anthropology* 1 (1942): 12–34.

Arrow, K. J. *Social Choice and Individual Values.* New Haven: Yale University Press, 1963.

Aspers, P. "Three Perspectives in Contemporary Economic Sociology." *British Journal of Sociology* 58 (1) (2007): 135–141.

Atkinson, P. *Language, Structure and Reproduction: An Introduction to the Sociology of Basil Bernstein.* London: Methuen, 1985.

Atkinson, D. & B. Davies, eds. *Discourse and Reproduction: Essays in honor of Basil Bernstein.* Cresskill, NJ: Hampton Press, 1995.

Axelrod, R. "Uncertainty, Evolution, and Economic Theory." *The American Political Science Review* 80 (4) (1986): 1095–1111.

Axelrod, R., R. O. Keohane "Games with Discounting or with Incomplete Information." *World Politics* 38 (1) (1985): 226–254.

Axelrod, R. & W. D. Hamilton. "Achieving Cooperation under Anarchy: Strategies and Institutions." *Science, New Series* 211 (4489) (1981): 1390–1396.

Babcock, L., X. Wang & G. Loewenstein. "Choosing the Wrong Pond: Social Comparisons in Negotiations That Reect a Self-Serving Bias." *Quarterly Journal of Economics* 111 (1996): 1–21.

Banerjee, AbhihitV. "Envy." In *Economic Theory and Policy, Essays in Honour of Dipak Banerjee*, edited by Dutta Bhaskaretal. Oxford University Press, 1990.

Bagwell, L. & D. Bernheim. "Veblen Effects In A Theory Of Conspicuous Consumption." *American Economic Review* 86 (1996): 349–373.

Bakshi, G. & Z. Chen. "The Spirit Of Capitalism And Stock-Market Prices." *American Economic Review* 86 (1996): 133–157.

Baker, W. "The Social Structure of a National Securities Market." *American Journal of Sociology* 89 (1984): 775–811.

Bainton, Roland. *The Reformation of the Sixteenth Century.* Boston: Beacon Press, 1952.

Banerski, G. Review of :. Tyszka, T. (ed.) Psychologia ekonomiczna, Gdańsk Decyzje. 2, 2004.

Banfield E. C. & J. Q. Wilson. *City Politics.* Cambridge: Harvard University Press, 1963.

Banfield, E. C. *Political Influence.* New York: The Free Press of Glencoe, 1982.

Banks, J., R. Blundell & S. Tanner. "Is There a Retirement-Savings Puzzle?" *American Economic Review* 88 (4) (1998): 769–88.

Barro, R. *Determinants of Economic Growth: A Cross-country Empirical Study*. Cambridge, MA: MIT Press, 1997.

Bartley, M. *Health Inequalities*. Oxford: Blackwells, 2004.

Bardsley, N. "Economic Theory: The Case of Public Goods." *Annals of Public and Cooperative Economics* 71 (2000): 2.

Baron, J. "Organizational Perspectives on Stratification," 1984 www.sociosite.net (accessed April 13, 2007)

Baron, J. & M. Hannan. "The Impact of Economics on Contemporary Sociology." *Journal of Economic Literature* 32 (1994): 1111–46.

Barry, N. P. "The Austrian Perspective." In *What Is Political Economy? Eight Perspectives*, edited by David K. Whynes, 33–5. New York, Blackwell, 1984.

Baums, T. Universal Banks and Investment Companies in Germany, Working paper. New York University Salomon Centre Conference on Universal Banking, 1995.

Bebchuk, L. A., J. M. Fried and D. I. Walker. "Executive Compensation in America: Optimal Contracting or Extraction of Rents?" Program in Law & Economics, Working Paper Series (University of California, Berkeley) Paper 50. posted at the eScholarship Repository, University of California, 2001. http://repositories.cdlib.org/blewp/50 (accessed July 7, 2009).

Becht, M., P. Bolton & A. Röell. "Corporate Governance and Control." Working Paper 9371, National Bureau Of Economic Research, 2002. http://www.nber.org/papers/w9371 (accessed September 17, 2005).

Beck, U. *Risk Society: Towards a New Modernity*. London: Sage, 1992.

—. "The Reinvention of Politics: Towards a Theory of Reflexive Modernization." In *Reflexive Modernization: Politics, Tradition and Aesthetics in the Modern Social Order*, edited by U.Beck, A. Giddens and S. Lash. Cambridge: Polity Press, 1994.

—. *Ecological Politics in an Age of Risk*. Cambridge: Polity Press, 1995.

—. *Democracy Without Enemies*. Cambridge: Polity Press, 1998.

—. *World Risk Society*. Cambridge: Polity Press, 1999.

—. *The Brave New World of Work*. Cambridge: Polity Press, 2000a.

—. *What is Globalization?* Cambridge: Polity Press, 2000b.

—. "Zombie Categories; Interview with Ulrich Beck." In *Individualisation*, edited by U. Beck, U. and E. Beck-Gernsheim. London: Sage, 2002.

Beck, H. & C. M. Tolbert. "Stratification in a Dual Economy: A Sectoral Model of Earnings Determination." *American Sociological Review* 43 (1978).

Becker, G. S. *The Economics of Discrimination*. The University of Chicago Press, 1971.

—. *A Treatise on the Family*. Harvard University Press, 1991.
—. *Human Capital: A Theoretical and Empirical Analysis, with Special Reference to Education*. The University of Chicago Press, 1993.
—. *Accounting for Tastes*, Harvard University Press, 1993.
—. "Public Policies, Pressure Groups, and Dead-weight Costs." *Journal of Public Economics* 28(3) (1985): 329–347.
—. *The Economic Approach to Human Behaviour*. Chicago: Chicago University Press, 1976.
—. *The Essence of Becker*. Palo Alto, 1996.
Beckert, J. "Economic Sociology in Germany." *Sociology European Electronic Newsletter* 1 (2) (2000).
—. "Interpenetration Versus Embeddedness: The Premature Dismissal of Talcott Parsons in the New Economic Sociology." *American Journal of Economics and Sociology* 65 (1) (2006): 161–188.
—. "What is Sociological about Economic Sociology? Uncertainty and the Embeddedness of Economic Action." *Theory and Society* 25 (1996): 803–840.
—. "Agency, Entrepreneurs, and Institutional Change. The Role of Strategic Choice and Institutionalized Practices in Organizations." *Organization Studies* 20 (5) (1999): 777– 799.
—. *Beyond the Market: The Social Foundations of Economic Efficiency*. Princeton: Princeton University Press, 2002.
—. "Economic Sociology and Embeddedness: The Problem of the Structure of Action." *Journal of Economic Issues* 37 (2003): 769–787.
—. "Trust and the Performative Construction of Markets." MPIfG Discussion Paper 05/8, Cologne: MPIfG, 2005.
—. "What Is Sociological about Economic Sociology? Uncertainty and the Embeddedness of Economic Action." *Theory and Society* 25 (1996): 803–840.
Belanger, J. "Technology and Work." In *Social Theory at Work*, edited by M. Korczynski R. Hodson P. K. Edwards. Oxford: Oxford University Press, 2006.
Bell, P. F. & H. Cleaver. Marx's Crisis Theory as a Theory of Class Struggle. In *Research in Political Economy*. Greenwich, CT: Jai Press, 1982.
Bendor J. & D. Mookherjee. "Finitely Repeated Games." *The American Political Science Review* 81 (1987): 129–154.
Benoit J. P. & V. Krishna. "Towards a Pure Theory of Threat Systems." *Econometrica* 53 (4) (1985): 905–922.
Berg, J., J. Dickhaut & K. McCabe. "Trust, Reciprocity and Social History." *Games and Economic Behavior* 10 (1995): 122–142.

Berglof, E. "Corporate Control and Capital Structure—Essays on Property Rights and Financial Contracts." A Dissertation for the Doctor's Degree in Business Administration, mimeo, 1990.

Beski, L. *Konsumpcja w rodzinach pracowniczych* Warsaw, 1977.

Besley, T. *Principled Agents?: The Political Economy of Good Government*. Oxford: Oxford University Press, 2006.

Bignami, Francesca. www.jeanmonnetprogram.org.

Brecher, J. & T. Costello. *Global Village or Global Pillage: Economic Reconstruction from the Bottom Up*. Boston : South End Press, 1994.

Bewley, T. "A Depressed Labor Market as Explained by Participants." *American Economic Review, Papers and Proceedings* 85 (1995): 250–254.

—. "Why not Cut Pay?" *European Economic Review* 42 (1998): 459–490.

Binmore, K. L., L.Samuelson & R.Vaughn. "Musical Chairs: Modelling Noisy Evolution." *Games and Economic Behavior* 11 (1) (1995): 1–35.

Biz/ed. "Public Choice Theory," 2009. www. Citilib.org (accessed October 20, 2009).

Black, D. "On the Rationale of Group Decision-Making." *Journal of Political Economy* 56 (1948): 23–34.

—. "The Theory of Committees and Elections." Cambridge: Cambridge University Press, 1958.

Blackburn, R. "Fin de Siecle: Socialism After the Crash." *New Left Review* 185 (1991).

Blau, P. *Exchange and Power in Social Life*. New York: Transacton, 1964.

—. "Comment." In *Explanation in the Behavioural Sciences*, edited by R. Borger & F. Ciofffi. Cambridge: Cambridge University Press, 1970.

—. *Exchange And Power In Social Life*. New York: John Wiley & Sons, 1964.

—. *Structural Contexts Of Opportunities*. Chicago: The University of Chicago Press, 1994.

Blau, M. & O. D. Duncan. *The American Occupational Structure*. New York: Wiley, 1967

Blauner, R. *Alienation and Freedom: The Factory Worker and His Industry*. Chicago, IL: The University of Chicago Press, 1964.

Blinder, A. "What Central Bankers Could Learn From Academics, And Vice Versa." *Journal of Economic Perspectives* 11 (1997): 3–19.

Blinder, A. S. & D. H. Choi. "A Shred of Evidence on Theories of Wage Stickness." *Quarterly Journal of Economics* 105 (1990): 1003–1016.

Blount, S. "When Social Outcomes Aren't Fair: The Effect of Causal Attributions on Preferences." *Organizational Behavior and Human Decision Processes* 63 (1995): 131–144.

Blume, L. E. "The Statistical Mechanics of Strategic Interaction." *Games and Economic Behavior* 4 (1993): 387–424.
—. "The Statistical Mechanics of Best Response Strategy Revision." *Games and Economic Behavior* 11 (1995): 111–45.
—. Evolutionary Equilibrium with Forward-Looking Players, Santa Fe University, 2004.
Blume, L. E. and D. Easley. "Rationality." The New Palgrave Dictionary of Economics, 2008.
Böhm-Bawerk von, E. "Positive Theory of Capital." 1889.
Boissonade, P. *Colbert: Le triomphe de l'Étatisme. La fondation de la suprématie industrielle de la France. La dictature du travail (1661-1683)*, 1932.
Bolle, F. & A. Kritikos. "Self-Centered Inequality, Reciprocity and Altruism." Discussion Paper, Europa-Universita Viadrina. Frankfurt (Oder), 1998.
Bolton, G. E. & A. Ockenfels. "A Theory of Equity, Reciprocity and Competition." Discussion Paper, Pennsylvania State University, 1997.
Bolton, G. E., J. Brandts & A. Ockenfels. "Measuring Motivations for Reciprocal Responses Observed in Simple Dilemma Games." Discussion Paper, Universitat Magdeburg, 1997.
Bolton, G. E., J. Brandts and E. Katok. "A Simple Test of Explanations for Contributions in Dilemma Game." Discussion Paper, Pennsylvania State University, 1997.
Bonacich, P. "Power And Centrality: A Family Of Measures." *American Journal of Sociology* 92 (1987): 1170–1182.
Bondt, D., F. M. Werner & R. Thaler. "Does the Stock Market Overreact?" *Journal of Finance* 40 (3) (1985): 793 –805.
Bongard, G. & G. Lewin. "Drewnjaja Indija." Moskwa, 1969.
Borkenau, F. *Der Übergang vom feudalen zum bürgerlichen Weltbild: Studien zur Geschichte der Philosophie der Manufakturperiode*. Paris: Alcan, 1971.
Boot A. W. "Relationship Banking: What Do We Know?" *Journal of Financial Intermediation* 9 (2000): 7–25.
Boot A. W. & A. V. Thakor. "Financial System Architecture." *Rev. of Financial Studies* 10 (1997): 693–733.
Boot A. W, S. I.Greenbaum and A. V.Thakor. "Reputation and Discretion in Financial Contracting." *American Economic Review* 83 (1993): 1165–83.
Borcherding, T. E., P. Dillon & T. D. Willett. "Henry George: Precursor to Public Choice Analysis." *The American Journal of Economics and Sociology* 57 (2) (1998): 173–182.

Börsch-Supan, A. & J. Köke. “An Applied Econometricians’ View of Empirical Corporate Governance Studies.” *German Economic Review* 3 (3) (1998): 295–326.

Boudon, R. *The Unintended Consequences Of Social Action*. New York: St. Martin’s Press, 1982.

Boulding K. E. “Revenge, and Warfare in a Tribal Population.” *The American Economic Review* 53 (2) (1963). Papers and Proceedings of the Seventy-Fifth Annual Meeting of the American Economic Association, 424–434.

Bourdieu, P. *The Social Structures of the Economy*. Cambridge: Polity, 2005.

—. *Distinctions. A Social Critique of the Judgment of Taste*. Translated by Richard Nice. Harvard University Press, 1984.

—. “The Forms of Capital.” In *Handbook of Theory and Research for the Sociology of Education*, edited by J. G. Richardson, 241–258. New York: Greenwood, 1986.

—. “The Social Space and the Genesis of Groups.” *Theory and Society* 14 (1985): 723–744.

—. *Distinction*. Translated by R. Nice. London: Routledge and Kegan Paul, 1986.

—. Pascalian mediations. Stanford: Stanford University Press, 2000.

Bourdieu, P., and Passeron, J.-C. (1970). La reproduction. Paris: Les Editions de Minuit.

Bourdieu, P. (1977) [1970], Reproduction in Education, Culture and Society. London: Sage.

Bowles, S. “Endogenous Preferences: The Cultural Consequences Of Markets And Other Economic Institutions.” Journal of Economic Literature 36 (1998): 75–111.

Bowles, S., H. Gintis & M. Osborne. “The Determinants of Earnings: A Behavioral Approach.” *Journal of Economic Literature* 39 (2001): 1137–1176.

Boyd, R., H. Gintis, S. Bowles & J. Richerson. “The Evolution of Altruistic Punishment.” Proceedings of the National Academy of Sciences of the United States of America 100 (6) (2003): 3531–3535.

Breen, R. & J. H. Goldthorpe. 'Class, Mobility and Merit: The Experience of Two British Birth Cohorts', European Sociological Review 17(2) (2001): 81–101.

Brennan G. and A. Hamlin. “The insufficiency of Public Choice critique of democracy.”

http://www.socialsciences.manchester.ac.uk/disciplines/politics/researchgroups/mancept/workingpapers/documents/revisionistpublicchoicetheorynpe.pdf.

Brennan G. and A. Hamlin. "Analytic Conservatism." *British Journal of Political Science* 34 (2004): 675–691.

Brennan, G. & A. Hamlin. "Conservatism, Idealism and Cardinality." *Analysis* 66 (2006): 286–295.

Brennan G. & J. M. Buchanan. *The Reason of Rules*. Cambridge: Cambridge University Press, 1985.

Brennan G. & J. M. Buchanan. *The Power to Tax*. Cambridge: Cambridge University Press, 1980. Also in Brennan G. and L. Lomasky. *Democracy and Decision*. Cambridge: Cambridge University Press, 1993.

Brennan, G. & A. Schuessler. *A Logic of Expressive Choice.* Princeton: Princeton University Press, 2000.

Brennan & Hamlin. *Democratic Devices and Desires*. Cambridge: Cambridge University Press, 2000.

Brennan G. & P. Pettit. *The Economy of Esteem*. Oxford: Oxford University Press, 2004.

Brennan, G. Public Choice Theory. 1968. http://www.socialsciences.manchester.ac.uk/disciplines/politics/researchgroups/mancept/workingpapers/documents/revisionistpublicchoicetheorynpe.

Brenner, R. *Merchants and Revolution: Commercial Change, Political Conflict and London's Overseas Traders, 1550-1653*. Cambridge: Cambridge University Press, 1993.

Brick, H. "Talcott Parsons's Shift Away from Economics 1937–1946." *Journal of American History* 87 (2000): 490–514.

Brittan, Leon. "Globalisation" vs Sovereignty? The European Response." Speech, Rede Lecture, Cambridge University, February 20, 1997. http://europa.eu.int/ (accessed May 19, 2009).

Broome, J. *Weighing Goods*. Blackwells, 1991.

Brownstein A. R. & M. J. Panner. "Who Should Set CEO Pay? The Press? Congress? Shareholders?" *Harvard Businnes Review* May / June (1992).

Brubaker, R. *The Limits of Rationality*. London: George Allen and Unwin, 1984.

Buchanan, J. M. *Collected Works*, Library of Economics and Liberty, 2000.

—. *The Demand and Supply of Public Goods*. Rand McNally, 1999.

—. “Public Choice: The Origins and Development of a Research Program,” Center for Study of Public Choice at George Mason University, Fairfax: Virginia, USA, 2003a.

—. Politics Without Romance, Policy, the quarterly review of The Centre for Independent Studies. Spring, 2003b. http://www.cis.org.au/policy/spr03/polspr03-2.htm (accessed February 22, 2009).

—. “What is Public Choice Theory?” *The Rational Argumentator A Journal for Western Man* 173 (2008).

Buchanan, J. M. and G.Tullock. *The Calculus of Consent*. Ann Arbor: University of Michigan Press, 1962.

Buckingham, W. S. *Theoretical Economic Systems: A Comparative Analysis*. New York: Ronald Press, 1958.

Bueno de Mesquita, B., R. Morrow, R. Siverson & A. Smith. “Testing the Selectorate Explanation of the Democratic Peace.” Yale University , 2011.

Burlando, R. & J. D. Hey. “Do Anglo-Saxons Free-Ride More?” *Journal of Public Economics* 64 (1997): 41–60,

Burke, P. J. “An Identity Model For Network Exchange.” *American Sociological Review* 62 (1997): 134–150.

Burt, R. *Toward a Structural Theory of Action*. New York: Academic Press, 1982.

—. *Structural Holes*. Cambridge, MA: Harvard University Press, 1992.

—. “The Stability Of American Markets.” *American Journal of Sociology* 94 (1988): 356–395.

Caffentzis, G. "The Fundamental Implications of the Debt Crisis for Social Reproduction in Africa." In *Paying The Price. Women and the Politics of International Economic Strategy*, edited by M. Dalla Costa and G. F. Dalla Costa. London: Zed Books, 1995.

Callon, M. “Some Elements of a Sociology of Translation: Domestication of the Scallops and the Fishermen of St Brieuc Bay.” In *Power, Action and Belief: A New Sociology of Knowledge*, edited by J. Law. London: Routledge & Kegan Paul, 1986.

Callon, M., ed. *The Laws of the Market*. Oxford: Blackwell Publishers, 1998.

Camerer, C. & R. Thaler “Ultimatums, Dictators and Manners.” *Journal of Economic Perspectives* 9 (1995): 209–219.

Camerer, C., et al. Labor Supply of New York City Cabdrivers: One Day at a Time, The Quarterly Journal of Economics, vol. 112 (2) (1997): 407–41.

Cameron, L. "Raising the Stakes in the Ultimatum Game: Experimental Evidence from Indonesia." Discussion Paper, Princeton University, 1995.

Camic, C. "The Making of a Method: A Historical Reinterpretation of the Early Parsons." American Sociological Review 52 (1987): 421–439.

—. "Introduction." In *Talcott Parsons: The Early Essays*. Edited by C. Camic. Chicago: University of Chicago Press, 1991.

Campbell, C. M., & K. Kamlani. "The Reasons for Wage Rigidity: Evidence from a Survey of Firms." *Quarterly Journal of Economics* 112 (1997): 759–789.

Charness, G. "Attribution and Reciprocity in a Labor Market: An Experimental Investigation." *Games and Economic Behavior*, forthcoming.

Canning, D. "Average Behavior in Learning Models." *Journal of Economic Theory* 57 (1992): 442–472.

Carchedi, G. *Logic and Contradiction in the Social Sciences: From the myth of logical inconsistency to the theory of knowledge in Marx*. London: Verso, 2010.

Carruthers, B. & W. Espeland. "Accounting For Rationality: Double-Entry Bookkeeping and the Rhetoric of Economic Rationality." *The American Journal of Sociology* 97(1991): 31–69.

Castells, M. *The Rise of the Network Society*. Oxford: Blackwells, 1996.

—. "Materials for an Exploratory Theory of the Network Society." *British Journal of Sociology* 51 (1) (2000a): 5–24.

—. *The Rise of the Network Society*. US: Blackwell Publishing, 2000b.

—. *The Internet Galaxy*. UK: Oxford University Press, 2001.

Chagnon N. A. "Rhetoric Of Economic Rationality." *Science* 239 (4843) (1988): 985–992.

Chan K. S., S. Mestelman, R. Moir and R. A. Muller. "The Voluntary Provision of Public Goods under Varying Income Distributions." *The Canadian Journal of Economics* 29 (1) (1996): 54–69.

Chernilo, D. "The Theorization of Social Co-ordinations in Differentiated Societies: the Theory of Generalized Symbolic Media." *British Journal of Sociology* 53 (3) (2002).

Choonara, J. "Marx or the multitude?" *International Socialism: A Quarterly Journal of Socialist Theory* 105 (2005).

Chossudovsky, M. *The Globalisation of Poverty*. London: Zed Book, 1997.

Cho, M. H. "Ownership Structure, Investment, and the Corporate Value: an Empirical Analysis." *Journal of Financial Economics* 47 (1998): 103–121.

Chung, K. H. & S. W. Pruitt. "A Simple Approximation of Tobin's q." *Financial Management* 23 (1994): 70–74.
Cilleuls, A. des. *Histoire et Régime de la Grande Industrie en France aux XVIIe et XVIIIe siècles*. Paris, Giard et Brière, 1898.
Ciscel D. H. "Determinants of Executive Compensation." *Southern Economic Journal* 40 (1974).
Ciscel D. H. & T. M. Caroll. "The Determinants of Executive Salaries: An Econometric Survey." *The Review of Economics and Statistics* 48 (1) (1980).
Clark J. R. & D. Lee. "Expressive Voting: How Special Interests Enlist their victims as Political Allies." In *Beyond Conventional Economics: The Limits of Rational Behaviour in Political Decision-Making*, edited by G. Eusepi and A. Hamlin, 17–32. Edward Elgar Publishing, 2006.
Cleaver, H. "Work is Still The Central Issue: New Words for New Worlds." In *The Labour Debate: An Investigation into the Theory and Reality of Capitalist Work*, edited by M. Neary and A. Dinerstein. London: Ashgate, 2002.
Cockshott, W. P. & A. Cottrell. "The Scientific Status of the Labour Theory of Value." March 1997. www.wfu.edu/~cottrell/eea97.pdf (accessed January 12, 2010).
—. "Labour Time versus Alternative Value Bases: A Research Note." *Cambridge Journal of Economics* 21 (4) (1997): 545.
Coase, R. "The Nature of the Firm." *Economica* 4 (16) (1937): 386–405
—. "The Problem of Social Cost." *Journal of Law and Economics* 3 (1960): 1–44.
Cornerhouse. No Patents of Life! September, Briefing N. 1, 1997.
—. The Myth of the Minimalist State, March, Briefing N. 5, 1998.
Coleman, J. The Mathematics of Collective Action, Chicago, 1973.
—. "Social Theory, Social Research, and a Theory of Action." *American Journal of Sociology* 91 (1986): 1309–1335.
—. "Social Capital In The Creation Of Human Capital." *American Journal of Sociology* 94 (1988): 95–120.
—. *Foundations Of Social Theory*. Cambridge: Belkhap Press, 1990.
—. "A Rational Choice Perspective On Economic Sociology." In *Handbook of Economic Sociology*, edited by N. Smelser and R. Swedberg, 166–182. Princeton: Princeton University Press, 1994.
Coles, J. L., M. L.Lemmon & J. F. Meschke. "Structural models and endogenity in corporate finance." Arizona State University Working Paper, Tempe, AZ, 2003.
Collins, R. *The Credential Society*. New York: Academic Press, 1977.

—. "Market Dynamics As The Engine Of Historical Change." *Sociological Theory* 8 (1990): 111–135.

Commons, J. *Legal Foundations of Capitalism*. New York, 1924.

—. "Institutional Economics." *American Economic Review* 21 (1931).

Congleton, R. "The Median Voter Model." In *The Encyclopedia of Public Choice*, edited by C. K. Rowley & F. Schneider, Kluwer Academic Press, 2002.

Conlisk, J. "Why Bounded Rationality?" *Journal of Economic Literature* 34 (2) (1996): 669–700.

Cook, K. "Linking Actors and Structures: An Exchange Network Perspective." In *Structures Of Power And Constraint*, 115 128. Calhoun, 1990.

—. "Charting Futures for Sociology: Structure and Action." *Contemporary Sociology* 29 (2000): 685–692.

—. ed. *Social Exchange Theory*. London, 1987.

—. ed. *Trust in Society*. New York: Russell Sage Foundation, 2003.

Cook, K. & T. Yamaguchi. "Power Relations In Exchange Networks." *American Sociological Review* 55 (1990): 297–300.

Cook, S. "The Obsolete Anti-Market Mentality: A Critique of the Substantive Approach to Economic Anthropology." *American Anthropologist* 68 (1966): 323–345.

Cooper R., D. V. DeJong, R.Forsythe and T. W. Ross. "The Commons and the Optimal Number of Firms." *The Quarterly Journal of Economics* 107 (2) (1992): 739–771.

Copeland, C. & D. Laband. "Expressiveness and Voting." *Public Choice* 110 (2002): 351–363;

Cornes R., C. F. Mason & T. Sandler. "Rational: Evolutionary Psychology and the Invisible Hand." *The Quarterly Journal of Economics* 101 (3) (1986): 641–646.

Cornwell, C. & P. Rupert. "Unobservable Individual Effects, Marriage and the Earnings of Young Men." *Economic Inquiry* 35 (1997): 285–294.

Cosmides L. & J. Tooby, "Papers and Proceedings of the Hundred and Sixth Annual Meeting of the American Economic Association." *The American Economic Review* 84 (2) (1994): 327–332.

Coughlin, R. M. *Probabilistic Voting Theory*. Cambridge: Cambridge University Press, 1991.

—. ed. *Rationality and Efficiency: New Perspectives on Socio-Economics*. Armonk, 1991.

Cox, D. "Motives for Private Income Transfers." *Journal of Political Economy* 93 (1987): 508–546.

—. "Intergenerational Transfers and Liquidity Constraints." *Quarterly Journal of Economics* 105 (1990): 187–217.

Cox, D. & M. R. Rank. "Intervivos Transfers and Intergenerational Exchange." *Review of Economics and Statistics* 74 (1992): 305–314.

Crawford, S. E S. & E. Ostrom, *The American Political Science Review* 89 (3) (1995): 582–600.

Croley, S. P. *Regulation and Public Interests: The Possibility of Good Regulatory Government*. Princeton: Princeton University Press, 2008.

Croson, R. "Expectations in Voluntary Contributions Mechanisms." Discussion Paper, Wharton School, University of Pennsylvania, 1995.

—. "Partners and Strangers Revisited." *Economics Letters* 53 (1996): 25–32.

Curtis, M. *Web of Deceit: Britain's Real Role in the World*. London: Vintage, 2003.

Curtis, R. "Household And Family In Theory Of Inequality." *American Sociological Review* 51 (1986): 168–183.

Dahl, R. E. *Polyarchy: Participation and Opposition*. New Haven: Yale University Press, 1972.

Davis, Mike. *City of Quartz*. New York: Vintage Books, 1992.

De Angelis, M. "Beyond the Technological and the Social Paradigms: A Political reading of Abstract Labour as the Substance of Value." *Capital and Class* 57 (1995).

—. "Globalisation, Work and Class: Some Research Notes." Paper presented at the conference "The Labour Debate," Centre for Comparative Studies, University of Warwick, February 24, 1999.

Deutsch, M. "Homans in the Skinner Box." In *Institutions and Social Exchange*, edited by T. Herman and R. Simpson, 87–108. Indianapolis: Bobbs-Merril. (1971),

Dahya, J., J, J. McConnell & Travlos, N. G. "The Cadbury Committee, Corporate Performance and Top Management Turnover." *Journal of Finance* 57 (1) (2002): 461–483.

Daily G. C. et al. The Value of Nature and the Nature of Value. Science 289 (5478) (2000): 395–96.

Darwin, C. D. *The Descent of Man*. Princeton: Princeton University Press, 1981.

Das, R. J. "Putting Social Capital in Its Place." *Capital and Class* 30 (3) (2006): 65–92.

Davis, J. A. "A Formal Interpretation of the Theory of Relative Deprivation." *Sociometry* 22 (1959): 280–296.

Davis, J., E. Fama, K. French. "Characteristics, Covariances and Average Returns." *Journal of Finance* 55 (2000): 389–406.

Dawes, R. M. & R. Thaler. "Cooperation." *Journal of Economic Perspectives* 2 (1988): 187–197.
Dawes, R. M., J. M. Orbell, R. T. Simmons, A. J. C. Van De Kragt. "Cheap Talk, Coordination, and Entry." *The American Political Science Review* 80 (4) (1986): 1171–1185.
Dawkins, R. *The Selfish Gene*. Oxford: Oxford University Press, 1976.
De Alessi, L. "Private Property and Dispersion of Ownership in Large Corporation." *Journal of Finance* 28, 4 (1973).
Deflen, M., "The Sociology of the Sociology of Money: Simmel and the Contemporary
Battle of the Classics." *Journal of Classical Sociology* 3(1) (2003): 67–96.
DeLong, B., A. Shleifer, L. Summers & R. Waldman. "Noise Trader Risk in Financial Markets." *Journal of Political Economy* 98 (4) (1990): 703–38.
Demsetz, H. "Toward a Theory of Property Rights." *American Economic Review* 47 (2) (1967).
—. "The Structure of Ownership and the Theory of the Firm." *Journal of Law and Economics* 26 (1983): 375–390.
Demsetz, H. & K. Lehn. "The Structure of Corporate Ownership: Causes and Consequences." *Journal of Political Economy* 93 (1985): 1155–1177.
Demsetz, H. & B. Villalonga. "Ownership Structure and Corporate Performance." *Journal of Corporate Finance* 7 (3) (2001): 209–233.
Denis, D. J. & A. Sarin. "Ownership and Board Structures in Publicly Traded Corporations." *Journal of Financial Economics* 52 (1999): 187–223.
Denis, D. J., D. K. Denis & A. Sarin. "Ownership Structure and Top Executive Turnover." *Journal of Financial Economics* 45 (2) (1997): 193–221.
Deutschmann, C. Die Verheissung des absoluten Reichtums. Zur religiösen Natur des Kapitalismus, Frankfurt: Campus Verlag, 1999.
Diamond, P. A. "Aggregate Demand Management in Search Equilibrium." *Journal of Political Economy* 90 (1982): 881–94.
DiMaggio, P. "Endogenizing Animal Spirits: Toward a Sociology of Collective Response to Uncertainty and Risk." In *The New Economic Sociology: Developments of an Emerging Field*, edited by M. F. Guillén, R. Collins, P. England & M. Meyer. New York: Russell Sage Foundation, 2003.
—. "Review Essay: On Pierre Bourdieu." *American Journal of Sociology* 84 (1979): 1460–1474.

DiMaggio, P. & J. Mohr. “Cultural Capital, Educational Attainment, and Marital Selectio.” *American Journal of Sociology* 90 (1985): 1231–1261.

DiMaggio, P. & W. Powell. “Introduction.” In *The New Institutionalism in Organizational Analysis*, edited by P. DiMaggio & W. Powell. Chicago: University of Chicago Press, 1991.

Dickson, T. & H. V. McLachlan. "In Search of 'The Spirit of Capitalism': Weber's Misinterpretation of Franklin." *Sociology* 23 (1) (1989): 81–89.

Dobb, M. *Studies in the Development of Capitalism*. London: Routledge, 1946.

Dodd, N. *The Sociology of Money: Economics, Reason and Contemporary Society*. Cambridge: Polity Press, 1994.

Doogan, K., ed. “Insecurity and Long-Term Employment.” *Work, Employment and Society* 15 (3) (2001): 419–442.

Dore, R. *Stock Market Capitalism: Welfare Capitalism. Japan and Germany versus the Anglo-Saxons*. Oxford University Press, Oxford, 2000.

Downs, A. *An Economic Theory of Democracy*. Cambridge: Cambridge University Press, 1957.

—. *Inside Bureaucracy*. Boston: Little, Brown and Company, 1967.

Dufwenberg, M. & G. Kirchsteiger. “A Theory of Sequential Reciprocity.” Discussion Paper, Center, Tilburg University, 1998.

Dunbar, R. “Coevolution of Neocortex Size, Group Size and Language in Humans.” *Behavioral and Brain Sciences* 16 (4) (1993): 681–735.

Duncan S. “The Evolution Of Reciprocal Altruism.” *The American Political Science Review* 79 (4) (1985): 923–942.

Dunleavy, P. *Democracy, Bureaucracy and Public Choice*. Brighton: Longman, 1991.

Durkheim, E. *The Rules of Sociological Method*. New York: The Free Press, 1982.

—. *Selected Writings.* Edited by A. Giddens. Cambridge: Cambridge University Press, 1972.

Durlauf, S. N. “Bowling Alone: A Review Essay.” *Journal of Economic Behavior and Organization* 47 (3) (2002): 259–73.

Egan, T. “No Degree and No Way Back to the Middle.” The New York Times, May 24, 2005.

Eccles, R. & H. White. “Price And Authority In Inter-Profit Center Transactions.” *American Journal of Sociology* 94 (1988): S17-S51.

Ellison, G. "Cooperation in the Prisoner's Dilemma with Anonymous Random Matching." *The Review of Economic Studies* 61 (1994): 567–88.
Elster, J. *The Cement of Society*. Cambridge: Cambridge University Press, 1989.
—. *Ulysses And The Sirens*. Cambridge: Cambridge University Press, 1979.
—. "Emotions And Economic Theory." *Journal of Economic Literature* 36 (1998): 47–74.
Emerson, R. "Power-Dependence Relations." *American Sociological Review* 27(1962): 31–41.
—. "Operant Psychology And Exchange Theory." In *Behavioral Sociology*, edited by R. Burgess & D. Bushell, 379–408. New York: Columbia University Press, 1969.
—. "Social Exchange Theory." *Annual Review of Sociology* 2 (1976): 335–362.
—. "Exchange Theory, Part I: A Psychological Basis for Social Exchange." In *Sociological Theories in Progress* Vol. 2, edited by J. Berger, M. Zelditch Jr., & B. Anderson, 38–57. Boston: Houghton Mifflin, 1972.
Emirbayer, M. & J. Goodwin. "Network Analysis, Culture and the Problem of Agency." *American Journal of Sociology* 99 (1994): 1411–1453..
Encyclopaedia of the Social Sciences (1930–1935), E. R. A. Seligman, ed. New York: The Macmillan Company.
Ernsberger, D. C. "The Labour Theory of Value", 1988. http://www.isil.org/resources/lit/labor-theory-val.html (accessed September 26, 2009).
Erikson, R. & J. H. Goldthorpe. *The Constant Flux*. Oxford: Clarendon, 1992.
Etzioni, A. "Policy Implications of Socio-Economics." *Policy Studies Review* 9 (3) (1990): 445–454
—. *Essays in Socio-Economics*. New York: Springer, 1999.
—. "Toward a New Socio-Economic Paradigm." *Socio-Economic Review* 1 (1) (2006).
Evans, P. "Introduction: Development Strategies Across the Public-Private Divide." In *State-Society Synergy* edited by P. Evans. University of California Press, 1997a.
—. "Government Action, Social Capital and Development." In *State-Society Synergy* edited by P. Evans. University of California Press, 1997a.

Evans, G., ed. *The End of Class Politics*. Oxford: Clarendon, 1999
Faccio, M. & M. Lasfer. "Managerial Ownership, Board Structure and Firm Value: The UK Evidence," Cass Business School Research Paper, 1999.
Fairchild, H. P. "Business as an Institution." *American Sociological Review* 2 (1937).
Falk, A. & U. Fischbacher. "A Theory of Reciprocity," Discussion Paper, University of Zurich, 1998.
Falkinger, J., E.Fehr, S. Ga¨chter & R. Winter-Ebmer, "A Simple Mechanism for the Efficient Provision of Public Goods—Experimental Evidence." *American Economic Review*, forthcoming.
Fama, E. "Agency Problems and the Theory of the Firm." *Journal of Political Economy* 88 (1980): 288–307.
Fama, E. & K. French. "Size and Book to Market Factors in Earnings and Returns." *Journal of Finance* 50 (1994): 131–156.
Fama, E. & M. Jensen. "Separation of Ownership and Control." *Journal of Law and Economics* 26 (1983): 301–325.
Fararo, T. *Social Action Systems*. Westport: Praeger, 2001.
Farrell, J. "Cheap Talk." *The Rand Journal of Economics* 18 (1) (1987): 34–39.
Farrell J. & M. Rabin. "Cheap Talk." *The Journal of Economic Perspectives* 10 (1996): 103–118.
—. "I Get by with a Little Help from my Friends." *The Journal of Economic Perspectives* 10 (3) (1996): 103-118.
Federici, S. "The Debt Crisis, Africa and the New Enclosures." In *Midnight Notes*, 1992.
Felkins, L. *Introduction to Public Choice Theory*. American Political Science Association, 1997.
Fehr, E. & S. Gachter "Cooperation and Punishment—An Experimental Analysis of Norm Formation and Norm Enforcement," Discussion Paper, Institute for Empirical Research in Economics, University of Zurich, 1996.
—. Altruistic punishment in humans. *Nature* 415 (6868) (2002): 137–140.
Fehr, E. & K. Schmidt. "A Theory of Fairness, Competition and Cooperation." *The Quarterly Journal of Economics* 114 (3) (1999): 817–868.
Fehr, E., G. Kirchsteiger & A. Riedl. "Does Fairness Prevent Market Clearing? An Experimental Investigation." *Quarterly Journal of Economics* 107 (1993): 437–460.
Fehr, E., S. & G. Kirchsteiger. "Reciprocity as a Contract Enforcement Device." *Econometrica* 65 (4) (1996): 833–860.

Fehr, E., A. Falk. "Wage Rigidity in a Competitive Incomplete Contract Market." *Journal of Political Economy* 107 (1999): 106–134.
Feldman, M., K. Aoki & J. Kumm."Individual Versus Social Learning: Evolutionary Analysis in a Fluctuating Environment." Anthropological Science 104 (3) (1996): 209–231.
Festinger, L. "A Theory of Social Comparison Processes." *Human Relations* 7 (1954): 117–140.
Field, J., T. Schuller, and S. Baron. 'Social capital and human capital revisited.' Pp. 243-264 in Social Capital: Critical Perspectives, edited by Tom Schuller. Oxford: Oxford University Press. 2000.
Fine, B. "Economics Imperialism and Intellectual Progress: The Present as History of Economic Thought?" *History of Economics Review* 32 (1999): 10–36.
—. *Social Capital versus Social Theory: Political Economy and Social Science at the Turn of the Millennium.* London: Routledge, 2001.
Firth, R. *We, The Tikopia*. London: Allen & Unwin, 1936.
Fischbacher, U., S. Gächter and E. Fehr (2001), Are people conditionally cooperative? Evidence from a public goods experiment, Economic Letters 71 (3): 397–404.
Fiske, A. *Structures Of Social Life*. New York: Free Press, 1991.
Fligstein, N. *The Transformation of Corporate Control*. Cambridge, MA: Harvard University Press, 1990.
—. *The Architecture of Markets*. Princeton: Princeton University Press, 2001.
Fligstein, N. & P. Brantley. "Bank Control, Owner Control, Or Organizational Dynamics: Who Controls The Large Modern Corporation." *American Journal of Sociology* 98 (1992): 280–307.
Foer, A. A. "Review of 'Money for Nothing: Politicians, Rent Extraction and Political Extraction'." *White House Weekly*, 1988.
Foreman-Peck, James. *A History of the World Economy*. London: Harvester Wheatsheaf, 1983.
Forsythe, R., N. E. Horowitz, L. H. Savin & M. Sefton. "Fairness in Simple Bargaining Games." *Games and Economic Behavior* 6 (1988): 347– 369.
Foster, D. & H. P. Young. "Stochastic Evolutionary Game Dynamics." *Theoretical Population Biology* 38 (1990): 219–232.
Franciosi, R., P. Kujal, R. Michelitsch, V. Smith & G.Deng. "Fairness: Effect on Temporary and Equilibrium Prices in Posted-Offer Markets." *Economic Journal* 105 (1995): 938–950.
Frank, R. "The Political Economy Of Preference Falsification." *Journal of Economic Literature* 34 (1996): 115–123.

—. *Choosing the Right Pond—Human Behavior and the Quest for Status.* Oxford: Oxford University Press, 1985.

Frankfurt, H. "Freedom of the Will and the Concept of a Person." *Journal of Philosophy* 68 (1971): 5–20.

Franks, J. & C. Mayer "Ownership and Control of German Corporations." *Review of Financial Studies* 14 (4) (2001): 943–977.

—. "Hostile Takeovers and the Correction of Management Failure." *Journal of Financial Economics* 40 (1996): 163–181.

—. "Ownership and Control in German Corporations," Working Paper, 2000.

Franks, J., C. Mayer & L. Renneboog. "Who disciplines management in poorly performing companies?" *Journal of Financial Intermediation* 10 (3– 4) (2001): 209–248.

Freeman, R. & W. Evan. "Corporate Governance: A Stakeholder Interpretation." *Journal of Behavioural Economics* 19 (4) (1990).

Frei, B. S. *Not Just For the Money. An Economic Theory of Personal Motivation*. Cheltenham: Edward Elgar Publishing, 1997.

Frey, B., & F. Oberholzer-Gee. "The Cost Of Price Incentives: An Empirical Analysis Of Motivation Crowing-Out." *American Economic Review* 87 (1997): 746–755.

Friedberg, E. Ordnung und Macht. Dynamiken organisierten Handelns. Frankfurt: Campus, 1995.

Friedkin, N. "Theoretical Foundations For Centrality Measures." *American Journal of Sociology* 96 (1991): 1478–1504.

—. "Choice Shift and Group Polarization." *American Sociological Review* 64 (1999): 856–876.

Friedman, D. & J. Rust. *The Double Auction Market—Institutions, Theories and Evidence*. Reading, MA: Addison-Wesley Publishing Company, 1993.

Friedman, J., ed. *The Rational Choice Controversy*. New Haven: Yale University Press, 1996.

Fries, Christopher J. Ethnocultural space and the symbolic negotiation of alternative as "cure". Canadian Ethnic Studies Journal. Spring, 2005.

Frohlich, N. & J. A. Oppenheimer. *World Politics* 23 (1) (1970): 104–120.

Froot, K. A. & E. M. Dabora. "How Are Stock Prices Affected by the Location of Trade? *Journal of Financial Economics* 53 (2) (1996): 189–216.

Fudenberg D. & E. Maskin. "Social Distance and Other—Regarding Behaviour in Dictator Games." *Econometrica* 54 (3) (1986): 533–554.

Fudenberg, D. & C. Harris. "Evolutionary Dynamics with Aggregate Shocks." *Journal of Economic Theory* 57 (2) (1992): 420–41.

Furst, S. & M. Sherman, eds. *The Strategy of Change for Business Success*. New York: Clarkson N. Potter, 1969.
Furst, S. & M. Sherman. "The Emergence of Consumerism." In *The Strategy of Change for Business Success*, edited by S. Furst & M. Sherman. New York: Clarkson N. Potter, 1969.
Frey, Donald. "Protestant Ethic Thesis". EH.Net Encyclopedia, edited by Robert Whaples, 2001. http://eh.net/encyclopedia/article/frey.protestant.ethic (accessed August 10, 2008).
Furubotn, E. G. and S. Pejovich, eds. *The Economics Of Property Rights*. Cambridge, Mass: Ballinger, 1974.
—. "Introduction." In *The Economics Of Property Rights*, edited by E. G. Furubotn & S. Pejovich. Cambridge, Mass: Ballinger, 1974.
—. "Property Rights and Economic Theory: A Survey of Recent literature." *The Journal of Economic Literature* 10 (4) (1972).
Galbraith, J. "Time to Ditch the NAIRU." *Journal of Economic Perspectives* 11 (1997): 93–108.
Gamble A. & G. Kelly. *Stakeholder Capitalism*. London: Macmillan Press, 1997.
Gannon, S. P. "The Popularity of Max Weber's The Protestant Ethic and the Spirit of Capitalism: An Analysis of Historical Trends of Scholarship." *Gateway: An Academic Journal on the Web*. Winter 2002–2003.
Ganssmann, H. "Money—A Symbollically Generalized Medium of Communication?" *Economy and Society* 20 (3) (1988).
—. *Geld und Arbeit*, Frankfurt: Campus, 1996.
Garfinkel, H. *Studies in Ethnomethodology*. Englewood Cliffs, NJ: Prentice-Hall, 1967.
Goswami, G. "Stock Market and Economic Forces: Evidence from Korea," with Sung-Chang Jung, the Proceedings of Global Finance Conference May 1998. http://www.bnet.fordham.edu/public/finance/goswami/eiteman_178963_im01.pdf. accessed April 11, 2008.
Geertz, C. "The Bazaar Economy: Information And Search In Peasant Marketing." In *Sociology Of Economic Life*, edited by M. Granovetter & R. Swedberg, 225–232. Boulder: Westview Press, 1992.
Gertler, M. & R. G. Hubbard. "Financial Factors in Business Fluctuations. Financial Market Volatility: Causes and Consequences." Federal Reserve Bank, Kansas City, MO, 1988.
Giddens, A. *Constitution of Society: Outline of the Theory of Structuration*. University of California Press, 1986

—. *Modernity and Self-Identity: Self and Society in the Late Modern Age*. Stanford: Stanford University Press, 1991.
—. *Runaway World: How Globalisation is Shaping Our Lives.* London: Profile, 1999.
—. *The consequences of Modernity*. London: Polity Press, 1990.
Gide, C., & C. Rist. *A History of Economic Doctrines*. Trans, R. Richards. London: George Harrap and Co, 1948.
Gintis, H. "Welfare Economics and Individual Development: A Reply to Talcott Parsons." *Quarterly Journal of Economics* 89 (1975): 291–302.
Goetz, D. "The Hitchhiker's Guide to Altruism: Gene Culture Coevolution, and the Internalization of Norms." *Journal of Theoretical Biology* 220 (4) (2003): 407–418.
Goetze D. & D. Fudenberg. "The Norm of Reciprocity: A Preliminary Statement." *The Journal of Conflict Resolution* 38 (1) (1994): 56-86.
Gompers, I. & J. Metrick. "Incentives vs. control: An analysis of U.S. dual class companies," NBER Working Paper 10240, Cambridge, MA, 2004.
Goodfellow, D. M. *Principles Of Economic Sociology*, London: Routledge, 1939.
Goodman, J. E. *Sociology Specific Aspects*. New York: Free Press, 1980.
Gordon, David. "The Global Economy: New Edifice or Crumbling Foundations?" *New Left Review* 168 (1988).
Gould, M. "Voluntarism Versus Utilitarianism: A Critique of Camic's History of Ideas." *Theory, Culture and Society* 6 (1989): 637–654.
—. "Parsons' Economic Sociology: A Failure of Will." *Sociological Inquiry* 61 (1991): 89–101.
Gouldner, A. *For Sociology*, Harmondsworth, 1973.
—. "Coordination, Commitment, and Enforcement: The Case of the Merchant Guild." *American Sociological Review* 25 (2) (1960): 161–178.
Graef C. S. "CEO Pay: How Much Is Enough?" Harvard Business Review, 1992.
Garnham, N. "Information Society as Theory or Ideology." In *Manuel Castells* Volume III, edited by F. Webster & B. Dimitriou, 185–196. London: Sage Publications, 2004.
Granovetter, M. "Economic Action and Social Structure: the Problem of Embeddedness." *The American Journal of Sociology Volume* 91 (3) (1985): 481–510.
—. "The Old and the New Economic Sociology: A History and an Agenda." In *Beyond the Marketplace: Rethinking Economy and*

Society, edited by R. Friedland & A. F. Robertson. New York: Aldine De Gruyter, 1990.

—. A Theoretical Agenda for Economic Sociology, In The New Economic Sociology: Developments of an Emerging Field, Eds. Mauro F.Guillén, Randall Collins, Paula England and Marshall Meyer, New York: Russell Sage Foundation, (2003),

—. "The Strength of Weak Ties." *American Journal of Sociology* 78 (6) (1973): 1360–1380.

Granovetter, M. & R. Swedberg, eds. *The Sociology of Economic Life*. Boulder, CO: Westview Press, 1992.

Gray, J. S. *Hayek on Liberty*. London: Blackwell, 1984.

—. "The Fall in Men's Return to Marriage: Declining Productivity Effects or Changing Selection?" *The Journal of Human Resources* 32 (3) (1997): 481–504.

Green, D. P. & I. Shapiro. *Pathologies of Rational Choice Theory*. New Haven, Yale University Press, 1994.

Griffin, L., M. Wallace & B. Rubin. "Capitalist Resistance to the Organization of Labor Before the New Deal: Why? How? Success?" American Sociological Review 51 (1986): 47–67.

Groethuysen, B. Origines de l'esprit bourgeois en France. I. L'Église et la bourgeoisie. Paris: Gallimard, 1927.

Grossman, H. "The Beginning of Capitalism and the Mass Morality" [Die Anfänge des Kapitalismus und die neue Massenmoral"]. Journal of Classical Sociology 6 (2) (2006).

Grossman S. J. & J. E. Stiglitz. "On the Impossibility of Informationally Efficient Markets." *American Economic Review* (1980): 393–408.

Gueltekin B. & M.Goldstein. "Privatization in Post-Communist Economies: A Theoretical Analysis." In *The New Economic Sociology: Developments of an Emerging Field*, edited by M. F. Guillén, R. Collins, P. England, and M. Meyer. New York: Russell Sage Foundation, 1994.

Guinnane, T., R. H. Naomi, R.Lamoreaux and J. L. Rosenthal. Putting the Corporation in its Place, Working Paper 13109, 2007. http://www.nber.org/papers/w13109 (accessedOctober 26, 2008).

Gurven, M. "To Give and to Give Not: The Behavioral Ecology of Human Food Transfers." *Behavioral and Brain Sciences* 27 (4) (2004): 543–583.

Güth, W. & H. Kliemt. "Competition or Cooperation: On the volutionary Economics of Trust, Exploitation and Moral Attitudes," *Metroeconomica* 45 (1994): 155–187.

Guzman, R. E., R. Andres & C. Rodrıguez-Sickert. Theories of the evolution of cooperative behaviour: A critical survey plus some new results, 2009. http://mpra.ub.uni-muenchen.de/12574/1/MPRA_paper_12574 (accessedMarch 30, 2010).

Guzmán, R. A, C. Rodriguez-Sickert & R. E. Rowthorn. "When in Rome, Do as the Romans: The Coevolution of Altruistic Punishment, Conformism and Cooperation." *Evolution and Human Behavior* 28 (2) (2007): 112–117.

Habermas, J. *Theory of Communicative Action* Vol. 2. Boston: Beacon Press, 1984.

Hall, P. & D. Soskice. *Varieties of Capitalism: The Institutional Foundations of Comparative Advantage*. Oxford: Oxford University Press, 2001.

Halpin, A. "Disproving the Coase Theorem." Economics & Philosophy 321 (2007).

Halsey, A. H., A. F. Heath & J. M. Ridge. *Origins and Destinations: Family, Class and Education in Britain*. Oxford: Clarendon Press, 1980.

Haltiwanger, J. & M. Waldman. "Rational Expectations and the Limits of Rationality: An Analysis of Heterogeneity." *American Economic Review* 75 (3) (1985): 326–40.

Hamblin, R. L. & J. Kunkel, eds. *Behavioural Theory in Sociology: Essays in Honour of George C. Homans.* Transaction Publishers, 1977.

Hasse, R & H. Lieulsfrud. "From Disorganized Capitalism to Transnational Fine Tuning?: Recent Trends in Wage Development, Industrial Relations, and 'Work' as a Sociological Category." The British Journal of Sociology 53 (1) (2002).

Hamilton, G. and N. Biggart. "Market, Culture, And Authority: A Comparative Analysis Of Management And Organization In The Far East." *American Journal of Sociology* 94 (1988): S52–S94.

Hamilton, W. D. "The Genetical Evolution of Social Behavior." *Journal of Theoretical Biology* 7 (1) (1964): 1–52.

Hamlin, A. "Political Dispositions and Dispositional Politics." In *Beyond Conventional Economics: The Limits of Rational Behaviour in Political Decision-Making*, edited by Giuseppe Eusepi and Alan Hamlin, 3–16. Edward Elgar Publishing, 2006.

Hamlin A. & C. Jennings. "Group Formation and Political Conflict: Instrumental and Expressive Approaches." *Public Choice* 118 (2004): 413–435.

—. "Leadership and Conflict." *Journal of Economic Behavior and Organization* 64 (2007): 49–68.
Hanke S. H., ed. *Privatization and Development*. San Francisco: Institute for Contemporary Studies Press, 1987.
Hansmann, H. & R. Kraakman. *The End Of History For Corporate Law*. Yale Law School, New Haven, 2000.
Hanson, R. C. & M. H. Song, "Managerial Ownership, Board Structure, and the Division of Gains in Divestitures." Paper presented at the Financial Management Association's annual meeting, 1997.
Hardin, G. "The Tragedy of the Commons." *Science* 162 (1968): 1243–1248.
—. Harisalo R. & E. Miettinen. "Trust Capital the Unrecognized Dimension of Management," 1968.
www.ensto. fi/enstogroup/trustcapital.html (accessed December 22, 2005)
Hardt, M. & N. Antonio. *Empire*. Cambridge, Mass: Harvard University Press, 2000.
Hart, O. D. "The Market Mechanism as an Incentive Scheme." *Bell Journal of Economics* 14 (1983): 366–382.
Hatch, D. L. "Changes in the Structure and Function of a Rural New England Community Since 1900." Ph.D. thesis, Harvard University, 1948.
Harvey, D. *Spaces of Global Capitalism: Towards a Theory of Uneven Development*. London: Verso, 2006.
—. *The Condition of Postmodernity*. Oxford, MA: Basil Blackwell, 1989.
Hauser, H. *Les Débuts du Capitalisme*. Paris: Alcan, 1927.
Hayashi, N., E. Ostrom, J. Walker & T.Yamagishi. "Reciprocity, Trust and the Sense of Control: A Cross-Societal Study," discussion paper. Indiana University, Bloomington, 1998.
Hayek, F. A. "The Pretense of Knowledge." In Unemployment and Monetary Policy, edited by F.A. Hayek. Washington, D.C.: Cato Institute, 1979.
—. *Individualism and Economic Order*. Chicago: University of Chicago Press, 1948.
—. Order With or Without Design?,: Selections from F.A. Hayek's Contributions to the Theory and Application of Spontaneous Order Compiled by Moldofsky. London: The Centre For Research into Communist Economies. (1989),
—. *The Constitution of Liberty*. London: Routledge, 1960.
—. *The Essence of Hayek*. Edited by C. Nishiyama & K. R. Leube. Stanford: Hoover, 1984.

—. "The Nature and History of the Problem." In *Collectivist Economic Planning*, edited by F. Hayek, 1935.
—. "The Non sequitur of the Dependence Effect." In *Private Wants and Public Needs*, edited by E. Phelps. New York: W. W. Norton, 1965.
—. *Collectivist Economic Planning*. London: George Routledge and Sons, 1935.
Haynes, M. "Capitalism, Class, Health and Medicine." *International Socialism Journal* issue 123.
Hechter. M. "The Attainment Of Solidarity." In *Intentional Communities, Rationality and Society* 2 (2) (1990): 142–155.
—. "Should Values Be Written Out Of The Social Scientist's Lexicon?" *Sociological Theory* 10 (1992): 214–230.
Hechter, M. & S. Kanazawa. "Sociological Rational Choice Theory." *Annual Review of Sociology* 23 (1997): 191–214.
Heckelman, J. C. "Comment: Explaining the rain: The Rise and Decline of Nations after 25 Years." *Southern Economic Journal* 74 (1) (2007).
Heiner, R. "The Origin of Predictable Behavior." *American Economic Review* 73 (1983): 560–595;
—. "The Origin of Predictable Dynamic Behavior." *Journal of Economic Behavior and Organization* 12 (1989): 233–257.
Helleiner, E. "Explaining the Globalisation of Financial Markets: Bringing States Back In." *Review of International Political Economy* 2 (2) (1995): 315–41.
Heller, M. *The Gridlock Economy*. New York: Basic, 2008.
Henrich, J. "Cultural Group Selection, Co-Evolutionary Processes and Large-Scale Cooperation." *Journal of Economic Behavior and Organization* 53 (1) (2004): 3–35.
Henrich, J. & R. Boyd. "The Evolution of Conformist Transmission and Between-Group Differences." *Evolution and Human Behavior* 19 (4) (1998): 215–242.
Henrich, J., R. Boyd, S. Bowles, C. Camerer, E. Fehr & H. Gintis. *Foundations of Human Sociality: Economic Experiments and Ethnographic Evidence from Fifteen Small-Scale Societies*. Oxford: Oxford University Press, 2004.
Hermalin B., & M. Weisbach. "The Effects of Board Composition and Direct Incentives on Firm Performance." *Financial Management* 20 (1991): 101–112.
Herman E. S. *Corporate Control, Corporate Power*. Cambridge: Cambridge University Press, 1981.

Hersh, S. & M. Statman. "The Disposition to Sell Winners Too Early and Ride Losers Too Long: Theory and Evidence." *Journal of Finance* 40 (3) (1985): 777–90.

Hilton, R., ed. *The Transition from Feudalism to Capitalism*. London: Aakar, 1976.

Himmelberg, C. P., R. G. Hubbard & D. Palia. "Understanding the Determinants of Ownership and the Link Between Ownership and Performance." *Journal of Financial Economics* 53 (1999): 353–384.

Hindley, B. "Separation of Ownership and Control in the Modern Corporation." *Journal of Law and Economics* 13 (1) (1970): 185–221.

Hirschman, A. "Against Parsimony: Three Easy Ways of Complicating Economic Discourse." *American Economic Review* 74 (1984): 89–96.

Hirst P. & G. Thompson. *Globalisation in Question: The International economy and the Possibilities of Governance*. London: Polity Press, 1996.

Hirshleifer, J. "The Expanding Domain of Economics." *American Economic Review* 75 (1985): 53–68.

Hobson, J. A. *Work and Wealth: A Human Valuation*. London: Macmillan, 1914.

Hodgson J. "Institutional Economics and Analysis of Work." In *Social Theory at Work*, edited by M. Korczynski, R. Hodson and P. Edwards, 208–233. Oxford: Oxford University Press, 2006.

Hodgson, G. "The Approach Of Institutional Economics." *Journal of Economic Literature* 36 (1998): 166–192.

Hodgson, G. & G. M. Hodgson. *How Economics Forgot History: The Problem of Historical Specificity in the Social Sciences*. London: Routledge, 2001.

—. *Economics and Institutions*. Cambridge: Polity Press, 1989.

Hodson, R. & R. Kaufman. "Economic Dualism." *American Sociological Review* 47 (1982): 727–739.

Hoffman E., K. McCabe & V. L. Smith. "Group Size Effects in Public Goods Provision: The Voluntary Contributions Mechanism R." *The American Economic Review* 86 (3) (1996): 653–660.

Hoffman, E. & M. Spitzer. "The Cease Theorem: Some Experimental Tests." *Journal of Law and Economics* 25 (1) (1982): 73–98.

Hoffman, E., K. McCabe, & V. Smith. "On Expectations and Monetary, Stakes in Ultimatum Games." *International Journal of Game Theory* 25 (1996): 289–301.

Holcombe, R. G. "The Median Voter Model in Public Choice Theory." *Public Choice* 61 (1989): 115–125.

Holderness, C. G., R. S. Kroszner & D. P. Sheehan. "Were the Good Old Days that Good?" *Journal of Finance* 54 (1999): 435–469.
Holloway, J. "Global Capital and the National State." In *Global Capital, National State and the Politics of Money*, edited by W. Bonefeld and J. Holloway. London: MacMillan, 1995.
Holmwood, J. "Economics, Sociology and the Professional Complex: Talcott Parsons and the Critique of Orthodox Economics." *American Journal of Economics and Sociology* 65 (1) (2006): 127–160.
—. *Founding Sociology? Talcott Parsons and the Idea of General Theory*. London: Longman, 1996.
Holton, R. J. "Talcott Parsons and the Theory of Economy and Society." In *Talcott Parsons on Economy and Society*, edited by R. J.Holton & B. S.Turner. New York: Routledge Kegan, 1986.
—. *Economy and Society*. London: Routledge, 1992.
Homans G. C. *The Nature of Social Science*. New York: Harcourt, Brace and World, 1967.
—. *Social Behavior: Its Elementary forms*. New York: Harcourt, Brace and World, 1961.
—. "The Sociological Relevance of Behaviorism." In *Behavioral Sociology*, edited by B. Robert and D. Bushell, 9–28. New York: Columbia University Press, 1969.
—. "Ogólne twierdzenia nauk społecznych" ["The Nature of Social Science"]. In Metodologiczne podstawy socjologii, edited by P. Sztompka. Craków, 1974.
—. "Zachowania społeczne jako wymiana dóbr." iElementy teorii socjologicznych, edited by W. Derczyński. Warsaw, 1975.
—. "Commentary." In *Institutions and Social Exchange*, edited by R. Simpson and H. Turk. Indianapolis: Bobbs-Merrill, 1971.
—. "Contemporary Theory in Sociology." In *Handbook of Modern Sociology*, edited by R. E. Faris. Chicago: Rand McNully, 1964.
—. "Bringing Men Back In." In "Institutions And Social Exchange," edited by T. Herman and R. Simpson, 109–127. Indianapolis: Bobbs-Merril, 1971.
—. "The Rational Choice Theory and Behavioral Psychology." In *Structures of Power and Constraint*, edited by C. Calhoun, M. Meyer and R. Scott, 77-90. Cambridge: Cambridge University Press, 1990.
—. "The Small Warship." *American Sociological Review* 11 (3) (1946): 294–300.
—. "A Conceptual Scheme for the Study of Social Organization." *American Sociological Review* 12 (1) (1947): 13–26.

—. "The Strategy of Industrial Sociology." *American Journal of Sociology* 54 4 (1949): 330–37.
—. *The Human Group*. New York: Harcourt, Brace and Company, 1950.
—. "Social Behaviour as Exchange." *American Journal of Sociology* 63 6 (1958): 597–606.
—. *Social Behaviour: Its Elementary Forms*. New York: Harcourt, Brace & World, Inc, 1961.
—. *Sentiments and Activities: Essays in Social Science*. Glencoe, IL: The Free Press of Glencoe, 1962.
—. "Bringing Men Back In." *American Sociological Review* 29 (5) (1964): 809–18.
—. "A Life of Synthesis." *American Behavioural Scientist* 12 1 (1968): 2–8.
—. *Social Behaviour: Its Elementary Forms*. New York: Harcourt Brace Jovanovich, Inc., 1974.
—. "Steps to a Theory of Social Behaviour: An Autobiographical Account." *Theory and Society* 12 1 (1983): 1–45.
—. *Coming to My Senses: The Autobiography of a Sociologist*. New Brunswick, NJ: Transaction Books, 1984.
—. *Certainties and Doubts: Collected Papers, 1962–1985*. New Brunswick, NJ: Transaction Books, 1987.
—. "Just Like the Rest." In *The Witch Hazel: Poems of a Lifetime*, 83–84. New Brunswick, NJ: Transaction Books, 1988.
—. "The Western Electric Researches." In *Fatigue of Workers: Its Relation to Industrial Production, by The Committee on Work in Industry of the National Research Council*, 56–107. New York: Reinhold Publishing Corporation, 1941.
—. "Status among Clerical Workers." *Human Organization* 12 (1953): 5–10.
—. "The Cash Posters: A Study of a Group of Working Girls." *American Sociological Review* 19 (6) (1954): 724–33.
—. "The Strategy of Small-Group Research." In Sentiments and Activities: Essays in Social Science, 269–77. Glencoe, IL: The Free Press of Glencoe, 1962.
—. "Small Groups." In *Sentiments and Activities: Essays in Social Science*, 294–302. Glencoe, IL: The Free Press of Glencoe, 1962.
—. "What Kind of a Myth is the Myth of a Value-Free Social Science?" *Social Science Quarterly* 58 (4) (1978): 530–41.
—. "My Meta-Sociology." In *The Study of Behaviour: Psychology as Science: Science as Psychology*, edited by Harold Miller, Jr., 13–23. Lexington, MA: Xerox Individualized Publishing, 1978.

—. "Skinner Again." *American Journal of Sociology* 86 (2) (1980): 389–93.
—. "Steps to a Theory of Social Behaviour: An Autobiographical Account." *Theory and Society* 12 (1) (1983): 1–45.
—. "Fifty Years of Sociology." Annual Review of Sociology 12 (1986): 13–30
Homans, G. C. & C. P. Curtis, Jr. "An Introduction to Pareto: His Sociology." New York: Knopf, 1934.
Hoover, K. & R. Plant. *Conservative Capitalism in Britain and the United States: A Critical Appraisal*. London: Routledge, 1989.
Hoshi T., A. Kashyap & D. Scharfstein. "The Role of Banks in Reducing the Costs of Financial Distress in Japan." *Journal of Financial Economics* 27 (1990): 67–88.
—. "Bank Monitoring and Investment: Evidence from the Changing Structure of Japanese Corporate Banking Relationships." In *Asymmetric Information, Corporate Finance, and Investment*, edited by R. Glenn Hubbard. University of Chicago Press, A National Bureau of Economic Research Project Report. Chicago and London, 1990.
Hubbard, R.G. & D. Palia. "Executive pay and performance: Evidence from the U.S. banking industry." *Journal of Financial Economics* 39 (1995): 105–130.
Huson, M., R. Parrino & L. T. Starks. "Internal Monitoring Mechanisms and CEO Turnover: A Long Term Perspective," unpublished manuscript. University of Alberta, Edmonton, AB. Investor Update, 1998. https://www.StreetAuthority.com (accessed July 10, 2003).
Hutchinson, T. W. *The Significance and Basic Postulates of Economics*. New York: Augustus M. Kelley, 1960.
—. *The Politics and Philosophy of Economics: Marxians, Keynesians and Austrians*. New York: New York University Press, 1984.
Hyde, A. "Notes on Human Capital," 2007. andromeda.rutgers.edu/~hyde/humancap.html (accessed August 25, 2010).
Hyun-Chin, L. "Globalizing Asia: Towards a New Development Paradigm." *Globality Studies Journal* 9 (2007).
Ingham, G. "Some Recent Changes in the Relationship Between Economics and Sociology." *Cambridge Journal of Economics* 20 (1996): 243–275.
Isaac, M. R. & J. M. Walker. "Group Size Effects in Public Goods Provision: The Voluntary Contribution Mechanism." *Quarterly Journal of Economics* 103 (1988): 179–199.

Isaac, M.R. & J. M.Walker. "Costly Communication: An Experiment in a Nested Public Goods Problem." In Laboratory Research in Political Economy, edited by Thomas R. Palfrey. Ann Arbor: University of Michigan Press, 1991.
Isaac, M. R., J. M. Walker & A. M. Williams. "Group Size and the Voluntary Provision of Public Goods: Experimental Evidence Utilizing Large Groups." *Journal of Public Economics* 1 (3) (1994): 191–206.
Iwanek, M. Analiza instytucji własności przedsiębiorstw. Przyczynek do roblematyki efektywności i usprawnienia przedsiębiorstw publicznych, Warsaw: Wydział Nauk Ekonomicznych Uniwersytetu Warszawskiego, 1996.
Jackson G. & R. Deeg. How many varieties of capitalism?, MPIfG Discussion Paper 2006, Max-Plank Institute for the Study of Societies, Bonn.
Jahmani, Y. & M.Ansari. "Managerial Ownership, Risk, and Corporate Performance." *International Journal of Commerce and Management* 16 (3) (2006): 212–221
Jaffe, A. J. & K. M. Lusht. "The History of the Value Theory: The Early Years." In *Essays in Honor of William N. Kinnard, Jr. Research Issues in Real Estate, Volume 9*, edited by C. F. Sirmans and E. Worzala. New York: Springer, 2003.
Jansen E. "Stockholder Capitalism. Fighting against Prejudice." In *De Facto*, November 2007.
Jasso, G. & K. D. Opp. "Probing the Character Of Norms. A Factorial Survey Analysis Of The Norms Of Political Action." *American Sociological Review* 62 (1997): 947–964.
Jensen, M. "Agency Costs of Free Cash Flow, Corporate Finance and Takeovers." *American Economic Review* 76 (1986): 323–329.
—. "Agency Costs of Overvalued Equity." *Financial Management* 34 (1) (2005).
Jensen, M., & K. J. Murphy. "Performance Pay and Top-Management Incentives." *Journal of Political Economy* 98 (2) (1990): 225–64.
Jensen, M., W. Meckling. "Theory of the Firm: Managerial Behavior, Agency Costs and Ownership Structure." *Journal of Financial Economics* 3 (1976): 305–360.
Jensen, M. & K. Murphy. "Remuneration: Where We've Been, How We Got To Here, What Are the Problems and How To Fix Them." Harvard Business School NOM Working Paper no. 04-28. Cambridge, MA., 2004.
Jensen, M., & R. Ruback. "The Market for Corporate Control: The Scientific Evidence." *Journal of Financial Economics* 11 (1983): 5–50.

Jonquières, G. Network Guerrillas." In *Financial Times*, April 30, 1998

Joas, H. & J.Beckert. "Action Theory." In *Handbook of Sociological Theory*, edited by Jonathan H.Turner. New York: Kluwer, 2001.

Jonassen, C. "The Protestant Ethic and the Spirit of Capitalism in Norway." *American Sociological Review* 12 (6) (1947): 676–686.

Jones, A.H.M. *The Roman Economy*, edited by P.A. Brunt. Oxford: Blackwell, 1974.

Kachelmeier, S. J. & M. Shehata. "Culture and Competition: A Laboratory Market Comparison between China and the West." *Journal of Economic Organization and Behavior* 19 (1992): 145–168.

Kahneman, D. & A. Tversky. "Judgement Under Uncertainty: Heuristics and Biases." *Science* 185 (1974): 1124–31.

Kahneman, D. & A. Tversky. "Prospect Theory: An Analysis of Decision Under Risk." *Econometrica* 47 (2) (1979): 263–91.

Kahneman, D. "Experiences Extended Across Time:Evaluation of Moments and Episodes." *Journal of Behavioral Decision Making* 5 (3) (1992): 169–185.

Kahneman, D., J. L. Knetsch & R. Thaler. "Fairness as a Constraint on Profit Seeking: Entitlements in the Market." *American Economic Review* 76 (1986): 728–741.

Kahneman, D., P. Slovic: & A. Tversky. *Judgement under Uncertainty: Heuristics and Biases*. Cambridge and New York: Cambridge University Press, 1982.

Kandori, M. "Social Norms and Community Enforcement." *The Review of Economic Studies* 59 (1992): 63–80.

Kandori, M., G. Mailath & R. Rob. "Learning, Mutation and Long Run Equilibrium in Games." *Econometrica* 61 (1993): 29–56.

Kang, J., & A. Shivdasani. "Firm Performance, Corporate Governance, and Top Executive Turnover in Japan." *Journal of Financial Economics* 38 (1995): 29–58.

Caplan, B. Why I Am Not an Austrian Economist. Bryan Caplan Home page, 1997. http://econfaculty.gmu.edu/bcaplan/whyaust.htm (accessed June 12, 2004).

Kaplan S. "Top Executive Rewards and Firm Performance: A Comparison of Japan and the US" *Journal of Political Economy* 102 (1994): 510–546.

Kaplan, S. & P. Stromberg. Venture capitalists as principals: Contracting, screening, and monitoring. American Economic Review 91(2001): 426–430.

Katona, G. *Psychological Analysis of Economic Behavior*. New York: McGraw-Hill, 1951.

Kaus, M. "Fifty-Fifty Forever." *Slate*, 2004. http://www.slate.com/id/2073262/ (accessed 18 September 18, 2010).

Kerr, C., J.T. Dunlop, F.H. Harbison & C. A. Myers. *Industrialism and Industrial Man: The Problems of Labor and Management in Economic Growth*. Cambridge, Mass: Harvard University Press, 1960.

Keser, C. & F. van Winden. "Partners Contribute More to Public Goods than Strangers: Conditional Cooperation," Discussion Paper, University of Karlsruhe, 1996.

Keynes, J. M. "The General Theory of Employment, Interest, and Money." London: Macmillan, 1949.

Khalil, E. "Two Kinds of Order: Thoughts on the Theory of the Firm." *Journal of Socio-Economics* 28 (1999): 157–173.

Killian, L. "Organization, Rationality and Spontaneity in the Civil Rights Movement." *American Sociological Review* 49 (1984): 770–783.

Khanna, A. Managerial ownership and firm value: Agency problems of empire building and overvalued equity, 2005. http://www.fma.org/SLC/Papers/ManagerialOwnership3.pdf (accessed March 11, 2008)

Kirzner, I. M. "Philosophical and Ethical Implications of Austrian Economics. In *The Foundations of Modern Austrian Economics*, edited by E. G. Dolan. Kansas City: Sheed and Ward, 1976c.

—. *Perception, Opportunity, and Profit*. Chicago: Chicago University Press, 1979.

—. "The Perils of Regulation: A Market Process Approach." Occasional Paper. The Law and Economics Center. University of Miami, 1978.

—. "Uncertainty, Discovery, and Human Action: A Study of the Entrepreneurial Profile in the Disesian System." In *Method, Process, and Austrian Economics: Essays in Honor of Ludwig von Mises*, edited by I. M. Kirzner. Lexington, Mass.: Heath, 1982.

—. ed. *Classics in Austrian Economics: A Sampling in the History of a Tradition*. London: Pickering & Chatto, 1994.

Kiyotaki, N. & R. Wright. "On Money as a Medium of Exchange." *Journal of Political Economy* 92 (1989): 927–54.

Klandermans, B. "Mobilization And Participation: Social-Psychological Expansions Of Resource Mobilization Theory." *American Sociological Review* 49 (1984): 583–600.

Klandermans, B. & D. Oegema. "Potentials, Networks, Motivations, and Barriers: Steps Toward Participation in Social Movements." *American Sociological Review* 52 (1987): 519–531.

Kloskowska, A. Przedmowa [Preface] in: T. Veblen, Teoria klasy próżniaczej. http://merlin.pl/Teoria-klasy-prozniaczej_Thorstein-Veblen/browse/product/1,120082.html (accessed December 15, 2011).

Knoke, D. "Incentives in Collective Action Organizations." *American Sociological Review* 53 (1988): 311–329.

Knorr C. K., & A. Preda. "The Sociology of Financial Markets." Oxford: Oxford University Press, 2004.

Kole, S. "Measuring Managerial Equity Ownership: A Comparison of Sources of Ownership Data." *Journal of Corporate Finance* 1(1995): 413–435.

Korenman, S. & D. Neumark. "Does Marriage Really Make Men More Productive?" *Journal of Human Resources* 26 (2) (1991): 282–307

Kowalczyk, K. Wikinomia – czy obserwujemy powstanie nowego modelu produkcji?, 2006. http://www.wiki.konferencja2006.pti.katowice.pl/images/9/91/0_Kowalczyk_Peer_Production.pdf (accessed December 15, 2008).

Kozyr-Kowalski, S. & J. Ładosz. *Dialektyka a społeczeństwo*. Warsaw: KiW, 2006.

Kranton, R. "Reciprocal Exchange: A Self-Sustaining System." *American Economic Review* 86 (1996): 830–851.

Kulischer, J. *Allgemeine Wirtschaftsgeschichte des Mittelalters und der Neuzeit: Band II Die Neuzeit*. München: Oldenbourg, 1929.

Kuszweyko, R. *Stara nowa gospodarka*. Biuletyn Zespołu Doradczego, Warsaw, 2001.

La Porta R., F. Lopez-de-Silanes & A. Shleifer. "Investor Protection and Corporate Valuation." *Journal of Finance* 58 (3) (2002): 145–168

La Porta R., F. López-de-Silanes, A. Shleifer & R. Vishny. "Corporate Ownership Around the World." Journal of Finance 54 (2) (1999): 471–520

—. "Law and Finance." *Journal of Political Economy* 106 (1998): 1113–55.

Lachmann, L. M. "On the Central Concept of Austrian Economics: Market Process." In *The Foundations of Modern Austrian Economics*, edited by E. G. Dolan. Kansas City: Sheed and Ward, 1976.

Laibson, D. "Golden Eggs and Hyperbolic Discounting." *The Quarterly Journal of Economics* 112 (2). (1997): 443–77.

Lakonishok, J., A. Shleifer & R. Vishny. "Contrarian Investment, Extrapolation, and Risk." *Journal of Finance* 49 (1994): 1541–1578.

Landier, A. & D. Thesmar. "Financial Contracting with Optimistic Entrepreneurs: Theory and Evidence," University of Chicago Working Paper, Chicago, IL. 2004.

Lane, R. "The Loss Of Happiness In Market Democracies." New Haven: Yale University Press, 2000.
Lange, O. *Ekonomia polityczna*. Warsaw, 1978.
Langlois, R. N., ed. *Economics as a Process*. Cambridge: Cambridge University Press, 1989.
Larner R. J. *Management Control and the Large Corporation*. New York: Dunellen, 1970.
Larson, M. S. *The Rise of Professionalism: A Sociological Analysis*. Berkeley: University of California Press, 1977.
Lawler, E. J. "An Affect Theory of Social Exchange." *American Journal of Sociology* 107 (2) (2001): 321–52.
Lawrer, S. "Rules of Disengagement: Habitus, Power and Resistance." *Sociological Review* 52 (S2) (2004).
LAUGIQ, J. Social Capital Trumping Class and Cultural Capital? Engagement in School among Immigrant Youth. in: Social Capital: Critical Perspectives, edited by Tom Schuller. Oxford: Oxford University Press. 2000.
Ledyard, J. "Public Goods: A Survey of Experimental Research." In *Handbook of Experimental Economics*, edited J. Kagel and A. Roth. Princeton: Princeton UniversityPress, 1995.
Lee, C. M C, A. Shleifer & R. H. Thaler. "Investor Sentiment and the Closed-End Fund Puzzle." *Journal of Finance* 46 (1) (1991): 75–109.
Lenin, V. I. "A great beginning." In *The Essentials of Lenin*. London: Lawrence and Wishart, 1947.
—. "How Bogdanov Corrects and 'Develops' Marx." In *Collected Works, vol.14*. Moscow, 1908.
Lewin, T. "When Richer Weds Poorer, Money Isn't the Only Difference." *The New York Times*, 2005.
Levine B & K. Ross. Bank-Based Or Market-Based Financial Systems: Which is Better? Working Paper 9138, 2002. National Bureau Of Economic Research at http://www.nber.org/papers/w9138 (accessed September 23, 2008).
Levine, D. K. "Modeling Altruism and Spite fullness in Experiments." *Review of Economic Dynamics* 1 (1997): 593–622.
Levi-Strauss, C. *Les structures elementaires de la parente*. Paris: Mouton & Co., 1971.
Levine, D. N. *Visions of the Sociological Tradition*. Chicago: The University of Chicago Press, 1995.
Lewellen W. *The Ownership Income of Management*. New York: National Bureau of Economic Research, 1971

Lord Roll of Ipsden, ed. The Mixed Economy: Proceedings of Section F (Economics) of the British Association for the Advancement of Science. Salford: Macmillan, 1982.
Lewellen W. G. Recent Evidence on Senior Executive Pay, National Tax Review (June), 1975.
Lewellen W. G. & B. Huntsman. "Managerial Pay and Corporate Performance." *American Economic Review* 50 (4) (1970).
Lewellen, W. G. & S. G. Badrinath. "On the Measurement of Tobin's q." *Journal of Financial Economics* 44 (1997): 77–122.
Lewin, S. "Economics And Psychology: Lessons For Our Own Day from the Early Twentieth Century." *Journal of Economic Literature* 34 (1996): 1293–1324.
Li Xing & Jacques. The Nexus between "Politics in Command" and Social Engineering, research center on development and international relations (dir), working paper no. 121, 2003.
Lie, J. "The Concept Of Mode Of Exchange." *American Sociological Review* 57 (1992): 508–523.
—. "Sociology Of Markets." *Annual Review of Sociology* 23 (1997): 341–360.
Lindenberg, E. & S. Ross, S. "Tobin's q Ratio and the Industrial Organization." *Journal of Business* 54 (1981): 1–33.
Littlechild, S. C. *The Fallacy of the Mixed Economy: An Austrian Critique of Recent Economic, Thinking and Policy*. London: The Institute of Economic Affairs, 1986.
—. Three Types of Market Process. In *Economics as a Process*, edited by R. N. Langlois. Cambridge: Cambridge University Press, 1989.
Loewenstein, G. F., L. Thompson & M. H. Bazerman. "Social Utility and Decision Making in Interpersonal Contexts." *Journal of Personality and Social Psychology* 57 (1989): 426–441.
Loh, E. S. "Productivity Differences and the Marriage Wage Premium for White Males." Journal of Economic Resources 31 (3) (1996): 566–590.
Lopes, H. "From Self-Interest Motives to Justice Motives: The Challenges of Some Experimental Results." *American Journal of Economics and Sociology* 67 (2) (2008).
Lawler, S. "Rules of Engagement:Habitus and Power." *Sociological Review* 52 (S2) (2004).
Luhmann, N. "Das sind Preise." *Soziale Welt* 2 (1983): 153–170.
—. Die Wirtschaft der Gesellschaft, Suhrkamp, Frankfurt a.M, 1994.
—. Die Wirtschaft der Gesellschaft, Frankfurt: Suhrkamp, 1998.
—. Social Systems, Stanford, CA: Stanford University Press, 1995.

—. "Knappheit, Geld und die bürgerliche Gesellschaft." *Jahrbuch f. Sozial wissenschaft* 23 (2) (1972): 186–210.

Lukes, S. *Individualism*. Oxford: Basil Blackwell, 1973.

MacKenzie, D. W. "The Use of Knowledge about Society." *Journal of Economic Behavior and Organization* (2008),

—. Politics and Knowledge: Expectations formation in Democracy. Working paper, Presented at the Southern Economics Association Conference in 2005.

Macmillan, P. A Reader with Institutions and Collective Choic`e in Developing Countries.

Maitland, I. & A. Martin. "EMU and Wage Bargaining: the Americanization of the European Labor Market." Center for European Studies, Harvard University, 1998.

Mandel, E. Marx's Labour Theory of Value – part IV. International Viewpoint www.internationalveiwpoint.org (accessed April 14, 2010).

Macy, M. & A. Flache. "Beyond Rationality In Models Of Choice." *Annual Review of Sociology* 21 (1995): 73–92.

Madrian, B. & D. Shea. *The Power of Suggestion: Inertia in 401(k) Savings Behavior*. Chicago: University of Chicago, 2000.

Mann, M. "Explaining the World as a System: Can it Be Done?" *British Journal of Sociology* 61 (1) (2010): 177–182.

Mailath, G., L. Samuelson & A. Shaked. "Endogenous Interactions." In *The Evolution of Economic Diversity*, edited by A. Nicita and U. Pagano. New York: Routledge, (2001): 300–324.

Menger, C. "On the Origin of Money." *Economic Journal* 2 (1892): 239–55.

Maitland, I. & M. Andrew. "EMU and Wage Bargaining: the Americanization of the European Labor Market," Center for European Studies, mimeograph, 1998.

Malik, M. "Hunger, Choice and Struggle for it." unpublished desertation on poverty in India, 2009.

Malmendier, U. & G. Tate. "Who Makes Acquisitions? CEO Overconfidence and the Market's Reaction." Stanford University Working Paper, Stanford, CA, 2004.

Mann, M. "Explaining the World as a System: Can it be Done?" *British Journal of Sociology* 61 (1) (2010): 177–182.

Marciniak S., ed. *Makro i Mikro EkonomiaPodstawowe Problemy*. Warsaw: PWE, 2001.

Mare, R. "Five Decades Of Educational Assortative Mating." *American Sociological Review* 56 (1991): 15–32.

Margolis, H. *Selfishness, Altruism and Rationality*. Cambridge: Cambridge University Press, 1982.

Mark I. & J. M. Walker. "An Eye for an Eye Leaves Everyone Blind: Cooperation and Accounting Systems." *The Quarterly Journal of Economics* 103 (1) (1988): 179–199.

Markovsky, B., D. Willer, B. Simpson & M. Lovardia. "Power In Exchange Networks." *American Sociological Review* 62 (1997): 833–837.

Markovsky, B., D.Willer & T. Patton. Theory, Evidence, And Intuition. American Sociological Review 55(1990): 300-304.

Markovsky, B., L. R. Smith and J. Berger. "Do Status Interventions Persist?" *American Sociological Review* 49 (1984): 373–382.

Marmot, M. "Social Differentials in Health Within and Between Populations." *Daedalus* 123 (4) (1994).

—. *Status Syndrome*. London: Bloomsbury, 2003.

—. "Social Determinants of Health Inequalities." *Lancet* 365 (1099) (2005).

Marmot, Michael, and Richard Wilkinson. "The Solid Facts (second edition)," World Health Organisation, 2003. www.euro.who.int/document/e81384.pdf (accessed November 10, 2009).

Manning, B. "The English Revolution and the Transition from Feudalism to Capitalism." *International Socialism Journal* 63 (1994).

Marquez, R., F. Allen & E. Carletti. "Stakeholder Capitalism, Corporate Governance and Firm Value," 2007. http://knowledge.wharton.upenn.edu/papers/1344.pdf (accessed February 1, 2009).

Martin, K. J., & J. J. McConnell. "Corporate Performance, Corporate Takeovers, and Management Turnover." *Journal of Finance* 46 (2) (1991): 671–687.

Martindale, D. C. "Talcott Parsons' Theoretical Metamorphosis from Social Behaviourism to Macro-Functionalism." In *Institutions and Exchange: The Sociologies of Talcott Parsons and George Caspar Homans*, edited by H. Turk and R. L. Simposon, New York: Bobbs-Merrill, 1971.

Marwell G. & R. E. Ames. "Experiments on the Provision of Public Goods. II. Provision Points, Stakes, Experience, and the Free-Rider Problem." *The American Journal of Sociology* 84 (6) (1979): 1335–1360.

—. "An Experimental Study of the Centipede Game." *The American Journal of Sociology* 85 (4) (1980): 926–937.

Marchand, G. & J. L. Rulliere. "On the Reliability of Reciprocal Fairness—An Experimental Study," Discussion Paper, Humboldt University Berlin, 1997.

Maryanski, A. & J. Turner. *The Social Cage: Human Nature and the Evolution of Society*. Stanford: Stanford University Press, 1992.

Marx, K. *Capital Vol. I*. New York: Progress Publishers, 1967.

—. *Capital: A Critique of Political Economy, Vol. 1*. Harmondsworth: Penguin, 1976

—. *A Contribution to the Critique of Political Economy*, Moscow: Progress Publishers , 1977, with some notes by R. Rojas.

—. "Economic and Philosophical Manuscripts." In *Early Writings*. New York: Vintage Book, 1844.

—. "Economic Manuscripts: Theories of Surplus-Value, Addenda to Part 1." *Theories of Surplus Value*, 1861–3.

—. "The Emancipation Question." *The New-York Daily Tribune*, January 17 and 22, 1859.

—. "Economic Works of Karl Marx 1857–61." *Grundrisse der Kritik der Politischen Ökonomie* [*Outlines of the Critique of Political Economy*], Moscow: Foreign Language Publishers, 1939.

—. *Soczienienia*. v. 49. Moscow, 1974.

—. *Ekonomiczeskije rukopisy* 1857–1861 godow. Part I. Moscow, 1980a.

—. *Ekonomicziskije*… Part II. Moscow, 1980b.

—. *Soczinienia*. vol. 48. Moscow, 1980c.

Mashaw, J. L. *Greed, Chaos, and Governance*. New Haven: Yale University Press, 1997.

Maskowitz, T. & M. Grinblatt. Do industries explain momentum? *Journal of Finance* 54 (1999): 1249–1290.

Mathiesen, H. "Managerial ownership and performance-Empirical studies." http://www.encycogov.com/A5OwnershipStructures.asp (accessed December 11, 2009).

Maton, K. "Recovering Pedagogic Discourse: A Bernsteinian Approach to the Sociology of Educational Knowledge." *Linguistics & Education* 11 (1) (2000): 79–98.

Mayer, H. "The Cognitive Value of Functional Theories of Price: Critical and Positive Investigations concerning the Price Problem." In *Classics in Austrian Economics: A Sampling in the History of a Tradition*, edited by I. M. Kirzner. William Pickering, 1994.

McAdam, D. & R. Paulsen. "Specifying The Relationship Between Social Ties And Activism." *American Journal of Sociology* 99 (1993): 640–667.

McChesney, F. S. *Money For Nothing: Politicians, Rent Extraction, And Political Extortion*. Cambridge, MA: Harvard University Press, 1997.
McConnell, J. J. and H. Servaes. "Additional Evidence on Equity Ownership and Corporate Value." *Journal of Financial Economics* 27 (1990): 595–612.
—. "Additional Evidence on Equity Ownership and Corporate Value." *Journal of Financial Economics* 27 (1990): 595–612.
—. "Equity Ownership and the Two Faces of Debt." *Journal of Financial Economics* 39 (1995): 131–157.
McConnell, J., H. Servaes, H. and K. Lins. Changes in equity ownership and changes in the market value of the firm, London Business School Working Paper, London, U.K., 2005.
McEachern, W.A. (1975), Managerial Control and Performance, Lexington: D.C. Heath.
McGahan, A. M. "The Performance of US Corporations: 1981-1994." *Journal of Industrial Economics* 47 (1999): 373–398.
McKelvey, R. D., & T. R. Palfrey. "Quantal Response Equilibria for Normal Form Games." *Games and Economic Behavior* 10 (1) (1995): 6–38.
McKelvey, R. D. "Intransitivities in Multi Dimensional Voting Models and Some Implications for Agenda Control." *Journal of Economic Theory* 12 (1976): 472–482.
Mas-Collel, A., M. D. Whinston & J. R. Green. *Microeconomic Theory*. Oxford: Oxford University Press, 1976.
McPherson, J. M. *Drawn with the Sword: Reflections on the American Civil War*. New York: Oxford University Press, 1996.
Mehran, H. "Executive Compensation Structure, Ownership, and Firm Performance." *Journal of Financial Economics* 38 (2) (1995): 163–185.
Mann, M. "Explaining the World as a System: Can it be Done?" *British Journal of Sociology* 61 (1) (2010): 177–182.
Menger, C. *Principles of Economics*, 1994
Menzies, K. *Talcott Parsons and the Social Image of Man*. London: Routledge and Kegan Paul, 1976.
Merton, R. "The Thomas Theorem And The Matthew Effect." *Social Forces* 74 (1995): 379–422.
Meyer, M. C. "A Test for Linear Versus Convex Regression Function Using Shape Restricted Regression." *Biometrika* 90 (2003): 223–232.
Michener, A., E. Cohen & A. Sorensen. "Social Exchange. Predicting Transactional Outcomes In Five-Event, Four-Person Systems." *American Sociological Review* 42 (1977): 522–535.
Millede N. *Nad rzekami Babilonu*. Warsaw, 2005.

Montgomery, D. "For many protesters, Bush isn't the main issue." *Washington Post*, January 20, 2001.
Mirowski, P. *More Heat than Light: Economics as Social Physics, Physics as Nature's Economics*. Cambridge: Cambridge University Press, 1989.
Mises, L. "Economic Calculation in the Socialist Commonwealth," 1920. Reprinted in *Individualism and Economic Order*, edited by F. A. Hayek. Chicago: University of Chicago Press, 1948.
Mises, L. von. Epistemological Problems of Economics, Princeton: D.Van Nostrand, 1960.
—. *Human Action: A Treatise on Economics*. New Haven: Yale University Press.
—. *Socialism: An Economic and Sociological Analysis*. London: Jonathan Cape, 1936.
—. *Human Action: A Treatise on Economics*. New Haven: Yale University Press, 1949.
Mitchell. M. "What is the right model for corporate governance in developing Asia?" *Asian Development Bank*, 2003.
Moldofsky, N. "The Problems Considered, 1920-1989." In "Order—With or Without Design? Excerpts from the Writings of Friedrich A. Hayek," edited by N. Moldofsky. London Centre for Research into Communist Economie, 1989.
Molm, L. "Punishment Power: A Balancing Process In Power-Dependence Relations." *American Journal of Sociology* 94 (1989): 1392–1418.
—. "Structure, Action, And Outcomes: The Dynamics Of Power In Social Exchange." *American Sociological Review* 55 (1990): 427–447.
—. "Affect And Social Exchange: Satisfaction In Power-Dependence Relations." *American Sociological, Review* 56 (1991): 475–493.
—. "Risk And Power Use: Constraints On The Use Of Coercion In Exchange." *American Sociological Review* 62 (1997): 113–133.
—. *Coercive Power in Social Exchange*. New York: Cambridge University Press, 1997.
Molm, L. & G. Peterson. "Power In Negotiated And Reciprocal Exchange." *American Sociological Review* 64 (1999): 876–891.
Molm, L., G. Peterson & N. Takahashi. "In The Eye Of The Beholder: Procedural Justice In Social Exchange." *American Sociological Review* 68 (2003): 128–152.
Molm, L., T. Quist & P. Wiseley. "Imbalanced Structures, Unfair Strategies: Power And Justice In Social Exchange." *American Sociological Review* 59 (1994): 98–121.

Montchrestien, A. De. *Traicté de l'économie politique*. Rouen: Osmont, 1615.

Moore, J. "Managerial Behavior in the Theory of Comparative Economic Systems. In *The Economics Of Property Rights*, edited by E. G. Furubotn & S. Pejovich. Cambridge, Mass: Ballinger, 1974.

Moore, R. & K. Maton. "Founding the Sociology of Knowledge: Basil Bernstein, Intellectual Fields and the Epistemic Device." In *Towards a Sociology of Pedagogy*, edited by A. Morais, I. Neves, B. Davies & H. Daniels, 153–182. New York, Peter Lang.

Moore, R., M. Arnot, J. Beck & H. Daniels, eds. *Knowledge, Power and Educational Reform: Applying the sociology of Basil Bernstein*. London: Routledge, 2006.

Morais, A., I. Neves, B. Davies & H. Daniels, eds. *Towards a Sociology of Pedagogy: The Contribution of Basil Bernstein to Research*. New York, Peter Lang, 2001.

Morishima, M. *The Introduction to Marx's Economics: A Dual Theory of Value and Growth*. Cambridge: Cambridge University Press, 1978.

Mork, R. "A Frog in a Well Knows Nothing of the Ocean: A history of Corporate Ownership in Japan," National Bureau of Economic Research Working Paper, 2004.

—. "Behavioral Finance in Corporate Governance," Independent Directors and Non-Executive Chairs, 2004.

—. "How to Eliminate Pyramidal Business Groups—The Double Taxation of Intercorporate Dividends and other Incisive Uses of Tax Policy," National Bureau of Economic Research Working Paper 106XX, 2004.

Morck R., D. A. Stangeland & Y. Bernard. "Inherited Wealth, Corporate Control, and Economic Growth: The Canadian Disease." In *Concentrated Corporate Ownership*, edited by R. Morck. Chicago: University of Chicago Press, 2000.

Morck R., D. Wolfenzon & B. Yeung. "Corporate Governance, Economic Entrenchment and Growth," National Bureau of Economic Research Working Paper 10692, 2004.

Morck R/ K., & L. Steier. "The Global History Of Corporate Governance An Introduction Working Paper," 11062 National Bureau Of Economic Research, 2005. http://www.nber.org/papers/w11062 (accessed November 29, 2007).

Morck, R. & M. Nakamura. "Banks and Corporate Control in Japan." *Journal of Finance* 54 (1) (1999): 319–340.

Morck, R., A. Shleifer & R. Vishny. "Management Ownership and Market Valuation: An Empirical Analysis." *Journal of Financial Economics* 20 (1) (1988): 293–315.

—. "The stock market and investment: Is the market a sideshow? *Brookings Papers on Economic Activity* 2 (1990): 157–215.

Morck, R., M. Percy, G. Tian & B. Yeung. "The Rise and Fall of the Widely Held Firm: A History of corporate Ownership in Canada." National Bureau of Economic Research Working Paper, 2004.

Morris, S. Contagion. *Review of Economic Studies* 67 (1) (2000): 57–78.

Müller, D. *Public Choice II*. Cambridge: Cambridge University Press, 1989.

—. *Public Choice III*. Cambridge: Cambridge University Press, 2003.

Münch, R. *Theorie des Handelns. Zur Rekonstruktion der Beiträge von Talcott Parsons, Emile Durkheim und Max Weber*. Frankfurt: Suhrkamp, 1988.

—. "Zahlung und Achtung. Die Interpenetration von Ökonomie und Moral." *Zeitschrift für Soziologie* 23 (1994): 388–411.

Muller, J., B. Davies & A. Morais, eds. *Reading Bernstein, Researching Bernstein*. London, Routledge Falmer, 2004.

Munn, P. Social Capital, Schools, and Exclusions. in: Social Capital: Critical Perspectives, edited by Tom Schuller. Oxford: Oxford University Press 2002.

Murphy, K. J. "Executive compensation." In *Handbook of Labor Economics, Vol. 3b*, edited by O. Ashenfelter & D. Card. Elsevier Science North Holland, 1999.

—. "The Control and Performance of State-Owned Enterprises: Comment." In Privatization and State Owned Enterprises, edited by P. W. MacAvoy et al. Kluwer Academic Publishers, 1989.

Muzaffar, A. I. "An Economic Approach to Politics in Developing Countries." Unpublished Ph.D. Dissertation, Georgetown University, Washington, D.C., 1982.

Myers, S. C. "Determinants of Corporate Borrowing." *Journal of Financial Economics* 5 (1977):147–175.

Mythen, G. "Employment, Individualization and Insecurity: Rethinking the Risk Society Perspective." *Sociological Review* 53 (1) (2005): 129–149.

Nader, R. & L. Wallach. "GATT, NAFTA, and the Subversion of the Democratic Process." In *The Case Against the Global Economy and For a Turn Towards the Local*, edited by J. Mander & E. Goldsmith. San Francisco: Sierra Club Books, 1996.

Nagel, T. *Mortal Questions*. Cambridge: Cambridge University Press, 1979.

Nineham, C. "Anti-Capitalism Ten Years after Seattle," 2010. www. Counterfire.org (accessed January 10, 2011).

National Consumer Council. “In the Absence of Competition.” London: HMSO, 1989.
Narayanan, M. P. “Managerial Incentives for Short-term Results.” *Journal of Finance* 40 (5) (1985): 1469–1484.
Niskanen, W. *Bureaucracy: Servant or Master?* London: Institute of Economic Affairs, 1974.
Nau, R. Criticism of Rational Choice Theory in Political Science,” Seminar on Choice Theory, Newbould G. D. Management and Merger Activity. Liverpool, 1970.
Nielsen, J. K. “The Political Orientation of Talcott Parsons: The Second World War and Its Aftermath.” In *Talcott Parsons: Theorist of Modernity*, edited by. R. Robertson & B. S. Turner. London: Sage, 1991.
Newman, F. W. *Lectures on Political Economy*. London, 1851.
Niskanen, W. A. “Bureaucracy.” In *Democracy and Public Choice*, edited by C. K. Rowley. Oxford: Basil Blackwell, 1987.
Niven, J. “Brain evolution: Getting Better all the Time?” *Current Biology* 15 (16) (2005): 624–626.
Nutter, G. “Markets without Property: A Grand Illusion.” In *The Economics Of Property Rights*, edited by E. G. Furubotn & S. Pejovich. Cambridge, Mass: Ballinger, 1974.
O’Driscoll, G. P. Competition as a Process: A Law and Economic Perspective. In *Economics as a Process*, edited by R. N. Langlois. Cambridge: Cambridge University Press, 1989.
O’Driscoll, G. P. & M. J. Rizzo. *The Economics of Time and Ignorance.* Oxford: Basil Blackwell, 1985.
Ockenfels, A. & J. Weimann. “Types and Patterns—An Experimental East-West Comparison of Cooperation and Solidarity,” Discussion Paper, Department of Economics, University of Magdeburg, 1996.
Odean, T. “Are Investors Reluctant to Realize Their Losses?” *Journal of Finance* 53 (5) (1998): 1775–98.
O'Donoghue, T. & R. Matthew. “Procrastination in Preparing for Retirement.” In *Behavioral Dimensions of Retirement Economics*, edited by H. Aaron. The Brookings Institution, 1999.
Oegema, D. & B. Klandermans. “Why Social Movement Sympathizers Don’t Participate: Erosion And Non-Conversion Of Support.” *American Journal of Sociology* 49 (1994): 703–722.
Oliver, P. “A Cognitive Miser Theory of Cooperators' Advantage.” *The American Journal of Sociology* 85 (6) (1980): 1356–1375.
Olsen, M. “Social Participation And Voting Turnout: A Multivariate Analysis.” *American Sociological Review* 37 (1972): 317–333.

—. *The Logic of Collective Action*. Cambridge, MA: Harvard, University Press, 1965.

—. *How bright are the northern lights? Some questions about Sweden*. Lund: Lund University Press, 1990.

—. "Autocracy, Democracy and Prosperity." In *Strategy and Choice*, edited by R. J. Zeckhauser, 131–57. Cambridge: MIT Press, 1991.

—. "Dictatorship, Democracy and Development." *American Political Science Review* 87 (1993): 567–76.

—. "The Devolution of the Nordic and Teutonic Economies." *American Economic Review, Papers and Proceedings* 85 (1995): 22–27.

—. "Why the Transition from Communism is So Difficult." *Eastern Economic Journal* 21 (1995): 437–61.

—. "Big Bills Left on the Sidewalk: Why Some Nations are Rich and Others Poor." *Journal of Economic Perspectives* 10 (2) (1996): 3–24.

—. The Logic of Collective Action. Cambridge: Harvard University Press, 1971

—. *The Rise and Decline of Nations: Economic Growth, Stagflation, and Social Rigidities*. New Haven: Yale University Press, 1982.

—. "The South will Fall Again: The South as Leader and Laggard in Economic Growth." *Southern Economic Journal* 49 (1983): 917–32.

—. *Power and prosperity: Outgrowing communist and capitalist dictatorships*. New York: Basic Books, 2000.

Olson, M. & R. Zeckhauser. "An Economic Theory of Alliances." *Review of Economics and Statistics* 48 (1966): 266–79.

—. "The Efficient Production of External Economies." *American Economic Review* 60 (1970): 512–17.

Opp, K. D. Grievances and Participation in Social Movements. American Sociological Review 53 (1988): 853–864.

—. *The Rationality Of Political Protest*. Boulder: Westview Press, 1989.

Orbell J. M., P. Schwartz-Shea & R. T. Simmons. "Covenants With and Without a Sword: Self-Governance is Possible." *The American Political Science Review* 78 (1) (1984): 147–162.

Orbell J. M., R. Dawes & A. van de Kragt. "A Grammar of Institutions." *Ethics* 100 (3) (1990): 616–627.

Orbell J. M. & R. M. Dawes. "Free Riding and Collective Action: An Experiment in Public Microeconomics." *American Sociological Review* 58 (6) (1993): 787–800.

—. "Do Cooperators Exit More Readily than Defectors?" *Ethics* 100 (3) (1990): 616–627.

—. “Social Welfare, Cooperators' Advantage and the Option of Not Playing the Game.” *The American Political Science Review* 85 (2) (1991): 515–528.

Ossowski, S. *Dzieła. vol. 4*. Warsaw: PWN, 1967.

Ostrom, E. *Governing the Commons: The Evolution of Institutions for Collective Action*. New York: Cambridge University Press, 1990.

—. “A Behavioral Approach to the Rational Choice Theory of Collective Action: Presidential Address, American Political Science Association, 1997.” *The American Political Science Review* 92 (1) (1998).

Ostrom E., J. Walker & R. Gardner. “Bargaining and Market Behavior in Jerusalem, Ljubljana, Pittsburgh, and Tokyo: An Experimental Study.” *The American Political Science Review* 86 (2) (1992): 404–417

Ostrom, E. and V. Ostrom “The Quest for Meaning in Public Choice.” *The American Journal of Economics and Sociology* 63 (1) (2004).

Ostrom, E., J. Walker & R. Gardner. “Covenants With and Without a Sword: Self-Governance Is Possible.” *American Political Science Review* 86 (2) (1992): 404–17.

Ostrom, E. & J. M. Walker. “Cooperation Without External Enforcement.” In *Laboratory Research in Political Economy*, edited by T. R.Palfrey. Ann Arbor: University of Michigan Press, 1964.

Ostrom, V. *The Theory of the Compound Republic*. Lincoln, Nebraska: University of Nebraska Press, 1986.

—. *Crafting Institutions for Self-Governing Irrigation Systems*. San Francisco: Institute for Contemporary Studies, 1992.

—. “Developments in the 'No-Name' Fields of Public Administration.” *Public Administration Review* 24 (1) (1964): 62–63.

—. "Artisanship and Artifact." *Public Administration Review* 40 (4) (1980): 309–317.

Ostrom, V. & Ostrom, E. “Public Choice: A Different Approach to the Study of Public Administration.” *Public Administration Review* 31 (2) (1971): 203–216.

Ott A.F. & K.Hartley, eds. *Privatization and Economic Efficiency: A Comparative Analysis of Developed and Developing Countries*. Edward Elgar Publishing, Aldershot, 1991.

Olsen, O. H. “Historians and the extent of slave ownership in the Southern United States.” Civil War History, 2004. http://www.southernhistory.net/modules.php?op=modload&name=News&file=article&sid=9406 (accessed November 23, 2007).

Ohmae, K. *The Borderless World: Power and Strategy in the Interlinked Economy*. New York: Harper Business, 1990.

Pappalardo, A. "The Rational Paradigm In Political Science: Persistent Anomalies And The Role Of Sociology." *Sociological Theory* 9 (1991): 228–231.
Parsons, T. "On the Concept of Political Power." In *Sociological Theory and Modern Society*. New York: The Free Press, 1967.
—. "The Levels of Organization and the Mediation of Social Interaction." In *Institutions and Social Exchange*, edited by R. Simnpson & H. Turk. Indianapolis-New York, 1971.
—. "On the Concept of Value-Commitments." In *Politics and Social Structure*, edited by T. Parsons. NY: Free Press, 1969.
—. "The Social Systems." In *Social Systems and the Evolution of Action Theory*, edited by T. Parsons. New York: Free Press, 1977.
—. "Social Structure and the Symbolic Media of Interchange." In *Social Systems and the Evolution of Action Theory*, edited by T. Parsons. New York: Free Press, 1977.
—. *The Structure of Social Action*. Glencoe, IL: Free Press, 1949a.
—. "The Professions and Social Structure." In *Essays in Sociological Theory.* Glencoe, Ill.: Free Press, 1954a.
—. "The Motivation of Economic Activities." In *Essays in Sociological Theory*. Glencoe, ILl: Free Press, 1954b.
—. "The Rise and Fall of Economic Man." *Journal for General Education* 4 (1949): 46–53.
—. *The Social System*. Glencoe, IL: Free Press, 1951.
—. *The Social System*. London: Routledge and Kegan Paul, 1951.
—. "On the Concept of Political Power." *Proceedings of the American Philosophical Society* 107 (1963): 232–262.
—. "Sociological Elements in Economic Thought". In *The Early Essays*, edited by C. Camic. Chicago: University of Chicago Press, 1991.
—. *The Structure of Social Action*. New York: Free Press, 1937.
—. "The Professions and Social Structure." In *Essays in Sociological Theory*. New York: Free Press, 1954.
—. "The Motivation of Economic Activities." In *Essays in Sociological Theory*. New York: Free Press, 1954.
—. "A Sociologist Looks at the Legal Profession." In *Essays in Sociological Theory*. New York: Free Press, 1954.
—. "A Revised Analytical Approach to the Social Stratification." In *Essays in Sociological Theory*. New York: Free Press, 1954.
—. "Some Problems Confronting Sociology as a Profession." *American Sociological Review* 24 (1959): 547– 558.
—. "Pattern Variables Revisited: A Response to Professor Dubin's Stimulus." *American Sociological Review* 25 (1960): 467– 483.

—. *Societies: Evolutionary and Comparative Perspectives*. Englewood Cliffs, NJ: Prentice-Hall, 1966.
—. *The System of Modern Societies*. Englewood Cliffs, NJ: Prentice-Hall, 1971.
—. "Commentary on Herbert Gintis, A Radical Analysis of Welfare Economics and Individual Development." *Quarterly Journal of Economics* 89 (1975): 280– 290.
—. "The Rise and Fall of Economic Man." *Journal for General Education* 4 (1949): 46–53.
—. "The Marshall Lectures." In *Research Reports from the Department of Sociology. Vol. 4*. Uppsala: Uppsala University, 1986.
—. "On the Concept of Political Power." *Proceedings of the American Philosophical Society* 107 (1963: 232– 262.
—. "On Building Social System Theory: A Personal History." In *Social Systems and the Evolution of Action Theory*. New York: Free Press, 1977.
Parsons, T. & R. F. Bales. *Family, Socialization and Interaction Process*. London: Routledge & Paul, 1956.
Parsons, T. & N. J. Smelser. *Economy and Society: A Study in the Integration of Economic and Social Theory*. London: Routledge and Kegan Paul, 1956.
Paul, A. *Die Gesellschaft des Geldes. Entwurf einer monetären Theorie der Moderne*. Wiesbaden: VS Verlag, 2004.
Pejovich S. "Karl Marx, Property rights school and the process of social change." *Kyklos* 35 (1982): 383–407.
—. *The Economics of Property Rights: Towards a Theory of Comparative Systems*. Kluwer : Dordrecht, 1990.
—. "Comment on Paper by Alchian and Demsetz." *The Journal of Economic History* 33 (1) (1973).
—. *The Economics of Property Rights: Towards a Theory of Comparative Systems*. Kluwer Academic Publishers, 1990
Perelman, M. *Classical Political Economy: Primitive Accumulation and the Social Division of Labour*. Durham, NC: Duke University Press, 1998.
Peukert, H. "Max Weber: Precursor of Economic Sociology and Heterodox Economics?" *American Journal of Economics and Sociology* 63 (5) (2004): 987–1020.
Perrone, L. "Positional Power, Strikes, and Wages." *American Sociological Review* 49 (1984): 412–426.
Perrow, C. *Organizing America: Wealth, Power and the Origins of American Capitalism*. Princeton: Princeton Un. Press, 2002.

Pierotti, S. “Backup of The Protestant Ethic and the Spirit of Capitalism: Criticisms of Weber's Thesis,” 2003. http://www.csudh.edu/dearhabermas/weberrelbk01.htm (accessed October 23, 2009).
Piven, F. F. & R. Cloward. *Regulating the Poor: The Functions of Public Welfare*. New York: Vintage, 1972.
Pigou,A. C. "Real and Money Wage Rates in Relation to Unemployment." *The Economic Journal* 47 (187) (1937): 405–422
—. *The Economics of Welfare*. London: Macmillon, 1920.
—. “Economic Progress in a Stable Environment." *Economica* 14 (55) (1947): 180–188.
Pescosolido, B. “Beyond Rational Choice: The Social Dynamics Of How People Seek Help.” *American Journal of Sociology* 97 (1992): 1096–1138.
Phelps, W., ed. *Private Wants and Public Needs*. New York: W.W. Norton, 1965.
Pluciński P. “Teoria systemu społecznego Juergena Habermasa.” Ph. D. Thesis written under the supervision of Professor Jacek Tittenbrun. Adam Mickiewicz University. Poznan, 2008.
Radnitzky, G. & H. Bouillon, eds. “Values and the Social Order, Vol. 1.” *Values and Society* (1995): 189–194.
Reich, R. Democratic Voters and Democratic Investors, November 30, 2002.
Rhodes, M. & B. van Apeldoorn. “The transformation of West European capitalism?” European University Institute, Working Papers No. 97/60, 1997.
Podolny, J. “A Status-Based Model Of Market Competition.” *American Journal of Sociology* 98 (1993): 829–872.
Polanyi, K., C. M. Arensberg & H. W. Pearson, eds. *Trade and Market in Early Empires: Economies in History and Theory*. New York: Free Press, 1957.
Pollis, N. P. “Reference Groups Re-examined.” *British Journal of Sociology* 19 (1968): 300–307.
Porter, M. E. *Competitive Strategy: Techniques for Analyzing Industries and Competitors*. New York: Free Press, 1980.
Portes, A. “Social Capital: Its Origins and Applications in Modern Sociology.” *Annual Review of Sociology* 24 (1998): 1–24.
Portes A. & P. Landolt. “The Downside of Social Capital.” *The American Prospect* 26 (1996): 18-21, 94.
Poulantzas, N. *Classes in Contemporary Capitalism*. London: Verso, 1979.

Putterman, L. "Human Nature, Communication and Trust." *Annals of Public and Cooperative Economics* 80 (1) (2009).

Rabin, M. "Incorporating Fairness into Game Theory and Economics." *American Economic Review* (1993).

Richter, R. "New Economic Sociology and New Institutional Economics." Paper presented at the Annual Conference of the International Society for New Institutional Economics (ISNIE) Berkeley, California, USA

September 13–15, 2001.

Ralston S. J. *The Collapse of Globalism and the Reinvention of the World*. Canada: Viking, 2005. Rapaczyński, Raub, W. & J. Weesie. "Reputation And Efficiency In Social Interactions: An Example Of Network Effects." *American Journal of Sociology* 96 (1990): 626–654.

Regan, M. C. *Alone Together: Law and the Meanings of Marriage*. New York: Cambridge University Press, 1999.

Rehder, R. "Japanese Transplants: After the Honeymoon." *Business Horizons* (1990): 87–98.

Reich R. "Democratic Voters and Democratic Investors." *Journal of Private Enterprise* (2002).

Rhodes M. & B. van Apeldoor. "The Transformation of West European Capitalism?" European University Institute, Working Papers No. 97, 60, 1997.

Riker, W. H. "The Theory of Political Coalitions." New Haven and London: Yale University Press, 1962.

Riker, W. H. & P. C. Ordeshook. "A Theory of the Calculus of Voting." *American Political Science Review* 62 (1) (1968): 25–42.

Roberts, D. R. *Executive Compensation*. The Free Press: Glencoe, Ill, 1959.

Rodriguez-Sickert, C., R. E. Rowthorn & R. A. Guzman. *The Social Benefit of Slow Learners*. University of Cambridge, mimeo, 2008.

Roe, M. J. "Political and Legal Restraints on Ownership and Control of Public Companies." *Journal of Financial Economics* 27 (1990):7–42.

Roethlisberger, F. J. & W. J. Dickson. *Management and the Worker*. Cambridge, MA: Harvard University Press, 1939.

Romano, R. "Corporate Law and Corporate Governance." *Industrial and Corporate Change* 5 (2) (1996): 277–339.

—. "Less is More: Making Institutional Investor Activism a Valuable Mechanism of Corporate Governance." *Yale Journal on Regulation* 18 (2001).

—. "Corporate Law and Corporate Governance." In *Firms, Markets and Hierarchies*, edited by G. R. Carroll and D. J. Teece. New York: Oxford University Press, 1999.

—. *The Genius of American Corporate Law*. Washington D.C.: AEI Press, 1993.

—. "The Shareholder Suit: Litigation without Foundation?" *Journal of Law, Economics and Organization* 7 (1991): 55–87.

—. "Empowering Investors: A Market Approach to Securities Regulation." *Yale Law Journal* 107 (1998): 2359–2430.

—. "Corporate Law and Corporate Governance." In *Firms, Markets and Hierarchies*, edited by G. R. Carroll, and D. J. Teece. Oxford University Press, New York Oxford, 1999.

Romer, T. & H. Rosenthal. "The Elusive Median Voter." *Journal of Public Economics* 12 (2) (1979): 143–170.

Ross, L. Bank-Based or Market-Based Financial Systems:Which is Better? Working Paper 9138, National Bureau of Economic Research, 2002. http://www.nber.org/papers/w9138 (accessed September 23, 2008).

Ross, S. A. "The Determination of Financial Structure: the Incentive-Signalling Approach." *Bell Journal of Economics* 8 (1977): 23–40.

Rosser, Jr., J. Barkley. "The Rise and Decline of Mancur Olson's viewof the Rise and Decline of Nations," 2007 http://cob.jmu.edu/rosserjb/RISE%20AND%20DECLINE%20OLSON 's%20RAND.doc (accessed February 19, 2011).

Roth, A., E., V. Prasnikar, M. Okuno-Fujiwara & S. Zamir. "Bargaining and Market Behavior in Jerusalem, Ljubljana, Pittsburgh and Tokyo: An Experimental Study." *American Economic Review* 81 (1991): 1068–1095.

Roth, A. E. & I. Erev. "Learning in Extensive-Form Games: Experimental Data and Simple Dynamic Models in the Intermediate Term." *Games and Economic Behavior* 8 (1) (1995): 64–212.

Roth, A. E. "Bargaining Experiments." In *Handbook of Experimental Economics*, edited by J. Kageland & A. Roth. Princeton: Princeton University Press, 1995.

Rowley, C. K. & F. Schneider, eds. *The Encyclopedia of Public Choice*. New York: Springer, 2004.

Rowthorn, B. & H. Chang. *Public Ownership and the Theory of the State*. St. Andrews: University of St. Andrews (unpublished), 1991.

Rowthorn, R. E., R. Guzman, C. Rodrıguez-Sickert, S. C. Rose & H. Hartmann. *Still a Man's Labor Market: The Long-Term Earnings Gap*. Washington, DC: Institute for Women's Policy Research, 2004.

Rowthorn, R. E., R. Guzman, C. Rodrıguez-Sickert. "Theories of the Evolution of Cooperative Behaviour: A Critical Survey Plus Some New Results," 2009.

http://mpra.ub.uni-muenchen.de/12574/1/MPRA_paper_1257 (accessed August 20, 2010).

Rozo C. A. Between The Stakeholder and The Stockholder Models of Capitalism. Working Paper 01.3, 2006. European Monetary Union at http://www.ces.fas.harvard.edu/publications/docs/pdfs/Rozo (accessed May 5, 2009).

Runciman, W. G. *Relative Deprivation and Social Justice*. NewYork: Penguin, 1966.

Russell, T. & R. Thaler. "The Relevance of Quasi Rationality in Competitive Markets." *American Economic Review* 75 (2006): 1071–1082.

Sachs, J. "The Social Welfare State, Beyond Ideology". Scientific American, November 2006. http://www.scientificamerican.com/article.cfm?id=the-social-welfare-state (accessed June 20, 2008).

Sadovnik, A. R., ed. *Knowledge and Pedagogy: The sociology of Basil Bernstein.* Norwood, NJ: Ablex, 1995.

Sakamato, A. & M. Chen. "Inequality And Attainment In A Dual Labor Market". *American Sociological Review* 56 (1991): 295–308.

Samuelsson, K. *Religion and Economic Action.* Toronto: University of Toronto Press, 1993.

Samuelson, P. *Economics*. New York: McGraw-Hill, 1964.

Samuelson P. A. "Cheap Talk, Coordination, and Entry." *The Review of Economics and Statistics* 36 (4) (1954): 387–389,

—. Foundations of Economic Analysis. Cambridge: Antheneum, 1947.

Samuelson, L. "Stochastic Stability in Games with Alternative Best Replies." *Journal of Economic Theory* 64 (1994): 35–65.

Saurwein, K. H. Ökonomie und soziologische Theoriekonstruktion. Zur Bedeutung ökonomischer Theorieelemente in der Sozialtheorie Talcott Parsons. Opladen: Westdeutscher Verlag, 1988.

Savage, M., A. Warde & F. Devine. "Capitals, Assets, and Resources: Some Critical Issues." 56 (1) (2005): 31–47.

Schap, D. *Independent review of: The Limits of Public Choice: A Sociological Critique of the Economic Theory of Politics.* New York: Routledge, 1996.

Scheidel, W. *The Roman Slave Supply*. Stanford: Stanford University Press, 2001.

Schluchter, W. *The Rise of Western Rationalism*. California: University of California Press, 1981.

Schneider F. & W. W. Pommerehne, "Exit Threats and Cooperation Under Anonymity." *The Quarterly Journal of Economics* 96 (4) (1981): 689–704.

Schneider, F. "Public Choice-Economic Theory Of Politics." In *Essays on Economic Psychology*, Edited by Hermann Brandstatter and Werner Guth. Berlin: Springer-Verlag, 1994.

Schneider, H. K. *Economic Man*. New York: Free Press, 1974.

Schotter, A. *The Economic Theory of Social Institutions*. New York, 1981.

Schram, A. & F. van Winden. "Why People Vote: The Role Of Inter-And Intragroup Interaction In The Turnout Decision." In *Essays on Economic Psychology*, edited by H. Brandstatter & W. Guth, 213–250. Berlin: Springer-Verlag, 1994.

Schram, S. F., & B. Caterino, eds. *Making Political Science Matter: Debating Knowledge, Research, and Method*. New York and London: New York University Press, 2006.

Schuessler, R. "Levels of Information and Contributions to Public Goods." *The Journal of Conflict Resolution* 33 (4) (1989): 728–749.

Schumpeter J. A., *History of Economic Analysis*. London: Routledge, 1996.

—. *Capitalism, Socialism, and Democracy*. New York: Harper, 1950.

Schutz, A. "Parsons' Theory of Social Action." In *The Theory of Social Action*: *The Correspondence of Alfred Schutz and Talcott Parsons*, edited by R. Grathoff. Bloomington, IN: Indiana University Press, 1978.

Schwartz Giron P. E. *New thinking in political economy series, Economies and Its Enemies: Two Centuries of Anti-economies, Economies and Its Enemies: Two Centuries of Anti-Economies*. New York: William Oliver Coleman, 2007.

Schwinn, T. "False Connections: Systems and Action Theories in Neo-functionalism and in Jürgen Habermas." Sociological Theory 16 (1) (1998): 75–95.

Scott, J. "Life at the Top in America isn't Just Better, It's Longer." *The New York Times*, May 16, 2005.

Scott, J. & D. Leonhardt. "Shadowy Lines that Still Divide." *The New York Times*, May 15, 2005.

Scott, J. *Understanding Contemporary Society: Theories of the Present*. New York: Sage, 2000.

Scott, J. F. "The Changing Foundations of the Parsonian Action Scheme." *American Sociological Review* 28 (1963): 716–735.

Sell J. & R. K. Wilson. "Levels of Information and Contributions to Public Goods." *Social Forces* 70 (1991): 107–124.

Selten R., M. Mitzkewitz, & G. R. Uhlich. "Duopoly Strategies Programmed by Experienced Players." *Econometrica* 65 (3) (1997): 517–555.

Sen, A. K. "Rational Fools: A Critique of the Behavioral Foundations of Economic Theory." *Philosophy and Public Affairs* 6 (4) (1977).

Sennet, R. *The Culture of the New Capitalism*. New Haven: Yale University Press, 2006

Sethi R. & E. Somanathan. "Human Nature in Politics: The Dialogue of Psychology with Political Science." *The American Economic Review* 86 (4) (1996): 766–788

Sewell, Jr., W. H.. "A Theory of Structure: Duality, Agency and Transformation." *The American Journal of Sociology* 98 (1) (1992):1–29.

Shackle, G. "Epistemics and Economics." Cambridge: Cambridge University Press, 1972.

Schluchter, W. *Paradoxes of Modernity*. California: Stanford University Press, 1996.

Shleifer A. & L. Summers. "Breach of Trust in Hostile Takeovers." In *Corporate Takeovers: Causes and Consequences*, edited by A. J. Auerbach. Chicago: University of Chicago Press, 1988.

Shleifer, A. *Inefficient Markets: An Introduction to Behavioral Finance. Clarendon Lectures*. Oxford University Press, 2000.

Shleifer A. & R. W. Vishny. "The Takeover Wave of the 1980s." In *Studies in International Corporate Finance and Governance Systems*, edited by D. H. Chew. Oxford: Oxford University Press, 1997.

—. "Large Shareholders and Corporate Control." *Journal of Political Economy* 94 (1986): 461–88.

—. "Value Maximization and the Acquisition Process." *Journal of Economic Perspectives* 2 (1988): 7–20.

—. "Equilibrium Short Horizons Of Investors And Firms." *American Economic Review* 80 (2) (1989): 148–153

—. "A Survey of Corporate Governance." *Journal of Finance* 52 (1997): 737–83

—. "The Limits of Arbitrage." *Journal of Finance* 52 (1) (1997): 35–55.

Shleifer, A., & L. H. Summers. "Breach of Trust." In *Corporate Takeovers: Causes and Consequences*, edited by A. J. Auerbach. Chicago: University of Chicago Press, 1988.

Schmittberger, W., R. & B. Schwarze. "An Experimental Analysis of Ultimatum Bargaining." *Journal of Economic Behavior and Organization* 3 (1982): 367–388.

Schmittberger, W. & R. Tietz. "Ultimatum Bargaining Behavior—A Survey and Comparison of Experimental Results." *Journal of Economic Psychology* 11 (1990): 417–449.
Shughart II, W. F. *Public Choice: The Concise Encyclopedia of Economics*. Library Fund, 2008.
Shughart II, W. F. & L. Razzolini, eds. *The Elgar Companion to Public Choice*. Northampton, MA, USA and Cheltenham, UK: Edward Elgar Publishing, 2001.
Scott, A. "Risk Society or Angst Society? Two Views of Risk, Consciousness and Community." In *The Risk Society and Beyond: Critical Issues for Social Theory*. London: Sage, 2000.
Shavit, Y. & H. P. Blossfeld, eds. *Persistent Inequality: Changing Educational Attainment in Thirteen Countries*. Boulder: Westview Press, 1993.
Short, H. & K. Keasey. "Managerial Ownership and the Performance of Firms: Evidence from the UK." *Journal of Corporate Finance* 5 (1999): 79–101.
Shortell, T. Weber's Theory of Class http://www.brooklynsoc.org/courses/43.1/weber.html (accessed December 11, 2007).
Siemionow, J. *Kak wozniklo czielowiieczestwo*. Moscow, 1966.
Simmel, G. "Money in Modern Culture." *Theory, Culture, Society* 8 (3) (1991): 17–31.
Simmel, G. *The Philosophy of Money*. London: Routledge, 1990.
Simon, H., "A Behavioral Model of Rational Choice." *Quarterly Journal of Economics* 69 (1955): 99–118.
—. "A Mechanism for Social Selection and Successful Altruism." *Science* 250 (4988) (1990): 1665–1668.
—. *Administrative Behavior*. New York: Free Press, 1976.
Simon, H. A. "A Behavioral Model of Rational Choice." *Quarterly Journal of Economics* 69 (1955): 99–118.
—. "Microeconomic Systems as an Experimental Science." *The American Political Science Review* 79 (2) (1985): 293–304.
Skidmore, W. *Sociology's Models of Man*. New York: Routledge, 1975
Skinner, B. F. *Science and Human Behaviour*. New York: Macmillan, 1953.
Skinner, J. & J. Slemrod. "An Economic Perspective on Tax Evasion." *National Tax Journal* 38 (1985): 345–353.
Skyrms, B. "Evolution of the Social Contract." Cambridge: Cambridge University Press, 1996.

Slonim, R. & A. E. Roth. "Financial Incentives and Learning in Ultimatum and Market Games: An Experiment in the Slovak Republic." *Econometrica* 66 (1997): 569–596.

Smelser, N. J. *Problematics Of Sociology*. Berkeley: University of California Press, 1997.

—. "On Collaborating with Talcott Parsons: Some Intellectual and Personal Notes." *Sociological Inquiry* 51(1981): 143–154.

Smelser, N. J., & R. Swedberg. *The Handbook of Economic Sociology*. Princeton: Princeton University Press, 1994.

—. *The Handbook of Economic Sociology*. Princeton, NJ: Russell Sage Foundation, 1994.

Smith, A. *The Wealth of Nations*. London: Penguin, 1982.

Smith V. L., Coordination versus Prisoners' Dilemma: Implications for International Cooperation and Regimes. , The American Economic Review 72 (5) (1982): 923–955.

Smith, K. "Operationalizing Weber's Concept of Social Class." *British Journal of Sociology* 58 (1) (2007).

—. "Operationalising Max Weber's Concept of Class Situation: the Concept of Social Class." *British Journal of Sociology* 46 (1) (2007)

Smith, M. "What Is New In New Structuralist Analyses Of Earnings." *American Sociological Review* 55 (1990): 827–841.

Smith, V. L. "An Experimental Study of Competitive Market." *Journal of Political Economy* 70 (2) (1962): 111–137.

—. "Microeconomic Systems: an Experimental Science." *American Economic Review* 72 (5) (1982): 923–955.

Smith, V. L. & A. W. Williams. "The Boundaries of Competitive Price Theory: Convergence Expectations and Transaction Costs." In *Advances in Behavioural Economics, Vol.2*, edited by L. Green and J. H. Kagel. Norwood, NJ: Ablex Publishing Corporation, 1990.

Snow, D., B. Rochford, S.Worden & R. Benford. "Frame Alignment Process, Micromobilization And Movement Participation." *American Sociological Review* 51 (1986): 464–481.

Snyder, D. "Institutional Setting And Industrial Conflict: Comparative Analyses of France, Italy and the US." *American Sociological Review* 40 (1975): 259–278.

So, A. *Social Change and Development*. Newbury Park: Sage Publications, 1990.

Soto de. J. H. Spór metodologiczny (Methodenstreit) Szkoły austriackiej. Mises Institute. Stanford: Hoover Institution Press spp. 184–208.

Sowa, J. *Ciesz się, późny wnuku! Kolonializm, globalizacja i demokracja, Krakow: radykalna* Korporacja Ha!art, 2008.

Sproule-Jones, M. “Public Choice Theory and Natural Resources: Methodological Explication and Critique.” *The American Political Science Review* 76 (4) (1982): 790–804.

Starmer, C. “Developments in Non-Expected Utility: The Hunt for a Descriptive Theory of Choice Under Risk.” *Journal of Economic Literature* 38 (2000): 332–82.

Steel, G. R. “Understanding Economic Man, Psychology, Rationality, and Values.” *American Journal of Economics and Sociology* 63 (5) (2004).

Steelman, Lall & B. Powell. “Sponsoring The Next Generation: Parental Willingness To Pay For Higher Education.” *American Journal of Sociology* 96 (1991): 1505–1529.

Steiner, P. “Le fait social économique chez Durkheim.” *Revue française de sociologie* 33(1992): 641–661.

Storper, M. & R.Salais. *Worlds of Production: The Action Framework of the Economy*. Cambridge: Harvard University Press, 1997.

Stigler, George J. & Gary S. Becker. *De Gustibus*, 1995.

Strumilin, S. Od Oktrabrja k komunizmu. Woprosy Ekonomii. nr 9, 1968.

Sułek, A. Eksperyment na zwierzętach jako narzędzie nauk o zachowaniu ludzkim, Studia Filozoficzne, 7, 1975.

Steuart, J. D. *An Inquiry into the Principles of Political Economy*. 1767.

Stiglitz J. “Credit Markets and the Control of Capital.” *Journal of Money, Credit and Banking* 17 (2) (1986).

Stinchcombe, A. “Comment.” *Rationality and Society* 2 (1990): 214–223.

Stolte, J., G. Fine & K. Cook. “Sociological Miniaturism: Seeing the Big Through the Small in Social Psychology.” *Annual Review of Sociology* 27 (2001): 387–413.

Stoney C. & N. Aylott. “Tomorrow’s Company ?” *Renewal* 2 (4) (1994).

Storper, M., & R. Salais. “Worlds of Production: The Action Framework of the Economy.” Cambridge: Harvard University Press, 1997.

Stouffer, S. A. *The American Soldier*. Princeton: Princeton University Press, 1949.

Stulz, L. H. P., Walkling, R. A. “Managerial Performance, Tobin’s q, and the Gains from Successful Tender Offers.” *Journal of Financial Economics* 24 (1989): 137–154.

Stulz, R. M. “Managerial Control of Voting Rights: Financing Policies and the Market for Corporate Control.” *Journal of Financial Economics* 20 (1988): 25–54.

Starr P. “The Meaning of Privatization.” In *Privatization and the Welfare State*, edited by A. Kahn and S. Kamerman. Princeton: Princeton University Press, 1989.

Sutcliffe, B. & A. Glyn. "Measures of Globalisation and their Misinterpretation." *The Handbook of Globalisation*. Edward Elgar Publlishing, 2003.

—. "Economic Sociology: Past and Present." *Current Sociology* 35 (1987): 1–221.

—. "Max Weber and the Idea of Economic Sociology." Princeton: Princeton University Press, 1998.

—. "Major Traditions of Economic Sociology." *Annual Review of Sociology* 17 (1991): 251–276.

Swidler, A. "Culture in Action: Symbols and Strategies." *American Sociological Review* 51 (1986): 273–286.

Swift, A. "Class Analysis from a Normative Perspective." *British Journal of Sociology* 51 (4) (2003).

Szczurkiewicz, T. Studia socjologiczne, Warsaw, 1969.

Szlendak, T. Bobo po polsku. Rzecz o zremasterowanej klasie próżniaczej. Odra 8, 1996.

Takeo, H., A. K. Kashyap & D. S. Scharfstein. "Bank Monitoring and Investment: Evidence from the Changing Structure of Japanese Corporate Banking Relationships." In *Asymmetric Information, Corporate Finance and Investment*, edited by R. G. Hubbard. Chicago: University of Chicago Press, 1990.

Takeo H., A. Kashyap & D. Scharfstein, "The Role of Banks in Reducing the Costs of Financial Distress in Japan." *Journal of Financial Economics* 27 (1990): 67–88.

Tawney, R. H. *Religion and the Rise of Capitalism*. New York: Harcourt, Brace & World, 1926.

Thaler R. H. Behavioral Economics. http://www.iies.su.se/nobel/papers/Encyclopedia%202.0.pdf (accessed November 24, 2007).

—. *Quasi-Rational Economics*. New York: Russell Sage Foundation, 1994.

—. "Mental Accounting and Consumer Choice." *Marketing Science* 4 (3) (1985): 199–214.

—. "The Ultimatum Game." *Journal of Economic Perspectives* 2 (1988): 195–206.

Thibaut, J. & H. Kelley. *The Social Psychology Of Groups*. New York: Willey, 1959.

Tiryakian, E. "Collective Effervescence, Social Change And Charisma: Durkheim, Weber and 1989." *International Sociology* 10 (1995): 269–279.

Titmuss, R. M. *The Gift Relationship*. London: Allen & Unwin, 1970.

Tittenbrun, J. "Ownership of Philanthropic Foundations." *Science and Society* 55 (1) (1991).
—. "Der polnische Weg zum Kapitalismus." *Prokla* 22 (4) (1992): 604–21.
—. "Between Dogmas and Realities: The Transition to a Market Economy in Poland." *Society and Change* 9 (1993): 39–70.
—. "The Managerial Revolution Revisited: The Case of Privatisation in Poland." *Capital and Class* 55 (1995): 21–328.
—. "Divide and Rule. Privatisation in Poland and the Working Class." *Critique* 1 (83) (2010).
—. *Private versus Public Enterprise: In Search of the Economic Rationale of Privatisation.* London, Janus Books, 1996.
—. Interakcjonizm we współczesnej socjologii amerykańskiej. Poznan, 1983.
—. Strukturalne antynomie. Kultura I Społeczeństwo. 3, 1983.
—. Nowi kapitaliści? Pracownicze fundusze emerytalne a własność kapitału akcyjnego. Poznan, 1991.
—. Społeczeństwo (Society) in Encyklopedia Britannica, 40. Poznań, 2005.
—. Struktura klasowo-stanowa spolecznosci Poznania(The Class and Estate Structure of the Poznan Community), Poznan: Nakom, 2010.
—. Shareholder Capitalism vs. Stakeholder Capitalism, in: Humanities and Education, in: Bondareva [ed.], Samara, 2011, ISBN 978-5-8428-0871-7
—. Z deszczu pod rynnę [*From the Frying Pan into the Fire*]. Poznan: Zysk and Co., 2008.
Treviño, A. J. "George C. Homans, The Human Group and Elementary Social Behaviour." The Encyclopaedia of Informal Education, 2009. www.infed.org/thinkers/george_homans.htm (accessed January 21, 2010).
—. ed. *George C. Homans: History, Theory and Method. Boulder*. CO: Paradigm Publishers, 2006.
Trivers, R. L. "The Evolution of Reciprocal Altruism." *Quarterly Review of Biology* 46 (1) (1971): 35–57.
Travers, R. "Experiments on the Provision of Public Goods. Resources, Interest, Group Size, and the Free-Rider Problem." *The Quarterly Review of Biology* 46 (1) (1971): 35–57.
Trotsky, L. "Engels's War Articles: Trotsky Reviews The General's Military Work." March 19, 1924. *The New International* 10 (86) (1944): 137–141.

Tullock, G. *The Economics of Special Privilege and Rent Seeking*. Boston & Dordrecht, Netherlands: Kluwer Academic Publishers, 1989.
—. *The Politics of Bureaucracy*. Washington, DC: Public Affairs Press, 1965.
—. "Public choice." *The New Palgrave: A Dictionary of Economics*. 2008.
—. *Toward a Mathematics of Politics*. Ann Arbor: University of Michigan Press, 1967.
Turk, H. & R. L. Simpson, eds. *Institutions and Social Exchange: The Sociologies of Talcott Parsons and George C. Homans*. Indianapolis: The Bobbs-Merril Company, 1971.
Turner, J. "Toward A Sociological Theory Of Motivation." *American Sociological Review* 52 (1987): 15–27.
Tversky, A. & D. Kahneman. "Loss Aversion in Riskless Choice: A Reference-Dependent Model." *Quarterly Journal of Economics* 106 (10) (1991): 39–1062.
—. "Belief in the Law of Small Numbers." *Psychological Bulletin* 2 (1972): 105–110.
—. "The Framing of Decisions and the Rationality of Choice." *Science* 211 (1981): 453–458.
—. "Extensional Versus Intuitive Reasoning: The Conjunction Fallacy in Probability Judgment." *Psychological Review* 90 (1983): 239–315.
Tym S. Znikomo szkodliwy społecznie. Wprost 15, 2001.
Tyran, J. R. "Voting When Money and Morals Conflict: An Experimental Test of Expressive Voting." *Journal of Public Economics* 88 (2004): 1645–1664.
Udehn, L. *Public Choice: A Sociological Critique of the Economic Theory of Politics.* New York: Routledge, 1996.
—. *The Limits of Public Choice: A Sociological Critique of the Economic Theory of Politics*. New York: Routledge, 1996.
Uehara, E. "Dual Exchange Theory, Social Networks and Informal Social Support." *American Journal of Sociology* 96 (1990): 521–557.
Umezu, M. "An Evaluation of Japan's Stakeholder Capitalism." *Journal of Private Enterprise* 3 (22) (2006).
Uzzi, B. "Social Structure and Competition in Interfirm Networks: The Paradox of Embeddedness." *Administrative Science Quarterly* 42 (1997): 35–67.
Veblen, T. *The Engineers and the Price System*. Kitchener, Ontario: General Books, 2001.
—. *The Theory of the Business Enterprise*. New York: Scribner, 1904.
Velthuis, O. "The Changing Relationship Between Economic Sociology and Institutional Economics: From Talcott Parsons to Mark

Granovetter." *American Journal of Economics and Sociology* 58 (1999): 629–649.

Vienneau, R. Frequently Asked Questions about The Labor Theory of Value. FAQ for alt.politics.socialism.trotsky, 2004.

Viner, J. "Religious Thought and Economic Society." Durham: Duke University Press, 1967.

Vroom, V. H. & E. L. Deci. eds. *Management and Motivation.* Harmondsworth: Penguin, 1970

Wallerstein, I. *The Modern World-System: Capitalist Agriculture and the Origins of the European World-Economy in the Sixteenth Century.* New York: Academic Press, 1976.

—. *World-Systems Analysis: An Introduction.* Durham: Duke University Press, 2004.

Wallace, M., L. Griffin & B. Rubin. "The Positional Power Of American Labor, 1963–1977." *American Sociological Review* 54 (1989): 197–214.

Wallace, S. Notes from Україна: A Blue Devil's Ukrainian experience, 2007. http://chernobyl-summer.blogspot.com/2007/07/chernobyl-liquidators-incredible-men.html (accessed December 11, 2009).

Walton, J. & D. Seddon. *Free Markets and Food Riots. The Politics of Global Adjustment.* Oxford: Blackwell.

Warner, R. S. "Toward a Redefinition of Action Theory: Paying the Cognitive Element its Due." *American Journal of Sociology* 83: 1317–1349.

Watabe, M. S., N. Terai, N. Hayashi & T. Yamagishi. "Cooperationinthe One-Shot Prisoner's Dilemma Based onExpectations of Reciprocity." *Japanese Journal of Experimental Social Psychology* 36 (1996: 183–196. Waterman, P. *Globalisation, Social Movements, and the New Internationalism*. Washington, D.C.: Mansell, 1998.

Wearne, B. *The Theory and Scholarship of Talcott Parsons to 1951: A Critical Commentary.* Cambridge: Cambridge University Press, 1989.

Weber, M. *Sociological Writings.* Continuum, Wrocław, 1984.

—. *The Theory of Social and Economic Organization*; Part I of Wirtschaft und Gesellschaft, translated from the German by A. R. Henderson and Talcott Parsons. London: W. Hodge, 1947.

—. *The Protestant Ethic and the Spirit of Capitalism.* London, 1930.

—. *Economy and Society.* New York, 1968.

Webster, F. *Theories of the Information Society*, London: Routledge, 1995.

Willer, D., B. Markovsky & T. Patton. "Power Structures: Derivations and Applications of Elementary Theory." In *Sociological Theories in Progress*, edited by B. Joseph, M. Zelditch & B. Anderson, 313–351. Newbury Park: Sage, 1989.

Weininger E. B. Foundations of Class Analysis in the work of Bourdieu, in: Alternative Foundations of class, 2002. http://www.ssc.wisc.edu/~wright/Found-all.pdf (accessed March 16, 2010).

Wenzel, H. Die Ordnung des Handelns, Frankfurt: Suhrkamp, 1990.

—. Die Abenteuer der Kommunikation, Weilerwist: Verlbrück Verlag, 2001.

White, H. *Identity and Control: A Structural Theory of a Social Action.* Princeton: Princeton University Press, 1992.

—. *Markets from Networks: Socioeconomic Models of Production.* Princeton: Princeton University Press, 2002.

White, J. D. *Greed, Chaos, And Governance: Using Public Choice To Improve Public Law*. New Haven, Connecticut: Yale University Press, 1997,

Whitford, J. "Pragmatism and the Untenable Dualism of Means and Ends: Why Rational Choice Theory Does Not Deserve Paradigmatic Privilege." *Theory and Society* 31(2002): 325–363.

Whynes, D., ed. *What Is Political Economy?* Oxford: Basil Blackwell, 1984.

Whyte, W. F. *Street Corner Society*. Chicago: University of Chicago Press, 1943.

—. *Money and Motivation*. NewYork: Harper and Brothers, 1955.

Wiliamson, O. *Corporate Control and Business Behavior*. Prentice-Hall: Englewood Cliffs, 1964

Willer, D. "The Principle Of Rational Choice And The Problem Of A Satisfactory Theory." In *Rational Choice Theory*, edited by C. James & T. Fararo, 49–77. Newbury Park: Sage Publications, 1992.

Williams H. M. "It's Time for a Takeover Moratorium." *Fortune*, July 22, 1985.

Williams, G. C. *Adaptation and Natural Selection*. Princeton: Princeton University Press, 1966.

Williams, M. "Primate Encephalization and Intelligence." *Medical Hypotheses* 58 (4) (2002): 284–290.

Williamson, O. E. *The Economic Institutions of Capitalism*. New York, Free Press, 1985.

—. *Markets and Hierarchies*. New York, 1975.

—. "Managerial Discretion and Business Behavior." *The American Economic Review* 53 (1963).

—. "The Evolving Science of Organization." *Journal of Institutional and Theoretical Economics* 149 (1993): 36–63.

—. "The Economics of Organization: The Transaction Cost Approach." *American Journal of Sociology* 87 (1981): 548–577.

Williamson, O. & W. Ouchi. "The Markets and Hierarchies and Visible Hand Perspectives." In *Perspectives on Organizational Design and Behavior*, edited by A. Van de Ven & W. Joyce, 347–70. New York, 1981.

Wilson, D. and W. Dixon. "Homo Economicus: A Contribution to the Critique of Economic Theory." *American Journal of Economics and Sociology* 67 (2) (2008).

Weiss, L. "Globalisation and the Myth of the Powerless State." *New Left Review*. September/October, 1997.

Wolfreys, J. "In perspective: Pierre Bourdieu." *International Socialism* 87 (2000).

Wright, E. O. *Class Structure and Income Determination*. New York: Harcourt, Brace and Jovanovich, 1979.

Wrong, D. "The Oversocialized Conception of Man in Modern Sociology." *American Sociological Review* 26 (1961): 183–193.

WSM (World Socialist Movement). An Introduction to Marxian Labour Theory of Value, 2006.

Wymeersch, E. "A Status Report on Corporate Governance Rules and Practices in Some Continental European States." In *Comparative Corporate Governance: The State of the Art and Emerging Research*, edited by K. Hopt, H. Kanda, M. Roe, E. Wymeersch & S. Prigge. Oxford: Clarendon Press, 1998.

Xenophon. *The Economist*. The Project Gutenberg EBook (EBook #1173), 2008.

Yamagishi, T. "Seriousness of Social Dilemmas and the Provision of a Sanctioning System." *Social Psychology Quarterly* 51 (3) (1988): 265–271.

Yamagishi T., M. Gilmore & K.Cook. "Network Connections And The Distribution Of Power In Exchange Networks." *American Journal of Sociology* 93 (1988): 833–851.

Yamaguchi, K. "Power in Networks Of Substitutable / Complementary Exchange Relations; A Rational Choice Model And An Analysis Of Power Centralization." *American Sociological Review* 6 (1996): 308–332.

—. "The Logic Of The New Theory And Misrepresentations Of The Logic." *American Sociological Review* 62 (1997): 838–841.

Yermack, D. "Higher Market Valuation of Companies with Small Board of Directors." *Journal of Financial Economics* 40 (1996): 185–212.

—. "Do corporations award CEO stock options effectively?" *Journal of Financial Economics* 39 (1995): 237–69.

Coles, J., M. Lemmon & F. Meschke. MPRA Paper No. 4374, 2007. http://mpra.ub.uni-muenchen.de/4374 (accessed April 19, 2010).

Yonay, Y. P. *The Struggle Over the Soul of Economics: Institutionalist and Neoclassical Economists in America Between the Wars*. Princeton: Princeton University Press, 1998.

Young, H. P. "The Evolution of Conventions." *Econometrica* 61–1 (1993): 57–84.

Yung-A. H. & D.Y. Liu. "Altruism versus Egoism in Human Behavior of Mixed Motives." *American Journal of Economics and Sociology* 62 (4) (2004),: 677–705.

Zafirovski, M. "The Social Construction of Production: An Application of Economic Sociology." *M@n@gement*, 5 (2) (2002): 147–174.

Zafirovski M. "Some Amendments to Social Exchange Theory: A Sociological Perspective." *Theory and Science* 4 (2) (2003).

Zelizer, V. *The Social Meaning of Money*. New York: Basic Books, 1994.

—. "Circuits in Economic Life." *Economic Sociology, The European Electronic Newsletter* 8 (1) (2006): 30–35.

—. The Social Meaning Of Money: Special Monies." *American Journal of Sociology* 95 (1989): 342–377.

Zhou, X. "Understanding the Determination of Managerial Ownership and its Relationship to Firm Performance: Comment." *Journal of Financial Economics* 62 (2001): 559–571.

Zukin, S. & P. Di Maggio "Introduction." In *Structures of Capital: The Social Organization of the Economy*, edited by S. Zukin and P. Di Maggio. Cambridge: Cambridge University Press, 1990.

INDEX